Karl Friedrich Keil, Franz Delitzsch

Biblical Commentary on the Books of Samuel

Karl Friedrich Keil, Franz Delitzsch

Biblical Commentary on the Books of Samuel

ISBN/EAN: 9783743329669

Manufactured in Europe, USA, Canada, Australia, Japa

Cover: Foto ©ninafisch / pixelio.de

Manufactured and distributed by brebook publishing software (www.brebook.com)

Karl Friedrich Keil, Franz Delitzsch

Biblical Commentary on the Books of Samuel

CLARK'S

FOREIGN

THEOLOGICAL LIBRARY

FOURTH SERIES.
VOL. IX.

Keil and Delitzsch on the Books of Samuel.

EDINBURGH:
T. & T. CLARK, 38, GEORGE STREET.
MDCCCLXXX.

PRINTED BY MORRISON AND GIBB,
FOR
T. & T. CLARK, EDINBURGH.

LONDON,	HAMILTON, ADAMS, AND CO.
DUBLIN, .	ROBERTSON AND CO.
NEW YORK,	SCRIBNER AND WELFORD.

BIBLICAL COMMENTARY

ON

THE BOOKS OF SAMUEL.

BY

C. F. KEIL, D.D., AND F. DELITZSCH, D.D.,
PROFESSORS OF THEOLOGY.

TRANSLATED FROM THE GERMAN
BY THE
REV. JAMES MARTIN, B.A.,
NOTTINGHAM.

EDINBURGH:
T. & T. CLARK, 38, GEORGE STREET.
MDCCCLXXX.

22214
K27

110921

MAR 18 1993

TABLE OF CONTENTS.

THE BOOKS OF SAMUEL.

INTRODUCTION.

	PAGE
TITLE, CONTENTS, CHARACTER, AND ORIGIN OF THE BOOKS OF SAMUEL,	1

EXPOSITION.

I. HISTORY OF THE PEOPLE OF ISRAEL UNDER THE PROPHET SAMUEL
   (1 SAM. I.–VII.), ... 13

   Samuel's Birth and Dedication to the Lord. Hannah's Song
   of Praise (Chap. i.–ii. 10), ... 14

   Samuel's Service before Eli. Ungodliness of Eli's Sons. Denunciation of Judgment upon Eli and his House (Chap.
   ii. 11–36), ... 34

   Samuel called to be a Prophet (Chap. iii.), . . . 48

   War with the Philistines. Loss of the Ark. Death of Eli and
   his Sons (Chap. iv.), ... 52

   Humiliation of the Philistines by means of the Ark of the
   Covenant (Chap. v.–vii. 1), ... 57

   Conversion of Israel to the Lord by Samuel. Victory over the
   Philistines. Samuel as Judge of Israel (Chap. vii. 2–17), 70

II. THE MONARCHY OF SAUL FROM HIS ELECTION TILL HIS ULTIMATE
    REJECTION (CHAP. VIII.–XV.), ... 77

   Israel's Prayer for a King (Chap. viii.), . . 81

   Anointing of Saul as King (Chap. ix.–x. 16), . . 86

	PAGE
Saul elected King. His Election confirmed (Chap. x. 17–xi. 15),	105
Samuel's Address at the Renewal of the Monarchy (Chap. xii.),	114
Saul's Reign, and his Unseasonable Sacrifice in the War against the Philistines (Chap. xiii.),	122
Jonathan's Heroic Act, and Israel's Victory over the Philistines. Saul's Wars and Family (Chap. xiv.),	136
War with Amalek. Saul's Disobedience and Rejection (Chap. xv.),	149

III. SAUL'S FALL AND DAVID'S ELECTION (CHAP. XVI.–XXXI.), 160

Anointing of David. His playing before Saul (Chap. xvi.),	167
David's Victory over Goliath (Chap. xvii. 1–54),	172
Jonathan's Friendship. Saul's Jealousy and Plots against David (Chap. xvii. 55–xviii. 30),	185
Jonathan's Intercession for David. Saul's renewed Attempts to murder him. David's Flight to Samuel (Chap. xix.),	194
Jonathan's last Attempt to reconcile his Father to David (Chap. xx.–xxi. 1),	206
David's Flight to Nob, and thence to Gath (Chap. xxi. 2–16),	216
David's Wanderings in Judah and Moab. Massacre of Priests by Saul (Chap. xxii.),	222
David delivers Keilah. He is betrayed by the Ziphites, and marvellously saved from Saul in the Desert of Maon (Chap. xxiii.),	228
David spares Saul in the Cave (Chap. xxiv.),	233
Death of Samuel. Nabal and Abigail (Chap. xxv.),	238
David is betrayed again by the Ziphites, and spares Saul a second time (Chap. xxvi.),	247
David at Ziklag in the Land of the Philistines (Chap. xxvii.),	254
David in the Army of the Philistines. Attack upon Israel. Saul and the Witch of Endor (Chap. xxviii.),	258
Removal of David from the Army of the Philistines (Chap. xxix.),	270
David avenges upon the Amalekites the plundering and burning of Ziklag (Chap. xxx.),	272
Death and Burial of Saul and his Sons (Chap. xxxi.),	278

THE SECOND BOOK OF SAMUEL.

	PAGE
I. DAVID KING OVER JUDAH, AND ISHBOSHETH KING OVER ISRAEL,	283
David's Conduct on hearing of Saul's Death. His Elegy upon Saul and Jonathan (Chap. i.),	284
David King over Judah, and Ishbosheth King over Israel. Battle at Gibeon (Chap. ii.),	292
David advances and Ishbosheth declines. Abner goes over to David, and is murdered by Joab (Chap. iii.),	299
Murder of Ishbosheth, and Punishment of the Murderers (Chap. iv.),	308
II. THE GOVERNMENT OF DAVID OVER ALL ISRAEL IN THE TIME OF ITS STRENGTH AND GLORY (CHAP. V.–IX.),	312
David anointed King over all Israel. Jerusalem taken, and made the Capital of the Kingdom. Victories over the Philistines (Chap. v.),	313
Removal of the Ark to Jerusalem (Chap. vi.),	326
David's Resolution to build a Temple. The promised Perpetuity of his Throne (Chap. vii.),	339
David's Wars, Victories, and Ministers of State (Chap. viii.),	354
David's Kindness towards Mephibosheth (Chap. ix.),	370
III. DAVID'S REIGN IN ITS DECLINE (CHAP. X.–XX.),	372
War with the Ammonites and Syrians (Chap. x.),	373
Siege of Rabbah. David's Adultery (Chap. xi.),	381
Nathan's Reproof and David's Repentance. Conquest of Rabbah (Chap. xii.),	388
Amnon's Incest, and Absalom's Fratricide (Chap. xiii.),	396
Absalom's Return, and Reconciliation to the King (Chap. xiv.),	405
Absalom's Rebellion and David's Flight (Chap. xv.–xvi. 14),	413
Absalom's Entrance into Jerusalem. Advice of Ahithophel and Hushai (Chap. xvi. 15–xvii. 23),	427
Absalom's Defeat and Death (Chap. xvii. 24–xix. 1),	433
David reinstated in his Kingdom (Chap. xix. 1–39),	442
Discontent in Israel, and Sheba's Rebellion (Chap. xix. 40–xx. 26),	451

		PAGE
IV. CLOSE OF DAVID'S REIGN (CHAP. XXI.–XXIV.),	.	458
Three Years' Famine. Heroic Acts performed in the Wars with the Philistines (Chap. xxi.),	. . . .	459
David's Psalm of Thanksgiving for Victory over all his Enemies (Chap. xxii.),	. . . . .	467
David's Last Words (Chap. xxiii. 1–7),		484
David's Heroes (Chap. xxiii. 8–39),	. . .	490
Numbering of the People, and Pestilence (Chap. xxiv.),		500

THE BOOKS OF SAMUEL.

INTRODUCTION.

TITLE, CONTENTS, CHARACTER, AND ORIGIN OF THE BOOKS OF SAMUEL.

THE books of Samuel originally formed one undivided work, and in the Hebrew MSS. they do so still. The division into two books originated with the Alexandrian translators (LXX.), and was not only adopted in the Vulgate and other versions, but in the sixteenth century it was introduced by Daniel Bomberg into our editions of the Hebrew Bible itself. In the Septuagint and Vulgate, these books are reckoned as belonging to the books of the Kings, and have the heading, Βασιλειῶν πρώτη, δευτέρα (*Regum*, i. *et* ii.). In the Septuagint they are called "books of the kingdoms," evidently with reference to the fact that each of these works contains an account of the history of a double kingdom, viz.: the books of Samuel, the history of the kingdoms of Saul and David; and the books of Kings, that of the kingdoms of Judah and Israel. This title does not appear unsuitable, so far as the books before us really contain an account of the rise of the monarchy in Israel. Nevertheless, we cannot regard it as the original title, or even as a more appropriate heading than the one given in the Hebrew canon, viz. "*the book of Samuel*," since this title not only originated in the fact that the first half (*i.e.* our first book) contains an account of the acts of the prophet Samuel, but was also intended to indicate that the spirit of Samuel formed the soul of the true kingdom in Israel, or that the earthly throne of the Israelitish kingdom of God derived its strength and perpetuity from the Spirit of the Lord which lived in the prophet. The division into two books answers to the contents, since the death of Saul, with which the first book closes, formed a turning-point in the development of the kingdom.

The books of Samuel contain the history of the kingdom of God in Israel, from the termination of the age of the judges to the close of the reign of king David, and embrace a period of about 125 years, viz. from about 1140 to 1015 B.C. The *first* book treats of the judgeship of the prophet Samuel and the reign of king Saul, and is divided into three sections, answering to the three epochs formed by the judicial office of Samuel (ch. i.–vii.), the reign of Saul from his election till his rejection (ch. viii.–xv.), and the decline of his kingdom during his conflict with David, whom the Lord had chosen to be the leader of His people in the place of Saul (ch. xvi.–xxxi.). The renewal of the kingdom of God, which was now thoroughly disorganized both within and without, commenced with Samuel. When the pious Hannah asked for a son from the Lord, and Samuel was given to her, the sanctuary of God at Shiloh was thoroughly desecrated under the decrepit high priest Eli by the base conduct of his worthless sons, and the nation of Israel was given up to the power of the Philistines. If Israel, therefore, was to be delivered from the bondage of the heathen, it was necessary that it should be first of all redeemed from the bondage of sin and idolatry, that its false confidence in the visible pledges of the gracious presence of God should be shaken by heavy judgments, and the way prepared for its conversion to the Lord its God by deep humiliation. At the very same time, therefore, at which Samuel was called to be the prophet of God, the judgment of God was announced upon the degraded priesthood and the desecrated sanctuary. The *first* section of our book, which describes the history of the renewal of the theocracy by Samuel, does not commence with the call of Samuel as prophet, but with an account on the one hand of the character of the national religion in the time of Eli, and on the other hand of the piety of the parents of Samuel, especially of his mother, and with an announcement of the judgment that was to fall upon Eli's house (ch. i. ii.). Then follow first of all the call of Samuel as prophet (ch. iii.), and the fulfilment of the judgment upon the house of

Eli and the house of God (ch. iv.); secondly, the manifestation of the omnipotence of God upon the enemies of His people, by the chastisement of the Philistines for carrying off the ark of the covenant, and the victory which the Israelites gained over their oppressors through Samuel's prayer (ch. v.–vii. 14); and lastly, a summary of the judicial life of Samuel (ch. vii. 15–17). The *second* section contains, first, the negotiations of the people with Samuel concerning the appointment of a king, the anointing of Saul by the prophet, and his election as king, together with the establishment of his kingdom (ch. viii.–xii.); and secondly, a brief survey of the history of his reign, in connection with which the only events that are at all fully described are his first successful conflicts with the Philistines, and the war against the Amalekites which occasioned his ultimate rejection (ch. xiii.–xv.). In the *third* section (ch. xvi.–xxxi.) there is a much more elaborate account of the history of Saul from his rejection till his death, since it not only describes the anointing of David and his victory over Goliath, but contains a circumstantial account of his attitude towards Saul, and the manifold complications arising from his long-continued persecution on the part of Saul, for the purpose of setting forth the gradual accomplishment of the counsels of God, both in the rejection of Saul and the election of David as king of Israel, to warn the ungodly against hardness of heart, and to strengthen the godly in their trust in the Lord, who guides His servants through tribulation and suffering to glory and honour. The *second* book contains the history of the reign of David, arranged in four sections: (1) his reign over Judah in Hebron, and his conflict with Ishbosheth the son of Saul, whom Abner had set up as king over the other tribes of Israel (ch. i.–iv.): (2) the anointing of David as king over all Israel, and the firm establishment of his kingdom through the conquest of the citadel of Zion, and the elevation of Jerusalem into the capital of the kingdom; the removal of the ark of the covenant to Jerusalem; the determination to build a temple to the Lord; the promise given him by the Lord of the everlasting duration of his dominion; and lastly, the subjugation of all the enemies of Israel (ch. v.–viii. 14), to which there is appended a list of the principal officers of state (ch. viii. 15–18), and an account of the favour shown to the house of Saul in the person of Mephibosheth (ch. ix.): (3) the disturbance of his reign through his adultery with Bathsheba during the Ammonitish and Syrian war, and the judgments which came upon his house in consequence of this sin through the wickedness of his sons, viz. the incest of Amnon and rebellion of Absalom, and the insurrection of Sheba (ch. x.-xx.): (4) the close of his reign, his song of thanksgiving for deliverance out of the hand of all his foes (ch. xxii.), and his last prophetic words concerning the just ruler in the fear of God (ch. xxiii. 1-7). The way is prepared for these, however, by an account of the expiation of Saul's massacre of the Gibeonites, and of various heroic acts performed by his generals during the wars with the Philistines (ch. xxi.); whilst a list of his several heroes is afterwards appended in ch. xxiii. 8-39, together with an account of the numbering of the people and consequent pestilence (ch. xxiv.), which is placed at the close of the work, simply because the punishment of this sin of David furnished the occasion for the erection of an altar of burnt-offering upon the site of the future temple. His death is not mentioned here, because he transferred the kingdom to his son Solomon before he died; and the account of this transfer forms the introduction to the history of Solomon in the first book of Kings, so that the close of David's life was most appropriately recorded there.

So far as the *character* of the historical writing in the books of Samuel is concerned, there is something striking in the contrast which presents itself between the fulness with which the writer has described many events of apparently trifling importance, in connection with the lives of persons through whom the Lord secured the deliverance of His people and kingdom from their foes, and the summary brevity with which he disposes of the greatest enterprises of Saul and David, and the fierce and for the most part tedious wars with the surrounding nations; so that, as Thenius says, "particular portions of the work differ in the most striking manner from all the rest, the one part being very brief, and written almost in the form of a chronicle, the other elaborate, and in one part composed with really biographical fulness." This peculiarity is not to be accounted for from the nature of the sources which the author had at his command; for even if we cannot define with precision the nature and extent of these sources, yet when we compare the accounts contained in these books of the wars between David and the Ammonites and Syrians with those in the books of Chronicles (2 Sam. viii. and x. with 1 Chron. xviii. xix.), we see clearly enough that the sources from which those accounts were derived embraced more than our books have given, since there are several places in which the chronicler gives fuller details of historical facts, the truth of which is universally allowed. The preparations for the building of the temple and the organization of the army, as well as the arrangement of the official duties of the Levites which David undertook, according to 1 Chron. xxii.-xxviii., in the closing years of his life, cannot possibly have been unknown to the author of our books. Moreover, there are frequent allusions in the books before us to events which are assumed as known, though there is no record of them in the writings which have been handed down to us, such as the removal of the tabernacle from Shiloh, where it stood in the time of Eli (1 Sam. i. 3, 9, etc.), to Nob, where David received the shewbread from the priests on his flight from Saul (ch. xxi. 1 sqq.); the massacre of the Gibeonites by Saul, which had to be expiated under David (2 Sam. xxi.); the banishment of the necromancers out of the land in the time of Saul (1 Sam. xxviii. 3); and the flight of the Beerothites to Gittaim (2 Sam. iv. 3). From this also we must conclude, that the author of our books knew more than he thought it necessary to mention in his work. But we certainly cannot infer from these peculiarities, as has often been done, that our books are to be regarded as a compilation. Such an inference as this simply arises from an utter disregard of the plan and object, which run through both books and regulate the selection and arrangement of the materials they contain. That the work has been composed upon a definite plan, is evident from the grouping of the historical facts, in favour of which the chronological order generally observed in both the books has now and then been sacrificed. Thus, in the history of Saul and the account of his wars (1 Sam. xiv. 47, 48), the fact is also mentioned, that he smote the Amalekites; whereas the war itself, in which he smote them, is first described in detail in ch. xv., because it was in that war that he forfeited his kingdom through his transgression of the divine command, and brought about his own rejection on the part of God. The sacrifice of the chronological order to the material grouping of kindred events, is still more evident in the history of David. In 2 Sam. viii. all his wars with foreign nations are collected together, and even the wars with the Syrians and Ammonites are included, together with an account of the booty taken in these wars; and then after this, viz. in ch. x.-xii., the war with the Ammonites and Syrians is more fully described, including the circumstances which occasioned it, the course which it took, and David's adultery which occurred during this war. Moreover, the history of Saul, as well as that of David, is divided into two self-contained periods, answering indeed to the historical course of the reigns of these two kings, but yet so distinctly marked off by the historian, that not only is the turning-point distinctly given in both instances, viz. the rejection of Saul and the grievous fall of David, but each of these periods is rounded off with a comprehensive account of the wars, the family, and the state officials of the two kings (1 Sam. xiv. 47-52, and 2 Sam. viii.). So likewise in the history of Samuel, after the victory which the Israelites obtained over the Philistines through his prayer, everything that had to be related concerning his life as judge is grouped together in ch. vii. 15-17, before the introduction of the monarchy is described; although Samuel himself lived till nearly the close of the reign of Saul, and not only instituted Saul as king, but afterwards announced his rejection, and anointed David as his successor. These comprehensive accounts are anything but proofs of compilations from sources of different kinds, which ignorance of the peculiarities of the Semitic style of writing history has led some to regard them as being; they simply serve to round off the different periods into which the history has been divided, and form resting-places for the historical review, which neither destroy the material connection of the several groups, nor throw any doubt upon the unity of the authorship of the books themselves. And even where separate incidents appear to be grouped together, without external connection or any regard to chronological order, on a closer inspection it is easy to discover the relation in which they stand to the leading purpose of the whole book, and the reason why they occupy this position and no other (see the introductory remarks to 2 Sam. ix. xxi.-xxiv.).

If we look more closely, however, at the contents of these books, in order to determine their character more precisely, we find at the very outset, in Hannah's song of praise, a prophetic glance at the anointed of the Lord (ch. ii. 10), which foretells the establishment of the monarchy that was afterwards accomplished under Saul and David. And with this there is associated the rise of the new name, *Jehovah Sabaoth*, which is never met with in the Pentateuch or in the books of Joshua and Judges; whereas it occurs in the books before us from the commencement (ch. i. 3, 11, etc.) to the close. (For further remarks on the origin and signification of this divine name, see at ch. i. 3.) When Israel received a visible representative of its invisible God-king in the person of an earthly monarch; Jehovah, the God of Israel, became the God of the heavenly hosts. Through the establishment of the monarchy, the people of Jehovah's possession became a "world-power;" the kingdom of God was elevated into a kingdom of the world, as distinguished from the other ungodly kingdoms of the world, which it was eventually to overcome in the power of its God. In this conflict Jehovah manifested himself as the Lord of hosts, to whom all the nations and kingdoms of this world were to become subject. Even in the times of Saul and David, the heathen nations were to experience a foretaste of this subjection. When Saul had ascended the throne of Israel, he fought against all his enemies round about, and extended his power in every direction in which he turned (ch. i. 14, 47, 48). But David made all the nations who bordered upon the kingdom of God tributary to the people of the Lord, as the Lord gave him victory wherever he went (ch. ii. 8, 14, 15); so that his son Solomon reigned over all the kingdoms, from the stream (the Euphrates) to the boundary of Egypt, and they all brought him presents, and were subject to him (1 Kings v. 1). But the Israelitish monarchy could never thus acquire the power to secure for the kingdom of God a victory over all its foes, except as the king himself was diligent in his endeavours to be at all times simply the instrument of the God-king, and exercise his authority solely in the name and according to the will of Jehovah. And as the natural selfishness and pride of man easily made this concentration of the supreme earthly power in a single person merely an occasion for self-aggrandisement, and therefore the Israelitish kings were exposed to the temptation to use the plenary authority entrusted to them even in opposition to the will of God; the Lord raised up for Himself organs of His own Spirit, in the persons of the prophets, to stand by the side of the kings, and make known to them the will and counsel of God. The introduction of the monarchy was therefore preceded by the development of the prophetic office into a spiritual power in Israel, in which the kingdom was to receive not only a firm support to its own authority, but a strong bulwark against royal caprice and tyranny. Samuel was called by the Lord to be His prophet, to convert the nation that was sunk in idolatry to the Lord its God, and to revive the religious life by the establishment of associations of prophets, since the priests had failed to resist the growing apostasy of the nation, and had become unfaithful to their calling to instruct and establish the congregation in the knowledge and fear of the Lord. Even before the call of Samuel as a prophet, there was foretold to the high priest Eli by a man of God, not only the judgment that would fall upon the degenerate priesthood, but the appointment of a faithful priest, for whom the Lord would build a permanent house, that he might ever walk before His anointed (1 Sam. ii. 27–36). And the first revelation which Samuel received from God had reference to the fulfilment of all that the Lord had spoken against the house of Eli (ch. iii. 11 sqq.). The announcement of a faithful priest, who would walk before the anointed of the Lord, also contained a prediction of the establishment of the monarchy, which foreshadowed its worth and great significance in relation to the further development of the kingdom of God. And whilst these predictions of the anointed of the Lord, before and in connection with the call of Samuel, show the deep spiritual connection which existed between the prophetic order and the regal office in Israel; the insertion of them in these books is a proof that from the very outset the author had this new organization of the Israelitish kingdom of God before his mind, and that it was his intention not simply to hand down biographies of Samuel, Saul, and David, but to relate the history of the Old Testament kingdom of God at the time of its elevation out of a deep inward and outward decline into the full authority and power of a kingdom of the Lord, before which all its enemies were to be compelled to bow.

Israel was to become a kingship of priests, *i.e.* a kingdom whose citizens were priests and kings. The Lord had announced this to the sons of Israel before the covenant was concluded at Sinai, as the ultimate object of their adoption as the people of His possession (Ex. xix. 5, 6). Now although this promise reached far beyond the times of the Old Covenant, and will only receive its perfect fulfilment in the completion of the kingdom of God under the New Covenant, yet it was to be realized even in the people of Israel so far as the economy of the Old Testament allowed. Israel was not only to become a priestly nation, but a royal nation also ; not only to be sanctified as a congregation of the Lord, but also to be exalted into a kingdom of God. The establishment of the earthly monarchy, therefore, was not only an eventful turning-point, but also an " epoch-making" advance in the development of Israel towards the goal set before it in its divine calling. And this advance became the pledge of the ultimate attainment of the goal, through the promise which David received from God (2 Sam. vii. 12-16), that the Lord would establish the throne of his kingdom for ever. With this promise God established for His anointed the eternal covenant, to which David reverted at the close of his reign, and upon which he rested his divine announcement of the just ruler over men, the ruler in the fear of God (2 Sam. xxiii. 1-7). Thus the close of these books points back to their commencement. The prophecy of the pious mother of Samuel, that the Lord would give strength unto His king, and exalt the horn of His anointed (1 Sam. ii. 10), found a fulfilment in the kingdom of David, which was at the same time a pledge of the ultimate completion of the kingdom of God under the sceptre of the Son of David, the promised Messiah.

This is one, and in fact the most conspicuous, arrangement of the facts connected with the history of salvation, which determined the plan and composition of the work before us. By the side of this there is another, which does not stand out so prominently indeed, but yet must not be overlooked. At the very beginning, viz. in ch. i., the inward decay of the house of God under the high priest Eli is exhibited ; and in the announcement of the judgment upon the house of Eli, a long-continued oppression of the dwelling-place (of God) is foretold (ch. ii. 32). Then, in the further course of the narrative, not only is the fulfilment of these threats pointed out, in the events described in 1 Sam. iv., vi. 19–vii. 2, and xxii. 11-19; but it is also shown how David first of all brought the ark of the covenant, about which no one had troubled himself in the time of Saul, out of its concealment, had a tent erected for it in the capital of his kingdom upon Mount Zion, and made it once more the central point of the worship of the congregation; and how after that, when God had given him rest from his enemies, he wished to build a temple for the Lord to be the dwelling-place of His name; and lastly, when God would not permit him to carry out this resolution, but promised that his son would build the house of the Lord, how, towards the close of his reign, he consecrated the site for the future temple by building an altar upon Mount Moriah (2 Sam. xxiv. 25). Even in this series of facts the end of the work points back to the beginning, so that the arrangement and composition of it according to a definite plan, which has been consistently carried out, are very apparent. If, in addition to this, we take into account the deep-seated connection between the building of the temple as designed by David, and the confirmation of his monarchy on the part of God as exhibited in 2 Sam. vii., we cannot fail to observe that the historical development of the true kingdom, in accordance with the nature and constitution of the Old Testament kingdom of God, forms the leading thought and purpose of the work to which the name of Samuel has been attached, and that it was by this thought and aim that the writer was influenced throughout in his selection of the historical materials which lay before him in the sources that he employed.

The full accounts which are given of the birth and youth of Samuel, and the life of David, are in the most perfect harmony with this design. The lives and deeds of these two men of God were of significance as laying the foundation for the development and organization of the monarchical kingdom in Israel. Samuel was the model and type of the prophets; and embodied in his own person the spirit and nature of the prophetic office, whilst his attitude towards Saul foreshadowed the position which the prophet was to assume in relation to the king. In the life of David, the Lord himself educated the king of His kingdom, the prince over His people, to whom He could continue His favour and grace even when he had fallen. so deeply that it was necessary that he should be chastised for his sins. Thus all the separate parts and sections are fused together as an organic whole in the fundamental thought of the work before us. And this unity is not rendered at all questionable by differences such as we find in the accounts of the mode of Saul's death as described in 1 Sam. xxxi. 4 and 2 Sam. i. 9, 10, or by such repetitions as the double account of the death of Samuel, and other phenomena of a similar kind, which can be explained without difficulty; whereas the assertion sometimes made, that there are some events of which we have two different accounts that contradict each other, has never yet been proved, and, as we shall see when we come to the exposition of the passages in question, has arisen partly from unscriptural assumptions, partly from ignorance of the formal peculiarities of the Hebrew mode of writing history, and partly from a mistaken interpretation of the passages themselves.

With regard to the *origin* of the books of Samuel, all that can be maintained with certainty is, that they were not written till after the division of the kingdom under Solomon's successor. This is evident from the remark in 1 Sam. xxvii. 6, that "*Ziklag pertaineth unto the kings of Judah unto this day.*" For although David was king over the tribe of Judah alone for seven years, it was not till after the falling away of the ten tribes from the house of David that there were really "kings of Judah." On the other hand, nothing can be inferred with certainty respecting the date of composition, either from the distinction drawn between Israel and Judah in 1 Sam. xi. 8, xvii. 52, xviii. 16, and 2 Sam. iii. 10, xxiv. 1, which evidently existed as early as the time of David, as we may see from 2 Sam. ii. 9, 10, v. 1–5, xix. 41, xx. 2; or from the formula "*to this day,*" which we find in 1 Sam. v. 5, vi. 18, xxx. 25, 2 Sam. iv. 3, vi. 18, xviii. 18, since the duration of the facts to which it is applied is altogether unknown; or lastly, from such passages as 1 Sam. ix. 9, 2 Sam. xiii. 18, where explanations are given of expressions and customs belonging to the times of Saul and David, as it is quite possible that they may have been altogether changed by the time of Solomon. In general, the contents and style of the books point to the earliest times after the division of the kingdom; since we find no allusions whatever to the decay of the kingdoms which afterwards took place, and still less to the captivity; whilst the style and language are classical throughout, and altogether free from Chaldaisms and later forms, such as we meet with in the writings of the Chaldean period, and even in those of the time of the captivity. The author himself is quite unknown; but, judging from the spirit of his writings, he was a prophet of the kingdom of Judah. It is unanimously admitted, however, that he made use of written documents, particularly of prophetic records made by persons who were contemporaries of the events described, not only for the history of the reigns of Saul and David, but also for the life and labours of Samuel, although no written sources are quoted, with the exception of the "book of Jasher," which contained the elegy of David upon Saul and Jonathan (2 Sam. i. 18); so that the sources employed by him cannot be distinctly pointed out. The different attempts which have been made to determine them minutely, from the time of Eichhorn down to G. Em. Karo (*de fontibus librorum qui feruntur Samuelis Dissert. Berol.* 1862), are lacking in the necessary proofs which hypotheses must bring before they can meet with adoption and support. If we confine ourselves to the historical evidence, according to 1 Chron. xxix. 29, the first and last acts of king David, *i.e.* the events of his entire reign, were recorded in the "*dibre* of Samuel the seer, of Nathan the prophet, and of Gad the seer." These prophetic writings formed no doubt the leading sources from which our books of Samuel were also drawn, since, on the one hand, apart from sundry deviations arising from differences in the plan and object of the two authors, the two accounts of the reign of David in 2 Sam. viii.–xxiv. and 1 Chron. xi.–xxi. agree for the most part so thoroughly word for word, that they are generally regarded as extracts from one common source; whilst, on the other hand, the prophets named not only lived in the time of David but throughout the whole of the period referred to in the books before us, and took a very active part in the progressive development of the history of those times (see not only 1 Sam. i.–iii. vii.–x. xii. xv. xvi., but also 1 Sam. xix. 18–24, xxii. 5, 2 Sam. vii. 12, xxiv. 11–18). Moreover, in 1 Chron. xxvii. 24, there are "chronicles (diaries or annals) of king David" mentioned, accompanied with the remark that the result of the census appointed by David was not inserted in them, from which we may infer that all the principal events of his reign were included in these chronicles. And they may also have formed one of the sources for our books, although nothing certain can be determined concerning the relation in which they stood to the writings of the three prophets that have been mentioned. Lastly, it is very evident from the character of the work before us, that the author had sources composed by eyewitnesses of the events at his command, and that these were employed with an intimate knowledge of the facts and with historical fidelity, inasmuch as the history is distinguished by great perspicuity and vividness of description, by a careful delineation of the characters of the persons engaged, and by great accuracy in the accounts of localities, and of subordinate circumstances connected with the historical events.

EXPOSITION.

I. HISTORY OF THE PEOPLE OF ISRAEL UNDER THE PROPHET SAMUEL.

1 Sam. I.–VII.

The call of Samuel to be the prophet and judge of Israel formed a turning-point in the history of the Old Testament kingdom of God. As the prophet of Jehovah, Samuel was to lead the people of Israel out of the times of the judges into those of the kings, and lay the foundation for a prosperous development of the monarchy. Consecrated like Samson as a Nazarite from his mother's womb, Samuel accomplished the deliverance of Israel out of the power of the Philistines, which had been only commenced by Samson; and that not by the physical might of his arm, but by the spiritual power of his word and prayer, with which he led Israel back from the worship of dead idols to the Lord its God. And whilst as one of the judges, among whom he classes himself in 1 Sam. xii. 11, he brought the office of judge to a close, and introduced the monarchy; as a prophet, he laid the foundation of the prophetic office, inasmuch as he was the first to naturalize it, so to speak, in Israel, and develope it into a power that continued henceforth to exert the strongest influence, side by side with the priesthood and monarchy, upon the development of the covenant nation and kingdom of God. For even if there were prophets before the time of Samuel, who revealed the will of the Lord at times to the nation, they only appeared sporadically, without exerting any lasting influence upon the national life; whereas, from the time of Samuel onwards, the prophets sustained and fostered the spiritual life of the congregation, and were the instruments through whom the Lord made known His purposes to the nation and its rulers. To exhibit in its origin and growth the new order of things which Samuel introduced, or rather the deliverance which the Lord sent to His people through this servant of His, the prophetic historian goes back to the time of Samuel's birth, and makes us acquainted not only with the religious condition of the nation, but also with the political oppression under which it was suffering at the close of the period of the judges, and during the high-priesthood of Eli. At the time when the pious parents of Samuel were going year by year to the house of God at Shiloh to worship and offer sacrifice before the Lord, the house of God was being profaned by the abominable conduct of Eli's sons (ch. i. ii.). When Samuel was called to be the prophet of Jehovah, Israel lost the ark of the covenant, the soul of its sanctuary, in the war with the Philistines (ch. iii. iv.). And it was not till after the nation had been rendered willing to put away its strange gods and worship Jehovah alone, through the influence of Samuel's exertions as prophet, that the faithful covenant God gave it, in answer to Samuel's intercession, a complete victory over the Philistines (ch. vii.). In accordance with these three prominent features, the history of the judicial life of Samuel may be divided into three sections, viz.: ch. i. ii.; iii.-vi.; and vii.

SAMUEL'S BIRTH AND DEDICATION TO THE LORD. HANNAH'S SONG OF PRAISE.—CHAP. I.-II. 10.

While Eli the high priest was judging Israel, and at the time when Samson was beginning to fight against the Philistines, a pious Israelitish woman prayed to the Lord for a son (vers

1-18). Her prayer was heard. She bore a son, to whom she gave the name of Samuel, because he had been asked for from the Lord. As soon as he was weaned, she dedicated him to the Lord for a lifelong service (vers. 19-28), and praised the Lord in a song of prophetic character for the favour which He had shown to His people through hearkening to her prayer (ch. ii. 1-10).

Vers. 1-8. *Samuel's pedigree.*—Ver. 1. His father was a man of Ramathaim-Zophim, on the mountains of Ephraim, and named Elkanah. *Ramathaim-Zophim*, which is only mentioned here, is the same place, according to ver. 3 (comp. with ver. 19 and ch. ii. 11), which is afterwards called briefly *ha-Ramah*, *i.e.* the height. For since Elkanah of Ramathaim-Zophim went year by year out of his city to Shiloh, to worship and sacrifice there, and after he had done this, returned to his house to Ramah (ver. 19, ch. ii. 11), there can be no doubt that he was not only a native of Ramathaim-Zophim, but still had his home there; so that Ramah, where his house was situated, is only an abbreviated name for Ramathaim-Zophim.[1] This Ramah (which is invariably written with the article, ha-Ramah), where Samuel was not only born (vers. 19 sqq.), but lived, laboured, died (ch. vii. 17, xv. 34, xvi. 13, xix. 18, 19, 22, 23), and was buried (ch. xxv. 1, xxviii. 3), is not a different place, as has been frequently assumed,[2] from the Ramah in Benjamin (Josh. xviii. 25), and is not to be sought for in Ramleh near Joppa (v. Schubert, etc.), nor in Soba on the north-west of Jerusalem (Robinson, *Pal.* ii. p. 329), nor three-quarters of an hour to the north of Hebron (Wolcott, v. de Velde), nor anywhere else in the tribe of Ephraim, but is identical with Ramah of Benjamin,

---

[1] The argument lately adduced by Valentiner in favour of the difference between these two names, viz. that " examples are not wanting of a person being described according to his original descent, although his dwelling-place had been already changed," and the instance which he cites, viz. Judg. xix. 16, show that he has overlooked the fact, that in the very passage which he quotes the temporary dwelling-place is actually mentioned along with the native town. In the case before us, on the contrary, Ramathaim-Zophim is designated, by the use of the expression " from his city," in ver. 3, as the place where Elkanah lived, and where " his house" (ver. 19) was still standing.

[2] For the different views which have been held upon this point, see the article " Ramah," by Pressel, in Herzog's *Cyclopædia*.

and was situated upon the site of the present village of er-Râm, two hours to the north-west of Jerusalem, upon a conical mountain to the east of the Nablus road (see at Josh. xviii. 25). This supposition is neither at variance with the account in ch. ix. x. (see the commentary upon these chapters), nor with the statement that Ramathaim-Zophim was upon the mountains of Ephraim, since the mountains of Ephraim extended into the tribe-territory of Benjamin, as is indisputably evident from Judg. iv. 5, where Deborah the prophetess is said to have dwelt between Ramah and Bethel in the mountains of Ephraim. The name Ramathaim-Zophim, *i.e.* " the two heights (of the) Zophites," appears to have been given to the town to distinguish it from other Ramahs, and to have been derived from the Levitical family of Zuph or Zophai (see 1 Chron. vi. 26, 35), which emigrated thither from the tribe of Ephraim, and from which Elkanah was descended. The full name, therefore, is given here, in the account of the descent of Samuel's father; whereas in the further history of Samuel, where there was no longer the same reason for giving it, the simple name Ramah is invariably used.[1] The connection between Zophim and Zuph is confirmed by the fact that Elkanah's ancestor, Zuph, is called Zophai in 1 Chron. vi. 26, and Zuph or Ziph in 1 Chron. vi. 35. Zophim therefore signifies the descendants of Zuph or Zophai, from which the name " land of Zuph," in ch. ix. 5, was also derived (see the commentary on this passage). The tracing back of Elkanah's family through four generations to Zuph agrees with the family registers in 1 Chron. vi., where the ancestors of Elkanah are mentioned twice,—first of all in the genealogy of the Kohathites (ver. 26), and then in that of Heman, the leader of the singers, a grandson of Samuel (ver.

---

[1] The fuller and more exact name, however, appears to have been still retained, and the use of it to have been revived after the captivity, in the Ῥαμαθίμ of 1 Macc. xi. 34, for which the Codd. have Ῥαθαμεῖν and Ῥαμαθαΐμ, and Josephus Ῥαμαθά, and in the Arimathæa of the gospel history (Matt. xxvii. 57). " For the opinion that this Ramathaim is a different place from the city of Samuel, and is to be sought for in the neighbourhood of Lydda, which Robinson advocates (*Pal.* iii. pp. 41 sqq.), is a hasty conclusion, drawn from the association of Ramathaim with Lydda in 1 Macc. xi. 34,—the very same conclusion which led the author of the *Onomasticon* to transfer the city of Samuel to the neighbourhood of Lydda" (Grimm on 1 Macc. xi. 34).

33),—except that the names Elihu, Tohu, and Zuph, are given as Eliab, Nahath, and Zophai in the first instance, and Eliel, Toah, and Ziph (according to the *Chethibh*) in the second,— various readings, such as often occur in the different genealogies, and are to be explained partly from the use of different forms for the same name, and partly from their synonymous meanings. *Tohu* and *Toah*, which occur in Arabic, with the meaning to press or sink in, are related in meaning to *nachath* or *nuach*, to sink or settle down. From these genealogies in the Chronicles, we learn that Samuel was descended from Kohath, the son of Levi, and therefore was a Levite. It is no valid objection to the correctness of this view, that his Levitical descent is never mentioned, or that Elkanah is called an Ephrathite. The former of these can very easily be explained from the fact, that Samuel's work as a reformer, which is described in this book, did not rest upon his Levitical descent, but simply upon the call which he had received from God, as the prophetic office was not confined to any particular class, like that of priest, but was founded exclusively upon the divine calling and endowment with the Spirit of God. And the difficulty which Nägelsbach expresses in Herzog's *Cycl.*, viz. that " as it was stated of those two Levites (Judg. xvii. 7, xix. 1), that they lived in Bethlehem and Ephraim, but only after they had been expressly described as Levites, we should have expected to find the same in the case of Samuel's father," is removed by the simple fact, that in the case of both those Levites it was of great importance, so far as the accounts which are given of them are concerned, that their Levitical standing should be distinctly mentioned, as is clearly shown by Judg. xvii. 10, 13, and xix. 18; whereas in the case of Samuel, as we have already observed, his Levitical descent had no bearing upon the call which he received from the Lord. The word *Ephrathite* does not belong, so far as the grammatical construction is concerned, either to *Zuph* or *Elkanah*, but to " *a certain man*," the subject of the principal clause, and signifies an Ephraimite, as in Judg. xii. 5 and 1 Kings xi. 26, and not an inhabitant of Ephratah, *i.e.* a Bethlehemite, as in ch. xvii. 12 and Ruth i. 2; for in both these passages the word is more precisely defined by the addition of the expression " of Bethlehem-Judah," whereas in this verse the explanation is to be found in the expression " of

B

Mount Ephraim." Elkanah the Levite is called an Ephraimite, because, so far as his civil standing was concerned, he belonged to the tribe of Ephraim, just as the Levite in Judg. xvii. 7 is described as belonging to the family of Judah. The Levites were reckoned as belonging to those tribes in the midst of which they lived, so that there were Judæan Levites, Ephraimitish Levites, and so on (see Hengstenberg, *Diss.* vol. ii. p. 50). It by no means follows, however, from the application of this term to Elkanah, that Ramathaim-Zophim formed part of the tribe-territory of Ephraim, but simply that Elkanah's family was incorporated in this tribe, and did not remove till afterwards to Ramah in the tribe of Benjamin. On the division of the land, dwelling-places were allotted to the Levites of the family of Kohath, in the tribes of Ephraim, Dan, and Manasseh (Josh. xxi. 5, 21 sqq.). Still less is there anything at variance with the Levitical descent of Samuel, as Thenius maintains, in the fact that he was dedicated to the Lord by his mother's vow, for he was not dedicated to the service of Jehovah generally through this vow, but was set apart to a lifelong service at the house of God as a Nazarite (vers. 11, 22); whereas other Levites were not required to serve till their twenty-fifth year, and even then had not to perform an uninterrupted service at the sanctuary. On the other hand, the Levitical descent of Samuel receives a very strong confirmation from his father's name. All the Elkanahs that we meet with in the Old Testament, with the exception of the one mentioned in 2 Chron. xxviii. 7, whose genealogy is unknown, can be proved to have been Levites; and most of them belong to the family of Korah, from which Samuel was also descended (see Simonis, *Onomast.* p. 493). This is no doubt connected in some way with the meaning of the name *Elkanah*, the man whom God has bought or acquired; since such a name was peculiarly suitable to the Levites, whom the Lord had set apart for service at the sanctuary, in the place of the first-born of Israel, whom He had sanctified to himself when He smote the first-born of Egypt (Num. iii. 13 sqq., 44 sqq.; see Hengstenberg, *ut sup.*).—Vers. 2, 3. Elkanah had two wives, Hannah (grace or gracefulness) and Peninnah (coral), the latter of whom was blessed with children, whereas the first was childless. He went with his wives year by year (מִיָּמִים יָמִימָה, as in Ex. xiii. 10, Judg. xi. 40), according to the instructions of the law (Ex. xxxiv. 23, Deut. xvi. 16), to the tabernacle at Shiloh (Josh. xviii. 1), to worship and sacrifice to the Lord of hosts. "*Jehovah Zebaoth*" is an abbreviation of "*Jehovah Elohe Zebaoth*," or יְהוָֹה אֱלֹהֵי הַצְּבָאוֹת ; and the connection of *Zebaoth* with *Jehovah* is not to be regarded as the construct state, nor is *Zebaoth* to be taken as a genitive dependent upon *Jehovah*. This is not only confirmed by the occurrence of such expressions as "*Elohim Zebaoth*" (Ps. lix. 6, lxxx. 5, 8, 15, 20, lxxxiv. 9) and "*Adonai Zebaoth*" (Isa. x. 16), but also by the circumstance that *Jehovah*, as a proper name, cannot be construed with a genitive. The combination "Jehovah Zebaoth" is rather to be taken as an ellipsis, where the general term Elohe (God of), which is implied in the word *Jehovah*, is to be supplied in thought (see Hengstenberg, *Christol*. i. p. 375, English translation) ; for frequently as this expression occurs, especially in the case of the prophets, *Zebaoth* is never used alone in the Old Testament as one of the names of God. It is in the Septuagint that the word is first met with occasionally as a proper name (Σαβαώθ), viz. throughout the whole of the first book of Samuel, very frequently in Isaiah, and also in Zech. xiii. 2. In other passages, the word is translated either κύριος, or θεὸς τῶν δυνάμεων, or παντοκράτωρ ; whilst the other Greek versions use the more definite phrase κύριος στρατιῶν instead.

This expression, which was not used as a divine name until the age of Samuel, had its roots in Gen. ii. 1, although the title itself was unknown in the Mosaic period, and during the times of the judges (see p. 7). It represented Jehovah as ruler over the heavenly hosts (*i.e.* the angels, according to Gen. xxxii. 2, and the stars, according to Isa. xl. 26), who are called the "armies" of Jehovah in Ps. ciii. 21, cxlviii. 2 ; but we are not to understand it as implying that the stars were supposed to be inhabited by angels, as Gesenius (*Thes. s. v.*) maintains, since there is not the slightest trace of any such notion in the whole of the Old Testament. It is simply applied to Jehovah as the God of the universe, who governs all the powers of heaven, both visible and invisible, as He rules in heaven and on earth. It cannot even be proved that the epithet Lord, or God of Zebaoth, refers chiefly and generally to the sun, moon, and stars, on account of their being so peculiarly adapted, through their visible splendour, to keep alive the consciousness of the omnipotence and glory of God (Hengstenberg on Ps. xxiv. 10). For even though the expression צְבָאָם (their host), in Gen. ii. 1, refers to the heavens only, since it is only to the heavens (*vid.* Isa. xl. 26), and never to the earth, that a "host" is ascribed, and in this particular passage it is probably only the stars that are to be thought of, the creation of which had already been mentioned in Gen. i. 14 sqq.; yet we find the idea of an army of angels introduced in the history of Jacob (Gen. xxxii. 2, 3), where Jacob calls the angels of God who appeared to him the "camp of God," and also in the blessing of Moses (Deut. xxxiii. 2), where the "ten thousands of saints" (*Kodesh*) are not stars, but angels, or heavenly spirits; whereas the fighting of the stars against Sisera in the song of Deborah probably refers to a natural phenomenon, by which God had thrown the enemy into confusion, and smitten them before the Israelites (see at Judg. v. 20). We must also bear in mind, that whilst on the one hand the tribes of Israel, as they came out of Egypt, are called Zebaoth Jehovah, "the hosts of Jehovah" (Ex. vii. 4, xii. 41), on the other hand the angel of the Lord, when appearing in front of Jericho in the form of a warrior, made himself known to Joshua as "the prince of the army of Jehovah," *i.e.* of the angelic hosts. And it is in this appearance of the heavenly leader of the people of God to the earthly leader of the hosts of Israel, as the prince of the angelic hosts, not only promising him the conquest of Jericho, but through the miraculous overthrow of the walls of this strong bulwark of the Canaanitish power, actually giving him at the same time a practical proof that the prince of the angelic hosts was fighting for Israel, that we have the material basis upon which the divine epithet " Jehovah God of hosts" was founded, even though it was not introduced immediately, but only at a later period, when the Lord began to form His people Israel into a kingdom, by which all the kingdoms of the heathen were to be overcome. It is certainly not without significance that this title is given to God for the first time in these books, which contain an account of the founding of the kingdom, and (as Auberlen has observed) that it was by Samuel's mother, the pious Hannah, when dedicating her son to the Lord, and prophesying of the king and anointed of the Lord in her song of praise (ch. ii. 10), that this name was employed for the first time, and that God was addressed in prayer as "Jehovah of hosts" (ver. 11). Consequently, if this name of God goes hand in hand with the prophetic announcement and the actual establishment of the monarchy in Israel, its origin cannot be attributed to any antagonism to Sabæism, or to the hostility of pious Israelites to the worship of the stars, which was gaining increasing ground in the age of David, as Hengstenberg (on Ps. xxiv. 10) and Strauss (on Zeph. ii. 9) maintain; to say nothing of the fact, that there is no historical foundation for such an assumption at all. It is a much more natural supposition, that when the invisible sovereignty of Jehovah received a visible manifestation in the establishment of the earthly monarchy, the sovereignty of Jehovah, if it did possess and was to possess any reality at all, necessarily claimed to be recognised in its all-embracing power and glory, and that in the title "God of (the heavenly) hosts" the fitting expression was formed for the universal government of the God-king of Israel,—a title which not only served as a bulwark against any eclipsing of the invisible sovereignty of God by the earthly monarchy in Israel, but overthrew the vain delusion of the heathen, that the God of Israel was simply the national deity of that particular nation.[1]

The remark introduced in ver. 3*b*, "*and there were the two sons of Eli, Hophni and Phinehas, priests of the Lord*," *i.e.* performing the duties of the priesthood, serves as a preparation for what follows. This reason for the remark sufficiently explains why the sons of Eli only are mentioned here, and not Eli himself, since, although the latter still presided over the sanctuary as high priest, he was too old to perform the duties connected with the offering of sacrifice. The addition made by the LXX., Ἠλὶ καὶ, is an arbitrary interpolation, occasioned by a misapprehension of the reason for mentioning the sons of Eli.—Vers. 4, 5. "*And it came to pass, the day, and he*

---

[1] This name of God was therefore held up before the people of the Lord even in their war-songs and pæans of victory, but still more by the prophets, as a banner under which Israel was to fight and to conquer the world. Ezekiel is the only prophet who does not use it, simply because he follows the Pentateuch so strictly in his style. And it is not met with in the book of Job, just because the theocratic constitution of the Israelitish nation is never referred to in the problem of that book.

offered sacrifice" (for, "on which he offered sacrifice"), that he gave to Peninnah and her children portions of the flesh of the sacrifice at the sacrificial meal; but to Hannah he gave מָנָה אַחַת אַפָּיִם, "*one portion for two persons*," *i.e.* a double portion, because he loved her, but Jehovah had shut up her womb: *i.e.* he gave it as an expression of his love to her, to indicate by a sign, "thou art as dear to me as if thou hadst born me a child" (O. v. Gerlach). This explanation of the difficult word אַפַּיִם, of which very different interpretations have been given, is the one adopted by Tanchum Hieros., and is the only one which can be grammatically sustained, or yields an appropriate sense. The meaning *face* (*facies*) is placed beyond all doubt by Gen. iii. 19 and other passages; and the use of לְאַפֵּי as a synonym for לִפְנֵי in ch. xxv. 23, also establishes the meaning "person," since פָּנִים is used in this sense in 2 Sam. xvii. 11. It is true that there are no other passages that can be adduced to prove that the singular אַף was also used in this sense; but as the word was employed promiscuously in both singular and plural in the derivative sense of anger, there is no reason for denying that the singular may also have been employed in the sense of *face* (πρόσωπον). The combination of אַפָּיִם with מָנָה אַחַת in the absolute state is supported by many other examples of the same kind (see Ewald, § 287, *h*). The meaning *double* has been correctly adopted in the Syriac, whereas Luther follows the *tristis* of the Vulgate, and renders the word *traurig*, or sad. But this meaning, which Fr. Böttcher has lately taken under his protection, cannot be philologically sustained either by the expression נָפְלוּ פָנֶיךָ (Gen. iv. 6), or by Dan. xi. 20, or in any other way. אַף and אַפַּיִם do indeed signify anger, but anger and sadness are two very different ideas. But when Böttcher substitutes "angrily or unwillingly" for sadly, the incongruity strikes you at once: "he gave her a portion unwillingly, because he loved her!" For the custom of singling out a person by giving double or even large portions, see the remarks on Gen. xliii. 34.—Ver. 6. "*And her adversary* (Peninnah) *also provoked her with provocation, to irritate her.*" The גַּם is placed before the noun belonging to the verb, to add force to the meaning. רָעַם (*Hiphil*), to excite, put into (inward) commotion, not exactly to make angry.—Ver. 7. "*So did he* (Elkanah) *from year to year* (namely give to Hannah a double portion at the sacrificial meal), *as often as she went up to the house of the Lord. So did she* (Peninnah) *provoke her* (Hannah), *so that she wept, and did not eat.*" The two מִן correspond to one another. Just as Elkanah showed his love to Hannah at every sacrificial festival, so did Peninnah repeat her provocation, the effect of which was that Hannah gave vent to her grief in tears, and did not eat.—Ver. 8. Elkanah sought to comfort her in her grief by the affectionate appeal: "*Am I not better to thee* (טוֹב, *i.e.* dearer) *than ten children?*" Ten is a round number for a large number.

Vers. 9-18. *Hannah's prayer for a son.*—Vers. 9-11. "*After the eating at Shiloh, and after the drinking,*" *i.e.* after the sacrificial meal was over, Hannah rose up with a troubled heart, to pour out her grief in prayer before God, whilst Eli was sitting before the door-posts of the palace of Jehovah, and vowed this vow: "*Lord of Zebaoth, if Thou regardest the distress of Thy maiden, and givest men's seed to Thy maiden, I will give him to the Lord all his life long, and no razor shall come upon his head.*" The choice of the infinitive absolute שָׁתֹה instead of the infinitive construct is analogous to the combination of two nouns, the first of which is defined by a suffix, and the second written absolutely (see *e.g.* עֳנִי וּמְרַת, Ex. xv. 2; cf. 2 Sam. xxiii. 5, and Ewald, § 339, *b*). The words from וְעֵלִי onwards to מָרַת נֶפֶשׁ form two circumstantial clauses inserted in the main sentence, to throw light upon the situation and the further progress of the affair. The tabernacle is called "*the palace of Jehovah*" (cf. ch. ii. 22), not on account of the magnificence and splendour of the building, but as the dwelling-place of Jehovah of hosts, the God-king of Israel, as in Ps. v. 8, etc. מְזוּזָה is probably a porch, which had been placed before the curtain that formed the entrance into the holy place, when the tabernacle was erected permanently at Shiloh. מָרַת נֶפֶשׁ, troubled in soul (cf. 2 Kings iv. 27). וּבָכֹה תִבְכֶּה is really subordinate to תִּתְפַּלֵּל, in the sense of "weeping much during her prayer." The depth of her trouble was also manifest in the crowding together of the words in which she poured out the desire of her heart before God: "*If Thou wilt look upon the distress of Thine handmaid, and remember and not forget,*" etc. "*Men's seed*" (*semen virorum*), *i.e.* a male child. אֲנָשִׁים

is the plural of אִישׁ, a man (see Ewald, § 186–7), from the root אוּשׁ, which combines the two ideas of fire, regarded as life, and giving life and firmness. The vow contained two points: (1) she would give the son she had prayed for to be the Lord's all the days of his life, *i.e.* would dedicate him to the Lord for a lifelong service, which, as we have already observed at p. 18, the Levites as such were not bound to perform; and (2) no razor should come upon his head, by which he was set apart as a Nazarite for his whole life (see at Num. vi. 2 sqq., and Judg. xiii. 5). The Nazarite, again, was neither bound to perform a lifelong service nor to remain constantly at the sanctuary, but was simply consecrated for a certain time, whilst the sacrifice offered at his release from the vow shadowed forth a complete surrender to the Lord. The second point, therefore, added a new condition to the first, and one which was not necessarily connected with it, but which first gave the true consecration to the service of the Lord at the sanctuary. At the same time, the qualification of Samuel for priestly functions, such as the offering of sacrifice, can neither be deduced from the first point in the vow, nor yet from the second. If, therefore, at a later period, when the Lord had called him to be a prophet, and had thereby placed him at the head of the nation, Samuel officiated at the presentation of sacrifice, he was not qualified to perform this service either as a Levite or as a lifelong Nazarite, but performed it solely by virtue of his prophetic calling.—Vers. 12–14. But when Hannah prayed much (*i.e.* a long time) before the Lord, and Eli noticed her mouth, and, as she was praying inwardly, only saw her lips move, but did not hear her voice, he thought she was drunken, and called out to her: "*How long dost thou show thyself drunken? put away thy wine from thee*," *i.e.* go away and sleep off thine intoxication (cf. ch. xxv. 37). מְדַבֶּרֶת עַל לִבָּהּ, *lit.* speaking to her heart. עַל is not to be confounded with אֶל (Gen. xxiv. 45), but has the subordinate idea of a comforting address, as in Gen. xxxiv. 3, etc.— Vers. 15, 16. Hannah answered: "*No, my lord, I am a woman of an oppressed spirit. I have not drunk wine and strong drink, but have poured out my soul before the Lord* (see Ps. xlii. 5). *Do not count thine handmaid for a worthless woman, for I have spoken hitherto out of great sighing and grief.*" נָתַן לִפְנֵי, to set or lay before a person, *i.e.* generally to give a person up to another; here to place him in thought in the position of another, *i.e.* to take him for another. שִׂיחַ, meditation, inward movement of the heart, sighing.—Ver. 17. Eli then replied : *"Go in peace, and the God of Israel give* (grant) *thy request* (שֵׁלָתֵךְ for שְׁאֵלָתֵךְ), *which thou hast asked of Him."* This word of the high priest was not a prediction, but a pious wish, which God in His grace most gloriously fulfilled.—Ver. 18. Hannah then went her way, saying, *"Let thine handmaid find grace in thine eyes,"* *i.e.* let me be honoured with thy favour and thine intercession, and was strengthened and comforted by the word of the high priest, which assured her that her prayer would be heard by God; and she did eat, *"and her countenance was no more,"* *sc.* troubled and sad, as it had been before. This may be readily supplied from the context, through which the word countenance (פָּנִים) acquires the sense of a troubled countenance, as in Job ix. 27.

Vers. 19–28. *Samuel's birth, and dedication to the Lord.*— Vers. 19, 20. The next morning Elkanah returned home to Ramah (see at ver. 1) with his two wives, having first of all worshipped before the Lord; after which he knew his wife Hannah, and Jehovah remembered her, *i.e.* heard her prayer. *"In the revolution of the days,"* *i.e.* of the period of her conception and pregnancy, Hannah conceived and bare a son, whom she called Samuel; *"for* (she said) *I have asked him of the Lord."* The name שְׁמוּאֵל (Σαμουήλ, LXX.) is not formed from שֵׁם=שְׁמוֹ and אֵל, name of God (Ges. *Thes.* p. 1434), but from שְׁמוּעַ אֵל, *heard of God, a Deo exauditus,* with an elision of the ע (see Ewald, § 275, *a,* Not. 2); and the words *"because I have asked him of the Lord"* are not an etymological explanation of the name, but an exposition founded upon the facts. Because Hannah had asked him of Jehovah, she gave him the name, *"the God-he d,"* as a memorial of the hearing of her prayer.— Vers. 21, 22. When Elkanah went up again with his family to Shiloh, to present his yearly sacrifice and his vow to the Lord, Hannah said to her husband that she would not go up till she had weaned the boy, and could present him to the Lord, that he might remain there for ever. זֶבַח הַיָּמִים, the sacrifice of the days, *i.e.* which he was accustomed to offer on the days when he went up to the sanctuary; really, therefore, the annual sacrifice. It follows from the expression *"and his vow,"* that Elkanah had also vowed a vow to the Lord, in case the beloved Hannah should have a son. The vow referred to the presentation of a sacrifice. And this explains the combination of אֶת־נִדְרוֹ with לְזָבֹחַ.[1] Weaning took place very late among the Israelites. According to 2 Macc. vii. 28, the Hebrew mothers were in the habit of suckling their children for three years. When the weaning had taken place, Hannah would bring her son up to the sanctuary, to appear before the face of the Lord, and remain there for ever, *i.e.* his whole life long. The Levites generally were only required to perform service at the sanctuary from their twenty-fifth to their fiftieth year (Num. viii. 24, 25), but Samuel was to be presented to the Lord immediately after his weaning had taken place, and to remain at the sanctuary for ever, *i.e.* to belong entirely to the Lord. To this end he was to receive his training at the sanctuary, that at the very earliest waking up of his spiritual susceptibilities he might receive the impressions of the sacred presence of God. There is no necessity, therefore, to understand the word גָּמַל (wean) as including what followed the weaning, namely, the training of the child up to

---

[1] The LXX. add to τὰς εὐχὰς αὐτοῦ the clause καὶ πάσας τὰς δεκάτας τῆς γῆς αὐτοῦ ("and all the tithes of his land"). This addition is just as arbitrary as the alteration of the singular נִדְרוֹ into the plural τὰς εὐχὰς αὐτοῦ. The translator overlooked the special reference of the word נִדְרוֹ to the child desired by Elkanah, and imagined—probably with Deut. xii. 26, 27 in his mind, where vows are ordered to be paid at the sanctuary in connection with slain offerings and sacrificial meals—that when Elkanah made his annual journey to the tabernacle he would discharge all his obligations to God, and consequently would pay his tithes. The genuineness of this additional clause cannot be sustained by an appeal to Josephus (*Ant.* v. 10, 3), who also has δεκάτας τε ἔφερον, for Josephus wrote his work upon the basis of the Alexandrian version. This statement of Josephus is only worthy of notice, inasmuch as it proves the incorrectness of the conjecture of Thenius, that the allusion to the tithes was intentionally dropped out of the Hebrew text by copyists, who regarded Samuel's Levitical descent as clearly established by 1 Chron. vi. 7-13 and 19-21. For Josephus (*l. c.* § 2) expressly describes Elkanah as a Levite, and takes no offence at the offering of tithes attributed to him in the Septuagint, simply because he was well acquainted with the law, and knew that the Levites had to pay to the priests a tenth of the tithes that they received from the other tribes, as a heave-offering of Jehovah (Num. xviii. 26 sqq.; cf. Neh. x. 38). Consequently the presentation of tithe on the part of Elkanah, if it were really well founded in the biblical text, would not furnish any argument against his Levitical descent.

his thirteenth year (Seb. Schmidt), on the ground that a child of three years old could only have been a burden to Eli : for the word never has this meaning, not even in 1 Kings xi. 20 ; and, as O. v. Gerlach has observed, his earliest training might have been superintended by one of the women who worshipped at the door of the tabernacle (ch. ii. 22).—Ver. 23. Elkanah expressed his approval of Hannah's decision, and added, "*only the Lord establish His word*," *i.e.* fulfil it. By "His word" we are not to understand some direct revelation from God respecting the birth and destination of Samuel, as the Rabbins suppose, but in all probability the word of Eli the high priest to Hannah, "The God of Israel grant thy petition" (ver. 17), which might be regarded by the parents of Samuel after his birth as a promise from Jehovah himself, and therefore might naturally excite the wish and suggest the prayer that the Lord would graciously fulfil the further hopes, which the parents cherished in relation to the son whom they had dedicated to the Lord by a vow. The paraphrase of דְּבָרוֹ in the rendering given by the LXX., τὸ ἐξελθὸν ἐκ τοῦ στόματός σου, is the subjective view of the translator himself, and does not warrant an emendation of the original text.—Vers. 24, 25. As soon as the boy was weaned, Hannah brought him, although still a נַעַר, *i.e.* a tender boy, to Shiloh, with a sacrifice of three oxen, an ephah of meal, and a pitcher of wine, and gave him up to Eli when the ox (bullock) had been slain, *i.e.* offered in sacrifice as a burnt-offering. The striking circumstance that, according to ver. 24, Samuel's parents brought three oxen with them to Shiloh, and yet in ver. 25 the ox (הַפָּר) alone is spoken of as being slain (or sacrificed), may be explained very simply on the supposition that in ver. 25 that particular sacrifice is referred to, which was associated with the presentation of the boy, that is to say, the burnt-offering by virtue of which the boy was consecrated to the Lord as a spiritual sacrifice for a lifelong service at His sanctuary, whereas the other two oxen served as the yearly festal offering, *i.e.* the burnt-offerings and thank-offerings which Elkanah pre sented year by year, and the presentation of which the writer did not think it needful to mention, simply because it followed partly from ver. 3 and partly from the Mosaic law.[1]—Vers.

---

[1] The interpretation of בְּפָרִים שְׁלֹשָׁה by ἐν μόσχῳ τριετίζοντι (LXX.), upon which Thenius would found an alteration of the text, is proved to be

26-28. When the boy was presented, his mother made herself known to the high priest as the woman who had previously prayed to the Lord at that place (see vers. 11 sqq.), and said, "*For this child I prayed; and the Lord hath granted me my request which I asked of Him: therefore I also make him one asked of the Lord all the days that he liveth; he is asked of the Lord.*" וְגַם אָנֹכִי: *I also; et ego vicissim* (Cler.). הִשְׁאִיל, to let a person ask, to grant his request, to give him what he asks (Ex. xii. 36), signifies here to make a person "asked" (שָׁאוּל). The meaning to lend, which the lexicons give to the word both here and Ex. xii. 36, has no other support than the false rendering of the LXX., and is altogether unsuitable both in the one and the other. Jehovah had not *lent* the son to Hannah, but had *given* him (see ver. 11); still less could a man *lend* his son to the Lord. The last clause of ver. 28, "*and he worshipped the Lord there,*" refers to Elkanah, *qui in votum Hannæ consenserat*, and not to Samuel. On a superficial glance, the plural יִשְׁתַּחֲווּ, which is found in some Codd., and in the Vulgate, Syriac, and Arabic, appears the more suitable; but when we look more closely at the connection in which the clause stands, we see at once that it does not wind up the foregoing account, but simply introduces the closing act of the transference of Samuel. Consequently the singular is perfectly appropriate; and notwithstanding the fact that the subject is not mentioned, the allusion to Samuel is placed beyond all doubt. When Hannah had given up her son to the high priest, his father Elkanah first of all worshipped before the Lord in the sanctuary, and then Hannah worshipped in the song of praise, which follows in ch. ii. 1-10.

both arbitrary and wrong by the fact that the translators themselves afterwards mention the θυσία, which Elkanah brought year by year, and the μόσχος, and consequently represent him as offering at least two animals, in direct opposition to the μόσχῳ τριετίζοντι. This discrepancy cannot be removed by the assertion that in ver. 24 the sacrificial animal intended for the dedication of the boy is the only one mentioned; and the presentation of the regular festal sacrifice is taken for granted, for an ephah of meal would not be the proper quantity to be offered in connection with a single ox, since, according to the law in Num. xv. 8, 9, only three-tenths of an ephah of meal were required when an ox was presented as a burnt-offering or slain offering. The presentation of an ephah of meal presupposes the offering of three oxen, and therefore shows that in ver. 24 the materials are mentioned for all the sacrifices that Elkanah was about to offer.

Chap. ii. 1-10. *Hannah's song of praise.*—The prayer in which Hannah poured out the feelings of her heart, after the dedication of her son to the Lord, is a song of praise of a prophetic and Messianic character. After giving utterance in the introduction to the rejoicing and exulting of her soul at the salvation that had reached her (ver. 1), she praises the Lord as the only holy One, the only rock of the righteous, who rules on earth with omniscience and righteousness, brings down the proud and lofty, kills and makes alive, maketh poor and maketh rich (vers. 2-8). She then closes with the confident assurance that He will keep His saints, and cast down the rebellious, and will judge the ends of the earth, and exalt the power of His king (vers. 9, 10).

This psalm is the mature fruit of the Spirit of God. The pious woman, who had gone with all the earnest longings of a mother's heart to pray to the Lord God of Israel for a son, that she might consecrate him to the lifelong service of the Lord, "discerned in her own individual experience the general laws of the divine economy, and its signification in relation to the whole history of the kingdom of God" (Auberlen, p. 564). The experience which she, bowed down and oppressed as she was, had had of the gracious government of the omniscient and holy covenant God, was a pledge to her of the gracious way in which the nation itself was led by God, and a sign by which she discerned how God not only delivered at all times the poor and wretched who trusted in Him out of their poverty and distress, and set them up, but would also lift up and glorify His whole nation, which was at that time so deeply bowed down and oppressed by its foes. Acquainted as she was with the destination of Israel to be a *kingdom*, from the promises which God had given to the patriarchs, and filled as she was with the longing that had been awakened in the nation for the realization of these promises, she could see in spirit, and through the inspiration of God, the *king* whom the Lord was about to give to His people, and through whom He would raise it up to might and dominion.

The refusal of modern critics to admit the genuineness of this song is founded upon an *a priori* and utter denial of the supernatural saving revelations of God, and upon a consequent inability to discern the prophetic illumination of the pious

Hannah, and a complete misinterpretation of the contents of her song of praise. The "proud and lofty," whom God humbles and casts down, are not the heathen or the national foes of Israel, and the "poor and wretched" whom He exalts and makes rich are not the Israelites as such; but the former are the *ungodly*, and the latter the *pious*, in Israel itself. And the description is so well sustained throughout, that it is only by the most arbitrary criticism that it can be interpreted as referring to definite historical events, such as the victory of David over Goliath (Thenius), or a victory of the Israelites over heathen nations (Ewald and others). Still less can any argument be drawn from the words of the song in support of its later origin, or its composition by David or one of the earliest of the kings of Israel. On the contrary, not only is its genuineness supported by the general consideration that the author of these books would never have ascribed a song to Hannah, if he had not found it in the sources he employed; but still more decisively by the circumstance that the songs of praise of Mary and Zechariah, in Luke i. 46 sqq. and 68 sqq., show, through the manner in which they rest upon this ode, in what way it was understood by the pious Israelites of every age, and how, like the pious Hannah, they recognised and praised in their own individual experience the government of the holy God in the midst of His kingdom.

The first verse forms the introduction to the song. Holy joy in the Lord at the blessing which she had received impelled the favoured mother to the praise of God:

> Ver. 1. My heart is joyful in the Lord,
> My horn is exalted in the Lord,
> My mouth is opened wide over mine enemies:
> For I rejoice in Thy salvation.

Of the four members of this verse, the first answers to the third, and the second to the fourth. The heart rejoices at the lifting up of her horn, the mouth opens wide to proclaim the salvation before which the enemies would be dumb. "*My horn is high*" does not mean 'I am proud' (Ewald), but "my power is great in the Lord." The horn is the symbol of strength, and is taken from oxen whose strength is in their horns (*vid.* Deut. xxxiii. 17; Ps. lxxv. 5, etc.). The power was high or exalted by the salvation which the Lord had manifested to her. To Him all the glory was due, because He had proved himself to be the holy One, and a rock upon which a man could rest his confidence.

> Ver. 2. None is holy as the Lord; for there is none beside Thee;
> And no rock is as our God.
> 3. Speak ye not much lofty, lofty;
> Let (not) insolence go out of thy mouth!
> For the Lord is an omniscient God,
> And with Him deeds are weighed.

God manifests himself as holy in the government of the kingdom of His grace by His guidance of the righteous to salvation (see at Ex. xix. 6). But holiness is simply the moral reflection of the glory of the one absolute God. This explains the reason given for His holiness, viz. "there is not one (a God) beside thee" (cf. 2 Sam. xxii. 32). As the holy and only One, God is the rock (vid. Deut. xxxii. 4, 15; Ps. xviii. 3) in which the righteous can always trust. The wicked therefore should tremble before His holiness, and not talk in their pride of the *lofty* things which they have accomplished or intend to perform. גְּבֹהָה is defined more precisely in the following clause, which is also dependent upon אַל by the word עָתָק, as insolent words spoken by the wicked against the righteous (see Ps. xxxi. 19). For Jehovah hears such words; He is "*a God of knowledge*" (*Deus scientiarum*), a God who sees and knows every single thing. The plural דֵעוֹת has an intensive signification. לֹא נִתְכְּנוּ עֲלִלוֹת might be rendered "deeds are not weighed, or equal" (cf. Ezek. xviii. 25, 26, xxxiii. 17). But this would only apply to the actions of men; for the acts of God are always just, or weighed. But an assertion respecting the actions of men does not suit the context. Hence this clause is reckoned in the Masora as one of the passages in which לֹא stands for לוֹ (see at Ex. xxi. 8). "*To Him* (with Him) *deeds are weighed:*" that is to say, the acts of God are weighed, *i.e.* equal or just. This is the real meaning according to the passages in Ezekiel, and not " the actions of men are weighed by Him" (De Wette, Maurer, Ewald, etc.): for God weighs the minds and hearts of men (Prov. xvi. 2, xxi. 2, xxiv. 12), not their actions. This expression never occurs. The weighed or righteous acts of God are described in vers. 4–8 in great and general traits, as displayed in the government of His kingdom through the marvellous changes which occur in the circumstances connected with the lives of the righteous and the wicked.

Ver. 4. Bow-heroes are confounded,
And stumbling ones gird themselves with strength;

5. Full ones hire themselves out for bread,
And hungry ones cease to be.
Yea, the barren beareth seven (children),
And she that is rich in children pines away.

6. The Lord kills and makes alive;
Leads down into hell, and leads up.

7. The Lord makes poor and makes rich,
Humbles and also exalts.

8. He raises mean ones out of the dust,
He lifts up poor ones out of the dunghill,
To set them beside the noble;
And He apportions to them the seat of glory:
For the pillars of the earth are the Lord's,
And He sets the earth upon them.

In ver. 4, the predicate חַתִּים is construed with the *nomen rectum* גִּבֹּרִים, not with the *nomen regens* קֶשֶׁת, because the former is the leading term (*vid.* Ges. § 148, 1, and Ewald, § 317, *d*). The thought to be expressed is, not that the bow itself is to be broken, but that the heroes who carry the bow are to be confounded or broken inwardly. "*Bows of the heroes*" stands for heroes carrying bows. For this reason the verb is to be taken in the sense of confounded, not broken, especially as, apart from Isa. li. 56, חָתַת is not used to denote the breaking of outward things, but the breaking of men.—Ver. 5. שְׂבֵעִים are the rich and well to do; these would become so poor as to be obliged to hire themselves out for bread. חָדֵל, to cease to be what they were before. The use of עַד as a conjunction, in the sense of "yea" or "in fact," may be explained as an elliptical expression, signifying "it comes to this, that." "*Seven children*" are mentioned as the full number of the divine blessing in children (see Ruth iv. 15). "The mother of many children" pines away, because she has lost all her sons, and with them her support in her old age (see Jer. xv. 9). This comes from the Lord, who kills, etc. (cf. Deut. xxxii. 39). The words of ver. 6 are figurative. God hurls down into death and the danger of death, and also rescues therefrom (see Ps. xxx. 3, 4).

The first three clauses of ver. 8 are repeated *verbatim* in Ps. cxiii. 7, 8. *Dust* and the *dunghill* are figures used to denote the deepest degradation and ignominy. The antithesis to this is, sitting upon the chair or throne of glory, the seat occupied by noble princes. The Lord does all this, for He is the creator and upholder of the world. *The pillars* (מְצֻקֵי, from צוּק = יָצַק) *of the earth are the Lord's;* i.e. they were created or set up by Him, and by Him they are sustained. Now as Jehovah, the God of Israel, the Holy One, governs the world with His almighty power, the righteous have nothing to fear. With this thought the last strophe of the song begins:

Ver. 9. The feet of His saints He will keep,
And the wicked perish in darkness;
For by power no one becomes strong.

10. The Lord—those who contend against Him are confounded.
He thunders above him in the heavens;
The Lord will judge the ends of the earth,
That He may lend might to His king,
And exalt the horn of His anointed.

The Lord keeps the feet of the righteous, so that they do not tremble and stumble, *i.e.* so that the righteous do not fall into adversity and perish therein (*vid.* Ps. lvi. 14, cxvi. 8, cxxi. 3). But the wicked, who oppress and persecute the righteous, will perish in darkness, *i.e.* in adversity, when God withdraws the light of His grace, so that they fall into distress and calamity. For no man can be strong through his own power, so as to meet the storms of life. All who fight against the Lord are destroyed. To bring out the antithesis between man and God, "Jehovah" is written absolutely at the commencement of the sentence in ver. 10: "*As for Jehovah, those who contend against Him are broken,*" both inwardly and outwardly (יֵחַתּוּ, as in ver. 4). The word עָלָיו, which follows, is not to be changed into עֲלֵיהֶם. There is simply a rapid alternation of the numbers, such as we frequently meet with in excited language. "*Above him,*" *i.e.* above every one who contends against God, He thunders. Thunder is a premonitory sign of the approach of the Lord to judgment. In the thunder, man is made to feel in an alarming way the presence of the omnipotent God. In the words, "*The Lord will judge the ends of the earth,*" *i.e.* the earth to its utmost extremities, or the whole world, Hannah's prayer rises up to a prophetic glance at the consummation of the kingdom of God. As certainly as the Lord God keeps the righteous at all times, and casts down the wicked, so certainly will He judge the whole world, to hurl down all His foes, and perfect His kingdom which He has founded in Israel. And as every kingdom culminates in its throne, or in the full might and government of a king, so the kingdom of God can only attain its full perfection in the king whom the Lord will give to His people, and endow with His might. *The king*, or the *anointed of the Lord*, of whom Hannah prophesies in the spirit, is not one single king of Israel, either David or Christ, but an ideal king, though not a mere personification of the throne about to be established, but the actual king whom Israel received in David and his race, which culminated in the Messiah. The exaltation of the horn of the anointed of Jehovah commenced with the victorious and splendid expansion of the power of David, was repeated with every victory over the enemies of God and His kingdom gained by the successive kings of David's house, goes on in the advancing spread of the kingdom of Christ, and will eventually attain to its eternal consummation in the judgment of the last day, through which all the enemies of Christ will be made His footstool.

SAMUEL'S SERVICE BEFORE ELI. UNGODLINESS OF ELI'S SONS. DENUNCIATION OF JUDGMENT UPON ELI AND HIS HOUSE. —CHAP. II. 11-36.

Vers. 11-17. *Samuel the servant of the Lord under Eli. Ungodliness of the sons of Eli.*—Ver. 11 forms the transition to what follows. After Hannah's psalm of thanksgiving, Elkanah went back with his family to his home at Ramah, and the boy (Samuel) was serving, *i.e.* ministered to the Lord, in the presence of Eli the priest. The fact that nothing is said about Elkanah's wives going with him, does not warrant the interpretation given by Thenius, that Elkanah went home alone. It was taken for granted that his wives went with him, according to ch. i. 21 (" all his house"). שָׁרֵת אֶת־יְהוָֹה, which signifies literally, both here and in ch. iii. 1, to serve the Lord, and which is used interchangeably with שָׁרֵת אֶת־פְּנֵי יי (ver. 18), to serve in the presence of the Lord, is used to denote the duties performed both by priests and Levites in connection with the worship of God, in which Samuel took part, as he grew up, under the superintendence of Eli and according to his instructions.—Ver. 12. But Eli's sons, Hophni and Phinehas (ver. 34), were בְּנֵי בְלִיָּעַל, *worthless fellows, and knew not the Lord*, sc. as He should be known, *i.e.* did not fear Him, or trouble themselves about Him (*vid.* Job xviii. 21 ; Hos. viii. 2, xiii. 4).— Vers. 13, 14. *"And the right of the priests towards the people was* (the following)." *Mishpat* signifies the right which they had usurped to themselves in relation to the people. *"If any one brought a sacrifice* (כָּל־אִישׁ זֹבֵחַ זֶבַח is placed first, and construed absolutely : ' as for every one who brought a slain-offering'), *the priest's servant* (*lit.* young man) *came while the flesh was boiling, with a three-pronged fork in his hand, and thrust into the kettle, or pot, or bowl, or saucepan. All that the fork brought up the priest took. This they did to all the Israelites who came thither to Shiloh."*—Vers. 15, 16. They did still worse. *" Even before the fat was consumed,"* i.e. before the fat portions of the sacrifice had been placed in the altar-fire for the Lord (Lev. iii. 3–5), the priest's servant came and demanded flesh of the person sacrificing, to be roasted for the priest; *" for he will not take boiled flesh of thee, but only* חַי, *raw, i.e.* fresh meat." And if the person sacrificing replied, *" They will burn the fat directly* (*lit.* ' at this time,' as in Gen. xxv. 31, 1 Kings xxii. 5), *then take for thyself, as thy soul desireth,"* he said, *" No* (לוֹ for לֹא), *but thou shalt give now ; if not, I take by force."* These abuses were practised by the priests in connection with the thank-offerings, with which a sacrificial meal was associated. Of these offerings, the portion which legally fell to the priest as his share was the heave-leg and wave-breast. And this he was to receive after the fat portions of the sacrifice had been burned upon the altar (see Lev. vii. 30–34). To take the flesh of the sacrificial animal and roast it before this offering had been made, was a crime which was equivalent to a robbery of God, and is therefore referred to here with the emphatic particle גַּם, as being the worst crime that the sons of Eli committed. Moreover, the priests could not claim any of the flesh which the offerer of the sacrifice boiled for the sacrificial meal, after burning the fat portions upon the altar and giving up the portions which belonged to them, to say nothing of their taking it forcibly out of the pots while it was being boiled.—Ver. 17. Such conduct as this on the part of the young men (the priests' servants), was a great sin in the sight of the Lord, as they thereby brought the sacrifice of the Lord into contempt. נִאֵץ, causative, to bring into contempt, furnish occasion for blaspheming (as in 2 Sam. xii. 14). "The robbery which they committed was a small sin in comparison with the contempt of the sacrifices themselves, which they were the means of spreading among the people" (O. v. Gerlach). *Minchah* does not refer here to the meat-offering as the accompaniment to the slain-offerings, but to the sacrificial offering generally, as a gift presented for the Lord.

Vers. 18–21. *Samuel's service before the Lord.*—Ver. 18. Samuel served as a boy before the Lord by the side of the worthless sons of Eli, girt with an ephod of white material (בַּד, see at Ex. xxviii. 42). The ephod was a shoulder-dress, no doubt resembling the high priest's in shape (see Ex. xxviii. 6 sqq.), but altogether different in the material of which it was made, viz. simple white cloth, like the other articles of clothing that were worn by the priests. At that time, according to ch. xxii. 18, all the priests wore clothing of this kind; and, according to 2 Sam. vi. 14, David did the same on the occasion of a religious festival. Samuel received a dress of this kind even when a boy, because he was set apart to a lifelong service before the Lord. חָגוּר is the technical expression for putting on the ephod, because the two pieces of which it was composed were girt round the body with a girdle.—Ver. 19. The small מְעִיל also (*Angl.* "coat"), which Samuel's mother made and brought him every year, when she came with her husband to Shiloh to the yearly sacrifice, was probably a coat resembling the *meïl* of the high priest (Ex. xxviii. 31 sqq.), but was made of course of some simpler material, and without the symbolical ornaments attached to the lower hem, by which that official dress was distinguished.—Ver. 20. The priestly clothing of the youthful Samuel was in harmony with the spiritual relation in which he stood to the high priest and to Jehovah. Eli blessed his parents for having given up the boy to the Lord, and expressed this wish to the father: "*The Lord lend thee seed of this woman in the place of the one asked for* (הַשְּׁאֵלָה), *whom they* (one) *asked for from the Lord.*" The striking use of the third pers. masc. שָׁאַל instead of the second singular or plural may be accounted for on the supposition that it is an indefinite form of speech, which the writer chose because, although it was Hannah who prayed to the Lord for Samuel in the sight of Eli, yet Eli might assume that the father, Elkanah, had shared the wishes of his pious wife. The apparent harshness disappears at once if we substitute the passive; whereas in Hebrew active constructions were always preferred to passive, wherever it was possible to employ them (Ewald, § 294, b). The singular suffix attached to לִמְקוֹמוֹ after the plural הָלְכוּ may be explained on the simple ground, that a dwelling-place is determined by the husband, or master of the house.—Ver. 21. The particle כִּי, "*for*" (Jehovah visited), does not mean *if*, *as*, or *when*, nor is it to be regarded as a copyist's error. It is only necessary to supply the thought contained in the words, "*Eli blessed Elkanah*," viz. that Eli's blessing was not an empty fruitless wish; and to understand the passage in some such way as this: Eli's word was fulfilled, or still more simply, *they went to their home blessed;* for *Jehovah visited Hannah*, blessed her with "*three sons and two daughters; but the boy Samuel grew up with the Lord*," i.e. near to Him (at the sanctuary), and under His protection and blessing.

Vers. 22–26. *Eli's treatment of the sins of his sons.*—Ver. 22. The aged Eli reproved his sons with solemn warnings on account of their sins; but without his warnings being listened to. From the reproof itself we learn, that beside the sin noticed in vers. 12–17, they also committed the crime of lying with the women who served at the tabernacle (see at Ex. xxxviii. 8), and thus profaned the sanctuary with whoredom. But Eli, with the infirmities of his old age, did nothing further to prevent these abominations than to say to his sons, "*Why do ye according to the sayings which I hear, sayings about you which are evil, of this whole people.*" אֶת־דִּבְרֵיכֶם רָעִים is inserted to make the meaning clearer, and מֵאֵת כָּל־ה' is dependent upon שֹׁמֵעַ. "*This whole people*" signifies all the people that came to Shiloh, and heard and saw the wicked doings there.—Ver. 24. אַל בָּנַי, "*not, my sons*," i.e. do not such things, "*for the report which I hear is not good; they make the people of Jehovah to transgress.*" מַעֲבִרִים is written without the pronoun אַתֶּם in an indefinite construction, like מִשְׁלְחִים in ch. vi. 3 (Maurer). Ewald's rendering as given by Thenius, "The report which I hear the people of God bring," is just as inadmissible as the one proposed by Böttcher, "The report which, as I hear, the people of God are spreading." The assertion made by Thenius, that הֶעֱבִיר, without any further definition, cannot mean to cause to sin or transgress, is correct enough no doubt; but it does not prove that this meaning is inadmissible in the passage before us, since the further definition is actually to be found in the context.—Ver. 25. "*If man sins against man, God judges him; but if a man sins against Jehovah, who can interpose with entreaty for him?*" In the use of פִלֵּל and יִתְפַּלֶּל־לוֹ there is a paronomasia which cannot be reproduced in our language. פִלֵּל signifies to decide or pass sentence (Gen. xlviii. 11), then to arbitrate, to settle a dispute as arbitrator (Ezek. xvi. 52, Ps. cvi. 30), and in the *Hithpael* to act as mediator, hence to entreat. And these meanings are applicable here. In the case of one man's sin against another, God settles the dispute as arbitrator through the proper authorities; whereas, when a man sins against God, no one can interpose as arbitrator. Such a sin cannot be disposed of by intercession. But Eli's sons did not listen to this admonition, which was designed to reform daring sinners with mild words and representations; "*for,*" adds the historian, "*Jehovah was resolved to slay them.*" The father's reproof made no impression upon them, because they were already given up to the judgment of hardening. (On hardening as a divine sentence, see the discussions at Ex. iv. 21.)—Ver. 26. The youthful Samuel, on the other hand, continued to grow in stature, and in favour with God and man (see Lev. ii. 52).

Vers. 27–36. *Announcement of the judgment upon Eli and his house.*—Ver. 27. Before the Lord interposed in judgment, He sent a prophet (a "*man of God,*" as in Judg. xiii. 6) to the aged Eli, to announce as a warning for all ages the judgment which was about to fall upon the worthless priests of his house. In order to arouse Eli's own conscience, he had pointed out to him, on the one hand, the grace manifested in the choice of his father's house, *i.e.* the house of Aaron, to keep His sanctuary (vers. 27*b* and 28), and, on the other hand, the desecration of the sanctuary by the wickedness of his sons (ver. 29). Then follows the sentence: The choice of the family of Aaron still stood fast, but the deepest disgrace would come upon the despisers of the Lord (ver. 30): the strength of his house would be broken; all the members of his house were to die early deaths. They were not, however, to be removed entirely from service at the altar, but to their sorrow were to survive the fall of the sanctuary (vers. 31-34). But the Lord would raise up a faithful priest, and cause him to walk before His anointed, and from him all that were left of the house of Eli would be obliged to beg their bread (vers. 35, 36). To arrive at the true interpretation of this announcement of punishment, we must picture to ourselves the historical circumstances that come into consideration here. Eli the high priest was a descendant of Ithamar, the younger son of Aaron, as we may see from the fact that his great-grandson Ahimelech was "of the sons of Ithamar" (1 Chron. xxiv. 3). In perfect agreement with this, Josephus (*Ant.* v. 11, 5) relates, that after the high priest Ozi of the family of Eleazar, Eli of the family of Ithamar received the high-priesthood. The circumstances which led to the transfer of this honour from the line of Eleazar to that of Ithamar are unknown. We cannot imagine it to have been occasioned by an extinction of the line of Eleazar, for the simple reason that, in the time of David, Zadok the descendant of Eleazar is spoken of as high priest along with Abiathar and Ahimelech, the descendants of Eli (2 Sam. viii. 17, xx. 25). After the deposition of Abiathar he was reinstated by Solomon as sole high priest (1 Kings ii. 27), and the dignity was transmitted to his descendants. This fact also overthrows the conjecture of Clericus, that the transfer of the high-priesthood to Eli took place by the command of God on account of the grievous sins of the high priests of the line of Eleazar; for in that case Zadok would not have received this office again in connection with Abiathar. We have, no doubt, to search for the true reason in the circumstances of the times of the later judges, namely in the fact that at the death of the last high priest of the family of Eleazar before the time of Eli, the remaining son was not equal to the occasion, either because he was still an infant, or at any rate because he was too young and inexperienced, so that he could not enter upon the office, and Eli, who was probably related by marriage to the high priest's family, and was no doubt a vigorous man, was compelled to take the oversight of the congregation; and, together with the supreme administration of the affairs of the nation as judge, received the post of high priest as well, and filled it till the time of his death, simply because in those troublous times there was not one of the descendants of Eleazar who was able to fill the supreme office of judge, which was combined with that of high priest. For we cannot possibly think of an unjust usurpation of the office of high priest on the part of Eli, since the very judgment denounced against him and his house presupposes that he had entered upon the office in a just and upright way, and that the wickedness of his sons was all that was brought against him. For a considerable time after the death of Eli the high-priesthood lost almost all its significance. All Israel turned to Samuel, whom the Lord established as His prophet by means of revelations, and whom He also chose as the deliverer of His people. The tabernacle at Shiloh, which ceased to be the scene of the gracious presence of God after the loss of the ark, was probably presided over first of all after Eli's death by his grandson Ahitub, the son of Phinehas, as his successor in the high-priesthood. He was followed in the time of Saul by his son Ahijah or Ahimelech, who gave David the shew-bread to eat at Nob, to which the tabernacle had been removed in the meantime, and was put to death by Saul in consequence, along with all the priests who were found there. His son Abiathar, however, escaped the massacre, and fled to David (ch. xxii. 9–20, xxiii. 6). In the reign of David he is mentioned as high priest along with Zadok; but he was afterwards deposed by Solomon (2 Sam. xv. 24, xvii. 15, xix. 12, xx. 25; 1 Kings ii. 27).

Different interpretations have been given of these verses. The majority of commentators understand them as signifying that the loss of the high-priesthood is here foretold to Eli, and also the institution of Zadok in the office. But such a view is too contracted, and does not exhaust the meaning of the words. The very introduction to the prophet's words points to something greater than this: "*Thus saith the Lord, Did I reveal myself to thy father's house, when they were in Egypt at the house of Pharaoh?*" The ה interrogative is not used for הלא (*nonne*), but is emphatic, as in Jer. xxxi. 20. The question is an appeal to Eli's conscience, which he cannot deny, but is obliged to confirm. By Eli's father's house we are not to understand Ithamar and his family, but Aaron, from whom Eli was descended through Ithamar. God revealed himself to the tribe-father of Eli by appointing Aaron to be the spokesman of Moses before Pharaoh (Ex. iv. 14 sqq. and 27), and still more by calling Aaron to the priesthood, for which the way was prepared by the fact that, from the very beginning, God made use of Aaron, in company with Moses, to carry out His purpose of delivering Israel out of Egypt, and entrusted Moses and Aaron with the arrangements for the celebration of the passover (Ex. xii. 1, 43). This occurred when they, the fathers of Eli, Aaron and his sons, were still in Egypt at the house of Pharaoh, *i.e.* still under Pharaoh's rule.—Ver. 28. "*And did I choose him out of all the tribes for a priest to myself.*" The interrogative particle is not to be repeated before וּבָחוֹר, but the construction becomes affirmative with the inf. abs. instead of the perfect. "*Him*" refers back to "*thy father*" in ver. 27, and signifies Aaron. The expression "*for a priest*" is still further defined by the clauses which follow : לַעֲלוֹת עַל מ׳, "*to ascend upon mine altar,*" *i.e.* to approach my altar of burnt-offering and perform the sacrificial worship ; "*to kindle incense,*" *i.e.* to perform the service in the holy place, the principal feature in which was the daily kindling of the incense, which is mentioned *instar omnium;* "*to wear the ephod before me,*" *i.e.* to perform the service in the holy of holies, which the high priest could only enter when wearing the ephod to represent Israel before the Lord (Ex. xxviii. 12). "*And have given to thy father's house all the firings of the children of Israel*" (see at Lev. i. 9). These words are to be understood, according to Deut. xviii. 1, as signifying that the Lord had given to the house of Aaron, *i.e.* to the priesthood, the sacrifices of Jehovah to eat in the place of any inheritance in the land, according to the portions appointed in the sacrificial law in Lev. vi. vii., and Num. xviii.—Ver. 29. With such distinction conferred upon the priesthood, and such careful provision made for it, the conduct of the priests under Eli was an inexcusable crime. "*Why do ye tread with your feet my slain-offerings and meat-offerings, which I have commanded in the dwelling-place?*" Slain-offering and meat-offering are general expressions embracing all the altar-sacrifices. מָעוֹן is an accusative ("*in the dwelling*"), like בַּיִת, in the house. "*The dwelling*" is the tabernacle. This reproof applied to the priests generally, including

Eli, who had not vigorously resisted these abuses. The words which follow, "*and thou honourest thy sons more than me,*" relate to Eli himself, and any other high priest who like Eli should tolerate the abuses of the priests. "*To fatten yourselves with the first of every sacrificial gift of Israel, of my people.*" לְעַמִּי serves as a periphrasis for the genitive, and is chosen for the purpose of giving greater prominence to the idea of עַמִּי (my people). רֵאשִׁית, the first of every sacrificial gift (*minchah*, as in ver. 17), which Israel offered as the nation of Jehovah, ought to have been given up to its God in the altar-fire because it was the best; whereas, according to vers. 15, 16, the sons of Eli took away the best for themselves.—Ver. 30. For this reason, the saying of the Lord, "*Thy house* (*i.e.* the family of Eli) *and thy father's house* (Eli's relations in the other lines, *i.e.* the whole priesthood) *shall walk before me for ever*" (Num. xxv. 13), should henceforth run thus: "*This be far from me; but them that honour me I will honour, and they that despise me shall be despised.*" The first declaration of the Lord is not to be referred to Eli particularly, as it is by C. a Lapide and others, and understood as signifying that the high-priesthood was thereby transferred from the family of Eleazar to that of Ithamar, and promised to Eli for his descendants for all time. This is decidedly at variance with the fact, that although "walking before the Lord" is not a general expression denoting a pious walk with God, as in Gen. xvii. 1, but refers to the service of the priests at the sanctuary as walking before the face of God, yet it cannot possibly be specially and exclusively restricted to the right of entering the most holy place, which was the prerogative of the high priest alone. These words of the Lord, therefore, applied to the whole priesthood, or the whole house of Aaron, to which the priesthood had been promised, "*for a perpetual statute*" (Ex. xxix. 9). This promise was afterwards renewed to Phinehas especially, on account of the zeal which he displayed for the honour of Jehovah in connection with the idolatry of the people at Shittim (Num. xxv. 13). But even this renewed promise only secured to him an eternal *priesthood* as a covenant of peace with the Lord, and not specially the high-priesthood, although that was included as the culminating point of the priesthood. Consequently it was not abrogated by the temporary transfer of the high-priesthood from the descendants of Phinehas to the priestly line of Ithamar, because even then they still retained the priesthood. By the expression "*be it far from me,*" *sc.* to permit this to take place, God does not revoke His previous promise, but simply denounces a false trust therein as irreconcilable with His holiness. That promise would only be fulfilled so far as the priests themselves honoured the Lord in their office, whilst despisers of God, who dishonoured Him by sin and presumptuous wickedness, would be themselves despised.

This contempt would speedily come upon the house of Eli. —Ver. 31. "*Behold, days come,*"—a formula with which prophets were accustomed to announce future events (see 2 Kings xx. 17; Isa. xxxix. 6; Amos iv. 2, viii. 11, ix. 13; Jer. vii. 32, etc.),—"*then will I cut off thine arm, and the arm of thy father's house, that there shall be no old man in thine house.*" To cut off the arm means to destroy the strength either of a man or of a family (see Job xxii. 9; Ps. xxxvii. 17). The strength of a family, however, consists in the vital energy of its members, and shows itself in the fact that they reach a good old age, and do not pine away early and die. This strength was to vanish in Eli's house; no one would ever again preserve his life to old age.—Ver. 32. "*And thou wilt see oppression of the dwelling in all that He has shown of good to Israel.*" The meaning of these words, which have been explained in very different ways, appears to be the following: In all the benefits which the Lord would confer upon His people, Eli would see only distress for the dwelling of God, inasmuch as the tabernacle would fall more and more into decay. In the person of Eli, the high priest at that time, the high priest generally is addressed as the custodian of the sanctuary; so that what is said is not to be limited to him personally, but applies to all the high priests of his house. מָעוֹן is not Eli's dwelling-place, but the dwelling-place of God, *i.e.* the tabernacle, as in ver. 29, and is a genitive dependent upon צַר. הֵיטִיב, in the sense of benefiting a person, doing him good, is construed with the accusative of the person, as in Deut. xxviii. 63, viii. 16, xxx. 5. The subject to the verb יֵיטִיב is *Jehovah*, and is not expressly mentioned, simply because it is so clearly implied in the words themselves. This threat began to be fulfilled even in Eli's own days. The distress or tribulation for the tabernacle began with the capture of the ark by the Philistines (ch. iv. 11), and continued during the time that the Lord was sending help and deliverance to His people through the medium of Samuel, in their spiritual and physical oppression. The ark of the covenant—the heart of the sanctuary—was not restored to the tabernacle in the time of Samuel; and the tabernacle itself was removed from Shiloh to Nob, probably in the time of war; and when Saul had had all the priests put to death (ch. xxi. 2, xxii. 11 sqq.), it was removed to Gibeon, which necessarily caused it to fall more and more into neglect. Among the different explanations, the rendering given by Aquila (καὶ ἐπιβλέψει (? ἐπιβλέψῃς) ἀντίζηλον κατοικητηρίου) has met with the greatest approval, and has been followed by Jerome (*et videbis æmulum tuum*), Luther, and many others, including De Wette. According to this rendering, the words are either supposed to refer to the attitude of Samuel towards Eli, or to the deposition of Abiathar, and the institution of Zadok by Solomon in his place (1 Kings ii. 27). But צַר does not mean the antagonist or rival, but simply the oppressor or enemy; and Samuel was not an enemy of Eli any more than Zadok was of Abiathar. Moreover, if this be adopted as the rendering of צַר, it is impossible to find any suitable meaning for the following clause. In the second half of the verse the threat of ver. 31 is repeated with still greater emphasis. כָּל־הַיָּמִים, all the time, *i.e.* so long as thine house shall exist.—Ver. 33. "*And I will not cut off every one to thee from mine altar, that thine eyes may languish, and thy soul consume away; and all the increase of thine house shall die as men.*" The two leading clauses of this verse correspond to the two principal thoughts of the previous verse, which are hereby more precisely defined and explained. Eli was to see the distress of the sanctuary; for to him, *i.e.* of his family, there would always be some one serving at the altar of God, that he might look upon the decay with his eyes, and pine away with grief in consequence. אִישׁ signifies every one, or any one, and is not to be restricted, as Thenius supposes, to Ahitub, the son of Phinehas, the brother of Ichabod; for it cannot be shown from ch. xiv. 3 and xxii. 20, that he was the only one that was left of the house of Eli. And secondly, there was to be no old man, no one advanced in life, in his house; but all the increase of the house was to die in the full bloom of manhood. אֲנָשִׁים, in contrast with זָקֵן, is used to denote men in the prime of life.

Ver. 34. "*And let this be the sign to thee, what shall happen to* (come upon) *thy two sons, Hophni and Phinehas; in one day they shall both die.*" For the fulfilment of this, see ch. iv. 11. This occurrence, which Eli lived to see, but did not long survive (ch. iv. 17 sqq.), was to be the sign to him that the predicted punishment would be carried out in its fullest extent.—Ver. 35. But the priesthood itself was not to fall with the fall of Eli's house and priesthood; on the contrary, the Lord would raise up for himself a tried priest, who would act according to His heart. "*And I will build for him a lasting house, and he will walk before mine anointed for ever.*"—Ver. 36. Whoever, on the other hand, should still remain of Eli's house, would come "*bowing before him* (to get) *a silver penny and a slice of bread,*" and would say, "*Put me, I pray, in one of the priests' offices, that I may get a piece of bread to eat.*" אֲגוֹרָה, *that which is collected,* signifies some small coin, of which a collection was made by begging single coins. Commentators are divided in their opinions as to the historical allusions contained in this prophecy. By the "tried priest," Ephraem Syrus understood both the prophet Samuel and the priest Zadok. "As for the facts themselves," he says, "it is evident that, when Eli died, Samuel succeeded him in the government, and that Zadok received the high-priesthood when it was taken from his family." Since his time, most of the commentators, including Theodoret and the Rabbins, have decided in favour of Zadok. Augustine, however, and in modern times Thenius and O. v. Gerlach, give the preference to Samuel. The fathers and earlier theologians also regarded Samuel and Zadok as the type of Christ, and supposed the passage to contain a prediction of the abrogation of the Aaronic priesthood by Jesus Christ.[1] This higher

---

[1] Theodoret, qu. vii. in 1 Reg. Οὐκοῦν ἡ πρόρρησις κυρίως μὲν ἁρμόττει τῷ σωτῆρι Χριστῷ. κατὰ δὲ ἱστορίαν τῷ Σαδούκ, ὃς ἐκ τοῦ Ἐλεάζαρ κατάγων τὸ γένος, τὴν ἀρχιερωσύνην διὰ τοῦ Σολομῶνος ἐδέξατο. Augustine says (*De civit. Dei* xvii. 5, 2): "Although Samuel was not of a different tribe from the one which had been appointed by the Lord to serve at the altar, he was not of the sons of Aaron, whose descendants had been set apart as priests; and thus the change is shadowed forth, which was afterwards to be introduced through Jesus Christ." And again, § 3: "What follows (ver. 35) refers to

reference of the words is in any case to be retained; for the rabbinical interpretation, by which Grotius, Clericus, and others abide,—namely, that the transfer of the high-priesthood from the descendants of Eli to Zadok, the descendant of Eleazar, is all that is predicted, and that the prophecy was entirely fulfilled when Abiathar was deposed by Solomon (1 Kings ii. 27),—is not in accordance with the words of the text. On the other hand, Theodoret and Augustine both clearly saw that the words of Jehovah, "I revealed myself to thy father's house in Egypt," and, "Thy house shall walk before me for ever," do not apply to Ithamar, but to Aaron. "Which of his fathers," says Augustine, "was in that Egyptian bondage, from which they were liberated when he was chosen to the priesthood, excepting Aaron? It is with reference to his posterity, therefore, that it is here affirmed that they would not be priests for ever; and this we see already fulfilled." The only thing that appears untenable is the manner in which the fathers combine this historical reference to Eli and Samuel, or Zadok, with the Messianic interpretation, viz. either by referring vers. 31–34 to Eli and his house, and then regarding the sentence pronounced upon Eli as simply a type of the Messianic fulfilment, or by admitting the Messianic allusion simply as an allegory. The true interpretation may be obtained from a correct insight into the relation in which the prophecy itself stands to its fulfilment. Just as, in the person of Eli and his sons, the threat announces deep degradation and even destruction to all the priests of the house of Aaron who should walk in the footsteps of the sons of Eli, and the death of the two sons of Eli in one day was to be merely a sign that the threatened punishment would be completely fulfilled upon the ungodly priests; so, on the other hand, the promise of the raising up of the tried priest, for whom God would build a lasting house, also refers to all the priests whom

that priest, whose figure was borne by Samuel when succeeding to Eli." So again in the Berleburger Bible, to the words, "I will raise me up a faithful priest," this note is added: "Zadok, of the family of Phinehas and Eleazar, whom king Solomon, as the anointed of God, appointed high priest by his ordinance, setting aside the house of Eli (1 Kings ii. 35; 1 Chron. xxix. 22). At the same time, just as in the person of Solomon the Spirit of prophecy pointed to the true Solomon and Anointed One, so in this priest did He also point to Jesus Christ the great High Priest."

the Lord would raise up as faithful servants of His altar, and only receives its complete and final fulfilment in Christ, the true and eternal High Priest. But if we endeavour to determine more precisely from the history itself, which of the Old Testament priests are included, we must not exclude either Samuel or Zadok, but must certainly affirm that the prophecy was partially fulfilled in both. Samuel, as the prophet of the Lord, was placed at the head of the nation after the death of Eli; so that he not only stepped into Eli's place as judge, but stood forth as priest before the Lord and the nation, and "had the important and sacred duty to perform of going before the anointed, the king, whom Israel was to receive through him; whereas for a long time the Aaronic priesthood fell into such contempt, that, during the general decline of the worship of God, it was obliged to go begging for honour and support, and became dependent upon the new order of things that was introduced by Samuel" (O. v. Gerlach). Moreover, Samuel acquired a strong house in the numerous posterity that was given to him by God. The grandson of Samuel was Heman, "the king's seer in the words of God," who was placed by David over the choir at the house of God, and had fourteen sons and three daughters (1 Chron. vi. 33, xxv. 4, 5). But the very fact that these descendants of Samuel did not follow their father in the priesthood, shows very clearly that a lasting house was not built to Samuel as a tried priest through them, and therefore that we have to seek for the further historical fulfilment of this promise in the priesthood of Zadok. As the word of the Lord concerning the house of Eli, even if it did not find its only fulfilment in the deposition of Abiathar (1 Kings ii. 27), was at any rate partially fulfilled in that deposition; so the promise concerning the tried priest to be raised up received a new fulfilment in the fact that Zadok thereby became the sole high priest, and transmitted the office to his descendants, though this was neither its last nor its highest fulfilment. This final fulfilment is hinted at in the vision of the new temple, as seen by the prophet Ezekiel, in connection with which the sons of Zadok are named as the priests, who, because they had not fallen away with the children of Israel, were to draw near to the Lord, and perform His service in the new organization of the kingdom of God as set forth in that vision

(Ezek. xl. 46, xliii. 19, xliv. 15, xlviii. 11). This fulfilment is effected in connection with Christ and His kingdom. Consequently, the anointed of the Lord, before whom the tried priest would walk for ever, is not Solomon, but rather David, and the Son of David, whose kingdom is an everlasting kingdom.

SAMUEL CALLED TO BE A PROPHET.—CHAP. III.

Vers. 1-9. At the time when Samuel served the Lord before Eli, both as a boy and as a young man (ch. ii. 11, 21, 26), the word of the Lord had become *dear, i.e.* rare, in Israel, and "*prophecy was not spread.*" נִפְרָץ, from פָּרַץ, to spread out strongly, to break through copiously (cf. Prov. iii. 10). The "*word of the Lord*" is the word of God announced by prophets: the "*vision*," "*visio prophetica*." It is true that Jehovah had promised His people, that He would send prophets, who should make known His will and purpose at all times (Deut. xviii. 15 sqq.; cf. Num. xxiii. 23); but as a revelation from God presupposed susceptibility on the part of men, the unbelief and disobedience of the people might restrain the fulfilment of this and all similar promises, and God might even withdraw His word to punish the idolatrous nation. Such a time as this, when revelations from God were universally rare, had now arisen under Eli, in whose days, as the conduct of his sons sufficiently proves, the priesthood had fallen into very deep corruption.—Vers. 2-4. The word of the Lord was then issued for the first time to Samuel. Vers. 2-4 form one period. The clause, "*it came to pass at that time*" (ver. 2a), is continued in ver. 4a, "*that the Lord called,*" etc. The intervening clauses from וְעֵלִי to אֲרוֹן אֱלֹהִים are circumstantial clauses, intended to throw light upon the situation. The clause, "*Eli was laid down in his place,*" etc., may be connected logically with "*at that time*" by the insertion of "*when*" (as in the English version: TR.). The dimness of Eli's eyes is mentioned, to explain Samuel's behaviour, as afterwards described. Under these circumstances, for example, when Samuel heard his own name called out in sleep, he might easily suppose that Eli was calling him to render some assistance. The "*lamp of God*" is the light of the candlestick in the tabernacle, the seven lamps of which were put up and lighted every evening, and burned through the night till all the oil was consumed (see Ex. xxx. 8, Lev. xxiv. 2, 2 Chron. xiii. 11, and the explanation given at Ex. xxvii. 21). The statement that this light was not yet extinguished, is equivalent to "before the morning dawn." "*And Samuel was lying* (sleeping) *in the temple of Jehovah, where the ark of God was.*" הֵיכָל does not mean the holy place, as distinguished from the "most holy," as in 1 Kings vi. 5, vii. 50,[1] but the whole tabernacle, the tent with its court, as the palace of the God-king, as in ch. i. 9, Ps. xi. 4. Samuel neither slept in the holy place by the side of the candlestick and table of shew-bread, nor in the most holy place in front of the ark of the covenant, but in the court, where cells were built for the priests and Levites to live in when serving at the sanctuary (see at ver. 15). *The ark of God, i.e.* the ark of the covenant, is mentioned as the throne of the divine presence, from which the call to Samuel proceeded.—Vers. 5-9. As soon as Samuel heard his name called out, he hastened to Eli to receive his commands. But Eli bade him lie down again, as he had not called him. At first, no doubt, he thought the call which Samuel had heard was nothing more than a false impression of the youth, who had been fast asleep. But the same thing was repeated a second and a third time; for, as the historian explains in ver. 6, "*Samuel had not yet known Jehovah, and* (for) *the word of Jehovah was not yet revealed to him.*" (The perfect יָדַע after טֶרֶם, though very rare, is fully supported by Ps. xc. 2 and Prov. viii. 25, and therefore is not to be altered into יֵדַע, as Dietrich and Böttcher propose.) He therefore imagined again that Eli had called him. But when he came to Eli after the third call, Eli perceived that the Lord was calling, and directed Samuel, if the call were repeated, to answer, "*Speak, Lord; for Thy servant heareth.*"

Vers. 10-18. When Samuel had lain down again, "*Jehovah came and stood,*" *sc.* before Samuel. These words show that the revelation of God was an objectively real affair, and not a mere dream of Samuel's. "*And he called to him as at*

---

[1] The Masoretes have taken הֵיכָל in this sense, and therefore have placed the *Athnach* under שֹׁכֵב, to separate וּשְׁמוּאֵל שֹׁכֵב from בְּהֵיכַל יְיָ, and thus to guard against the conclusion, which might be drawn from this view of הֵיכָל, that Samuel slept in the holy place.

other times" (see Num. xxiv. 1; Judg. xvi. 20, etc.) When Samuel replied in accordance with Eli's instructions, the Lord announced to him that He would carry out the judgment that had been threatened against the house of Eli (vers. 11-14). "*Behold, I do a thing in Israel, at which both the ears of every one that heareth it shall tingle,*" sc. with horror (see 2 Kings xxi. 12; Jer. xix. 3; Hab. i. 5).—Ver. 12. "*On that day I will perform against Eli all that I have spoken concerning his house* (see ch. ii. 30 sqq.), *beginning and finishing it,*" *i.e.* completely. הָקִים אֶת־אֲשֶׁר דִּבֶּר, to set up the word spoken, *i.e.* to carry it out, or accomplish it. In ver. 13 this word is communicated to Samuel, so far as its essential contents are concerned. God would judge "*the house of Eli for ever because of the iniquity, that he knew his sons were preparing a curse for themselves and did not prevent them.*" To judge on account of a crime, is the same as to punish it. עַד־עוֹלָם, *i.e.* without the punishment being ever stopped or removed. מְקַלְלִים לָהֶם, cursing themselves, *i.e.* bringing a curse upon themselves. "*Therefore I have sworn to the house of Eli, that the iniquity of the house of Eli shall not* (אִם, a particle used in an oath, equivalent to assuredly not) *be expiated by slain-offerings and meat-offerings* (through any kind of sacrifice) *for ever.*" The oath makes the sentence irrevocable. (On the facts themselves, see the commentary on ch. ii. 27-36.) —Ver. 15. Samuel then slept till the morning; and when he opened the doors of the house of Jehovah, he was afraid to tell Eli of the revelation which he had received. Opening the doors of the house of God appears to have been part of Samuel's duty. We have not to think of doors opening into the holy place, however, but of doors leading into the court. Originally, when the tabernacle was simply a tent, travelling with the people from place to place, it had only curtains at the entrance to the holy place and court. But when Israel had become possessed of fixed houses in the land of Canaan, and the dwelling-place of God was permanently erected at Shiloh, instead of the tents that were pitched for the priests and Levites, who encamped round about during the journey through the desert, there were erected fixed houses, which were built against or inside the court, and not only served as dwelling-places for the priests and Levites who were officiating, but were also used for the reception and custody of the gifts that were brought as offerings to the sanctuary. These buildings in all probability supplanted entirely the original tent-like enclosure around the court; so that instead of the curtains at the entrance, there were folding doors, which were shut in the evening and opened again in the morning. It is true that nothing is said about the erection of these buildings in our historical books, but the fact itself is not to be denied on that account. In the case of Solomon's temple, notwithstanding the elaborate description that has been given of it, there is nothing said about the arrangement or erection of the buildings in the court; and yet here and there, principally in Jeremiah, the existence of such buildings is evidently assumed. מַרְאָה, *visio*, a sight or vision. This expression is applied to the word of God which came to Samuel, because it was revealed to him through the medium of an inward sight or intuition.—Vers. 16-18. When Samuel was called by Eli and asked concerning the divine revelation that he had received, he told him all the words, without concealing anything; whereupon Eli bowed in quiet resignation to the purpose of God: "*It is the Lord; let Him do what seemeth Him good.*" Samuel's communication, however, simply confirmed to the aged Eli what God had already made known to him through a prophet. But his reply proves that, with all his weakness and criminal indulgence towards his wicked sons, Eli was thoroughly devoted to the Lord in his heart. And Samuel, on the other hand, through his unreserved and candid communication of the terribly solemn word of God with regard to the man, whom he certainly venerated with filial affection, not only as high priest, but also as his own parental guardian, proved himself to be a man possessing the courage and the power to proclaim the word of the Lord without fear to the people of Israel.

Vers. 19-21. Thus Samuel grew, and Jehovah was with him, and let none of his words fall to the ground, *i.e.* left no word unfulfilled which He spoke through Samuel. (On הִפִּיל, see Josh. xxi. 45, xxiii. 14, 1 Kings viii. 56.) By this all Israel from Dan to Beersheba (see at Judg. xx. 1) perceived that Samuel was found trustworthy, or approved (see Num xii. 7) as a prophet of Jehovah. And the Lord continued to appear at Shiloh; for He revealed himself there to Samuel "*in the word of Jehovah,*" *i.e.* through a prophetic announcement of

His word. These three verses form the transition from the call of Samuel to the following account of his prophetic labours in Israel. At the close of ver. 21, the LXX. have appended a general remark concerning Eli and his sons, which, regarded as a deduction from the context, answers no doubt to the paraphrastic treatment of our book in that version, but in a critical aspect is utterly worthless.

WAR WITH THE PHILISTINES. LOSS OF THE ARK. DEATH OF ELI AND HIS SONS.—CHAP. IV.

At Samuel's word, the Israelites attacked the Philistines, and were beaten (vers. 1, 2). They then fetched the ark of the covenant into the camp according to the advice of the elders, that they might thereby make sure of the help of the almighty covenant God ; but in the engagement which followed they suffered a still greater defeat, in which Eli's sons fell and the ark was taken by the Philistines (vers. 3-11). The aged Eli, terrified at such a loss, fell from his seat and broke his neck (vers. 12-18); and his daughter-in-law was taken in labour, and died after giving birth to a son (vers. 19-22). With these occurrences the judgment began to burst upon the house of Eli. But the disastrous result of the war was also to be a source of deep humiliation to all the Israelites. Not only were the people to learn that the Lord had departed from them, but Samuel also was to make the discovery that the deliverance of Israel from the oppression and dominion of its foes was absolutely impossible without its inward conversion to its God.

Vers. 1, 2. The two clauses, "*The word of Samuel came to all Israel*," and "*Israel went out*," etc., are to be logically connected together in the following sense: "At the word or instigation of Samuel, Israel went out against the Philistines to battle." The Philistines were ruling over Israel at that time. This is evident, apart from our previous remarks concerning the connection between the commencement of this book and the close of the book of Judges (see vol. iv. pp. 280 sqq.), from the simple fact that the land of Israel was the scene of the war, and that nothing is said about an invasion on the part of the Philistines. The Israelites encamped at Ebenezer, and the Philistines were encamped at Aphek. The name *Ebenezer* ("the stone of help") was not given to the place so designated till a later period, when Samuel set up a memorial stone there to commemorate a victory that was gained over the Philistines upon the same chosen battle-field after the lapse of twenty years (ch. vii. 12). According to this passage, the stone was set up between *Mizpeh* and *Shen*. The former was not the Mizpeh in the lowlands of Judah (Josh. xv. 38), but the *Mizpeh* of Benjamin (Josh. xviii. 26), *i.e.*, according to Robinson, the present *Neby Samwil*, two hours to the north-west of Jerusalem, and half an hour to the south of Gibeon (see at Josh. xviii. 26). The situation of *Aphek* has not been discovered. It cannot have been far from Mizpeh and Ebenezer, however, and was probably the same place as the Canaanitish capital mentioned in Josh. xii. 18, and is certainly different from the *Aphekah* upon the mountains of Judah (Josh. xv. 53); for this was on the south or south-west of Jerusalem, since, according to the book of Joshua, it belonged to the towns that were situated in the district of Gibeon.—Ver. 2. When the battle was fought, the Israelites were defeated by the Philistines, and in battle-array four thousand men were smitten upon the field. עָרַךְ, *sc.* מִלְחָמָה, as in Judg. xx. 20, 22, etc. בַּמַּעֲרָכָה, in battle-array, *i.e.* upon the field of battle, not in flight. "*In the field*," *i.e.* the open field where the battle was fought.

Vers. 3-11. On the return of the people to the camp, the elders held a council of war as to the cause of the defeat they had suffered. "*Why hath Jehovah smitten us to-day before the Philistines?*" As they had entered upon the war by the word and advice of Samuel, they were convinced that Jehovah had smitten them. The question presupposes at the same time that the Israelites felt strong enough to enter upon the war with their enemies, and that the reason for their defeat could only be that the Lord, their covenant God, had withdrawn His help. This was no doubt a correct conclusion; but the means which they adopted to secure the help of their God in continuing the war were altogether wrong. Instead of feeling remorse and seeking the help of the Lord their God by a sincere repentance and confession of their apostasy from Him, they resolved to fetch the ark of the covenant out of the tabernacle at Shiloh into the camp, with the delusive idea that God had so inseparably bound up His gracious presence in the midst of His people with this holy ark, which He had selected as the throne of His gracious appearance, that He would of necessity come with it into the camp and smite the foe. In ver. 4, the ark is called "*the ark of the covenant of Jehovah of hosts, who is enthroned above the cherubim,*" partly to show the reason why the people had the ark fetched, and partly to indicate the hope which they founded upon the presence of this sacred object. (See the commentary on Ex. xxv. 20–22.) The remark introduced here, "*and the two sons of Eli were there with the ark of the covenant of God,*" is not merely intended to show who the guardians of the ark were, viz. priests who had hitherto disgraced the sanctuary, but also to point forward at the very outset to the result of the measures adopted.—Ver. 5. On the arrival of the ark in the camp, the people raised so great a shout of joy that the earth rang again. This was probably the first time since the settlement of Israel in Canaan, that the ark had been brought into the camp, and therefore the people no doubt anticipated from its presence a renewal of the marvellous victories gained by Israel under Moses and Joshua, and for that reason raised such a shout when it arrived.—Vers. 6–8. When the Philistines heard the noise, and learned on inquiry that the ark of Jehovah had come into the camp, they were thrown into alarm, for "*they thought (lit. said), God (Elohim) is come into the camp, and said, "Woe unto us! For such a thing has not happened yesterday and the day before (i.e. never till now). Woe to us! Who will deliver us from the hand of these mighty gods? These are the very gods that smote Egypt with all kinds of plagues in the wilderness.*" The Philistines spoke of the God of Israel in the plural, הָאֱלֹהִים הָאַדִּירִים, as heathen who only knew of *gods*, and not of one Almighty God. Just as all the heathen feared the might of the gods of other nations in a certain degree, so the Philistines also were alarmed at the might of the God of the Israelites, and that all the more because the report of His deeds in the olden time had reached their ears (see Ex. xv. 14, 15). The expression "*in the wilderness*" does not compel us to refer the words "smote with all the plagues" exclusively to the destruction of Pharaoh and his army in the Red Sea (Ex. xiv. 23 sqq.). "*All the plagues*" include the rest of the plagues which God inflicted upon Egypt, without there being any necessity to supply the copula וְ before בַּמִּדְבָּר, as in the LXX. and Syriac.

By this addition an antithesis is introduced into the words, which, if it really were intended, would require to be indicated by a previous בָּאָרֶץ or בְּאַרְצָם. According to the notions of the Philistines, all the wonders of God for the deliverance of Israel out of Egypt took place in the desert, because even when Israel was in Goshen they dwelt on the border of the desert, and were conducted thence to Canaan.—Ver. 9. But instead of despairing, they encouraged one another, saying, "*Show yourselves strong, and be men, O Philistines, that we may not be obliged to serve the Hebrews, as they have served you; be men, and fight!*"—Vers. 10, 11. Stimulated in this way, they fought and smote Israel, so that every one fled home ("to his tent," see at Josh. xxii. 8), and 30,000 men of Israel fell. The ark also was taken, and the two sons of Eli died, *i.e.* were slain when the ark was taken,—a practical proof to the degenerate nation, that Jehovah, who was enthroned above the cherubim, had departed from them, *i.e.* had withdrawn His gracious presence.[1]

Vers. 12-22. The tidings of this calamity were brought by a Benjaminite, who came as a messenger of evil tidings, with his clothes rent, and earth upon his head—a sign of the deepest mourning (see Josh. vii. 6)—to Shiloh, where the aged Eli was sitting upon a seat by the side (יָד is a copyist's error for יַד) of the way watching; for his heart trembled for the ark of God, which had been taken from the sanctuary into the camp without the command of God. At these tidings the whole city cried out with terror, so that Eli heard the sound of the cry, and asked the reason of this loud noise (or tumult), whilst the messenger was hurrying towards him with the news.—Ver. 15. Eli was ninety-eight years old, and "*his eyes stood*," *i.e.* were

---

[1] "It is just the same now, when we take merely a historical Christ outside us for our Redeemer. He must prove His help chiefly internally by His Holy Spirit, to redeem us out of the hand of the Philistines; though externally He must not be thrown into the shade, as accomplishing our justification. If we had not Christ, we could never stand. For there is no help in heaven and on earth beside Him. But if we have Him in no other way than merely without us and under us, if we only preach about Him, teach, hear, read, talk, discuss, and dispute about Him, take His name into our mouth, but will not let Him work and show His power in us, He will no more help us than the ark helped the Israelites."—*Berleburger Bible.*

stiff, so that he could no more see (*vid.* 1 Kings xiv. 4). This is a description of the so-called black cataract (*amaurosis*), which generally occurs at a very great age from paralysis of the optic nerves.—Vers. 16 sqq. When the messenger informed him of the defeat of the Israelites, the death of his sons, and the capture of the ark, at the last news Eli fell back from his seat by the side of the gate, and broke his neck, and died. The loss of the ark was to him the most dreadful of all—more dreadful than the death of his two sons. Eli had judged Israel forty years. The reading *twenty* in the Septuagint does not deserve the slightest notice, if only because it is perfectly incredible that Eli should have been appointed judge of the nation in his seventy-eighth year.—Vers. 19–22. The judgment which fell upon Eli through this stroke extended still further. His daughter-in-law, the wife of Phinehas, was with child (near) to be delivered. לָלַת, contracted from לָלֶדֶת (from יָלַד: see Ges. § 69, 3, note 1; Ewald, § 238, *c*). When she heard the tidings of the capture (אֶל־הִלָּקַח, "*with regard to the being taken away*") of the ark of God, and the death of her father-in-law and husband, she fell upon her knees and was delivered, for her pains had fallen upon her (*lit.* had turned against her), and died in consequence. Her death, however, was but a subordinate matter to the historian. He simply refers to it casually in the words, "*and about the time of her death*," for the purpose of giving her last words, in which she gave utterance to her grief at the loss of the ark, as a matter of greater importance in relation to his object. As she lay dying, the women who stood round sought to comfort her, by telling her that she had brought forth a son; but "*she did not answer, and took no notice* (שׂוּם לֵב = שִׁית לֵב, *animum advertere;* cf. Ps. lxii. 11), *but called to the boy* (*i.e.* named him), *Ichabod* (אִי כָבוֹד, no glory), saying, *The glory of Israel is departed*," referring to the capture of the ark of God, and also to her father-in-law and husband. She then said again, "*Gone* (גָּלָה, wandered away, carried off) *is the glory of Israel, for the ark of God is taken.*" The repetition of these words shows how deeply the wife of the godless Phinehas had taken to heart the carrying off of the ark, and how in her estimation the glory of Israel had departed with it. Israel could not be brought lower. With the surrender of the earthly throne of His glory, the Lord appeared to have abolished

His covenant of grace with Israel.; for the ark, with the tables of the law and the capporeth, was the visible pledge of the covenant of grace which Jehovah had made with Israel.

HUMILIATION OF THE PHILISTINES BY MEANS OF THE ARK OF THE COVENANT.—CHAP. V.–VII. 1.

Whilst the Israelites were mourning over the loss of the ark of God, the Philistines were also to derive no pleasure from their booty, but rather to learn that the God of Israel, who had given up to them His greatest sanctuary to humble His own degenerate nation, was the only true God, beside Whom there were no other gods. Not only was the principal deity of the Philistines thrown down into the dust and dashed to pieces by the glory of Jehovah; but the Philistines themselves were so smitten, that their princes were compelled to send back the ark into the land of Israel, together with a trespass-offering, to appease the wrath of God, which pressed so heavily upon them.

Chap. v. THE ARK IN THE LAND OF THE PHILISTINES.— Vers. 1–6. The Philistines carried the ark from Ebenezer, where they had captured it, into their capital, Ashdod (*Esdud;* see at Josh. xiii. 3), and placed it there in the temple of Dagon, by the side of the idol Dagon, evidently as a dedicatory offering to this god of theirs, by whose help they imagined that they had obtained the victory over both the Israelites and their God. With regard to the image of *Dagon*, compounded of man and fish, *i.e.* of a human body, with head and hands, and a fish's tail, see, in addition to Judg. xvi. 23, Stark's *Gaza*, pp. 248 sqq., 308 sqq., and Layard's *Nineveh and its Remains*, pp. 466–7, where there is a bas-relief from Khorsabad, in which " a figure is seen swimming in the sea, with the upper part of the body resembling a bearded man, wearing the ordinary conical tiara of royalty, adorned with elephants' tusks, and the lower part resembling the body of a fish. It has the hand lifted up, as if in astonishment or fear, and is surrounded by fishes, crabs, and other marine animals" (Stark, p. 308). As this bas-relief represents, according to Layard, the war of an Assyrian king with the inhabitants of the coast of Syria, most probably of Sargon, who had to carry on a long conflict with the Philistian towns, more especially with Ashdod, there can hardly be any doubt that we have a representation of the Philistian Dagon here. This deity was a personification of the generative and vivifying principle of nature, for which the fish with its innumerable multiplication was specially adapted, and set forth the idea of the giver of all earthly good.—Ver. 3. The next morning the Ashdodites found Dagon lying on his face upon the ground before the ark of Jehovah, and restored him to his place again, evidently supposing that the idol had fallen or been thrown down by some accident.—Ver. 4. But they were obliged to give up this notion when they found the god lying on his face upon the ground again the next morning in front of the ark of Jehovah, and in fact broken to pieces, so that Dagon's head and the two hollow hands of his arms lay severed upon the threshold, and nothing was left but the trunk of the fish (דָּגוֹן). The word *Dagon*, in this last clause, is used in an appellative sense, viz. the fishy part, or fish's shape, from דָּג, a fish. הַמִּפְתָּן is no doubt the threshold of the door of the recess in which the image was set up. We cannot infer from this, however, as Thenius has done, that with the small dimensions of the recesses in the ancient temples, if the image fell forward, the pieces named might easily fall upon the threshold. This naturalistic interpretation of the miracle is not only proved to be untenable by the word בְּרֻתוֹת, since כָּרוּת means *cut off*, and not broken off, but is also precluded by the improbability, not to say impossibility, of the thing itself. For if the image of Dagon, which was standing by the side of the ark, was thrown down towards the ark, so as to lie upon its face in front of it, the pieces that were broken off, viz. the head and hands, could not have fallen sideways, so as to lie upon the threshold. Even the first fall of the image of Dagon was a miracle. From the fact that their god Dagon lay upon its face before the ark of Jehovah, *i.e.* lay prostrate upon the earth, as though worshipping before the God of Israel, the Philistines were to learn, that even their supreme deity had been obliged to fall down before the majesty of Jehovah, the God of the Israelites. But as they did not discern the meaning of this miraculous sign, the second miracle was to show them the annihilation of their idol through the God of Israel, in such a way as to preclude every thought of accident. The disgrace attending the annihilation of their idol was probably to be heightened by the fact, that the pieces of Dagon that were smitten off were lying upon the threshold, inasmuch as what lay upon the threshold was easily trodden upon by any one who entered the house. This is intimated in the custom referred to in ver. 5, that in consequence of this occurrence, the priests of Dagon, and all who entered the temple of Dagon at Ashdod, down to the time of the historian himself, would not step upon the threshold of Dagon, *i.e.* the threshold where Dagon's head and hands had lain, but stepped over the threshold (not " leaped over," as many commentators assume on the ground of Zeph. i. 9, which has nothing to do with the matter), that they might not touch with their feet, and so defile, the place where the pieces of their god had lain.—Ver. 6. The visitation of God was not restricted to the demolition of the statue of Dagon, but affected the people of Ashdod as well. " *The hand of Jehovah was heavy upon the Ashdodites, and laid them waste.*" הֵשַׁם, from שָׁמֵם, when applied to men, as in Micah vi. 13, signifies to make desolate not only by diseases, but also by the withdrawal or diminution of the means of subsistence, the devastation of the fields, and such like. That the latter is included here, is evident from the dedicatory offerings with which the Philistines sought to mitigate the wrath of the God of the Israelites (ch. vi. 4, 5, 11, 18), although the verse before us simply mentions the diseases with which God visited them.[1] " *And He smote them with* עֳפָלִים, *i.e. boils :*" according to the Rabbins, swellings on the anus, *mariscæ* (see at Deut. xxviii. 27). For עֳפָלִים the Masoretes have invariably substituted טְחֹרִים,

---

[1] At the close of vers. 3 and 6 the Septuagint contains some comprehensive additions; viz. at the close of ver. 3 : Καὶ ἐβαρύνθη χεὶρ Κυρίου ἐπὶ τοὺς Ἀζωτίους καὶ ἐβασάνιζεν αὐτούς, καὶ ἐπάταξεν αὐτοὺς εἰς τὰς ἕδρας αὐτῶν, τὴν Ἄζωτον καὶ τὰ ὅρια αὐτῆς ; and at the end of ver. 6 : Καὶ μέσον τῆς χώρας αὐτῆς ἀνεφύησαν μύες καὶ ἐγένετο σύγχυσις θανάτου μεγάλη ἐν τῇ πόλει. This last clause we also find in the Vulgate, expressed as follows : *Et eballiverunt villæ et agri in medio regionis illius, et nati sunt mures, et facta est confusio mortis magnæ in civitate.* Ewald's decision with regard to these clauses (*Gesch.* ii. p. 541) is, that they are not wanted at ch. v 3, 6, but that they are all the more necessary at ch. vi. 1 ; whereas at ch. v. 3, 6, they would rather injure the sense. Thenius admits that the clause appended to ver. 3 is nothing more than a second translation of our sixth verse, which has been interpolated by a copyist of the Greek in the wrong place ; whereas that of ver. 6 contains the original though somewhat

which is used in ch. vi. 11, 17, and was probably regarded as more decorous. *Ashdod* is a more precise definition of the word *them*, viz. Ashdod, *i.e.* the inhabitants of Ashdod and its territory.

Vers. 7-12. " *When the Ashdodites saw that it was so,*" they were unwilling to keep the ark of the God of Israel any longer, because the hand of Jehovah lay heavy upon them and their god Dagon ; whereupon the princes of the Philistines (סַרְנֵי, as in Josh. xiii. 3, etc.) assembled together, and came to the resolution to " *let the ark of the God of Israel turn* (*i.e.* be taken) *to Gath*" (ver. 8). The princes of the Philistines probably imagined that the calamity which the Ashdodites attributed to the ark of God, either did not proceed from the ark, *i.e.* from the God of Israel, or if actually connected with the presence of the ark, simply arose from the fact that the city itself was hateful to the God of the Israelites, or that the Dagon of Ashdod was weaker than the Jehovah of Israel : they therefore resolved to let the ark be taken to Gath in order to pacify the Ashdodites. According to our account, the city of *Gath* seems to have stood between Ashdod and Ekron (see at Josh. xiii. 3). —Ver. 9. But when the ark was brought to Gath, the hand of Jehovah came upon that city also with very great alarm. מְהוּמָה גְדוֹלָה is subordinated to the main sentence either adverbially or in the accusative. Jehovah smote the people of the city, small and great, so that boils broke out upon their hinder parts.—Vers. 10-12. They therefore sent the ark of God to *Ekron*, *i.e. Akir*, the north-western city of the Philistines (see

corrupt text, according to which the Hebrew text should be emended. But an impartial examination would show very clearly, that all these additions are nothing more than paraphrases founded upon the context. The last part of the addition to ver. 6 is taken *verbatim* from ver. 11, whilst the first part is a conjecture based upon ch. vi. 4, 5. Jerome, if indeed the addition in our text of the Vulgate really originated with him, and was not transferred into his version from the Itala, did not venture to suppress the clause interpolated in the Alexandrian version. This is very evident from the words *confusio mortis magnæ*, which are a literal rendering of σύγχυσις θανάτου μεγάλη ; whereas in ver. 11, Jerome has given to מְהוּמַת מָוֶת, which the LXX. rendered σύγχυσις θανάτου, the much more accurate rendering *pavor mortis*. Moreover, neither the Syriac nor Targum Jonath. has this clause ; so that long before the time of Jerome, the Hebrew text existed in the form in which the Masoretes have handed it down to us.

at Josh. xiii. 3). But the Ekronites, who had been informed of what had taken place in Ashdod and Gath, cried out, when the ark came into their city, "*They have brought the ark of the God of Israel to me, to slay me and my people*" (these words are to be regarded as spoken by the whole town) ; and they said to all the princes of the Philistines whom they had called together, "*Send away the ark of the God of Israel, that it may return to its place, and not slay me and my people. For deadly alarm* (מְהוּמַת מָוֶת, *confusion of death, i.e.* alarm produced by many sudden deaths) *ruled in the whole city ; very heavy was the hand of God there. The people who did not die were smitten with boils, and the cry of the city ascended to heaven.*" From this description, which simply indicates briefly the particulars of the plagues that God inflicted upon Ekron, we may see very clearly that Ekron was visited even more severely than Ashdod and Gath. This was naturally the case. The longer the Philistines resisted and refused to recognise the chastening hand of the living God in the plagues inflicted upon them, the more severely would they necessarily be punished, that they might be brought at last to see that the God of Israel, whose sanctuary they still wanted to keep as a trophy of their victory over that nation, was the omnipotent God, who was able to destroy His foes.

Chap. vi.–vii. 1. THE ARK OF GOD SENT BACK.—Vers. 1–3. The ark of Jehovah was in the land (*lit.* the fields, as in Ruth i. 2) of the Philistines for seven months, and had brought destruction to all the towns to which it had been taken. At length the Philistines resolved to send it back to the Israelites, and therefore called their priests and diviners (see at Num. xxiii. 23) to ask them, "*What shall we do with regard to the ark of God; tell us, with what shall we send it to its place?*" "*Its place*" is the land of Israel, and בַּמֶּה does not mean "in what manner" (*quomodo:* Vulgate, Thenius), but *with what, wherewith* (as in Micah vi. 6). There is no force in the objection brought by Thenius, that if the question had implied with what presents, the priests would not have answered, "*Do not send it without a present;*" for the priests did not confine themselves to this answer, in which they gave a general assent, but proceeded at once to define the present more minutely. They replied, "*If they send away the ark of the God of Israel* (מְשַׁלְּחִים is to be

taken as the third person in an indefinite address, as in ch. ii.
24, and not to be construed with אֹתָם supplied), *do not send it
away empty* (*i.e.* without an expiatory offering), *but return Him*
(*i.e.* the God of Israel) *a trespass-offering.*" אָשָׁם, *lit.* guilt, then
the gift presented as compensation for a fault, the trespass-
offering (see at Lev. v. 14-26). The gifts appointed by the
Philistines as an *asham* were to serve as a compensation and
satisfaction to be rendered to the God of Israel for the robbery
committed upon Him by the removal of the ark of the covenant, and were therefore called *asham*, although in their nature
they were only expiatory offerings. For the same reason the
verb הֵשִׁיב, to return or repay, is used to denote the presentation
of these gifts, being the technical expression for the payment of
compensation for a fault in Num. v. 7, and in Lev. v. 23 for
compensation for anything belonging to another, that had been
unjustly appropriated. "*Are ye healed then, it will show you why
His hand is not removed from you,*" *sc.* so long as ye keep back the
ark. The words אָז תֵּרָפְאוּ are to be understood as conditional,
even without אִם, which the rules of the language allow (see
Ewald, § 357, *b*); this is required by the context. For, according to ver. 9, the Philistine priests still thought it a possible
thing that any misfortune which had befallen the Philistines
might be only an accidental circumstance. With this view,
they could not look upon a cure as certain to result from the
sending back of the ark, but only as possible; consequently
they could only speak conditionally, and with this the words
"*we shall know*" agree.

Vers. 4-6. The trespass-offering was to correspond to the
number of the princes of the Philistines. מִסְפַּר is an accusative
employed to determine either measure or number (see Ewald,
§ 204, *a*), lit. "*the number of their princes:*" the compensations
were to be the same in number as the princes. "*Five golden
boils, and five golden mice,*" *i.e.*, according to ver. 5, images
resembling their boils, and the field-mice which overran the
land; the same gifts, therefore, for them all, "*for one plague is
to all and to your princes,*" *i.e.* the same plague has fallen upon
all the people and their princes. The change of person in the
two words, לְכֻלָּם, "*all of them,*" *i.e.* the whole nation of the
Philistines, and לְסַרְנֵיכֶם, "*your princes,*" appears very strange to
us with our modes of thought and speech, but it is by no means

unusual in Hebrew. The selection of this peculiar kind of expiatory present was quite in accordance with a custom, which was not only widely spread among the heathen but was even adopted in the Christian church, viz. that after recovery from an illness, or rescue from any danger or calamity, a representation of the member healed or the danger passed through was placed as an offering in the temple of the deity, to whom the person had prayed for deliverance;[1] and it also perfectly agrees with a custom which has prevailed in India, according to Tavernier (Ros. *A. u. N. Morgenland* iii. p. 77), from time immemorial down to the present day, viz. that when a pilgrim takes a journey to a pagoda to be cured of a disease, he offers to the idol a present either in gold, silver, or copper, according to his ability, of the shape of the diseased or injured member, and then sings a hymn. Such a present passed as a practical acknowledgment that the god had inflicted the suffering or evil. If offered after recovery or deliverance, it was a public expression of thanksgiving. In the case before us, however, in which it was offered before deliverance, the presentation of the images of the things with which they had been chastised was probably a kind of fine or compensation for the fault that had been committed against the Deity, to mitigate His wrath and obtain a deliverance from the evils with which they had been smitten. This is contained in the words, "Give glory unto the God of Israel! peradventure He will lighten His (punishing) hand from off you, and from off your

---

[1] Thus, after a shipwreck, any who escaped presented a tablet to Isis, or Neptune, with the representation of a shipwreck upon it; gladiators offered their weapons, and emancipated slaves their fetters. In some of the nations of antiquity even representations of the private parts, in which a cure had been obtained from the deity, were hung up in the temples in honour of the gods (see Schol. ad Aristoph. *Acharn.* 243, and other proofs in Winer's *Real-wörterbuch*, ii. p. 255). Theodoret says, concerning the Christians of the fourth century (*Therapeutik. Disp.* viii.): Ὅτι δὲ τυγχάνουσιν ὧνπερ αἰτοῦσιν οἱ πιστῶς ἐπαγγέλλοντες, ἀναφανδὸν μαρτυρεῖ τὰ τούτων ἀναθήματα, τὴν ἰατρείαν δηλοῦντα, οἱ μὲν γὰρ ὀφθαλμῶν, οἱ δὲ ποδῶν, ἄλλοι δὲ χειρῶν προσφέρουσιν ἐκτυπώματα· καὶ οἱ μὲν ἐκ χρυσοῦ, οἱ δὲ ἐξ ὕλης ἀργύρου πεποιημένα. δέχεται γὰρ ὁ τούτων Δεσπότης καὶ τὰ σμικρά τε καὶ εὔωνα, τῇ τοῦ προσφέροντος δυνάμει τὸ δῶρον μετρῶν. δηλοῖ δὲ ταῦτα προκείμενα τῶν παθημάτων τὴν λύσιν, ἧς ἀνετέθη μνημεῖα παρὰ τῶν ἀρτίων γεγενημένων. And at Rome they still hang up a picture of the danger, from which deliverance had been obtained after a vow, in the church of the saint invoked in the danger

gods, and from off your land." The expression is a pregnant one for "make His heavy hand light and withdraw it," *i.e.* take away the punishment. In the allusion to the representations of the field-mice, the words "that devastate the land" are added, because in the description given of the plagues in ch. v. the devastation of the land by mice is not expressly mentioned. The introduction of this clause after עַכְבְּרֵיכֶם, when contrasted with the omission of any such explanation after עָפְלֵיכֶם, is a proof that the plague of mice had not been described before, and therefore that the references made to these in the Septuagint at ch. v. 3, 6, and ch. vi. 1, are nothing more than explanatory glosses. It is a well-known fact that field-mice, with their enormous rate of increase and their great voracity, do extraordinary damage to the fields. In southern lands they sometimes destroy entire harvests in a very short space of time (Aristot. *Animal.* vi. 37 ; Plin. *h. n.* x. c. 65 ; Strabo, iii. p. 165 ; Ælian, etc., in Bochart, *Hieroz.* ii. p. 429, ed. Ros.).—Ver. 6. "*Wherefore,*" continued the priests, "*will ye harden your heart, as the Egyptians and Pharaoh hardened their hearts?*" (Ex. vii. 13 sqq.) *Was it not the case, that when He* (Jehovah) *had let out His power upon them* (בְּ הִתְעַלֵּל, as in Ex. x. 2), *they* (the Egyptians) *let them* (the Israelites) *go, and they departed?*" There is nothing strange in this reference, on the part of the Philistian priests, to the hardening of the Egyptians, and its results, since the report of those occurrences had spread among all the neighbouring nations (see at ch. iv. 8). And the warning is not at variance with the fact that, according to ver. 9, the priests still entertained some doubt whether the plagues really did come from Jehovah at all : for their doubts did not preclude the possibility of its being so ; and even the possibility might be sufficient to make it seem advisable to do everything that could be done to mitigate the wrath of the God of the Israelites, of whom, under existing circumstances, the heathen stood not only no less, but even more, in dread, than of the wrath of their own gods.

Vers. 7-12. Accordingly they arranged the sending back in such a manner as to manifest the reverence which ought to be shown to the God of Israel as a powerful deity (vers. 7-9). The Philistines were to take a new cart and make it ready (עָשָׂה), and to yoke two milch cows to the cart upon which no yoke had ever come, and to take away their young ones (calves) from them into the house, *i.e.* into the stall, and then to put the ark upon the cart, along with the golden things to be presented as a trespass-offering, which were to be in a small chest by the side of the ark, and to send it (*i.e.* the ark) away, that it might go, viz. without the cows being either driven or guided. From the result of these arrangements, they were to learn whether the plague had been sent by the God of Israel, or had arisen accidentally. "*If it* (the ark) *goeth up by the way to its border towards Bethshemesh, He* (Jehovah) *hath done us this great evil; but if not, we perceive that His hand hath not touched us. It came to us by chance,*" *i.e.* the evil came upon us merely by accident. In עֲלֵיהֶם, בְּנֵיהֶם, and מֵאַחֲרֵיהֶם (ver. 7), the masculine is used in the place of the more definite feminine, as being the more general form. This is frequently the case, and occurs again in vers. 10 and 12. אַרְנִי, which only occurs again in vers. 8, 11, and 15, signifies, according to the context and the ancient versions, a chest or little case. The suffix to אֹתוֹ refers to the ark, which is also the subject to יַעֲלֶה (ver. 9). גְּבוּלוֹ, the territory of the ark, is the land of Israel, where it had its home. מִקְרֶה is used adverbially: by chance, or accidentally. The new cart and the young cows, which had never worn a yoke, corresponded to the holiness of the ark of God. To place it upon an old cart, which had already been used for all kinds of earthly purposes, would have been an offence against the holy thing; and it would have been just the same to yoke to the cart animals that had already been used for drawing, and had had their strength impaired by the yoke (see Deut. xxi. 3). The reason for selecting cows, however, instead of male oxen, was no doubt to be found in the further object which they hoped to attain. It was certainly to be expected, that if suckling cows, whose calves had been kept back from them, followed their own instincts, without any drivers, they would not go away, but would come back to their young ones in the stall. And if the very opposite should take place, this would be a sure sign that they were driven and guided by a divine power, and in fact by the God whose ark they were to draw into His own land. From this they would be able to draw the conclusion, that the plagues which had fallen upon the Philistines were also sent by this God. There was no special sagacity in this advice of the priests; it was nothing more than a cleverly devised attempt to put the power of the God of the Israelites to the test, though they thereby unconsciously and against their will furnished the occasion for the living God to display His divine glory before those who did not know Him.—Vers. 10–12. The God of Israel actually did what the idolatrous priests hardly considered possible. When the Philistines, in accordance with the advice given them by their priests, had placed the ark of the covenant and the expiatory gifts upon the cart to which the two cows were harnessed, " *the cows went straight forward on the way to Bethshemesh; they went along a road going and lowing* (i.e. lowing the whole time), *and turned not to the right or to the left; and the princes of the Philistines went behind them to the territory of Bethshemesh.*" יִשַּׁרְנָה בַדֶּרֶךְ, lit. "*they were straight in the way*," i.e. they went straight along the road. The form יִשַּׁרְנָה for תִּישַׁרְנָה is the imperf. *Kal*, third pers. plur. fem., with the preformative י instead of ת, as in Gen. xxx. 38 (see Ges. § 47, Anm. 3; Ewald, § 191, *b*). *Bethshemesh*, the present *Ain-shems*, was a priests' city on the border of Judah and Dan (see at Josh. xv. 10).

Vers. 13–18. The inhabitants of Bethshemesh were busy with the wheat-harvest in the valley (in front of the town), when they unexpectedly saw the ark of the covenant coming, and rejoiced to see it. The cart had arrived at the field of Joshua, a Bethshemeshite, and there it stood still before a large stone. And they (the inhabitants of Bethshemesh) chopped up the wood of the cart, and offered the cows to the Lord as a burnt-offering. In the meantime the Levites had taken off the ark, with the chest of golden presents, and placed it upon the large stone; and the people of Bethshemesh offered burnt-offerings and slain-offerings that day to the Lord. The princes of the Philistines stood looking at this, and then returned the same day to Ekron. That the Bethshemeshites, and not the Philistines, are the subject to וַיְבַקְּעוּ, is evident from the correct interpretation of the clauses; viz. from the fact that in ver. 14*a* the words from וְהָעֲגָלָה to אֶבֶן גְּדוֹלָה are circumstantial clauses introduced into the main clause, and that וַיְבַקְּעוּ is attached to וַיִּשְׂמְחוּ לִרְאוֹת, and carries on the principal clause.—Ver. 15*a* contains a supplementary remark, therefore הוֹרִידוּ is to be translated as a pluperfect. After sacrificing the cart, with the cows, as a burnt-offering to the Lord, the inhabitants of Bethshemesh gave a further practical expression to their joy at the return of the ark, by offering burnt-offerings and slain-offerings in praise of God. In the burnt-offerings they consecrated themselves afresh, with all their members, to the service of the Lord ; and in the slain-offerings, which culminated in the sacrificial meals, they sealed anew their living fellowship with the Lord. The offering of these sacrifices at Bethshemesh was no offence against the commandment, to sacrifice to the Lord at the place of His sanctuary alone. The ark of the covenant was the throne of the gracious presence of God, before which the sacrifices were really offered at the tabernacle. The Lord had sanctified the ark afresh as the throne of His presence, by the miracle which He had wrought in bringing it back again.—In vers. 17 and 18 the different atoning presents, which the Philistines sent to Jehovah as compensation, are enumerated once more : viz. five golden boils, one for each of their five principal towns (see at Josh. xiii. 3), and "*golden mice, according to the number of all the Philistian towns of the five princes, from the fortified city to the village of the inhabitants of the level land*" (*perazi;* see at Deut. iii. 5). The priests had only proposed that five golden mice should be sent as compensation, as well as five boils (ver. 4). But the Philistines offered as many images of mice as there were towns and villages in their five states, no doubt because the plague of mice had spread over the whole land, whereas the plague of boils had only fallen upon the inhabitants of those towns to which the ark of the covenant had come. In this way the apparent discrepancy between ver. 4 and ver. 18 is very simply removed. The words which follow, viz. אֲשֶׁר הִנִּיחוּ עָלֶיהָ וגו׳, "*upon which they had set down the ark,*" show unmistakeably, when compared with vers. 14 and 15, that we are to understand by אָבֵל הַגְּדוֹלָה the great stone upon which the ark was placed when it was taken off the cart. The conjecture of Kimchi, that this stone was called *Abel* (*luctus*), on account of the mourning which took place there (see ver. 19), is extremely unnatural. Consequently there is no other course left than to regard אבל as an error in writing for אֶבֶן, according to the reading, or at all events the rendering, adopted by the LXX. and *Targum.* But וְעַד (even unto) is quite unsuitable here, as no further local definition is required after the foregoing וְעַד כֹּפֶר הַפְּרָזִי, and it is impossible to suppose that the

Philistines offered a golden mouse as a trespass-offering for the great stone upon which the ark was placed. We must therefore alter וָעַד into וְעֵד: "*And the great stone is witness* (for וְעֵד in this sense, see Gen. xxxi. 52) *to this day in the field of Joshua the Bethshemeshite*," sc. of the fact just described.

Ver. 19-ch. vii. 1. DISPOSAL OF THE ARK OF GOD.—
Ver. 19. As the ark had brought evil upon the Philistines, so the inhabitants of Bethshemesh were also to be taught that they could not stand in their unholiness before the holy God: "*And He* (God) *smote among the men of Bethshemesh, because they had looked at the ark of Jehovah, and smote among the people seventy men, fifty thousand men.*" In this statement of numbers we are not only struck by the fact that the 70 stands before the 50,000, which is very unusual, but even more by the omission of the copula ו before the second number, which is altogether unparalleled. When, in addition to this, we notice that 50,000 men could not possibly live either in or round Bethshemesh, and that we cannot conceive of any extraordinary gathering having taken place out of the whole land, or even from the immediate neighbourhood; and also that the words חֲמִשִּׁים אֶלֶף אִישׁ are wanting in several Hebrew MSS., and that Josephus, in his account of the occurrence, only speaks of *seventy* as having been killed (*Ant.* vi. 1, 4); we cannot come to any other conclusion than that the number 50,000 is neither correct nor genuine, but a gloss which has crept into the text through some oversight, though it is of great antiquity, since the numbers stood in the text employed by the Septuagint and Chaldee translators, who attempted to explain them in two different ways, but both extremely forced. Apart from this number, however, the verse does not contain anything either in form or substance that could furnish occasion for well-founded objections to its integrity. The repetition of וַיַּךְ simply resumes the thought that had been broken off by the parenthetical clause כִּי רָאוּ בַּאֲרוֹן יְיָ; and בָּעָם is only a general expression for בְּאַנְשֵׁי ב"ש. The stroke which fell upon the people of Bethshemesh is sufficiently accounted for in the words, "*because they had looked*," etc. There is no necessity to understand these words, however, as many Rabbins do, as signifying " they looked *into* the ark," *i.e.* opened it and looked in; for if this had been the meaning, the

opening would certainly not have been passed over without notice. רָאָה with בְּ means to look *upon* or *at* a thing with lust or malicious pleasure; and here it no doubt signifies a foolish staring, which was incompatible with the holiness of the ark of God, and was punished with death, according to the warning expressed in Num. iv. 20. This severe judgment so alarmed the people of Bethshemesh, that they exclaimed, " *Who is able to stand before Jehovah, this holy God!*" Consequently the Bethshemeshites discerned correctly enough that the cause of the fatal stroke, which had fallen upon them, was the unholiness of their own nature, and not any special crime which had been committed by the persons slain. They felt that they were none of them any better than those who had fallen, and that sinners could not approach the holy God. Inspired with this feeling, they added, " *and to whom shall He go away from us?*" The subject to יַעֲלֶה is not the ark, but Jehovah who had chosen the ark as the dwelling-place of His name. In order to avert still further judgments, they sought to remove the ark from their town. They therefore sent messengers to Kirjath-jearim to announce to the inhabitants the fact that the ark had been sent back by the Philistines, and to entreat them to fetch it away.

Ch. vii. 1. The inhabitants of Kirjath-jearim complied with this request, and brought the ark into the house of Abinadab upon the height, and sanctified Abinadab's son Eleazar to be the keeper of the ark. *Kirjath-jearim*, the present *Kuryet el Enab* (see at Josh. ix. 17), was neither a priestly nor a Levitical city. The reason why the ark was taken there, is to be sought for, therefore, in the situation of the town, *i.e.* in the fact that Kirjath-jearim was the nearest large town on the road from Bethshemesh to Shiloh. We have no definite information, however, as to the reason why it was not taken on to Shiloh, to be placed in the tabernacle, but was allowed to remain in the house of Abinadab at Kirjath-jearim, where a keeper was expressly appointed to take charge of it; so that we can only confine ourselves to conjectures. Ewald's opinion (*Gesch.* ii. 540), that the Philistines had conquered Shiloh after the victory described in ch. iv., and had destroyed the ancient sanctuary there, *i.e.* the tabernacle, is at variance with the accounts given in ch. xxi. 6, 1 Kings iii. 4, 2 Chron. i. 3, respecting the continuance of worship in the tabernacle at Nob and Gibeon. There is much more to be said in support of the conjecture, that the carrying away of the ark by the Philistines was regarded as a judgment upon the sanctuary, which had been desecrated by the reckless conduct of the sons of Eli, and consequently, that even when the ark itself was recovered, they would not take it back without an express declaration of the will of God, but were satisfied, as a temporary arrangement, to leave the ark in Kirjath-jearim, which was farther removed from the cities of the Philistines. And there it remained, because no declaration of the divine will followed respecting its removal into the tabernacle, and the tabernacle itself had to be removed from Shiloh to Nob, and eventually to Gibeon, until David had effected the conquest of the citadel of Zion, and chosen Jerusalem as 'his capital, when it was removed from Kirjath-jearim to Jerusalem (2 Sam. vi.). It is not stated that Abinadab was a Levite; but this is very probable, because otherwise they would hardly have consecrated his son to be the keeper of the ark, but would have chosen a Levite for the office.

CONVERSION OF ISRAEL TO THE LORD BY SAMUEL. VICTORY OVER THE PHILISTINES. SAMUEL AS JUDGE OF ISRAEL.—CHAP. VII. 2-17.

Vers. 2-4. *Purification of Israel from idolatry.*—Twenty years passed away from that time forward, while the ark remained at Kirjath-jearim, and all Israel mourned after Jehovah. Then Samuel said to them, "*If ye turn to the Lord with all your heart, put away the strange gods from the midst of you, and the Astartes, and direct your heart firmly upon the Lord, and serve Him only, that He may save you out of the hand of the Philistines.*" And the Israelites listened to this appeal. The single clauses of vers. 2 and 3 are connected together by *vav consec.*, and are not to be separated from one another. There is no gap between these verses; but they contain the same closely and logically connected thought,[1] which may be arranged in

---

[1] There is no force at all in the proofs which Thenius has adduced of a gap between vers. 2 and 3. It by no means follows, that because the Philistines had brought back the ark, their rule over the Israelites had ceased, so as to make the words "he will deliver you," etc., incomprehensible. Moreover, the appearance of Samuel as *judge* does not presuppose

one period in the following manner: "And it came to pass, when the days multiplied from the time that the ark remained at Kirjath-jearim, and grew to twenty years, and the whole house of Israel mourned after Jehovah, that Samuel said," etc. The verbs וַיִּרְבּוּ, וַיְהִי, and וַיִּנָּהוּ, are merely continuations of the infinitive שֶׁבֶת, and the main sentence is resumed in the words וַיֹּאמֶר שְׁמוּאֵל. The contents of the verses require that the clauses should be combined in this manner. The statement that twenty years had passed can only be understood on the supposition that some kind of turning-point ensued at the close of that time. The complaining of the people after Jehovah was no such turning-point, but became one simply from the fact that this complaining was followed by some result. This result is described in ver. 3. It consisted in the fact that Samuel exhorted the people to put away the strange gods (ver. 3); and that when the people listened to his exhortation (ver. 4), he helped them to gain a victory over the Philistines (vers. 5 sqq.). יִנָּהוּ, from נָהָה, to lament or complain (Micah ii. 4; Ezek. xxxii. 18). "The phrase, *to lament after God*, is taken from human affairs, when one person follows another with earnest solicitations and complaints, until he at length assents. We have an example of this in the Syrophenician woman in Matt. xv." (Seb. Schmidt). The meaning "to assemble together," which is the one adopted by Gesenius, is forced upon the word from the Chaldee אִתְנְהִי, and it cannot be shown that the word was ever used in this sense in Hebrew. Samuel's appeal in ver. 3 recalls to mind Josh. xxiv. 14, and Gen. xxxv. 2; but the words, "*If ye do return unto the Lord with all your hearts,*" assume that the turning of the people to the Lord their God had already inwardly commenced, and indeed,

that his assumption of this office must necessarily have been mentioned before. As a general rule, there was no such formal assumption of the office, and this would be least of all the case with Samuel, who had been recognised as an accredited prophet of Jehovah (ch. iii. 19 sqq.). And lastly, the reference to idols, and to their being put away in consequence of Samuel's appeal, is intelligible enough, without any express account of their falling into idolatry, if we bear in mind, on the one hand, the constant inclination of the people to serve other gods, and if we observe, on the other hand, that Samuel called upon the people to turn to the Lord with all their heart and serve Him alone, which not only does not preclude, but actually implies, the outward continuance of the worship of Jehovah.

as the participle שָׁבִים expresses duration, had commenced as a permanent thing, and simply demand that the inward turning of the heart to God should be manifested outwardly as well, by the putting away of all their idols, and should thus be carried out to completion. The "strange gods" (see Gen. xxxv. 2) are described in ver. 4 as "*Baalim.*" On *Baalim* and *Ashtaroth*, see at Judg. ii. 11, 13. הָכִין לֵב, to direct the heart firmly, see Ps. lxxviii. 8; 2 Chron. xxx. 19.

Vers. 5–14. *Victory obtained over the Philistines through Samuel's prayer.*—Vers. 5, 6. When Israel had turned to the Lord with all its heart, and had put away all its idols, Samuel gathered together all the people at Mizpeh, to prepare them for fighting against the Philistines by a solemn day for penitence and prayer. For it is very evident that the object of calling all the people to Mizpeh was that the religious act performed there might serve as a consecration for battle, not only from the circumstance that, according to ver. 7, when the Philistines heard of the meeting, they drew near to make war upon Israel, but also from the contents of ver. 5: "*Samuel said* (sc. to the heads or representatives of the nation), *Gather all Israel to Mizpeh, and I will pray for you unto the Lord.*" His intention could not possibly have been any other than to put the people into the right relation to their God, and thus to prepare the way for their deliverance out of the bondage of the Philistines. Samuel appointed *Mizpeh, i.e. Nebi Samwil*, on the western boundary of the tribe of Benjamin (see at Josh. xviii. 26), as the place of meeting, partly no doubt on historical grounds, viz. because it was there that the tribes had formerly held their consultations respecting the wickedness of the inhabitants of Gibeah, and had resolved to make war upon Benjamin (Judg. xx. 1 sqq.), but still more, no doubt, because Mizpeh, on the western border of the mountains, was the most suitable place for commencing the conflict with the Philistines.— Ver. 6. When they had assembled together here, "*they drew water and poured it out before Jehovah, and fasted on that day, and said there, We have sinned against the Lord.*" Drawing water and pouring it out before Jehovah was a symbolical act, which has been thus correctly explained by the Chaldee, on the whole: "They poured out their heart like water in penitence before the Lord." This is evident from the figurative expressions, "poured out like water," in Ps. xxii. 15, and " pour out thy heart like water," in Lam. ii. 19, which are used to denote inward dissolution through pain, misery, and distress (see 2 Sam. xiv. 14). Hence the pouring out of water before God was a symbolical representation of the temporal and spiritual distress in which they were at the time,—a practical confession before God, "Behold, we are before Thee like water that has been poured out;" and as it was their own sin and rebellion against God that had brought this distress upon them, it was at the same time a confession of their misery, and an act of the deepest humiliation before the Lord. They gave a still further practical expression to this humiliation by fasting (צוֹם), as a sign of their inward distress of mind on account of their sin, and an oral confession of their sin against the Lord. By the word שָׁם, which is added to וַיֹּאמְרוּ, "they said *there*," *i.e.* at Mizpeh, the oral confession of their sin is formally separated from the two symbolical acts of humiliation before God, though by this very separation it is practically placed on a par with them. What they did symbolically by the pouring out of water and fasting, they explained and confirmed by their verbal confession. שָׁם is never an adverb of time signifying "*then;*" neither in Ps. xiv. 5, cxxxii. 17, nor Judg. v. 11. "*And thus Samuel judged the children of Israel at Mizpeh.*" וַיִּשְׁפֹּט does not mean "he became judge" (Mich. and others), any more than "he punished every one according to his iniquity" (Thenius, after David Kimchi). Judging the people neither consisted in a censure pronounced by Samuel afterwards, nor in absolution granted to the penitent after they had made a confession of their sin, but in the fact that Samuel summoned the nation to Mizpeh to humble itself before Jehovah, and there secured for it, through his intercession, the forgiveness of its sin, and a renewal of the favour of its God, and thus restored the proper relation between Israel and its God, so that the Lord could proceed to vindicate His people's rights against their foes.

When the Philistines heard of the gathering of the Israelites at Mizpeh (vers. 7, 8), their princes went up against Israel to make war upon it; and the Israelites, in their fear of the Philistines, entreated Samuel, "*Do not cease to cry for us to the Lord our God, that He may save us out of the hand of the Philistines.*"—Ver. 9. "*And Samuel took a milk-lamb* (a lamb that was still sucking, probably, according to Lev. xxii. 27, a lamb seven days old), *and offered it whole as a burnt-offering to the Lord.*" כָּלִיל is used adverbially, according to its original meaning as an adverb, "*whole.*" The Chaldee has not given the word at all, probably because the translators regarded it as pleonastic, since every burnt-offering was consumed upon the altar whole, and consequently the word כָּלִיל was sometimes used in a substantive sense, as synonymous with עוֹלָה (Deut. xxxiii. 10; Ps. li. 21). But in the passage before us, כָּלִיל is not synonymous with עוֹלָה, but simply affirms that the lamb was offered upon the altar without being cut up or divided. Samuel selected a young lamb for the burnt-offering, not "as being the purest and most innocent kind of sacrificial animal,"—for it cannot possibly be shown that very young animals were regarded as purer than those that were full-grown,—but as being the most suitable to represent the nation that had wakened up to new life through its conversion to the Lord, and was, as it were, new-born. For the burnt-offering represented the man, who consecrated therein his life and labour to the Lord. The sacrifice was the substratum for prayer. When Samuel offered it, he cried to the Lord for the children of Israel; and the Lord "*answered,*" *i.e.* granted, his prayer.—Ver. 10. When the Philistines advanced during the offering of the sacrifice to fight against Israel, "*Jehovah thundered with a great noise,*" *i.e.* with loud peals, against the Philistines, and threw them into confusion, so that they were smitten before Israel. The thunder, which alarmed the Philistines and threw them into confusion (יְהֻמֵּם, as in Josh. x. 10), was the answer of God to Samuel's crying to the Lord.—Ver. 11. As soon as they took to flight, the Israelites advanced from Mizpeh, and pursued and smote them to below *Beth-car*. The situation of this town or locality, which is only mentioned here, has not yet been discovered. Josephus (*Ant.* vi. 2, 2) has μέχρι Κορραίων.—Ver. 12. As a memorial of this victory, Samuel placed a stone between Mizpeh and Shen, to which he gave the name of *Eben-ha-ezer*, *i.e.* stone of help, as a standing memorial that the Lord had thus far helped His people. The situation of *Shen* is also not known. The name *Shen* (*i.e.* tooth) seems to indicate a projecting point of rock (see ch. xiv. 4), but may also signify a place situated upon such a point.—Ver. 13. Through this victory which was

obtained by the miraculous help of God, the Philistines were so humbled, that they no more invaded the territory of Israel, *i.e.* with lasting success, as they had done before. This limitation of the words "*they came no more*" (*lit.* "they did not add again to come into the border of Israel"), is implied in the context; for the words which immediately follow, "*and the hand of Jehovah was against the Philistines all the days of Samuel*," show that they made attempts to recover their lost supremacy, but that so long as Samuel lived they were unable to effect anything against Israel. This is also manifest from the successful battles fought by Saul (ch. xiii. and xiv.), when the Philistines had made fresh attempts to subjugate Israel during his reign. The defeats inflicted upon them by Saul also belong to the days of Samuel, who died but a very few years before Saul himself. Because of these battles which Saul fought with the Philistines, Lyra and Brentius understand the expression "all the days of Samuel" as referring not to the lifetime of Samuel, but simply to the duration of his official life as judge, viz. till the commencement of Saul's reign. But this is at variance with ver. 15, where Samuel is said to have judged Israel all the days of his life. Seb. Schmidt has given, on the whole, the correct explanation of ver. 13: "They came no more so as to obtain a victory and subdue the Israelites as before; yet they did return, so that the hand of the Lord was against them, *i.e.* so that they were repulsed with great slaughter, although they were not actually expelled, or the Israelites delivered from tribute and the presence of military garrisons, and that all the days that the judicial life of Samuel lasted, in fact all his life, since they were also smitten by Saul."
—Ver. 14. In consequence of the defeat at Ebenezer, the Philistines were obliged to restore to the Israelites the cities which they had taken from them, "*from Ekron to Gath.*" This definition of the limits is probably to be understood as *exclusive, i.e.* as signifying that the Israelites received back their cities up to the very borders of the Philistines, measuring these borders from Ekron to Gath, and not that the Israelites received Ekron and Gath also. For although these chief cities of the Philistines had been allotted to the tribes of Judah and Dan in the time of Joshua (Josh. xiii. 3, 4, xv. 45, 46), yet, notwithstanding the fact that Judah and Simeon conquered Ekron,

together with Gaza and Askelon, after the death of Joshua (Judg. i. 18), the Israelites did not obtain any permanent possession. "*And their territory*" (coasts), *i.e.* the territory of the towns that were given back to Israel, not that of Ekron and Gath, "*did Israel deliver out of the hands of the Philistines. And there was peace between Israel and the Amorites;*" *i.e.* the Canaanitish tribes also kept peace with Israel after this victory of the Israelites over the Philistines, and during the time of Samuel. The Amorites are mentioned, as in Josh. x. 6, as being the most powerful of the Canaanitish tribes, who had forced the Danites out of the plain into the mountains (Judg. i. 34, 35).

Vers. 15-17. *Samuel's judicial labours.*—With the calling of the people to Mizpeh, and the victory at Ebenezer that had been obtained through his prayer, Samuel had assumed the government of the whole nation; so that his office as judge dates from this period, although he had laboured as prophet among the people from the death of Eli, and had thereby prepared the way for the conversion of Israel to the Lord. As his prophetic labours were described in general terms in ch. iii. 19-21, so are his labours as judge in the verses before us: viz. in ver. 15 their duration,—"*all the days of his life,*" as his activity during Saul's reign and the anointing of David (ch. xv. xvi.) sufficiently prove; and then in vers. 16, 17 their general character,—"*he went round from year to year*" (וְסָבַב serves as a more precise definition of וְהָלַךְ, he went and travelled round) *to Bethel, i.e.* Beitin (see at Josh. vii. 2), *Gilgal, and Mizpeh* (see at ver. 5), and judged Israel at all these places. Which Gilgal is meant, whether the one situated in the valley of the Jordan (Josh. iv. 19), or the *Jiljilia* on the higher ground to the southwest of Shiloh (see at Josh. viii. 35), cannot be determined with perfect certainty. The latter is favoured partly by the order in which the three places visited by Samuel on his circuits occur, since according to this he probably went first of all from Ramah to Bethel, which was to the north-east, then farther north or north-west to Jiljilia, and then turning back went towards the south-east to Mizpeh, and returning thence to Ramah performed a complete circuit; whereas, if the Gilgal in the valley of the Jordan had been the place referred to, we should expect him to go there first of all from Ramah, and then towards the north-east to Bethel, and from that to the south-west to Mizpeh; and partly also by the circumstance that, according to 2 Kings ii. 1 and iv. 38, there was a school of the prophets at Jiljilia in the time of Elijah and Elisha, the founding of which probably dated as far back as the days of Samuel. If this conjecture were really a well-founded one, it would furnish a strong proof that it was in this place, and not in the Gilgal in the valley of the Jordan, that Samuel judged the people. But as this conjecture cannot be raised into a certainty, the evidence in favour of Jiljilia is not so conclusive as I myself formerly supposed (see also the remarks on ch. ix. 14). אֵת כָּל־הַמְּקוֹמוֹת is grammatically considered an accusative, and is in apposition to אֶת־יִשְׂרָאֵל, *lit. Israel,* viz. all the places named, *i.e.* Israel which inhabited all these places, and was to be found there. "*And his return was to Ramah;*" *i.e.* after finishing the annual circuit he returned to Ramah, where he had his house. There he judged Israel, and also built an altar to conduct the religious affairs of the nation. Up to the death of Eli, Samuel lived and laboured at Shiloh (ch. iii. 21). But when the ark was carried away by the Philistines, and consequently the tabernacle at Shiloh lost what was most essential to it as a sanctuary, and ceased at once to be the scene of the gracious presence of God, Samuel went to his native town Ramah, and there built an altar as the place of sacrifice for Jehovah, who had manifested himself to him. The building of the altar at Ramah would naturally be suggested to the prophet by these extraordinary circumstances, even if it had not been expressly commanded by Jehovah.

II. THE MONARCHY OF SAUL FROM HIS ELECTION TILL HIS ULTIMATE REJECTION.

CHAP. VIII.-XV.

The earthly monarchy in Israel was established in the time of Samuel, and through his mediation. At the pressing desire of the people, Samuel installed the Benjaminite Saul as king, according to the command of God. The reign of Saul may be divided into two essentially different periods: viz. (1) the establishment and vigorous development of his regal supremacy (ch. viii.-xv.); (2) the decline and gradual overthrow of his monarchy (ch. xvi.-xxxi.). The establishment of the monarchy is introduced by the negotiations of the elders of Israel with Samuel concerning the appointment of a king (ch. viii.). This is followed by (1) the account of the anointing of Saul as king (ch. ix. 1-x. 16), of his election by lot, and of his victory over the Ammonites and the confirmation of his monarchy at Gilgal (ch. x. 17-xi. 15), together with Samuel's final address to the nation (ch. xii.); (2) the history of Saul's reign, of which only his earliest victories over the Philistines are given at all elaborately (ch. xiii. 1-xiv. 46), his other wars and family history being disposed of very summarily (ch. xiv. 47-52); (3) the account of his disobedience to the command of God in the war against the Amalekites, and the rejection on the part of God with which Samuel threatened him in consequence (ch. xv.). The brevity with which the history of his actual reign is treated, in contrast with the elaborate account of his election and confirmation as king, may be accounted for from the significance and importance of Saul's monarchy in relation to the kingdom of God in Israel.

The people of Israel traced the cause of the oppression and distress, from which they had suffered more and more in the time of the judges, to the defects of their own political constitution. They wished to have a king, like all the heathen nations, to conduct their wars and conquer their enemies. Now, although the desire to be ruled by a king, which had existed in the nation even from the time of Gideon, was not in itself at variance with the appointment of Israel as a kingdom of God, yet the motive which led the people to desire it was both wrong and hostile to God, since the source of all the evils and misfortunes from which Israel suffered was to be found in the apostasy of the nation from its God, and its coquetting with the gods of the heathen. Consequently their self-willed obstinacy in demanding a king, notwithstanding the warnings of Samuel, was an actual rejection of the sovereignty of Jehovah, since He had always manifested himself to His people as their king by delivering them out of the power of their foes, as soon as they returned to Him with simple penitence of heart. Samuel pointed this out to the elders of Israel, when they laid their petition before him that he would choose them a king. But Jehovah fulfilled their desires. He directed Samuel to appoint them a king, who possessed all the qualifications that were necessary to secure for the nation what it looked for from a king, and who therefore might have established the monarchy in Israel as foreseen and foretold by Jehovah, if he had not presumed upon his own power, but had submitted humbly to the will of God as made known to him by the prophet. Saul, who was chosen from Benjamin, the smallest but yet the most warlike of all the tribes, a man in the full vigour of youth, and surpassing all the rest of the people in beauty of form as well as bodily strength, not only possessed "warlike bravery and talent, unbroken courage that could overcome opposition of every kind, a stedfast desire for the well-being of the nation in the face of its many and mighty foes, and zeal and pertinacity in the execution of his plans" (Ewald), but also a pious heart, and an earnest zeal for the maintenance of the provisions of the law, and the promotion of the religious life of the nation. He would not commence the conflict with the Philistines until sacrifice had been offered (ch. xiii. 9 sqq.); in the midst of the hot pursuit of the foe he opposed the sin committed by the people in eating flesh with the blood (ch. xiv. 32, 33); he banished the wizards and necromancers out of the land (ch. xxviii. 3, 9); and in general he appears to have kept a strict watch over the observance of the Mosaic law in his kingdom. But the consciousness of his own power, coupled with the energy of his character, led him astray into an incautious disregard of the commands of God; his zeal in the prosecution of his plans hurried him on to reckless and violent measures; and success in his undertakings heightened his ambition into a haughty rebellion against the Lord, the God-king of Israel. These errors come out very conspicuously in the three great events of his reign which are the most circumstantially described. When Saul was preparing for war against the Philistines, and Samuel did not appear at once on the day appointed, he presumptuously disregarded the prohibition of the prophet, and offered the sacrifice himself without waiting for Samuel to arrive (ch. xiii. 7 sqq.). In the engagement with the Philistines, he attempted to force on the annihilation of the foe by pronouncing the ban upon any one in his army who should eat bread before the evening, or till he had avenged himself upon his foes. Consequently, he not only diminished the strength of the people, so that the overthrow of the enemy was not great, but he also prepared humiliation for himself, inasmuch as he was not able to carry out his vow (ch. xiv. 24 sqq.). But he sinned still more grievously in the war with the Amalekites, when he violated the express command of the Lord by only executing the ban upon that nation as far as he himself thought well, and thus by such utterly unpardonable conduct altogether renounced the obedience which he owed to the Lord his God (ch. xv.). All these acts of transgression manifest an attempt to secure the unconditional gratification of his own self-will, and a growing disregard of the government of Jehovah in Israel; and the consequence of the whole was simply this, that Saul not only failed to accomplish that deliverance of the nation out of the power of its foes which the Israelites had anticipated from their king, and was unable to inflict any lasting humiliation upon the Philistines, but that he undermined the stability of his monarchy, and brought about his own rejection on the part of God.

From all this we may see very clearly, that the reason why the occurrences connected with the election of Saul as king are fully described on the one hand, and on the other only such incidents connected with his enterprises after he began to reign as served to bring out the faults and crimes of his monarchy, was, that Israel might learn from this, that royalty itself could never secure the salvation it expected, unless the occupant of the throne submitted altogether to the will of the Lord. Of the other acts of Saul, the wars with the different nations round about are only briefly mentioned, but with this remark, that he displayed his strength and gained the victory in whatever direction he turned (ch. xiv. 47), simply because this statement was sufficient to bring out the brighter side of his reign, inasmuch as this clearly showed that it might have been a source of blessing to the people of God, if the king had only studied how to govern his people in the power and according to the will of Jehovah. If we examine the history of Saul's reign from this point of view, all the different points connected with it exhibit the greatest harmony. Modern critics, however, have discovered irreconcilable contradictions in the history, simply because, instead of studying it for the purpose of fathoming the plan and purpose which lie at the foundation, they have entered upon the inquiry with a twofold assumption : viz. (1) that the government of Jehovah over Israel was only a subjective idea of the Israelitish nation, without any objective reality; and (2) that the human monarchy was irreconcilably opposed to the government of God. Governed by these axioms, which are derived not from the Scriptures, but from the philosophical views of modern times, the critics have found it impossible to explain the different accounts in any other way than by the purely external hypothesis, that the history contained in this book has been compiled from two different sources, in one of which the establishment of the earthly monarchy was treated as a violation of the supremacy of God, whilst the other took a more favourable view. From the first source, ch. viii., x. 17–27, xi., xii., and xv. are said to have been derived; and ch. ix.–x. 17, xiii., and xiv. from the second.

ISRAEL'S PRAYER FOR A KING.—CHAP. VIII.

As Samuel had appointed his sons as judges in his old age, and they had perverted justice, the elders of Israel entreated him to appoint them a king after the manner of all the nations (vers. 1–5). This desire not only displeased Samuel, but Jehovah also saw in it a rejection of His government; nevertheless He commanded the prophet to fulfil the desire of the people, but at the same time to set before them as a warning the prerogatives of a king (vers. 6–9). This answer from God, Samuel made known to the people, describing to them the prerogatives which the king would assume to himself above the rest of the people (vers. 10–18). As the people, however, persisted in their wish, Samuel promised them, according to the direction of God, that their wishes should be gratified (vers. 19–22).

Vers. 1–5. The reason assigned for the appointment of Samuel's sons as judges is his own advanced age. The inference which we might draw from this alone, namely, that they were simply to support their father in the administration of justice, and that Samuel had no intention of laying down his office, and still less of making the supreme office of judge hereditary in his family, is still more apparent from the fact that they were stationed as judges of the nation in Beersheba, which was on the southern border of Canaan (Judg. xx. 1, etc.; see at Gen. xxi. 31). The sons are also mentioned again in 1 Chron. vi. 13, though the name of the elder has either been dropped out of the Masoretic text or has become corrupt.—Ver. 3. The sons, however, did not walk in the ways of their father, but set their hearts upon gain, took bribes, and perverted justice, in opposition to the command of God (see Ex. xxiii. 6, 8; Deut. xvi. 19).—Vers. 4, 5. These circumstances (viz. Samuel's age and the degeneracy of his sons) furnished the elders of Israel with the opportunity to apply to Samuel with this request: "*Appoint us a king to judge us, as all the nations*" (the heathen), *sc.* have kings. This request resembles so completely the law of the king in Deut. xvii. 14 (observe, for example, the expression כְּכָל־הַגּוֹיִם), that the distinct allusion to it is unmistakeable. The custom of expressly quoting the book of the law is met with for the first time in the writings of the period of the captivity. The elders simply desired what Jehovah had foretold through His servant Moses, as a thing that would take place in the future and for which He had even made provision.

Vers. 6–9. Nevertheless "*the thing displeased Samuel when they said*," etc. This serves to explain הַדָּבָר, and precludes the supposition that Samuel's displeasure had reference to what they had said concerning his own age and the conduct of his sons. At the same time, the reason why the petition for a king displeased the prophet, was not that he regarded the earthly monarchy as irreconcilable with the sovereignty of God, or even as untimely; for in both these cases he would not have entered into the question at all, but would simply have refused the request as ungodly or unseasonable. But "*Samuel prayed to the Lord*," *i.e.* he laid the matter before the Lord in prayer, and the Lord said (ver. 7): "*Hearken unto the voice of the people in all that they say unto thee.*" This clearly implies, that not only in Samuel's opinion, but also according to the counsel of God, the time had really come for the establishment of the earthly sovereignty in Israel. In this respect the request of the elders for a king to reign over them was perfectly justifiable; and there is no reason to say, with Calvin, "they ought to have had regard to the times and conditions prescribed by God, and it would no doubt have come to pass that the regal power would have grown up in the nation. Although, therefore, it had not yet been established, they ought to have waited patiently for the time appointed by God, and not to have given way to their own reasons and counsels apart from the will of God." For God had not only appointed no particular time for the establishment of the monarchy; but in the introduction to the law for the king, "When thou shalt say, I will set a king over me," He had ceded the right to the representatives of the nation to deliberate upon the matter. Nor did they err in this respect, that while Samuel was still living, it was not the proper time to make use of the permission that they had received; for they assigned as the reason for their application, that Samuel had grown old: consequently they did not petition for a king instead of the prophet who had been appointed and so gloriously accredited by God, but simply that Samuel himself would give them a king in consideration of his own age, in order that when he should become feeble or die, they might have a judge and leader of the nation. Nevertheless the Lord declared, "*They have not rejected thee, but they have rejected me, that I should not reign over them. As they have always done from the day that I brought them up out of Egypt unto this day, that they have forsaken me and served other gods, so do they also unto thee.*" This verdict on the part of God refers not so much to the desire expressed, as to the feelings from which it had sprung. Externally regarded, the elders of Israel had a perfect right to present the request; the wrong was in their hearts.[1] They not only declared to the prophet their confidence in his administration of his office, but they implicitly declared him incapable of any further superintendence of their civil and political affairs. This mistrust was founded upon mistrust in the Lord and His

---

[1] Calvin has correctly pointed out how much would have been warrantable under the circumstances: "They might, indeed, have reminded Samuel of his old age, which rendered him less able to attend to the duties of his office, and also of the avarice of his sons and the corruptness of the judges; or they might have complained that his sons did not walk in his footsteps, and have asked that God would choose suitable men to govern them, and thus have left the whole thing to His will. And if they had done this, there can be no doubt that they would have received a gracious and suitable answer. But they did not think of calling upon God; they demanded that a king should be given them, and brought forward the customs and institutions of other nations."

guidance. In the person of Samuel they rejected the Lord and His rule. They wanted a king, because they imagined that Jehovah their God-king was not able to secure their constant prosperity. Instead of seeking for the cause of the misfortunes which had hitherto befallen them in their own sin and want of fidelity towards Jehovah, they searched for it in the faulty constitution of the nation itself. In such a state of mind as this, their desire for a king was a contempt and rejection of the kingly government of Jehovah, and was nothing more than forsaking Jehovah to serve other gods. (See ch. x. 18, 19, and ch. xii. 7 sqq., where Samuel points out to the people still more fully the wrong that they have committed.)—Ver. 9. In order to show them wherein they were wrong, Samuel was instructed to bear witness against them, by proclaiming the right of the king who would rule over them. הָעֵד תָּעִיד בָּהֶם neither means "warn them earnestly" (De Wette), nor "explain and solemnly expound to them" (Thenius). הָעִיד בְּ means *to bear witness*, or give testimony against a person, *i.e.* to point out to him his wrong. The following words, וְהִגַּדְתָּ וגו׳, are to be understood as explanatory, in the sense of "*by proclaiming to them.*" "*The manner (mishpat) of the king*" is the *right* or *prerogative* which the king would claim, namely, such a king as was possessed by all the other nations, and such an one as Israel desired in the place of its own God-king, *i.e.* a king who would rule over his people with arbitrary and absolute power.

Vers. 10–18. In accordance with the instructions of God, Samuel told the people all the words of Jehovah, *i.e.* all that God had said to him, as related in vers. 7–9, and then proclaimed to them the right of the king.—Ver. 11. "*He will take your sons, and set them for himself upon his chariots, and upon his saddle-horses, and they will run before his chariot;*" *i.e.* he will make the sons of the people his retainers at court, his charioteers, riders, and runners. The singular suffix attached to בְּמֶרְכַּבְתּוֹ is not to be altered, as Thenius suggests, into the plural form, according to the LXX., Chald., and Syr., since the word refers, not to war-chariots, but to the king's state-carriage; and פָּרָשׁ does not mean a rider, but a saddle-horse, as in 2 Sam. i. 6, 1 Kings v. 6, etc.—Ver. 12. "*And to make himself chiefs over thousands and over fifties;*"—the greatest and smallest military officers are mentioned, instead of all the soldiers and officers (comp. Num. xxxi. 14, 2 Kings i. 9 sqq., with Ex. xviii. 21, 25). וְלָשׁוּם is also dependent upon יִקַּח (ver. 11),—" *and to plough his field* (חָרִישׁ, *lit.* the ploughed), *and reap his harvest, and make his instruments of war and instruments of his chariots.*"—Ver. 13. " *Your daughters he will take as preparers of ointments, cooks, and bakers,*" *sc.* for his court.—Vers. 14 sqq. All their possessions he would also take to himself: the good (*i.e.* the best) fields, vineyards, and olive-gardens, he would take away, and give to his servants; he would tithe the sowings and vineyards (*i.e.* the produce which they yielded), and give them to his courtiers and servants. סָרִים, *lit.* the eunuch; here it is used in a wider sense for the *royal chamberlains.* Even their *slaves* (men-servants and maid-servants) and their *beasts of draught and burden* he would take and use for his own work, and *raise the tithe of the flock.* The word בַּחוּרֵיכֶם, between the slaves (men-servants and maid-servants) and the asses, is very striking and altogether unsuitable; and in all probability it is only an ancient copyist's error for בְּקַרְכֶם, your oxen, as we may see from the LXX. rendering, τὰ βουκόλια. The servants and maids, oxen and asses, answer in that case to one another; whilst the young men are included among the sons in vers. 11, 12. In this way the king would make all the people into his servants or slaves. This is the meaning of the second clause of ver. 17; for the whole are evidently summed up in conclusion in the expression, " *and ye shall be his servants.*"—Ver. 18. Israel would then cry out to God because of its king, but the Lord would not hear it then. This description, which contains a fearful picture of the tyranny of the king, is drawn from the despotic conduct of the heathen kings, and does not presuppose, as many have maintained, the times of the later kings, which were so full of painful experiences.

Vers. 19–22. With such a description of the " *right of the king*" as this, Samuel had pointed out to the elders the dangers connected with a monarchy in so alarming a manner, that they ought to have been brought to reflection, and to have desisted from their demand. " *But the people refused to hearken to the voice of Samuel.*" They repeated their demand, " *We will have a king over us, that we also may be like all the nations, and that our king may judge us, and go out before us, and conduct our battles.*"—Vers. 21, 22. These words of the people were laid by Samuel before the Lord, and the Lord commanded him to give the people a king. With this answer Samuel sent the men of Israel, *i.e.* the elders, away. This is implied in the words, " *Go ye every man unto his city*," since we may easily supply from the context, " till I shall call you again, to appoint you the king you desire."

ANOINTING OF SAUL AS KING.—CHAP. IX.-X. 16.

When the Lord had instructed Samuel to appoint a king over the nation, in accordance with its own desire, He very speedily proceeded to show him the man whom He had chosen. Saul the Benjaminite came to Samuel, to consult him as a seer about his father's she-asses, which had been lost, and for which he had been seeking in all directions in vain (ch. ix. 1–14). And the Lord had already revealed to the prophet the day before, that He would send him the man who had been set apart by Him as the king of Israel; and when Samuel met with Saul, He pointed him out as the man to whom He had referred (vers. 15–17). Accordingly, Samuel invited Saul to be his guest at a sacrificial meal, which he was about to celebrate (vers. 18–24). After the meal he made known to him the purpose of God, anointed him as king (vers. 25–27, ch. x. 1), and sent him away, with an announcement of three signs, which would serve to confirm his election on the part of God (ch. x. 2–16). This occurrence is related very circumstantially, to bring out distinctly the miraculous interposition of God, and to show that Saul did not aspire to the throne; and also that Samuel did not appoint of his own accord the man whom he was afterwards obliged to reject, but that Saul was elected by God to be king over His people, without any interference on the part of either Samuel or himself.[1]

Ch. ix. 1–10. *Saul searches for his father's asses.*—Vers. 1, 2. The elaborate genealogy of the Benjaminite Kish, and the minute description of the figure of his son Saul, are in-

---

[1] There is no tenable ground for the assumption of Thenius and others, that this account was derived from a different source from ch. viii., x. 17–27, and xi. sqq.; for the assertion that ch. x. 17–27 connects itself in the most natural way with ch. viii. is neither well-founded nor correct. In the first place, it was certainly more natural that Samuel, who was to place a king over the nation according to the appointment of God, should be

tended to indicate at the very outset the importance to which Saul attained in relation to the people of Israel. *Kish* was the son of *Abiel*: this is in harmony with ch. xiv. 51. But when, on the other hand, it is stated in 1 Chron. viii. 33, ix. 39, that *Ner* begat *Kish*, the difference may be reconciled in the simplest manner, on the assumption that the *Ner* mentioned there is not the father, but the grandfather, or a still more remote ancestor of *Kish*, as the intervening members are frequently passed over in the genealogies. The other ancestors of *Kish* are never mentioned again. גִּבּוֹר חַיִל refers to *Kish*, and signifies not a brave man, but a man of property, as in Ruth ii. 1. This son Saul (*i.e.* "*prayed for:*" for this meaning of the word, comp. ch. i. 17, 27) was "*young and beautiful.*" It is true that even at that time Saul had a son grown up (viz. Jonathan), according to ch. xiii. 2; but still, in contrast with his father, he was "a young man," *i.e.* in the full vigour of youth, probably about forty or forty-five years old. There is no necessity, therefore, to follow the Vulgate rendering *electus*. No one equalled him in beauty. "*From his shoulder upwards he was higher than any of the people.*" Such a figure as this was well adapted to commend him to the people as their king (cf. ch. x. 24), since size and beauty were highly valued in rulers, as signs of manly strength (see Herod. iii. 20, vii. 187; Aristot. *Polit.* iv. c. 24).—Vers. 3–5. Having been sent out by his father to search for his she-asses which had strayed, Saul went with his servant through the mountains of Ephraim, which ran southwards into the tribe-territory of Benjamin (see at ch. i. 1), then through the land of Shalishah and the land of Shaalim, and after that through the land of Benjamin, without finding the asses; and at length, when he had reached the land of Zuph, he determined to return, because he was afraid that his father might turn his mind from the asses, and trouble himself about them (the son and servant). חָדַל מִן, to desist from a thing, to give it up or renounce it.

made acquainted with the man whom God had appointed, before the people elected him by lot. And secondly, Saul's behaviour in hiding himself when the lots were cast (ch. x. 21 sqq.), can only be explained on the supposition that Samuel had already informed him that he was the appointed king; whereas, if this had not been the case, it would be altogether incomprehensible.

As Saul started in any case from Gibeah of Benjamin, his own home (ch. x. 10 sqq., 26, xi. 4, xv. 34, xxiii. 19, xxvi. 1), *i.e.* the present *Tuleil el Phul*, which was an hour or an hour and a half to the north of Jerusalem (see at Josh. xviii. 28), and went thence into the mountains of Ephraim, he no doubt took a north-westerly direction, so that he crossed the boundary of Benjamin somewhere between Bireh and Atarah, and passing through the crest of the mountains of Ephraim, on the west of Gophnah (Jifna), came out into the land of Shalishah. *Shalishah* is unquestionably the country round (or of) *Baal-shalishah* (2 Kings iv. 42), which was situated, according to Eusebius (*Onom. s.v.* Βαιθσαρισάθ: *Beth-sarisa* or *Beth-salisa*), *in regione Thamnitica*, fifteen Roman miles to the north of Diospolis (Lydda), and was therefore probably the country to the west of Jiljilia, where three different wadys run into one large wady, called Kurawa; and according to the probable conjecture of Thenius, it was from this fact that the district received the name of *Shalishah*, or *Three-land*. They proceeded thence in their search to the land of *Shaalim*: according to the *Onom.* (*s.v.*), " a village seven miles off, *in finibus Eleutheropoleos contra occidentem*." But this is hardly correct, and is most likely connected with the mistake made in transposing the town of Samuel to the neighbourhood of Diospolis (see at ch. i. 1). For since they went on from Shaalim into the land of Benjamin, and then still further into the land of Zuph, on the south-west of Benjamin, they probably turned eastwards from Shalishah, into the country where we find *Beni Mussah* and *Beni Salem* marked upon Robinson's and v. de Velde's maps, and where we must therefore look for the land of *Shaalim*, that they might proceed thence to explore the land of Benjamin from the northeast to the south-west. If, on the contrary, they had gone from Shaalim in a southerly or south-westerly direction, to the district of Eleutheropolis, they would only have entered the land of Benjamin at the south-west corner, and would have had to go all the way back again in order to go thence to the land of Zuph. For we may infer with certainty that the land of Zuph was on the south-west of the tribe-territory of Benjamin, from the fact that, according to ch. x. 2, Saul and his companion passed Rachel's tomb on their return thence to their own home, and then came to the border of

Benjamin. On the name *Zuph*, see at ch. i. 1 —Ver. 6. When Saul proposed to return home from the land of Zuph, his servant said to him, " *Behold, in this city* (' *this*,' referring to the town which stood in front of them upon a hill) *is a man of God, much honoured; all that he saith cometh surely to pass: now we will go thither; perhaps he will tell us our way that we have to go*" (*lit.* have gone, and still go, *sc.* to attain the object of our journey, viz. to find the asses). The name of this town is not mentioned either here or in the further course of this history. Nearly all the commentators suppose it to have been Ramah, Samuel's home. But this assumption has no foundation at all in the text, and is irreconcilable with the statements respecting the return in ch. x. 2–5. The servant did not say there *dwells* in this city, but there is in this city (ver. 6; comp. with this ver. 10, " They went into the city where the man of God was," not " dwelt "). It is still more evident, from the answer given by the drawers of water, when Saul asked them, " *Is the seer here?*" (ver. 11),—viz. " *He came to-day to the city, for the people have a great sacrifice upon the high place*" (ver. 12),—that the seer (Samuel) did not live in the town, but had only come thither to a sacrificial festival. Moreover, "every impartial man will admit, that the fact of Samuel's having honoured Saul as his guest at the sacrificial meal of those who participated in the sacrifice, and of their having slept under the same roof, cannot possibly weaken the impression that Samuel was only there in his peculiar and official capacity. It could not be otherwise than that the presidency should be assigned to him at the feast itself as priest and prophet, and therefore that the appointments mentioned should proceed from him. And it is but natural to assume that he had a house at his command for any repetition of such sacrifices, which we find from 2 Kings iv. to have been the case in the history of Elisha" (Valentiner). And lastly, the sacrificial festival itself does not point to Ramah; for although Samuel had built an altar to the Lord at Ramah (ch. vii. 17), this was by no means the only place of sacrifice in the nation. If Samuel offered sacrifice at Mizpeh and Gilgal (ch. vii. 9, x. 8, xiii. 8 sqq.), he could also do the same at other places. What the town really was in which Saul met with him, cannot indeed be determined, since all that we can gather from ch. x. 2 is, that it was situated on the south-west of Bethlehem.

—Vers. 7-10. Saul's objection, that they had no present to bring to the man of God, as the bread was gone from their vessels, was met by the servant with the remark, that he had a quarter of a shekel which he would give.—Ver. 9. Before proceeding with the further progress of the affair, the historian introduces a notice, which was required to throw light upon what follows; namely, that beforetime, if any one wished to inquire of God, *i.e.* to apply to a prophet for counsel from God upon any matter, it was customary in Israel to say, We will go to the seer, because "*he that is now called a prophet was beforetime called a seer.*" After this parenthetical remark, the account is continued in ver. 10. Saul declared himself satisfied with the answer of the servant; and they both went into the town, to ask the man of God about the asses that were lost.

Vers. 11-17. As they were going up to the high place of the town, they met maidens coming out of the town to draw water; and on asking them whether the seer was there, they received this answer: "*Yes; behold, he is before thee: make haste now, for he has come into the town to-day; for the people have a sacrifice to-day upon the high place.*" *Bamah* (in the singular) does not mean the height or hill generally; but throughout it signifies *the high place*, as a place of sacrifice or prayer.— Ver. 13. "*When ye come into the city, ye will find him directly, before he goes up to the high place to eat.*" כְּ not only introduces the apodosis, but corresponds to כְּ, *as, so:* here, however, it is used with reference to time, in the sense of our "immediately." "*For the people are not accustomed to eat till he comes, for he blesses the sacrifice,*" etc. בָּרֵךְ, like εὐλογεῖν, refers to the thanksgiving prayer offered before the sacrificial meal. "*Go now for him; ye will meet him even to-day.*" The first אֹתוֹ is placed at the beginning for the sake of emphasis, and then repeated at the close. כְּהַיּוֹם, "*Even to-day.*"—Ver. 14. When they went into the town, Samuel met them on his way out to go to the high place of sacrifice. Before the meeting itself is described, the statement is introduced in vers. 15-17, that the day before Jehovah had foretold to Samuel that the man was coming to him whom he was to anoint as captain over his people. גָּלָה אֹזֶן, to *open any one's ear*, equivalent to *reveal* something to him (ch. xx. 12; 2 Sam. vii. 27, etc.). אֶשְׁלַח, *I will send thee, i.e.* "I will so direct his way in my overruling providence, that he shall come to thee" (J. H. Mich.). The words, "*that he may save my people out of the hand of the Philistines; for I have looked upon my people, for their cry is come unto me,*" are not at all at variance with ch. vii. 13. In that passage there is simply the assertion, that there was no more any permanent oppression on the part of the Philistines in the days of Samuel, such as had taken place before; but an attempt to recover their supremacy over Israel is not only not precluded, but is even indirectly affirmed (see the comm. on ch. vii. 13). The words before us simply show that the Philistines had then begun to make a fresh attempt to contend for dominion over the Israelites. "*I have looked upon my people:*" this is to be explained like the similar passage in Ex. ii. 25, "God looked upon the children of Israel," and Ex. iii. 7, "I have looked upon the misery of my people." God's looking was not a quiet, inactive looking on, but an energetic look, which brought help in trouble. "*Their cry is come unto me:*" this is word for word the same as in Ex. iii. 9. As the Philistines wanted to tread in the footsteps of the Egyptians, it was necessary that Jehovah should also send His people a deliverer from these new oppressors, by giving them a king. The reason here assigned for the establishment of a monarchy is by no means at variance with the displeasure which God had expressed to Samuel at the desire of the people for a king (ch. viii. 7 sqq.); since this displeasure had reference to the state of heart from which the desire had sprung.—Ver. 17. When Samuel saw Saul, the Lord answered him, *sc.* in reply to the tacit inquiry, '*Is this he?*' "*Behold, this is the man of whom I spake to thee.*" עָצַר, *coercere imperio.*

Vers. 18–24. The thread of the narrative, which was broken off in ver. 15, is resumed in ver. 18. Saul drew near to Samuel in the gate, and asked him for the seer's house. The expression בְּתוֹךְ הַשַּׁעַר is used to define more precisely the general phrase in ver. 14, בָּאִים בְּתוֹךְ הָעִיר; and there is no necessity to alter הָעִיר in ver. 14 into הַשַּׁעַר, as Thenius proposes, for בּוֹא בְּתוֹךְ הָעִיר does not mean to go (or be) in the middle of the town, as he imagines, but to *go into,* or enter, *the town;* and the entrance to the town was through the gate.—Ver. 19. Samuel replied, "*I am the seer: go up before me to the high place, and eat with me to-day; and to-morrow I will send thee away, and make known to thee all that is in thy heart.*" Letting a person go in front was a sign of great esteem. The change from the singular עֲלֵה to the plural אֲכָלְתֶּם may be explained on the ground that, whilst Samuel only spoke to Saul, he intended expressly to invite his servant to the meal as well as himself. "*All that is in thine heart*" does not mean "all that thou hast upon thy heart," *i.e.* all that troubles thee, for Samuel relieved him of all anxiety about the asses at once by telling him that they were found; but simply the thoughts of thy heart generally. Samuel would make these known to him, to prove to him that he was a prophet. He then first of all satisfied him respecting the asses (ver. 20): "*As for the asses that were lost to thee to-day three days* (three days ago), *do not set thy heart upon them* (*i.e.* do not trouble thyself about them), *for they are found.*" After this quieting announcement, by which he had convinced Saul of his seer's gift, Samuel directed Saul's thoughts to that higher thing which Jehovah had appointed for him: "*And to whom does all that is worth desiring of Israel belong? is it not to thee, and to all thy father's house?*" "The desire of Israel" (*optima quæque Israel,* Vulg.; "the best in Israel," Luther) is not all that Israel desires, but all that Israel possesses of what is precious or *worth desiring* (see Hag. ii. 7). "The antithesis here is between the asses and every desirable thing" (Seb. Schmidt). Notwithstanding the indefinite character of the words, they held up such glorious things as in prospect for Saul, that he replied in amazement (ver. 21), "*Am not I a Benjaminite, of the smallest of the tribes of Israel? and my family is the least of all the families of the tribe of Benjamin* (שִׁבְטֵי בנ׳ is unquestionably a copyist's error for שֵׁבֶט בנ׳); *and how speakest thou such a word to me?*" Samuel made no reply to this, as he simply wanted first of all to awaken the expectation in Saul's mind of things that he had never dreamt of before.—Ver. 22. When they arrived at the high place, he conducted Saul and his servant into the cell (the apartment prepared for the sacrificial meal), and gave them (the servant as well as Saul, according to the simple customs of antiquity, as being also his guest) a place at the upper end among those who had been invited. There were about thirty persons present, no doubt the most distinguished men of the city, whilst the rest of the people probably encamped in the open air.—Vers. 23, 24. He then ordered the cook to bring the piece which he had directed him to set aside, and to place it before Saul, namely the leg and הֶעָלֶיהָ (the article in the place of the relative; see Ewald, § 331, *b*); *i.e.* not what was over it, viz. the broth poured upon it (Dathe and Maurer), but what was attached to it (Luther). The reference, however, is not to the kidney as the choicest portion (Thenius), for the kidneys were burned upon the altar in the case of all the slain sacrifices (Lev. iii. 4), and only the flesh of the animals offered in sacrifice was applied to the sacrificial meal. What was attached to the leg, therefore, can only have been such of the fat upon the flesh as was not intended for the altar. Whether the right or left leg, is not stated: the earlier commentators decide in favour of the left, because the right leg fell to the share of the priests (Lev. vii. 32 sqq.). But as Samuel conducted the whole of the sacrificial ceremony, he may also have offered the sacrifice itself by virtue of his prophetic calling, so that the right leg would fall to his share, and he might have it reserved for his guest. In any case, however, the leg, as the largest and best portion, was to be a piece of honour for Saul (see Gen. xliii. 34). There is no reason to seek for any further symbolical meaning in it. The fact that it was Samuel's intention to distinguish and honour Saul above all his other guests, is evident enough from what he said to Saul when the cook had brought the leg: "*Behold, that which is reserved is set before thee* (שִׂים is the passive participle, as in Num. xxiv. 21); *for unto this time hath it been kept for thee, as I said I have invited the people.*" לַמּוֹעֵד is either "*to the appointed time of thy coming,*" or possibly, "*for the* (this) *meeting together.*" Samuel mentions this to give Saul his guest to understand that he had foreseen his coming in a supernatural way. לֵאמֹר, *saying*, *i.e.* as I said (to the cook).

Vers. 25-27. When the sacrificial meal was over, Samuel and Saul went down from the high place into the town, and he (Samuel) talked with him upon the roof (of the house into which Samuel had entered). The flat roofs of the East were used as places of retirement for private conversation (see at Deut. xxii. 8). This conversation did not refer of course to the call of Samuel to the royal dignity, for that was not made known to him as a word of Jehovah till the following day (ver. 27); but it was intended to prepare him for that announcement: so that O. v. Gerlach's conjecture is probably the correct one, viz. that Samuel "talked with Saul concerning the deep religious and political degradation of the people of God, the oppression of the heathen, the causes of the inability of the Israelites to stand against these foes, the necessity for a conversion of the people, and the want of a leader who was entirely devoted to the Lord."[1]—Ver. 26. "*And they rose up early in*

---

[1] For וַיְדַבֵּר עִם־שָׁאוּל עַל הַגָּג the LXX. have καὶ διέστρωσαν τῷ Σαοὺλ ἐπὶ τῷ δώματι καὶ ἐκοιμήθη, "they prepared Saul a bed upon the house, and he slept," from which Clericus conjectured that these translators had read (וַיִּרְבְּדוּ) וַיִּרְבְּדוּ or וַיִּרְבְּדוּ לְשָׁאוּל; and Ewald and Thenius propose to alter the Hebrew text in this way. But although וַיַּשְׁכִּימוּ וגו' (ver. 26) no doubt presupposes that Saul had slept in Samuel's house, and in fact upon the roof, the remark of Thenius, "that the private conversation upon the roof (ver. 25) comes too early, as Saul did not yet know, and was not to learn till the following day, what was about to take place," does not supply any valid objection to the correctness of the Masoretic text, or any argument in favour of the Septuagint rendering or interpretation, since it rests upon an altogether unfounded and erroneous assumption, viz. that Samuel had talked with Saul about his call to the throne. Moreover, "the strangeness" of the statement in ver. 26, "they rose up early," and then "when the morning dawned, Samuel called," etc., cannot possibly throw any suspicion upon the integrity of the Hebrew text, as this "strangeness" vanishes when we take וַיְהִי כַּעֲלוֹת וגו' as a more precise definition of וַיַּשְׁכִּימוּ. The Septuagint translators evidently held the same opinion as their modern defenders. They took offence at Samuel's private conversation with Saul, because he did not make known to him the word of God concerning his call to the throne till the next morning; and, on the other hand, as their rising the next morning is mentioned in ver. 26, they felt the absence of any allusion to their sleeping, and consequently not only interpreted ידבר by a conjectural emendation as standing for ירבד, because רְבַד מַרְבַדִּים is used in Prov. vii. 16 to signify the spreading of mats or carpets for a bed, but also identified וישכמו with ישכבו, and rendered it ἐκοιμήθη. At the same time, they did not reflect that the preparation of the bed and their sleeping during the night were both of them matters of course, and there was consequently no necessity to mention them; whereas Samuel's talking with Saul upon the roof was a matter of importance in relation to the whole affair, and one which could not be passed over in silence. Moreover, the correctness of the Hebrew text is confirmed by all the other ancient versions. Not only do the Chaldee, Syriac, and Arabic follow the Masoretic text, but Jerome does the same in the rendering adopted by him, "*Et locutus est cum Saule in solario. Cumque mane surrexissent;*" though the words "*stravitque Saul in solario et dormivit*" have been interpolated probably from the Itala into the text of the Vulgate which has come down to us

the morning: namely, when the morning dawn arose, Samuel called to Saul upon the roof (*i.e.* he called from below within the house up to the roof, where Saul was probably sleeping upon the balcony; cf. 2 Kings iv. 10), *Get up, I will conduct thee.*" As soon as Saul had risen, "*they both* (*both Samuel and Saul*) *went out* (into the street)." And when they had gone down to the extremity of the town, *Samuel said to Saul,* "*Let the servant pass on before us* (*and he did so*), *and do thou remain here for the present; I will show thee a word of God.*"

Ch. x. 1. Samuel then took the oil-flask, poured it upon his (Saul's) head, kissed him, and said, "*Hath not Jehovah* (equivalent to 'Jehovah assuredly hath') *anointed thee to be captain over His inheritance?*" הֲלוֹא, as an expression of lively assurance, receives the force of an independent clause through the following כִּי, "*is it not so?*" *i.e.* "yea, it is so, that," etc., just as it does before אִם in Gen. iv. 7. נַחֲלָתוֹ, His (Jehovah's) possession, was the nation of Israel, which Jehovah had acquired as the people of His own possession through their deliverance out of Egypt (Deut. iv. 20, ix. 26, etc.). Anointing with oil was a symbol of endowment with the Spirit of God; as the oil itself, by virtue of the strength which it gives to the vital spirits, was a symbol of the Spirit of God as the principle of divine and spiritual power (see at Lev. viii. 12). Hitherto there had been no other anointing among the people of God than that of the priests and sanctuary (Ex. xxx. 23 sqq.; Lev. viii. 10 sqq.). When Saul, therefore, was consecrated as king by anointing, the monarchy was inaugurated as a divine institution, standing on a par with the priesthood; through which henceforth the Lord would also bestow upon His people the gifts of His Spirit for the building up of His kingdom. As the priests were consecrated by anointing to be the media of the ethical blessings of divine grace for Israel, so the king was consecrated by anointing to be the vehicle and medium of all the blessings of grace which the Lord, as the God-king, would confer upon His people through the institution of a civil government. Through this anointing, which was performed by Samuel under the direction of God, the king was set apart from the rest of the nation as "anointed of the Lord" (cf. ch. xii. 3, 5, etc.), and sanctified as the נָגִיד, *i.e.* its captain, its leader and commander. *Kissing* was probably not a sign of homage or reverence towards the anointed of the Lord, so much as "a kiss of affection, with which the grace of God itself was sealed" (Seb. Schmidt).[1]

Vers. 2–7. To confirm the consecration of Saul as king over Israel, which had been effected through the anointing, Samuel gave him three more signs which would occur on his journey home, and would be a pledge to him that Jehovah would accompany his undertakings with His divine help, and practically accredit him as His anointed. These signs, therefore, stand in the closest relation to the calling conveyed to Saul through his anointing.—Ver. 2. *The first sign:* "*When thou goest away from me to-day* (*i.e.* now), *thou wilt meet two men at Rachel's sepulchre, on the border of Benjamin at Zelzah; and they will say unto thee, The asses of thy father, which thou wentest to seek, are found. Behold, thy father hath given up* אֶת־דִּבְרֵי הָאֲתֹנוֹת, *the words* (*i.e.* talking) *about the asses, and troubleth himself about you, saying, What shall I do about my son?*" According to Gen. xxxv. 16 sqq., Rachel's sepulchre was on the way from Bethel

---

[1] The LXX. and Vulgate have expanded the second half of this verse by a considerable addition, which reads as follows in the LXX.: οὐχὶ κέχρικέ σε κύριος εἰς ἄρχοντα ἐπὶ τὸν λαὸν αὐτοῦ ἐπὶ Ἰσραήλ; καὶ σὺ ἄρξεις ἐν λαῷ κυρίου, καὶ σὺ σώσεις αὐτὸν ἐκ χειρὸς ἐχθρῶν αὐτοῦ κυκλόθεν, καὶ τοῦτο σοι τὸ σημεῖον ὅτι ἔχρισέ σε κύριος ἐπὶ κληρονομίαν αὐτοῦ εἰς ἄρχοντα. And in the Vulgate: *Ecce, unxit te Dominus super hæreditatem suam in principem, et liberabis populum suum de manibus inimicorum ejus, qui in circuitu ejus sunt. Et hoc tibi signum, quia unxit te Deus in principem.* A comparison of these two texts will show that the LXX. interpolated their addition between הֲלוֹא and כִּי, as the last clause, ὅτι ἔχρισέ σε κύριος ἐπὶ κληρονομίαν αὐτοῦ εἰς ἄρχοντα, is a verbal translation of כִּי מְשָׁחֲךָ יְהוָה עַל־נַחֲלָתוֹ לְנָגִיד. In the Vulgate, on the other hand, the first clause, *ecce unxit—in principem*, corresponds word for word with the Hebrew text, from which we may see that Jerome translated our present Hebrew text; and the addition, *et liberabis*, etc., was interpolated into the Vulgate from the Itala. The text of the Septuagint is nothing more than a gloss formed from ch. ix. 16, 17, which the translator thought necessary, partly because he could not clearly see the force of הֲלוֹא כִּי, but more especially because he could not explain the fact that Samuel speaks to Saul of signs, without having announced them to him as such. But the author of the gloss has overlooked the fact that Samuel does not give Saul a σημεῖον, but three σημεῖα, and describes the object of them in ver. 7 as being the following, namely, that Saul would learn when they took place what he had to do, for Jehovah was with him, and not that they would prove that the Lord had anointed him to be captain.

to Bethlehem, only a short distance from the latter place, and therefore undoubtedly on the spot which tradition has assigned to it since the time of Jerome, viz. on the site of the *Kubbet Rahil*, half an hour to the north-west of Bethlehem, on the left of the road to Jerusalem, about an hour and a half from the city (see at Gen. xxxv. 20). This suits the passage before us very well, if we give up the groundless assumption that Saul came to Samuel at Ramah and was anointed by him there, and assume that the place of meeting, which is not more fully defined in ch. ix., was situated to the south-west of Bethlehem.[1] The expression "in the border of Benjamin" is not at variance with this. It is true that *Kubbet Rahil* is about an hour and a quarter from the southern boundary of Benjamin, which ran past the *Rogel* spring, through the valley of Ben-Hinnom (Josh. xviii. 16); but the expression עִם קְבֻרָה must not be so pressed as to be restricted to the actual site of the grave, since otherwise the further definition "*at Zelzah*" would be superfluous, as Rachel's tomb was unquestionably a well-known locality at that time. If we suppose the place called Zelzah, the situation of which has not yet been discovered,[2] to have been about midway between Rachel's tomb and the *Rogel* spring, Samuel could very well describe the spot where Saul would meet the

[1] As the account of Saul's meeting with Samuel, in ch. ix., when properly understood, is not at variance with the tradition concerning the situation of Rachel's tomb, and the passage before us neither requires us on the one hand to understand the Ephratah of Gen. xxxv. 19 and xlviii. 7 as a different place from Bethlehem, and erase "*that is Bethlehem*" from both passages as a gloss that has crept into the text, and then invent an *Ephratah* in the neighbourhood of Bethel between Benjamin and Ephraim, as Thenius does, nor warrants us on the other hand in transferring Rachel's tomb to the neighbourhood of Bethel, in opposition to the ordinary tradition, as Kurtz proposes; so the words of Jer. xxxi. 15, " A voice was heard in Ramah, lamentation and bitter weeping, Rachel weeping for her children," etc., furnish no evidence that Rachel's tomb was at Ramah (*i.e. er Râm*). " For here (in the cycle of prophecy concerning the restoration of all Israel, Jer. xxx.-xxxiii.) Rachel's weeping is occasioned by the fact of the exiles of Benjamin having assembled together in Ramah (Jer. xl. 1), without there being any reason why Rachel's tomb should be sought for in the neighbourhood of this Ramah " (Delitzsch on Gen. xxxv. 20).

[2] Ewald (*Gesch*. iii. p. 29) supposes Zelzah to be unsuitable to the context, if taken as the name of a place, and therefore follows the ἀλλομένους μεγάλα of the LXX., and renders the word "in great haste;" but he has neither given any reason why the name of a place is unsuitable here, nor

two men in the way that he has done. This sign, by confirming the information which Samuel had given to Saul with reference to the asses, was to furnish him with a practical proof that what Samuel had said to him with regard to the monarchy would quite as certainly come to pass, and therefore not only to deliver him from all anxiety as to the lost animals of his father, but also to direct his thoughts to the higher destiny to which God had called him through Samuel's anointing.

The second sign (vers. 3, 4): "*Then thou shalt go on forward from thence, and thou shalt come to the terebinth of Tabor; and there shall meet thee there three men going up to God to Bethel, carrying one three kids, one three loaves of bread, and one a bottle of wine. They will ask thee after thy welfare, and give thee two loaves; receive them at their hands.*" The terebinth of *Tabor* is not mentioned anywhere else, and nothing further can be determined concerning it, than that it stood by the road leading from Rachel's tomb to Gibeah.[1] The fact that the three men were going up to God at Bethel, shows that there was still a place of sacrifice consecrated to the Lord at Bethel, where Abraham and Jacob had erected altars to the Lord who had appeared to them there (Gen. xii. 8, xiii. 3, 4, xxviii. 18, 19, xxxv. 7); for the kids and loaves and wine were sacrificial gifts which they were about to offer. שָׁאַל לְשָׁלוֹם, to ask after one's welfare, *i.e.* to greet in a friendly manner (cf. Judg. xviii. 15; Gen. xliii. 27). The meaning of this double sign consisted in the fact that these men gave Saul two loaves from their sacrificial offerings. In this he was to

---

considered that the Septuagint rendering is merely conjectural, and has nothing further to support it than the fact that the translators rendered צָלַח ἐφήλατο, "he sprang upon him," in ver. 6 and ch. xi. 6, and took צָלְחָה to be an emphatic form of צָלַח.

[1] The opinion expressed by Ewald and Thenius, that Deborah's mourning oak (Gen. xxxv. 8) is intended, and that *Tabor* is either a different form of *Deborah*, or that *Tabor* should be altered into Deborah, has no foundation to rest upon; for the fact that the oak referred to stood below (*i.e.* to the south of) Bethel, and the three men whom Saul was to meet at the terebinth of *Tabor* were going to Bethel, by no means establishes the identity of the two, as their going up to Bethel does not prove that they were already in the neighbourhood of Bethel. Moreover, the Deborah oak was on the north of Gibeah, whereas Saul met the three men between Rachel's tomb and Gibeah, *i.e.* to the south of Gibeah.

discern a homage paid to the anointed of the Lord; and he was therefore to accept the gift in this sense at their hand.

The third sign (vers. 5, 6) Saul was to receive at Gibeah of God, where posts of the Philistines were stationed. *Gibeath ha-Elohim* is not an appellative, signifying a high place of God, *i.e.* a high place dedicated to God, but a proper name referring to *Gibeah* of Benjamin, the native place of Saul, which was called *Gibeah of Saul* from the time when Saul resided there as king (ver. 16 : cf. ch. xi. 4, xv. 34 ; 2 Sam. xxi. 6 ; Isa. x. 29). This is very apparent from the fact that, according to vers. 10 sqq., all the people of Gibeah had known Saul of old, and therefore could not comprehend how he had all at once come to be among the prophets. The name *Gibeah of God* is here given to the town on account of a *bamah* or sacrificial height which rose within or near the town (ver. 13), and which may possibly have been renowned above other such heights, as the seat of a society of prophets. נְצִבֵי פְלִשְׁתִּים are not bailiffs of the Philistines, still less columns erected as signs of their supremacy (Thenius), but military posts of the Philistines, as ch. xiii. 3, 4, and 2 Sam. viii. 6, 14, clearly show. The allusion here to the posts of the Philistines at Gibeah is connected with what was about to happen to Saul there. At the place where the Philistines, those severe oppressors of Israel, had set up military posts, the Spirit of God was to come upon Saul, and endow him with the divine power that was required for his regal office. *"And it shall come to pass, when thou comest to the town there, thou wilt light upon a company of prophets coming down from the high place (bamah, the sacrificial height), before them lyre and tambourin, and flute, and harp, and they prophesying."* חֶבֶל signifies a rope or cord, then a *band* or *company* of men. It does not follow that because this band of prophets was coming down from the high place, the high place at Gibeah must have been the seat of a school of the prophets. They might have been upon a pilgrimage to Gibeah. The fact that they were preceded by musicians playing, seems to indicate a festal procession. *Nebel* and *kinnor* are stringed instruments which were used after David's time in connection with the psalmody of divine worship (1 Chron. xiii. 8, xv. 20, 21 ; Ps. xxxiii. 2, xliii. 4, etc.). The *nebel* was an instrument resembling a *lyre*, the *kinnor* was more like a *guitar* than a harp. *Toph :* the *tambourin,* which was played by Miriam at the Red Sea (Ex. xv. 20). *Chalil*, the *flute*; see my *Bibl. Archæology*, ii. § 137. By the prophesying of these prophets we are to understand an ecstatic utterance of religious feelings to the praise of God, as in the case of the seventy elders in the time of Moses (Num. xi. 25). Whether it took the form of a song or of an enthusiastic discourse, cannot be determined; in any case it was connected with a very energetic action indicative of the highest state of mental excitement. (For further remarks on these societies of prophets, see at ch. xix. 18 sqq.)—Ver. 6. "*And the Spirit of Jehovah will come upon thee, and thou wilt prophesy with them, and be changed into another man.*" "Ecstatic states," says Tholuck (*die Propheten*, p. 53), "have something infectious about them. The excitement spreads involuntarily, as in the American revivals and the preaching mania in Sweden, even to persons in whose state of mind there is no affinity with anything of the kind." But in the instance before us there was something more than psychical infection. The Spirit of Jehovah, which manifested itself in the prophesying of the prophets, was to pass over to Saul, so that he would prophesy along with them (הִתְנַבִּיתָ formed like a verb ל״ה for הִתְנַבֵּאת; so again in ver. 13), and was entirely to transform him. This transformation is not to be regarded indeed as regeneration in the Christian sense, but as a change resembling regeneration, which affected the entire disposition of mind, and by which Saul was lifted out of his former modes of thought and feeling, which were confined within a narrow earthly sphere, into the far higher sphere of his new royal calling, was filled with kingly thoughts in relation to the service of God, and received "*another heart*" (ver. 9). *Heart* is used in the ordinary scriptural sense, as the centre of the whole mental and psychical life of will, desire, thought, perception, and feeling (see Delitzsch, *Bibl. Psychol.* pp. 248 sqq., ed. 2). Through this sign his anointing as king was to be inwardly sealed.—Ver. 7. "*When these signs are come unto thee* (the *Kethibh* תבאינה is to be read תְּבֹאֶינָה, as in Ps. xlv. 16 and Esther iv. 4; and the *Keri* תְּבֹאנָה is a needless emendation), *do to thee what thy hand findeth*, *i.e.* act according to the circumstances (for this formula, see Judg. ix. 33); *for God will be with thee.*" The occurrence of the signs mentioned was to assure him of the certainty that

God would assist him in all that he undertook as king. The first opportunity for action was afforded him by the Ammonite Nahash, who besieged Jabesh-gilead (ch. xi.).

Ver. 8. In conclusion, Samuel gave him an important hint with regard to his future attitude : " *And goest thou before me down to Gilgal; and, behold, I am coming down to thee, to offer burnt-offerings, and to sacrifice peace-offerings: thou shalt wait seven days, till I come to thee, that I may show thee what thou art to do.*" The infinitive clause לְהַעֲלוֹת וגו׳ is undoubtedly dependent upon the main clause וְיָרַדְתָּ, and not upon the circumstantial clause which is introduced as a parenthesis. The thought therefore is the following: If Saul went down to Gilgal to offer sacrifice there, he was to wait till Samuel arrived. The construction of the main clause itself, however, is doubtful, since, grammatically considered, יָרַדְתָּ can either be a continuation of the imperative עָשֵׂה (ver. 7), or can be regarded as independent, and in fact conditional. The latter view, according to which יָרַדְתָּ supposes his going down as a possible thing that may take place at a future time, is the one required by the circumstantial clause which follows, and which is introduced by וְהִנֵּה; for if וְיָרַדְתָּ were intended to be a continuation of the imperative which precedes it, so that Samuel commanded Saul to go down to Gilgal before him, he would have simply announced his coming, that is to say, he would either have said וְיָרַדְתִּי or וַאֲנִי אֵרֵד. The circumstantial clause " *and behold I am coming down to thee*" evidently presupposes Saul's going down as a possible occurrence, in the event of which Samuel prescribes the course he is to pursue. But the conditional interpretation of וְיָרַדְתָּ is still more decidedly required by the context. For instance, when Samuel said to Saul that after the occurrence of the three signs he was to do what came to his hand, he could hardly command him immediately afterwards to go to Gilgal, since the performance of what came to his hand might prevent him from going to Gilgal. If, however, Samuel meant that after Saul had finished what came to his hand he was to go down to Gilgal, he would have said, "And after thou hast done this, go down to Gilgal," etc. But as he does not express himself in this manner, he can only have referred to Saul's going to Gilgal as an occurrence which, as he foresaw, would take place at some time or other. And to Saul himself this must not only have presented itself as a possible occurrence, but under the existing circumstances as one that was sure to take place; so that the whole thing was not so obscure to him as it is to us, who are only able to form our conclusions from the brief account which lies before us. If we suppose that in the conversation which Samuel had with Saul upon the roof (ch. ix. 25), he also spoke about the manner in which the Philistines, who had pushed their outposts as far as Gibeah, could be successfully attacked, he might also have mentioned that Gilgal was the most suitable place for gathering an army together, and for making the necessary preparations for a successful engagement with their foes. If we just glance at the events narrated in the following chapters, for the purpose of getting a clear idea of the thing which Samuel had in view; we find that the three signs announced by Samuel took place on Saul's return to Gibeah (vers. 9–16). Samuel then summoned the people to Mizpeh, where Saul was elected king by lot (vers. 17–27); but Saul returned to Gibeah to his own house even after this solemn election, and was engaged in ploughing the field, when messengers came from Jabesh with the account of the siege of that town by the Ammonites. On receiving this intelligence the Spirit of Jehovah came upon him, so that he summoned the whole nation with energy and without delay to come to battle, and proceeded to Jabesh with the assembled army, and smote the Ammonites (ch. xi. 1–11). Thereupon Samuel summoned the people to come to Gilgal and renew the monarchy there (ch. xi. 12–15); and at the same time he renewed his office of supreme judge (ch. xii.), so that now for the first time Saul actually commenced his reign, and began the war against the Philistines (ch. xiii. 1), in which, as soon as the latter advanced to Michmash with a powerful army after Jonathan's victorious engagement, he summoned the people to Gilgal to battle, and after waiting there seven days for Samuel in vain, had the sacrifices offered, on which account as soon as Samuel arrived he announced to him that his rule would not last (ch. xiii. 13 sqq.). Now, it cannot have been the first of these two gatherings at Gilgal that Samuel had in his mind, but must have been the second. The first is precluded by the simple fact that Samuel summoned the people to go to Gilgal for the purpose of renewing the monarchy; and therefore, as the words "come and let us go to Gilgal" (ch. xi. 14) unquestionably imply, he must have gone thither himself along with the people and the king, so that Saul was never in a position to have to wait for Samuel's arrival. The second occurrence at Gilgal, on the other hand, is clearly indicated in the words of ch. xiii. 8, "*Saul tarried seven days, according to the set time that Samuel had appointed*," in which there is almost an express allusion to the instructions given to Saul in the verse before us. But whilst we cannot but regard this as the only true explanation, we cannot agree with Seb. Schmidt, who looks upon the instructions given to Saul in this verse as "a rule to be observed throughout the whole of Samuel's life," that is to say, who interprets יֵרַדְתָּ in the sense of "as often as thou goest down to Gilgal." For this view cannot be grammatically sustained, although it is founded upon the correct idea, that Samuel's instructions cannot have been intended as a solitary and arbitrary command, by which Saul was to be kept in a condition of dependence. According to our explanation, however, this is not the case; but there was an inward necessity for them, so far as the government of Saul was concerned. Placed as he was by Jehovah as king over His people, for the purpose of rescuing them out of the power of those who were at that time its most dangerous foes, Saul was not at liberty to enter upon the war against these foes simply by his own will, but was directed to wait till Samuel, the accredited prophet of Jehovah, had completed the consecration through the offering of a solemn sacrifice, and had communicated to him the requisite instructions from God, even though he should have to wait for seven days.[1]

Vers. 9–16. When Saul went away from Samuel, to return to Gibeah, "*God changed to him another heart*,"—a pregnant expression for "God changed him, and gave him another heart"

[1] The difficulty in question has been solved on the whole quite correctly by Brentius. "It is not to be supposed," he says, "that Samuel was directing Saul to go at once to Gilgal as soon as he should go away from him, and wait there for seven days; but that he was to do this after he had been chosen king by public lot, and having conquered the Ammonites and been confirmed in the kingdom, was about to prepare to make war upon the Philistines, on whose account chiefly it was that he had been called to the kingdom. For the Lord had already spoken thus to Samuel concerning Saul: 'He will save my people from the hands of the Phili-

(see at ver. 6); and all these signs (the signs mentioned by Samuel) happened on that very day. As he left Samuel early in the morning, Saul could easily reach Gibeah in one day, even if the town where he had met with Samuel was situated to the south-west of Rachel's tomb, as the distance from that tomb to Gibeah was not more than three and a half or four hours.— Ver. 10. The third sign is the only one which is minutely described, because this caused a great sensation at Gibeah, Saul's home. "*And they* (Saul and his attendant) *came thither to Gibeah.*" "*Thither*" points back to "thither to the city" in ver. 5, and is defined by the further expression "to Gibeah" (Eng. version, "to the hill :" Tr.). The rendering ἐκεῖθεν (LXX.) does not warrant us in changing שָׁם into מִשָּׁם; for the latter would be quite superfluous, as it was self-evident that they came to Gibeah from the place where they had been in the company of Samuel.—Ver. 11. When those who had known Saul of old saw that he prophesied with the prophets, the people said one to another, "*What has happened to the son of Kish? Is Saul also among the prophets?*" This expression presupposes that Saul's previous life was altogether different from that of the disciples of the prophets.—Ver. 12. And one from thence (*i.e.* from Gibeah, or from the crowd that was gathered round the prophets) answered, "*And who is their father?*" *i.e.* not "who is their president?" which would be a very gratuitous question; but, "is *their* father a prophet then?" *i.e.*, according to the explanation given by Oehler (Herzog's *Real. Enc.* xii. p. 216), "have they the prophetic spirit by virtue of their birth?" Understood in this way, the retort forms a very appropriate "answer" to the expression of surprise and the inquiry, how it came to pass that Saul was among the prophets. If those prophets had not obtained the gift of prophecy by inheritance, but as a free gift of the Lord, it was equally possible for the Lord to communi-

stines, because I have looked upon my people.' This is the meaning therefore of Samuel's command: Thou hast been called to the kingdom chiefly for this purpose, that thou mayest deliver Israel from the tyranny of the Philistines. When therefore thou shalt enter upon this work, go down into Gilgal and wait there seven days, until I shall come to thee: for thou shalt then offer a holocaust, though not before I come to thee, and I will show thee what must be done in order that our enemies the Philistines may be conquered. The account of this is given below in ch. xiii., where we learn that Saul violated this command."

cate the same gift to Saul. On the other hand, the alteration of the text from אֲבִיהֶם (their father) into אָבִיהוּ (his father), according to the LXX., Vulg., Syr., and Arab., which is favoured by Ewald, Thenius, and others, must be rejected, for the simple reason that the question, Who is his father? in the mouth of one of the inhabitants of Gibeah, to whom Saul's father was so well known that they called Saul the son of Kish at once, would have no sense whatever. From this the proverb arose, "Is Saul also among the prophets?"—a proverb which was used to express astonishment at the appearance of any man in a sphere of life which had hitherto been altogether strange to him.—Vers. 13 sqq. When Saul had left off prophesying, and came to Bamah, his uncle asked him and his attendant where they had been; and Saul told him, that as they had not found the asses anywhere, they had gone to Samuel, and had learned from him that the asses were found. But he did not relate the words which had been spoken by Samuel concerning the monarchy, from unambitious humility (cf. vers. 22, 23) and not because he was afraid of unbelief and envy, as Thenius follows Josephus in supposing. From the expression "he came to Bamah" (Eng. ver. "to the high place"), we must conclude, that not only Saul's uncle, but his father also, lived in Bamah, as we find Saul immediately afterwards in his own family circle (see vers. 14 sqq.).

SAUL ELECTED KING. HIS ELECTION CONFIRMED.—
CHAP. X. 17–XI. 15.

Vers. 17-27. SAUL'S ELECTION BY LOT.—After Samuel had secretly anointed Saul king by the command of God, it was his duty to make provision for a recognition of the man whom God had chosen on the part of the people also. To this end he summoned the people to Mizpeh, and there instructed the tribes to choose a king by lot. As the result of the lot was regarded as a divine decision, not only was Saul to be accredited by this act in the sight of the whole nation as the king appointed by the Lord, but he himself was also to be more fully assured of the certainty of his own election on the part of God.[1]—Ver. 17.

[1] Thenius follows De Wette, and adduces the incompatibility of ch. viii. and ch. x. 17-27 with ch. ix. 1-10, 16, as a proof that in vers. 17-27 we

הָעָם is the nation in its heads and representatives. *Samuel* selected *Mizpeh* for this purpose, because it was there that he had once before obtained for the people, by prayer, a great victory over the Philistines (ch. vii. 5 sqq.).—Vers. 18, 19. "But before proceeding to the election itself, Samuel once more charged the people with their sin in rejecting God, who had brought them out of Egypt, and delivered them out of the hand of all their oppressors, by their demand for a king, that he might show them how dangerous was the way which they were taking now, and how bitterly they would perhaps repent of what they had now desired" (O. v. Gerlach; see the commentary on ch. viii.). The masculine הַלְּחָצִים is construed *ad sensum* with הַמַּמְלָכוֹת. In וַיֹּאמְרוּ לוֹ the early translators have taken לוֹ for לֹא, which is the actual reading in some of the Codices. But although this reading is decidedly favoured by the parallel passages, ch. viii. 19, xii. 12, it is not necessary; since כִּי is used to introduce a direct statement, even in a declaration of the opposite, in the sense of our "*no but*" (*e.g.* in Ruth i. 10, where לָהּ precedes). There is, therefore, no reason for exchanging לוֹ for לֹא.—Vers. 20, 21. After this warning, Samuel directed the assembled Israelites to come before Jehovah (*i.e.* before the altar of Jehovah which stood at Mizpeh, according to ch. vii. 9) according to their tribes and families (*alaphim*: see at Num i. 16); "*and there was taken* (by lot) *the tribe of Benjamin.*"

have a different account of the manner in which Saul became king from that given in ch. ix. 1-10, 16, and one which continues the account in ch. viii. 22. "It is thoroughly inconceivable," he says, "that Samuel should have first of all anointed Saul king by the instigation of God, and then have caused the lot to be cast, as it were, for the sake of further confirmation; for in that case either the prophet would have tempted God, or he would have made Him chargeable before the nation with an unworthy act of jugglery." Such an argument as this could only be used by critics who deny not only the inspiration of the prophets, but all influence on the part of the living God upon the free action of men, and cannot therefore render the truth of the biblical history at all doubtful. Even Ewald sees no discrepancy here, and observes in his history (*Gesch.* iii. p. 32): "If we bear in mind the ordinary use made of the sacred lot at that time, we shall find that there is nothing but the simple truth in the whole course of the narrative. The secret meeting of the seer with Saul was not sufficient to secure a complete and satisfactory recognition of him as king; it was also necessary that the Spirit of Jehovah should single him out publicly in a solemn assembly of the nation, and point him out as the man of Jehovah."

הִלָּכֵד, *lit.* to be snatched out by Jehovah, namely, through the lot (see Josh. vii. 14, 16). He then directed the tribe of Benjamin to draw near according to its families, *i.e.* he directed the heads of the families of this tribe to come before the altar of the Lord and draw lots; and *the family of Matri was taken.* Lastly, when the heads of the households in this family came, and after that the different individuals in the household which had been taken, the lot fell upon *Saul the son of Kish.* In the words, "*Saul the son of Kish was taken,*" the historian proceeds at once to the final result of the casting of the lots, without describing the intermediate steps any further.[1] When the lot fell upon Saul, they sought him, and he could not be found.—Ver. 22. Then they inquired of Jehovah, "*Is any one else come hither?*" and Jehovah replied, "*Behold, he* (whom ye are seeking) *is hidden among the things.*" The inquiry was made through the high priest, by means of the Urim and Thummim, for which שָׁאַל בַּיהוָה was the technical expression, according to Num. xxvii. 21 (see Judg. xx. 27, 28, i. 1, etc.). There can be no doubt, that in a gathering of the people for so important a purpose as the election of a king, the high priest would also be present, even though this is not expressly stated. Samuel presided over the meeting as the prophet of the Lord. The answer given by God, "*Behold, he is hidden,*" etc., appears to have no relation to the question, "*Is any one else come?*" The Sept. and Vulg. have therefore altered the question into εἰ ἔτι ἔρχεται ὁ ἀνήρ, *utrumnam venturus esset;* and Thenius would adopt this

---

[1] It is true the Septuagint introduces the words καὶ προσάγουσι τὴν φυλὴν Ματταρὶ εἰς ἄνδρας before וַיִּלָּכֵד, and this clause is also found in a very recent Hebrew MS. (viz. 451 in Kennicott's *dissert. gener.* p. 491). But it is very evident that these words did not form an integral part of the original text, as Thenius supposes, but were nothing more than an interpolation of the Sept. translators, from the simple fact that they do not fill up the supposed gap at all completely, but only in a very partial, and in fact a very mistaken manner; for the *family of Matri* could not come to the lot εἰς ἄνδρας (man by man), but only κατ' οἴκους (by households: Josh. vii. 14). Before the household (*beth-aboth,* father's house) of Saul could be taken, it was necessary that the גְּבָרִים (ἄνδρες), *i.e.* the different heads of households, should be brought; and it was not till then that Kish, or his son Saul, could be singled out as the appointed of the Lord. Neither the author of the gloss in the LXX., nor the modern defender of the gloss, has thought of this.

as an emendation. But he is wrong in doing so; for there was no necessity to ask whether Saul would still come: they might at once have sent to fetch him. What they asked was rather, whether any one else had come besides those who were present, as Saul was not to be found among them, that they might know where they were to look for Saul, whether at home or anywhere else. And to this question God gave the answer, "He is present, only hidden among the things." By כֵּלִים (the *things* or *vessels*, Eng. ver. the stuff) we are to understand the *travelling baggage* of the people who had assembled at Mizpeh. Saul could neither have wished to avoid accepting the monarchy, nor have imagined that the lot would not fall upon him if he hid himself. For he knew that God had chosen him; and Samuel had anointed him already. He did it therefore simply from humility and modesty. "In order that he might not appear to have either the hope or desire for anything of the kind, he preferred to be absent when the lots were cast" (Seb. Schmidt).— Vers. 23, 24. He was speedily fetched, and brought into the midst of the (assembled) people; and when he came, he was a head taller than all the people (see ch. ix. 2). And Samuel said to all the people, "*Behold ye whom the Lord hath chosen! for there is none like him in all the nation.*" Then all the people shouted aloud, and cried, "*Let the king live!*" Saul's bodily stature won the favour of the people (see the remarks on ch. ix. 2).

Samuel then communicated to the people the right of the monarchy, and laid it down before Jehovah. "*The right of the monarchy*" (*meluchah*) is not to be identified with the right of the king (*melech*), which is described in ch. viii. 11 and sets forth the right or prerogative which a despotic king would assume over the people; but it is the right which regulated the attitude of the earthly monarchy in the theocracy, and determined the duties and rights of the human king in relation to Jehovah the divine King on the one hand, and to the nation on the other. This right could only be laid down by a prophet like Samuel, to raise a wholesome barrier at the very outset against all excesses on the part of the king. Samuel therefore wrote it in a document which was laid down before Jehovah, *i.e.* in the sanctuary of Jehovah; though certainly not in the sanctuary at Bamah in Gibeah, as Thenius supposes, for nothing is known respecting any such sanctuary. It was no doubt placed in the tabernacle, where the law of Moses was also deposited, by the side of the fundamental law of the divine state in Israel. When the business was all completed, Samuel sent the people away to their own home.—Ver. 26. Saul also returned to his house at Gibeah, and there went with him the crowd of the men whose hearts God had touched, *sc.* to give him a royal escort, and show their readiness to serve him. הַחַיִל is not to be altered into בְּנֵי הַחַיִל, according to the free rendering of the LXX., but is used as in Ex. xiv. 28; with this difference, however, that here it does not signify a large military force, but a crowd of brave men, who formed Saul's escort of honour. —Ver. 27. But as it generally happens that, where a person is suddenly lifted up to exalted honours or office, there are sure to be envious people found, so was it here: there were בְּנֵי בְלִיַּעַל, *worthless people*, even among the assembled Israelites, who spoke disparagingly of Saul, saying, "*How will this man help us?*" and who brought him no present. *Minchah:* the present which from time immemorial every one has been expected to bring when entering the presence of the king; so that the refusal to bring a present was almost equivalent to rebellion. But Saul was "*as being deaf*," *i.e.* he acted as if he had not heard. The objection which Thenius brings against this view, viz. that in that case it would read וְהוּא הָיָה כְמ׳, exhibits a want of acquaintance with the Hebrew construction of a sentence. There is no more reason for touching וַיְהִי than וַיֵּלְכוּ in ver. 26. In both cases the apodosis is attached to the protasis, which precedes it in the form of a circumstantial clause, by the *imperfect*, with *vav consec.* According to the genius of our language, these protases would be expressed by the conjunction *when*, viz.: "*when Saul also went home*, . . . *there went with him*," etc.; and "*when loose* (or idle) *people said*, etc., *he was as deaf.*"

Ch. xi. SAUL'S VICTORY OVER THE AMMONITES.—Even after the election by lot at Mizpeh, Saul did not seize upon the reins of government at once, but returned to his father's house in Gibeah, and to his former agricultural occupation; not, however, merely from personal humility and want of ambition, but rather from a correct estimate of the circumstances. The monarchy was something so new in Israel, that the king could not expect a general and voluntary recognition of his regal dignity and authority, especially after the conduct of the worthless people mentioned in ch. x. 27, until he had answered their expectations from a king (ch. viii. 6, 20), and proved himself a deliverer of Israel from its foes by a victorious campaign. But as Jehovah had chosen him ruler over his people without any seeking on his part, he would wait for higher instructions to act, before he entered upon the government. The opportunity was soon given him.

Vers. 1-5. Nahash, the king of the Ammonites (cf. ch. xii. 12; 2 Sam. x. 2), attacked the tribes on the east of the Jordan, no doubt with the intention of enforcing the claim to a part of Gilead asserted by his ancestor in the time of Jephthah (Judg. xi. 13), and besieged *Jabesh* in Gilead,[1]—according to Josephus the metropolis of Gilead, and probably situated by the Wady Jabes (see at Judg. xxi. 8); from which we may

---

[1] The time of this campaign is not mentioned in the Hebrew text. But it is very evident from ch. xii. 12, where the Israelites are said to have desired a king, when they saw that Nahash had come against them, that Nahash had invaded Gilead before the election of Saul as king. The Septuagint, however, renders the words וַיְהִי כְּמַחֲרִישׁ (ch. x. 27) by καὶ ἐγενήθη ὡς μετὰ μῆνα, and therefore the translators must have read בְּמֵחֹדֶשׁ, which Ewald and Thenius would adopt as an emendation of the Hebrew text. But all the other ancient versions give the Masoretic text, viz. not only the Chaldee, Syriac, and Arabic, but even Jerome, who renders it *ille vero dissimulabat se audire*. It is true that in our present Vulgate text these words are followed by *et factum est quasi post mensem;* but this addition has no doubt crept in from the Itala. With the general character of the Septuagint, the rendering of כְּמַחֲרִישׁ by ὡς μετὰ μῆνα is no conclusive proof that the word in their Hebrew Codex was בְּמֵחֹדֶשׁ; it simply shows that this was the interpretation which they gave to כמחריש. And Josephus (vi. 5, 1), who is also appealed to, simply establishes the fact that ὡς μετὰ μῆνα stood in the Sept. version of his day, since he made use of this version and not of the original text. Moreover, we cannot say with Ewald, that this was the last place in which the time could be overlooked; for it is perfectly evident that Nahash commenced the siege of Jabesh shortly after the election of Saul at Mizpeh, as we may infer from the verb וַיַּעַל, when taken in connection with the fact implied in ch. xii. 12, that he had commenced the war with the Israelites before this. And lastly, it is much more probable that the LXX. changed כמחריש into כמחדש, than that the Hebrew readers of the Old Testament should have altered במחדש into במחריש, without defining the time more precisely by אֶחָד, or some other number.

see that he must have penetrated very far into the territory of the Israelites. The inhabitants of Jabesh petitioned the Ammonites in their distress, "*Make a covenant with us, and we will serve thee;*" i.e. grant us favourable terms, and we will submit.—Ver. 2. But Nahash replied, "*On this condition* (בְּזֹאת, *lit.* at this price, ב *pretii*) *will I make a covenant with you, that I may put out all your right eyes, and so bring a reproach upon all Israel.*" From the fact that the infinitive נְקוֹר is continued with וְשַׂמְתִּי, it is evident that the subject to נְקוֹר is Nahash, and not the Israelites, as the Syriac, Arabic, and others have rendered it. The suffix to שַׂמְתִּיהָ is neuter, and refers to the previous clause: "*it*," i.e. the putting out of the right eye. This answer on the part of Nahash shows unmistakeably that he sought to avenge upon the people of Israel the shame of the defeat which Jephthah had inflicted upon the Ammonites.—Ver. 3. The elders of Jabesh replied: "*Leave us seven days, that we may send messengers into all the territory of Israel; and if there is no one who saves us, we will come out to thee,*" i.e. will surrender to thee. This request was granted by Nahash, because he was not in a condition to take the town at once by storm, and also probably because, in the state of internal dissolution into which Israel had fallen at that time, he had no expectation that any vigorous help would come to the inhabitants of Jabesh. From the fact that the messengers were to be sent into all the territory of Israel, we may conclude that the Israelites had no central government at that time, and that neither Nahash nor the Jabeshites had heard anything of the election that had taken place; and this is still more apparent from the fact that, according to ver. 4, their messengers came to Gibeah of Saul, and laid their business before the people generally, without applying at once to Saul. —Ver. 5. Saul indeed did not hear of the matter till he came (returned home) from the field behind the oxen, and found the people weeping and lamenting at these mournful tidings. "*Behind the oxen,*" i.e., judging from the expression "yoke of oxen" in ver. 7, the pair of oxen with which he had been ploughing.

Vers. 6-11. When the report of the messengers had been communicated to him, "*the Spirit of Jehovah came upon him, and his anger was kindled greatly,*" sc. at the shame which the

Ammonites had resolved to bring upon all Israel.—Ver. 7. He took a yoke of oxen, cut them in pieces, and sent (the pieces) into every possession of Israel by messengers, and said, " *Whoever cometh not forth after Saul and Samuel, so shall it be done unto his oxen.*" The introduction of Samuel's name after that of Saul, is a proof that Saul even as king still recognised the authority which Samuel possessed in Israel as the prophet of Jehovah. This symbolical act, like the cutting up of the woman in Judg. xix. 29, made a deep impression. "*The fear of Jehovah fell upon the people, so that they went out as one man.*" By " the fear of Jehovah " we are not to understand δεῖμα πανικόν (Thenius and Böttcher), for *Jehovah* is not equivalent to *Elohim*, nor the fear of Jehovah in the sense of fear of His punishment, but a fear inspired by Jehovah. In Saul's energetic appeal the people discerned the power of Jehovah, which inspired them with fear, and impelled them to immediate obedience.—Ver. 8. Saul held a muster of the people of war, who had gathered together at (or near) *Bezek*, a place which was situated, according to the *Onom.* (*s. v. Bezek*), about seven hours to the north of Nabulus towards Beisan (see at Judg. i. 4). The number assembled were 300,000 men of Israel, and 30,000 of Judah. These numbers will not appear too large, if we bear in mind that the allusion is not to a regular army, but that Saul had summoned all the people to a general levy. In the distinction drawn between the children of Judah and the children of Israel we may already discern a trace of that separation of Judah from the rest of the tribes, which eventually led to a formal secession on the part of the latter.— Ver. 9. The messengers from Jabesh, who had been waiting to see the result of Saul's appeal, were now despatched with this message to their fellow-citizens : " *To-morrow you will have help, when the sun shines hot,*" *i.e.* about noon.—Ver. 10. After receiving these joyful news, the Jabeshites announced to the Ammonites : " *To-morrow we will come out to you, and ye may do to us what seemeth good to you,*"—an untruth by which they hoped to assure the besiegers, so that they might be fallen upon unexpectedly by the advancing army of Saul, and thoroughly beaten.—Ver. 11. The next day Saul arranged the people in three divisions (רָאשִׁים, as in Judg. vii. 16), who forced their way into the camp of the foe from three different sides, in the morning watch (between three and six o'clock in the morning), smote the Ammonites "*till the heat of the day*," and routed them so completely, that those who remained were all scattered, and there were not two men left together.

Vers. 12–15. RENEWAL OF THE MONARCHY.—Saul had so thoroughly acted the part of a king in gaining this victory, and the people were so enthusiastic in his favour, that they said to Samuel, viz. after their return from the battle, "*Who is he that said, Saul should reign over us!*" The clause שָׁאוּל יִמְלֹךְ עָלֵינוּ contains a question, though it is indicated simply by the tone, and there is no necessity to alter שָׁאוּל into הֲשָׁאוּל. These words refer to the exclamation of the worthless people in ch. x. 27. "*Bring the men* (who spoke in this manner), *that we may put them to death.*" But Saul said, "*There shall not a man be put to death this day; for to-day Jehovah hath wrought salvation in Israel;*" and proved thereby not only his magnanimity, but also his genuine piety.[1]—Ver. 14. Samuel turned this victory to account, by calling upon the people to go with him to Gilgal, and there renew the monarchy. In what the renewal consisted is not clearly stated; but it is simply recorded in ver. 15 that "*they* (the whole people) *made Saul king there before the Lord in Gilgal.*" Many commentators have supposed that he was anointed afresh, and appeal to David's second anointing (2 Sam ii. 4 and v. 3). But David's example merely proves, as Seb. Schmidt has correctly observed, that the anointing could be repeated under certain circumstances; but it does not prove that it was repeated, or must have been repeated, in the case of Saul. If the ceremony of anointing had been performed, it would no doubt have been mentioned, just as it is in 2 Sam. ii. 4 and v. 3. But יַמְלִכוּ does not mean "they anointed," although the LXX. have rendered it ἔχρισε Σαμουήλ, according to their own subjective interpretation. The renewal of the monarchy may very well have consisted in nothing more than

---

[1] "Not only signifying that the public rejoicing should not be interrupted, but reminding them of the clemency of God, and urging that since Jehovah had shown such clemency upon that day, that He had overlooked their sins, and given them a glorious victory, it was only right that they should follow His example, and forgive their neighbours' sins without bloodshed."—*Seb. Schmidt.*

a solemn confirmation of the election that had taken place at Mizpeh, in which Samuel once more laid before both king and people the right of the monarchy, receiving from both parties in the presence of the Lord the promise to observe this right, and sealing the vow by a solemn sacrifice. The only sacrifices mentioned are *zebachim shelamim*, *i.e.* peace-offerings. These were thank-offerings, which were always connected with a sacrificial meal, and when presented on joyous occasions, formed a feast of rejoicing for those who took part, since the sacrificial meal shadowed forth a living and peaceful fellowship with the Lord. *Gilgal* is in all probability the place where Samuel judged the people every year (ch. vii. 16). But whether it was the Gilgal in the plain of the Jordan, or Jiljilia on higher ground to the south-west of Shiloh, it is by no means easy to determine. The latter is favoured, apart from the fact that Samuel did not say "Let us go down," but simply "Let us go" (cf. ch. x. 8), by the circumstance that the solemn ceremony took place after the return from the war at Jabesh; since it is hardly likely that the people would have gone down into the valley of the Jordan to Gilgal, whereas Jiljilia was close by the road from Jabesh to Gibeah and Ramah.

SAMUEL'S ADDRESS AT THE RENEWAL OF THE MONARCHY.—
CHAP. XII.

Samuel closed this solemn confirmation of Saul as king with an address to all Israel, in which he handed over the office of judge, which he had hitherto filled, to the king, who had been appointed by God and joyfully recognised by the people. The good, however, which Israel expected from the king depended entirely upon both the people and their king maintaining that proper attitude towards the Lord with which the prosperity of Israel was ever connected. This truth the prophet felt impelled to impress most earnestly upon the hearts of all the people on this occasion. To this end he reminded them, that neither he himself, in the administration of his office, nor the Lord in His guidance of Israel thus far, had given the people any reason for asking a king when the Ammonites invaded the land (vers. 1-12). Nevertheless the Lord had given them a king, and would not withdraw His hand from them, if they would only fear Him and confess their sin (vers. 13-15). This address was then confirmed by the Lord at Samuel's desire, through a miraculous sign (vers. 16-18); whereupon Samuel gave to the people, who were terrified by the miracle and acknowledged their sin, the comforting promise that the Lord would not forsake His people for His great name's sake, and then closed his address with the assurance of his continued intercession, and a renewed appeal to them to serve the Lord with faithfulness (vers. 19-25). With this address Samuel laid down his office as judge, but without therefore ceasing as prophet to represent the people before God, and to maintain the rights of God in relation to the king. In this capacity he continued to support the king with his advice, until he was compelled to announce his rejection on account of his repeated rebellion against the commands of the Lord, and to anoint David as his successor.

Vers. 1-6. The time and place of the following address are not given... But it is evident from the connection with the preceding chapter implied in the expression וַיֹּאמֶר, and still more from the introduction (vers. 1, 2) and the entire contents of the address, that it was delivered on the renewal of the monarchy at Gilgal.—Vers. 1, 2. Samuel starts with the fact, that he had given the people a king in accordance with their own desire, who would now walk before them. הִנֵּה with the participle expresses what is happening, and will happen still. הִתְהַלֵּךְ לִפְנֵי must not be restricted to going at the head in war, but signifies the general direction and government of the nation, which had been in the hands of Samuel as judge before the election of Saul as king. "*And I have grown old and grey* (שַׂבְתִּי from שִׂיב); *and my sons, behold, they are with you.*" With this allusion to his sons, Samuel simply intended to confirm what he had said about his own age. By the further remark, "*and I have walked before you from my childhood unto this day,*" he prepares the way for the following appeal to the people to bear witness concerning his conduct in office.—Ver. 3. "*Bear witness against me before the Lord,*" i.e. looking up to the Lord, the omnipotent and righteous God-king, "*and before His anointed,*" the visible administrator of His divine government, whether I have committed any injustice in my office of judge, by appropriating another's property, or by oppression and violence (רָצַץ, to pound or crush in pieces, when used to denote an act of violence, is stronger than עֹשֶׁק, with which it is connected here and in many other passages, *e.g.* Deut. xxviii. 33; Amos iv. 1), or by taking atonement money (כֹּפֶר, redemption or atonement money, is used, as in Ex. xxi. 30 and Num. xxxv. 31, to denote a payment made by a man to redeem himself from capital punishment), "*so that I had covered my eyes with it*," viz. to exempt from punishment a man who was worthy of death. The בּוֹ, which is construed with הֶעְלִים, is the בְּ *instrumenti*, and refers to כֹּפֶר; consequently it is not to be confounded with מִן, "to hide from," which would be quite unsuitable here. The thought is not that the judge covers his eyes from the *copher*, that he may not see the bribe, but that he covers his eyes with the money offered him as a bribe, so as not to see and not to punish the crime committed. —Ver. 4. The people answered Samuel, that he had not done them any kind of injustice.—Ver. 5. To confirm this declaration on the part of the people, he then called Jehovah and His anointed as witnesses against the people, and they accepted these witnesses. כָּל־יִשְׂרָאֵל is the subject to וַיֹּאמֶר; and the *Keri* וַיֹּאמְרוּ, though more simple, is by no means necessary. Samuel said, "*Jehovah be witness against you*," because with the declaration which the people had made concerning Samuel's judicial labours they had condemned themselves, inasmuch as they had thereby acknowledged on oath that there was no ground for their dissatisfaction with Samuel's administration, and consequently no well-founded reason for their request for a king.— Ver. 6. But in order to bring the people to a still more thorough acknowledgment of their sin, Samuel strengthened still more their assent to his solemn appeal to God, as expressed in the words "*He is witness*," by saying, "*Jehovah* (*i.e.* yea, the witness is Jehovah), *who made Moses and Aaron, and brought your fathers out of the land of Egypt.*" The context itself is sufficient to show that the expression "is witness" is understood; and there is no reason, therefore, to assume that the word has dropped out of the text through a copyist's error. עָשָׂה, to make, in a moral and historical sense, *i.e.* to make a person what he is to be; it has no connection, therefore, with his physical birth, but simply relates to his introduction upon the stage of history, like ποιεῖν, Heb. iii. 2. But if Jehovah, who redeemed Israel out of Egypt by the hands of Moses and Aaron, and exalted it into His own nation, was witness of the unselfishness and impartiality of Samuel's conduct in his office of judge, then Israel had grievously sinned by demanding a king. In the person of Samuel they had rejected Jehovah their God, who had given them their rulers (see ch. viii. 7). Samuel proves this still further to the people from the following history.

Vers. 7-12. "*And now come hither, and I will reason with you before the Lord with regard to all the righteous acts which He has shown to you and your fathers.*" צִדְקוֹת, righteous acts, is the expression used to denote the benefits which Jehovah had conferred upon His people, as being the results of His covenant fidelity, or as acts which attested the righteousness of the Lord in the fulfilment of the covenant grace which He had promised to His people.—Ver. 8. The first proof of this was furnished by the deliverance of the children of Israel out of Egypt, and their safe guidance into Canaan ("*this place*" is the land of Canaan). The second was to be found in the deliverance of the people out of the power of their foes, to whom the Lord had been obliged to give them up on account of their apostasy from Him, through the judges whom He had raised up for them, as often as they turned to Him with penitence and cried to Him for help. Of the hostile oppressions which overtook the Israelites during this period of the judges, the following are singled out in ver. 9: (1) that by Sisera, the commander-in-chief of Hazor, *i.e.* that of the Canaanitish king Jabin of Hazor (Judg. iv. 2 sqq.); (2) that of the Philistines, by which we are to understand not so much the hostilities of that nation described in Judg. iii. 31, as the forty years' oppression mentioned in Judg. x. 2 and xiii. 1; and (3) the Moabitish oppression under Eglon (Judg. iii. 12 sqq.). The first half of ver. 10 agrees almost word for word with Judg. x. 10, except that, according to Judg. x. 6, the Ashtaroth are added to the Baalim (see at ch. vii. 4 and Judg. ii. 13). Of the judges whom God sent to the people as deliverers, the following are named, viz. Jerubbaal (see at Judg. vi. 32), *i.e.* Gideon (Judg. vi.), and Bedan, and Jephthah (see Judg. xi.), and Samuel. There is no judge named *Bedan* mentioned either in the book of Judges or anywhere else. The name *Bedan* only occurs again in 1 Chron. vii. 17, among the descendants of Machir the Manassite: consequently some of the commentators suppose *Jair* of Gilead to be the judge intended. But such a supposition is perfectly arbitrary, as it is not rendered probable by any identity in the two names, and Jair is not described as having delivered Israel from any hostile oppression. Moreover, it is extremely improbable that Samuel should have mentioned a judge here, who had been passed over in the book of Judges on account of his comparative insignificance. There is also just as little ground for rendering *Bedan* as an appellative, *e.g.* the Danite (*ben-Dan*), as Kimchi suggests, or *corpulentus* as Böttcher maintains, and so connecting the name with Samson. There is no other course left, therefore, than to regard *Bedan* as an old copyist's error for *Barak* (Judg. iv.), as the LXX., Syriac, and Arabic have done,—a conclusion which is favoured by the circumstance that Barak was one of the most celebrated of the judges, and is placed by the side of Gideon and Jephthah in Heb. xi. 32. The Syriac, Arabic, and one Greek MS. (see Kennicott in the *Addenda* to his *Dissert. Gener.*), have the name of *Samson* instead of *Samuel*. But as the LXX., Chald., and Vulg. all agree with the Hebrew text, there is no critical ground for rejecting Samuel, the more especially as the objection raised to it, viz. that Samuel would not have mentioned himself, is far too trivial to overthrow the reading supported by the most ancient versions; and the assertion made by Thenius, that Samuel does not come down to his own times until the following verse, is altogether unfounded. Samuel could very well class himself with the deliverers of Israel, for the simple reason that it was by him that the people were delivered from the forty years' tyranny of the Philistines, whilst Samson merely commenced their deliverance and did not bring it to completion. Samuel appears to have deliberately mentioned his own name along with those of the other judges who were sent by God, that he might show the people in the most striking manner (ver. 12) that they had no reason whatever for saying to him, "*Nay, but a king shall reign over us,*" as soon as the Ammonites invaded Gilead. "*As Jehovah your God is your King,*" *i.e.* has ever proved himself to be your King by sending judges to deliver you.

Vers. 13–18*a*. After the prophet had thus held up before the people their sin against the Lord, he bade them still further consider, that the king would only procure for them the anticipated deliverance if they would fear the Lord, and give up their rebellion against God.—Ver. 13. "*But now behold the king whom ye have chosen, whom ye have asked for! behold, Jehovah hath set a king over you.*" By the second וְהִנֵּה, the thought is brought out still more strongly, that Jehovah had fulfilled the desire of the people. Although the request of the people had been an act of hostility to God, yet Jehovah had fulfilled it. The word בְּחַרְתֶּם, relating to the choice by lot (ch. x. 17 sqq.), is placed before אֲשֶׁר שְׁאֶלְתֶּם, to show that the demand was the strongest act that the people could perform. They had not only chosen the king with the consent or by the direction of Samuel; they had even demanded a king of their own self-will.—Ver. 14. Still, since the Lord had given them a king, the further welfare of the nation would depend upon whether they would follow the Lord from that time forward, or whether they would rebel against Him again. "*If ye will only fear the Lord, and serve Him, . . . and ye as well as the king who rules over you will be after Jehovah your God.*" אִם, in the sense of *modo*, if only, does not require any apodosis, as it is virtually equivalent to the wish, "*O that ye would only!*" for which אִם with the imperfect is commonly used (*vid.* 2 Kings xx. 19; Prov. xxiv. 11, etc.; and Ewald, § 329, *b*). There is also nothing to be supplied to אַחַר יְהוָֹה . . . וִהְיִיתֶם, since הָיָה אַחַר, to be after or behind a person, is good Hebrew, and is frequently met with, particularly in the sense of attaching one's self to the king, or holding to him (*vid.* 2 Sam. ii. 10; 1 Kings xii. 20, xvi. 21, 22). This meaning is also at the foundation of the present passage, as Jehovah was the God-king of Israel.—Ver. 15. "*But if ye do not hearken to the voice of Jehovah, and strive against His commandment, the hand of Jehovah will be heavy upon you, as upon your fathers.*" וְ in the sense of *as, i.e.* used in a comparative sense, is most frequently placed before whole sentences (see Ewald, § 340, *b*); and the use of it here may be explained, on the ground that בַּאֲבֹתֵיכֶם contains the force of an entire sentence: "*as it was upon your fathers.*" The allusion to the fathers is very suitable here, because the people were looking to the king for the removal of all the calamities, which had fallen upon them from time immemorial. The paraphrase of this word, which is adopted in the Septuagint, ἐπὶ τὸν βασιλέα ὑμῶν, is a very unhappy conjecture, although Thenius proposes to alter the text to suit it.—Ver. 16. In order to give still greater emphasis to his words, and to secure their lasting, salutary effect upon the people, Samuel added still further: Even now ye may see that ye have acted very wickedly in the sight of Jehovah, in demanding a king. This chain of thought is very clearly indicated by the words גַּם־עַתָּה, "*yea, even now.*" "*Even now come hither, and see this great thing which Jehovah does before your eyes.*" The words גַּם־עַתָּה, which are placed first, belong, so far as the sense is concerned, to רְאוּ אֶת־הַד׳; and הִתְיַצְּבוּ ("*place yourselves,*" *i.e.* make yourselves ready) is merely inserted between, to fix the attention of the people more closely upon the following miracle, as an event of great importance, and one which they ought to lay to heart. "*Is it not now wheat harvest? I will call to Jehovah, that He may give thunder* (קֹלוֹת, as in Ex. ix. 23, etc.) *and rain. Then perceive and see, that the evil is great which ye have done in the eyes of Jehovah, to demand a king.*" The wheat harvest occurs in Palestine between the middle of May and the middle of June (see my *Bibl. Arch.* i. § 118). And during this time it scarcely ever rains. Thus Jerome affirms (*ad Am.* c. 4): "*Nunquam in fine mensis Junii aut in Julio in his provinciis maximeque in Judæa pluvias vidimus.*" And Robinson also says in his *Palestine* (ii. p. 98): "In ordinary seasons, from the cessation of the showers in spring until their commencement in October and November, rain never falls, and the sky is usually serene" (see my *Arch.* i. § 10). So that when God sent thunder and rain on that day in answer to Samuel's appeal to him, this was a miracle of divine omnipotence, intended to show to the people that the judgments of God might fall upon the sinners at any time. Thunderings, as "the voices of God" (Ex. ix. 28), are harbingers of judgment.

Vers. 18b–25. This miracle therefore inspired the people with a salutary terror. "*All the people greatly feared the Lord and Samuel,*" and entreated the prophet, "*Pray for thy servants to the Lord thy God, that we die not, because we have added to all our sins the evil thing, to ask us a king.*"—Vers. 20, 21 Samuel thereupon announced to them first of all, that the Lord would not forsake His people for His great name's sake, if they would only serve Him with uprightness. In order, however, to give no encouragement to any false trust in the covenant faithfulness of the Lord, after the comforting words, "*Fear not*," he told them again very decidedly that they had done wrong, but that now they were not to turn away from the Lord, but to serve Him with all their heart, and not go after vain idols. To strengthen this admonition, he repeats the לֹא תָסוּרוּ in ver. 21, with the explanation, that in turning from the Lord they would fall away to idols, which could not bring them either help or deliverance. To the כִּי after תָּסוּרוּ the same verb must be supplied from the context: "*Do not turn aside (from the Lord), for* (ye turn aside) *after that which is vain.*" הַתֹּהוּ, the vain, worthless thing, signifies the *false gods*. This will explain the construction with a plural: "*which do not profit and do not save, because they are emptiness*" (*tohu*), *i.e.* worthless beings (*elilim*, Lev. xix. 4 ; cf. Isa. xliv. 9 and Jer. xvi. 19).—Ver. 22. "*For* (כִּי gives the reason for the main thought of the previous verse, 'Fear not, but serve the Lord,' etc.) *the Lord will not forsake His people for His great name's sake ; for it hath pleased the Lord* (for הוֹאִיל, see at Deut. i. 5) *to make you His people.*" The emphasis lies upon *His*. This the Israelites could only be, when they proved themselves to be the people of God, by serving Jehovah with all their heart. "*For His great name's sake,*" *i.e.* for the great name which He had acquired in the sight of all the nations, by the marvellous guidance of Israel thus far, to preserve it against misapprehension and blasphemy (see at Josh. vii. 9).—Ver. 23. Samuel then promised the people his constant intercession : "*Far be it from me to sin against the Lord, that I should cease to pray for you, and to instruct you in the good and right way,*" *i.e.* to work as prophet for your good. " In this he sets a glorious example to all rulers, showing them that they should not be led astray by the ingratitude of their subordinates or subjects, and give up on that account all interest in their welfare, but should rather persevere all the more in their anxiety for them" (*Berleb. Bible*).—Vers. 24, 25. Lastly, he repeats once more his admonition, that they would continue stedfast in the fear of God, threatening at the same time the destruction of both king and people if they should do wrong (on ver. 24*a*, see ch. vii. 3 and Josh. xxiv. 14, where the form יְראוּ is also found). " *For see what great things He has done for you*" (shown to you), not by causing it to thunder and rain at Samuel's prayer, but by giving them a king. הִגְדִּיל עִם, as in Gen. xix. 19.

SAUL'S REIGN, AND HIS UNSEASONABLE SACRIFICE IN THE WAR AGAINST THE PHILISTINES.—CHAP. XIII.

The history of the reign of Saul commences with this chapter;[1] and according to the standing custom in the history of the kings, it opens with a statement of the age of the king when he began to reign, and the number of years that his reign lasted. If, for example, we compare the form and contents of this verse with 2 Sam. ii. 10, v. 4, 1 Kings xiv. 21,

---

[1] The connection of vers. 8-11 of this chapter with ch. x. 8 is adduced in support of the hypothesis that ch. xiii. forms a direct continuation of the account that was broken off in ch. x. 16. This connection must be admitted; but it by no means follows that in the source from which the books before us were derived, ch. xiii. was directly attached to ch. viii. 16, and that Samuel intended to introduce Saul publicly as king here in Gilgal immediately before the attack upon the Philistines, to consecrate him by the solemn presentation of sacrifices, and to connect with this the religious consecration of the approaching campaign. For there is not a word about any such intention in the chapter before us or in ch. x. 8, nor even the slightest hint at it. Thenius has founded this view of his upon his erroneous interpretation of יָרַדְתָּ in ch. x. 8 as an imperative, as if Samuel intended to command Saul to go to Gilgal immediately after the occurrence of the signs mentioned in ch. x. 2 sqq.: a view which is at variance with the instructions given to him, to do what his hand should find after the occurrence of those signs (see p. 101). To this we may also add the following objections: How is it conceivable that Saul, who concealed his anointing even from his own family after his return from Samuel to Gibeah (ch. x. 16), should have immediately after chosen 3000 men of Israel to begin the war against the Philistines? How did Saul attain to any such distinction, that at his summons all Israel gathered round him as their king, even before he had been publicly proclaimed king in the presence of the people, and before he had secured the confidence of the people by any kingly heroic deed? The fact of his having met with a band of prophets, and even prophesied in his native town of Gibeah after his departure from Samuel, and that this had become a proverb, is by no means enough to explain the enterprises described in ch. xiii. 1-7, which so absolutely demand the incidents that occurred in the meantime as recorded in ch. x. 17-xii. 25 even to make them intelligible, that any writing in which ch. xiii. 2 sqq. followed directly upon ch. x. 16 would necessarily be regarded as utterly faulty. This fact, which I have already adduced in my examination of the hypothesis defended by Thenius in my *Introduction to the Old Testament* (p. 168), retains its force undiminished, even though, after a renewed investigation of the question, I have given up the supposed connection between ch. x. 8 and the proclamation mentioned in ch. xi. 14 sqq., which I defended there.

xxii. 42, 2 Kings viii. 26, and other passages, where the age is given at which Ishbosheth, David, and many of the kings of Judah began to reign, and also the number of years that their reign lasted, there can be no doubt that our verse was also intended to give the same account concerning Saul, and therefore that every attempt to connect this verse with the one which follows is opposed to the uniform historical usage. Moreover, even if, as a matter of necessity, the second clause of ver. 1 could be combined with ver. 2 in the following manner: He was two years king over Israel, then Saul chose 3000 men, etc.; the first half of the verse would give no reasonable sense, according to the Masoretic text that has come down to us. בֶּן־שָׁנָה שָׁאוּל בְּמָלְכוֹ cannot possibly be rendered "*jam per annum regnaverat Saul*," "Saul had been king for a year," or "Saul reigned one year," but can only mean "*Saul was a year old when he became king*." This is the way in which the words have been correctly rendered by the Sept. and Jerome; and so also in the Chaldee paraphrase ("Saul was an innocent child when he began to reign") this is the way in which the text has been understood. It is true that this statement as to his age is obviously false; but all that follows from that is, that there is an error in the text, namely, that between בֶּן and שָׁנָה the age has fallen out,—a thing which could easily take place, as there are many traces to show that originally the numbers were not written in words, but only in letters that were used as numerals. This gap in the text is older than the Septuagint version, as our present text is given there. There is, it is true, an *anonymus* in the *hexapla*, in which we find the reading υἱὸς τριάκοντα ἐτῶν Σαούλ; but this is certainly not according to ancient MSS., but simply according to a private conjecture, and that an incorrect one. For since Saul already had a son, Jonathan, who commanded a division of the army in the very first years of his reign, and therefore must have been at least twenty years of age, if not older, Saul himself cannot have been less than forty years old when he began to reign. Moreover, in the second half of the verse also, the number given is evidently a wrong one, and the text therefore equally corrupt; for the rendering "*when he had reigned two years over Israel*" is opposed both by the parallel passages already quoted, and also by the introduction of the name Saul as the subject in ver. 2*a*, which shows very clearly that ver. 2 commences a fresh sentence, and is not merely the apodosis to ver. 1b. But Saul's reign must have lasted longer than two years, even if, in opposition to all analogies to be found elsewhere, we should understand the two years as merely denoting the length of his reign up to the time of his rejection (ch. xv.), and not till the time of his death. Even then he reigned longer than that; for he could not possibly have carried on all the wars mentioned in ch. xiv. 47, with Moab, Ammon, Edom, the kings of Zobah and the Philistines, in the space of two years. Consequently a numeral, say ב, twenty, must also have dropped out before שְׁתֵּי שָׁנִים (two years); since there are cogent reasons for assuming that his reign lasted as long as twenty or twenty-two years, reckoning to the time of his death. We have given the reasons themselves in connection with the chronology of the period of the judges (vol. iv. pp. 283-4).[1]

Vers. 2-7. *The war with the Philistines* (ch. xiii. xiv.) certainly falls, at least so far as the commencement is concerned, in the very earliest part of Saul's reign. This we must infer partly from the fact, that at the very time when Saul was seeking for his father's asses, there was a military post of the Philistines at Gibeah (ch. x. 5), and therefore the Philistines had already occupied certain places in the land; and partly also from the fact, that according to this chapter Saul selected an army of 3000 men out of the whole nation, took up his post at Michmash with 2000 of them, placing the other thousand at Gibeah under his son Jonathan, and sent the rest of the people home (ver. 2), because his first intention was simply to check the further advance of the Philistines. The dismission of the rest of the people to their own homes presupposes that the whole of the fighting men of the nation were assembled together. But as no other summoning together of the people has been

---

[1] The traditional account that Saul reigned forty years (Acts xiii. 24, and Josephus, *Ant.* vi. 14, 9) is supposed to have arisen, according to the conjecture of Thenius (on 2 Sam. ii. 10), from the fact that his son Ishbosheth was forty years old when he began to reign, and the notion that as he is not mentioned among the sons of Saul in 1 Sam. xiv. 49, he must have been born after the commencement of Saul's own reign. This conjecture is certainly a probable one; but it is much more natural to assume that as David and Solomon reigned forty years, it arose from the desire to make Saul's reign equal to theirs.

mentioned before, except to the war upon the Ammonites at Jabesh (ch. xi. 6, 7), where all Israel gathered together, and at the close of which Samuel had called the people and their king to Gilgal (ch. xi. 14), the assumption is a very probable one, that it was there at Gilgal, after the renewal of the monarchy, that Saul formed the resolution at once to make war upon the Philistines, and selected 3000 fighting men for the purpose out of the whole number that were collected together, and then dismissed the remainder to their homes. In all probability Saul did not consider that either he or the Israelites were sufficiently prepared as yet to undertake a war upon the Philistines generally, and therefore resolved, in the first place, only to attack the outpost of the Philistines, which was advanced as far as Gibeah, with a small number of picked soldiers. According to this simple view of affairs, the war here described took place at the very commencement of Saul's reign; and the chapter before us is closely connected with the preceding one.—Ver. 2. Saul posted himself at Michmash and on the mount of Bethel with his two thousand men. *Michmash*, the present *Mukhmas*, a village in ruins upon the northern ridge of the Wady *Suweinit*, according to the *Onom.* (*s. v. Machmas*), was only nine Roman miles to the north of Jerusalem, whereas it took Robinson three hours and a half to go from one to the other (*Pal.* ii. p. 117). *Bethel* (*Beitin;* see at Josh. vii. 2) is to the north-west of this, at a distance of two hours' journey, if you take the road past Deir-Diwan. The mountain (הַר) of Bethel cannot be precisely determined. Bethel itself was situated upon very high ground; and the ruins of Beitin are completely surrounded by heights (Rob. ii. p. 126; and v. Raumer, *Pal.* pp. 178-9). Jonathan stationed himself with his thousand men at (by) Gibeah of Benjamin, the native place and capital of Saul, which was situated upon *Tell el Phul* (see at Josh. xviii. 28), about an hour and a half from Michmas.—Ver. 3. "*And Jonathan smote the garrison of the Philistines that was at Geba,*" probably the military post mentioned in ch. x. 5, which had been advanced in the meantime as far as Geba. For *Geba* is not to be confounded with *Gibeah*, from which it is clearly distinguished in ver. 16 as compared with ver. 15, but is the modern *Jeba*, between the Wady *Suweinit* and Wady *Fara*, to the north-west of Ramah (er-Râm; see at Josh. xviii. 24). "*The Philistines* heard this. *And Saul had the trumpet blown throughout the whole land, and proclamation made: let the Hebrews hear it."* לֵאמֹר after תָּקַע בַּשּׁוֹפָר points out the proclamation that was made after the alarm given by the *shophar* (see 2 Sam. xx. 1; 1 Kings i. 34, 39, etc.). The object to "let them hear" may be easily supplied from the context, viz. Jonathan's feat of arms. Saul had this trumpeted in the whole land, not only as a joyful message for the Hebrews, but also as an indirect summons to the whole nation to rise and make war upon the Philistines. In the word שָׁמַע (hear), there is often involved the idea of observing, laying to heart that which is heard. If we understand יִשְׁמְעוּ in this sense here, and the next verse decidedly hints at it, there is no ground whatever for the objection which Thenius, who follows the LXX., has raised to יִשְׁמְעוּ הָעִבְרִים. He proposes this emendation, יִפְשְׁעוּ הָעִבְרִים, "let the Hebrews fall away," according to the Alex. text ἠθετήκασιν οἱ δοῦλοι, without reflecting that the very expression οἱ δοῦλοι is sufficient to render the Alex. reading suspicious, and that Saul could not have summoned the people in *all* the land to fall away from the Philistines, since they had not yet conquered and taken possession of the whole. Moreover, the correctness of יִשְׁמְעוּ is confirmed by וְכָל־יִשְׂרָאֵל שָׁמְעוּ in ver. 4. "*All Israel heard,*" not the call to fall away, but the news, "*Saul has smitten a garrison of the Philistines, and Israel has also made itself stinking with the Philistines,*" *i.e.* hated in consequence of the bold and successful attack made by Jonathan, which proved that the Israelites would no longer allow themselves to be oppressed by the Philistines. "*And the people let themselves be called together after Saul to Gilgal.*" הִצָּעֵק, to permit to summon to war (as in Judg. vii. 23, 24). The words are incorrectly rendered by the Vulgate, "*clamavit ergo populus post Saul,*" and by Luther, "Then the people cried after Saul to Gilgal." Saul drew back to Gilgal, when the Philistines advanced with a large army, to make preparations for the further conflict (see at ver. 13).—Ver. 5. The Philistines also did not delay to avenge the defeat at Geba. They collected an innumerable army: 30,000 chariots, 6000 horsemen, and people, *i.e.* foot-soldiers, without number (as the sand by the sea-shore; cf. Judg. vii. 12, Josh. xi. 4, etc.). רֶכֶב by the side of פָּרָשִׁים can only mean war chariots. 30,000 war chariots, however, bear no proportion whatever to 6000 horsemen, not only because the number of war chariots is invariably smaller than that of the horsemen (cf. 2 Sam. x. 18; 1 Kings x. 26; 2 Chron. xii. 3), but also, as Bochart observes in his *Hieroz.* p. i. lib. ii. c. 9, because such a number of war chariots is never met with either in sacred or profane history, not even in the case of nations that were much more powerful than the Philistines. The number is therefore certainly corrupt, and we must either read 3000 (שְׁלֹשֶׁת אֲלָ׳) instead of שְׁלֹשִׁים אֲלָ׳), according to the Syriac and Arabic, or else simply 1000; and in the latter case the origin of the number thirty must be attributed to the fact, that through the oversight of a copyist the ל of the word יִשְׂרָאֵל was written twice, and consequently the second ל was taken for the numeral thirty. This army was encamped " *at Michmash, before* (i.e. in the front, or on the western side of) *Bethaven:*" for, according to Josh. vii. 2, Bethaven was to the east of Michmash; and קִדְמַת, when it occurs in geographical accounts, does not " always mean to the east," as Thenius erroneously maintains, but invariably means simply " in front " (see at Gen. ii. 14).[1]—Vers. 6, 7. When the Israelites saw that they had come into a strait (צַר לוֹ), for the people were oppressed (by the Philistines), they hid themselves in the caves, thorn-bushes, rocks (*i.e.* clefts of the rocks), fortresses (צְרִחִים; see at Judg. ix. 46), and pits (which were to be found in the land); and Hebrews also went over the Jordan into the land of Gad and Gilead, whilst Saul was still at Gilgal; and all the people (the people of war who had been called together, ver. 4) trembled behind him, *i.e.* were gathered together in his train, or assembled round him as leader, trembling or in despair.

The *Gilgal* mentioned here cannot be Jiljilia, which is situated upon the high ground, as assumed in the *Comm. on Joshua*, p. 94, but must be the Gilgal in the valley of the Jordan. This is not only favoured by the expression יֵרְדוּ (the Philistines will come *down* from Michmash to Gilgal, ver. 12),

---

[1] Consequently there is no ground whatever for altering the text according to the confused rendering of the LXX., ἐν Μαχμάς ἐξ ἐναντίας Βαιθωρὼν κατὰ νότου, for the purpose of substituting for the correct statement in the text a description which would be geographically wrong, viz. to the south-east of Beth-horon, since Michmash was neither to the south nor to the south-east, but to the east of Beth-horon.

but also by וַיַּעַל (Samuel went *up* from Gilgal to Gibeah, ver. 15), and by the general attitude of Saul and his army towards the Philistines. As the Philistines advanced with a powerful army, after Jonathan's victory over their garrison at Geba (to the south of Michmash), and encamped at Michmash (ver. 5); and Saul, after withdrawing from Gilgal, where he had gathered the Israelites together (vers. 4, 8, 12), with Jonathan and the six hundred men who were with him when the muster took place, took up his position at Geba (vers. 15, 16), from which point Jonathan attacked the Philistine post in the pass of Michmash (ver. 23, and ch. xiv. 1 sqq.): Saul must have drawn back from the advancing army of the Philistines to the Gilgal in the Jordan valley, to make ready for the battle by collecting soldiers and presenting sacrifices, and then, after this had been done, must have advanced once more to Gibeah and Geba to commence the war with the army of the Philistines that was encamped at Michmash. If, on the other hand, he had gone northwards to Jiljilia from Michmash, where he was first stationed, to escape the advancing army of the Philistines; he would have had to attack the Philistines from the north when they were encamped at Michmash, and could not possibly have returned to Geba without coming into conflict with the Philistines, since Michmash was situated between Jiljilia and Geba.

Vers. 8–15. *Saul's untimely sacrifice.*—Vers. 8, 9. Saul waited seven days for Samuel's coming, according to the time appointed by Samuel (see at ch. x. 8), before proceeding to offer the sacrifices through which the help of the Lord was to be secured for the approaching campaign (see ver. 12); and as Samuel did not come, the people began to disperse and leave him. The *Kethib* וייחל is either the *Niphal* וַיִּיָּחֶל, as in Gen. viii. 12, or *Piel* וַיְיַחֵל; and the *Keri* וַיּוֹחֶל (*Hiphil*) is unnecessary. The verb יָעַד may easily be supplied to אֲשֶׁר שְׁמוּאֵל from the word לַמּוֹעֵד (see *Ges. Lehrgeb.* p. 851).—Ver. 9. Saul then resolved, in his anxiety lest the people should lose all heart and forsake him altogether if there were any further delay, that he would offer the sacrifice without Samuel. וַיַּעַל הָעֹלָה does not imply that Saul offered the sacrifice with his own hand, *i.e.* that he performed the priestly function upon this occasion. The co-operation of the priests in performing the duties belonging to them on such an occasion is taken for granted, just as in the case of the sacrifices offered by David and Solomon (2 Sam. xxiv. 25; 1 Kings iii. 4, viii. 63).—Vers. 10 sqq. The offering of the sacrifice was hardly finished when Samuel came and said to Saul, as he came to meet him and salute him, " *What hast thou done?* " Saul replied, "*When I saw that the people were scattered away from me, and thou camest not at the time appointed, and the Philistines were assembled at Michmash, I thought the Philistines will come down to me to Gilgal now* (to attack me), *before I have entreated the face of Jehovah ; and I overcame myself, and offered the burnt-offering.*" חִלָּה פְּנֵי יי׳: see Ex. xxxii. 11.—Ver. 13. Samuel replied, " *Thou hast acted foolishly,* (and) *not kept the commandment of Jehovah thy God, which He commanded thee: for now* (sc. if thou hadst obeyed His commandment) *Jehovah would have established thy sovereignty over Israel for ever ; but now* (sc. since thou hast acted thus) *thy sovereignty shall not continue.*" The antithesis of עַתָּה הֵכִין and וְעַתָּה לֹא תָקוּם requires that we should understand these two clauses conditionally. The conditional clauses are omitted, simply because they are at once suggested by the tenor of the address (see Ewald, § 358, a). The כִּי (for) assigns the reason, and refers to נִסְכַּלְתָּ ("thou hast done foolishly"), the לֹא שָׁמַרְתָּ וגו׳ being merely added as explanatory. The non-continuance of the sovereignty is not to be regarded as a rejection, or as signifying that Saul had actually lost the throne so far as he himself was concerned; but לֹא תָקוּם (shall not continue) forms the antithesis to הֵכִין עַד־עוֹלָם (established for ever), and refers to the fact that it was not established in perpetuity by being transmitted to his descendants. It was not till his second transgression that Saul was rejected, or declared unworthy of being king over the people of God (ch. xv.). We are not compelled to assume an immediate rejection of Saul even by the further announcement made by Samuel, " *Jehovah hath sought him a man after his own heart ; him hath Jehovah appointed prince over His people ;*" for these words merely announce the purpose of God, without defining the time of its actual realization. Whether it would take place during Saul's reign, or not till after his death, was known only to God, and was made contingent upon Saul's further behaviour. But if Saul's sin did not consist, as we have observed above, in his having interfered with the prerogatives of the priests by offering the sacrifice

I

himself, but simply in the fact that he had transgressed the commandment of God as revealed to him by Samuel, to postpone the sacrifice until Samuel arrived, the punishment which the prophet announced that God would inflict upon him in consequence appears a very severe one, since Saul had not come to the resolution either frivolously or presumptuously, but had been impelled and almost forced to act as he did by the difficulties in which he was placed in consequence of the prophet delaying his coming. But wherever, as in the present instance, there is a definite command given by the Lord, a man has no right to allow himself to be induced to transgress it, by fixing his attention upon the earthly circumstances in which he is placed. As Samuel had instructed Saul, as a direct command from Jehovah, to wait for his arrival before offering sacrifice, Saul might have trusted in the Lord that he would send His prophet at the right time and cause His command to be fulfilled, and ought not to have allowed his confidence to be shaken by the pressing danger of delay. The interval of seven days and the delay in Samuel's arrival were intended as a test of his faith, which he ought not to have lightly disregarded. Moreover, the matter in hand was the commencement of the war against the principal enemies of Israel, and Samuel was to tell him what he was to do (ch. x. 8). So that when Saul proceeded with the consecrating sacrifice for that very conflict, without the presence of Samuel, he showed clearly enough that he thought he could make war upon the enemies of his kingdom without the counsel and assistance of God. This was an act of rebellion against the sovereignty of Jehovah, for which the punishment announced was by no means too severe.—Ver. 15. After this occurrence Samuel went up to Gibeah, and Saul mustered the people who were with him, about six hundred men. Consequently Saul had not even accomplished the object of his unseasonable sacrifice, namely, to prevent the dispersion of the people. With this remark the account of the occurrence that decided the fate of Saul's monarchy is brought to a close.

Vers. 16-23. *Disarming of Israel by the Philistines.*—The following account is no doubt connected with the foregoing, so far as the facts are concerned, inasmuch as Jonathan's brave heroic deed, which brought the Israelites a splendid victory over the Philistines, terminated the war for which Saul had entreated the help of God by his sacrifice at Gilgal; but it is not formally connected with it, so as to form a compact and complete account of the successive stages of the war. On the contrary, the 16th verse, where we have an account of the Israelitish warriors and their enemies, commences a new section of the history, in which the devastating march of the Philistines through the land, and the disarming of the Israelites by these their enemies, are first of all depicted (vers. 17-23); and then the victory of the Israelites through Jonathan's daring and heroic courage, notwithstanding their utter prostration, is recorded (ch. xiv. 1-46), for the purpose of showing how the Lord had miraculously helped His people.[1]

Ver. 16. The two clauses of this verse are circumstantial clauses: "*But Saul, and Jonathan his son, and the people that were with him, were sitting, i.e.* tarrying, *in Geba of Benjamin* (the present Jeba; see at ver. 3); *and the Philistines had encamped at Michmash.*" Just as in vers. 2-4 it is not stated when or why Saul went from Michmash or Geba to Gilgal,

---

[1] From this arrangement of the history, according to which the only two points that are minutely described in connection with the war with the Philistines are those which bring out the attitude of the king, whom the nation had desired to deliver it from its foes, towards Jehovah, and the way in which Jehovah acted towards His people, whilst all the rest is passed over, we may explain the absence of any closer connection between ver. 15 and ver. 16, and not from a gap in the text. The LXX., however, adopted the latter supposition, and according to the usual fashion filled up the gap by expanding ver. 15 in the following thoughtless manner: καὶ ἀνέστη Σαμουὴλ καὶ ἀπῆλθεν ἐκ Γαλγάλων· καὶ τὸ κατάλειμμα τοῦ λαοῦ ἀνέβη ὀπίσω Σαοὺλ εἰς ἀπάντησιν ὀπίσω τοῦ λαοῦ τοῦ πολεμιστοῦ· αὐτῶν παραγενομένων ἐκ Γαλγάλων εἰς Γαβαὰ Βενιαμὶν καὶ ἐπεσκέψατο Σαούλ, κ.τ.λ. For there is no sense in εἰς ἀπάντησιν ὀπίσω, and the whole thought, that the people who were left went up after Saul to meet the people of war, is unintelligible, since it is not stated whence the people of war had come, who are said to have met with those who had remained behind with Saul, and to have gone up with him from Gilgal to Gibeah. If, however, we overlook this, and assume that when Saul returned from Gilgal to Gibeah a further number of fighting men came to him from different parts of the land, how does this assumption agree with the account which follows, viz. that when Saul mustered the people he found only six hundred men,—a statement which is repeated again in ch. xiv. 2? The discrepancy remains even if we adopt Ewald's conjecture (*Gesch.* iii. 43), that εἰς ἀπάντησιν is a false rendering of לַקְרָב, "to the conflict." Moreover, even with the Alexandrian filling up, no natural connection is secured between vers. 15 and 16, unless we identify *Geba* of Ben-

but this change in his position is merely hinted at indirectly at the close of ver. 4; so here Saul's return from Gilgal to Geba with the fighting men who remained with him is not distinctly mentioned, but simply taken for granted as having already occurred.—Vers. 17, 18. Then the spoiler went out of the camp of the Philistines in three companies. שְׁלֹשָׁה רָאשִׁים is made subject to the verb to define the mode of action (see Ewald, § 279, c); and *rashim* is used here, as in ch. xi. 11. הַמַּשְׁחִית, according to the context, is a hostile band that went out to devastate the land. The definite article points it out as well known. One company took the road to *Ophrah* into the land of *Shual, i.e.* went in a north-easterly direction, as, according to the *Onom., Ophrah* of Benjamin was five Roman miles to the east of Bethel (see at Josh. xviii. 23). Robinson supposes it to have been on the site of *Tayibeh*. The land of Shual (fox-land) is unknown; it may possibly have been identical with the land of *Saalim* (ch. ix. 5). The other company turned on the road to Beth-horon (Beit-ur: see at Josh. x. 11), that is to say, towards the west; the third, "the way to the territory that rises above the valley of *Zeboim* towards the

---

jamin with *Gibeah*, as the Septuagint and its latest defenders have done, and not only change the participle יֹשְׁבִים (ver. 16) into the aorist ἐκάθισαν, but interpolate καὶ ἔκλαιον after "at *Geba* of Benjamin;" whereas the statement of the text "at *Geba* in Benjamin" is proved to be correct by the simple fact that Jonathan could only attempt or carry out the heroic deed recorded in ch. xiv. from *Geba* and not from *Gibeah;* and the alteration of the participle into the aorist is just as arbitrary as the interpolation of καὶ ἔκλαιον. From all this it follows that the Septuagint version has not preserved the original reading, as Ewald and Thenius suppose, but contains nothing more than a mistaken attempt to restore the missing link. It is true the Vulgate contains the same filling up as the Septuagint, but with one alteration, which upsets the assertion made by Thenius, that the repetition of the expression מִן הַגִּלְגָּל, ἐκ Γαλγάλων, caused the reading contained in the Septuagint to be dropped out of the Hebrew text. For the text of the Vulgate runs as follows: *Surrexit autem Samuël et ascendit de Galgalis in Gabaa Benjamin. Et reliqui populi ascenderunt post Saul obviam populo, qui expugnabant eos venientes de Galgala in Gabaa in colle Benjamin. Et recensuit Saul, etc.* Jerome has therefore rendered the first two clauses of ver. 15 in perfect accordance with the Hebrew text; and the addition which follows is nothing more than a gloss that has found its way into his translation from the Itala, and in which *de Galgala in colle Benjamin* is still retained, whereas Jerome himself rendered מִן הַגִּלְגָּל *de Galgalis.*

desert." These descriptions are obscure; and the valley of *Zeboim* altogether unknown. There is a town of this name (צְבֹעִים, different from צְבֹיִים, Deut. xxix. 22, Gen. xiv. 2, 8; or צְבֹאִים, Hos. xi. 8, in the vale of Siddim) mentioned in Neh. xi. 34, which was inhabited by Benjaminites, and was apparently situated in the south-eastern portion of the land of Benjamin, to the north-east of Jerusalem, from which it follows that the third company pursued its devastating course in a south easterly direction from Michmash towards Jericho. " *The wilderness*" is probably the desert of Judah. The intention of the Philistines in carrying out these devastating expeditions, was no doubt to entice the men who were gathered round Saul and Jonathan out of their secure positions at Gibeah and Geba, and force them to fight.—Vers. 19 sqq. The Israelites could not offer a successful resistance to these devastating raids, as there was no smith to be found in the whole land: "*For the Philistines thought the Hebrews might make themselves sword or spear*" (אָמַר followed by פֶּן, " to say, or think, that not," equivalent to being unwilling that it should be done). Consequently (as the words clearly imply) when they proceeded to occupy the land of Israel as described in ver. 5, they disarmed the people throughout, *i.e.* as far as they penetrated, and carried off the smiths, who might have been able to forge weapons; so that, as is still further related in ver. 20, all Israel was obliged to go to the Philistines, every one to sharpen his edge-tool, and his ploughshare, and his axe, and his chopper. According to Isa. ii. 4, Micah iv. 3, and Joel iv. 10, אֵת is an iron instrument used in agriculture; the majority of the ancient versions render it *ploughshare*. The word מַחֲרֵשְׁתוֹ is striking after the previous מַחֲרַשְׁתּוֹ (from מַחֲרֶשֶׁת); and the meaning of both words is uncertain. According to the etymology, מַחֲרֶשֶׁת might denote any kind of edge-tool, even the ploughshare. The second מַחֲרֵשְׁתוֹ is rendered τὸ δρέπανον αὐτοῦ (his sickle) by the LXX., and *sarculum* by Jerome, a small garden hoe for loosening and weeding the soil. The fact that the word is connected with קַרְדֹּם, the axe or hatchet, favours the idea that it signifies a *hoe* or *spade* rather than a sickle. Some of the words in ver. 21 are still more obscure. וְהָיְתָה, which is the reading adopted by all the earlier translators, indicates that the result is about to be given of the facts mentioned before: "*And there came to* pass," i.e. so that there came to pass (or arose), הַפְּצִירָה פִים, "*a blunting of the edges.*" פְּצִירָה, bluntness, from פָּצַר, to tear, hence to make blunt, is confirmed by the Arabic نظل, *gladius fissuras habens, obtusus ensis*, whereas the meaning to hammer, *i.e.* to sharpen by hammering, cannot be established. The insertion of the article before פְּצִירָה is as striking as the omission of it before פִים; also the *stat. abs.* instead of the construct פְּצִירַת. These anomalies render it a very probable conjecture that the reading may have been הַפְצִיר הַפִּים (*inf. Hiph. nomin.*). Accordingly the rendering would be, "*so that bluntness of the edges occurred in the edge-tools, and the ploughshares, and the trident, and the axes, and the setting of the goad.*" שְׁלֹשׁ קִלְּשׁוֹן is to be regarded as a *nom. comp.* like our trident, denoting an instrument with three prongs, according to the Chaldee and the Rabbins (see Ges. *Thes.* p. 1219). דָּרְבָן, *stimulus*, is probably a pointed instrument generally, since the meaning goad is fully established in the case of דָּרְבֹן by Eccl. xii. 11.[1]—Ver. 22. On the day of battle, therefore, the people with Saul and Jonathan were without either sword or spear; Saul and Jonathan were the only persons provided with them. The account of the expedition of the Israelites, and their victory over the Ammonites, given in ver. 11, is apparently at variance with this description of the situation of the Israelites, since the

---

[1] Ver. 21 runs very differently in the LXX., namely, καὶ ἦν ὁ τρυγητός ἕτοιμος τοῦ θερίζειν, τὰ δὲ σκεύη ἦν τρεῖς σίκλοι εἰς τὸν ὀδόντα, καὶ τῇ ἀξίνῃ καὶ τῷ δρεπάνῳ ὑπόστασις ἦν ἡ αὐτή; and Thenius and Böttcher propose an emendation of the Hebrew text accordingly, so as to obtain the following meaning: " And the sharpening of the edges in the case of the spades and ploughshares was done at three shekels a tooth (*i.e.* three shekels each), and for the axe and sickle it was the same" (Thenius); or, " and the same for the sickles, and for the axes, and for setting the prong" (Böttcher). But here also it is easy enough to discover that the LXX. had not another text before them that was different from the Masoretic text, but merely confounded הַפְצִיר with הַבְּצִיר, τρυγητός, and took שְׁלֹשׁ קִלְּשׁוֹן, which was unintelligible to them, *e conjectura* for שְׁלֹשׁ שֶׁקֶל שֵׁן, altogether regardless of the sense or nonsense of their own translation. The latest supporters of this senseless rendering, however, have neither undertaken to prove the possibility of translating ὀδόντα (ὀδούς), "each single piece" (*i.e.* each), or inquired into the value of money at that time, so as to see whether three shekels would be an unexampled charge for the sharpening of an axe or sickle.

war in question not only presupposes the possession of weapons by the Israelites, but must also have resulted in their capturing a considerable quantity. The discrepancy is very easily removed, however, when we look carefully at all the circumstances. For instance, we can hardly picture the Israelites to ourselves as amply provided with ordinary weapons in this expedition against the Ammonites. Moreover, the disarming of the Israelites by the Philistines took place for the most part if not entirely after this expedition, viz. at the time when the Philistines swept over the land with an innumerable army after Jonathan had smitten their garrison at Geba (vers. 3, 5), so that the fighting men who gathered round Saul and Jonathan after that could hardly bring many arms with them. Lastly, the words "there was neither sword nor spear found in the hands of all the people with Saul and Jonathan" must not be too closely pressed, but simply affirm that the 600 fighting men of Saul and Jonathan were not provided with the necessary arms, because the Philistines had prevented the possibility of their arming themselves in the ordinary way by depriving the people of all their smiths.

Ver. 23 forms the transition to the heroic act of Jonathan described in ch. xiv.: "*An outpost of the Philistines went out to the pass of Michmash;*" *i.e.* the Philistines pushed forward a company of soldiers to the pass (מַעֲבַר, the crossing place) of Michmash, to prevent an attack being made by the Israelites upon their camp. Between *Geba* and *Michmash* there runs the great deep Wady *es Suweinit,* which goes down from Beitin and Bireh (Bethel and Beeroth) to the valley of the Jordan, and intersects the ridge upon which the two places are situated, so that the sides of the wady form very precipitous walls. When Robinson was travelling from Jeba to Mukhmas he had to go down a very steep and rugged path into this deep wady (*Pal.* ii. p. 116). "The way," he says in his *Biblical Researches,* p. 289, "was so steep, and the rocky steps so high, that we were compelled to dismount; while the baggage mules got along with great difficulty. Here, where we crossed, several short side wadys came in from the south-west and north-west. The ridges between these terminate in elevating points projecting into the great wady; and the most easterly of these bluffs on each side were probably the outposts of the two garrisons of Israel and the Philistines. The road passes around the eastern side of the southern hill, the post of Israel, and then strikes up over the western part of the northern one, the post of the Philistines, and the scene of Jonathan's adventure."

JONATHAN'S HEROIC ACT, AND ISRAEL'S VICTORY OVER THE PHILISTINES. SAUL'S WARS AND FAMILY.—CHAP XIV.

Vers. 1–15. *Jonathan's heroic act.*—With strong faith and confidence in the might of the Lord, that He could give the victory even through the hands of very few, Jonathan resolved to attack the outpost of the Philistines at the pass of Mukhmas, accompanied by his armour-bearer alone, and the Lord crowned his enterprise with a marvellous victory.—Ver. 1. Jonathan said to his armour-bearer, "*We will go over to the post of the Philistines, that is over there.*" To these words, which introduce the occurrences that followed, there are attached from וּלְאָבִיו to ver. 5 a series of sentences introduced to explain the situation, and the thread of the narrative is resumed in ver. 6 by a repetition of Jonathan's words. It is first of all observed that Jonathan did not disclose his intentions to his father, who would hardly have approved of so daring an enterprise. Then follows a description of the place where Saul was stationed with the six hundred men, viz. "*at the end of Gibeah* (*i.e.* the extreme northern end), *under the pomegranate-tree* (*Rimmon*) *which is by Migron.*" *Rimmon* is not the rock Rimmon (Judg. xx. 45), which was on the north-east of Michmash, but is an appellative noun, signifying *a pomegranate-tree*. *Migron* is a locality with which we are not acquainted, upon the north side of Gibeah, and a different place from the Migron which was on the north or north-west of Michmash (Isa. x. 28). *Gibeah* (*Tuleil el Phul*) was an hour and a quarter from *Geba*, and from the pass which led across to Michmash. Consequently, when Saul was encamped with his six hundred men on the north of Gibeah, he may have been hardly an hour's journey from Geba.—Ver. 3. Along with Saul and his six hundred men, there was also *Ahiah*, the son of Ahitub, the (elder) brother of Ichabod, the son of Phinehas, the son of Eli, the priest at Shiloh, and therefore a great-grandson of Eli, wearing the ephod, *i.e.* in the high priest's robes. *Ahiah* is generally supposed to be the same person as *Ahimelech*, the son of Ahitub (ch. xxii. 9 sqq.), in which case *Ahiah* (אֲחִיָּה, brother, *i.e.* friend of Jehovah) would be only another form of the name Ahimelech (*i.e.* brother or friend of the King, viz. Jehovah). This is very probable, although Ahimelech might have been Ahiah's brother, who succeeded him in the office of high priest on account of his having died without sons, since there is an interval of at least ten years between the events related in this chapter and those referred to in ch. xxii. Ahimelech was afterwards slain by Saul along with the priests of Nob (ch. xxii. 9 sqq.); the only one who escaped being his son Abiathar, who fled to David and, according to ch. xxx. 7, was invested with the ephod. It follows, therefore, that Ahiah (or Ahimelech) must have had a son at least ten years old at the time of the war referred to here, viz. the Abiathar mentioned in ch. xxx. 7, and must have been thirty or thirty-five years old himself, since Saul had reigned at least twenty-two years, and Abiathar had become high priest a few years before the death of Saul. These assumptions may be very easily reconciled with the passage before us. As Eli was ninety-eight years old when he died, his son Phinehas, who had been killed in battle a short time before, might have been sixty or sixty-five years old, and have left a son of forty years of age, namely Ahitub. Forty years later, therefore, *i.e.* at the beginning of Saul's reign, Ahitub's son Ahiah (Ahimelech) might have been about fifty years old; and at the death of Ahimelech, which took place ten or twelve years after that, his son Abiathar might have been as much as thirty years of age, and have succeeded his father in the office of high priest. But Abiathar cannot have been older than this when his father died, since he was high priest during the whole of David's forty years' reign, until Solomon deposed him soon after he ascended the throne (1 Kings ii. 26 sqq.). Compare with this the remarks on 2 Sam. viii. 17. Jonathan had also refrained from telling the people anything about his intentions, so that they did not know that he had gone.

In vers. 4, 5, the locality is more minutely described. Between the passes, through which Jonathan endeavoured to cross over to go up to the post of the Philistines, there was a sharp rock on this side, and also one upon the other. One of these was called *Bozez*, the other *Seneh*; one (formed) a pillar (מָצוּק), *i.e.* a steep height towards the north opposite to Michmash, the other towards the south opposite to Geba. The expression "*between the passes*" may be explained from the remark of Robinson quoted above, viz. that at the point where he passed the Wady Suweinit, side wadys enter it from the south-west and north-west. These side wadys supply so many different crossings. Between them, however, on the north and south walls of the deep valley, were the jagged rocks *Bozez* and *Seneh*, which rose up like pillars to a great height. These were probably the "hills" which Robinson saw to the left of the pass by which he crossed: "Two hills of a conical or rather spherical form, having steep rocky sides, with small wadys running up behind so as almost to isolate them. One is on the side towards Jeba, and the other towards Mukhmas" (*Pal.* ii. p. 116).—Ver. 6. And Jonathan said to his armour-bearer, "*Come, we will go over to the post of these uncircumcised; it may be that Jehovah will work for us; for* (there is) *no hindrance for Jehovah to work salvation by many or few.*" Jonathan's resolution arose from the strong conviction that Israel was the nation of God, and possessed in Jehovah an omnipotent God, who would not refuse His help to His people in their conflict with the foes of His kingdom, if they would only put their whole trust in Him.—Ver. 7. As the armour-bearer approved of Jonathan's resolution (נְטֵה לָךְ, *turn thither*), and was ready to follow him, Jonathan fixed upon a sign by which he would ascertain whether the Lord would prosper his undertaking.— Vers. 8 sqq. "*Behold, we go over to the people and show ourselves to them. If they say to us, Wait* (דֹּמּוּ, *keep quiet*) *till we come to you, we will stand still in our place, and not go up to them; but if they say thus, Come up unto us, then we will go up, for Jehovah hath* (in that case) *delivered them into our hand.*" The sign was well chosen. If the Philistines said, "Wait till we come," they would show some courage; but if they said, "Come up to us," it would be a sign that they were cowardly, and had not courage enough to leave their position and attack the Hebrews. It was not tempting God for Jonathan to fix upon such a sign by which to determine the success of his enterprise; for he did it in the exercise of his calling, when fighting not for personal objects, but for the kingdom of God, which the uncircumcised were threatening to annihilate, and in the most confident belief that the Lord would deliver and preserve His people. Such faith as this God would not put to shame.—Vers. 11 sqq. When the two showed themselves to the garrison of the Philistines, they said, "*Behold, Hebrews come forth out of the holes in which they have hidden themselves.*" And the men of the garrison cried out to Jonathan and his armour-bearer, "*Come up to us, and we will tell you a word,*" *i.e.* we will communicate something to you. This was ridicule at the daring of the two men, whilst for all that they had not courage enough to meet them bravely and drive them back. In this Jonathan received the desired sign that the Lord had given the Philistines into the hand of the Israelites: he therefore clambered up the rock on his hands and feet, and his armour-bearer after him; and "*they* (the Philistines) *fell before Jonathan,*" *i.e.* were smitten down by him, "*and his armour-bearer was slaying behind him.*"—Ver. 14. The first stroke that Jonathan and his armour-bearer struck was (amounted to) about twenty men "*on about half a furrow of an acre of field.*" מַעֲנָה, *a furrow*, as in Ps. cxxix. 3, is in the absolute state instead of the construct, because several nouns follow in the construct state (cf. Ewald, § 291, *a*). צֶמֶד, *lit.* things bound together, then a pair; here it signifies a pair or *yoke of oxen*, but in the transferred sense of a piece of land that could be ploughed in one morning with a yoke of oxen, like the Latin *jugum, jugerum*. It is called the furrow of an acre of land, because the *length* only of half an acre of land was to be given, and not the breadth or the entire circumference. The Philistines, that is to say, took to flight in alarm as soon as the brave heroes really ascended, so that the twenty men were smitten one after another in the distance of half a rood of land. Their terror and flight are perfectly conceivable, if we consider that the outpost of the Philistines was so stationed upon the top of the ridge of the steep mountain wall, that they could not see how many were following, and the Philistines could not imagine it possible that two Hebrews would have ventured to climb the rock alone and make an attack upon them. Sallust relates a similar occurrence in connection with the scaling of a castle in the Numidian war (*Bell. Jugurth*. c. 89, 90).—Ver. 15. And there arose a *terror in the camp upon the field* (*i.e.* in the principal camp) *as well as among all the people* (of the advanced outpost of the Philistines); *the garrison* (*i.e.* the army that was encamped at Michmash), *and the spoilers, they also trembled, and the earth quaked, sc.* with the noise and tumult of the frightened foe; "*and it grew into a trembling of God*," *i.e.* a supernatural terror miraculously infused by God into the Philistines. The subject to the last וַתְּהִי is either חֲרָדָה, the alarm in the camp, or all that has been mentioned before, *i.e.* the alarm with the noise and tumult that sprang out of it.

Vers. 16–23. *Flight and defeat of the Philistines.*—Ver. 16. The spies of Saul at Gibeah saw how the multitude (in the camp of the Philistines) melted away and was beaten more and more. The words וַיֵּלֶךְ וַהֲלֹם are obscure. The Rabbins are unanimous in adopting the explanation *magis magisque frangebatur*, and have therefore probably taken הֲלֹם as an inf. absol. הָלוֹם, and interpreted הָלַם according to Judg. v. 26. This was also the case with the Chaldee; and Gesenius (*Thes.* p. 383) has adopted the same rendering, except that he has taken הֲלֹם in the sense of *dissolutus, dissipatus est.* Others take הֲלֹם as adverbial ("*and thither*"), and supply the correlate הֲלֹם (hither), so as to bring out the meaning "*hither and thither.*" Thus the LXX. render it ἔνθεν καὶ ἔνθεν, but they have not translated וַיֵּלֶךְ at all.—Ver. 17. Saul conjectured at once that the excitement in the camp of the Philistines was occasioned by an attack made by Israelitish warriors, and therefore commanded the people: פִּקְדוּ־נָא, "*Muster* (number) *now, and see who has gone away from us;*" and "*Jonathan and his armour-bearer were not there,*" *i.e.* they were missing.—Vers. 18 sqq. Saul therefore resolved to ask God, through the priest Ahiah, what he should do; whether he should go out with his army against the Philistines or no. But whilst he was talking with the priest, the tumult in the camp of the Philistines became greater and greater, so that he saw from that what ought to be done under the circumstances, and stopped the priest's inquiring of God, and set out with his people without delay. We are struck, however, with the expression in ver. 18, "*Bring hither the ark of God,*" and the explanation which follows, "*for the ark of God was at that time with the children of Israel,*" inasmuch as the ark was then deposited at Kirjath-jearim, and it is a very improbable thing that it should have been in the little camp of Saul. Moreover, in other cases where the high priest is spoken of as inquiring the will of God, there is no mention made of the ark, but only of the ephod, the high priest's shoulder-dress, upon which there were fastened the Urim and Thummim, through which inquiry was made of God. And in addition to this, the verb הַגִּישָׁה is not really applicable to the ark, which was not an object that could be carried about at will; whereas this verb is the current expression used to signify the fetching of the ephod (vid. ch. xxiii. 9, xxx. 7). All these circumstances render the correctness of the Masoretic text extremely doubtful, notwithstanding the fact that the Chaldee, the Syriac, the Arabic, and the Vulgate support it, and recommend rather the reading adopted by the LXX., προσάγαγε τὸ 'Εφούδ· ὅτι αὐτὸς ἦρεν τὸ 'Εφοὺδ ἐν τῇ ἡμέρᾳ ἐκείνῃ ἐνώπιον 'Ισραήλ, which would give as the Hebrew text, הַגִּישָׁה הָאֵפוֹד כִּי הוּא נָשָׂא הָאֵפוֹד בַּיּוֹם הַהוּא לִפְנֵי יִשְׂרָאֵל. In any case, וּבְנֵי יִשְׂרָאֵל at the end of the verse should be read לִפְנֵי or לִבְנֵי יִשׂ׳, since ו gives no sense at all.—Ver. 19. "*It increased more and more;*" lit. increasing and becoming greater. The subject וְהֶהָמוֹן וגו׳ is placed absolutely at the head, so that the verb וַיֵּלֶךְ is appended in the form of an apodosis. אֱסֹף יָדְךָ, "*draw thy hand in*" (back); *i.e.* leave off now. —Ver. 20. "*And* (*i.e.* in consequence of the increasing tumult in the enemy's camp) *Saul had himself, and all the people with him, called,*" *i.e.* called together for battle; and when they came to the war, *i.e.* to the place of conflict, "*behold, there was the sword of the one against the other, a very great confusion,*" in consequence partly of terror, and partly of the circumstance alluded to in ver. 21.—Ver. 21. "*And the Hebrews were with the Philistines as before* (yesterday and the day before yesterday), *who had come along with them in the camp round about; they also came over to Israel, which was with Saul and Jonathan.*" סָבִיב means distributed round about among the Philistines. Those Israelites whom the Philistines had incorporated into their army are called *Hebrews*, according to the name which was current among foreigners, whilst those who were with Saul are called *Israel*, according to the sacred name of the nation. The difficulty which many expositors have found in the word לִהְיוֹת has been very correctly solved, so far as the sense is concerned, by the earlier translators, by the interpolation of "*they returned:*" תָּבוּ (Chald.), ἐπεστράφησαν (LXX.), *reversi sunt* (Vulg.), and similarly the Syriac and Arabic. We are not at liberty, however, to amend the Hebrew text in this manner, as nothing more is omitted than the finite verb הָיוּ before the infinitive לִהְיוֹת (for this construction, see Gesenius, *Gramm.* § 132, 3, Anm. 1), and this might easily be left out here, since it stands at the beginning of the verse in the main clause. The literal rendering would be, they were to be with Israel, *i.e.* they came over to Israel. The fact that the Hebrews who were serving in the army of the Philistines came over to Saul and his host, and turned their weapons against their oppressors, naturally heightened the confusion in the camp of the Philistines, and accelerated their defeat; and this was still further increased by the fact that the Israelites who had concealed themselves on the mountains of Ephraim also joined the Israelitish army, as soon as they heard of the flight of the Philistines (ver. 22).—Ver. 23. " *Thus the Lord helped Israel that day, and the conflict went out beyond Bethaven.*" Bethaven was on the east of Michmash, and, according to ver. 31, the Philistines fled westwards from Michmash to Ajalon. But if we bear in mind that the camp of the Philistines was on the eastern side of Michmash before Bethaven, according to ch. xiii. 5, and that the Israelites forced their way into it from the south, we shall see that the battle might easily have spread out beyond Bethaven, and that eventually the main body of the enemy might have fled as far as Ajalon, and have been pursued to that point by the victorious Israelites.

Vers. 24–31. *Saul's precipitate haste.*—Ver. 24. The men of Israel *were pressed* (*i.e.* fatigued) *on that day, sc.* through the military service and fighting. Then Saul adjured the people, saying, " *Cursed be the man that eateth bread until the evening, and* (till) *I have avenged myself upon mine enemies.*" אִיָּאֵל, *fut. apoc.* of יֹאאֶלָה for יַאֲלֶה, from אָלָה, to swear, *Hiphil* to adjure or require an oath of a person. The people took the oath by saying " *amen*" to what Saul had uttered. This command of Saul did not proceed from a proper attitude towards the Lord, but was an act of false zeal, in which Saul had more regard to himself and his own kingly power than to the cause of the kingdom of Jehovah, as we may see at once from the expression נִקַּמְתִּי וגו׳, " till *I* have avenged *myself* upon mine enemies." It was a despotic measure which not only failed to accomplish its object (see vers. 30, 31), but brought Saul into the unfortunate position of being unable to carry out the oath (see ver. 45). All the people kept the command. "*They tasted no bread.*" וְלֹא־טָעַם is not to be connected with וְנִקְמְתִּי as an apodosis.—Ver. 25. "*And all the land* (*i.e.* all the people of the land who had gathered round Saul : *vid.* ver. 29) *came into the woody country; there was honey upon the field.*" יַעַר signifies here a woody district, in which forests alternated with tracts of arable land and meadows.—Ver. 26. When the people came into the wood and saw *a stream of honey* (of wild or wood bees), "*no one put his hand to his mouth* (*sc.* to eat of the honey), *because they feared the oath.*"—Ver. 27. But Jonathan, who had not heard his father's oath, dipped (in the heat of pursuit, that he might not have to stop) the point of his staff in the new honey, and put it to his mouth, "*and his eyes became bright;*" his lost strength, which is reflected in the eye, having been brought back by this invigorating taste. The *Chethibh* תראנה is probably to be read תֵּרְאֶנָה, the eyes became seeing, received their power of vision again. The Masoretes have substituted as the *Keri* תָּאֹרְנָה, from אוֹר, to become bright, according to ver. 29; and this is probably the correct reading, as the letters might easily be transposed. —Vers. 28 sqq. When one of the people told him thereupon of his father's oath, in consequence of which the people were exhausted (וַיָּעַף הָעָם belongs to the man's words ; and וַיָּעַף is the same as in Judg. iv. 21), Jonathan condemned the prohibition. "*My father has brought the land* (*i.e.* the people of the land, as in ver. 25) *into trouble* (עָכַר, see at Gen. xxxiv. 30) : *see how bright mine eyes have become because I tasted a little of this honey. How much more if the people had eaten to-day of the booty of its enemies, would not the overthrow among the Philistines truly have then become great?*" אַף כִּי, *lit.* to this (there comes) also that = not to mention how much more ; and כִּי עַתָּה is an emphatic introduction of the apodosis, as in Gen. xxxi. 42, xliii. 10, and other passages, and the apodosis itself is to be taken as a question.

Vers. 31–46. *Result of the battle, and consequences of Saul's rashness.*—Ver. 31. "*On that day they smote the Philistines from Michmash to Ajalon,*" which has been preserved in the village of *Yâlo* (see at Josh. xix. 42), and was about three geographical miles to the south-west of Michmash ; "*and the people were very faint,*" because Saul had forbidden them to eat before the evening (ver. 24).—Ver. 32. They therefore "*fell voraciously upon the booty*"—(the *Chethibh* וַיַּעַשׂ is no doubt merely an error in writing for וַיַּעַט, *imperf. Kal* of עִיט with *Dagesh forte implic.* instead of וַיָּעָט, as we may see from ch. xv. 19, since the meaning required by the context, viz. to fall upon a thing, cannot be established in the case of עָשָׂה with אֶל. On the other hand, there does not appear to be any necessity to supply the article before שָׁלָל, and this *Keri* seems only to have been taken from the parallel passage in ch. xv. 19),—"*and took sheep, and oxen, and calves, and slew them on the ground* (אַרְצָה, *lit.* to the earth, so that when they were slaughtered the animal fell upon the ground, and remained lying in its blood, and was cut in pieces), *and ate upon the blood*" (עַל הַדָּם, with which אֶל הַדָּם, "*lying to the blood*," is interchanged in ver. 34), *i.e.* the flesh along with the blood which adhered to it, by doing which they sinned against the law in Lev. xix. 26. This sin had been occasioned by Saul himself through the prohibition which he issued.—Vers. 33, 34. When this was told to Saul, he said, "*Ye act faithlessly towards Jehovah*" by transgressing the laws of the covenant; "*roll me now* (*lit.* this day) *a large stone. Scatter yourselves among the people, and say to them, Let every one bring his ox and his sheep to me, and slay here*" (upon the stone that has been rolled up), viz. so that the blood could run off properly upon the ground, and the flesh be separated from the blood. This the people also did.—Ver. 35. As a thanksgiving for this victory, Saul built an altar to the Lord. אֹתוֹ הֵחֵל לִבְנוֹת, "*he began to build it*," *i.e.* he built this altar at the beginning, or as the first altar. This altar was probably not intended to serve as a place of sacrifice, but simply to be a memorial of the presence of God, or the revelation of God which Saul had received in the marvellous victory.—Ver. 36. After the people had strengthened themselves in the evening with food, Saul wanted to pursue the Philistines still farther during the night, and to plunder among them until the light (*i.e.* till break of day), and utterly destroy them. The people assented to this proposal, but the priest (Ahiah) wished first of all to obtain the decision of God upon the matter. "*We will draw near to God here*" (before the altar which has just been built).—Ver. 37. But when Saul inquired of God (through the Urim and Thummim of the high priest), "*Shall I go down after the Philistines? wilt Thou deliver them into the hand of Israel?"* God did not answer him. Saul was to perceive from this, that the guilt of some sin was resting upon the people, on account of which the Lord had turned away His countenance, and was withdrawing His help.—Vers. 38, 39. When Saul perceived this, he directed all the heads of the people (*pinnoth*, as in Judg. xx. 2) to draw near to learn whereby (wherein) the sin had occurred that day, and declared, *"As truly as Jehovah liveth, who has brought salvation to Israel, even if it were upon Jonathan my son, he shall die."* The first כִּי in ver. 39 is explanatory; the second and third serve to introduce the words, like ὅτι, *quod*; and the repetition serves to give emphasis, *lit.* *" that even if it were upon my son, that he shall die."* *" And of all the people no one answered him,"* from terror at the king's word.—Ver. 40. In order to find out the guilt, or rather the culprit, Saul proceeded to the lot; and for this purpose he made all the people stand on one side, whilst he and his son Jonathan went to the other, and then solemnly addressed Jehovah thus: *"God of Israel, give innocence* (of mind, *i.e.* truth). *And the lot fell upon Saul and Jonathan* (יִלָּכֵד, as in ch. x. 20, 21); *and the people went out,"* sc. without the lot falling upon them, *i.e.* they went out free.—Ver. 42. When they proceeded still further to cast lots between Saul and his son (הַפִּילוּ, sc. גּוֹרָל; cf. 1 Chron. xxvi. 14, Neh. xi. 11, etc.), *Jonathan was taken.*[1]—Vers. 43,

---

[1] In the Alex. version, vers. 41 and 42 are lengthened out with long paraphrases upon the course pursued in casting the lots: καὶ εἶπε Σαούλ, Κύριε ὁ θεὸς Ἰσραήλ τί ὅτι οὐκ ἀπεκρίθης τῷ δούλῳ σου σήμερον; εἰ ἐν ἐμοὶ ἢ ἐν Ἰωνάθαν τῷ υἱῷ μου ἡ ἀδικία; κύριε ὁ θεός Ἰσραήλ δὸς δήλους· καὶ ἐὰν τάδε εἴπῃ, δὸς δὴ τῷ λαῷ σου Ἰσραήλ, δὸς δὴ ὁσιότητα, καὶ κληροῦται Ἰωνάθαν καὶ Σαούλ, καὶ ὁ λαὸς ἐξῆλθε. Ver. 42: Καὶ εἶπε Σαούλ, Βάλλετε ἀνὰ μέσον ἐμοῦ καὶ ἀνὰ μέσον Ἰωνάθαν τοῦ υἱοῦ μου· ὃν ἂν κατακληρώσηται Κύριος ἀποθανέτω. Καὶ εἶπεν ὁ λαὸς πρὸς Σαούλ, Οὐκ ἔστι τὸ ῥῆμα τοῦτο. Καὶ κατεκράτησε Σαοὺλ τοῦ λαοῦ, καὶ βάλλουσιν ἀνὰ μέσον αὐτοῦ καὶ ἀνὰ μέσον Ἰωνάθαν τοῦ υἱοῦ αὐτοῦ, καὶ κατακληροῦται Ἰωνάθαν. One portion of these additions is also found in the text of our present Vulgate, and reads as follows: *Et dixit Saul ad Dominum Deum Israel: Domine Deus Israel, da indicium! quid est quod non responderis servo tuo hodie? Si in me aut in Jonatha filio meo est iniquitas, da ostensionem; aut si hæc iniquitas est in populo tuo, da sanctitatem. Et deprehensus est Jonathas et Saul, populus autem exivit.* The beginning and end of this verse, as well as ver. 42, agree here most accurately with the Hebrew text. But the words from *quid est quod to da sanctitatem* are interpolated, so that הָבָה תָמִים are translated twice;

44. When Saul asked him what he had done, Jonathan confessed that he had tasted a little honey (see ver. 27), and resigned himself to the punishment suspended over him, saying, "*Behold, I shall die;*" and Saul pronounced sentence of death upon him, accompanying it with an oath ("*God do so,*" etc.: *vid.* Ruth i. 17).—Ver. 45. But the people interposed, "*Shall Jonathan die, who has achieved this great salvation* (victory) *in Israel? God forbid! As truly as Jehovah liveth, not a hair shall fall from his head upon the ground; for he hath wrought* (the victory) *with God to-day.*" Thus the people delivered Jonathan from death. The objection raised by the people was so conclusive, that Saul was obliged to yield.

What Jonathan had done was not wrong in itself, but became so simply on account of the oath with which Saul had first in the words *da indicium*, and then in the interpolation *da ostensionem*. This repetition of the same words, and that in different renderings, when taken in connection with the agreement of the Vulgate with the Hebrew text at the beginning and end of the verse, shows clearly enough, that the interpolated clauses did not originate with Jerome, but are simply inserted in his translation from the Itala. The additions of the LXX., in which τάδε εἴπη is evidently only a distortion of ἡ ἀδικία, are regarded by Ewald (*Gesch.* iii. p. 48) and Thenius as an original portion of the text which has dropped out from the Masoretic text. They therefore infer, that instead of תָּמִים we ought to read תֻּמִּים (*Thummim*), and that we have here the full formula used in connection with the use of the Urim and Thummim, from which it may be seen, that this mode of divine revelation consisted simply in a sacred lot, or in the use of two dice, the one of which was fixed upon at the outset as meaning *no*, and the other as meaning *yes*. So much at any rate is indisputable, that the Septuagint translator took תמים in the sense of *thummim*, and so assumed that Saul had the guilty person discovered by resorting to the Urim and Thummim. But this assumption is also decidedly erroneous, together with all the inferences based upon it. For, in the first place, the verbs הִפִּיל and יָלְכֵד can be proved to be never used throughout the whole of the Old Testament to signify the use of the Urim and Thummim, and to be nothing more than technical expressions used to denote the casting of a simple lot (see the passages cited above in the text). Moreover, such passages as ch. x. 22, and ii. 5, 23, show most unmistakeably that the divine oracle of the Urim and Thummim did not consist merely in a sacred lot with yes and no, but that God gave such answers through it as could never have been given through the lots. The Septuagint expansions of the text are nothing more, therefore, than a subjective and really erroneous interpretation on the part of the translators, which arose simply from the mistaken idea that תמים was *thummim*, and which is therefore utterly worthless.

forbidden it. But Jonathan did not hear the oath, and therefore had not even consciously transgressed. Nevertheless a curse lay upon Israel, which was to be brought to light as a warning for the culprit. Therefore Jehovah had given no reply to Saul. But when the lot, which had the force of a divine verdict, fell upon Jonathan, sentence of death was not thereby pronounced upon him by God; but it was simply made manifest, that through his transgression of his father's oath, with which he was not acquainted, guilt had been brought upon Israel. The breach of a command issued with a solemn oath, even when it took place unconsciously, excited the wrath of God, as being a profanation of the divine name. But such a sin could only rest as guilt upon the man who had committed, or the man who occasioned it. Now where the command in question was one of God himself, there could be no question, that even in the case of unconscious transgression the sin fell upon the transgressor, and it was necessary that it should either be expiated by him or forgiven him. But where the command of a man had been unconsciously transgressed, the guilt might also fall upon the man who issued the command, that is to say, if he did it without being authorized or empowered by God. In the present instance, Saul had issued the prohibition without divine authority, and had made it obligatory upon the people by a solemn oath. The people had conscientiously obeyed the command, but Jonathan had transgressed it without being aware of it. For this Saul was about to punish him with death, in order to keep his oath. But the people opposed it. They not only pronounced Jonathan innocent, because he had broken the king's command unconsciously, but they also exclaimed that he had gained the victory for Israel "*with God.*" In this fact (Jonathan's victory) there was a divine verdict. And Saul could not fail to recognise now, that it was not Jonathan, but he himself, who had sinned, and through his arbitrary and despotic command had brought guilt upon Israel, on account of which God had given him no reply.—Ver. 46. With the feeling of this guilt, Saul gave up any further pursuit of the Philistines: he "*went up*" (*sc.* to Gibeah) "*from behind the Philistines,*" *i.e.* desisting from any further pursuit. But the Philistines went to their place, *i.e.* back into their own land.

Vers. 47–52. GENERAL SUMMARY OF SAUL'S OTHER WARS, AND ACCOUNT OF HIS FAMILY.—Ver. 47. "*But Saul had taken the sovereignty.*" As Saul had first of all secured a recognition of himself as king on the part of all the tribes of Israel, through his victory over the Ammonites at Jabesh (ch. xi. 12 sqq.), so it was through the victory which he had gained over the Philistines, and by which these obstinate foes of Israel were driven back into their own land, that he first acquired the kingship over Israel, *i.e.* first really secured the regal authority over the Israelites. This is the meaning of לָכַד הַמְּלוּכָה; and this statement is not at variance either with the election of Saul by lot (ch. x. 17 sqq.), or with his confirmation at Gilgal (ch. xi. 14, 15). But as Saul had to fight for the sovereignty, and could only secure it by successful warfare, his other wars are placed in the foreground in the summary account of his reign which follows (vers. 47, 48), whilst the notices concerning his family, which stand at the very beginning in the case of the other kings, are not mentioned till afterwards (vers. 49-51). Saul fought successfully against all the enemies of Israel round about; against Moab, the Ammonites, Edom, the kings of Zobah, a district of Syria on this side the Euphrates (see at 2 Sam. viii. 3), and against the Philistines. The war against the Ammonites is described in ch. xi.; but with the Philistines Saul had to wage repeated war all the days of his life (ver. 52). The other wars are none of them more fully described, simply because they were of no importance to the history of the kingdom of God, having neither furnished occasion for any miraculous displays of divine omnipotence, nor brought about the subjection of hostile nations to the power of Israel. "*Whithersoever he turned, he inflicted punishment.*" This is the rendering which Luther has very aptly given to יַרְשִׁיעַ; for הִרְשִׁיעַ signifies to declare wrong, hence to condemn, more especially as applied to judges: here it denotes sentence or condemnation *by deeds*. Saul chastised these nations for their attacks upon Israel.— Ver. 48. "*And he acquired power;*" עָשָׂה חַיִל (as in Num. xxiv. 18) does not merely signify he proved himself brave, or he formed an army, but denotes the development and unfolding of power in various respects. Here it relates more particularly to the development of strength in the war against Amalek, by virtue of which Saul smote this arch-enemy of Israel, and put an end

to their depredations. This war is described more fully in ch.
xv., on account of its consequences in relation to Saul's own sovereignty.—Vers. 49-51. *Saul's family.*—Ver. 49. Only three of
his sons are mentioned, namely those who fell with him, according to ch. xxxi. 2, in the war with the Philistines. *Jisvi* is
only another name for Abinadab (ch. xxxi. 2; 1 Chron. viii. 33,
ix. 39). In these passages in the Chronicles there is a fourth
mentioned, *Esh-baal,* i.e. the one who is called *Ish-bosheth* in
2 Sam. ii. 8, etc., and who was set up by Abner as the antagonist of David. The reason why he is not mentioned here it is
impossible to determine. It may be that the name has fallen
out simply through some mistake in copying: the daughters
Michal and *Merab* are mentioned, with special reference to the
occurrence described in ch. xviii. 17 sqq.—Vers. 50, 51. *Abner*
the general was also Saul's cousin. For "*son of Abiel*" (*ben
Abiel*) we must read "*sons of Abiel*" (*bne Abiel:* see ch. ix. 1).
—Ver. 52. The statement, "*and the war was hard* (severe)
against the Philistines as long as Saul lived," merely serves to
explain the notice which follows, namely, that Saul took or drew
to himself every strong man and every brave man that he saw
If we observe this, which is the true relation between the two
clauses in this verse, the appearance of abruptness which we
find in the first notice completely vanishes, and the verse follows
very suitably upon the allusion to the general. The meaning
might be expressed in this manner : And as Saul had to carry
on a severe war against the Philistines his whole life long, he
drew to himself every powerful man and every brave man that
he met with.

WAR WITH AMALEK. SAUL'S DISOBEDIENCE AND REJECTION.—CHAP. XV.

As Saul had transgressed the commandment of God which
was given to him through Samuel, by the sacrifice which he
offered at Gilgal in the war with the Philistines at the very
commencement of his reign, and had thereby drawn upon himself the threat that his monarchy should not be continued in
perpetuity (ch. xiii. 13, 14); so his disobedience in the war
against the Amalekites was followed by his rejection on the
part of God. The Amalekites were the first heathen nation to

attack the Israelites after their deliverance out of Egypt, which they did in the most treacherous manner on their journey from Egypt to Sinai; and they had been threatened by God with extermination in consequence. This Moses enjoined upon Joshua, and also committed to writing, for the Israelites to observe in all future generations (Ex. xvii. 8-16). As the Amalekites afterwards manifested the same hostility to the people of God which they had displayed in this first attack, on every occasion which appeared favourable to their ravages, the Lord instructed Samuel to issue the command to Saul, to wage war against Amalek, and to smite man and beast with the ban, *i.e.* to put all to death (vers. 1-3). But when Saul had smitten them, he not only left Agag the king alive, but spared the best of the cattle that he had taken as booty, and merely executed the ban upon such animals as were worthless (vers. 4-9). He was rejected by the Lord for this disobedience, so that he was to be no longer king over Israel. His rejection was announced to him by Samuel (vers. 10-23), and was not retracted in spite of his prayer for the forgiveness of his sin (vers. 24-35). In fact, Saul had no excuse for this breach of the divine command; it was nothing but open rebellion against the sovereignty of God in Israel; and if Jehovah would continue King of Israel, He must punish it by the rejection of the rebel. For Saul no longer desired to be the medium of the sovereignty of Jehovah, or the executor of the commands of the God-king, but simply wanted to reign according to his own arbitrary will. Nevertheless this rejection was not followed by his outward deposition. The Lord merely took away His Spirit, had David anointed king by Samuel, and thenceforward so directed the steps of Saul and David, that as time advanced the hearts of the people were turned away more and more from Saul to David; and on the death of Saul, the attempt of the ambitious Abner to raise his son Ishbosheth to the throne could not possibly have any lasting success.

Vers. 1-3. The account of the war against the Amalekites is a very condensed one, and is restricted to a description of the conduct of Saul on that occasion. Without mentioning either the time or the immediate occasion of the war, the narrative commences with the command of God which Samuel solemnly communicated to Saul, to go and exterminate that people

Samuel commenced with the words, "*Jehovah sent me to anoint thee to be king over His people, over Israel*," in order to show to Saul the obligation which rested upon him to receive his commission as coming from God, and to proceed at once to fulfil it. The allusion to the anointing points back not to ch. xi. 15, but to ch. x. 1.—Ver. 2. "*Thus saith the Lord of Zebaoth, I have looked upon what Amalek did to Israel, that it placed itself in his way when he came up out of Egypt*" (Ex. xvii. 8). Samuel merely mentions this first outbreak of hostility on the part of Amalek towards the people of Israel, because in this the same disposition was already manifested which now made the people ripe for the judgment of extermination (*vid.* Ex. xvii. 14). The hostility which they had now displayed, according to ver. 33, there was no necessity for the prophet to mention particularly, since it was well known to Saul and all Israel. When God looks upon a sin, directs His glance towards it, He must punish it according to His own holiness. This פָּקַדְתִּי points at the very outset to the punishment about to be proclaimed.—Ver. 3 Saul is to smite and ban everything belonging to it without reserve, *i.e.* to put to death both man and beast. The last clause וְהֵמַתָּה וגו׳ is only an explanation and exemplification of וְהַחֲרַמְתֶּם וגו׳. "*From man to woman,*" etc., *i.e.* men and women, children and sucklings, etc.

Vers. 4-9. Saul summoned the people to war, and mustered them (those who were summoned) at *Telaim* (this was probably the same place as the *Telem* mentioned in Josh. xv. 24, and is to be looked for in the eastern portion of the Negeb). "*Two hundred thousand foot, and ten thousand of the men of Judah:*" this implies that the two hundred thousand were from the other tribes. These numbers are not too large; for a powerful Bedouin nation, such as the Amalekites were, could not possibly be successfully attacked with a small army, but only by raising the whole of the military force of Israel.—Ver. 5. He then advanced as far as the city of the Amalekites, the situation of which is altogether unknown, and placed an ambush in the valley. וַיָּרֶב does not come from רִיב, to fight, *i.e.* to quarrel, not to give battle, but was understood even by the early translators as a contracted form of וַיֶּאֱרֹב, the *Hiphil* of אָרַב. And modern commentators have generally understood it in the same way; but Olshausen (*Hebr. Gramm.* p. 572) questions the correctness of the reading, and Thenius proposes to alter מֵרִיב בַּנַּחַל into וַיָּעֶרֹךְ מִלְחָמָה. נַחַל refers to a valley in the neighbourhood of the city of the Amalekites.—Ver. 6. Saul directed the Kenites to come out from among the Amalekites, that they might not perish with them (אֹסִפְךָ, *imp. Kal* of אָסַף), as they had shown affection to the Israelites on their journey out of Egypt (compare Num. x. 29 with Judg. i. 16). He then smote the Amalekites from Havilah in the direction towards Shur, which lay before (to the east of) Egypt (cf. Gen. xxv. 18). *Shur* is the desert of Jifar, *i.e.* that portion of the desert of Arabia which borders upon Egypt (see at Gen. xvi. 7). *Havilah*, the country of the *Chaulotæans*, on the border of Arabia Petræa towards Yemen (see at Gen. x. 29).—Vers. 8, 9. Their king, *Agag*, he took alive (on the name, see at Num. xxiv. 7), but all the people he banned with the edge of the sword, *i.e.* he had them put to death without quarter. "*All*," *i.e.* all that fell into the hands of the Israelites. For it follows from the very nature of the case that many escaped, and consequently there is nothing striking in the fact that Amalekites are mentioned again at a later period (ch. xxvii. 8, xxx. 1; 2 Sam. viii. 12). The last remnant was destroyed by the Simeonites upon the mountains of Seir in the reign of Hezekiah (1 Chron. iv. 43). Only, king Agag did Saul and the people (of Israel) spare, also "*the best of the sheep and oxen, and the animals of the second birth, and the lambs and everything good; these they would not ban.*" מִשְׁנִים, according to D. Kimchi and R. Tanch., are שנים לבטן, *i.e. animalia secundo partu edita*, which were considered superior to the others (*vid.* Roediger in *Ges. Thes.* p. 1451); and כָּרִים, pasture lambs, *i.e.* fat lambs. There is no necessity, therefore, for the conjecture of Ewald and Thenius, מִשְׁמַנִּים, fattened, and כְּרָמִים, vineyards; nor for the far-fetched explanation given by Bochart, viz. camels with two humps and camel-saddles, to say nothing of the fact that camel-saddles and vineyards are altogether out of place here. In "*all that was good*" the things already mentioned singly are all included. הַמְּלָאכָה, the property; here it is applied to cattle, as in Gen. xxxiii. 14. נְמִבְזָה = נְבִזָה, despised, undervalued. The form of the word is not contracted from a noun מִבְזָה and the participle נִבְזֶה (*Ges. Lehrgeb.* p. 463), but seems to be a *participle Niph.* formed from a noun מִבְזֶה. But as such a form is contrary to all analogy, Ewald and Olshausen regard the reading as corrupt. נָמֵס (from מָסַס): flowing away; used with reference to diseased cattle, or such as have perished. The reason for sparing the best cattle is very apparent, namely selfishness. But it is not so easy to determine why Agag should have been spared by Saul. It is by no means probable that he wished thereby to do honour to the royal dignity. O. v. Gerlach's supposition, that vanity or the desire to make a display with a royal slave was the actual reason, is a much more probable one.

Vers. 10–23. The word of the Lord came to Samuel: "*It repenteth me that I have made Saul king, for he hath turned away from me, and not set up* (carried out) *my word.*" (On the repentance of God, see the remarks on Gen. vi. 6.) That this does not express any changeableness in the divine nature, but simply the sorrow of the divine love at the rebellion of sinners, is evident enough from ver. 29. שׁוּב מֵאַחֲרֵי יְיָ, to turn round from following God, in order to go his own ways. This was Saul's real sin. He would no longer be the follower and servant of the Lord, but would be absolute ruler in Israel. Pride arising from the consciousness of his own strength, led him astray to break the command of God. What more God said to Samuel is not communicated here, because it could easily be gathered and supplied from what Samuel himself proceeded to do (see more particularly vers. 16 sqq.). In order to avoid repetitions, only the principal feature in the divine revelation is mentioned here, and the details are given fully afterwards in the account of the fulfilment of the instructions. Samuel was deeply agitated by this word of the Lord. "*It burned* (in) *him,*" sc. wrath (אַף, compare Gen. xxxi. 36 with xxx. 2), not on account of the repentance to which God had given utterance at having raised up Saul as king, nor merely at Saul's disobedience, but at the frustration of the purpose of God in calling him to be king in consequence of his disobedience, from which he might justly dread the worst results in relation to the glory of Jehovah and his own prophetic labours.[1] The opinion

---

[1] "Many grave thoughts seem to have presented themselves at once to Samuel and disturbed his mind, when he reflected upon the dishonour which might be heaped upon the name of God, and the occasion which the rejection and deposition of Saul would furnish to wicked men for blaspheming God. For Saul had been anointed by the ministry of Samuel, and he

that לְ יָחַר is also used to signify deep distress cannot be established from 2 Sam. iv. 8. "*And he cried to Jehovah the whole night*," sc. praying for Saul to be forgiven. But it was in vain. This is evident from what follows, where Samuel maintains the cause of his God with strength and decision, after having wrestled with God in prayer.—Ver. 12. The next morning, after receiving the revelation from God (ver. 11), Samuel rose up early, to go and meet Saul as he was returning from the war. On the way it was told him, "*Saul has come to Carmel*"—*i.e. Kurmul*, upon the mountains of Judah to the south-east of Hebron (see at Josh. xv. 55)—"*setting himself a memorial*" (יָד, a hand, then a memorial or monument, inasmuch as the hand calls attention to anything: see 2 Sam. xviii. 18), "*and has turned and proceeded farther, and gone down to Gilgal*" (in the valley of the Jordan, as in ch. xiii. 4).—Ver. 13. When Samuel met him there, Saul attempted to hide his consciousness of guilt by a feigned friendly welcome. "*Blessed be thou of the Lord*" (*vid.* Ruth ii. 20, Gen. xiv. 19, etc.) was his greeting to the prophet; "*I have set up the word of Jehovah.*"—Vers. 14, 15. But the prophet stripped his hypocrisy at once with the question, "*What then is this bleating of sheep in my ears, and a lowing of oxen that I hear?*" Saul replied (ver. 15), "*They have brought them from the Amalekites, because the people spared the best sheep and oxen, to sacrifice them to the Lord thy God; and the rest we have banned.*" So that it was not Saul, but the people, who had transgressed the command of the Lord, and that with the most laudable intention, viz. to offer the best of the cattle that had been taken, as a thank-offering to the Lord. The falsehood and hypocrisy of these words lay upon the very surface; for even if the cattle spared were really intended as sacrifices to the Lord, not only the people, but Saul also, would have had their own interests in view (*vid.* ver. 9), since the flesh of thank-offerings was appropriated to sacrificial meals.—Vers. 16 sqq.

had been chosen by God himself from all the people, and called by Him to the throne. If, therefore, he was nevertheless deposed, it seemed likely that so much would be detracted from the authority of Samuel and the confidence of the people in his teaching, and, moreover, that the worship of God would be overturned, and the greatest disturbance ensue; in fact, that universal confusion would burst upon the nation. These were probably the grounds upon which Samuel's great indignation rested."—*Calvin.*

Samuel therefore bade him be silent. הֶרֶף, "*leave off*," excusing thyself any further. "*I will tell thee what Jehovah hath said to me this night.*" (The *Chethibh* וַיֹּאמְרוּ is evidently a copyist's error for וַיֹּאמֶר.) "*Is it not true, when thou wast little in thine eyes* (a reference to Saul's own words, ch. ix. 21), *thou didst become head of the tribes of Israel? and Jehovah anointed thee king over Israel, and Jehovah sent thee on the way, and said, Go and ban the sinners, the Amalekites, and make war against them, until thou exterminatest them. And wherefore hast thou not hearkened to the voice of Jehovah, and hast fallen upon the booty,*" etc. ? (חָטַט, see at ch. xiv. 32.)

Even after this Saul wanted to justify himself, and to throw the blame of sparing the cattle upon the people.—Ver. 20. "*Yea, I have hearkened to the voice of Jehovah* (אֲשֶׁר serving, like כִּי, to introduce the reply: here it is used in the sense of asseveration, *utique*, yea), *and have brought Agag the king of the Amalekites, and banned Amalek.*" Bringing Agag he mentioned probably as a practical proof that he had carried out the war of extermination against the Amalekites.—Ver. 21. Even the sparing of the cattle he endeavoured to defend as the fulfilment of a religious duty. The people had taken sheep and oxen from the booty, "*as firstlings of the ban,*" to sacrifice to Jehovah. Sacrificing the best of the booty taken in war as an offering of first-fruits to the Lord, was not indeed prescribed in the law, but was a praiseworthy sign of piety, by which all honour was rendered to the Lord as the giver of the victory (see Num. xxxi. 48 sqq.). This, Saul meant to say, was what the people had done on the present occasion; only he overlooked the fact, that what was banned to the Lord could not be offered to Him as a burnt-offering, because, being most holy, it belonged to Him already (Lev. xxvii. 29), and according to Deut. xiii. 16, was to be put to death, as Samuel had expressly said to Saul (ver. 3).—Vers. 22, 23. Without entering, therefore, into any discussion of the meaning of the ban, as Saul only wanted to cover over his own wrong-doings by giving this turn to the affair, Samuel put a stop to any further excuses, by saying, "*Hath Jehovah delight in burnt-offerings and slain-offerings as in hearkening to the voice of Jehovah?* (*i.e.* in obedience to His word.) *Behold, hearing* (obeying) *is better than slain-offerings, attending better than fat of rams.*" By saying this, Samuel did

not reject sacrifices as worthless; he did not say that God took
no pleasure in burnt-offerings and slain-offerings, but simply
compared sacrifice with obedience to the command of God, and
pronounced the latter of greater worth than the former. "It
was as much as to say that the sum and substance of divine
worship consisted in obedience, with which it should always
begin, and that sacrifices were, so to speak, simple appendices,
the force and worth of which were not so great as of obedience
to the precepts of God" (Calvin). But it necessarily follows
that sacrifices without obedience to the commandments of God
are utterly worthless; in fact, are displeasing to God, as Ps. l.
8 sqq., Isa. i. 11 sqq., lxvi. 3, Jer. vi. 20, and all the prophets,
distinctly affirm. There was no necessity, however, to carry
out this truth any further. To tear off the cloak of hypocrisy,
with which Saul hoped to cover his disobedience, it was quite
enough to affirm that God's first demand was obedience, and
that observing His word was better than sacrifice; because, as
the *Berleb. Bible* puts it, " in sacrifices a man offers only the
strange flesh of irrational animals, whereas in obedience he
offers his own will, which is rational or spiritual worship"
(Rom. xii. 8). This spiritual worship was shadowed forth in
the sacrificial worship of the Old Testament. In the sacrificial
animal the Israelite was to give up and sanctify his own person
and life to the Lord. (For an examination of the meaning of
the different sacrifices, see *Pent.* vol. ii. pp. 274 sqq., and Keil's
Bibl. Archäol. i. § 41 sqq.) But if this were the design of
the sacrifices, it was clear enough that God did not desire the
animal sacrifice in itself, but first and chiefly obedience to His
own word. In ver. 22, טוֹב is not to be connected as an adjective with זֶבַח, " more than good sacrifice," as the Sept. and
Thenius render it; it is rather to be taken as a predicate,
" *better than slain-offerings*," and מִזֶּבַח is placed first simply
for the sake of emphasis. Any contrast between good and bad
sacrifices, such as the former construction would introduce into
the words, is not only foreign to the context, but also opposed
to the parallelism. For חֵלֶב אֵילִים does not mean fat rams, but
the fat of rams; the fat portions taken from the ram, which
were placed upon the altar in the case of the slain-offerings, and
for which חֵלֶב is the technical expression (compare Lev. iii. 9,
16, with vers. 4, 11, etc.). " *For,*" continued Samuel (ver. 23),

" *rebellion is the sin of soothsaying, and opposition is heathenism and idolatry.*" מְרִי and הַפְצַר are the subjects, and synonymous in their meaning. חַטַּאת קֶסֶם, the sin of soothsaying, *i.e.* of divination in connection with the worship of idolatrous and demoniacal powers. In the second clause idols are mentioned instead of idolatry, and compared to resistance, but without any particle of comparison. Opposition is keeping idols and teraphim, *i.e.* it is like worshipping idols and teraphim. אָוֶן, nothingness, then an idol or image (*vid.* Isa. lxvi. 3; Hos. iv. 15, x. 5, 8). On the *teraphim* as domestic and oracular deities, see at Gen. xxxi. 19. Opposition to God is compared by Samuel to soothsaying and oracles, because idolatry was manifested in both of them. All conscious disobedience is actually idolatry, because it makes self-will, the human I, into a god. So that all manifest opposition to the word and commandment of God is, like idolatry, a rejection of the true God. "*Because thou hast rejected the word of Jehovah, He hath rejected thee, that thou mayst be no longer king.*" מִהְיוֹת מֶלֶךְ = מִמְּלֹךְ (ver. 26), away from being king.

Vers. 24–35. This sentence made so powerful an impression upon Saul, that he confessed, "*I have sinned: for I have transgressed the command of the Lord and thy words, because I feared the people, and hearkened to their voice.*" But these last words, with which he endeavoured to make his sin appear as small as possible, show that the consciousness of his guilt did not go very deep. Even if the people had really desired that the best of the cattle should be spared, he ought not as king to have given his consent to their wish, since God had commanded that they should all be banned (*i.e.* destroyed); and even though he had yielded from weakness, this weakness could not lessen his guilt before God. This repentance, therefore, was rather the effect of alarm at the rejection which had been announced to him, than the fruit of any genuine consciousness of sin. "It was not true and serious repentance, or the result of genuine sorrow of heart because he had offended God, but was merely repentance of the lips arising from fear of losing the kingdom, and of incurring public disgrace" (C. v. Lapide). This is apparent even from ver. 25, but still more from ver. 30. In ver. 25 he not only entreats Samuel for the forgiveness of his sin, but says, "*Return with me, that I may pray to the Lord.*"

The שָׁב presupposes that Samuel was about to go away after executing his commission. Saul entreated him to remain that he might pray, *i.e.* not only in order to obtain for him the forgiveness of his sin through his intercession, but, according to ver. 30, to show him honour before the elders of the people and before Israel, that his rejection might not be known.—Vers. 26, 27. This request Samuel refused, repeating at the same time the sentence of rejection, and turned to depart. " *Then Saul laid hold of the lappet of his mantle (i.e.* his upper garment), *and it tore*" (lit. was torn off). That the *Niphal* וַיִּקָּרַע is correct, and is not to be altered into וַיִּקְרַע אֹתָהּ, " Saul tore off the lappet," according to the rendering of the LXX., as Thenius supposes, is evident from the explanation which Samuel gave of the occurrence (ver. 28) : "*Jehovah hath torn the sovereignty of Israel from thee to-day, and given it to thy neighbour, who is better than thou.*" As Saul was about to hold back the prophet by force, that he might obtain from him a revocation of the divine sentence, the tearing of the mantle, which took place accidentally, and evidently without any such intention on the part of Saul, was to serve as a sign of the rending away of the sovereignty from him. Samuel did not yet know to whom Jehovah would give it; he therefore used the expression לְרֵעֶךָ, as רֵעַ is applied to any one with whom a person associates. To confirm his own words, he adds in ver. 29 : " *And also the Trust of Israel doth not lie and doth not repent, for He is not a man to repent.*" נֵצַח signifies constancy, endurance, then confidence, trust, because a man can trust in what is constant. This meaning is to be retained here, where the word is used as a name for God, and not the meaning *gloria*, which is taken in 1 Chron. xxix. 11 from the Aramæan usage of speech, and would be altogether unsuitable here, where the context suggests the idea of unchangeableness. For a man's repentance or regret arises from his changeableness, from the fluctuations in his desires and actions. This is never the case with God; consequently He is נֵצַח יִשְׂרָאֵל, *the unchangeable One, in whom Israel can trust, since He does not lie or deceive, or repent of His purposes.* These words are spoken θεοπρεπῶς (theomorphically), whereas in ver. 11 and other passages, which speak of God as repenting, the words are to be understood ἀνθρωποπαθῶς (anthropomorphically; cf. Num. xxiii. 19).—Vers. 30,

31. After this declaration as to the irrevocable character of the determination of God to reject Saul, Samuel yielded to the renewed entreaty of Saul, that he would honour him by his presence before the elders and the people, and remained whilst Saul worshipped, not merely " for the purpose of preserving the outward order until a new king should take his place" (O. v. Gerlach), but also to carry out the ban upon Agag, whom Saul had spared.—Ver. 32. After Saul had prayed, Samuel directed him to bring Agag the king of the Amalekites. Agag came מַעֲדַנֹּת, *i.e.* in a contented and joyous state of mind, and said (in his heart), *" Surely the bitterness of death is vanished,"* not from any special pleasure at the thought of death, or from a heroic contempt of death, but because he thought that his life was to be granted him, as he had not been put to death at once, and was now about to be presented to the prophet (Clericus).—Ver. 33. But Samuel pronounced the sentence of death upon him : *" As thy sword hath made women childless, so be thy mother childless before women !"* מִנָּשִׁים is to be understood as a comparative : more childless than (other) women, *i.e.* the most childless of women, namely, because her son was the king. From these words of Samuel, it is very evident that Agag had carried on his wars with great cruelty, and had therefore forfeited his life according to the *lex talionis*. Samuel then hewed him in pieces *" before the Lord at Gilgal,"* *i.e.* before the altar of Jehovah there ; for the slaying of Agag being the execution of the ban, was an act performed for the glory of God.—Vers. 34, 35. After the prophet had thus maintained the rights of Jehovah in the presence of Saul, and carried out the ban upon Agag, he returned to his own home at Ramah ; and Saul went to his house at Gibeah. From that time forward Samuel broke off all intercourse with the king whom Jehovah had rejected. *" For Samuel was grieved for Saul, and it repented the Lord that he had made Saul king,"* *i.e.* because Samuel had loved Saul on account of his previous election ; and yet, as Jehovah had rejected him unconditionally, he felt that he was precluded from doing anything to effect a change of heart in Saul, and his reinstatement as king.

III. SAUL'S FALL AND DAVID'S ELECTION.

Chap. XVI.–XXXI.

Although the rejection of Saul on the part of God, which was announced to him by Samuel, was not followed by immediate deposition, but Saul remained king until his death, the consequences of his rejection were very speedily brought to light. Whilst Samuel, by the command of God, was secretly anointing David, the youngest son of Jesse, at Bethlehem, as king (ch. xvi. 1–13), the Spirit of Jehovah departed from Saul, and an evil spirit began to terrify him, so that he fell into melancholy; and his servants fetched David to the court, as a man who could play on stringed instruments, that he might charm away the king's melancholy by his playing (ch. xvi. 14–23). Another war with the Philistines soon furnished David with the opportunity for displaying his heroic courage, by the defeat of the giant Goliath, before whom the whole army of the Israelites trembled; and to attract the eyes of the whole nation to himself, as the deliverer of Israel from its foes (ch. xvii. 1–54), in consequence of which Saul placed him above the men of war, whilst Saul's brave son Jonathan formed a bond of friendship with him (ch. xvii. 55–xviii. 5). But this victory, in commemorating which the women sang, "Saul hath slain a thousand, David ten thousand" (ch. xviii. 7), excited the jealousy of the melancholy king, so that the next day, in an attack of madness, he threw his spear at David, who was playing before him, and after that not only removed him from his presence, but by elevating him to the rank of chief captain, and by the promise to give him his daughter in marriage for the performance of brave deeds, endeavoured to entangle him in such conflicts with the Philistines as should cost him his life. And when this failed, and David prospered in all his undertakings, he began to be afraid of him, and cherished a lifelong hatred towards him (ch. xviii. 6–30). Jonathan did indeed try to intercede and allay his father's suspicions, and effect a reconciliation between Saul and David; but the evil spirit soon drove the jealous king to a fresh attack upon David's life, so that he was obliged to flee not only from the presence of Saul, but from his own house also, and went to Ramah, to the prophet Samuel, whither, however, Saul soon followed him, though he was so overpowered by the Spirit of the prophets, that he could not do anything to David (ch. xix.). Another attempt on the part of Jonathan to change his father's mind entirely failed, and so excited the wrath of Saul, that he actually threw the spear at his own son; so that no other course now remained for David, than to separate himself from his noble friend Jonathan, and seek safety in flight (ch. xx.). He therefore fled with his attendant first of all to Nob, where Ahimelech the high priest gave him some of the holy loaves and the sword of Goliath, on his representing to him that he was travelling hastily in the affairs of the king. He then proceeded to Achish, the king of the Philistines, at Gath; but having been recognised as the conqueror of Goliath, he was obliged to feign madness in order to save his life; and being driven away by Achish as a madman, he went to the cave of Adullam, and thence into the land of Moab. But he was summoned by the prophet to return to his own land, and went into the wood Hareth, in the land of Judah; whilst Saul, who had been informed by the Edomite Doeg of the occurrence at Nob, ordered all the priests who were there to be put to death, and the town itself to be ruthlessly destroyed, with all the men and beasts that it contained. Only one of Ahimelech's sons escaped the massacre, viz. Abiathar; and he took refuge with David (ch. xxi. xxii.). Saul now commenced a regular pursuit of David, who had gradually collected around him a company of 600 men. On receiving intelligence that David had smitten a marauding company of Philistines at Keilah, Saul followed him, with the hope of catching him in this fortified town; and when this plan failed, on account of the flight of David into the wilderness of Ziph, because the high priest had informed him of the intention of the inhabitants to deliver him up, Saul pursued him thither, and had actually surrounded David with his warriors, when a messenger arrived with the intelligence of an invasion of the land by the Philistines, and he was suddenly called away to make war upon these foes (ch. xxiii.). But he had no sooner returned from the attack upon the Philistines, than he pursued David still farther into the wilderness of Engedi, where he entered into a large cave,

L

behind which David and his men were concealed, so that he actually fell into David's hands, who might have put him to death. But from reverence for the anointed of the Lord, instead of doing him any harm, David merely cut off a corner of his coat, to show his pursuer, when he had left the cave, in what manner he had acted towards him, and to convince him of the injustice of his hostility. Saul was indeed moved to tears; but he was not disposed for all that to give up any further pursuit (ch. xxiv.). David was still obliged to wander about from place to place in the wilderness of Judah; and at length he was actually in want of the necessaries of life, so that on one occasion, when the rich Nabal had churlishly turned away the messengers who had been sent to him to ask for a present, he formed the resolution to take bloody revenge upon this hard-hearted fool, and was only restrained from carrying the resolution out by the timely and friendly intervention of the wise Abigail (ch. xxv.). Soon after this Saul came a second time into such a situation, that David could have killed him; but during the night, whilst Saul and all his people were sleeping, he slipped with Abishai into the camp of his enemy and carried off as booty the spear that was at the king's head, that he might show him a second time how very far he was from seeking to take his life (ch. xxvi.). But all this only made David's situation an increasingly desperate one; so that eventually, in order to save his life, he resolved to fly into the country of the Philistines, and take refuge with Achish, the king of Gath, by whom he was now received in the most friendly manner, as a fugitive who had been proscribed by the king of Israel. At his request Achish assigned him the town of Ziklag as a dwelling-place for himself and his men, whence he made sundry excursions against different Bedouin tribes of the desert. In consequence of this, however, he was brought into a state of dependence upon this Philistian prince (ch. xxvii.); and shortly afterwards, when the Philistines made an attack upon the Israelites, he would have been perfectly unable to escape the necessity of fighting in their ranks against his own people and fatherland, if the other princes of the Philistines had not felt some mistrust of " these Hebrews," and compelled Achish to send David and his fighting men back to Ziklag (ch. xxix.). But this was also to put an end to his prolonged flight.

Saul's fear of the power of the Philistines, and the fact that he could not obtain any revelation from God, induced him to have recourse to a necromantist woman, and he was obliged to hear from the mouth of Samuel, whom she had invoked, not only the confirmation of his own rejection on the part of God, but also the announcement of his death (ch. xxviii.). In the battle which followed on the mountains of Gilboa, after his three sons had been put to death by his side, he fell upon his own sword, that he might not fall alive into the hands of the archers of the enemy, who were hotly pursuing him (ch. xxxi.), whilst David in the meantime chastised the Amalekites for their attack upon Ziklag (ch. xxx.).

It is not stated anywhere how long the pursuit of David by Saul continued; the only notice given is that David dwelt a year and four months in the land of the Philistines (ch. xxvii. 7). If we compare with this the statement in 2 Sam. v. 4, that David was thirty years old when he became king (over Judah), the supposition that he was about twenty years old when Samuel anointed him, and therefore that the interval between Saul's rejection and his death was about ten years, will not be very far from the truth. The events which occurred during this interval are described in the most elaborate way, on the one hand because they show how Saul sank deeper and deeper, after the Spirit of God had left him on account of his rebellion against Jehovah, and not only was unable to procure any longer for the people that deliverance which they had expected from the king, but so weakened the power of the throne through the conflict which he carried on against David, whom the Lord had chosen ruler of the nation in his stead, that when he died the Philistines were able to inflict a total defeat upon the Israelites, and occupy a large portion of the land of Israel; and, on the other hand, because they teach how, after the Lord had anointed David ruler over His people, and had opened the way to the throne through the victory which he gained over Goliath, He humbled him by trouble and want, and trained him up as king after His own heart. On a closer examination of these occurrences, which we have only briefly hinted at, giving their main features merely, we see clearly how, from the very day when Samuel announced to Saul his rejection by God, he hardened himself more and more against the leadings of divine grace, and continued steadily ripening for the judgment of death. Immediately after this announcement an evil spirit took possession of his soul, so that he fell into trouble and melancholy; and when jealousy towards David was stirred up in his heart, he was seized with fits of raving madness, in which he tried to pierce David with a spear, and thus destroy the man whom he had come to love on account of his musical talent, which had exerted so beneficial an influence upon his mind (ch. xvi. 23, xviii. 10, 11, xix. 9, 10). These attacks of madness gradually gave place to hatred, which developed itself with full consciousness, and to a most deliberately planned hostility, which he concealed at first not only from David but also from all his own attendants, with the hope that he should be able to put an end to David's life through his stratagems, but which he afterwards proclaimed most openly as soon as these plans had failed. When his hostility was first openly declared, his eagerness to seize upon his enemy carried him to such a length that he got into the company of prophets at Ramah, and was so completely overpowered by the Spirit of God dwelling there, that he lay before Samuel for a whole day in a state of prophetic ecstasy (ch. xix. 22 sqq.). But this irresistible power of the Spirit of God over him produced no change of heart. For immediately afterwards, when Jonathan began to intercede for David, Saul threw the spear at his own son (ch. xx. 33), and this time not in an attack of madness or insanity, but in full consciousness; for we do not read in this instance, as in ch. xviii. xix., that the evil spirit came upon him. He now proceeded to a consistent carrying out of his purpose of murder. He accused his courtiers of having conspired against him like Jonathan, and formed an alliance with David (ch. xxii. 6 sqq.), and caused the priests at Nob to be murdered in cold blood, and the whole town smitten with the edge of the sword, because Ahimelech had supplied David with bread; and this he did without paying any attention to the conclusive evidence of his innocence (ch. xxii. 11 sqq.). He then went with 3000 men in pursuit of David; and even after he had fallen twice into David's hands, and on both occasions had been magnanimously spared by him, he did not desist from plotting for his life until he had driven him out of the land; so that we may clearly see how each fresh proof of the righteousness of David's cause only increased his hatred, until at length, in the war against the Philistines, he rashly resorted to the godless arts of a necromancer which he himself had formerly prohibited, and eventually put an end to his own life by falling upon his sword.

Just as clearly may we discern in the guidance of David, from his anointing by Samuel to the death of Saul, how the Lord, as King of His people, trained him in the school of affliction to be His servant, and led him miraculously on to the goal of his divine calling. Having been lifted up as a young man by his anointing, and by the favour which he had acquired with Saul through his playing upon the harp, and still more by his victory over Goliath, far above the limited circumstances of his previous life, he might very easily have been puffed up in the consciousness of the spiritual gifts and powers conferred upon him, if God had not humbled his heart by want and tribulation. The first outbursts of jealousy on the part of Saul, and his first attempts to get rid of the favourite of the people, only furnished him with the opportunity to distinguish himself still more by brave deeds, and to make his name still dearer to the people (ch. xviii. 30). When, therefore, Saul's hostility was openly displayed, and neither Jonathan's friendship nor Samuel's prophetic authority could protect him any longer, he fled to the high priest Ahimelech, and from him to king Achish at Gath, and endeavoured to help himself through by resorting to falsehood. He did save himself in this way no doubt, but he brought destruction upon the priests at Nob. And he was very soon to learn how all that he did for his people was rewarded with ingratitude. The inhabitants of Keilah, whom he had rescued from their plunderers, wanted to deliver him up to Saul (ch. xxiii. 5, 12); and even the men of his own tribe, the Ziphites, betrayed him twice, so that he was no longer sure of his life even in his own land. But the more this necessarily shook his confidence in his own strength and wisdom, the more clearly did the Lord manifest himself as his faithful Shepherd. After Ahimelech had been put to death, his son Abiathar fled to David with the light and right of the high priest, so that he was now in a position to inquire the will and counsel of God in any difficulty into which he might be brought (ch. xxiii. 6). On two occasions God brought his mortal foe Saul into his hand, and David's conduct in both these cases shows how the deliverance of God which he had hitherto experienced had strengthened his confidence in the Lord, and in the fulfilment of His promises (compare ch. xxiv. with ch. xxvi.). And his gracious preservation from carrying out his purposes of vengeance against Nabal (ch. xxv.) could not fail to strengthen him still more. Nevertheless, when his troubles threatened to continue without intermission, his courage began to sink and his faith to waver, so that he took refuge in the land of the Philistines, where, however, his wisdom and cunning brought him into a situation of such difficulty that nothing but the grace and fidelity of his God could possibly extricate him, and out of which he was delivered without any act of his own.

In this manner was the divine sentence of rejection fulfilled upon Saul, and the prospect which the anointing of David had set before him, of ascending the throne of Israel, carried out to completion. The account before us of the events which led to this result of the various complications, bears in all respects so thoroughly the stamp of internal truth and trustworthiness, that even modern critics are unanimous in acknowledging the genuine historical character of the biblical narrative upon the whole. At the same time, there are some things, such as the supposed irreconcilable discrepancy between ch. xvi. 14-23 and ch. xvii. 55-58, and certain repetitions, such as Saul's throwing the spear at David (ch. xviii. 10 and xix. 9, 10), the treachery of the Ziphites (ch. xxiii. 19 sqq. and xxvi. 1 sqq.), David's sparing Saul (ch. xxiv. 4 sqq. and xxvi. 5 sqq.), which they cannot explain in any other way than by the favourite hypothesis that we have here divergent accounts, or legendary traditions derived from two different sources that are here woven together; whereas, as we shall see when we come to the exposition of the chapters in question, not only do the discrepancies vanish on a more thorough and minute examination of the matter, but the repetitions are very clearly founded on facts.

ANOINTING OF DAVID. HIS PLAYING BEFORE SAUL.—
CHAP. XVI.

After the rejection of Saul, the Lord commanded Samuel the prophet to go to Bethlehem and anoint one of Jesse's sons as king; and when he went to carry out this commission, He pointed out David, the youngest of eight sons, as the chosen one, whereupon the prophet anointed him (vers. 1-13). Through the overruling providence of God, it came to pass after this, that David was brought to the court of Saul, to play upon the harp, and so cheer up the king, who was troubled with an evil spirit (vers. 14-23).

Vers. 1-13. ANOINTING OF DAVID.—Ver. 1. The words in which God summoned Samuel to proceed to the anointing of another king, "*How long wilt thou mourn for Saul, whom I have rejected, that he may not be king over Israel?*" show that the prophet had not yet been able to reconcile himself to the hidden ways of the Lord; that he was still afraid that the people and kingdom of God would suffer from the rejection of Saul; and that he continued to mourn for Saul, not merely from his own personal attachment to the fallen king, but also, or perhaps still more, from anxiety for the welfare of Israel. He was now to put an end to this mourning, and to fill his horn with oil and go to Jesse the Bethlehemite, for the Lord had chosen a king from among his sons.—Ver. 2. But Samuel replied, "*How shall I go? If Saul hear it, he will kill me.*" This fear on the part of the prophet, who did not generally show himself either hesitating or timid, can only be explained, as we may see from ver. 14, on the supposition that Saul was already given up to the power of the evil spirit, so that the very worst might be dreaded from his madness, if he discovered that Samuel had anointed another king. That there was some foundation for Samuel's anxiety, we may infer from the fact that the Lord did not blame him for his fear, but pointed out the way by which he might anoint David without attracting attention (vers. 2, 3) "*Take a young heifer with thee, and say* (sc. if any one ask the reason for your going to Bethlehem), *I am come to sacrifice to the Lord.*" There was no untruth in this, for Samuel was really about to conduct a sacrificial festival, and was to invite Jesse's family to it, and then anoint the one whom Jehovah should point out to him as the chosen one. It was simply a concealment of the principal object of his mission from any who might make inquiry about it, because they themselves had not been invited. "There was no dissimulation or falsehood in this, since God really wished His prophet to find safety under the pretext of the sacrifice. A sacrifice was therefore really offered, and the prophet was protected thereby, so that he was not exposed to any danger until the time of full revelation arrived" (Calvin).—Ver. 4. When Samuel arrived at Bethlehem, the elders of the city came to meet him in a state of the greatest anxiety, and asked him whether his coming was peace, or promised good. The singular וַיֹּאמֶר may be explained on the ground that one of the elders spoke for the rest. The anxious inquiry of the elders presupposes that even in the time of Saul the prophet Samuel was frequently in the habit of coming unexpectedly to one place and another, for the purpose of reproving and punishing wrong-doing and sin.—Ver. 5. Samuel quieted them with the reply that he was come to offer sacrifice to the Lord, and called upon them to sanctify themselves and take part in the sacrifice. It is evident from this that the prophet was accustomed to turn his visits to account by offering sacrifice, and so building up the people in fellowship with the Lord. The reason why sacrifices were offered at different places was, that since the removal of the ark from the tabernacle, this sanctuary had ceased to be the only place of the nation's worship. הִתְקַדֵּשׁ, to sanctify one's self by washings and legal purifications, which probably preceded every sacrificial festival (*vid.* Ex. xix. 10, 22). The expression, "*Come with me to the sacrifice,*" is *constructio prægnans* for "Come and take part in the sacrifice." "*Call to the sacrifice*" (ver. 3) is to be understood in the same way. זֶבַח is the slain-offering, which was connected with every sacrificial meal. It is evident from the following words, "*and he sanctified Jesse and his sons,*" that Samuel addressed the general summons to sanctify themselves more especially to Jesse and his sons. For it was with them that he was about to celebrate the sacrificial meal.—Vers. 6 sqq. When they came, *sc.* to the sacrificial meal, which was no doubt held in Jesse's house, after the sacrifice had been presented upon an altar, and when Samuel saw the eldest son Eliab, who was tall and handsome according to ver. 7, "*he thought* (*lit.* he said, *sc.* in his heart), *Surely His anointed is before Jehovah*," *i.e.* surely the man is now standing before Jehovah whom He hath chosen to be His anointed. But Jehovah said to him in the spirit, "*Look not at his form and the height of his stature, for I have rejected him: for not as man seeth* (*sc.* do I see); *for man looketh at the eyes, and Jehovah looketh at the heart.*" The eyes, as contrasted with the heart, are figuratively employed to denote the outward form.—Vers. 8 sqq. When Jesse thereupon brought up his other sons, one after another, before Samuel, the prophet said in the case of each, "*This also Jehovah hath not chosen.*" As Samuel must be the subject to the verb וַיֹּאמֶר in vers. 8–10, we may assume that he had communicated the object of his coming to Jesse.—Ver. 11. After the seventh had been presented, and the Lord had not pointed any one of them out as the chosen one, "*Samuel said to Jesse, Are these all the boys?*" When Jesse replied that there was still *the smallest, i.e.* the youngest, left, and he was keeping the sheep, he directed him to fetch him; "*for,*" said he, "*we will not sit down till he has come hither.*" סָבַב, to surround, *sc.* the table, upon which the meal was arranged. This is implied in the context.—Vers. 12, 13. When David arrived,—and he was *ruddy*, also *of beautiful eyes and good looks* (אַדְמוֹנִי, used to denote the reddish colour of the hair, which was regarded as a mark of beauty in southern lands, where the hair is generally black. עִם is an adverb here = therewith), and therefore, so far as his looks and figure were concerned, well fitted, notwithstanding his youth, for the office to which the Lord had chosen him, since corporeal beauty was one of the outward distinctions of a king,—the Lord pointed him out to the prophet as the chosen one; whereupon he anointed him in the midst of his brethren. Along with the anointing the Spirit of Jehovah came upon David from that day forward. But Samuel returned to Ramah when the sacrificial meal was over. There is nothing recorded concerning any words of Samuel to David at the time of the anointing and in explanation of its meaning, as in the case of Saul (ch. x. 1). In all probability Samuel said nothing at the time, since, according to ver. 2, he had good reason for keeping the matter secret, not only on his own account, but still more for David's sake; so that even the brethren of David who were present knew nothing about the meaning and object of the anointing, but may have imagined that Samuel merely intended to consecrate David as a pupil of the prophets. At the same time, we can hardly suppose that Samuel left Jesse, and even David, in uncertainty as to the object of his mission, and of the anointing which he had performed. He may have communicated all this to both of them, without letting the other sons know. It by no means follows, that because David remained with his father and kept the sheep as before, therefore his calling to be king must have been unknown to him; but only that in the anointing which he had received he did not discern either the necessity or obligation to appear openly as the anointed of the Lord, and that after receiving the Spirit of the Lord in consequence of the anointing, he left the further development of the matter to the Lord in childlike submission, assured that He would prepare and show him the way to the throne in His own good time.

Vers. 14–23. DAVID'S INTRODUCTION TO THE COURT OF SAUL.—Ver. 14. With the rejection of Saul on the part of God, the Spirit of Jehovah had departed from him, and an evil spirit from Jehovah had come upon him, who filled him with fear and anguish. The "*evil spirit from Jehovah*" which came into Saul in the place of the Spirit of Jehovah, was not merely an inward feeling of depression at the rejection announced to him, which grew into melancholy, and occasionally broke out in passing fits of insanity, but a higher evil power, which took possession of him, and not only deprived him of his peace of mind, but stirred up the feelings, ideas, imagination, and thoughts of his soul to such an extent that at times it drove him even into madness. This demon is called "*an evil spirit* (coming) *from Jehovah*," because Jehovah had sent it as a punishment, or "*an evil spirit of God*" (*Elohim*: ver. 15), or briefly "*a spirit of God*" (*Elohim*), or "*the evil spirit*" (ver. 23, compare ch. xviii. 10), as being a supernatural, spiritual, evil power; but never "the Spirit of Jehovah," because this is the Spirit proceeding from the holy God, which works upon men as the spirit of strength, wisdom, and knowledge, and generates and fosters the spiritual or divine life. The expression רוּחַ יְהוָֹה רָעָה (ch. xix. 9) is an abbreviated form for רוּחַ רָעָה מֵאֵת יְהוָֹה, and is to be interpreted accordingly.—Ver.

15. When Saul's attendants, *i.e.* his officers at court, perceived the mental ailment of the king, they advised him to let the evil spirit which troubled him be charmed away by instrumental music. "*Let our lord speak* (command) ; *thy servants are before thee* (*i.e.* ready to serve thee) : *they will seek a man skilled in playing upon the harp; so will it be well with thee when an evil spirit of God comes upon thee, and he* (the man referred to) *plays with his hand.*" The powerful influence exerted by music upon the state of the mind was well known even in the earliest times; so that the wise men of ancient Greece recommended music to soothe the passions, to heal mental diseases, and even to check tumults among the people. From the many examples collected by Grotius, Clericus, and more especially Bochart in the *Hieroz.* P. i. l. 2, c. 44, we will merely cite the words of Censorinus (*de die natali*, c. 12) : "*Pythagoras ut animum sua semper divinitate imbueret, priusquam se somno daret et cum esset expergitus, cithara ut ferunt cantare consueverat, et Asclepiades medicus phreneticorum mentes morbo turbatas sæpe per symphoniam suæ naturæ reddidit.*"—Vers. 17, 18. When Saul commanded them to seek out a good player upon a stringed instrument in accordance with this advice, one of the youths (נְעָרִים, a lower class of court servants) said, "*I have seen a son of Jesse the Bethlehemite, skilled in playing, and a brave man, and a man of war, eloquent, and a handsome man, and Jehovah is with him.*" The description of David as "*a mighty man*" and "*a man of war*" does not presuppose that David had already fought bravely in war, but may be perfectly explained from what David himself afterwards affirmed respecting his conflicts with lions and bears (ch. xvii. 34, 35). The courage and strength which he had then displayed furnished sufficient proofs of heroism for any one to discern in him the future warrior.—Vers. 19, 20. Saul thereupon sent to ask Jesse for his son David; and Jesse sent him with a present of an ass's burden of bread, a bottle of wine, and a buck-kid. Instead of the singular expression חֲמוֹר לֶחֶם, an ass with bread, *i.e.* laden with bread, the LXX. read חֹמֶר לֶחֶם, and rendered it γόμορ ἄρτων, but this is certainly wrong, as they were not accustomed to measure bread in bushels. These presents show how simple were the customs of Israel and in the court of Saul at that time.—Ver. 21. When David came to Saul and stood before

him, *i.e.* served him by playing upon his harp, Saul took a great liking to him, and nominated him his armour-bearer, *i.e.* his adjutant, as a proof of his satisfaction with him, and sent to Jesse to say, "*Let David stand before me*," *i.e.* remain in my service, "*for he has found favour in my sight.*" The historian then adds (ver. 23) : " *When the* (evil) *spirit of God came to Saul* (אֶל, as in ch. xix. 9, is really equivalent to עַל), *and David took the harp and played, there came refreshing to Saul, and he became well, and the evil spirit departed from him.*" Thus David came to Saul's court, and that as his benefactor, without Saul having any suspicion of David's divine election to be king of Israel. This guidance on the part of God was a school of preparation to David for his future calling. In the first place, he was thereby lifted out of his quiet and homely calling in the country into the higher sphere of court-life; and thus an opportunity was afforded him not only for intercourse with men of high rank, and to become acquainted with the affairs of the kingdom, but also to display those superior gifts of his intellect and heart with which God had endowed him, and thereby to gain the love and confidence of the people. But at the same time he was also brought into a severe school of affliction, in which his inner man was to be trained by conflicts from without and within, so that he might become a man after God's heart, who should be well fitted to found the true monarchy in Israel.

DAVID'S VICTORY OVER GOLIATH.—CHAP. XVII. 1-54.

A war between the Philistines and the Israelites furnished David with the opportunity of displaying before Saul and all Israel, and greatly to the terror of the enemies of his people, that heroic power which was firmly based upon his bold and pious trust in the omnipotence of the faithful covenant God (vers. 1-3). A powerful giant, named Goliath, came forward from the ranks of the Philistines, and scornfully challenged the Israelites to produce a man who would decide the war by a single combat with him (vers. 4-11). David, who had returned home for a time from the court of Saul, and had just been sent into the camp by his father with provisions for his elder brothers who were serving in the army, as soon as he heard the challenge and the scornful words of the Philistine, offered to fight with him (vers. 15-37), and killed the giant with a stone from a sling; whereupon the Philistines took to flight, and were pursued by the Israelites to Gath and Ekron (vers. 38-54).

Vers. 1-11. Some time after David first came to Saul for the purpose of playing, and when he had gone back to his father to Bethlehem, probably because Saul's condition had improved, the Philistines made a fresh attempt to subjugate the Israelites. They collected their army together (*machaneh*, as in Ex. xiv. 24, Judg. iv. 16) to war at *Shochoh*, the present *Shuweikeh*, in the Wady *Sumt*, three hours and a half to the south-west of Jerusalem, in the hilly region between the mountains of Judah and the plain of Philistia (see at Josh. xv. 35), and encamped between *Shochoh* and *Azekah*, at *Ephes-dammim*, which has been preserved in the ruins of *Damûm*, about an hour and a half east by north of Shuweikeh; so that *Azekah*, which has not yet been certainly traced, must be sought for to the east or north-east of Damûm (see at Josh. x. 10).— Vers. 2, 3. Saul and the Israelites encamped opposite to them in the *terebinth* valley (*Emek ha-Elah*), *i.e.* a plain by the Wady *Musur*, and stood in battle array opposite to the Philistines, in such order that the latter stood *on that side against the mountain* (on the slope of the mountain), and the Israelites *on this side against the mountain; and the valley* (הַגַּיְא, the deeper cutting made by the brook in the plain) *was between them.*—Vers. 4 sqq. And *the* (well-known) *champion* came out of the camps of the Philistines (אִישׁ הַבֵּנַיִם, the middle-man, who decides a war between two armies by a single combat; Luther, "*the giant*," according to the ἀνὴρ δυνατός of the LXX., although in ver. 23 the Septuagint translators have rendered the word correctly ἀνὴρ ὁ ἀμεσσαῖος, which is probably only another form of ὁ μεσαῖος), named *Goliath* of Gath, one of the chief cities of the Philistines, where there were Anakim still left, according to Josh. xi. 22. His height was *six cubits and a span* (6¼ cubits), *i.e.*, according to the calculation made by Thenius, about nine feet two inches Parisian measure,—a great height no doubt, though not altogether unparalleled, and hardly greater than that of the great uncle of Iren, who came to Berlin in the year 1857 (see Pentateuch, vol. iii. p. 303, note).[1] The armour

[1] According to Pliny (*h. n.* vii. 16), the giant *Pusio* and the giantess *Secundilla*, who lived in the time of Augustus, were ten feet three inches

of Goliath corresponded to his gigantic stature: "*a helmet of brass upon his head, and clothed in scale armour, the weight of which was five thousand shekels of brass.*" The meaning *scales* is sustained by the words קַשְׂקֶשֶׂת in Lev. xi. 9, 10, and Deut. xiv. 9, 10, and קַשְׂקְשׂוֹת in Ezek. xxix. 4. שִׁרְיוֹן קַשְׂקַשִּׂים, therefore, is not θώραξ ἁλυσιδωτός (LXX.), a coat of mail made of rings worked together like chains, such as were used in the army of the Seleucidæ (1 Macc. vi. 35), but according to Aquila's φολιδωτόν (scaled), a coat made of plates of brass lying one upon another like scales, such as we find upon the old Assyrian sculptures, where the warriors fighting in chariots, and in attendance upon the king, wear coats of scale armour, descending either to the knees or ankles, and consisting of scales of iron or brass, which were probably fastened to a shirt of felt or coarse linen (see Layard, *Nineveh and its Remains*, vol. ii. p. 335). The account of the weight, 5000 shekels, *i.e.* according to Thenius, 148 Dresden pounds, is hardly founded upon the actual weighing of the coat of mail, but probably rested upon a general estimate, which may have been somewhat too high, although we must bear in mind that the coat of mail not only covered the chest and back, but, as in the case of the Assyrian warriors, the lower part of the body also, and therefore must have been very large and very heavy.[1]—Ver. 6. And "*greaves of brass upon his feet, and a brazen lance* (hung) *between his shoulders,*" *i.e.* upon his back. כִּידוֹן signifies a lance, or small spear. The LXX. and Vulgate, however, adopt the rendering ἀσπὶς χαλκῆ, *clypeus æneus;* and Luther has followed them, and translates

(Roman) in height; and a Jew is mentioned by Josephus (*Ant.* xviii. 4, 5), who was seven cubits in height, *i.e.* ten Parisian feet, or if the cubits are Roman, nine and a half.

[1] According to Thenius, the cuirass of *Augustus* the Strong, which has been preserved in the historical museum at Dresden, weighed fifty-five pounds; and from that he infers, that the weight given as that of Goliath's coat of mail is by no means too great. Ewald, on the other hand, seems to have no idea of the nature of the Hebrew weights, or of the bodily strength of a man, since he gives 5000 lbs. of brass as the weight of Goliath's coat of mail (*Gesch.* iii. p. 90), and merely observes that the pounds were of course much smaller than ours. But the shekel did not even weigh so much as our full ounce. With such statements as these you may easily turn the historical character of the scriptural narrative into incredible myths; but they cannot lay any claim to the name of science.

it a brazen shield. Thenius therefore proposes to alter בְּידוֹ into מִגֵּו, because the expression "between his shoulders" does not appear applicable to a spear or javelin, which Goliath must have suspended by a strap, but only to a small shield slung over his back, whilst his armour-bearer carried the larger צִנָּה in front of him. But the difficulty founded upon the expression "*between his shoulders*" has been fully met by Bochart (*Hieroz.* i. 2, c. 8), in the examples which he cites from Homer, Virgil, etc., to prove that the ancients carried their own swords slung over their shoulders (ἀμφὶ δ' ὤμοισιν: *Il.* ii. 45, etc.). And Josephus understood the expression in this way (*Ant.* vi. 9, 1). Goliath had no need of any shield to cover his back, as this was sufficiently protected by the coat of mail. Moreover, the allusion to the בְּידוֹ in ver. 45 points to an offensive weapon, and not to a shield.—Ver. 7. "*And the shaft of his spear was like a weaver's beam, and the point of it six hundred shekels of iron*" (about seventeen pounds). For חֵץ, according to the *Keri* and the parallel passages, 2 Sam. xxi. 19, 1 Chron. xx. 5, we should read עֵץ, wood, *i.e.* a shaft. Before him went the bearer of the *zinnah*, *i.e.* the great shield.—Ver. 8. This giant stood and cried to the ranks of the Israelites, "*Why come ye out to place yourselves in battle array? Am I not the Philistine, and ye the servants of Saul? Choose ye out a man who may come down to me*" (into the valley where Goliath was standing). The meaning is: "Why would you engage in battle with us? I am the man who represents the strength of the Philistines, and ye are only servants of Saul. If ye have heroes, choose one out, that we may decide the matter in a single combat."—Ver. 9. "*If he can fight with me, and kill me, we will be your servants; if I overcome him, and slay him, ye shall be our servants, and serve us.*" He then said still further (ver. 10), "*I have mocked the ranks of Israel this day* (the mockery consisted in his designating the Israelites as servants of Saul, and generally in the triumphant tone in which he issued the challenge to single combat); *give me a man, that we may fight together!*"—Ver. 11. At these words Saul and all Israel were dismayed and greatly afraid, because not one of them dared to accept the challenge to fight with such a giant.

Vers. 12-31. *David's arrival in the camp, and wish to fight with Goliath.*—David had been dismissed by Saul at that time, and having returned home, he was feeding his father's sheep once more (vers. 12–15). Now, when the Israelites were standing opposite to the Philistines, and Goliath was repeating his challenge every day, David was sent by his father into the camp to bring provisions to his three eldest brothers, who were serving in Saul's army, and to inquire as to their welfare (vers. 16–19). He arrived when the Israelites had placed themselves in battle array; and running to his brethren in the ranks, he saw Goliath come out from the ranks of the Philistines, and heard his words, and also learned from the mouth of an Israelite what reward Saul would give to any one who would defeat this Philistine (vers. 20–25). He then inquired more minutely into the matter; and having thereby betrayed his own intention of trying to fight with him (vers. 26, 27), he was sharply reproved by his eldest brother in consequence (vers. 28, 29). He did not allow this to deter him, however, but turned to another with the same question, and received a similar reply (ver. 30); whereupon his words were told to the king, who ordered David to come before him (ver. 31). This is, in a condensed form, the substance of the section, which introduces the conquest of Goliath by David in the character of an episode. This first heroic deed was of the greatest importance to David and all Israel, for it was David's first step on the way to the throne, to which Jehovah had resolved to raise him. This explains the fulness and circumstantiality of the narrative, in which the intention is very apparent to set forth most distinctly the marvellous overruling of all the circumstances by God himself. And this circumstantiality of the account is closely connected with the form of the narrative, which abounds in repetitions, that appear to us tautological in many instances, but which belong to the characteristic peculiarities of the early Hebrew style of historical composition.[1]

[1] On account of these repetitions and certain apparent differences, the LXX. (*Cod. Vat.*) have omitted the section from ver. 12 to ver. 31, and also that from ver. 55 to ch. xviii. 5; and on the ground of this omission, Houbigant, Kennicott, Michaelis, Eichhorn, Dathe, Bertheau, and many others, have pronounced both these sections later interpolations; whereas the more recent critics, such as De Wette, Thenius, Ewald, Bleek, Stähelin, and others, reject the hypothesis that they are interpolations, and infer from the supposed discrepancies that ch. xvii. and xviii. were written by some one who was ignorant of the facts mentioned in ch. xvi., and was

Vers. 12–15 are closely connected with the preceding words, "*All Israel was alarmed at the challenge of the Philistine; but David the son of that Ephratite (Ephratite, as in* Ruth i. 1, 2) *of Bethlehem in Judah, whose name was Jesse*," etc. The verb and predicate do not follow till ver. 15; so that the words occur here in the form of an anacolouthon. The traditional introduction of the verb הָיָה between וְדָוִד and בֶּן־אִישׁ (David was the son of that Ephratite) is both erroneous and misleading. If the words were to be understood in this way, הָיָה could no more be omitted here than הָיְתָה in 2 Chron. xxii. 3, 11. The true explanation is rather, that vers. 12–15 form one period expanded by parentheses, and that the historian lost sight of

altogether a different person from the author of this chapter. According to ch. xvi. 21 sqq., they say, David was Saul's armour-bearer already, and his family connections were well known to the king, whereas, according to ch. xvii. 15, David was absent just at the time when he ought as armour-bearer to have been in attendance upon Saul; whilst in ch. xvii. 33 he is represented as a shepherd boy who was unaccustomed to handle weapons, and as being an unauthorized spectator of the war, and, what is still more striking, even his lineage is represented in vers. 55 sqq. as unknown both to Abner and the king. Moreover, in ver. 12 the writer introduces a notice concerning David with which the reader must be already well acquainted from ch. xvi. 5 sqq., and which is therefore, to say the least, superfluous; and in ver. 54 Jerusalem is mentioned in a manner which does not quite harmonize with the history, whilst the account of the manner in which he disposed of Goliath's armour is apparently at variance with ch. xxi. 9. But the notion, that the sections in question are interpolations that have crept into the text, cannot be sustained on the mere authority of the Septuagint version; since the arbitrary manner in which the translators of this version made omissions or additions at pleasure is obvious to any one. Again, the assertion that these sections cannot well be reconciled with ch. xvi., and emanated from an author who was unacquainted with the history in ch. xvi., is overthrown by the unquestionable reference to ch. xvi. which we find in ver. 12, "David the son of *that* Ephratite,"—where Jerome has correctly paraphrased הַנֶּה, *de quo supra dictum est*,—and also by the remark in ver. 15, that David went backwards and forwards from Saul to feed his father's sheep in Bethlehem. Neither of these can be pronounced interpolations of the compiler, unless the fact can be established that the supposed discrepancies are really well founded. But it by no means follows, that because Saul loved David on account of the beneficial effect which his playing upon the harp produced upon his mind, and appointed him his armour-bearer, therefore David had really to carry the king's armour in time of war. The appointment of armour-bearer was nothing more than conferring upon him the title of aide-de-camp, from which it cannot be the construction with which he commenced in the intermediate clauses; so that he started afresh with the subject וְדָוִד in ver. 15, and proceeded with what he had to say concerning David, doing this at the same time in such a form that what he writes is attached, so far as the sense is concerned, to the parenthetical remarks concerning Jesse's eldest sons. To bring out distinctly the remarkable chain of circumstances by which David was led to undertake the conflict with Goliath, he links on to the reference to his father certain further notices respecting David's family and his position at that time. Jesse had eight sons and was an old man in the time of Saul. בָּא בַאֲנָשִׁים, "*come among the weak*." אֲנָשִׁים generally means, no doubt,

inferred that David had already become well known to the king through the performance of warlike deeds. If Joab, the commander-in-chief, had *ten* armour-bearers (2 Sam. xviii. 15, compare ch. xxiii. 37), king Saul would certainly have other armour-bearers besides David, and such as were well used to war. Moreover, it is not stated anywhere in ch. xvi. that Saul took David at the very outset into his regular and permanent service, but, according to ver. 22, he merely asked his father Jesse that David might stand before him, *i.e.* might serve him; and there is no contradiction in the supposition, that when his melancholy left him for a time, he sent David back to his father to Bethlehem, so that on the breaking out of the war with the Philistines he was living at home and keeping sheep, whilst his three eldest brothers had gone to the war. The circumstance, however, that when David went to fight with Goliath, Saul asked Abner his captain, "Whose son is this youth?" and Abner could give no explanation to the king, so that after the defeat of Goliath, Saul himself asked David, "Whose son art thou?" (vers. 55-58), can hardly be comprehended, if all that Saul wanted to ascertain was the name of David's father. For even if Abner had not troubled himself about the lineage of Saul's harpist, Saul himself could not well have forgotten that David was a son of the Bethlehemite Jesse. But there was much more implied in Saul's question. It was not the name of David's father alone that he wanted to discover, but what kind of man the father of a youth who possessed the courage to accomplish so marvellous a heroic deed really was; and the question was put not merely in order that he might grant him an exemption of his house from taxes as the reward promised for the conquest of Goliath (ver. 25), but also in all probability that he might attach such a man to his court, since he inferred from the courage and bravery of the son the existence of similar qualities in the father. It is true that David merely replied, "The son of thy servant Jesse of Bethlehem;" but it is very evident from the expression in ch. xviii. 1, "when he had made an end of speaking unto Saul," that Saul conversed with him still further about his family affairs, since the very words imply a lengthened conversation. The other difficulties are very trivial, and will be answered in connection with the exposition of the passages in question.

people or men. But this meaning does not give any appropriate sense here; and the supposition that the word has crept in through a slip of the pen for בַּשָּׁנִים, is opposed not only by the authority of the early translators, all of whom read אֲנָשִׁים, but also by the circumstance that the expression בּוֹא בַשָּׁנִים does not occur in the whole of the Old Testament, and that בּוֹא בַיָּמִים alone is used with this signification.—Ver. 13. *"The three great (i.e. eldest) sons of Jesse had gone behind Saul into the war."* הָלְכוּ, which appears superfluous after the foregoing וַיֵּלְכוּ, has been defended by Böttcher, as necessary to express the pluperfect, which the thought requires, since the *imperfect consec.* וַיֵּלְכוּ, when attached to a substantive and participial clause, merely expresses the force of the aorist. Properly, therefore, it reads thus: *"And then* (in Jesse's old age) *the three eldest sons followed, had followed, Saul;"* a very ponderous construction indeed, but quite correct, and even necessary, with the great deficiency of forms, to express the pluperfect. The names of these three sons agree with ch. xvi. 6-9, whilst the third, *Shammah,* is called *Shimeah* (שִׁמְעָה) in 2 Sam. xiii. 3, 32, שִׁמְעִי in 2 Sam. xxi. 21, and שִׁמְעָא in 1 Chron. ii. 13, xx. 7.—Ver. 15. *"But David was going and returning away from Saul:"* i.e. he went backwards and forwards from Saul to feed his father's sheep in Bethlehem; so that he was not in the permanent service of Saul, but at that very time was with his father. The latter is to be supplied from the context.—Ver. 16. The Philistine drew near (to the Israelitish ranks) morning and evening, and stationed himself for forty days (in front of them). This remark continues the description of Goliath's appearance, and introduces the account which follows. Whilst the Philistine was coming out every day for forty days long with his challenge to single combat, Jesse sent his son David into the camp. *"Take now for thy brethren this ephah of parched grains* (see Lev. xxiii. 14), *and these ten loaves, and bring them quickly into the camp to thy brethren."*—Ver. 18. *"And these ten slices of soft cheese* (so the ancient versions render it) *bring to the chief captain over thousand, and visit thy brethren to inquire after their welfare, and bring with you a pledge from them"*—a pledge that they are alive and well. This seems the simplest explanation of the word עֲרֻבָּתָם, of which very different renderings were given by the early translators.—Ver. 19. *"But Saul and they* (the brothers), *and the whole of the men of Israel, are in the terebinth valley,"* etc. This statement forms part of Jesse's words.—Vers. 20, 21. In pursuance of this commission, David went in the morning *to the waggon-rampart,* when the army, which was going out (of the camp) into battle array, raised the war-cry, and Israel and the Philistines placed themselves *battle-array against battle-array.* וְהֵחָיִל וגו׳ is a circumstantial clause, and the predicate is introduced with וְהֵרֵעוּ, as וְהֵחָיִל וגו׳ is placed at the head absolutely: "*and as for the army which,* etc., *it raised a shout.*" הָרֵעַ בַּמִּלְחָמָה, *lit.* to make a noise in war, *i.e.* to raise a war-cry.—Ver. 22. David left the vessels with the provisions in the charge of the keeper of the vessels, and ran into the ranks to inquire as to the health of his brethren.—Ver. 23. Whilst he was talking with them, the champion (middle-man) Goliath drew near, and spoke according to those words (the words contained in vers. 8 sqq.), and David heard it. מִמַּעֲרוֹת פְּלִ׳ is probably an error for מִמַּעַרְכוֹת פְּלִ׳ (*Keri,* LXX., Vulg.; cf. ver. 26). If the *Chethibh* were the proper reading, it would suggest an Arabic word signifying a crowd of men (Dietrich on *Ges. Lex.*).—Vers. 24, 25. All the Israelites fled from Goliath, and were sore afraid. They said (אִישׁ יִשְׂרָאֵל is a collective noun), "*Have ye seen this man who is coming?* (הַרְאִיתֶם, with *Dagesh dirim.* as in ch. x. 24.) *Surely to defy Israel is he coming; and whoever shall slay him, the king will enrich him with great wealth, and give him his daughter, and make his father's house (i.e.* his family) *free in Israel,*" viz. from taxes and public burdens. There is nothing said afterwards about the fulfilment of these promises. But it by no means follows from this, that the statement is to be regarded as nothing more than an exaggeration, that had grown up among the people, of what Saul had really said. There is all the less probability in this, from the fact that, according to ver. 27, the people assured him again of the same thing. In all probability Saul had actually made some such promises as these, but did not feel himself bound to fulfil them afterwards, because he had not made them expressly to David himself.—Ver. 26. When David heard these words, he made more minute inquiries from the bystanders about the whole matter, and dropped some words which gave rise to the supposition that he wanted to go and fight with this Philistine himself. This is implied in the words, "*For who is the Philistine, this uncircumcised one* (i.e. standing as he does outside the covenant with Jehovah), *that he insults the ranks of the living God!*" whom he has defied in His army. "He must know," says the *Berleburger Bible,* "that he has not to do with men, but with God. With a living God he will have to do, and not with an idol."—Ver. 28. David's eldest brother was greatly enraged at his talking thus with the men, and reproved David : " *Why hast thou come down* (from Bethlehem, which stood upon high ground, to the scene of the war), *and with whom hast thou left those few sheep in the desert?*" *'Those few sheep,*" the loss of only one of which would be a very great loss to our family. " *I know thy presumption, and the wickedness of thy heart; for thou hast come down to look at the war;*" i.e. thou art not contented with thy lowly calling, but aspirest to lofty things; it gives thee pleasure to look upon bloodshed. Eliab sought for the splinter in his brother's eye, and was not aware of the beam in his own. The very things with which he charged his brother—presumption and wickedness of heart—were most apparent in his scornful reproof.— Vers. 29, 30. David answered very modestly, and so as to put the scorn of his reprover to shame : " *What have I done, then ? It was only a word*"—a very allowable inquiry certainly. He then turned from him (Eliab) to another who was standing by; and having repeated his previous words, he received the same answer from the people.—Ver. 31. David's words were told to Saul, who had him sent for immediately.

Vers. 32-40. *David's resolution to fight with Goliath; and his equipment for the conflict.*—Ver. 32. When in the presence of Saul, David said, "*Let no man's heart* (i.e. courage) *fail on his account* (on account of the Philistine, about whom they had been speaking) : *thy servant will go and fight with this Philistine.*"—Vers. 33 sqq. To Saul's objection that he, a mere youth, could not fight with this Philistine, a man of war from his youth up, David replied, that as a shepherd he had taken a sheep out of the jaws of a lion and a bear, and had also slain them both. The article before אֲרִי and דּוֹב points out these animals as the *well-known* beasts of prey. By the expression וְאֶת־הַדּוֹב the bear is subordinated to the lion, or rather placed afterwards, as something which came in addition to it; so that אֵת is to be taken as a *nota accus.* (*vid.* Ewald, § 277, *a*), though it is not to be understood as implying that the lion and the bear went together in search of prey. The subordination or addition is merely a logical one: not only the lion, but also the bear, which seized the sheep, did David slay. זֶה, which we find in most of the editions since the time of Jac. Chayim, 1525, is an error in writing, or more correctly in hearing, for שֶׂה, a sheep. *"And I went out after it; and when it rose up against me, I seized it by its beard, and smote it, and killed it."* זָקָן, beard and chin, signifies *the bearded chin*. Thenius proposes, though without any necessity, to alter בִּזְקָנוֹ into בְּגָרוֹנוֹ, for the simple but weak reason, that neither lions nor bears have any actual beard. We have only to think, for example, of the λῖς ἠϋγένειος in Homer (*Il.* xv. 275, xvii. 109), or the *barbam vellere mortuo leoni* of Martial (x. 9). Even in modern times we read of lions having been killed by Arabs with a stick (see Rosenmüller, *Bibl. Althk.* iv. 2, pp. 132-3). The constant use of the *singular* suffix is sufficient to show, that when David speaks of the lion and the bear, he connects together two different events, which took place at different times, and then proceeds to state how he smote both the one and the other of the two beasts of prey.—Ver. 36. *"Thy servant slew both the lion and the bear; and the Philistine, this uncircumcised one, shall become like one of them* (*i.e.* the same thing shall happen to him as to the lion and the bear), *because he has defied the ranks of the living God."* "And," he continued (ver. 37), *"the Lord who delivered me out of the hand* (the power) *of the lion and the bear, he will deliver me out of the hand of this Philistine."* David's courage rested, therefore, upon his confident belief that the living God would not let His people be defied by the heathen with impunity. Saul then desired for him the help of the Lord in carrying out his resolution, and bade him put on his own armour-clothes, and gird on his armour. מַדָּיו (his clothes) signifies probably a peculiar kind of clothes which were worn under the armour, a kind of armour-coat to which the sword was fastened.—Vers. 39, 40. When he was thus equipped with brazen helmet, coat of mail, and sword, David began to walk, but soon found that he could do nothing with these. He therefore said to Saul, *"I cannot go in these things, for I have not tried them;"* and having taken them off, he took his shepherd's staff in his hand, sought out five smooth stones from the brook-valley, and put them in the shepherd's thing that he had, namely his shepherd's bag. He then took the sling in his hand, and went up to the Philistine. In the exercise of his shepherd's calling he may have become so skilled in the use of the sling, that, like the Benjaminites mentioned in Judg. xx. 16, he could sling at a hair's-breadth, and not miss.

Vers. 41-54. *David and Goliath: fall of Goliath, and flight of the Philistines.*—Ver. 41. The Philistine came closer and closer to David.—Vers. 42 sqq. When he saw David, "*he looked at him, and despised him*," *i.e.* he looked at him contemptuously, because he was a youth (as in ch. xvi. 12); "*and then said to him, Am I a dog, that thou comest to me with sticks?*" (the plural מַקְלוֹת is used in contemptuous exaggeration of the armour of David, which appeared so thoroughly unfit for the occasion); "*and cursed David by his God* (*i.e.* making use of the name of Jehovah in his cursing, and thus defying not David only, but the God of Israel also), *and finished with the challenge, Come to me, and I will give thy flesh to the birds of heaven and the beasts of the field*" (to eat). It was with such threats as these that Homer's heroes used to defy one another (*vid.* Hector's threat, for example, in *Il.* xiii. 831-2).—Vers. 45 sqq. David answered this defiance with bold, believing courage: "*Thou comest to me with sword, and javelin, and lance; but I come to thee in the name of the Lord of Sabaoth, the God of the ranks of Israel, whom thou hast defied. This day will Jehovah deliver thee into my hand; and I shall smite thee, and cut off thine head, and give the corpse of the army of the Philistines to the birds this day. . . . And all the world shall learn that Israel hath a God; and this whole assembly shall discover that Jehovah bringeth deliverance* (victory) *not by sword and spear: for war belongeth to Jehovah, and He will give you into our hand.*" Whilst Goliath boasted of his strength, David founded his own assurance of victory upon the Almighty God of Israel, whom the Philistine had defied. פְּנֵי is to be taken collectively. יֵשׁ אֱלֹהִים לְיִשְׂרָאֵל does not mean "God is for Israel," but "Israel hath a God," so that *Elohim* is of course used here in a pregnant sense. This *God* is Jehovah; war is his, *i.e.* He is the Lord of war, who has both war and its results in His power.—Vers. 48, 49. When the Philistine rose up, drawing near towards David (קָם and יֵלֶךְ simply serve to set forth the occurrence in a more pictorial manner), *David hastened and ran to the battle array to meet him,* took a stone out of his pocket, hurled it, and hit the Philistine on his temples, so that the stone entered them, and Goliath fell upon his face to the ground.—Ver. 50 contains a remark by the historian with reference to the result of the conflict : " *Thus was David stronger than the Philistine, with sling and stone, and smote the Philistine, and slew him without a sword in his hand.*" And then in ver. 51 the details are given, namely, that David cut off the head of the fallen giant with his own sword. Upon the downfall of their hero the Philistines were terrified and fled; whereupon the Israelites rose up with a cry to pursue the flying foe, and pursued them "*to a valley, and to the gates of Ekron.*" The first place mentioned is a very striking one. The " *valley* " cannot mean the one which divided the two armies, according to ver. 3, not only because the article is wanting, but still more from the facts themselves. For it is neither stated, nor really probable, that the Philistines had crossed that valley, so as to make it possible to pursue them into it again. But if the word refers to some other valley, it seems very strange that nothing further should be said about it. Both these circumstances render the reading itself, גיא, suspicious, and give great probability to the conjecture that גיא is only a copyist's error for *Gath*, which is the rendering given by the LXX., especially when taken in connection with the following clause, " *to Gath and to Ekron* " (ver. 52).—Ver. 52. " *And wounded of the Philistines fell on the way to Shaaraim, and to Gath and to Ekron.*" Shaaraim is the town of *Saarayim*, in the lowland of Judah, and has probably been preserved in the Tell *Kefr Zakariya* (see at Josh. xv. 36). On *Gath* and *Ekron*, see at Josh. xiii. 3.—Ver. 53. After returning from the pursuit of the flying foe, the Israelites plundered the camp of the Philistines. דָּלַק אַחֲרֵי, to pursue hotly, as in Gen. xxxi. 36.—Ver. 54. But David took the head of Goliath and brought it to Jerusalem, and put his armour in his tent. אֹהֶל is an antiquated term for a dwelling-place, as in ch. iv. 10, xiii. 2, etc. The reference is to David's house at Bethlehem, to which he returned with the booty after the defeat of Goliath, and that by the road which ran past Jerusalem, where he left the head of Goliath. There is no anachronism in these statements ; for the assertion made by some, that Jerusalem was not yet in the possession of the Israelites, rests upon a confusion between the citadel of Jebus upon Zion, which was still in the hands of the Jebusites, and the city of Jerusalem, in which Israelites had dwelt for a long time (see at Josh. xv. 63, and Judg. i. 8). Nor is there any contradiction between this statement and ch. xxi. 9, where Goliath's sword is said to have been preserved in the tabernacle at Nob : for it is not affirmed that David *kept* Goliath's armour in his own home, but only that he took it thither ; and the supposition that Goliath's sword was afterwards deposited by him in the sanctuary in honour of the Lord, is easily reconcilable with this. Again, the statement in ch. xviii. 2, to the effect that, after David's victory over Goliath, Saul did not allow him to return to his father's house any more, is by no means at variance with this explanation of the verse before us. For the statement in question must be understood in accordance with ch. xvii. 15, viz. as signifying that from that time forward Saul did not allow David to return to his father's house to keep the sheep as he had done before, and by no means precludes his paying brief visits to Bethlehem.

JONATHAN'S FRIENDSHIP. SAUL'S JEALOUSY AND PLOTS AGAINST DAVID.—CHAP. XVII. 55–XVIII. 30.

David's victory over Goliath was a turning-point in his life, which opened the way to the throne. But whilst this heroic deed brought him out of his rural shepherd life to the scene of Israel's conflict with its foes, and in these conflicts Jehovah crowned all his undertakings with such evident success, that the Israelites could not fail to discern more and more clearly in him the man whom God had chosen as their future king; it brought him, on the other hand, into such a relation to the royal house, which had been rejected by God, though it still continued to reign, as produced lasting and beneficial results in connection with his future calling. In the king himself, from whom the Spirit of God had departed, there was soon stirred up such jealousy of David as his rival to whom the kingdom would one day come, that he attempted at first to get rid of him by stratagem; and when this failed, and David's renown steadily increased, he proceeded to open hostility and persecution. On the other hand, the heart of Jonathan clung more and more firmly to David with self-denying love and sacrifice. This friendship on the part of the brave and noble son of the king, not only helped David to bear the more easily all the enmity and persecution of the king when plagued by his evil spirit, but awakened and strengthened in his soul that pure feeling of unswerving fidelity towards the king himself, which amounted even to love of his enemy, and, according to the marvellous counsel of the Lord, contributed greatly to the training of David for his calling to be a king after God's own heart. In the account of the results which followed David's victory over Goliath, not only for himself but also for all Israel, the friendship of Jonathan is mentioned first (ver. 55–ch. xviii. 5); and this is followed by an account of the growing jealousy of Saul in its earliest stages (vers. 6-30).

Ch. xvii. 55–xviii. 5. *Jonathan's friendship.*—Vers. 55-58. The account of the relation into which David was brought to Saul through the defeat of Goliath is introduced by a supplementary remark, in vers. 55, 56, as to a conversation which took place between Saul and his commander-in-chief Abner concerning David, whilst he was fighting with the giant. So far, therefore, as the actual meaning is concerned, the verbs in vers. 55 and 56 should be rendered as pluperfects. When Saul saw the youth walk boldly up to meet the Philistine, he asked Abner whose son he was; whereupon Abner assured him with an oath that he did not know. In our remarks concerning the integrity of this section (p. 177) we have already observed, with regard to the meaning of the question put by Saul, that it does not presuppose an actual want of acquaintance with the person of David and the name of his father, but only ignorance of the social condition of David's family, with which both Abner and Saul may hitherto have failed to make themselves more fully acquainted.[1]—Vers. 57, 58. When David returned "*from the slaughter of the Philistine,*" *i.e.* after the defeat of Goliath, and when Abner, who probably went as commander to meet the brave hero and congratulate him upon his victory, had brought him to Saul, the king addressed the same question to David, who immediately gave him the information he desired. For it is evident that David said more than is

[1] The common solutions of this apparent discrepancy, such as that Saul pretended not to know David, or that his question is to be explained on the supposition that his disease affected his memory, have but little probability in them, although Karkar still adheres to them.

here communicated, viz. "*the son of thy servant Jesse the Bethlehemite,*" as we have already observed, from the words of ch. xviii. 1, which presuppose a protracted conversation between Saul and David. The only reason, in all probability, why this conversation has not been recorded, is that it was not followed by any lasting results either for Jesse or David.

Ch. xviii. 1-5. The bond of friendship which Jonathan formed with David was so evidently the main point, that in ver. 1 the writer commences with the love of Jonathan to David, and then after that proceeds in ver. 2 to observe that Saul took David to himself from that day forward; whereas it is very evident that Saul told David, either at the time of his conversation with him or immediately afterwards, that he was henceforth to remain with him, *i.e.* in his service. "*The soul of Jonathan bound itself* (lit. chained itself; cf. Gen. xliv. 30) *to David's soul, and Jonathan loved him as his soul.*" The *Chethibh* וַיֶּאֱהָבוֹ with the suffix ו attached to the imperfect is very rare, and hence the *Keri* וַיֶּאֱהָבֵהוּ (*vid.* Ewald, § 249, *b*, and Olshausen, *Gramm.* p. 469). לָשׁוּב, to return to his house, viz. to engage in his former occupation as shepherd.—Ver. 3. Jonathan *made a covenant* (*i.e.* a covenant of friendship) *and* (*i.e.* with) *David, because he loved him as his soul.*—Ver. 4. As a sign and pledge of his friendship, Jonathan gave David *his clothes and his armour. Meil*, the upper coat or cloak. *Maddim* is probably the *armour coat* (*vid.* ch. xvii. 39). This is implied in the word עַד, which is repeated three times, and by which the different arms were attached more closely to מַדָּיו. For the act itself, compare the exchange of armour made by Glaucus and Diomedes (Hom. *Il.* vi. 230). This seems to have been a common custom in very ancient times, as we meet with it also among the early Celts (see Macpherson's *Ossian*).—Ver. 5. And David *went out, sc.* to battle; *whithersoever Saul sent him, he acted wisely and prosperously* (יַשְׂכִּיל, as in Josh. i. 8: see at Deut. xxix. 8). Saul placed him above the men of war in consequence, made him one of their commanders; and he pleased all the people, and the servants of Saul also, *i.e.* the courtiers of the king, who are envious as a general rule.

Vers. 6-16. *Saul's jealousy towards David.*[1]—Saul had no

---

[1] The section vers. 6-14 is supposed by Thenius and others to have been taken by the compiler from a different source from the previous one, and

sooner attached the conqueror of Goliath to his court, than he began to be jealous of him. The occasion for his jealousy was the celebration of victory at the close of the war with the Philistines.—Vers. 6, 7. "*When they came,*" *i.e.* when the warriors returned with Saul from the war, "*when* (as is added to explain what follows) *David returned from the slaughter,*" *i.e.* from the war in which he had slain Goliath, the women came out of all the towns of Israel, "*to singing and dancing,*" *i.e.* to celebrate the victory with singing and choral dancing (see the remarks on Ex. xv. 20), "*to meet king Saul with tambourines, with joy, and with triangles.*" שִׂמְחָה is used here to signify expressions of joy, a *fête,* as in Judg. xvi. 23, etc. The striking position in which the word stands, viz. between two musical instruments, shows that the word is to be understood here as referring specially to songs of rejoicing, since according to ver. 7 their playing was accompanied with singing. The women who "*sported*" (מְשַׂחֲקוֹת), *i.e.* performed mimic dances, sang in alternate choruses ("*answered,*" as in Ex. xv. 21), "*Saul hath slain*

not to have been written by the same author: (1) because the same thing is mentioned in vers. 13, 14, as in ver. 5, though in a somewhat altered form, and vers. 10, 11 occur again in ch. xix. 9, 10, with a few different words, and in a more appropriate connection; (2) because the contents of ver. 9, and the word מִמָּחֳרָת in ver. 10, are most directly opposed to vers. 2 and 5. On these grounds, no doubt, the LXX. have not only omitted the beginning of ver. 6 from their version, but also vers. 9-11. But the supposed discrepancy between vers. 9 and 10 and vers. 2 and 5,—viz. that Saul could not have kept David by his side from attachment to him, or have placed him over his men of war after several prosperous expeditions, as is stated in vers. 2 and 5, if he had looked upon him with jealous eyes from the very first day, or if his jealousy had broken out on the second day in the way described in vers. 10, 11,—is founded upon two erroneous assumptions; viz. (1) that the facts contained in vers. 1-5 were contemporaneous with those in vers. 6-14; and (2) that everything contained in these two sections is to be regarded as strictly chronological. But the fact recorded in ver. 2, namely, that Saul took David to himself, and did not allow him to go back to his father's house any more, occurred unquestionably some time earlier than those mentioned in vers. 6 sqq. with their consequences. Saul took David to himself immediately after the defeat of Goliath, and before the war had been brought to an end. But the celebration of the victory, in which the pæan of the women excited jealousy in Saul's mind, did not take place till the return of the people and of the king at the close of the war. How long the war lasted we do not know; but from the fact that the Israelites pursued the flying Philistines to Gath *his thousands, and David his ten thousands."*—Ver. 8. Saul was enraged at this. The words displeased him, so that he said, *" They have given David ten thousands, and to me thousands, and there is only the kingdom more for him"* (*i.e.* left for him to obtain). " In this foreboding utterance of Saul there was involved not only a conjecture which the result confirmed, but a deep inward truth: if the king of Israel stood powerless before the subjugators of his kingdom at so decisive a period as this, and a shepherd boy came and decided the victory, this was an additional mark of his rejection" (O. v. Gerlach).— Ver. 9. From that day forward Saul *was looking askance* at David. עָוַן, a denom. verb, from עַיִן, an eye, looking askance, is used for עוֹיֵן (*Keri*).—Vers. 10, 11. The next day the evil spirit fell upon Saul (*" the evil spirit of God;"* see at ch. xvi. 14), so that he raved *in his house,* and threw his javelin at David, who played before him *"as day by day,"* but did not hit him, because David *turned away before him twice.* הִתְנַבֵּא does not

and Ekron, and then plundered the camp of the Philistines after that (ch. xvii. 52, 53), it certainly follows that some days, if not weeks, must have elapsed between David's victory over Goliath and the celebration of the triumph, after the expulsion of the Philistines from the land. Thus far the events described in the two sections are arranged in their chronological order; but for all the rest the facts are arranged antithetically, according to their peculiar character, whilst the consequences, which reached further than the facts that gave rise to them, and were to some extent contemporaneous, are appended immediately to the facts themselves. Thus David's going out whithersoever Saul sent him (ver. 5) may indeed have commenced during the pursuit of the flying Philistines; but it reached far beyond this war, and continued even while Saul was looking upon him with jealous eyes. Ver. 5 contains a general remark, with which the historian brings to a close one side of the relation between David and Saul, which grew out of David's victory. He then proceeds in ver. 6 to give the other side, and rounds off this paragraph also (vers. 14–16) with a general remark, the substance of which resembles, in the main, the substance of ver. 5. At the same time it implies some progress, inasmuch as the delight of the people at the acts performed by David (ver. 5) grew into love to David itself. This same progress is also apparent in ver. 13 (*" Saul made him captain over a thousand"*), as compared with ver. 5 (*" Saul set him over the men of war"*). Whether the elevation of David into a captain over a thousand was a higher promotion than his appointment over the men of war, or the latter expression is to be taken as simply a more general or indefinite term, denoting his promotion to the rank of commander-in-chief, is a point which can hardly be determined with certainty.

mean to prophesy in this instance, but "*to rave.*" This use of the word is founded upon the ecstatic utterances, in which the supernatural influence of the Spirit of God manifested itself in the prophets (see at ch. x. 5). וַיָּטֶל, from טוּל, he hurled the javelin, and said (to himself), "*I will pierce David and the wall.*" With such force did he hurl his spear; but David turned away from him, *i.e.* eluded it, twice. His doing so a second time presupposes that Saul hurled the javelin twice; that is to say, he probably swung it twice without letting it go out of his hand,—a supposition which is raised into certainty by the fact that it is not stated here that the javelin entered the wall, as in ch. xix. 10. But even with this view יָטֶל is not to be changed into יִטֹּל, as Thenius proposes, since the verb נָטַל cannot be proved to have ever the meaning to swing. Saul seems to have held the javelin in his hand as a sceptre, according to ancient custom.—Vers. 12, 13. "*And Saul was afraid of David, because the Spirit of Jehovah was with him, and had departed from Saul;*" he "*removed him therefore from him,*" *i.e.* from his immediate presence, by appointing him chief captain over thousand. In this fear of David on the part of Saul, the true reason for his hostile behaviour is pointed out with deep psychological truth. The fear arose from the consciousness that the Lord had departed from him,—a consciousness which forced itself involuntarily upon him, and drove him to make the attempt, in a fit of madness, to put David to death. The fact that David did not leave Saul immediately after this attempt upon his life, may be explained not merely on the supposition that he looked upon this attack as being simply an outburst of momentary madness, which would pass away, but still more from his firm believing confidence, which kept him from forsaking the post in which the Lord had placed him without any act of his own, until he saw that Saul was plotting to take his life, not merely in these fits of insanity, but also at other times, in calm deliberation (*vid.* ch. xix. 1 sqq.).—Vers. 14 sqq. As chief commander over thousand, he went out and in before the people, *i.e.* he carried out military enterprises, and that so wisely and prosperously, that the blessing of the Lord rested upon all he did. But these successes on David's part increased Saul's fear of him, whereas all Israel and Judah came to love him as their leader. David's success in all that he took in hand compelled Saul to promote him; and his standing with the people increased with his promotion. But as the Spirit of God had departed from Saul, this only filled him more and more with dread of David as his rival. As the hand of the Lord was visibly displayed in David's success, so, on the other hand, Saul's rejection by God was manifested in his increasing fear of David.

Vers. 17-30. *Craftiness of Saul in the betrothal of his daughters to David.*—Vers. 17 sqq. As Saul had promised to give his daughter for a wife to the conqueror of Goliath (ch. xvii. 25), he felt obliged, by the growing love and attachment of the people to David, to fulfil this promise, and told him that he was ready to do so, with the hope of finding in this some means of destroying David. He therefore offered him his elder daughter *Merab* with words that sounded friendly and kind: "*Only be a brave man to me, and wage the wars of the Lord.*" He called the wars with the Philistines "*wars of Jehovah,*" *i.e.* wars for the maintenance and defence of the kingdom of God, to conceal his own cunning design, and make David feel all the more sure that the king's heart was only set upon the welfare of the kingdom of God. Whoever waged the wars of the Lord might also hope for the help of the Lord. But Saul had intentions of a very different kind. He thought ("said," *sc.* to himself), "*My hand shall not be upon him, but let the hand of the Philistines be upon him;*" *i.e.* I will not put him to death; the Philistines may do that. When Saul's reason had returned, he shrank from laying hands upon David again, as he had done before in a fit of madness. He therefore hoped to destroy him through the medium of the Philistines.—Ver. 18. But David replied with true humility, without suspecting the craftiness of Saul: "*Who am I, and what is my condition in life, my father's family in Israel, that I should become son-in-law to the king?*" מִי חַיַּי is a difficult expression, and has been translated in different ways, as the meaning which suggests itself first (viz. "*what is my life*") is neither reconcilable with the מִי (the interrogative personal pronoun), nor suitable to the context. Gesenius (*Thes.* p. 471) and Böttcher give the meaning "*people*" for חַיִּים, and Ewald (*Gramm.* § 179, *b*) the meaning "*family.*" But neither of these meanings can be established. חַיִּים seems evidently to signify the condition in life, the relation in which a person stands to others, and מִי is to be explained on the ground that David referred to the persons who formed the class to which he belonged. "*My father's family*" includes all his relations. David's meaning was, that neither on personal grounds, nor on account of his social standing, nor because of his lineage, could he make the slightest pretension to the honour of becoming the son-in-law of the king.—Ver. 19. But Saul did not keep his promise. When the time arrived for its fulfilment, *he gave his daughter to Adriel the Meholathite,* a man of whom nothing further is known.[1]—Vers. 20-24. *Michal is married to David.*—The pretext under which Saul broke his promise is not given, but it appears to have been, at any rate in part, that Merab had no love to David. This may be inferred from vers. 17, 18, compared with ver. 20. *Michal, the younger daughter of Saul, loved David.* When Saul was told this, the thing was quite right in his eyes. He said, "*I will give her to him, that she may become a snare to him, and the hand of the Philistines may come upon him*" (*sc.* if he tries to get the price which I shall require as dowry; cf. ver. 25). He therefore said to David, "*In a second way* (בִּשְׁתַּיִם, as in Job xxxiii. 14) *shalt thou become my son-in-law.*" Saul said this casually to David; but he made no reply, because he had found out the fickleness of Saul, and therefore put no further trust in his words.—Ver. 22. Saul therefore employed his courtiers to persuade David to accept his offer. In this way we may reconcile in a very simple manner the apparent discrepancy, that Saul is said to have offered his daughter to David himself, and yet he commissioned his servants to talk to David privately of the king's willingness to give him his daughter. The omission of ver. 21*b* in the Septuagint is to be explained partly from the fact that בִּשְׁתַּיִם points back to vers. 17-19, which are wanting in this version, and partly also in all probability from the idea entertained by the translators that the statement itself is at variance with vers. 22 sqq. The courtiers were to talk to David בַּלָּט, "*in private,*" *i.e.* as though they were doing it behind the king's back.—Ver. 23. David replied to the courtiers, "*Does it seem to you a little thing to become son-in-law to the king, seeing that I*

---

[1] Vers. 17-19 are omitted from the Septuagint version; but they are so, no doubt, only because Saul's first promise was without result so far as David was concerned.

am a poor and humble man?" "*Poor,*" *i.e.* utterly unable to offer anything like a suitable dowry to the king. This reply was given by David in perfect sincerity, since he could not possibly suppose that the king would give him his daughter without a considerable marriage portion.—Vers. 24 sqq. When this answer was reported to the king, he sent word through his courtiers what the price was for which he would give him his daughter. He required no dowry (see at Gen. xxxiv. 12), but only a hundred foreskins of the Philistines, *i.e.* the slaughter of a hundred Philistines, and the proof that this had been done, to avenge himself upon the enemies of the king; whereas, as the writer observes, Saul supposed that he should thus cause David to fall, *i.e.* bring about his death by the hand of the Philistines. —Vers. 26, 27. But David was satisfied with Saul's demand, since he had no suspicion of his craftiness, and loved Michal. Even before the days were full, *i.e.* before the time appointed for the delivery of the dowry and for the marriage had arrived, he rose up with his men, smote two hundred Philistines, and brought their foreskins, which were placed in their full number before the king; whereupon Saul was obliged to give him Michal his daughter to wife. The words "*and the days were not full*" (ver. 26) form a circumstantial clause, which is to be connected with the following sentence, "*David arose,*" etc. David delivered twice the price demanded. "*They made them full to the king,*" *i.e.* they placed them in their full number before him.—Vers. 28, 29. The knowledge of the fact that David had carried out all his enterprises with success had already filled the melancholy king with fear. But when the failure of this new plan for devoting David to certain death had forced the conviction upon him that Jehovah was with David, and that he was miraculously protected by Him; and when, in addition to this, there was the love of his daughter Michal to David; his fear of David grew into a lifelong enmity. Thus his evil spirit urged him ever forward to greater and greater hardness of heart.—Ver. 30. The occasion for the practical manifestation of this enmity was the success of David in all his engagements with the Philistines. As often as the princes of the Philistines went out (*sc.* to war with Israel), David acted more wisely and prosperously than all the servants of Saul, so that his name was held in great honour. With this general remark the way is prepared for the further history of Saul's conduct towards David.

JONATHAN'S INTERCESSION FOR DAVID. SAUL'S RENEWED ATTEMPTS TO MURDER HIM. DAVID'S FLIGHT TO SAMUEL. —CHAP. XIX.

Vers. 1-7. Jonathan warded off the first outbreak of deadly enmity on the part of Saul towards David. When Saul spoke to his son Jonathan and all his servants about his intention to kill David (לְהָמִית אֶת־דָּוִד, *i.e.* not that they should kill David, but *"that he intended to kill him"*), Jonathan reported this to David, because he was greatly attached to him, and gave him this advice: *"Take heed to thyself in the morning; keep thyself in a secret place, and hide thyself. I will go out and stand beside my father in the field where thou art, and I will talk to my father about thee* (דִּבֶּר בְּ, as in Deut. vi. 7, Ps. lxxxvii. 3, etc., to talk of or about a person), *and see what* (*sc.* he will say), *and show it to thee."* David was to conceal himself in the field near to where Jonathan would converse with his father about him; not that he might hear the conversation in his hiding-place, but that Jonathan might immediately report to him the result of his conversation, without there being any necessity for going far away from his father, so as to excite suspicion that he was in league with David.—Vers. 4, 5. Jonathan then endeavoured with all the modesty of a son to point out most earnestly to his father the grievous wickedness involved in his conduct towards David. *"Let not the king sin against his servant, against David; for he hath not sinned against thee, and his works are very good* (*i.e.* very useful) *to thee. He hath risked his life* (see at Judg. xii. 3), *and smitten the Philistines, and Jehovah hath wrought a great salvation of all Israel. Thou hast seen it, and rejoiced; and wherefore wilt thou sin against innocent blood, to slay David without a cause?"*—Vers. 6, 7. These words made an impression upon Saul. He swore, *"As Jehovah liveth, he* (David) *shall not be put to death;"* whereupon Jonathan reported these words to David, and brought him to Saul, so that he was with him again as before. But this reconciliation, unfortunately, did not last long.

Vers. 8-17. Another great defeat which David had inflicted

upon the Philistines excited Saul to such an extent, that in a fit of insanity he endeavoured to pierce David with his javelin as he was playing before him. The words *Ruach Jehovah* describe the attack of madness in which Saul threw the javelin at David according to its higher cause, and that, as implied in the words *Ruach Jehovah* in contrast with *Ruach Elohim* (ch. xviii. 10, xvi. 15), as inflicted upon him by Jehovah. The thought expressed is, that the growth of Saul's melancholy was a sign of the hardness of heart to which Jehovah had given him up on account of his impenitence. David happily escaped this javelin also. He slipped away from Saul, so that he hurled the javelin into the wall; whereupon David fled and escaped the same night, *i.e.* the night after this occurrence. This remark somewhat anticipates the course of the events, as the author, according to the custom of Hebrew historians, gives the result at once, and then proceeds to describe in detail the more exact order of the events.—Ver. 11. " *Saul sent messengers to David's house*," to which David had first fled, "*to watch him* (that he might not get away again), *and to put him to death in the* (next) *morning.*" Michal made him acquainted with this danger, and then let him down through the window, so that he escaped. The danger in which David was at that time is described by him in Ps. lix., from which we may see how Saul was surrounded by a number of cowardly courtiers, who stirred up his hatred against David, and were busily engaged in getting the dreaded rival out of the way.—Vers. 13, 14. Michal then took the *teraphim*,—*i.e.* in all probability an image of the household gods of the size of life, and, judging from what follows, in human form,—laid it in the bed, and put a piece of woven goats' hair *at his head, i.e.* either round or over the head of the image, and *covered it with the garment* (*beged,* the upper garment, which was generally only a square piece of cloth for wrapping round), and told the messengers whom Saul had sent to fetch him that he was ill. Michal probably kept *teraphim* in secret, like Rachel, because of her barrenness (see at Gen. xxxi. 19). The meaning of כְּבִיר הָעִזִּים is doubtful. The earlier translators took it to mean goat-skin, with the exception of the Seventy, who confounded כְּבִיר with כָּבֵד, *liver,* upon which Josephus founds his account of Michal having placed a still moving goat's liver in the bed, to make the messengers believe that there was a breathing invalid beneath. כְּבִיר, from כָּבַר, signifies something woven, and עִזִּים goats' hair, as in Ex. xxv. 4. But it is impossible to decide with certainty what purpose the cloth of goats' hair was to serve; whether it was merely to cover the head of the teraphim with hair, and so make it like a human head, or to cover the head and face as if of a person sleeping. The definite article not only before תְּרָפִים and בֶּגֶד, but also with כְּבִיר הָעִזִּים, suggests the idea that all these things belonged to Michal's house furniture, and that כְּבִיר עִזִּים was probably a counterpane made of goats' hair, with which persons in the East are in the habit of covering the head and face when sleeping.—Vers. 15 sqq. But when Saul sent the messengers again to see David, and that with the command, "*Bring him up to me in the bed*," and when they only found the teraphim in the bed, and Saul charged Michal with this act of deceit, she replied, "*He* (David) *said to me, Let me go; why should I kill thee?*"—"*Behold, teraphim were* (laid) *in the bed.*" The verb can be naturally supplied from ver. 13. In the words "*Why should I kill thee?*" Michal intimates that she did not mean to let David escape, but was obliged to yield to his threat that he would kill her if she continued to refuse. This prevarication she seems to have considered perfectly justifiable.

Vers. 18-24. David fled to Samuel at Ramah, and reported to him all that Saul had done, partly to seek for further advice from the prophet who had anointed him, as to his further course, and partly to strengthen himself, by intercourse with him, for the troubles that still awaited him. He therefore went along with Samuel, and dwelt with him in *Naioth*. נוית (to be read נָיִת according to the *Chethibh*, for which the Masoretes have substituted the form נָיוֹת, vers. 19, 23, and xx. 1), from נָוֶה or נָוָה, signifies dwellings; but here it is in a certain sense a proper name, applied to the *coenobium* of the pupils of the prophets, who had assembled round Samuel in the neighbourhood of Ramah. The plural נָיִת points to the fact, that this coenobium consisted of a considerable number of dwelling-places or houses, connected together by a hedge or wall.—Vers. 19, 20. When Saul was told where this place was, he sent messengers to fetch David. But as soon as the messengers saw the company of prophets prophesying, and Samuel standing there as their leader, the Spirit of God came upon them, so that they also prophesied. The singular וַיַּרְא is certainly very striking here; but it is hardly to be regarded as merely a copyist's error for the plural וַיִּרְאוּ, because it is extremely improbable that such an error as this should have found universal admission into the mss.; so that it is in all probability to be taken as the original and correct reading, and understood either as relating to the leader of the messengers, or as used because the whole company of messengers were regarded as one body. The ἀπ. λεγ. לַהֲקָה signifies, according to the ancient versions, an assembly, equivalent to קְהִלָּה, from which it arose according to Kimchi and other Rabbins by simple inversion.—Ver. 21. The same thing happened to a second and third company of messengers, whom Saul sent one after another when the thing was reported to him.—Vers. 22 sqq. Saul then set out to Ramah himself, and inquired, as soon as he had arrived at the great pit at *Sechu* (a place near Ramah with which we are not acquainted), where Samuel and David were, and went, according to the answer he received, to the Naioth at Ramah. There the Spirit of God came upon him also, so that he went along prophesying, until he came to the Naioth at Ramah; and there he even took off his clothes, and prophesied before Samuel, and lay there naked all that day, and the whole night as well. עָרוֹם, γυμνός, does not always signify complete nudity, but is also applied to a person with his upper garment off (cf. Isa. xx. 2; Micah i. 8; John xxi. 7). From the repeated expression "*he also,*" in vers. 23, 24, it is not only evident that Saul came into an ecstatic condition of prophesying as well as his servants, but that the prophets themselves, and not merely the servants, took off their clothes like Saul when they prophesied. It is only in the case of וַיִּפֹּל עָרֹם that the expression "he also" is not repeated; from which we must infer, that Saul alone lay there the whole day and night with his clothes off, and in an ecstatic state of external unconsciousness; whereas the ecstasy of his servants and the prophets lasted only a short time, and the clear self-consciousness returned earlier than with Saul. This difference is not without significance in relation to the true explanation of the whole affair. Saul had experienced a similar influence of the Spirit of God before, namely, immediately after his anointing by Samuel, when he met a company of prophets who were prophesying at Gibeah, and he had been thereby changed into another man (ch. x. 6 sqq.). This miraculous seizure by the Spirit of God was repeated again here, when he came near to the seat of the prophets; and it also affected the servants whom he had sent to apprehend David, so that Saul was obliged to relinquish the attempt to seize him. This result, however, we cannot regard as the principal object of the whole occurrence, as Vatablus does when he says, " The spirit of prophecy came into Saul, that David might the more easily escape from his power." Calvin's remarks go much deeper into the meaning: "God," he says, "changed their (the messengers') thoughts and purpose, not only so that they failed to apprehend David according to the royal command, but so that they actually became the companions of the prophets. And God effected this, that the fact itself might show how He holds the hearts of men in His hand and power, and turns and moves them according to His will." Even this, however, does not bring out the full meaning of the miracle, and more especially fails to explain why the same thing should have happened to Saul in an intensified degree. Upon this point Calvin simply observes, that " Saul ought indeed to have been strongly moved by these things, and to have discerned the impossibility of his accomplishing anything by fighting against the Lord; but he was so hardened that he did not perceive the hand of God: for he hastened to Naioth himself, when he found that his servants mocked him;" and in this proceeding on Saul's part he discovers a sign of his increasing hardness of heart. Saul and his messengers, the zealous performers of his will, ought no doubt to have learned, from what happened to them in the presence of the prophets, that God had the hearts of men in His power, and guided them at His will; but they were also to be seized by the might of the Spirit of God, which worked in the prophets, and thus brought to the consciousness, that Saul's raging against David was fighting against Jehovah and His Spirit, and so to be led to give up the evil thoughts of their heart. Saul was seized by this mighty influence of the Spirit of God in a more powerful manner than his servants were, both because he had most obstinately resisted the leadings of divine grace, and also in order that, if it were possible, his hard heart might be broken and subdued by the power of grace. If, however, he should nevertheless continue obstinately in his rebellion against God, he would then fall under the judgment of hardening, which would be speedily followed by his destruction. This new occurrence in Saul's life occasioned a renewal of the proverb : " *Is Saul also among the prophets ?*" The words " *wherefore they say*" do not imply that the proverb was first used at this time, but only that it received a new exemplification and basis in the new event in Saul's experience. The origin of it has been already mentioned in ch. x. 12, and the meaning of it was there explained.

This account is also worthy of note, as having an important bearing upon the so-called *Schools of the Prophets* in the time of Samuel, to which, however, we have only casual allusions. From the passage before us we learn that there was a company of prophets at Ramah, under the superintendence of Samuel, whose members lived in a common building (נוית), and that Samuel had his own house at Ramah (ch. vii. 17), though he sometimes lived in the *Naioth* (cf. vers. 18 sqq.). The origin and history of these schools are involved in obscurity. If we bear in mind, that, according to ch. iii. 1, before the call of Samuel as prophet, the prophetic word was very rare in Israel, and prophecy was not widely spread, there can be no doubt that these unions of prophets arose in the time of Samuel, and were called into existence by him. The only uncertainty is whether there were other such unions in different parts of the land beside the one at Ramah. In ch. x. 5, 10, we find a band of prophesying prophets at Gibeah, coming down from the sacrificial height there, and going to meet Saul ; but it is not stated there that this company had its seat at Gibeah, although it may be inferred as probable, from the name " *Gibeah of God*" (see the commentary on ch. x. 5, 6). No further mention is made of these in the time of Samuel ; nor do we meet with them again till the times of Elijah and Elisha, when we find them, under the name of *sons of the prophets* (1 Kings xx. 35), living in considerable numbers at Gilgal, Bethel, and Jericho (*vid.* 2 Kings iv. 38, ii. 3, 5, 7, 15, iv. 1, vi. 1, ix. 1). According to ch. iv. 38, 42, 43, about a hundred sons of the prophets sat before Elisha at Gilgal, and took their meals together. The number at Jericho may have been quite as great; for fifty men of the sons of the prophets went with Elijah and Elisha to the Jordan (comp. ch. ii. 7 with vers. 16, 17). These passages render it very probable that the sons of the prophets also lived in a common house. And this conjecture is raised into a certainty by ch. vi. 1 sqq. In this passage, for example, they are represented as saying to Elisha: "The place where we sit before thee is too strait for us; let us go to the Jordan, and let each one fetch thence a beam, and build ourselves a place to dwell in there." It is true that we might, if necessary, supply לְפָנֶיךָ from ver. 1, after לָשֶׁבֶת שָׁם, "to sit before thee," and so understand the words as merely referring to the erection of a more commodious place of meeting. But if they built it by the Jordan, we can hardly imagine that it was merely to serve as a place of meeting, to which they would have to make pilgrimages from a distance, but can only assume that they intended to live there, and assemble together under the superintendence of a prophet. In all probability, however, only such as were unmarried lived in a common building. Many of them were married, and therefore most likely lived in houses of their own (2 Kings iv. 1 sqq.). We may also certainly assume the same with reference to the unions of prophets in the time of Samuel, even if it is impossible to prove that these unions continued uninterruptedly from the time of Samuel down to the times of Elijah and Elisha. Oehler argues in support of this, " that the historical connection, which can be traced in the influence of prophecy from the time of Samuel forwards, may be most easily explained from the uninterrupted continuance of these supports; and also that the large number of prophets, who must have been already there according to 1 Kings xviii. 13 when Elijah first appeared, points to the existence of such unions as these." But the historical connection in the influence of prophecy, or, in other words, the uninterrupted succession of prophets, was also to be found in the kingdom of Judah both before and after the times of Elijah and Elisha, and down to the Babylonian captivity, without our discovering the slightest trace of any schools of the prophets in that kingdom. All that can be inferred from 1 Kings xviii. is, that the large number of prophets mentioned there (vers. 4 and 13) were living in the time of Elijah, but not that they were there when he first appeared. The first mission of Elijah to king Ahab (ch. xvii.) took place about three years before the events described in 1 Kings xviii., and even this first appearance of the prophet in the presence of the king is not to be regarded as the commencement of his prophetic labours

How long Elijah had laboured before he announced to Ahab the judgment of three years' drought, cannot indeed be decided; but if we consider that he received instructions to call Elisha to be his assistant and successor not very long after this period of judgment had expired (1 Kings xix. 16 sqq.), we may certainly assume that he had laboured in Israel for many years, and may therefore have founded unions of the prophets. In addition, however, to the absence of any allusion to the continuance of these schools of the prophets, there is another thing which seems to preclude the idea that they were perpetuated from the time of Samuel to that of Elijah, viz. the fact that the schools which existed under Elijah and Elisha were only to be found in the kingdom of the ten tribes, and never in that of Judah, where we should certainly expect to find them if they had been handed down from Samuel's time. Moreover, Oehler also acknowledges that "the design of the schools of the prophets, and apparently their constitution, were not the same under Samuel as in the time of Elijah." This is confirmed by the fact, that the members of the prophets' unions which arose under Samuel are never called " sons of the prophets," as those who were under the superintendence of Elijah and Elisha invariably are (see the passages quoted above). Does not this peculiar epithet seem to indicate, that the " sons of the prophets" stood in a much more intimate relation to Elijah and Elisha, as their spiritual fathers, than the חֶבֶל הַנְּבִיאִים or לַהֲקַת הַנְּבִיאִים did to Samuel as their president? (1 Sam. xix. 20.) בְּנֵי הַנְּבִיאִים does not mean *filii prophetæ*, *i.e.* sons who are prophets, as some maintain, though without being able to show that בְּנֵי is ever used in this sense, but *filii prophetarum*, disciples or scholars of the prophets, from which it is very evident that these sons of the prophets stood in a relation of dependence to the prophets (Elijah and Elisha), *i.e.* of subordination to them, and followed their instructions and admonitions. They received commissions from them, and carried them out (*vid.* 2 Kings ix. 1). On the other hand, the expressions חֶבֶל and לַהֲקָה simply point to combinations for common working under the presidency of Samuel, although the words נִצָּב עֲלֵיהֶם certainly show that the direction of these unions, and probably the first impulse to form them, proceeded from Samuel, so that we might also call these societies schools of the prophets.

The opinions entertained with regard to the nature of these unions, and their importance in relation to the development of the kingdom of God in Israel, differ very widely from one another. Whilst some of the fathers (Jerome for example) looked upon them as an Old Testament order of monks; others, such as Tennemann, Meiners, and Winer, compare them to the Pythagorean societies. Kranichfeld supposes that they were free associations, and chose a distinguished prophet like Samuel as their president, in order that they might be able to cement their union the more firmly through his influence, and carry out their vocation with the greater success.[1] The truth lies between these two extremes. The latter view, which precludes almost every relation of dependence and community, is not reconcilable with the name "sons of the prophets," or with ch. xix. 20, where Samuel is said to have stood at the head of the prophesying prophets as נִצָּב עֲלֵיהֶם, and has no support whatever in the Scriptures, but is simply founded upon the views of modern times and our ideas of liberty and equality. The prophets' unions had indeed so far a certain resemblance to the monastic orders of the early church, that the members lived together in the same buildings, and performed certain sacred duties in common; but if we look into the aim and purpose of monasticism, they were the very opposite of those of the prophetic life. The prophets did not wish to withdraw from the tumult of the world into solitude, for the purpose of carrying on a contemplative life of holiness in this retirement from the earthly life and its affairs; but their unions were associations formed for the purpose of mental and spiritual training, that they might exert a more powerful influence upon their contemporaries. They were called into existence by chosen instruments of the Lord, such as Samuel, Elijah, and Elisha, whom the Lord had called to be His prophets, and endowed with a peculiar measure of His Spirit for this particular calling, that they might check the decline of religious life in the nation, and bring back the rebellious "to the law and the testimony."

---

[1] Compare Jerome (*Epist.* iv. *ad Rustic. Monach.* c. 7): "The sons of the prophets, whom we call the monks of the Old Testament, built themselves cells near the streams of the Jordan, and, forsaking the crowded cities, lived on meal and wild herbs." Compare with this his *Epist.* xiii. *ad Paulin*, c. 5.

Societies which follow this as their purpose in life, so long as they do not lose sight of it, will only separate and cut themselves off from the external world, so far as the world itself opposes them, and pursues them with hostility and persecution. The name "schools of the prophets" is the one which expresses most fully the character of these associations; only we must not think of them as merely educational institutions, in which the pupils of the prophets received instruction in prophesying or in theological studies.[1] We are not in possession indeed of any minute information concerning their constitution. Prophesying could neither be taught nor communicated by instruction, but was a gift of God which He communicated according to His free will to whomsoever He would. But the communication of this divine gift was by no means an arbitrary thing, but presupposed such a mental and spiritual disposition on the part of the recipient as fitted him to receive it; whilst the exercise of the gift required a thorough acquaintance with the law and the earlier revelations of God, which the schools of the prophets were well adapted to promote. It is therefore justly and generally assumed, that the study of the law and of the history of the divine guidance of Israel formed a leading feature in the occupations of the pupils of the prophets, which also included the cultivation of sacred poetry and music, and united exercises for the promotion of the prophetic inspiration. That the study of the earlier revelations of God was carried on, may be very safely inferred from the fact that from the time of Samuel downwards the writing of sacred history formed an essential part of the prophet's labours, as has been already observed at vol. iv. pp. 9, 10 (translation). The cultivation of sacred music and poetry may be inferred partly from the fact that, according to ch. x. 5, musicians walked in front of the

---

[1] Thus the Rabbins regarded them as בָּתֵּי מִדְרָשׁ; and the earlier theologians as colleges, in which, as Vitringa expresses it, "philosophers, or if you please theologians, and candidates or students of theology, assembled for the purpose of devoting themselves assiduously to the study of divinity under the guidance of some one who was well skilled as a teacher;" whilst others regarded them as schools for the training of teachers for the people, and leaders in the worship of God. The English Deists—Morgan for example—regarded them as seats of scientific learning, in which the study of history, rhetoric, poetry, natural science, and moral philosophy was carried on.

prophesying prophets, playing as they went along, and partly also from the fact that sacred music not only received a fresh impulse from David, who stood in a close relation to the association of prophets at Ramah, but was also raised by him into an integral part of public worship. At the same time, music was by no means cultivated merely that the sons of the prophets might employ it in connection with their discourses, but also as means of awakening holy susceptibilities and emotions in the soul, and of lifting up the spirit to God, and so preparing it for the reception of divine revelations (see at 2 Kings iii. 15). And lastly, we must include among the spiritual exercises prophesying in companies, as at Gibeah (ch. x. 5) and Ramah (ch. xix. 20).

The outward occasion for the formation of these communities we have to seek for partly in the creative spirit of the prophets Samuel and Elijah, and partly in the circumstances of the times in which they lived. The time of Samuel forms a turning-point in the development of the Old Testament kingdom of God. Shortly after the call of Samuel the judgment fell upon the sanctuary, which had been profaned by the shameful conduct of the priests: the tabernacle lost the ark of the covenant, and ceased in consequence to be the scene of the gracious presence of God in Israel. Thus the task fell upon Samuel, as prophet of the Lord, to found a new house for that religious life which he had kindled, by collecting together into closer communities, those who had been awakened by his word, not only for the promotion of their own faith under his direction, but also for joining with him in the spread of the fear of God and obedience to the law of the Lord among their contemporaries. But just as, in the time of Samuel, it was the fall of the legal sanctuary and priesthood which created the necessity for the founding of schools of the prophets; so in the times of Elijah and Elisha, and in the kingdom of the ten tribes, it was the utter absence of any sanctuary of Jehovah which led these prophets to found societies of prophets, and so furnish the worshippers of Jehovah, who would not bend their knees to Baal, with places and means of edification, as a substitute for what the righteous in the kingdom of Judah possessed in the temple and the Levitical priesthood. But the reasons for the establishment of prophets' schools were not to be found merely in the circumstances of the times. There was a higher reason still, which must not be overlooked in our examination of these unions, and their importance in relation to the theocracy. We may learn from the fact that the disciples of the prophets who were associated together under Samuel are found prophesying (ch. x. 10, xix. 20), that they were also seized by the Spirit of God, and that the Divine Spirit which moved them exerted a powerful influence upon all who came into contact with them. Consequently the founding of associations of prophets is to be regarded as an operation of divine grace, which is generally manifested with all the greater might where sin most mightily abounds. As the Lord raised up prophets for His people at the times when apostasy had become great and strong, that they might resist idolatry with almighty power; so did He also create for himself organs of His Spirit in the schools of the prophets, who united with their spiritual fathers in fighting for His honour. It was by no means an accidental circumstance, therefore, that these unions are only met with in the times of Samuel and of the prophets Elijah and Elisha. These times resembled one another in the fact, that in both of them idolatry had gained the upper hand; though, at the same time, there were some respects in which they differed essentially from one another. In the time of Samuel the people did not manifest the same hostility to the prophets as in the time of Elijah. Samuel stood at the head of the nation as judge even during the reign of Saul; and after the rejection of the latter, he still stood so high in authority and esteem, that Saul never ventured to attack the prophets even in his madness. Elijah and Elisha, on the other hand, stood opposed to a royal house which was bent upon making the worship of Baal the leading religion of the kingdom; and they had to contend against priests of calves and prophets of Baal, who could only be compelled by hard strokes to acknowledge the Lord of Sabaoth and His prophets. In the case of the former, what had to be done was to bring the nation to a recognition of its apostasy, to foster the new life which was just awakening, and to remove whatever hindrances might be placed in its way by the monarchy. In the time of the latter, on the contrary, what was needed was "a compact phalanx to stand against the corruption which had penetrated so deeply into the nation." These differences in the times would certainly not be without their influence upon the constitution and operations of the schools of the prophets.

JONATHAN'S LAST ATTEMPT TO RECONCILE HIS FATHER TO DAVID.—CHAP. XX.–XXI. 1.

Vers. 1–11. After the occurrence which had taken place at Naioth, David fled thence and met with Jonathan, to whom he poured out his heart.[1] Though he had been delivered for the moment from the death which threatened him, through the marvellous influence of the divine inspiration of the prophets upon Saul and his messengers, he could not find in this any lasting protection from the plots of his mortal enemy. He therefore sought for his friend Jonathan, and complained to him, "What have I done? what is my crime, my sin before thy father, that he seeks my life?"—Ver. 2. Jonathan endeavoured to pacify him: "*Far be it! thou shalt not die: behold, my father does nothing great or small (i.e.* not the smallest thing; cf. ch. xxv. 36 and Num. xxii. 18) *that he does not reveal to me; why should my father hide this thing from me? It is not so.*" The לֹא after הִנֵּה stands for לֹא: the *Chethibh* עָשָׂה is probably to be preferred to the *Keri* יַעֲשֶׂה, and to be understood in this sense: "My father has (hitherto) done nothing at all, which he has not told to me." This answer of Jonathan does not presuppose that he knew nothing of the occurrences described in ch. xix. 9–24, although it is possible enough that he might not have been with his father just at that time; but it is easily explained from the fact that Saul had made the fresh attack upon David's life in a state of madness, in which he was no longer master of himself; so that it could not be inferred with certainty from this that he would

---

[1] According to Ewald and Thenius, this chapter was not written by the author of the previous one, but was borrowed from an earlier source, and ver. 1 was inserted by the compiler to connect the two together. But the principal reason for this conjecture—namely, that David could never have thought of sitting at the royal table again after what had taken place, and that Saul would still less have expected him to come—is overthrown by the simple suggestion, that all that Saul had hitherto attempted against David, according to ch. xix. 8 sqq., had been done in fits of insanity (cf. ch. xix. 9 sqq.), which had passed away again; so that it formed no criterion by which to judge of Saul's actual feelings towards David when he was in a state of mental sanity.

still plot against David's life in a state of clear consciousness. Hitherto Saul had no doubt talked over all his plans and undertakings with Jonathan, but he had not uttered a single word to him about his deadly hatred, or his intention of killing David; so that Jonathan might really have regarded his previous attacks upon David's life as nothing more than symptoms of temporary aberration of mind.—Ver. 3. But David had looked deeper into Saul's heart. He replied with an oath ("he sware again," *i.e.* a second time), "*Thy father knoweth that I have found favour in thine eyes* (*i.e.* that thou art attached to me); *and thinketh Jonathan shall not know this, lest he be grieved. But truly, as surely as Jehovah liveth, and thy soul liveth, there is hardly a step* (*lit.* about a step) *between me and death.*" כִּי introduces the substance of the oath, as in ch. xiv. 44, etc.—Ver. 4. When Jonathan answered, "*What thy soul saith, will I do to thee,*" *i.e.* fulfil every wish, David made this request, "*Behold, to-morrow is new moon, and I ought to sit and eat with the king: let me go, that I may conceal myself in the field* (*i.e.* in the open air) *till the third evening.*" This request implies that Saul gave a feast at the new moon, and therefore that the new moon was not merely a religious festival, according to the law in Num. x. 10, xxviii. 11-15, but that it was kept as a civil festival also, and in the latter character for two days; as we may infer both from the fact that David reckoned to the third evening, *i.e.* the evening of the third day from the day then present, and therefore proposed to hide himself on the new moon's day and the day following, and also still more clearly from vers. 12, 27, and 34, where Saul is said to have expected David at table on the day after the new moon. We cannot, indeed, conclude from this that there was a religious festival of two days' duration; nor does it follow, that because Saul supposed that David might have absented himself on the first day on account of Levitical uncleanness (ver. 26), therefore the royal feast was a sacrificial meal. It was evidently contrary to social propriety to take part in a public feast in a state of Levitical uncleanness, even though it is not expressly forbidden in the law.—Ver. 6. *ᵏ If thy father should miss me, then say, David hath asked permission of me to hasten to Bethlehem, his native town; for there is a yearly sacrifice for the whole family there.*" This ground of excuse shows that families and households were accustomed to keep united sacrificial feasts once a year. According to the law in Deut. xii. 5 sqq., they ought to have been kept at the tabernacle; but at this time, when the central sanctuary had fallen into disuse, they were held in different places, wherever there were altars of Jehovah—as, for example, at Bethlehem (cf. ch. xvi. 2 sqq.). We see from these words that David did not look upon prevarication as a sin.—Ver. 7. "*If thy father says, It is well, there is peace to thy servant* (*i.e.* he cherishes no murderous thoughts against me); *but if he be very wroth, know that evil is determined by him.*" כָּלָה, to be completed; hence to be firmly and unalterably determined (cf. ch. xxv. 17; Esther vii. 7). Seb. Schmidt infers from the closing words that the fact was certain enough to David, but not to Jonathan. Thenius, on the other hand, observes much more correctly, that "it is perfectly obvious from this that David was not quite clear as to Saul's intentions," though he upsets his own previous assertion, that after what David had gone through, he could never think of sitting again at the king's table as he had done before.—Ver. 8. David made sure that Jonathan would grant this request on account of his friendship, as he had *brought him into a covenant of Jehovah with himself*. David calls the covenant of friendship with Jonathan (ch. xviii. 3) a *covenant of Jehovah*, because he had made it with a solemn invocation of Jehovah. But in order to make quite sure of the fulfilment of his request on the part of Jonathan, David added, "*But if there is a fault in me, do thou kill me* (אַתָּה used to strengthen the suffix); *for why wilt thou bring me to thy father?*" sc. that he may put me to death.— Ver. 9. Jonathan replied, "*This be far from thee!*" sc. that I should kill thee, or deliver thee up to my father. חָלִילָה points back to what precedes, as in ver. 2. "*But* (כִּי after a previous negative assertion) *if I certainly discover that evil is determined by my father to come upon thee, and I do not tell it thee*," sc. "may God do so to me," etc. The words are to be understood as an asseveration on oath, in which the formula of an oath is to be supplied in thought. This view is apparently a more correct one, on account of the cop. ו before לֹא, than to take the last clause as a question, "Shall I not tell it thee?"—Ver. 10. To this friendly assurance David replied, "*Who will tell me?*" sc. how thy father expresses himself concerning me; "*or what will thy father answer thee roughly?*" sc. if thou shouldst attempt to do it thyself. This is the correct explanation given by De Wette and Maurer. Gesenius and Thenius, on the contrary, take אִם in the sense of "*if perchance.*" But this is evidently incorrect; for even though there are certain passages in which אִם may be so rendered, it is only where some other case is supposed, and therefore the meaning *or* still lies at the foundation. These questions of David were suggested by a correct estimate of the circumstances, namely, that Saul's suspicions would leave him to the conclusion that there was some understanding between Jonathan and David, and that he would take steps in consequence to prevent Jonathan from making David acquainted with the result of his conversation with Saul.—Ver. 11. Before replying to these questions, Jonathan asked David to go with him to the field, that they might there fix upon the sign by which he would let him know, in a way in which no one could suspect, what was the state of his father's mind.

Vers. 12–23. In the field, where they were both entirely free from observation, Jonathan first of all renewed his covenant with David, by vowing to him on oath that he would give him information of his father's feelings towards him (vers. 12, 13); and then entreated him, with a certain presentiment that David would one day be king, even then to maintain his love towards him and his family for ever (vers. 14–16); and lastly, he made David swear again concerning his love (ver. 17), and then gave him the sign by which he would communicate the promised information (vers. 18–23).—Vers. 12 and 13*a* are connected. Jonathan commences with a solemn invocation of God: "*Jehovah, God of Israel!*" and thus introduces his oath. We have neither to supply "Jehovah is *witness*," nor "as truly as Jehovah *liveth*," as some have suggested. "*When I inquire of my father about this time to-morrow, the day after to-morrow* (a concise mode of saying 'to-morrow or the day after'), *and behold it is* (stands) *well for David, and then I do not send to thee and make it known to thee, Jehovah shall do so to Jonathan,*" etc. ("The Lord do so," etc., the ordinary formula used in an oath: see ch. xiv. 44). The other case is then added without an adversative particle: "*If it should please my father evil against thee* (lit. as regards evil), *I will make it known to thee, and let thee go, that thou mayest go in peace; and Jehovah be with thee, as He has been with my father.*" In this wish there is expressed the presentiment that David would one day occupy that place in Israel which Saul occupied then, *i.e.* the throne. —In vers. 14 and 15 the Masoretic text gives no appropriate meaning. Luther's rendering, in which he follows the Rabbins and takes the first וְלֹא (ver. 14) by itself, and then completes the sentence from the context ("but if I do it not, show me no mercy, because I live, not even if I die"), contains indeed a certain permissible sense when considered in itself; but it is hardly reconcilable with what follows, "*and do not tear away thy compassion for ever from my house.*" The request that he would show no compassion to him (Jonathan) even if he died, and yet would not withdraw his compassion from his house for ever, contains an antithesis which would have been expressed most clearly and unambiguously in the words themselves, if this had been really what Jonathan intended to say. De Wette's rendering gives a still more striking contradiction: "*But let not* (Jehovah be with thee) *if I still live, and thou showest not the love of Jehovah to me, that I die not, and thou withdrawest not thy love from my house for ever.*" There is really no other course open than to follow the Syriac and Arabic, as Maurer, Thenius, and Ewald have done, and change the וְלֹא in the first two clauses of ver. 14 into וְלִי or וְלֻא, according to the analogy of the form לוּא (ch. xiv. 30), and to render the passage thus: "And mayest thou, if I still live, mayest thou show to me the favour of the Lord, and not if I die, not withdraw thy favour from my house for ever, not even (וְלֹא) when Jehovah shall cut off the enemies of David, every one from the face of the earth!" "*The favour of Jehovah*" is favour such as Jehovah shows to His people. The expression "when Jehovah shall cut off," etc., shows very clearly Jonathan's conviction that Jehovah would give to David a victory over all his enemies.—Ver. 16. Thus Jonathan concluded a covenant with the house of David, namely, by bringing David to promise kindness to his family for ever. The word בְּרִית must be supplied in thought to יִכְרֹת, as in ch. xxii. 8 and 2 Chron. vii. 18. "*And Jehovah required it* (what Jonathan had predicted) *at the hand of David's enemies.*" Understood in this manner, the second clause contains a remark of the historian himself, namely, that Jonathan's words were really fulfilled in due time. The traditional rendering of וּבִקֵּשׁ as a relative preterite, with אָמַר

understood, "*and said, Let Jehovah take vengeance,*" is not only precluded by the harshness of the introduction of the word "saying," but still more by the fact, that if אָמַר (saying) is introduced between the copula *vav* and the verb בִּקֵּשׁ, the perfect cannot stand for the optative יְבַקֵּשׁ, as in Josh. xxii. 23. —Ver. 17. "*And Jonathan adjured David again by his love to him, because he loved him as his own soul*" (cf. ch. xviii. 1, 3); *i.e.* he once more implored David most earnestly with an oath to show favour to him and his house.—Vers. 18 sqq. He then discussed the sign with him for letting him know about his father's state of mind: "*To-morrow is new moon, and thou wilt be missed, for thy seat will be empty,*" *sc.* at Saul's table (see at ver. 5). "*And on the third day come down quickly* (from thy sojourning place), *and go to the spot where thou didst hide thyself on the day of the deed, and place thyself by the side of the stone Ezel.*" The first words in this (19th) verse are not without difficulty. The meaning "on the third day" for the verb שִׁלֵּשׁ cannot be sustained by parallel passages, but is fully established, partly by הַשְּׁלִשִׁית, the third day, and partly by the Arabic usage (*vid.* Ges. *Thes. s. v.*). מְאֹד after תֵּרֵד, lit. "*go violently down,*" is more striking still. Nevertheless the correctness of the text is not to be called in question, since שִׁלַּשְׁתָּ is sustained by τρισσεύσει in the Septuagint, and תֵּרֵד מְאֹד by *descende ergo festinus* in the Vulgate, and also by the rendering in the Chaldee, Arabic, and Syriac versions, "and on the third day thou wilt be missed still more," which is evidently merely a conjecture founded upon the context. The meaning of בְּיוֹם הַמַּעֲשֶׂה is doubtful. Gesenius, De Wette, and Maurer render it "on the day of the deed," and understand it as referring to Saul's deed mentioned in ch. xix. 2, viz. his design of killing David; others render it "on the day of business," *i.e.* the working day (Luther, after the LXX. and Vulgate), but this is not so good a rendering. The best is probably that of Thenius, "on the day of the business" (which is known to thee). Nothing further can be said concerning the stone Ezel than that Ezel is a proper name.—Ver. 20. "*And I will shoot off three arrows to the side of it* (the stone Ezel), *to shoot for me at the mark,*" *i.e.* as if shooting at the mark. The article attached to הַחִצִּים is either to be explained as denoting that the historian assumed the thing as already well known, or on the supposition that Jonathan went to the field armed, and when giving the sign pointed to the arrows in his quiver. In the word צִדָּה the *Raphe* indicates that the suffix of ‏ָה‎ is not a mere toneless ה, although it has no mappik, having given up its strong breathing on account of the harsh צ sound.—Ver. 21. "*And, behold* (הִנֵּה, directing attention to what follows as the main point), *I will send the boy* (saying), *Go, get the arrows. If I shall say to the boy, Behold, the arrows are from thee hitherwards, fetch them; then come, for peace is to thee, and it is nothing, as truly as Jehovah liveth.*"—Ver. 22. "*But if I say to the youth, Behold, the arrows are from thee farther off; then go, for Jehovah sendeth thee away,*" *i.e.* bids thee flee. The appointment of this sign was just as simple as it was suitable to the purpose.—Ver. 23. This arrangement was to remain an eternal secret between them. "*And* (as for) *the word that we have spoken, I and thou, behold, the Lord is between me and thee for ever,*" namely, a witness and judge in case one of us two should break the covenant (*vid.* Gen. xxxi. 48, 49). This is implied in the words, without there being any necessity to assume that עֵד had dropped out of the text. "*The word*" refers not merely to the sign agreed upon, but to the whole matter, including the renewal of the bond of friendship.

Vers. 24–34. David thereupon concealed himself in the field, whilst Jonathan, as agreed upon, endeavoured to apologize for his absence from the king's table.—Vers. 24, 25. On the new moon's day Saul sat at table, and as always, *at his seat by the wall, i.e.* at the top, just as, in eastern lands at the present day, the place of honour is the seat in the corner (see *Harmar Beobachtungen* ii. pp. 66 sqq.). "*And Jonathan rose up, and Abner seated himself by the side of Saul, and David's place remained empty.*" The difficult passage, "*And Jonathan rose up,*" etc., can hardly be understood in any other way than as signifying that, when Abner entered, Jonathan rose from his seat by the side of Saul, and gave up the place to Abner, in which case all that is wanting is an account of the place to which Jonathan moved. Every other attempted explanation is exposed to much graver difficulties. The suggestion made by Gesenius, that the cop. ו should be supplied before אַבְנֵר, and וַיֵּשֶׁב referred to Jonathan ("and Jonathan rose up and sat down, and Abner (sat down) by the side of Saul"), as in the Syriac, is open to this objection, that in addition to the necessity of supplying וֹ, it is impossible to see why Jonathan should have risen up for the purpose of sitting down again. The rendering " and Jonathan came," which is the one adopted by Maurer and De Wette, cannot be philologically sustained; inasmuch as, although קוּם is used to signify rise up, in the sense of the occurrence of important events, or the appearance of celebrated persons, it never means simply "to come." And lastly, the conjecture of Thenius, that וַיָּקָם should be altered into וַיְקַדֵּם, according to the senseless rendering of the LXX., προέφθασε τὸν Ἰονάθαν, is overthrown by the fact, that whilst קִדֵּם does indeed mean to anticipate or come to meet, it never means to sit in front of, *i.e.* opposite to a person.—Ver. 26. On this (first) day Saul said nothing, *sc.* about David's absenting himself, *" for he thought there has* (something) *happened to him, that he is not clean; surely* (כִּי) *he is not clean"* (vid. Lev. xv. 16 sqq.; Deut. xxiii. 11).—Vers. 27 sqq. But on the second day, the day after the new moon (*lit. the morrow after the new moon, the second day:* הַשֵּׁנִי is a nominative, and to be joined to וַיְהִי, and not a genitive belonging to הַחֹדֶשׁ), when David was absent from table again, Saul said to Jonathan, *" Why is the son of Jesse not come to meat, neither yesterday nor to-day?"* Whereupon Jonathan answered, as arranged with David (compare vers. 28 and 29 with ver. 6). *" And my brother, he hath commanded me,"* i.e. ordered me to come. צִוָּה as in Ex. vi. 13, and אָחִי, the elder brother, who was then at the head of the family, and arranged the sacrificial meal.—Vers. 30, 31. Saul was greatly enraged at this, and said to Jonathan, *" Son of a perverse woman* (נַעֲוַת is a participle, Niph. fem. from עָוָה) *of rebellion,"*—i.e. son of a perverse and rebellious woman (an insult offered to the mother, and therefore so much the greater to the son), hence the meaning really is, "Thou perverse, rebellious fellow,"—*"do I not know that thou hast chosen the son of Jesse to thine own shame, and to the shame of thy mother's nakedness?"* בָּחַר, to choose a person out of love, to take pleasure in a person; generally construed with בְּ *pers.*, here with לְ, although many Codd. have בְּ here also. *" For as long as the son of Jesse liveth upon the earth, thou and thy kingdom* (kingship, throne) *will not stand."* Thus Saul evidently suspected David as his rival, who would either wrest the government from him, or at any rate after his death from his son. "*Now send and fetch him to me, for he is a child of death*," *i.e.* he has deserved to die, and shall be put to death.—Vers. 32 sqq. When Jonathan replied, "*My father, why shall he die? what has he done?*" Saul was so enraged that he hurled his javelin at Jonathan (cf. ch. xviii. 11). Thus Jonathan saw that his father had firmly resolved to put David to death, and rose up from the table in fierce anger, and did not eat that day; for he was grieved concerning David, because his father had done him shame. כָּלָה is a substantive in the sense of unalterable resolution, like the verb in ver. 9. בְּיוֹם־הַחֹדֶשׁ הַשֵּׁנִי, on the second day of the new moon or month.

Vers. 35–42. The next morning Jonathan made David acquainted with what had occurred, by means of the sign agreed upon with David. The account of this, and of the meeting between Jonathan and David which followed, is given very concisely, only the main points being touched upon. In the morning (after what had occurred) Jonathan went to the field, לְמוֹעֵד דָּוִד, either "*at the time agreed upon with David*," or "*to the meeting with David*," or perhaps better still, "*according to the appointment* (agreement) *with David*," and a small boy with him.—Ver. 36. To the latter he said, namely as soon as they had come to the field, Run, get the arrows which I shoot. The boy ran, and he shot off the arrows, "*to go out beyond him*," *i.e.* so that the arrows flew farther than the boy had run. The form חֵצִי for חֵץ only occurs in connection with disjunctive accents; beside the present chapter (vers. 36, 37, 38, *Chethibh*) we find it again in 2 Kings ix. 24. The singular is used here with indefinite generality, as the historian did not consider it necessary to mention expressly, after what he had previously written, that Jonathan shot off three arrows one after another.—Ver. 37. When the boy came to the place of the shot arrow (*i.e.* to the place to which the arrow had flown), Jonathan called after him, "*See, the arrow is* (lies) *away from thee, farther off;*" and again, "*Quickly, haste, do not stand still,*" that he might not see David, who was somewhere near; and the boy picked up the arrow and came to his lord. The *Chethibh* הַחֵצִי is evidently the original reading, and the singular is to be understood as in ver. 37; the *Keri* הַחִצִּים is an emendation, according to the meaning of the words. The writer here introduces the remark in ver. 39, that the boy knew nothing of what had been arranged between Jonathan and David.—Ver. 40. Jonathan then gave the boy his things (bow, arrows, and quiver), and sent him with them to the town, that he might be able to converse with David for a few seconds after his departure, and take leave of him unobserved.—Ver. 41. When the boy had gone, *David rose* (from his hiding-place) *from the south side, fell down upon his face to the ground, and bowed three times* (before Jonathan); they then kissed each other, and wept for one another, "*till David wept strongly,*" *i.e.* to such a degree that David wept very loud. מֵאֵצֶל הַנֶּגֶב, "*from the side of the south*," which is the expression used to describe David's hiding-place, according to its direction in relation to the place where Jonathan was standing, has not been correctly rendered by any of the early translators except Aquila and Jerome. In the Septuagint, the Chaldee, the Syriac, and the Arabic, the statement in ver. 19 is repeated, simply because the translators could not see the force of מֵאֵצֶל הַנֶּגֶב, although it is intelligible enough in relation to what follows, according to which David fled from thence *southwards to Nob.*—Ver. 42. All that is given of the conversation between the two friends is the parting word spoken by Jonathan to David: "*Go in peace. What we two have sworn in the name of the Lord, saying, The Lord be between me and thee, and between my seed and thy seed for ever:*" *sc.* let it stand, or let us abide by it. The clause contains an aposiopesis, which may be accounted for from Jonathan's deep emotion, and in which the apodosis may be gathered from the sense. For it is evident, from a comparison of ver. 23, that the expression "for ever" must be understood as forming part of the oath.—Ch. xxi. 1. David then set out upon his journey, and Jonathan returned to the town. This verse ought, strictly speaking, to form the conclusion of ch. xx.[1] The subject to "*arose*" is David; not because Jonathan was the last one spoken of (Thenius), but because the following words, "and Jonathan came," etc., are in evident antithesis to "he arose and went."

---

[1] In our English version it does; but in the Hebrew, which is followed here, it forms the opening verse of ch. xxi. In the exposition of the following chapter it has been thought better to follow the numbering of the verses in our version rather than that of the original, although the latter is conformed to the Hebrew.—TR.

DAVID'S FLIGHT TO NOB, AND THENCE TO GATH.—CHAP. XXI. 2–16.

After the information which David had received from Jonathan, nothing remained for him in order to save his life but immediate flight. He could not return to the prophets at Ramah, where he had been miraculously preserved from the first outbreak of Saul's wrath, because they could not ensure him permanent protection against the death with which he was threatened. He therefore fled first of all to Nob, to Ahimelech the high priest, to inquire the will of God through him concerning his future course (ch. xxii. 10, 15), and induced him to give him bread and the sword of Goliath also, under the pretext of having to perform a secret commission from the king with the greatest speed; for which Saul afterwards took fearful vengeance upon the priests at Nob when he was made acquainted with the affair through the treachery of Doeg (vers. 1–9). David then fled to Gath to the Philistian king Achish; but here he was quickly recognised as the conqueror of Goliath, and obliged to feign insanity in order to save his life, and then to flee still farther (vers. 10–15). The state of his mind at this time he poured out before God in the words of Ps. lvi., lii., and xxxiv.

Vers. 1–9. *David at Nob.*—The town of *Nob* or *Nobeh* (unless indeed the form נֹבֶה stands for נֹבָה here and in ch. xxii. 9, and the ה attached is merely ה local, as the name is always written נֹב in other places: *vid.* ch. xxii. 11, 32; 2 Sam. xxi. 16; Isa. x. 32; Neh. xi. 32) was at that time a priests' city (ch. xxii. 19), in which, according to the following account, the tabernacle was then standing, and the legal worship carried on. According to Isa. x. 30, 32, it was between Anathoth (*Anata*) and Jerusalem, and in all probability it has been preserved in the village of *el-Isawiyeh*, *i.e.* probably the village of Esau or Edom, which is midway between Anata and Jerusalem, an hour from the latter, and the same distance to the south-east of Gibeah of Saul (Tell el Phul), and which bears all the marks of an ancient place, partly in its dwellings, the stones of which date from a great antiquity, and partly in many marble columns which are found there (*vid.* Tobler, *Topogr. v. Jerusalem* ii. p. 720). Hence v. Raumer (*Pal.* p. 215, ed. 4) follows Kiepert in the map which he has appended to Robinson's *Biblical Researches*, and set down this place as the ancient *Nob*, for which Robinson indeed searched in vain (see *Pal.* ii. p. 150). Ahimelech, the son of Ahitub, most probably the same person as Ahiah (ch. xiv. 3), was "*the priest*," *i.e.* the high priest (see at ch. xiv. 3). When David came to him, the priest "*went trembling to meet him*" (יֶחֱרַד לִקְרַאת) with the inquiry, " *Why art thou alone, and no one is with thee ?*" The unexpected appearance of David, the son-in-law of the king, without any attendants, alarmed Ahimelech, who probably imagined that he had come with a commission from the king which might involve him in danger. David had left the few servants who accompanied him in his flight somewhere in the neighbourhood, as we may gather from ver. 2, because he wished to converse with the high priest alone. Ahimelech's anxious inquiry led David to resort to the fabrication described in ver. 2 : " *The king hath commanded me a business, and said to me, No one is to know anything of this matter, in which* (*lit.* in relation to the matter with regard to which) *I send thee, and which I have entrusted to thee* (*i.e.* no one is to know either the occasion or the nature of the commission); *and the servants I have directed to such and such a place.*" יוֹדַע, *Poel*, to cause to know, point, show. Ahimelech had received no information as yet concerning the most recent occurrences between Saul and David ; and David would not confess to him that he was fleeing from Saul, because he was evidently afraid that the high priest would not give him any assistance, lest he should draw down the wrath of the king. This falsehood brought the greatest calamities upon Ahimelech and the priests at Nob (ch. xxii. 9-19), and David was afterwards obliged to confess that he had occasioned it all (ch. xxii. 22).— Ver. 3. " *And now what is under thy hand ? give into my hand* (*i.e.* hand me) *five loaves, or whatever* (else) *is to be found.*" David asked for five loaves, because he had spoken of several attendants, and probably wanted to make provision for two or three days (Thenius).—Ver. 4. The priest answered that he had no common bread, but only holy bread, viz., according to ver. 6, shew-bread that had been removed, which none but priests were allowed to eat, and that in a sacred place ; but that he was willing to give him some of these loaves, as David had said that he was travelling upon an important mission from the king, provided only that "*the young men had kept themselves at least from women,*" *i.e.* had not been defiled by sexual intercourse (Lev. xv. 18). If they were clean at any rate in this respect, he would in such a case of necessity depart from the Levitical law concerning the eating of the shew-bread, for the sake of observing the higher commandment of love to a neighbour (Lev. xix. 18 ; cf. Matt. xii. 5, 6, Mark ii. 25, 26).[1]—Ver. 5. David quieted him concerning this scruple, and said, "*Nay, but women have been kept from us since yesterday and the day before.*" The use of כִּי אִם may be explained from the fact, that in David's reply he paid more attention to the sense than to the form of the priest's scruple, and expressed himself as concisely as possible. The words, "if the young men have only kept themselves from women," simply meant, if only they are not unclean ; and David replied, That is certainly not the case, *but* women have been kept from us ; so that כִּי אִם has the meaning *but* in this passage also, as it frequently has after a previous negative, which is implied in the thought here as in 2 Sam. xiii. 33. "*When I came out, the young men's things were holy* (Levitically clean) ; *and if it is an unholy way, it becomes even holy through the instrument.*" David does not say that the young men were clean when he came out (for the rendering given to כְּלֵי הַנְּעָרִים in the Septuagint, πάντα τὰ παιδάρια, is without any critical value, and is only a mistaken attempt to explain the word כְּלִי, which was unintelligible to the translator), but simply affirms that כְּלֵי הַנְּעָרִים קֹדֶשׁ, *i.e.*, according to Luther's rendering (*der Knaben Zeug war heilig*), the young men's things (clothes, etc.) were holy. כֵּלִים does not mean merely vessels, arms, or tools, but also the dress (Deut. xxii. 5), or rather the clothes as well as such things as were most necessary to meet the wants of life. By the *coitus*, or strictly speaking, by the *emissio seminis* in connection with the *coitus*, not only were the persons themselves defiled, but also every article of clothing or leather upon which any of the *semen* fell (Lev. xv. 18) ; so that it was necessary for the purpose of purification that the things which a man had on should all be washed. David explains, with evident allusion to this provision, that the young

[1] When Mark (ii. 26) assigns this action to the days of Abiathar the high priest, the statement rests upon an error of memory, in which Ahimelech is confounded with Abiathar.

men's things were holy, *i.e.* perfectly clean, for the purpose of assuring the priest that there was not the smallest Levitical uncleanness attaching to them. The clause which follows is to be taken as conditional, and as supposing a possible case : "*and if it is an unholy way.*" דֶּרֶךְ, the way that David was going with his young men, *i.e.* his purpose or enterprise, by which, however, we are not to understand his request of holy bread from Ahimelech, but the performance of the king's commission of which he had spoken. וְאַף כִּי, *lit.* besides (there is) also that, = moreover there is also the fact, that it becomes holy through the instrument; *i.e.*, as O. v. Gerlach has correctly explained it, "on the supposition of the important royal mission, upon which David pretended to be sent, *through me* as an ambassador of the anointed of the Lord," in which, at any rate, David's meaning really was, "the way was sanctified before God, when he, as His chosen servant, the preserver of the true kingdom of God in Israel, went to him in his extremity." That כְּלִי in the sense of instrument is also applied to *men*, is evident from Isa. xiii. 5 and Jer. l. 25.—Ver. 6. The priest then gave him (what was) holy, namely the shew-loaves "*that were taken from before Jehovah,*" *i.e.* from the holy table, upon which they had lain before Jehovah for seven days (*vid.* Lev. xxiv. 6-9).—In ver. 7 there is a parenthetical remark introduced, which was of great importance in relation to the consequences of this occurrence. There at the sanctuary there was a man of Saul's servants, נֶעְצָר, *i.e.* "*kept back* (shut off) *before Jehovah :*" *i.e.* at the sanctuary of the tabernacle, either for the sake of purification or as a proselyte, who wished to be received into the religious communion of Israel, or because of supposed leprosy, according to Lev. xiii. 4. His name was Doeg the Edomite, אַבִּיר הָרֹעִים, "*the strong one* (*i.e.* the overseer) *of the herdsmen of Saul.*"[1]—Ver. 8.

---

[1] The Septuagint translators have rendered these words νέμων τὰς ἡμιόνους, "feeding the mules of Saul;" and accordingly in ch. xxii. 9 also they have changed Saul's servants into mules, in accordance with which Thenius makes Doeg the upper herdsman of Saul. But it is very evident that the text of the LXX. is nothing more than a subjective interpretation of the expression before us, and does not presuppose any other text, from the simple fact that all the other ancient versions are founded upon the Hebrew text both here and in ch. xxii. 9, including even the Vulgate (*potentissimus pastorum*) ; and the clause contained in some of the MSS. of the Vulgate (*hic pascebat mulas Saul*) is nothing more than a gloss that has

David also asked Ahimelech whether he had not a sword or a javelin at hand; "*for I have neither brought my sword nor my (other) weapons with me, because the affair of the king was pressing,*" *i.e.* very urgent, נָחוּץ, ἀπ. λεγ., literally, compressed.—Ver. 9. The priest replied, that there was only the sword of Goliath, whom David slew in the terebinth valley (ch. xvii. 2), wrapped up in a cloth hanging behind the ephod (the high priest's shoulder-dress),—a sign of the great worth attached to this dedicatory offering. He could take that. David accepted it, as a weapon of greater value to him than any other, because he had not only taken this sword as booty from the Philistine, but had cut off the head of Goliath with it (see ch. xvii. 51). When and how this sword had come into the tabernacle is not known (see the remarks on ch. xvii. 54). The form בָּזֶה for בְּזֶה is only met with here. On the *Piska*, see at Josh. iv. 1.

Vers. 10-15. *David with Achish at Gath.*—David fled from Nob to Achish of Gath. This Philistian king is called *Abimelech* in the heading of Ps. xxxiv., according to the standing title of the Philistian princes at Gath. The fact that David fled at once out of the land, and that to the Philistines at Gath, may be accounted for from the great agitation into which he had been thrown by the information he had received from Jonathan concerning Saul's implacable hatred. As some years had passed since the defeat of Goliath, and the conqueror of Goliath was probably not personally known to many of the Philistines, he might hope that he should not be recognised in Gath, and that he might receive a welcome there with his few attendants, as a fugitive who had been driven away by Saul, the leading foe of the Philistines.[1] But in this he

---

crept in from the Itala; and this is still more obvious in ch. xxii. 9, where וְהוּא נִצָּב is applicable enough to עַבְדֵי, but is altogether unsuitable in connection with פָּרְדֵי, since נָצַב is no more applied in Hebrew to herdsmen or keepers of animals, than we should think of speaking of presidents of asses, horses, etc. Moreover, it is not till the reign of David that we read of mules being used as riding animals by royal princes (2 Sam. xiii. 29, xviii. 9); and they are mentioned for the first time as beasts of burden, along with asses, camels, and oxen, in 1 Chron. xii. 40, where they are said to have been employed by the northern tribes to carry provisions to Hebron to the festival held at the recognition of David as king. Before David's time the sons of princes rode upon asses (*vid.* Judg. x. 4, xii. 14).

This removes the objection raised by modern critics to the historical

was mistaken. He was recognised at once by the courtiers of Achish. They said to their prince, "*Is not this David the king of the land? Have they not sung in circles, Saul hath slain his thousands, and David his ten thousands?*" (cf. ch. xviii. 6, 7.) "*King of the land*" they call David, not because his anointing and divine election were known to them, but on account of his victorious deeds, which had thrown Saul entirely into the shade. Whether they intended by these words to celebrate David as a hero, or to point him out to their prince as a dangerous man, cannot be gathered from the words themselves, nor can the question be decided with certainty at all (cf. ch. xxix. 5).—Ver. 12. But David took these words to heart, and was in great fear of Achish, lest he should treat him as an enemy, and kill him. In order to escape this danger, "*he disguised his understanding* (*i.e.* pretended to be out of his mind) *in their eyes* (*i.e.* before the courtiers of Achish), *behaved insanely under their hands* (when they tried to hold him as a madman), *scribbled upon the door-wings, and let his spittle run down into his beard.*" The suffix to וַיְשַׁנּוֹ is apparently superfluous, as the object, אֶת־טַעְמוֹ, follows immediately afterwards. But it may be accounted for from the circumstantiality of the conversation of every-day life, as in 2 Sam. xiv. 6, and (though these cases are not perfectly parallel) Ex. ii. 6, Prov. v. 22, Ezek. x. 3 (cf. Gesenius' *Gramm.* § 121, 6, Anm. 3). וַיְתָו, from תָּוָה, to make signs, *i.e.* to scribble. The Sept.

credibility of the narrative before us, namely, that David would certainly not have taken refuge at once with the Philistines, but would only have gone to them in the utmost extremity (Thenius). It is impossible to see how the words "he fled *that day for fear of Saul*" (ver. 11) are to prove that this section originally stood in a different connection, and are only arbitrarily inserted here (Thenius). Unless we tear away the words in the most arbitrary manner from the foregoing word וַיִּבְרַח, they not only appear quite suitable, but even necessary, since David's journey to Abimelech was not a flight, or at all events it is not described as a flight in the text; and David's flight from Saul really began with his departure from Nob. Still less can the legendary origin of this account be inferred from the fact that some years afterwards David really did take refuge with Achish in the Philistian country (ch. xxvii. and xxix.), or the conjecture sustained that this is only a distorted legend of that occurrence. For if the later sojourn of David with Achish be a historical fact, the popular legend could not possibly have assumed a form so utterly different as the account before us, to say nothing of the fact that this occurrence has a firm historical support in Ps. xxxiv. 1.

and Vulgate render it ἐτυμπανίζειν, *impingebat, he drummed,* smote with his fists upon the wings of the door, which would make it appear as if they had read וַיְתָו (from תָּפַף), which seems more suitable to the condition of a madman whose saliva ran out of his mouth.—Vers. 14, 15. By this dissimulation David escaped the danger which threatened him; for Achish thought him mad, and would have nothing to do with him. "*Wherefore do ye bring him to me? Have I need of madmen, that ye have brought this man hither to rave against me? Shall this man come into my house?*" Thus Achish refused to receive him into his house. But whether he had David taken over the border, or at any rate out of the town; or whether David went away of his own accord; or whether he was taken away by his servants, and then hurried as quickly as possible out of the land of the Philistines, is not expressly mentioned, as being of no importance in relation to the principal object of the narrative. All that is stated is, that he departed thence, and escaped to the cave Adullam.

DAVID'S WANDERINGS IN JUDAH AND MOAB. MASSACRE OF PRIESTS BY SAUL.—CHAP. XXII.

Vers. 1–5. Having been driven away by Achish, the Philistian king at Gath, David took refuge in the cave Adullam, where his family joined him. The cave *Adullam* is not to be sought for in the neighbourhood of Bethlehem, as some have inferred from 2 Sam. xxiii. 13, 14, but near the town *Adullam*, which is classed in Josh. xv. 35 among the towns in the lowlands of Judah, and at the foot of the mountains; though it has not yet been traced with any certainty, as the caves of *Deir Dubban*, of which Van de Velde speaks, are not the only large caves on the western slope of the mountains of Judah. When his brethren and his father's house, *i.e.* the rest of his family, heard of his being there, they came down to him, evidently because they no longer felt themselves safe in Bethlehem from Saul's revenge. The cave Adullam cannot have been more than three hours from Bethlehem, as Socoh and Jarmuth, which were near to Adullam, were only three hours and a half from Jerusalem (see at Josh. xii. 15).—Ver. 2. There a large number of malcontents gathered together round David, viz. all who were in distress, and all who had creditors, and all who were embittered in spirit (bitter of soul), *i.e.* people who were dissatisfied with the general state of affairs or with the government of Saul,—about four hundred men, whose leader he became. David must in all probability have stayed there a considerable time. The number of those who went over to him soon amounted to six hundred men (xxiii. 13), who were for the most part brave and reckless, and who ripened into heroic men under the command of David during his long flight. A list of the bravest of them is given in 1 Chron. xii., with which compare 2 Sam. xxiii. 13 sqq. and 1 Chron. xi. 15 sqq. — Vers. 3-5. David proceeded thence to *Mizpeh* in Moab, and placed his parents in safety with the king of the Moabites. His ancestress Ruth was a Moabitess. *Mizpeh*: literally a watch-tower or mountain height commanding a very extensive prospect. Here it is probably a proper name, belonging to a mountain fastness on the high land, which bounded the Arboth Moab on the eastern side of the Dead Sea, most likely on the mountains of Abarim or Pisgah (Deut. xxxiv. 1), and which could easily be reached from the country round Bethlehem, by crossing the Jordan near the point where it entered the Dead Sea. As David came to the king of Moab, the Moabites had probably taken possession of the most southerly portion of the eastern lands of the Israelites; we may also infer this from the fact that, according to ch. xiv. 47, Saul had also made war upon Moab, for *Mizpeh Moab* is hardly to be sought for in the actual land of the Moabites, on the south side of the Arnon (Mojeb). יֵצֵא־נָא ... אִתְּכֶם, "*May my father and my mother go out with you.*" The construction of יָצָא with אֵת is a pregnant one: to go out of their home and stay with you (Moabites). "*Till I know what God will do to me.*" Being well assured of the justice of his cause, as contrasted with the insane persecutions of Saul, David confidently hoped that God would bring his flight to an end. His parents remained with the king of Moab as long as David was בַּמְּצוּדָה, *i.e.* upon the mountain height, or citadel. This can only refer to the place of refuge which David had found at Mizpeh Moab. For it is perfectly clear from ver. 5, where the prophet Gad calls upon David not to remain any longer בַּמְּצוּדָה, but to return to the land of Judah, that the expression cannot refer either to the cave Adullam, or to any other place of refuge in the neighbourhood of Bethlehem. The prophet *Gad* had probably come to David from Samuel's school of prophets; but whether he remained with David from that time forward to assist him with his counsel in his several undertakings, cannot be determined, on account of our want of information. In 1 Chron. xxi. 9 he is called David's seer. In the last year of David's reign he announced to him the punishment which would fall upon him from God on account of his sin in numbering the people (2 Sam. xxiv. 11 sqq.); and according to 1 Chron. xxix. 29 he also wrote the acts of David. In consequence of this admonition, David returned to Judah, and went into the wood *Hareth*, a woody region on the mountains of Judah, which is never mentioned again, and the situation of which is unknown. According to the counsels of God, David was not to seek for refuge outside the land; not only that he might not be estranged from his fatherland and the people of Israel, which would have been opposed to his calling to be the king of Israel, but also that he might learn to trust entirely in the Lord as his only refuge and fortress.

Vers. 6–23. MURDER OF THE PRIESTS BY SAUL.—Vers. 6 sqq. When Saul heard that David and the men with him *were known*, *i.e.* that information had been received as to their abode or hiding-place, he said to his servants when they were gathered round him, "*Hear*," etc. The words, "*and Saul was sitting at Gibeah under the tamarisk upon the height*," etc., show that what follows took place in a solemn conclave of all the servants of Saul, who were gathered round their king to deliberate upon the more important affairs of the kingdom. This sitting took place at Gibeah, the residence of Saul, and in the open air "*under the tamarisk.*" בָּרָמָה, *upon the height*, not "under a grove at Ramah" (*Luther*); for *Ramah* is an appellative, and בָּרָמָה, which belongs to תַּחַת הָאֵשֶׁל, is a more minute definition of the locality, which is indicated by the definite article (*the* tamarisk upon *the* height) as the well-known place where Saul's deliberative assemblies were held. From the king's address ("*hear, ye Benjaminites; will the son of Jesse also give you all fields and vineyards?*") we perceive that Saul had chosen his immediate attendants from the members of his own tribe, and had rewarded their services right royally.

גַּם־לְכֻלְּכֶם is placed first for the sake of emphasis, "*You Benjaminites also*," and not rather to Judahites, the members of his own tribe. The second לְכֻלְּכֶם (before יִתֵּן) is not a dative; but ל merely serves to give greater prominence to the object which is placed at the head of the clause: *As for all of you, will he make* (you: see Ewald, § 310, *a*).—Ver. 8. "*That you have all of you conspired against me, and no one informs me of it, since my son makes a covenant with the son of Jesse.*" בִּכְרֹת, lit. at the making of a covenant. Saul may possibly have heard something of the facts related in ch. xx. 12–17; at the same time, his words may merely refer to Jonathan's friendship with David, which was well known to him. וְאֵין־חֹלֶה, "*and no one of you is grieved on my account . . . that my son has set my servant* (David) *as a lier in wait against me*," *i.e.* to plot against my life, and wrest the throne to himself. We may see from this, that Saul was carried by his suspicions very far beyond the actual facts. "*As at this day:*" cf. Deut. viii. 18, etc.—Vers. 9, 10. The Edomite Doeg could not refrain from yielding to this appeal, and telling Saul what he had seen when staying at Nob; namely, that Ahimelech had inquired of God for David, and given him food as well as Goliath's sword. For the fact itself, see ch. xxi. 1–10, where there is no reference indeed to his inquiring of God; though it certainly took place, as Ahimelech (ver. 15) does not disclaim it. Doeg is here designated נִצָּב, "*the superintendent of Saul's servants*," so that apparently he had been invested with the office of marshal of the court.—Vers. 11 sqq. On receiving this information, Saul immediately summoned the priest Ahimelech and "*all his father's house*," *i.e.* the whole priesthood, to Nob, to answer for what they had done. To Saul's appeal, "*Why have ye conspired against me, thou and the son of Jesse, by giving him bread?*" Ahimelech, who was not conscious of any such crime, since David had come to him with a false pretext, and the priest had probably but very little knowledge of what took place at court, replied both calmly and worthily (ver. 14): "*And who of all thy servants is so faithful* (proved, attested, as in Num. xii. 7) *as David, and son-in-law of the king, and having access to thy private audience, and honoured in thy house?*" The true explanation of סָר אֶל־מִשְׁמַעְתֶּךָ may be gathered from a comparison of 2 Sam. xxiii. 23 and 1 Chron. xi. 25, where מִשְׁמַעַת occurs again, as the context clearly shows, in the sense of a privy councillor of the king, who hears his personal revelations and converses with him about them, so that it corresponds to our "*audience.*" סוּר, *lit.* to turn aside from the way, to go in to any one, or to look after anything (Ex. iii. 3; Ruth iv. 1, etc.); hence in the passage before us "*to have access*," to be attached to a person. This is the explanation given by Gesenius and most of the modern expositors, whereas the early translators entirely misunderstood the passage, though they have given the meaning correctly enough at 2 Sam. xxiii. 23. But if this was the relation in which David stood to Saul,—and he had really done so for a long time,—there was nothing wrong in what the high priest had done for him; but he had acted according to the best of his knowledge, and quite conscientiously as a faithful subject of the king. Ahimelech then added still further (ver 15): "*Did I then begin to inquire of God for him this day?*" *i.e.* was it the first time that I had obtained the decision of God for David concerning important enterprises, which he had to carry out in the service of the king? "*Far be from me,*" *sc.* any conspiracy against the king, like that of which I am accused. "*Let not the king lay it as a burden upon thy servant, my whole father's house* (the omission of the *cop.* ו before בְּכָל־בֵּית may be accounted for from the excitement of the speaker); *for thy servant knows not the least of all this.*" בְּכָל־זֹאת, of all that Saul had charged him with.—Vers. 16, 17. Notwithstanding this truthful assertion of his innocence, Saul pronounced sentence of death, not only upon the high priest, but upon all the priests at Nob, and commanded his רָצִים, "*runners,*" *i.e.* halberdiers, to put the priests to death, because, as he declared in his wrath, "*their hand is with David* (*i.e.* because they side with David), *and because they knew that he fled and did not tell me.*" Instead of the *Chethibh* וְאָזְנוּ, it is probably more correct to read אָזְנִי, according to the *Keri*, although the *Chethibh* may be accounted for if necessary from a sudden transition from a direct to an indirect form of address: "*and* (as he said) *had not told him.*" This sentence was so cruel, and so nearly bordering upon madness, that the halberdiers would not carry it out, but refused to lay hands upon "*the priests of Jehovah.*"—Ver. 18. Saul then commanded Doeg to cut down the priests, and he at once performed the bloody deed. On the expression "*wearing the linen ephod*," compare the remarks at ch. ii. 18. The allusion to the priestly clothing, like the repetition of the expression "*priests of Jehovah*," serves to bring out into its true light the crime of the bloodthirsty Saul and his executioner Doeg. The very dress which the priests wore, as the consecrated servants of Jehovah, ought to have made them shrink from the commission of such a murder.—Ver. 19. But not content with even this revenge, Saul had the whole city of Nob destroyed, like a city that was laid under the ban (*vid.* Deut. xiii. 13 sqq.). So completely did Saul identify his private revenge with the cause of Jehovah, that he avenged a supposed conspiracy against his own person as treason against Jehovah the God-king.—Vers. 20–23. The only one of the whole body of priests who escaped this bloody death was a son of Ahimelech, named Abiathar, who "*fled after David*," *i.e.* to David the fugitive, and informed him of the barbarous vengeance which Saul had taken upon the priests of the Lord. Then David recognised and confessed his guilt. "*I knew that day that the Edomite Doeg was there, that he* (*i.e.* that as the Edomite Doeg was there, he) *would tell Saul: I am the cause of all the souls of thy father's house,*" *i.e.* of their death. סָבַב is used here in the sense of being the cause of a thing, which is one of the meanings of the verb in the Arabic and Talmudic (*vid.* Ges. *Lex. s.v.*). "*Stay with me, fear not; for he who seeks my life seeks thy life: for thou art safe with me.*" The abstract *mishmereth*, protection, keeping (Ex. xii. 6, xvi. 33, 34), is used for the concrete, in the sense of protected, well kept. The thought is the following: As no other is seeking thy life than Saul, who also wants to kill me, thou mayest stay with me without fear, as I am sure of divine protection. David spoke thus in the firm belief that the Lord would deliver him from his foe, and give him the kingdom. The action of Saul, which had just been reported to him, could only strengthen him in this belief, as it was a sign of the growing hardness of Saul, which must accelerate his destruction.

DAVID DELIVERS KEILAH. HE IS BETRAYED BY THE ZIPHITES, AND MARVELLOUSLY SAVED FROM SAUL IN THE DESERT OF MAON.—CHAP. XXIII.

The following events show how, on the one hand, the Lord gave pledges to His servant David that he would eventually become king, but yet on the other hand plunged him into deeper and deeper trouble, that He might refine him and train him to be a king after His own heart. Saul's rage against the priests at Nob not only drove the high priest into David's camp, but procured for David the help of the "light and right" of the high priest in all his undertakings. Moreover, after the prophet Gad had called David back to Judah, an attack of the Philistines upon Keilah furnished him with the opportunity to show himself to the people as their deliverer. And although this enterprise of his exposed him to fresh persecutions on the part of Saul, who was thirsting for revenge, he experienced in connection therewith not only the renewal of Jonathan's friendship on this occasion, but a marvellous interposition on the part of the faithful covenant God.

Vers. 1-14. RESCUE OF KEILAH.—After his return to the mountains of Judah, David received intelligence that Philistines, *i.e.* a marauding company of these enemies of Israel, were fighting against Keilah, and plundering the threshing-floors, upon which the corn that had been reaped was lying ready for threshing. *Keilah* belonged to the towns of the lowlands of Judah (Josh. xv. 44); and although it has not yet been discovered, was certainly very close to the Philistian frontier.— Ver. 2. After receiving this information, David inquired of the Lord (through the Urim and Thummim of the high priest) whether he should go and smite these Philistines, and received an affirmative answer.—Vers. 3-5. But his men said to him, "*Behold, here in Judah we are in fear* (*i.e.* are not safe from Saul's pursuit); *how shall we go to Keilah against the ranks of the Philistines?*" In order, therefore, to infuse courage into them, he inquired of the Lord again, and received the assurance from God, "*I will give the Philistines into thy hand.*" He then proceeded with his men, fought against the Philistines, drove off their cattle, inflicted a severe defeat upon them, and thus delivered the inhabitants of Keilah. In ver. 6 a supplementary remark is added in explanation of the expression "*inquired of the Lord*," to the effect that, when Abiathar fled to David to Keilah, the ephod had come to him. The words "*to David to Keilah*" are not to be understood as signifying that Abiathar did not come to David till he was in Keilah, but that when he fled after David (ch. xxii. 20), he met with him as he was already preparing for the march to Keilah, and immediately proceeded with him thither. For whilst it is not stated in ch. xxii. 20 that Abiathar came to David in the wood of Hareth, but the place of meeting is left indefinite, the fact that David had already inquired of Jehovah (*i.e.* through the oracle of the high priest) with reference to the march to Keilah, compels us to assume that Abiathar had come to him before he left the mountains for Keilah. So that the brief expression "to David to Keilah," which is left indefinite because of its brevity, must be interpreted in accordance with this fact.—Vers. 7-9. As soon as Saul received intelligence of David's march to Keilah, he said, "*God has rejected him* (and delivered him) *into my hand.*" נִכַּר does not mean simply to look at, but also to find strange, and treat as strange, and then absolutely *to reject* (Jer. xix. 4, as in the Arabic in the fourth conjugation). This is the meaning here, where the construction with בְּיָדִי is to be understood as a pregnant expression : "*rejected and delivered into my hand*" (*vid. Ges. Lex. s. v.*). The early translators have rendered it quite correctly according to the sense מָכַר, πέπρακεν, *tradidit*, without there being any reason to suppose that they read מָכַר instead of נִכַּר. "*For he hath shut himself in, to come* (= coming, or by coming) *into a city with gates and bolts.*"— Ver. 8. He therefore called all the people (*i.e.* men of war) together to war, to go down to Keilah, and to besiege David and his men.—Vers. 9 sqq. But David heard that Saul was *preparing mischief against him* (*lit.* forging, הֶחֱרִישׁ, from חָרַשׁ : Prov. iii. 29, vi. 14, etc.), and he inquired through the oracle of the high priest whether the inhabitants of Keilah would deliver him up to Saul, and whether Saul would come down ; and as both questions were answered in the affirmative, he departed from the city with his six hundred men, before Saul carried out his plan. It is evident from vers. 9-12, that when the will of God was sought through the Urim and Thummim, the person making the inquiry placed the matter before God in prayer, and received an answer; but always to *one* particular question. For when David had asked the two questions given in ver. 11, he received the answer to the second question only, and had to ask the first again (ver. 12).—Ver. 13. " *They went whithersoever they could go*" (lit. " they wandered about where they wandered about"), *i.e.* wherever they could go without danger. —Ver. 14. David retreated into the desert (of Judah), to the mountain heights (that were to be found there), and remained on the mountains in the desert of Ziph. The "*desert of Judah*" is the desert tract between the mountains of Judah and the Dead Sea, in its whole extent, from the northern boundary of the tribe of Judah to the Wady Fikreh in the south (see at Josh. xv. 61). Certain portions of this desert, however, received different names of their own, according to the names of different towns on the border of the mountains and desert. The desert of *Ziph* was that portion of the desert of Judah which was near to and surrounded the town of *Ziph*, the name of which has been retained in the ruins of *Tell Zif*, an hour and three-quarters to the south-east of Hebron (see at Josh. xv. 55). —Ver. 14*b*. " *And Saul sought him all the days, but God delivered him not into his hand.*" This is a general remark, intended to introduce the accounts which follow, of the various attempts made by Saul to get David into his power. " *All the days,*" *i.e.* as long as Saul lived.

Vers. 15–28. DAVID IN THE DESERTS OF ZIPH AND MAON. —The history of David's persecution by Saul is introduced in vers. 15–18, with the account of an attempt made by the noble-minded prince Jonathan, in a private interview with his friend David, to renew his bond of friendship with him, and strengthen David by his friendly words for the sufferings that yet awaited him. Vers. 15, 16 are to be connected together so as to form one period: " *When David saw that Saul was come out . . . and David was in the desert of Ziph, Jonathan rose up and went to David into the wood.*" חֹרְשָׁה, from חֹרֶשׁ, with ה paragogic, signifies a wood or thicket; here, however, it is probably a proper name for a district in the desert of Ziph that was overgrown with wood or bushes, and where David was stopping at that time. " There is no trace of this wood now. The land lost its ornament of trees centuries ago through the desolating hand of man" (v. de Velde). "*And strengthened his hand in God,*" *i.e.* strengthened his heart, not by supplies, or by money, or any subsidy of that kind, but by consolation drawn from his innocence, and the promises of God (*vid.* Judg. ix. 24 ; Jer. xxiii. 14). "*Fear not,*" said Jonathan to him, "*for the hand of Saul my father will not reach thee ; and thou wilt become king over Israel, and I will be the second to thee ; and Saul my father also knows that it is so.*" Even though Jonathan had heard nothing from David about his anointing, he could learn from David's course thus far, and from his own father's conduct, that David would not be overcome, but would possess the sovereignty after the death of Saul. Jonathan expresses here, as his firm conviction, what he has intimated once before, in ch. xx. 13 sqq.; and with the most loving self-denial entreats David, when he shall be king, to let him occupy the second place in the kingdom. It by no means follows from the last words ("*Saul my father knoweth*"), that Saul had received distinct information concerning the anointing of David, and his divine calling to be king. The words merely contain the thought, he also sees that it will come. The assurance of this must have forced itself involuntarily upon the mind of Saul, both from his own rejection, as foretold by Samuel, and also from the marvellous success of David in all his undertakings.—Ver. 18. After these encouraging words, they two made a covenant before Jehovah : *i.e.* they renewed the covenant which they had already made by another solemn oath ; after which Jonathan returned home, but David remained in the wood.

The *treachery of the Ziphites* forms a striking contrast to Jonathan's treatment of David. They went up to Gibeah to betray to Saul the fact that David was concealed in the wood upon their mountain heights, and indeed "*upon the hill Hachilah, which lies to the south of the waste.*" The hill of *Ziph* is a flattened hill standing by itself, of about a hundred feet in height. " There is no spot from which you can obtain a better view of David's wanderings backwards and forwards in the desert than from the hill of *Ziph*, which affords a true panorama. The Ziphites could see David and his men moving to and fro in the mountains of the desert of *Ziph*, and could also perceive how he showed himself in the distance upon the hill *Hachilah* on the south side of *Ziph* (which lies to the right by the desert); whereupon they sent as quickly as possible to Saul, and betrayed to him the hiding-place of his enemy" (v. de Velde, ii. pp. 104–5). *Jeshimon* does not refer here to the waste land on the north-eastern coast of the Dead Sea, as in Num. xxi. 20, xxiii. 28, but to the western side of that sea, which is also desert.—Ver. 20 reads literally thus: "*And now, according to all the desire of thy soul, O king, to come down* (from Gibeah, which stood upon higher ground), *come down, and it is in us to deliver him* (David) *into the hand of the king.*" —Ver. 21. For this treachery Saul blessed them: "*Be blessed of the Lord, that ye have compassion upon me.*" In his evil conscience he suspected David of seeking to become his murderer, and therefore thanked God in his delusion that the Ziphites had had compassion upon him, and shown him David's hiding-place.—Ver. 22. In his anxiety, however, lest David should escape him after all, he charged them, "*Go, and give still further heed* (הָכִין without בֵל, as in Judg. xii. 6), *and reconnoitre and look at his place where his foot cometh* (this simply serves as a more precise definition of the pronominal suffix in מְקוֹמוֹ, his place), *who hath seen him there* (*sc.* let them inquire into this, that they may not be deceived by uncertain or false reports): *for it is told me that he dealeth very subtilly.*"—Ver. 23. They were to search him out in every corner (the object to רְאוּ must be supplied from the context). "*And come ye again to me with the certainty* (*i.e.* when you have got some certain intelligence concerning his hiding-place), *that I may go with you; and if he is in the land, I will search him out among all the thousands* (*i.e.* families) *of Judah.*"—Ver. 24. With this answer the Ziphites arose and "*went to Ziph before Saul*" (who would speedily follow with his warriors); but David had gone farther in the meantime, and was with his men "*in the desert of Maon, in the steppe to the south of the wilderness.*" Maon, now *Maïn*, is about three hours and three-quarters s.s.e. of Hebron (see at Josh. xv. 55), and therefore only two hours from Ziph, from which it is visible. "The table-land appears to terminate here; nevertheless the principal ridge of the southern mountains runs for a considerable distance towards the south-west, whereas towards the south-east the land falls off more and more into a lower table-land." This is the *Arabah* or steppe on the right of the wilderness (v. de Velde, ii. pp. 107-8).—Ver. 25. Having been informed of the arrival of Saul and his men (warriors), David went down the rock, and remained in the desert of Maon. *"The rock"* is probably the conical mountain of *Main* (*Maon*), the top of which is now surrounded with ruins, probably remains of a tower (Robinson, *Pal.* ii. p. 194), as the rock from which David came down can only have been the mountain (ver. 26), along one side of which David went with his men whilst Saul and his warriors went on the other, namely when Saul pursued him into the desert of Maon.—Vers. 26, 27. *"And David was anxiously concerned to escape from Saul, and Saul and his men were encircling David and his men to seize them; but a messenger came to Saul. . . . Then Saul turned from pursuing David."* The two clauses, "for Saul and his men" (ver. 26b), and "there came a messenger" (ver. 27), are the circumstantial clauses by which the situation is more clearly defined: the apodosis to וַיְהִי דָוִד does not follow till וַיָּשָׁב in ver. 28. The apodosis cannot begin with וּמַלְאָךְ, because the verb does not stand at the head. David had thus almost inextricably fallen into the hands of Saul; but God saved him by the fact that at that very moment a messenger arrived with the intelligence, "Hasten and go (come), for Philistines have fallen into the land," and thus called Saul away from any further pursuit of David.—Ver. 28. From this occurrence the place received the name of *Sela-hammahlekoth,* "*rock of smoothnesses,*" *i.e.* of slipping away or escaping, from חָלַק, in the sense of being smooth. This explanation is at any rate better supported than "rock of divisions, *i.e.* the rock at which Saul and David were separated" (Clericus), since חָלַק does not mean to separate.

DAVID SPARES SAUL IN THE CAVE.—CHAP. XXIV.

Vers. 1-8. Whilst Saul had gone against the Philistines, David left this dangerous place, and went to the mountain heights of *Engedi, i.e.* the present *Ain-jidy* (goat-fountain), in the middle of the western coast of the Dead Sea (see at Josh. xv. 62), which he could reach from Maon in six or seven hours. The soil of the neighbourhood consists entirely of limestone; but the rocks contain a considerable admixture of chalk and flint. Round about there rise bare conical mountains, and even ridges of from two to four hundred feet in height, which mostly run down to the sea. The steep mountains are intersected by wadys running down in deep ravines to the sea. " On all sides the country is full of caverns, which might then serve as lurking-places for David and his men, as they do for outlaws at the present day" (Rob. *Pal.* p. 203).—Vers. 1, 2. When Saul had returned from his march against the Philistines, and was informed of this, he set out thither with three thousand picked men to search for David and his men in the wild-goat rocks. The expression *" rocks of the wild goats "* is probably not a proper name for some particular rocks, but a general term applied to the rocks of that locality on account of the number of wild goats and chamois that were to be found in all that region, as mountain goats are still (Rob. *Pal.* ii. p. 204). —Ver. 3. When Saul came to the sheep-folds by the way, where there was a cave, he entered it to cover his feet, whilst David and his men sat behind in the cave. V. de Velde (*R.* ii. p. 74) supposes the place, where the sheep-folds by the roadside were, to have been the Wady *Chareitun*, on the south-west of the Frank mountain, and to the north-east of Tekoah, a very desolate and inaccessible valley. " Rocky, precipitous walls, which rise up one above another for many hundred feet, form the sides of this defile. Stone upon stone, and cliff above cliff, without any sign of being habitable, or of being capable of affording even a halting-place to anything but wild goats." Near the ruins of the village of *Chareitun*, hardly five minutes' walk to the east, there is a large cave or chamber in the rock, with a very narrow entrance entirely concealed by stones, and with many side vaults in which the deepest darkness reigns, at least to any one who has just entered the limestone vaults from the dazzling light of day. It may be argued in favour of the conjecture that this is the cave which Saul entered, and at the back of which David and his men were concealed, that this cave is on the road from Bethlehem to Ain-jidy, and one of the largest caves in that district, if not the largest of all, and that, according to Pococke (*Beschr. des Morgenl.* ii. p. 61), the Franks call it a labyrinth, the Arabs *Elmauma*, *i.e.* hiding-place, whilst the latter relate how at one time thirty thousand people hid themselves in it " to escape an evil wind," in all probability the simoom. . The only difficulty connected with this supposition is the distance from Ain-jidy, namely about four or five German miles (fifteen or twenty English), and the nearness of Tekoah, according to which it belongs to the desert of Tekoah rather than to that of Engedi. *"To cover his feet"* is a euphemism according to most of the ancient versions, as in Judg. iii. 24, for performing the necessities of nature, as it is a custom in the East to cover the feet. It does not mean "to sleep," as it is rendered in this passage in the *Peschito*, and also by Michaelis and others; for although what follows may seem to favour this, there is apparently no reason why any such euphemistic expression should have been chosen for sleep. "*The sides of the cave:*" *i.e.* the outermost or farthest sides. —Ver. 4. Then David's men said to him, "*See, this is the day of which Jehovah hath said to thee, Behold, I give thine enemy into thy hand, and do to him what seemeth good to thee.*" Although these words might refer to some divine oracle which David had received through a prophet, Gad for example, what follows clearly shows that David had received no such oracle; and the meaning of his men was simply this, " Behold, to-day is the day when God is saying to thee:" that is to say, the speakers regarded the leadings of providence by which Saul had been brought into David's power as a divine intimation to David himself to take this opportunity of slaying his deadly enemy, and called this intimation a word of Jehovah. *David then rose up, and cut off the edge of Saul's cloak privily.* Saul had probably laid the *meil* on one side, which rendered it possible for David to cut off a piece of it unobserved.—Ver. 5. But *his heart smote him* after he had done it; *i.e.* his conscience reproached him, because he regarded this as an injury done to the king himself.—Ver. 6. With all the greater firmness, therefore, did he repel the suggestions of his men: "*Far be it to me from Jehovah* (on Jehovah's account: see at Josh. xxii. 29), *that* (אִם, a particle denoting an oath) *I should do such a thing to my lord, the anointed of Jehovah, to stretch out my hand against him.*" These words of David show clearly enough that no word of Jehovah had come to him to do as he liked with Saul.—Ver. 7. Thus he kept back his people with words (שִׁסַּע, *verbis dilacere*), and did not allow them to rise up against Saul, *sc.* to slay him.

Vers. 8–16. But when Saul had gone out of the cave, David

went out, and called, "*My lord king*," that when the king looked round he might expostulate with him, with the deepest reverence, but yet with earnest words, that should sharpen his conscience as to the unfounded nature of his suspicion and the injustice of his persecution. "*Why dost thou hearken to words of men, who say, Behold, David seeketh thy hurt? Behold, this day thine eyes have seen that Jehovah hath given thee to-day into my hand in the cave, and they said* (אָמַר, thought) *to kill thee, and I spared thee:*" lit. it (mine eye) spared thee (cf. Gen. xlv. 20, Deut. vii. 16, etc., which show that עֵינִי is to be supplied).— Ver. 11. To confirm what he said, he then showed him the lappet of his coat which he had cut off, and said, "*My father, see.*" In these words there is an expression of the childlike reverence and affection which David cherished towards the anointed of the Lord. "*For that I cut off the lappet and did not kill thee, learn and see* (from this) *that* (there is) *not evil in my hand* (*i.e.* that I do not go about for the purpose of injury and crime), *and that I have not sinned against thee, as thou nevertheless layest wait for my soul to destroy it.*"—Vers. 12, 13. After he had proved to the king in this conclusive manner that he had no reason whatever for seeking his life, he invoked the Lord as judge between him and his adversary: "*Jehovah will avenge me upon thee, but my hand will not be against thee. As the proverb of the ancients* (הַקַּדְמֹנִי is used collectively) *says, Evil proceedeth from the evil, but my hand shall not be upon thee.*" The meaning is this: Only a wicked man could wish to avenge himself; I do not.—Ver. 14. And even if he should wish to attack the king, he did not possess the power. This thought introduces ver. 14: "*After whom is the king of Israel gone out? After whom dost thou pursue? A dead dog, a single flea.*" By these similes David meant to describe himself as a perfectly harmless and insignificant man, of whom Saul had no occasion to be afraid, and whom the king of Israel ought to think it beneath his dignity to pursue. A dead dog cannot bite or hurt, and is an object about which a king ought not to trouble himself (cf. 2 Sam. ix. 8 and xvi. 9, where the idea of something contemptible is included). The point of comparison with a flea is the insignificance of such an animal (cf. ch. xxvi. 20).—Ver. 15. As Saul had therefore no good ground for persecuting David, the latter could very calmly commit his cause to the Lord God, that He might decide it as judge, and deliver him out of the hand of Saul : " *Let Him look at it, and conduct my cause*," etc.

Vers. 16–22 These words made an impression upon Saul. David's conduct went to his heart, so that he wept aloud, and confessed to him : " *Thou art more righteous than I, for thou hast shown me good, and I* (have shown) *thee evil;* and thou hast given me a proof of this to-day."—Ver. 19. " *If a man meet with his enemy, will he send him* (let him go) *in peace?*" This sentence is to be regarded as a question, which requires a negative reply, and expresses the thought: When a man meets with an enemy, he does not generally let him escape without injury. But thou hast acted very differently towards me. This thought is easily supplied from the context, and what follows attaches itself to this : " *The Lord repay thee good for what thou hast done to me this day.*"—Vers. 20, 21. This wish was expressed in perfect sincerity. David's behaviour towards him had conquered for the moment the evil demon of his heart, and completely altered his feelings. In this better state of mind he felt impelled even to give utterance to these words, " *I know that thou wilt be king, and the sovereignty will have perpetuity in thy hand.*" Saul could not prevent this conviction from forcing itself upon him, after his own rejection and the failure of all that he attempted against David ; and it was this which drove him to persecute David whenever the evil spirit had the upper hand in his soul. But now that better feelings had arisen in his mind, he uttered it without envy, and merely asked David to promise on oath that he would not cut off his descendants after his death, and seek to exterminate his name from his father's house. A name is exterminated when the whole of the descendants are destroyed,—a thing of frequent occurrence in the East in connection with a change of dynasties, and one which occurred again and again even in the kingdom of the ten tribes (*vid.* 1 Kings xv. 28 sqq., xvi. 11 sqq. ; 2 Kings x.). —Ver. 22. When David had sworn this, Saul returned home. But David remained upon the mountain heights, because he did not regard the passing change in Saul's feelings as likely to continue. הַמְּצוּדָה (translated " *the hold*") is used here to denote the mountainous part of the desert of Judah. It is different in ch. xxii. 5.

DEATH OF SAMUEL. NABAL AND ABIGAIL.—CHAP. XXV.

Ver. 1. The *death of Samuel* is inserted here, because it occurred at that time. The fact that all Israel assembled together to his burial, and lamented him, *i.e.* mourned for him, was a sign that his labours as a prophet were recognised by the whole nation as a blessing for Israel. Since the days of Moses and Joshua, no man had arisen to whom the covenant nation owed so much as to Samuel, who has been justly called the reformer and restorer of the theocracy. They buried him "*in his house at Ramah.*" The expression "his house" does not mean his burial-place or family tomb, nor his native place, but the house in which he lived, with the court belonging to it, where Samuel was placed in a tomb erected especially for him. After the death of Samuel, David went down into the desert of *Paran*, *i.e.* into the northern portion of the desert of Arabia, which stretches up to the mountains of Judah (see at Num. x. 12); most likely for no other reason than because he could no longer find sufficient means of subsistence for himself and his six hundred men in the desert of Judah.

Vers. 2–44. The following history of *Nabal's* folly, and of the wise and generous behaviour of his pious and intelligent wife Abigail towards David, shows how Jehovah watched over His servant David, and not only preserved him from an act of passionate excitement, which might have endangered his calling to be king of Israel, but turned the trouble into which he had been brought into a source of prosperity and salvation.

Vers. 2–13. At *Maon*, *i.e.* Main or the mountains of Judah (see at Josh. xv. 55), there lived a rich man (גָּדוֹל, *great* through property and riches), who had his establishment at *Carmel*. מַעֲשֶׂה, work, occupation, then establishment, possessions (*vid.* Ex. xxiii. 16). *Carmel* is not the promontory of that name (Thenius), but the present *Kurmul* on the mountains of Judah, scarcely half an hour's journey to the north-west of Maon (see at Josh. xv. 55). This man possessed three thousand sheep and a thousand goats, and was at the sheep-shearing at Carmel. His name was *Nabal* (*i.e.* fool): this was hardly his proper name, but was a surname by which he was popularly designated on account of his folly. His wife *Abigail* was "*of good understanding,*" *i.e.* intelligent, "*and of beautiful figure;*"

but the husband was "*harsh and evil in his doings.*" He sprang from the family of *Caleb*. This is the rendering adopted by the Chaldee and Vulgate, according to the *Keri* כָּלִבִּי. The *Chethibh* is to be read כְּלִבּוֹ, "according to his heart;" though the LXX. (ἄνθρωπος κυνικός) and Josephus, as well as the Arabic and Syriac, derive it from כֶּלֶב, and understand it as referring to the dog-like, or shameless, character of the man.—Vers. 4, 5. When David heard in the desert (cf. ver. 1) that Nabal was shearing his sheep, which was generally accompanied with a festal meal (see at Gen. xxxviii. 12), he sent ten young men up to Carmel to him, and bade them wish him peace and prosperity in his name, and having reminded him of the friendly services rendered to his shepherds, solicit a present for himself and his people. שְׁאַל־לוֹ לְשָׁלוֹם, ask him after his welfare, *i.e.* greet him in a friendly manner (cf. Ex. xviii. 7). The word לֶחָי is obscure, and was interpreted by the early translators merely according to uncertain conjectures. The simplest explanation is apparently *in vitam*, long *life*, understood as a wish in the sense of "good fortune to you" (Luther, Maurer, etc.); although the word חַי in the singular can only be shown to have the meaning *life* in connection with the formula used in oaths, חֵי נַפְשְׁךָ, etc. But even if חַי must be taken as an adjective, it is impossible to explain לֶחָי in any other way than as an elliptical exclamation meaning "good fortune to the living man." For the idea that the word is to be connected with אֲמַרְתֶּם, "say to the living man," *i.e.* to the man if still alive, is overthrown by the fact that David had no doubt that Nabal was still living. The words which follow are also to be understood as a wish, "*May thou and thy house, and all that is thine, be well!*" After this salutation they were to proceed with the object of their visit: "*And now I have heard that thou hast sheep-shearers. Now thy shepherds have been with us; we have done them no harm* (הֶכְלַמְנוּם, as in Judg. xviii. 7: on the form, see Ges. § 53, 3, Anm. 6), *and nothing was missed by them so long as they were in Carmel.*" When living in the desert, David's men had associated with the shepherds of Nabal, rendered them various services, and protected them and their flocks against the southern inhabitants of the desert (the Bedouin Arabs); in return for which they may have given them food and information. Thus David proved himself a protector of his people even in his banishment. וְאָמַרְתֶּם, "*so may the young men* (those sent by David) *find favour in thine eyes! for we have come to a good* (*i.e.* a festive) *day. Give, I pray, what thy hand findeth* (*i.e.* as much as thou canst) *to thy servant, and to thy son David.*" With the expression "*thy son*" David claims Nabal's fatherly goodwill. So far as the fact itself is concerned, "on such a festive occasion near a town or village even in our own time, an Arab sheikh of the neighbouring desert would hardly fail to put in a word either in person or by message; and his message both in form and substance would be only the transcript of that of David" (Robinson, *Palestine*, p. 201).—Ver. 9. David's messengers delivered their message to Nabal, וַיָּנוּחוּ, "*and sat down,*" *sc.* awaiting the fulfilment of their request. The rendering given by the Chaldee (פָּסְקוּ, *cessaverunt loqui*) and the Vulgate (*siluerunt*) is less suitable, and cannot be philologically sustained. The Septuagint, on the other hand, has καὶ ἀνεπήδησε, "and he (Nabal) sprang up," as if the translators had read וַיָּקָם (*vid.* LXX. at ch. xx. 34). This rendering, according to which the word belongs to the following clause, gives a very appropriate sense, if only, supposing that וַיָּקָם really did stand in the text, the origin and general adoption of וַיָּנוּחוּ could in any way be explained.—Ver. 10. Nabal refused the petitioners in the most churlish manner: "*Who is David? who the son of Jesse?*" *i.e.* what have I to do with David? "*There be many servants now-a-days who tear away every one from his master.*" Thus, in order to justify his own covetousness, he set down David as a vagrant who had run away from his master.—Ver. 11. "*And I should take my bread and my water* (*i.e.* my food and drink), *and my cattle,* . . . *and give them to men whom I do not know whence they are?*" וְלָקַחְתִּי is a perfect with vav consec., and the whole sentence is to be taken as a question.—Vers. 12, 13. The messengers returned to David with this answer. The churlish reply could not fail to excite his anger. He therefore commanded his people to gird on the sword, and started with 400 men to take vengeance upon Nabal, whilst 200 remained behind with the things.

Vers. 14-31. However intelligible David's wrath may appear in the situation in which he was placed, it was not right before God, but a sudden burst of sinful passion, which was unseemly in a servant of God. By carrying out his intention, he would have sinned against the Lord and against His people. But the Lord preserved him from this sin by the fact that, just at the right time, Abigail, the intelligent and pious wife of Nabal, heard of the affair, and was able to appease the wrath of David by her immediate and kindly interposition.—Vers. 14, 15. Abigail heard from one of (Nabal's) servants what had taken place (בֵּרֵךְ, to wish any one prosperity and health, *i.e.* to salute, as in ch. xiii. 10; and עִיט, from עוּט, to speak wrath fully: on the form, see at ch. xv. 19 and xiv. 32), and also what had been praiseworthy in the behaviour of David's men towards Nabal's shepherds; how they had not only done them no injury, had not robbed them of anything, but had defended them all the while. "*They were a wall* (*i.e.* a firm protection) *round us by night and by day, as long as we were with them feeding the sheep,*" *i.e.* a wall of defence against attacks from the Bedouins living in the desert.—Ver. 17. "*And now,*" continued the servant, "*know and see what thou doest; for evil is determined* (cf. ch. xx. 9) *against our master and all his house: and he* (Nabal) *is a wicked man, that one cannot address him.*"—Vers. 18, 19. Then Abigail took as quickly as possible a bountiful present of provisions,—*two hundred loaves, two bottles of wine, five prepared* (*i.e.* slaughtered) *sheep* (עֲשׂוּוֹת, a rare form for עֲשׂוּיֹת: see Ewald, § 189, *a*), *five seahs* (an ephah and two-thirds) *of roasted grains* (*Kali:* see ch. xvii. 17), *a hundred* צִמֻּקִים (dried grapes, *i.e.* raisin-cakes: Ital. *simmuki*), *and two hundred fig-cakes* (consisting of pressed figs joined together),—and sent these gifts laden upon asses on before her to meet David, whilst she herself followed behind to appease his anger by coming to meet him in a friendly manner, but without saying a word to her husband about what she intended to do.—Ver. 20. When she came down riding upon the ass by a hidden part of the mountain, David and his men came to meet her, so that she lighted upon them. סֵתֶר הָהָר, a hidden part of the mountain, was probably a hollow between two peaks of a mountain. This would explain the use of the word יָרַד, to come down, with reference both to Abigail, who approached on the one side, and David, who came on the other. —Vers. 21 and 22 contain a circumstantial clause introduced parenthetically to explain what follows: but David had said,

Only for deception (i.e. for no other purpose than to be deceived in my expectation) *have I defended all that belongs to this man* (Nabal) *in the desert, so that nothing of his was missed,* and (for) *he hath repaid me evil for good. God do so to the enemies of David, if I leave,* etc.; *i.e.* " as truly as God will punish the enemies of David, so certainly will I not leave till the morning light, of all that belongeth to him, one that pisseth against the wall." This oath, in which the punishment of God is not called down upon the swearer himself (God do so *to me*), as it generally is, but upon the enemies of David, is analogous to that in ch. iii. 17, where punishment is threatened upon the person addressed, who is there made to swear; except that here, as the oath could not be uttered in the ears of the person addressed, upon whom it was to fall, the enemies generally are mentioned instead of "*to thee.*" There is no doubt, therefore, as to the correctness of the text. The substance of this imprecation may be explained from the fact that David is so full of the consciousness of fighting and suffering for the cause of the kingdom of God, that he discerns in the insult heaped upon him by Nabal an act of hostility to the Lord and the cause of His kingdom. The phrase מַשְׁתִּין בְּקִיר, *mingens in parietem,* is only met with in passages which speak of the destruction of a family or household to the very last man (viz., besides this passage, 1 Kings xiv. 10, xvi. 11, xxi. 21 ; 2 Kings ix. 8), and neither refers primarily to dogs, as Ephraem Syrus, Juda ben Karish, and others maintain ; nor to the lowest class of men, as Winer, Maurer, and others imagine ; nor to little boys, as L. de Dieu, Gesenius, etc., suppose ; but, as we may see from the explanatory clause appended to 1 Kings xiv. 10, xxi. 21, 2 Kings ix. 8, to every male (*quemcumque masculi generis hominem : vid.* Bochart, *Hieroz.* i. pp. 776 sqq., and Rödiger on Ges. *Thes.* pp. 1397-8).—Ver. 23 is connected with ver. 20.

When Abigail saw David, she descended hastily from the ass, fell upon her face before him, bowed to the ground, and fell at his feet, saying, " *Upon me, me, my lord, be the guilt; allow thy handmaid to reveal the thing to thee.*" She takes the guilt upon herself, because she hopes that David will not avenge it upon her.—Ver. 25. She prayed that David would take no notice of Nabal, for he was what his name declared—*a fool, and folly in him;* but she (Abigail) had not seen the messengers of David. "The prudent woman uses a good argument; for a wise man should pardon a fool" (Seb. Schmidt). She then endeavours to bring David to a friendly state of mind by three arguments, introduced with וְעַתָּה (vers. 26, 27), before asking for forgiveness (ver. 28). She first of all pointed to the leadings of God, by which David had been kept from committing murder through her coming to meet him.[1] "*As truly as Jehovah liveth, and by the life of thy soul! yea, the Lord hath kept thee, that thou camest not into blood-guiltiness, and thy hand helped thee*" (*i.e.* and with thy hand thou didst procure thyself help). אֲשֶׁר, introducing her words, as in ch. xv. 20, *lit.* " as truly as thou livest, (so true is it) that," etc. In the second place, she points to the fact that God is the avenger of the wicked, by expressing the wish that all the enemies of David may become fools like Nabal; in connection with which it must be observed, in order to understand her words fully, that, according to the Old Testament representation, folly is a correlate of ungodliness, which inevitably brings down punishment.[2] The predicate to the sentence "*and they that seek evil to my lord*" must be supplied from the preceding words, viz. " *may they become just such fools.*"— Ver. 27. It is only in the third line that she finally mentions the present, but in such a manner that she does not offer it directly to David, but describes it as a gift for the men in his train. "*And now this blessing* (בְּרָכָה here and ch. xxx. 26, as in Gen. xxxiii. 11 : cf. ἡ εὐλογία, 2 Cor. ix. 5, 6), *which thine handmaid hath brought, let it be given to the young men in my lord's train*" (*lit.* " at the feet of :" cf. Ex. xi. 8 ; Judg. iv. 10, etc.).— Ver. 28. The shrewd and pious woman supports her prayer for

---

[1] "She founds her argument upon their meeting, which was so marvellously seasonable, that it might be easily and truly gathered from this fact that it had taken place through the providence of God; *i.e.* And now, because I meet thee so seasonably, do thou piously acknowledge with me the providence of God, which has so arranged all this, that innocent blood might not by chance be shed by thee."—*Seb. Schmidt.*

[2] Seb. Schmidt has justly observed, that "she reminds David of the promise of God. Not that she prophesies, but that she has gathered it from the general promises of the word of God. The promise referred to is, that whoever does good to his enemies, and takes no vengeance upon them, God himself will avenge him upon his enemies ; according to the saying, *Vengeance is mine, I will repay.* And this is what Abigail says : And now thine enemies shall be as Nabal."

forgiveness of the wrong, which she takes upon herself, by promises of the rich blessing with which the Lord would recompense David. She thereby gives such clear and distinct expression to her firm belief in the divine election of David as king of Israel, that her words almost amount to prophecy: "*For Jehovah will make my lord a lasting house* (cf. ch. ii. 35; and for the fact itself, 2 Sam. vii. 8 sqq., where the Lord confirms this pious wish by His own promises to David himself); *for my lord fighteth the wars of Jehovah* (*vid.* ch. xviii. 17), *and evil is not discovered in thee thy whole life long.*" רָעָה, evil, *i.e.* misfortune, mischief; for the thought that he might also be preserved from wrong-doing is not expressed till ver. 31. "*All thy days,*" *lit.* " from thy days," *i.e.* from the beginning of thy life.—Ver. 29. "*And should any one rise up to pursue thee, . . . the soul of my lord will be bound up in the bundle of the living with the Lord thy God.*" The metaphor is taken from the custom of binding up valuable things in a bundle, to prevent their being injured. The words do not refer primarily to eternal life with God in heaven, but only to the safe preservation of the righteous on this earth in the grace and fellowship of the Lord. But whoever is so hidden in the gracious fellowship of the Lord in this life, that no enemy can harm him or injure his life, the Lord will not allow to perish, even though temporal death should come, but will then receive him into eternal life. "*But the soul of thine enemies, He will hurl away in the cup of the sling.*" "*The cup* (*caph* : cf. Gen. xxxii. 26) *of the sling*" was the cavity in which the stone was placed for the purpose of hurling.—Vers. 30, 31. Abigail concluded her intercession with the assurance that the forgiveness of Nabal's act would be no occasion of anguish of heart to David when he should have become prince over Israel, on account of his having shed innocent blood and helped himself, and also with the hope that he would remember her. From the words, "*When Jehovah shall do to my lord according to all the good that He hath spoken concerning him, and shall make thee prince over Israel,*" it appears to follow that Abigail had received certain information of the anointing of David, and his designation to be the future king, probably through Samuel, or one of the pupils of the prophets. There is nothing to preclude this assumption, even if it cannot be historically sustained. Abigail manifests such an advance and maturity in the life of faith, as could only have been derived from intercourse with prophets. It is expressly stated with regard to Elijah and Elisha, that at certain times the pious assembled together around the prophets. What prevents us from assuming the same with regard to Samuel? The absence of any distinct testimony to that effect is amply compensated for by the brief, and for the most part casual, notices that are given of the influence which Samuel exerted upon all Israel.— Ver. 31 introduces the apodosis to ver. 30 : *So will this* (*i.e.* the forgiveness of Nabal's folly, for which she had prayed in ver. 28) *not be a stumbling-block* (*pukah:* anything in the road which causes a person to stagger) *and anguish of heart* (*i.e.* conscientious scruple) *to thee, and shedding innocent blood, and that my lord helps himself.* וְלִשְׁפֹּךְ וגו׳ is perfectly parallel to לְפוּקָה וגו׳, and cannot be taken as subordinate, as it is in the Vulgate, etc., in the sense of " that thou hast not shed blood innocently," etc. In this rendering not only is the *vav cop.* overlooked, but " not" is arbitrarily interpolated, to obtain a suitable sense, which the Vulgate rendering, *quod effuderis sanguinem innoxiam,* does not give. וְהֵיטִב is to be taken conditionally : " *and if Jehovah shall deal well with my lord,* then," etc.

Vers. 32–38. These words could not fail to appease David's wrath. In his reply he praised the Lord for having sent Abigail to meet him (ver. 32), and then congratulated Abigail upon her understanding and her actions, that she had kept him from bloodshed (ver. 33); otherwise he would certainly have carried out the revenge which he had resolved to take upon Nabal (ver. 34). וְאוּלָם is strongly adversative : *nevertheless.* מֵהָרַע, *inf. constr. Hiph.* of רָעַע. כִּי, ὅτι, introduces the substance of the affirmation, and is repeated before the oath : כִּי אִם . . . כִּי לוּלֵי, (that) *if thou hadst not,* etc., (that) *truly there would not have been left* (cf. 2 Sam. ii. 27). The very unusual form תְּבָאתִי, an imperfect with the termination of the perfect, might indeed possibly be a copyist's error for תָּבֹאִי (Olsh. *Gr.* pp. 452, 525), but in all probability it is only an intensified form of the second pers. fem. imperf., like תְּבוֹאָתָה (Deut. xxxiii. 16 ; cf. Ewald, § 191, *c*).—Ver. 35. David then received the gifts brought for him, and bade Abigail return to her house, with the assurance that he had granted her request for pardon. נָשָׂא פָנִים, as in Gen.

xix. 21, etc.—Ver. 36. When Abigail returned home, she found her husband *at a great feast, like a king's feast, very merry* (עָלָיו, "therewith," refers to מִשְׁתֶּה: cf. Prov. xxiii. 30), *and drunken above measure*, so that she told him nothing of what had occurred until the break of day.—Ver. 37. Then, "*when the wine had gone from Nabal*," *i.e.* when he had become sober, she related the matter to him; whereat he was so terrified, that he was smitten with a stroke. This is the meaning of the words, "*his heart died within him, and it became as stone.*" The cause of it was not his anger at the loss he had sustained, or merely his alarm at the danger to which he had been exposed, and which he did not believe to be over yet, but also his vexation that his wife should have made him humble himself in such a manner; for he is described as a hard, *i.e.* an unbending, self-willed man.—Ver. 38. About ten days later *the Lord smote him so that he died*, *i.e.* the Lord put an end to his life by a second stroke.

Vers. 39–44. When David heard of Nabal's death, he praised Jehovah that He had avenged his shame upon Nabal, and held him back from self-revenge. אֲשֶׁר רָב וגו׳, "*who hath pleaded the cause of my reproach* (the disgrace inflicted upon me) *against Nabal.*" "*Against Nabal*" does not belong to "*my reproach,*" but to "*pleaded the cause.*" The construction of רִיב with מִן is a pregnant one, to fight (and deliver) out of the power of a person (*vid.* Ps. xliii. 1); whereas here the fundamental idea is that of taking vengeance upon a person.— Ver. 40. He then sent messengers to Abigail, and conveyed to her his wish to marry her, to which she consented without hesitation. With deep reverence she said to the messengers (ver. 41), "*Behold, thy handmaid as servant* (*i.e.* is ready to become thy servant) *to wash the feet of the servants of my lord;*" *i.e.*, in the obsequious style of the East, "I am ready to perform the humblest possible services for thee."—Ver. 42. She then rose up hastily, and went after the messengers to David with five damsels in her train, and became his wife.— Ver. 43. The historian appends a few notices here concerning David's wives: "*And David had taken Ahinoam from Jezreel; thus they also both became his wives.*" The expression "*also*" points to David's marriage with Michal, the daughter of Saul (ch. xviii. 28). *Jezreel* is not the city of that name in the tribe of Issachar (Josh. xix. 18), but the one in the mountains of Judah (Josh. xv. 56).—Ver. 44. But Saul had taken his daughter Michal away from David, and given her to *Palti* of Gallim. *Palti* is called *Paltiel* in 2 Sam. iii. 15. According to Isa. x. 30, *Gallim* was a place between Gibeah of Saul and Jerusalem. Valentiner supposes it to be the hill to the south of *Tuleil el Phul* (Gibeah of Saul) called *Khirbet el Jisr*. After the death of Saul, however, David persuaded Ishbosheth to give him Michal back again (see 2 Sam. iii. 14 sqq.).

DAVID IS BETRAYED AGAIN BY THE ZIPHITES, AND SPARES SAUL A SECOND TIME.—CHAP. XXVI.

The repetition not only of the treachery of the Ziphites, but also of the sparing of Saul by David, furnishes no proof in itself that the account contained in this chapter is only another legend of the occurrences already related in ch. xxiii. 19-xxiv. 23. As the pursuit of David by Saul lasted for several years, in so small a district as the desert of Judah, there is nothing strange in the repetition of the same scenes. And the assertion made by Thenius, that "Saul would have been a moral monster, which he evidently was not, if he had pursued David with quiet deliberation, and through the medium of the same persons, and had sought his life again, after his own life had been so magnanimously spared by him," not only betrays a superficial acquaintance with the human heart, but is also founded upon the mere assertion, for which there is no proof, that Saul was *evidently* not so; and it is proved to be worthless by the fact, that after the first occasion on which his life was so magnanimously spared by David, he did not leave off seeking him up and down in the land, and that David was obliged to seek refuge with the Philistines in consequence, as may be seen from ch. xxvii., which Thenius himself assigns to the same source as ch. xxiv. The agreement between the two accounts reduces it entirely to outward and unessential things. It consists chiefly in the fact that the Ziphites came twice to Saul at Gibeah, and informed him that David was stopping in their neighbourhood, in the hill *Hachilah*, and also that Saul went out twice in pursuit of David with 3000 men. But the three thousand were the standing body of men that Saul had raised from the very beginning of his reign out of the whole number of those who were capable of bearing arms, for the purpose of carrying on his smaller wars (ch. xiii. 2); and the hill of *Hachilah* appears to have been a place in the desert of Judah peculiarly well adapted for the site of an encampment. On the other hand, all the details, as well as the final results of the two occurrences, differ entirely from one another. When David was betrayed the first time, he drew back into the desert of Maon before the advance of Saul; and being completely surrounded by Saul upon one of the mountains there, was only saved from being taken prisoner by the circumstance that Saul was compelled suddenly to relinquish the pursuit of David on account of the report that the Philistines had invaded the land (ch. xxiii. 25-28). But on the second occasion Saul encamped upon the hill of Hachilah, whilst David had drawn back into the adjoining desert, from which he crept secretly into Saul's encampment, and might, if he had chosen, have put his enemy to death (ch. xxvi. 3 sqq.). There is quite as much difference in the minuter details connected with the sparing of Saul. On the first occasion, Saul entered a cave in the desert of Engedi, whilst David and his men were concealed in the interior of the cave, without having the smallest suspicion that they were anywhere near (ch. xxiv. 2-4). The second time David went with Abishai into the encampment of Saul upon the hill of Hachilah, while the king and all his men were sleeping (ch. xxvi. 3, 5). It is true that on both occasions David's men told him that God had given his enemy into his hand; but the first time they added, Do to him what seemeth good in thy sight; and David cut off the lappet of Saul's coat, whereupon his conscience smote him, and he said, "Far be it from me to lay my hand upon the Lord's anointed" (ch. xxiv. 5-8). In the second instance, on the contrary, when David saw Saul in the distance lying by the carriage rampart and the army sleeping round him, he called to two of his heroes, Ahimelech and Abishai, to go with him into the camp of the sleeping foe, and then went thither with Abishai, who thereupon said to him, " God hath delivered thine enemy into thy hand: let me alone, that I may pierce him with the spear." But David rejected this proposal, and merely took away the spear and water-bowl that were at Saul's head (ch. xxvi. 6-12). And lastly, notwithstanding the fact that the words of David and replies of Saul agree in certain general thoughts, yet they differ entirely in the main. On the first occasion David showed the king that his life had been in his power, and yet he had spared him, to dispel the delusion that he was seeking his life (ch. xxiv. 10-16). On the second occasion he asked the king why he was pursuing him, and called to him to desist from his pursuit (ch. xxvi. 18 sqq.). But Saul was so affected the first time that he wept aloud, and openly declared that David would obtain the kingdom; and asked him to promise on oath, that when he did, he would not destroy his family (ch. xxiv. 17-23). The second time, on the contrary, he only declared that he had sinned and acted foolishly, and would do David no more harm, and that David would undertake and prevail; but he neither shed tears, nor brought himself to speak of David's ascending the throne, so that he was evidently much more hardened than before (ch. xxvi. 21-25). These decided differences prove clearly enough that the incident described in this chapter is not the same as the similar one mentioned in ch. xxiii. and xxiv., but belongs to a later date, when Saul's enmity and hardness had increased.

Vers. 1-12. The second betrayal of David by the Ziphites occurred after David had married Abigail at Carmel, and when he had already returned to the desert of Judah. On vers. 1 and 2 compare the explanations of ch. xxiii. 19 and xxiv. 3. Instead of "*before* (in the face of) *Jeshimon*" (*i.e.* the wilderness), we find the situation defined more precisely in ch. xxiii. 19, as "*to the right* (*i.e.* on the south) *of the wilderness*" (Jeshimon).—Vers. 3, 4. When David saw (*i.e.* perceived) in the desert that Saul was coming behind him, he sent out spies, and learned from them *that he certainly had come* (אֶל־נָכוֹן, for a certainty, as in ch. xxiii. 23).—Vers. 5 sqq. Upon the receipt of this information, David rose up with two attendants (mentioned in ver. 6) to reconnoitre the camp of Saul. When he saw the place where Saul and his general Abner were lying—Saul was lying *by the waggon rampart*, and the fighting men were encamped round about him—he said to Ahimelech and Abishai, "*Who will go down with me into the camp to Saul?*" Whereupon Abishai declared himself ready to do so; and they both went by night, and found Saul sleeping with all the people. *Ahimelech* the Hittite is never mentioned again; but *Abishai* the son of

Zeruiah, David's sister (1 Chron. ii. 16), and a brother of Joab, was afterwards a celebrated general of David, as was also his brother Joab (2 Sam. xvi. 9, xviii. 2, xxi. 17). Saul's spear was *pressed* (stuck) *into the ground at his head*, as a sign that the king was sleeping there, for the spear served Saul as a sceptre (cf. ch. xviii. 10).—Ver. 8. When Abishai exclaimed, "*God hath delivered thine enemy into thy hand: now will I pierce him with the spear into the ground with a stroke, and will give no second*" (sc. stroke: the Vulgate rendering gives the sense exactly: *et secundo non opus erit*, there will be no necessity for a second), David replied, "*Destroy him not; for who hath stretched out his hand against the anointed of the Lord, and remained unhurt?*" נִקָּה, as in Ex. xxi. 19, Num. v. 31. He then continued (in vers. 10, 11): "*As truly as Jehovah liveth, unless Jehovah smite him* (i.e. carry him off with a stroke; cf. ch. xxv. 38), *or his day cometh that he dies* (i.e. or he dies a natural death; 'his day' denoting the day of death, as in Job xiv. 6, xv. 32), *or he goes into battle and is carried off, far be it from me with Jehovah* (מֵיְהוָֹה, as in ch. xxiv. 7) *to stretch forth my hand against Jehovah's anointed*." The apodosis to ver. 10 commences with חָלִילָה, "far be it," or "the Lord forbid," in ver. 11. "*Take now the spear which is at his head, and the pitcher, and let us go*." —Ver. 12. They departed with these trophies, without any one waking up and seeing them, because they were all asleep, as a deep sleep from the Lord had fallen upon them. מְרַאֲשֹׁתֵי שָׁאוּל stands for מִמְּרַאֲשֹׁתֵי שׁ׳, "from the head of Saul," with מ dropped. The expression "*a deep sleep of Jehovah*," i.e. a deep sleep sent or inflicted by Jehovah, points to the fact that the Lord favoured David's enterprise.

Vers. 13–20. "*And David went over to the other side, and placed himself upon the top of the mountain afar off* (*the space between them was great*), *and cried to the people*," etc. Saul had probably encamped with his fighting men on the slope of the hill Hachilah, so that a valley separated him from the opposite hill, from which David had no doubt reconnoitred the camp and then *gone down* to it (ver. 6), and to which he returned after the deed was accomplished. The statement that this mountain was far off, so that there was a great space between David and Saul, not only favours the accuracy of the historical tradition, but shows that David reckoned far less now upon any change in the state of Saul's mind than he had done before, when he followed Saul without hesitation from the cave and called after him (ch. xxiv. 9), and that in fact he rather feared lest Saul should endeavour to get him into his power as soon as he woke from his sleep.—Ver. 14. David called out to Abner, whose duty it was as general to defend the life of his king. And Abner replied, " *Who art thou, who criest out to the king?*" *i.e.* offendest the king by thy shouting, and disturbest his rest.—Vers. 15, 16. David in return taunted Abner with having watched the king carelessly, and made himself chargeable with his death. "*For one of the people came to destroy thy lord the king.*" As a proof of this, he then showed him the spear and pitcher that he had taken away with him. רְאֵה is to be repeated in thought before אֶת־צַפַּחַת : "*look where the king's spear is; and* (look) *at the pitcher at his head,*" sc. where it is. These reproaches that were cast at Abner were intended to show to Saul, who might at any rate possibly hear, and in fact did hear, that David was the most faithful defender of his life, more faithful than his closest and most zealous servants.—Vers. 17, 18. When Saul heard David's voice (for he could hardly have seen David, as the occurrence took place before daybreak, at the latest when the day began to dawn), and David had made himself known to the king in reply to his inquiry, David said, " *Why doth my lord pursue his servant? for what have I done, and what evil is in my hand?*" He then gave him the well-meant advice, to seek reconciliation for his wrath against him, and not to bring upon himself the guilt of allowing David to find his death in a foreign land. The words, "*and now let my lord the king hear the saying of his servant,*" serve to indicate that what follows is important, and worthy of laying to heart. In his words, David supposes two cases as conceivable causes of Saul's hostility : (1) if Jehovah hath stirred thee up against me; (2) if men have done so. In the first case, he proposes as the best means of overcoming this instigation, that He (Jehovah) should smell an offering. The *Hiphil* יָרַח only means to smell, not to cause to smell. The subject is Jehovah. Smelling a sacrifice is an anthropomorphic term, used to denote the divine satisfaction (cf. Gen. viii. 21). The meaning of the words, "*let Jehovah smell sacrifice,*" is therefore, " let Saul appease the wrath of God by the presentation of acceptable sacrifices." What sacrifices they are which please God, is shown in Ps. li. 18, 19; and it is certainly not by accident merely that David uses the word *minchah*, the technical expression in the law for the blood less sacrifice, which sets forth the sanctification of life in good works. The thought to which David gives utterance here, namely, that God instigates a man to evil actions, is met with in other passages of the Old Testament. It not only lies at the foundation of the words of David in Ps. li. 6 (cf. Hengstenberg on *Psalms*), but is also clearly expressed in 2 Sam. xxiv. 1, where Jehovah instigates David to number the people, and where this instigation is described as a manifestation of the anger of God against Israel; and in 2 Sam. xvi. 10 sqq., where David says, with regard to Shimei, that God had bade him curse him. These passages also show that God only instigates those who have sinned against Him to evil deeds; and therefore that the instigation consists in the fact that God impels sinners to manifest the wickedness of their hearts in deeds, or furnishes the opportunity and occasion for the unfolding and practical manifestation of the evil desires of the heart, that the sinner may either be brought to the knowledge of his more evil ways and also to repentance, through the evil deed and its consequences, or, if the heart should be hardened still more by the evil deed, that it may become ripe for the judgment of death. The instigation of a sinner to evil is simply one peculiar way in which God, as a general rule, punishes sins through sinners; for God only instigates to evil actions such as have drawn down the wrath of God upon themselves in consequence of their sin. When David supposes the fact that Jehovah has instigated Saul against him, he acknowledges, implicitly at least, that he himself is a sinner, whom the Lord may be intending to punish, though without lessening Saul's wrong by this indirect confession.

The second supposition is: "*if, however, children of men*" (*sc* have instigated thee against me); in which case "*let them be cursed before the Lord; for they drive me now* (this day) *that I dare not attach myself to the inheritance of Jehovah* (*i.e.* the people of God), *saying, Go, serve other gods.*" The meaning is this: They have carried it so far now, that I am obliged to separate from the people of God, to fly from the land of the Lord, and, because far away from His sanctuary, to serve other gods The idea implied in the closing words was, that Jehovah could only be worshipped in Canaan, at the sanctuary consecrated to Him, because it was only there that He manifested himself to His people, and revealed His face or gracious presence (*vid.* Ps. xlii. 2, 3, lxxxiv. 11, cxliii. 6 sqq.). " We are not to understand that the enemies of David were actually accustomed to use these very words, but David was thinking of deeds rather than words" (Calvin).—Ver. 20. *" And now let not my blood fall to the earth far away from the face of the Lord,"* i.e. do not carry it so far as to compel me to perish in a foreign land. *" For the king of Israel has gone out to seek a single flea* (*vid.* ch. xxiv. 15), *as one hunts a partridge upon the mountains."* This last comparison does not of course refer to the first, so that " the object of comparison is compared again with something else," as Thenius supposes, but it refers rather to the whole of the previous clause. The king of Israel is pursuing something very trivial, and altogether unworthy of his pursuit, just as if one were hunting a partridge upon the mountains. " No one would think it worth his while to hunt a single partridge that had flown to the mountains, when they may be found in coveys in the fields" (Winer, *Bibl. R. W.* ii. p. 307). This comparison, therefore, does not presuppose that קֹרֵא must be a bird living upon the mountains, as Thenius maintains, so as to justify his altering the text according to the Septuagint. These words of David were perfectly well adapted to sharpen Saul's conscience, and induce him to desist from his enmity, if he still had an ear for the voice of truth.

Vers. 21-25. Moreover, Saul could not help confessing, *" I have sinned: return, my son David; I will do thee harm no more, because my life was precious in thine eyes that day."* A good intention, which he never carried out. " He declared that he would never do any more what he had already so often promised not to do again; and yet he did not fail to do it again and again. He ought rather to have taken refuge with God, and appealed to Him for grace, that he might not fall into such sins again; yea, he should have entreated David himself to pray for him" (*Berleb. Bible*). He adds still further, *" Behold, I have acted foolishly, and have gone sore astray;"* but yet he persists in this folly. " There is no sinner so hardened, but that God gives him now and then some rays of light, which show him all his error. But, alas! when they are awakened by such divine movings, it is only for a few moments; and such impulses are no sooner past, than they fall back again immediately into their former life, and forget all that they have promised."—Vers. 22, 23. David then bade the king send a servant to fetch back the spear and pitcher, and reminded him again of the recompense of God: "*Jehovah will recompense His righteousness and His faithfulness to the man into whose hand Jehovah hath given thee to-day; and* (for) *I would not stretch out my hand against the anointed of the Lord.*"—Ver. 24. "*Behold, as thy soul has been greatly esteemed in my eyes to-day, so will my soul be greatly esteemed in the eyes of Jehovah, that He will save me out of all tribulation.*" These words do not contain any "sounding of his own praises" (Thenius), but are merely the testimony of a good conscience before God in the presence of an enemy, who is indeed obliged to confess his wrong-doing, but who no longer feels or acknowledges his need of forgiveness. For even Saul's reply to these words in ver. 25 ("*Blessed art thou, my son David: thou wilt undertake, and also prevail:*" יָכֹל תּוּכָל, *lit.* to vanquish, *i.e.* to carry out what one undertakes) does not express any genuine goodwill towards David, but only an acknowledgment, forced upon him by this fresh experience of David's magnanimity, that God was blessing all his undertakings, so that he would prevail. Saul had no more thoughts of any real reconciliation with David. "*David went his way, and Saul turned to his place*" (cf. Num. xxiv. 25). Thus they parted, and never saw each other again. There is nothing said about Saul returning to his house, as there was when his life was first spared (ch. xxiv. 23). On the contrary, he does not seem to have given up pursuing David; for, according to ch. xxvii., David was obliged to take refuge in a foreign land, and carry out what he had described in ver. 19 as his greatest calamity.

DAVID AT ZIKLAG IN THE LAND OF THE PHILISTINES.—CHAP. XXVII.

In his despair of being able permanently to escape the plots of Saul in the land of Israel, David betook himself, with his attendants, to the neighbouring land of the Philistines, to king Achish of Gath, and received from him the town of Ziklag, which was assigned him at his own request as a dwelling-place (vers. 1-7). From this point he made attacks upon certain tribes on the southern frontier of Canaan which were hostile to Israel, but described them to Achish as attacks upon Judah and its dependencies, that he might still retain the protection of the Philistian chief (vers. 8-12). David had fled to Achish at Gath once before; but on that occasion he had been obliged to feign insanity in order to preserve his life, because he was recognised as the conqueror of Goliath. This act of David was not forgotten by the Philistines even now. But as David had been pursued by Saul for many years, Achish did not hesitate to give a place of refuge in his land to the fugitive who had been outlawed by the king of Israel, the arch-enemy of the Philistines, possibly with the hope that if a fresh war with Saul should break out, he should be able to reap some advantage from David's friendship.

Vers. 1-7. The result of the last affair with Saul, after his life had again been spared, could not fail to confirm David in his conviction that Saul would not desist from pursuing him, and that if he stayed any longer in the land, he would fall eventually into the hands of his enemy. With this conviction, he formed the following resolution: "*Now shall I be consumed one day by the hand of Saul: there is no good to me* (*i.e.* it will not be well with me if I remain in the land), *but* (כִּי after a negative) *I will flee into the land of the Philistines; so will Saul desist from me to seek me further* (*i.e.* give up seeking me) *in the whole of the territory of Israel, and I shall escape his hand.*"— Ver. 2. Accordingly he went over with the 600 men who were with him to Achish, the king of Gath. *Achish*, the son of *Maoch*, is in all probability the same person not only as the king *Achish* mentioned in ch. xxi. 11, but also as *Achish* the son of *Maachah* (1 Kings ii. 39), since *Maoch* and *Maachah* are certainly only different forms of the same name; and a fifty years' reign, which we should have in that case to ascribe to Achish, is not impossible.—Vers. 3, 4. Achish allotted dwelling-places in his capital, Gath, for David and his wives, and for all his retinue; and Saul desisted from any further pursuit of David when he was informed of his flight to Gath. The *Chethibh* ויסף is apparently only a copyist's error for יסף.— Vers. 5 sqq. In the capital of the kingdom, however, David felt cramped, and therefore entreated Achish to assign him one of the land (or provincial) towns to dwell in; whereupon he gave him *Ziklag* for that purpose. This town was given to the Simeonites in the time of Joshua (Josh. xix. 5), but was afterwards taken by the Philistines, probably not long before the time of David, and appears to have been left without inhabitants in consequence of this conquest. The exact situation, in the western part of the Negeb, has not been clearly ascertained (see at Josh. xv. 31). Achish appears to have given it to David. This is implied in the remark, " *Therefore Ziklag came to the kings of Judah* (*i.e.* became their property) *unto this day*."—Ver. 7. The statement that David remained a year and four months in the land of the Philistines, is a proof of the historical character of the whole narrative. The יָמִים before the "four months" signifies *a year;* strictly speaking, a term of days which amounted to a full year (as in Lev. xxv. 29: see also 1 Sam. i. 3, 20, ii. 19).

Vers. 8–12. From Ziklag David made an attack upon the Geshurites, Gerzites, and Amalekites, smote them without leaving a man alive, and returned with much booty. The occasion of this attack is not mentioned, as being a matter of indifference in relation to the chief object of the history; but it is no doubt to be sought for in plundering incursions made by these tribes into the land of Israel. For David would hardly have entered upon such a war in the situation in which he was placed at that time without some such occasion, seeing that it would be almost sure to bring him into suspicion with Achish, and endanger his safety. וַיַּעַל, " *he advanced*," the verb being used, as it frequently is, to denote the advance of an army against a people or town (see at Josh. viii. 1). At the same time, the tribes which he attacked may have had their seat upon the mountain plateau in the northern portion of the desert of Paran, so that David was obliged to march *up* to reach them. פָּשַׁט, *to invade* for the purpose of devastation and plunder. *Geshuri* is a tribe mentioned in Josh. xiii. 2 as living in the south of the territory of the Philistines, and is a different tribe from the Geshurites in the north-east of Gilead (Josh. xii. 5, xiii. 11, 13; Deut. iii. 14). These are the only passages in which they are mentioned. The *Gerzites*, or *Gizrites* according to the *Keri*, are entirely unknown. Bonfrere and Clericus suppose them to be the *Gerreni* spoken of in 2 Macc. xiii. 24, who inhabited the town of *Gerra*, between Rhinocolura and Pelusium (Strabo, xvi. 760), or *Gerron* (Ptol. iv. 5). This conjecture is a possible one, but is very uncertain nevertheless, as the Gerzites certainly dwelt somewhere in the desert of Arabia. At any rate Grotius and Ewald cannot be correct in their opinion that they were the inhabitants of *Gezer* (Josh. x. 33). The *Amalekites* were the remnant of this old hereditary foe of the Israelites, who had taken to flight on Saul's war of extermination, and had now assembled again (see at ch. xv. 8, 9). " *For they inhabit the land, where you go from of old to Shur, even to the land of Egypt.*" The אֲשֶׁר before מֵעוֹלָם may be explained from the fact that בּוֹאֲךָ is not adverbial here, but is construed according to its form as an infinitive: literally, "*where from of old thy coming is to Shur.*" אֲשֶׁר cannot have crept into the text through a copyist's mistake, as such a mistake would not have found its way into all the MSS. The fact that the early translators did not render the word proves nothing against its genuineness, but merely shows that the translators regarded it as superfluous. Moreover, the Alexandrian text is decidedly faulty here, and עוֹלָם is confounded with עֵלָם, ἀπὸ Γελάμ. *Shur* is the desert of *Jifar*, which is situated in front of Egypt (as in ch. xv. 7). These tribes were nomads, and had large flocks, which David took with him as booty when he had smitten the tribes themselves. After his return, David betook himself to Achish, to report to the Philistian king concerning his enterprise, and deceive him as to its true character.—Ver. 10. Achish said, " *Ye have not made an invasion to-day, have ye ?*" אַל, like μή, in an interrogative sense; the ה has dropped out: *vid.* Ewald, § 324, *b*. David replied, "*Against the south of Judah, and the south of the Jerahmeelites, and into the south of the Kenites,*" *sc.* we have made an incursion. This reply shows that the Geshurites, Gerzites, and Amalekites dwelt close to the southern boundary of Judah, so that David was able to represent the march against these tribes to Achish as a march against the south of Judah, to make him believe that he had been making an attack upon the southern territory of Judah and its dependencies. The *Negeb* of Judah is the land between the mountains of Judah and the desert of Arabia (see at Josh. xv. 21). The *Jerahmeelites* are the descendants of

R

Jerahmeel, the first-born of Hezron (1 Chron. ii. 9, 25, 26), and therefore one of the three large families of Judah who sprang from Hezron. They probably dwelt on the southern frontier of the tribe of Judah (*vid.* ch. xxx. 29). The *Kenites* were *protégés* of Judah (see at ch. xv. 6, and Judg. i. 16). In ver. 11 the writer introduces the remark, that in his raid David left neither man nor woman of his enemies alive, to take them to Gath, because he thought "*they might report against us, and say, Thus hath David done.*" There ought to be a major point under עָשָׂה דָוִד, as the following clause does not contain the words of the slaughtered enemies, but is a clause appended by the historian himself, to the effect that David continued to act in that manner as long as he dwelt in the land of the Philistines. מִשְׁפָּט, the mode of procedure; *lit.* the right which he exercised (see ch. viii. 9).—Ver. 12 is connected with ver. 10; Achish believed David's words, and said (to himself), "*He hath made himself stinking (i.e.* hated) *among his own people, among Israel, and will be my servant (i.e.* subject to me) *for ever.*"

DAVID IN THE ARMY OF THE PHILISTINES. ATTACK UPON ISRAEL. SAUL AND THE WITCH OF ENDOR.—CHAP. XXVIII.

Vers. 1, 2. The danger into which David had plunged through his flight into the land of the Philistines, and still more through the artifice with which he had deceived king Achish as to his real feelings, was to be very soon made apparent to him. For example, when the Philistines went to war again with Israel, Achish summoned him to go with his men in the army of the Philistines to the war against his own people and land, and David could not disregard the summons. But even if he had not brought himself into this danger without some fault of his own, he had at any rate only taken refuge with the Philistines in the greatest extremity; and what further he had done, was only done to save his own life. The faithful covenant God helped him therefore out of this trouble, and very soon afterwards put an end to his persecution by the fact that Saul lost his life in the war.—Ver. 1. "*In those days,*" *i.e.* whilst David was living in the land of the Philistines, it came to pass that the Philistines gathered their armies together for a campaign against Israel. And Achish sent word to David that he was to go with him in his army along with his men; and David answered (ver. 2), "*Thereby* (on this occasion) *thou shalt learn what thy servant will do*." This reply was ambiguous. The words "what thy servant will do" contained no distinct promise of faithful assistance in the war with the Israelites, as the expression "*thy servant*" is only the ordinary periphrasis for "*I*" in conversation with a superior. And there is just as little ground for inferring from ch. xxix. 8 that David was disposed to help the Philistines against Saul and the Israelites; for, as Calovius has observed, even there he gives no such promise, but "merely asks for information, that he may discover the king's intentions and feelings concerning him: he simply protests that he has done nothing to prevent his placing confidence in him, or to cause him to shut him out of the battle." Judging from his previous acts, it would necessarily have been against his conscience to fight against his own people. Nevertheless, in the situation in which he was placed he did not venture to give a distinct refusal to the summons of the king. He therefore gave an ambiguous answer, in the hope that God would show him a way out of this conflict between his inmost conviction and his duty to obey the Philistian king. He had no doubt prayed earnestly for this in his heart. And the faithful God helped His servant: first of all by the fact that Achish accepted his indefinite declaration as a promise of unconditional fidelity, as his answer "*so* (לָכֵן, *itaque, i.e.* that being the case, if thy conduct answers to thy promise) *I will make thee the keeper of my head*" (*i.e.* of my person) implies; and still more fully by the fact that the princes of the Philistines overturned the decision of their king (ch. xxix. 3 sqq.).

Vers. 3–25. *Saul with the witch at Endor.*—The invasion of Israel by the Philistines, which brought David into so difficult a situation, drove king Saul to despair, so that in utter helplessness he had recourse to ungodly means of inquiring into the future, which he himself had formerly prohibited, and to his horror had to hear the sentence of his own death. This account is introduced with the remark in ver. 3 that Samuel was dead and had been buried at Ramah (cf. ch. xxv. 1; וּבְעִירוֹ, with an explanatory *vav*, and indeed in his own city), and that Saul had expelled "*those that had familiar spirits and the wizards out of the land*" (on the terms employed, *oboth* and *yiddonim*, see at Lev. xix. 31). He had done this in accordance with the law in Lev. xix. 31, xx. 27, and Deut. xviii. 10 sqq.—Vers. 4, 5. When the Philistines advanced and encamped at *Shunem*, Saul brought all Israel together and encamped at *Gilboa, i.e.* upon the mountain of that name on the north-eastern edge of the plain of Jezreel, which slopes off from a height of about 1250 feet into the valley of the Jordan, and is not far from Beisan. On the north of the western extremity of this mountain was *Shunem*, the present *Sulem* or *Solam* (see at Josh. xix. 18); it was hardly two hours distant, so that the camp of the Philistines might be seen from Gilboa. When Saul saw this, he was thrown into such alarm that his heart greatly trembled. As Saul had been more than once victorious in his conflicts with the Philistines, his great fear at the sight of the Philistian army can hardly be attributed to any other cause than the feeling that God had forsaken him, by which he was suddenly overwhelmed.—Ver. 6. In his anxiety he inquired of the Lord; but the Lord neither answered him by dreams, nor by Urim, nor by prophets, that is to say, not by any of the three media by which He was accustomed to make known His will to Israel. שָׁאַל בַּיהוָה is the term usually employed to signify inquiring the will and counsel of God through the Urim and Thummim of the high priest (see at Judg. i. 1); and this is the case here, with the simple difference that here the other means of inquiring the counsel of God are also included. On dreams, see at Num. xii. 6. According to Num. xxvii. 21, *Urim* denotes divine revelation through the high priest *by means of the ephod.* But the high priest Abiathar had been with the ephod in David's camp ever since the murder of the priests at Nob (ch. xxii. 20 sqq., xxiii. 6, xxx. 7). How then could Saul inquire of God through the Urim? This question, which was very copiously discussed by the earlier commentators, and handled in different ways, may be decided very simply on the supposition, that after the death of Ahimelech and the flight of his son, another high priest had been appointed at the tabernacle, and another ephod made for him, with the *choshen* or breastplate, and the Urim and Thummim. It is no proof to the contrary that there is nothing said about this. We have no continuous history of the worship at the tabernacle, but only occasional notices. And from these it is perfectly clear that the public worship at the tabernacle was not suspended on the murder of the priests, but was continued still. For in the first years of David's reign we find the tabernacle at Gibeon, and Zadok the son of Ahitub, of the line of Eleazar, officiating there as high priest (1 Chron. xvi. 39, compared with ch. v. 38 and vi. 38); from which it follows with certainty, that after the destruction of Nob by Saul the tabernacle was removed to Gibeon, and the worship of the congregation continued there. From this we may also explain in a very simple manner the repeated allusions to two high priests in David's time (2 Sam. viii. 17, xv. 24, 29, 35; 1 Chron. xv. 11, xviii. 16). The reason why the Lord did not answer Saul is to be sought for in the wickedness of Saul, which rendered him utterly unworthy to find favour with God.

Vers. 7-14. Instead of recognising this, however, and searching his own heart, Saul attempted to obtain a revelation of the future in ungodly ways. He commanded his servants (ver. 7) to seek for a woman that had a familiar spirit. *Baalath-ob:* the mistress (or possessor) of a conjuring spirit, *i.e.* of a spirit with which the dead were conjured up, for the purpose of making inquiry concerning the future (see at Lev. xix. 31) There was a woman of this kind at *Endor,* which still exists as a village under the old name upon the northern shoulder of the *Duhy* or Little Hermon (see at Josh. xvii. 11), and therefore only two German (ten English) miles from the Israelitish camp at Gilboa.—Ver. 8. Saul went to this person by night and in disguise, that he might not be recognised, accompanied by two men ; and said to her, "*Divine to me through necromancy, and bring me up whomsoever I tell thee.*" The words "bring me up," etc., are an explanation or more precise definition of "divine unto me," etc. Prophesying by the *Ob* was probably performed by calling up a departed spirit from Sheol, and obtaining prophecies, *i.e.* disclosures concerning one's own fate, through the medium of such a spirit. On the form קסומי (*Chethibh*), see at Judg. ix. 8.—Ver. 9. Such a demand placed the woman in difficulty. As Saul had driven the necromantists out of the land, she was afraid that the unknown visitor (for it is evident from ver. 12 that she did not recognise Saul at first) might be laying a snare for her soul with his request, to put her to death, *i.e.* might have come to her merely for the purpose of spying her out as a conjurer of the dead, and then inflicting capital punishment upon her according to the law (Lev. xx. 27). —Vers. 10, 11. But when Saul swore to her that no punishment should fall upon her on that account (אִם־יִקְּרֵךְ, "*shall assuredly not fall upon thee*"), an oath which showed how utterly hardened Saul was, she asked him, "*Whom shall I bring up to thee?*" and Saul replied, "*Bring me up Samuel,*" *sc.* from the region of the dead, or *Sheol*, which was thought to be under the ground. This idea arose from the fact that the dead were buried in the earth, and was connected with the thought of heaven as being above the earth. Just as heaven, regarded as the abode of God and the holy angels and blessed spirits, is above the earth; so, on the other hand, the region of death and the dead is beneath the ground. And with our modes of thought, which are so bound up with time and space, it is impossible to represent to ourselves in any other way the difference and contrast between blessedness with God and the shade-life in death.—Ver. 12. The woman then commenced her conjuring arts. This must be supplied from the context, as ver. 12 merely states what immediately ensued. "*When the woman saw Samuel, she cried aloud,*" *sc.* at the form which appeared to her so unexpectedly. These words imply most unquestionably that the woman saw an apparition which she did not anticipate, and therefore that she was not really able to conjure up departed spirits or persons who had died, but that she either merely pretended to do so, or if her witchcraft was not mere trickery and delusion, but had a certain demoniacal background, that the appearance of Samuel differed essentially from everything she had experienced and effected before, and therefore filled her with alarm and horror. The very fact, however, that she recognised Saul as soon as Samuel appeared, precludes us from declaring her art to have been nothing more than jugglery and deception; for she said to him, "*Why hast thou cheated me, as thou art certainly Saul?*" *i.e.* why hast thou deceived me as to thy person? why didst thou not tell me that thou wast king Saul? Her recognition of Saul when Samuel appeared may be easily explained, if we assume that the woman had fallen into a state of *clairvoyance*, in which she recognised persons who, like Saul in his disguise, were unknown to her by face.—Ver. 13. The king quieted her fear, and then asked her what she had seen; whereupon she gave him a fuller description of the apparition: "*I saw a celestial being come up from the earth.*" *Elohim* does not signify gods here, nor yet God; still less an angel or a ghost, or even a person of superior rank, but a celestial (super-terrestrial), heavenly, or spiritual being.— Ver. 14. Upon Saul's further inquiry as to his form, she replied, "*An old man is ascending, and he is wrapped in a mantle.*" *Meïl* is the prophet's mantle, such as Samuel was accustomed to wear when he was alive (see ch. xv. 27). Saul recognised from this that the person who had been called up was Samuel, and he fell upon his face to the ground, to give expression to his reverence. Saul does not appear to have seen the apparition itself. But it does not follow from this that there was no such apparition at all, and the whole was an invention on the part of the witch. It needs an opened eye, such as all do not possess, to see a departed spirit or celestial being. The eyes of the body are not enough for this.

Vers. 15–22. Then Samuel said, "*Why hast thou disturbed me* (sc. from my rest in Hades; cf. Isa. xiv. 9), *to bring me up?*" It follows, no doubt, from this that Samuel had been disturbed from his rest by Saul; but whether this had been effected by the conjuring arts of the witch, or by a miracle of God himself, is left undecided. Saul replied, "*I am sore oppressed, for the Philistines fight against me, and God has departed from me, and answers me no more, either by prophets or by dreams; then I had thee called* (on the intensified form וָאֶקְרָאֶה, *vid.* Ewald, § 228, *c*), *to make known to me what I am to do.*" The omission of any reference to the Urim is probably to be interpreted very simply from the brevity of the account, and not from the fact that Saul shrank from speaking about the oracle of the high priest, on account of the massacre of the priests which had taken place by his command. There is a contradiction, however, in Saul's reply: for if God had forsaken him, he could not expect any answer from Him; and if God did not reply to his inquiry through the regularly appointed media of His revelation, how could he hope to obtain any divine revelation through the help of a witch? "When living prophets gave no answer, he thought that a dead one might be called up, as if a dead one were less dependent upon God than the living, or that, even in opposition to the will of God, he might reply through the arts of a conjuring woman. Truly, if he perceived that God was hostile to him, he ought to have been all the more afraid, lest His enmity should be increased by his breach of His laws. But fear and superstition never reason" (Clericus). Samuel points out this contradiction (ver. 16): "*Why dost thou ask me, since Jehovah hath departed from thee, and is become thine enemy?*" The meaning is: How canst thou expect an answer under these circumstances from me, the prophet of Jehovah? עָרֶךָ, from עָר, signifies an enemy here (from עִיר, *fervour*); and this meaning is confirmed by Ps. cxxxix. 20 and Dan. iv. 16 (Chald.). There is all the less ground for any critical objection to the reading, as the Chaldee and Vulgate give a periphrastic rendering of "enemy," whilst the Sept., Syr., and Arab. have merely paraphrased according to conjectures. Samuel then announced his fate (vers. 17–19): "*Jehovah hath performed for himself, as He spake by me* (לוֹ, for himself, which the LXX. and Vulg. have arbitrarily altered into לְךָ, σοί, *tibi* (to thee), is correctly explained by Seb. Schmidt, 'according to His grace, or to fulfil and prove His truth'); *and Jehovah hath rent the kingdom out of thy hand, and given it to thy neighbour David.*" The perfects express the purpose of God, which had already been formed, and was now about to be fulfilled.—Ver. 18. The reason for Saul's rejection is then given, as in ch. xv. 23: "*Because* (בַּאֲשֶׁר, according as) *thou . . . hast not executed the fierceness of His anger upon Amalek, therefore hath Jehovah done this thing to thee this day.*" "*This thing*" is the distress of which Saul had complained, with its consequences. וְיִתֵּן, *that Jehovah may give* (= for He will give) *Israel also with thee into the hand of the Philistines.* "*To-morrow wilt thou and thy sons be with me* (*i.e.* in Sheol, with the dead); *also the camp of Israel will Jehovah give into the hand of the Philistines,*" *i.e.* give up to them to plunder. The overthrow of the people was to heighten Saul's misery, when he saw the people plunged with him into ruin through his sin (O. v. Gerlach). Thus was the last hope taken from Saul. His day of grace was gone, and judgment was now to burst upon him without delay.—Ver. 20. These words so alarmed him, that he fell his whole length upon the ground; for he had been kneeling hitherto (ver. 14). He "*fell straightway* (lit. he hastened and fell) *upon the ground. For he was greatly terrified at the words of Samuel: there was also no strength in him, because he had eaten no food the whole day and the whole night,*" sc. from mental perturbation or inward excitement. Terror and bodily exhaustion caused him to fall powerless to the ground.—Vers. 21, 22. The woman then came to him and persuaded him to strengthen himself with food for the journey which he had to take. It by no means follows from the expression "*came unto Saul*," that the woman was in an adjoining room during the presence of the apparition, and whilst Samuel was speaking, but only that she was standing at some distance off, and came up to him to speak to him when he had fallen fainting to the ground. As she had fulfilled his wish at the risk of her own life, she entreated him now to gratify her wish, and let her set a morsel of bread before him and eat. "*That strength may be in thee when thou goest thy way*" (*i.e.* when thou returnest).

This narrative, when read without prejudice, makes at once and throughout the impression conveyed by the Septuagint at 1 Chron. x. 13: ἐπηρώτησε Σαοὺλ ἐν τῷ ἐγγαστριμύθῳ τοῦ ζητῆσαι, καὶ ἀπεκρίνατο αὐτῷ Σαμουὴλ ὁ προφήτης; and still more clearly at Ecclus. xlvi. 20, where it is said of Samuel: "And after his death he prophesied, and showed the king his end, and lifted up his voice from the earth in prophecy, to blot out the wickedness of the people." Nevertheless the fathers, reformers, and earlier Christian theologians, with very few exceptions, assumed that there was not a real appearance of Samuel, but only an imaginary one. According to the explanation given by Ephraem Syrus, an apparent image of Samuel was presented to the eye of Saul through demoniacal arts. Luther and Calvin adopted the same view, and the earlier Protestant theologians followed them in regarding the apparition as nothing but a diabolical spectre, a phantasm, or diabolical spectre in the form of Samuel, and Samuel's announcement as nothing but a diabolical revelation made by divine permission, in which truth is mixed with falsehood.[1] It was not till the

[1] Thus Luther says (in his work upon the abuses of the Mass, 1522): "The raising of Samuel by a soothsayer or witch, in 1 Sam. xxviii. 11, 12, was certainly merely a spectre of the devil; not only because the Scriptures state that it was effected by a woman who was full of devils (for who could believe that the souls of believers, who are in the hand of God, Ecclus. iii. 1, and in the bosom of Abraham, Luke xvi. 32, were under the power of the devil, and of simple men?), but also because it was evidently in opposition to the command of God that Saul and the woman inquired of the dead. The Holy Ghost cannot do anything against this himself, nor can He help

seventeenth century that the opinion was expressed, that the apparition of Samuel was merely a delusion produced by the witch, without any real background at all. After Reginald Scotus and Balth. Becker had given expression to this opinion, it was more fully elaborated by Ant. van Dale, in his *dissert. de divinationibus idololatricis sub V. T.;* and in the so-called age of enlightenment this was the prevailing opinion, so that Thenius still regards it as an established fact, not only that the woman was an impostor, but that the historian himself regarded the whole thing as an imposture. There is no necessity to refute this opinion at the present day. Even Fr. Boettcher (*de inferis*, pp. 111 sqq.), who looks upon the thing as an imposture, admits that the first recorder of the occurrence " believed that Samuel appeared and prophesied, *contrary to the expectation* of the witch ;" and that the author of the books of Samuel was convinced that the prophet was raised up and prophesied, so that after his death he was proved to be the true prophet of Jehovah, although through the intervention of ungodly arts (cf. Ezek. xiv. 7, 9). But the view held by the early church does not do justice to the scriptural narrative; and hence the more modern orthodox commentators are unanimous in the opinion that the departed prophet did really appear and announce the destruction of Saul, not, however, in consequence of the magical arts of the witch, but through a miracle wrought by the omnipotence of God. This is most decidedly favoured by the fact, that the prophetic historian speaks throughout of the appearance, not of

those who act in opposition to it." Calvin also regards the apparition as only a spectre (Hom. 100 in 1 Sam.) : " It is certain," he says, " that it was not really Samuel, for God would never have allowed His prophets to be subjected to such diabolical conjuring. For here is a sorceress calling up the dead from the grave. Does any one imagine that God wished His prophet to be exposed to such ignominy ; as if the devil had power over the bodies and souls of the saints which are in His keeping? The souls of the saints are said to rest and live in God, waiting for their happy resurrection. Besides, are we to believe that Samuel took his cloak with him into the grave? For all these reasons, it appears evident that the apparition was nothing more than a spectre, and that the senses of the woman herself were so deceived, that she thought she saw Samuel, whereas it really was not he." The earlier orthodox theologians also disputed the reality of the appearance of the departed Samuel on just the same grounds ; *e.g.* Seb. Schmidt (*Comm.*) ; Aug. Pfeiffer ; Sal. Deyling ; and Buddeus, *Hist. Eccl. V. T.* ii. p. 243, and many more a ghost, but of Samuel himself. He does this not only in ver. 12, " When the woman saw Samel she cried aloud," but also in vers. 14, 15, 16, and 20. It is also sustained by the circumstance, that not only do the words of Samuel to Saul, in vers. 16-19, create the impression that it is Samuel himself who is speaking; but his announcement contains so distinct a prophecy of the death of Saul and his sons, that it is impossible to imagine that it can have proceeded from the mouth of an impostor, or have been an inspiration of Satan. On the other hand, the remark of Calvin, to the effect that " God sometimes gives to devils the power of revealing secrets to us, which they have learned from the Lord," could only be regarded as a valid objection, provided that the narrative gave us some intimation that the apparition and the speaking were nothing but a diabolical delusion. But it does nothing of the kind. It is true, the opinion that the witch conjured up the prophet Samuel was very properly disputed by the early theologians, and rejected by Theodoret as " unholy, and even impious ;" and the text of Scripture indicates clearly enough that the very opposite was the case, by the remark that the witch herself was terrified at the appearance of Samuel (ver. 12). Shöbel is therefore quite correct in saying : " It was not at the call of the idolatrous king, nor at the command of the witch,—neither of whom had the power to bring him up, or even to make him hear their voice in his rest in the grave,—that Samuel came ; nor was it merely by divine ' permission,' which is much too little to say. No, rather it was by the special command of God that he left his grave (?), like a faithful servant whom his master arouses at midnight, to let in an inmate of the house who has wilfully stopped out late, and has been knocking at the door. ' Why do you disturb me out of my sleep ?' would always be the question put to the unwelcome comer, although it was not by his noise, but really by his master's command, that he had been aroused. Samuel asked the same question." The prohibition of witchcraft and necromancy (Deut. xviii. 11 ; Isa. viii. 19), which the earlier writers quote against this, does not preclude the possibility of God having, for His own special reasons, caused Samuel to appear. On the contrary, the appearance itself was of such a character, that it could not fail to show to the witch and the king, that God does not allow His prohibitions to be infringed with impunity. The very same thing occurred here, which God threatened to idolaters through the medium of Ezekiel (ch. xiv. 4, 7, 8): "If they come to the prophet, I will answer them in my own way." Still less is there any force in the appeal to Luke xvi. 27 sqq., where Abraham refuses the request of the rich man in Hades, that he would send Lazarus to his father's house to preach repentance to his brethren who were still living, saying, "They have Moses and the prophets, let them hear them. If they hear not Moses and the prophets, neither will they be persuaded though one rose from the dead." For this does not affirm that the appearance of a dead man is a thing impossible in itself, but only describes it as useless and ineffectual, so far as the conversion of the ungodly is concerned.

The reality of the appearance of Samuel from the kingdom of the dead cannot therefore be called in question, especially as it has an analogon in the appearance of Moses and Elijah at the transfiguration of Christ (Matt. xvii. 3; Luke ix. 30, 31); except that this difference must not be overlooked, namely, that Moses and Elijah appeared " in glory," *i.e.* in a glorified form, whereas Samuel appeared in earthly corporeality with the prophet's mantle which he had worn on earth. Just as the transfiguration of Christ was a phenomenal anticipation of His future heavenly glory, into which He was to enter after His resurrection and ascension, so may we think of the appearance of Moses and Elijah " in glory" upon the mount of transfiguration as an anticipation of their heavenly transfiguration in eternal life with God. It was different with Samuel, whom God brought up from Hades through an act of His omnipotence. This appearance is not to be regarded as the appearance of one who had risen in a glorified body; but though somewhat spirit-like in its external manifestation, so that it was only to the witch that it was visible, and not to Saul, it was merely an appearance of the soul of Samuel, that had been at rest in Hades, in the clothing of the earthly corporeality and dress of the prophet, which were assumed for the purpose of rendering it visible. In this respect the appearance of Samuel rather resembled the appearances of incorporeal angels in human form and dress, such as the three angels who came to Abraham in the grove at Mamre (Gen. xviii.), and the angel who appeared to Manoah (Judg. xiii.); with this exception, however, that these angels manifested themselves in a human form, which was visible to the ordinary bodily eye, whereas Samuel appeared in the spirit-like form of the inhabitants of Hades. In all these cases the bodily form and clothing were only a dress assumed for the soul or spirit, and intended to facilitate perception, so that such appearances furnish no proof that the souls of departed men possess an immaterial corporeality.[1]

Vers. 23-25. On Saul's refusing to take food, his servants (*i.e.* his two attendants) also pressed him, so that he yielded, rose up from the ground, and sat down upon the bed (*mittah*: *i.e.* a bench by the wall of the room provided with pillows); whereupon the woman quickly sacrificed (served up) a stalled calf, baked unleavened cakes, and set the food she had prepared before the king and his servants. The woman did all this from natural sympathy for the unhappy king, and not, as Thenius supposes, to remove all suspicion of deception from Saul's mind; for she had not deceived the king at all.—Ver. 25. When Saul and his servants had eaten, they started upon their way, and went back that night to Gilboa, which was about ten miles distant, where the battle occurred the next day, and Saul and his sons fell. " Saul was too hardened in his sin to express any grief or pain, either on his own account or because of the

---

[1] Delitzsch (*bibl. Psychol.* pp. 427 sqq.) has very properly rejected, not only the opinion that Samuel and Moses were raised up from the dead for the purpose of a transient appearance, and then died again, but also the idea that they appeared in their material bodies, a notion upon which Calvin rests his argument against the reality of the appearance of Samuel. But when he gives it as his opinion, that the angels who appeared in human form assumed this form by virtue of their own power, inasmuch as they can make themselves visible to whomsoever they please, and infers still further from this, " that the outward form in which Samuel and Moses appeared (which corresponded to their form when on this side the grave) was the immaterial production of their spiritual and psychical nature," he overlooks the fact, that not only Samuel, but the angels also, in the cases referred to, appeared in men's clothing, which cannot possibly be regarded as a production of their spiritual and psychical nature. The earthly dress is not indispensable to a man's existence. Adam and Eve had no clothing before the Fall, and there will be no material clothing in the kingdom of glory; for the " fine linen, pure and white," with which the bride adorns herself for the marriage supper of the Lamb, is " the righteousness of saints" (Rev. xix. 8).

fate of his sons and his people. In stolid desperation he went to meet his fate. This was the terrible end of a man whom the Spirit of God had once taken possession of and turned into another man, and whom he had endowed with gifts to be the leader of the people of God" (O. v. Gerlach).

REMOVAL OF DAVID FROM THE ARMY OF THE PHILISTINES.—CHAP. XXIX.

Vers. 1–5. Whilst Saul derived no comfort from his visit to the witch at Endor, but simply heard from the mouth of Samuel the confirmation of his rejection on the part of God, and an announcement of his approaching fate, David was delivered, through the interposition of God, from the danger of having to fight against his own people.—Ver. 1. The account of this is introduced by a fuller description of the position of the hostile army. "*The Philistines gathered all their armies together towards Aphek, but Israel encamped at the fountain in* (at) *Jezreel.*" This fountain is the present *Ain Jalûd* (or *Ain Jalût, i.e.* Goliath's fountain, probably so called because it was regarded as the scene of the defeat of Goliath), a very large fountain, which issues from a cleft in the rock at the foot of the mountain on the north-eastern border of Gilboa, forming a beautifully limpid pool of about forty or fifty feet in diameter, and then flowing in a brook through the valley (Rob. *Pal.* iii. p. 168). Consequently *Aphek*, which must be carefully distinguished from the towns of the same name in Asher (Josh. xix. 30; Judg. i. 31) and upon the mountains of Judah (Josh. xv. 53) and also at Ebenezer (1 Sam. iv. 1), is to be sought for not very far from *Shunem*, in the plain of Jezreel ; according to Van de Velde's *Mem.*, by the side of the present *el Afûleh*, though the situation has not been exactly determined. The statement in the *Onom.*, "near Endor of Jezreel where Saul fought," is merely founded upon the Septuagint, in which בעין is erroneously rendered ἐν 'Ενδώρ.—Vers. 2, 3. When the princes of the Philistines (*sarne*, as in Josh. xiii. 3) advanced by hundreds and thousands (*i.e.* arranged in companies of hundreds and thousands), and David and his men came behind with Achish (*i.e.* forming the rear-guard), the (other) princes pronounced against their allowing David and his men to go with them.

This did not occur at the time of their setting out, but on the road, when they had already gone some distance (compare ver. 11 with ch. xxx. 1), probably when the five princes (Josh. xiii. 3) of the Philistines had effected a junction. To the inquiry, "*What are these Hebrews doing?*" Achish replied, "*Is not this David, the servant of Saul the king of Israel, who has been with me days already, or years already? and I have found nothing in him since his coming over unto this day.*" מְאוּמָה, anything at all that could render him suspicious, or his fidelity doubtful. נָפַל, to fall away and go over to a person; generally construed with אֶל (Jer. xxxvii. 13, xxxviii. 19, etc.) or עַל (Jer. xxi. 9, xxxvii. 14; 1 Chron. xii. 19, 20), but here absolutely, as the more precise meaning can be gathered from the context.—Ver. 4. But the princes, *i.e.* the four other princes of the Philistines, not the courtiers of Achish himself, were angry with Achish, and demanded, "*Send the man back, that he may return to his place, which thou hast assigned him; that he may not go down with us into the war, and may not become an adversary (satan) to us in the war; for wherewith could he show himself acceptable to his lord* (viz. Saul), *if not with the heads of these men?*" הֲלוֹא, *nonne*, strictly speaking, introduces a new question to confirm the previous question. "*Go down to the battle:*" this expression is used as in ch. xxvi. 10, xxx. 24, because battles were generally fought in the plains, into which the Hebrews were obliged to come down from their mountainous land. "*These men,*" *i.e.* the soldiers of the Philistines, to whom the princes were pointing.— Ver. 5. To justify their suspicion, the princes reminded him of their song with which the women in Israel had celebrated David's victory over Goliath (ch. xviii. 7).

Vers. 6-11. After this declaration on the part of the princes, Achish was obliged to send David back.—Vers. 6, 7. With a solemn assertion,—swearing by Jehovah to convince David all the more thoroughly of the sincerity of his declaration,—Achish said to him, "*Thou art honourable, and good in my eyes* (*i.e.* quite right in my estimation) *are thy going out and coming in* (*i.e.* all thy conduct) *with me in the camp, for I have not found anything bad in thee; but in the eyes of the princes thou art not good* (*i.e.* the princes do not think thee honourable, do not trust thee). *Turn now, and go in peace, that thou mayest do nothing displeasing to the princes of the Philistines.*"—Ver. 8. Partly for the sake of vindicating himself against this suspicion, and partly to put the sincerity of Achish's words to the test, David replied, "*What have I done, and what hast thou found in thy servant, since I was with thee till this day, that I am not to come and fight against the enemies of my lord the king?*" These last words are also ambiguous, since the king whom David calls his lord might be understood as meaning either Achish or Saul. Achish, in his goodness of heart, applies them without suspicion to himself; for he assures David still more earnestly (ver. 9), that he is firmly convinced of his uprightness. "*I know that thou art good in my eyes as an angel of God,*" *i.e.* I have the strongest conviction that thou hast behaved as well towards me as an angel could; but the princes have desired thy removal.—Ver. 10. "*And now get up early in the morning with the servants of thy lord* (*i.e.* Saul, whose subjects David's men all were), *who have come with thee; get ye up in the morning when it gets light for you* (so that ye can see), *and go.*"—Ver. 11. In accordance with this admonition, David returned the next morning into the land of the Philistines, *i.e.* to Ziklag; no doubt very light of heart, and praising God for having so graciously rescued him out of the disastrous situation into which he had been brought and not altogether without some fault of his own, rejoicing that "he had not committed either sin, *i.e.* had neither violated the fidelity which he owed to Achish, nor had to fight against the Israelites" (Seb. Schmidt).

DAVID AVENGES UPON THE AMALEKITES THE PLUNDERING AND BURNING OF ZIKLAG.—CHAP. XXX.

Vers. 1-10. During David's absence the Amalekites had invaded the south country, smitten Ziklag and burnt it down, and carried off the women and children whom they found there; whereat not only were David and his men plunged into great grief on their return upon the third day, but David especially was involved in very great trouble, inasmuch as the people wanted to stone him. But he strengthened himself in the Lord his God (vers. 1-6).—Vers. 1-4 form one period, which is expanded by the introduction of several circumstantial clauses. The apodosis to "It came to pass, when," etc. (ver. 1), does not follow till ver. 4, "Then David and the people," etc. But this is formally attached to ver. 3, "so David and his men came," with which the protasis commenced in ver. 1 is resumed in an altered form. "*It came to pass, when David and his men came to Ziklag . . . the Amalekites had invaded . . . and had carried off the wives . . . and had gone their way, and David and his men came into the town* (for 'when David and his men came,' etc.), *and behold it was burned. . . . Then David and the people with him lifted up their voice.*" "*On the third day :*" after David's dismission by Achish, not after David's departure from Ziklag. David had at any rate gone with Achish beyond Gath, and had not been sent back till the whole of the princes of the Philistines had united their armies (ch. xxix. 2 sqq.), so that he must have been absent from Ziklag more than two days, or two days and a half. This is placed beyond all doubt by vers. 11 sqq., since the Amalekites are there described as having gone off with their booty three days before David followed them, and therefore they had taken Ziklag and burned it three days before David's return. These foes had therefore taken advantage of the absence of David and his warriors, to avenge themselves for David's invasions and plunderings (ch. xxvii. 8). Of those who were carried off, "*the women*" alone are expressly mentioned in ver. 2, although the female population and all the children had been removed, as we may see from the expression "*small and great*" (vers. 3, 6). The LXX. were therefore correct, so far as the sense is concerned, in introducing the words καὶ πάντα before אֲשֶׁר בָּהּ. "*They had killed no one, but* (only) *carried away.*" נָהַג, to carry away captive, as in Isa. xx. 4. Among those who had been carried off were David's two wives, Ahinoam and Abigail (*vid.* ch. xxv. 42, 43, xxvii. 3).—Ver. 6. David was greatly distressed in consequence; "*for the people thought* ('said,' *sc.* in their hearts) *to stone him,*" because they sought the occasion of their calamity in his connection with Achish, with which many of his adherents may very probably have been dissatisfied. "*For the soul of the whole people was embittered* (*i.e.* all the people were embittered in their souls) *because of their sons and daughters,*" who had been carried away into slavery. "*But David strengthened himself in the Lord his God,*" *i.e.* sought consolation and strength in prayer and believing confidence in the Lord (vers. 7 sqq.). This strength he manifested in the resolution to follow the foes and rescue their booty from them. To this end he had the ephod brought by the high priest Abiathar (cf. ch. xxiii. 9), and inquired by means of the Urim of the Lord, "*Shall I pursue this troop? Shall I overtake it?*" These questions were answered in the affirmative; and the promise was added, "*and thou wilt rescue.*" So David pursued the enemy with his six hundred men as far as the brook *Besor*, where the rest, *i.e.* two hundred, remained standing (stayed behind). The words וְהַנּוֹתָרִים עָמָדוּ, which are appended in the form of a circumstantial clause, are to be connected, so far as the facts are concerned, with what follows: whilst the others remained behind, David pursued the enemy still farther with four hundred men. By the word הַנּוֹתָרִים the historian has somewhat anticipated the matter, and therefore regards it as necessary to define the expression still further in ver. 10*b*. We are precluded from changing the text, as Thenius suggests, by the circumstance that all the early translators read it in this manner, and have endeavoured to make the expression intelligible by paraphrasing it. These two hundred men were too tired to cross the brook and go any farther. (פָּגַר, which only occurs here and in ver. 21, signifies, in Syriac, to be weary or exhausted.) As Ziklag was burnt down, of course they found no provisions there, and were consequently obliged to set out in pursuit of the foe without being able to provide themselves with the necessary supplies. The brook *Besor* is supposed to be the Wady *Sheriah*, which enters the sea below Ashkelon (see v. Raumer, *Pal.* p. 52).

Vers. 11–20. On their further march they found an Egyptian lying exhausted upon the field; and having brought him to David, they gave him food and drink, namely "*a slice of fig-cake* (cf. ch. xxv. 18), *and raisin-cakes to eat; whereupon his spirit of life returned* (*i.e.* he came to himself again), *as he had neither eaten bread nor drunk water for three days.*"—Ver. 13. When David asked him whence he had come (*to whom, i.e.* to what people or tribe, *dost thou belong?*), the young man said that he was an Egyptian, and servant of an Amalekite, and that he had been left behind by his master when he fell sick three days before ("to-day three," *sc.* days): he also said, "*We invaded the south of the Crethites, and what belongs to Judah, and the south of Caleb, and burned Ziklag with fire.*" הַכְּרֵתִי, identical with כְּרֵתִים (Ezek. xxv. 16; Zeph. ii. 5), denotes those tribes of the Philistines who dwelt in the south-west of Canaan, and is used by Ezekiel and Zephaniah as synonymous with Philistim. The origin of the name is involved in obscurity, as the explanation which prevailed for a time, viz. that it was derived from *Creta*, is without sufficient foundation (*vid.* Stark, *Gaza*, pp. 66 and 99 sqq.). The Negeb "belonging to Judah" is the eastern portion of the Negeb. One part of it belonged to the family of Caleb, and was called Caleb's Negeb (*vid.* ch. xxv. 3).—Vers. 15, 16. This Egyptian then conducted David, at his request, when he had sworn that he would neither kill him nor deliver him up to his master, down to the hostile troops, who were spread over the whole land, eating, drinking, and making merry, on account of all the great booty which they had brought out of the land of the Philistines and Judah. —Ver. 17. David surprised them in the midst of their security, and smote them from the evening twilight till the evening of the next day, so that no one escaped, with the exception of four hundred young men, who fled upon camels. *Nesheph* signifies the evening twilight here, not the dawn,—a meaning which is not even sustained by Job vii. 4. The form מָחֳרָתָם appears to be an adverbial formation, like יוֹמָם.—Vers. 18, 19. Through this victory David rescued all that the Amalekites had taken, his two wives, and all the children great and small; also the booty that they had taken with them, so that nothing was missing.—Ver. 20 is obscure: "*And David took all the sheep and the oxen: they drove them before those cattle, and said, This is David's booty.*" In order to obtain any meaning whatever from this literal rendering of the words, we must understand by the sheep and oxen those which belonged to the Amalekites, and the flocks taken from them as booty; and by "*those cattle,*" the cattle belonging to David and his men, which the Amalekites had driven away, and the Israelites had now recovered from them: so that David had the sheep and oxen which he had taken from the Amalekites as booty driven in front of the rest of the cattle which the Israelites had recovered; whereupon the drovers exclaimed, "*This* (the sheep and oxen) *is David's booty.*" It is true that there is nothing said in what goes before about any booty that David had taken from the Amalekites, in addition to what they had taken from the Israelites; but the fact that David had really taken such booty is perfectly obvious from vers. 26-31, where he is said to have sent portions of the booty of the enemies of Jehovah to different places in the land. If this explanation be not accepted, there is no other course open than to follow the Vulgate, alter לִפְנֵי into לִפָנָיו, and render the middle clause thus : " *they drove those cattle* (viz. the sheep and oxen already mentioned) *before him*," as Luther has done. But even in that case we could hardly understand anything else by the sheep and oxen than the cattle belonging to the Amalekites, and taken from them as booty.

Vers. 21-31. When David came back to the two hundred men whom he had left by the brook Besor (יֹשִׁיבֻם, they made them sit, remain), they went to meet him and his warriors, and were heartily greeted by David.—Ver. 22. Then all kinds of evil and worthless men of those who had gone with David to the battle replied : " *Because they have not gone with us* (lit. with me, the person speaking), *we will not give them any of the booty that we have seized, except to every one his wife and his children : they may lead them away, and go.*"—Vers. 23, 24. David opposed this selfish and envious proposal, saying, " *Do not so, my brethren, with that* (אֵת, the sign of the accusative, not the preposition ; see Ewald, § 329, a : lit. with regard to that) *which Jehovah hath done to us, and He hath guarded us* (since He hath guarded us), *and given this troop which came upon us into our hand. And who will hearken to you in this matter ?* But (כִּי; according to the negation involved in the question) *as the portion of him that went into the battle, so be the portion of him that stayed by the things ; they shall share together.*" הורד is a copyist's error for הַיֹּרֵד.—Ver. 25. So was it from that day and forward ; and he (David) made it (this regulation as to the booty) " *the law and right for Israel unto this day.*"—Vers. 26-31. When David returned to Ziklag, he sent portions of the booty to the elders of Judah, to his friends, with this message : " *Behold, here ye have a blessing of the booty of the enemies of Jehovah*" (which we took from the enemies of Jehovah) ; and this he did, according to ver. 31, to all the places in which he had wandered with his men, *i.e.* where he had wandered about during his flight from Saul, and in which he had no doubt received assistance. Sending these gifts could not fail to make the elders of these cities well disposed towards him, and so to facilitate his recognition as king after the death of Saul, which occurred immediately afterwards. Some of these places may have been plundered by the Amalekites, since they had invaded the *Negeb* of Judah (ver. 14). The cities referred to were *Bethel*,—not the Bethel so often mentioned, the present *Beitin*, in the tribe of Benjamin, but *Bethuel* (1 Chron. iv. 30) or *Bethul*, in the tribe of Simeon (Josh. xix. 4), which Knobel supposes to be *Elusa* or *el Khalasa* (see at Josh. xv. 30). The reading Βαιθσούρ in the Septuagint is a worthless conjecture. *Ramah* of the south, which was allotted to the tribe of Simeon, has not yet been discovered (see at Josh. xix. 8). *Jattir* has been preserved in the ruins of *Attir*, on the southern portion of the mountains of Judah (see at Josh. xv. 48). *Aroër* is still to be seen in ruins, viz. in the foundations of walls built of enormous stones in Wady Arara, where there are many cavities for holding water, about three hours E.S.E. of Bersaba, and twenty miles to the south of Hebron (*vid.* Rob. *Pal.* ii. p. 620, and v. de Velde, *Mem.* p. 288). *Siphmoth* (or *Shiphmoth*, according to several MSS.) is altogether unknown. It may probably be referred to again in 1 Chron. xxvii. 27, where Zabdi is called the *Shiphmite;* but it is certainly not to be identified with *Sepham*, on the north-east of the sea of Galilee (Num. xxxiv. 10, 11), as Thenius supposes. *Eshtemoa* has been preserved in the village of *Semua*, with ancient ruins, on the south-western portion of the mountains of Judah (see at Josh. xv. 50). *Racal* is never mentioned again, and is entirely unknown. The LXX. have five different names instead of this, the last being *Carmel*, into which Thenius proposes to alter *Racal*. But this can hardly be done with propriety, as the LXX. also introduced the Philistian *Gath*, which certainly does not belong here; whilst in ver. 30 they have totally different names, some of which are decidedly wrong. The cities of the *Jerahmeelites* and *Kenites* were situated in the Negeb of Judah (ch. xxvii. 10), but their names cannot be traced.—Ver. 30. *Hormah* in the Negeb (Josh. xv. 30) is *Zephath*, the present *Zepáta*, on the western slope of the *Rakhma* plateau (see at Josh. xii. 14). *Cor-ashan*, probably the same place as *Ashan* in the *Shephelah*, upon the border of the Negeb, has not yet been discovered (see at Josh. xv. 42). *Athach* is only mentioned here, and quite unknown. According to Thenius, it is probably a mistaken spelling for *Ether* in the tribe of Simeon

(Josh. xix. 7, xv. 43). *Hebron,* the present *el Khulil,* Abraham's city (see at Josh. x. 3; Gen. xxiii. 17).

DEATH AND BURIAL OF SAUL AND HIS SONS.—CHAP. XXXI.

The end of the unhappy king corresponded to his life ever since the day of his rejection as king. When he had lost the battle, and saw his three sons fallen at his side, and the archers of the enemy pressing hard upon him, without either repentance or remorse he put an end to his life by suicide, to escape the disgrace of being wounded and abused by the foe (vers. 1-7). But he did not attain his object; for the next day the enemy found his corpse and those of his sons, and proceeded to plunder, mutilate, and abuse them (vers. 8-10). However, the king of Israel was not to be left to perish in utter disgrace. The citizens of Jabesh remembered the deliverance which Saul had brought to their city after his election as king, and showed their gratitude by giving an honourable burial to Saul and his sons (vers. 11-13). There is a parallel to this chapter in 1 Chron. x., which agrees exactly with the account before us, with very few deviations indeed, and those mostly verbal, and merely introduces a hortatory clause at the end (vers. 13, 14).

Vers. 1-7. The account of the war between the Philistines and Israel, the commencement of which has already been mentioned in ch. xxviii. 1, 4 sqq., and xxix. 1, is resumed in ver. 1 in a circumstantial clause; and to this there is attached a description of the progress and result of the battle, more especially with reference to Saul. Consequently, in 1 Chron. x. 1, where there had been no previous allusion to the war, the participle נִלְחָמִים is changed into the perfect. The following is the way in which we should express the circumstantial clause: "Now when the Philistines were fighting against Israel, the men of Israel fled before the Philistines, and slain men fell in the mountains of Gilboa" (*vid.* ch. xxviii. 4). The principal engagement took place in the plain of Jezreel. But when the Israelites were obliged to yield, they fled up the mountains of Gilboa, and were pursued and slain there.—Vers. 2-4. The Philistines followed Saul, smote (*i.e.* put to death) his three sons (see at ch. xiv. 49), and fought fiercely against Saul himself. *When the archers* (אֲנָשִׁים בַּקָּשֶׁת is an explanatory apposition to הַמּוֹרִים) *hit him, i.e.* overtook him, *he was greatly alarmed at them* (יָחֶל, from חִיל or חוּל),[1] and called upon his armour-bearer to pierce him with the sword, "*lest these uncircumcised come and thrust me through, and play with me,*" *i.e.* cool their courage upon me by maltreating me. But as the armour-bearer would not do this, because he was very much afraid, since he was supposed to be answerable for the king's life, Saul inflicted death upon himself with his sword; whereupon the armour-bearer also fell upon his sword and died with his king, so that on that day Saul and his three sons and his armour-bearer all died; also "*all his men*" (for which we have "all his house" in the Chronicles), *i.e.* not all the warriors who went out with him to battle, but all the king's servants, or all the members of his house, *sc.* who had taken part in the battle. Neither Abner nor his son Ishbosheth was included, for the latter was not in the battle; and although the former was Saul's cousin and commander-in-chief (see ch. xiv. 50, 51), he did not belong to his house or servants.—Ver. 7. When the men of Israel upon the sides that were opposite to the valley (Jezreel) and the Jordan saw that the Israelites (the Israelitish troop) fled, and Saul and his sons were dead, they took to flight out of the cities, whereupon the Philistines took possession of them. עֵבֶר is used here to signify the side opposite to the place of conflict in the valley of Jezreel, which the writer assumed as his stand-

---

[1] The LXX. have adopted the rendering καὶ ἐτραυμάτισαν εἰς τὰ ὑποχόνδρια, they wounded him in the abdomen, whilst the Vulgate rendering is *vulneratus est vehementer a sagittariis*. In 1 Chron. x. 3 the Sept rendering is καὶ ἐπόνεσεν ἀπὸ τῶν τόξων, and that of the Vulgate *et vulneraverunt jaculis*. The translators have therefore derived יָחֶל from חָלַל = חָלָה, and then given a free rendering to the other words. But this rendering is overthrown by the word מְאֹד, very, vehemently, to say nothing of the fact that the verb חָלַל or חָלָה cannot be proved to be ever used in the sense of wounding. If Saul had been so severely wounded that he could not kill himself, and therefore asked his armour-bearer to slay him, as Thenius supposes, he would not have had the strength to pierce himself with his sword when the armour-bearer refused. The further conjecture of Thenius, that the Hebrew text should be read thus, in accordance with the LXX., וַיָּחֶל אֶל הַמֹּרְדִים, "he was wounded in the region of the gall," is opposed by the circumstance that ὑποχόνδρια is not the gall or region of the gall, but what is under the χόνδρος, or breast cartilage, viz. the abdomen and bowels.

point (cf. ch. xiv. 40); so that עֵבֶר הָעֵמֶק is the country to the west of the valley of Jezreel, and עֵבֶר הַיַּרְדֵּן the country to the west of the Jordan, *i.e.* between Gilboa and the Jordan. These districts, *i.e.* the whole of the country round about the valley of Jezreel, the Philistines took possession of, so that the whole of the northern part of the land of Israel, in other words the whole land with the exception of Peræa and the tribe-land of Judah, came into their hands when Saul was slain.

Vers. 8–10. On the day following the battle, when the Philistines stripped the slain, they found Saul and his three sons lying upon Gilboa; and having cut off their heads and plundered their weapons, they sent them (the heads and weapons) as trophies into the land of the Philistines, *i.e.* round about to the different towns and hamlets of their land, to announce the joyful news in their idol-temples (the writer of the Chronicles mentions the idols themselves) and to the people, and then deposited their weapons (the weapons of Saul and his sons) in the Astarte-houses. But the corpses they fastened to the town-wall of Beth-shean, *i.e.* Beisan, in the valley of the Jordan (see at Josh. xvii. 11). *Beth-azabbim* and *Beth-ashtaroth* are composite words; the first part is indeclinable, and the plural form is expressed by the second word: *idol-houses* and *Astarte-houses*, like *beth-aboth* (father's-houses: see at Ex. vi. 14). On the *Astartes*, see at Judg. ii. 13. It is not expressly stated indeed in vers. 9, 10, that the Philistines plundered the bodies of Saul's sons as well, and mutilated them by cutting off their heads; but רֹאשׁוֹ and כֵּלָיו, *his* (*i.e.* Saul's) *head* and *his weapons*, alone are mentioned. At the same time, it is very evident from ver. 12, where the Jabeshites are said to have taken down from the wall of Beth-shean not Saul's body only, but the bodies of his sons also, that the Philistines had treated the corpses of Saul's sons in just the same manner as that of Saul himself. The writer speaks distinctly of the abuse of Saul's body only, because it was his death that he had chiefly in mind at the time. To the word וַיְשַׁלְּחוּ we must supply in thought the object רֹאשׁוֹ and כֵּלָיו from the preceding clause. גְּוִיַּת and גְּוִיֹּת (vers. 10 and 12) are the corpses without the heads. The fact that the Philistines nailed them to the town-wall of Beth-shean presupposes the capture of that city, from which it is evident that they had occupied the land as far as the Jordan. The definite word

Beth-ashtaroth is changed by the writer of the Chronicles into *Beth-elohim*, temples of the gods; or rather he has interpreted it in this manner without altering the sense, as the Astartes are merely mentioned as the principal deities for the idols generally. The writer of the Chronicles has also omitted to mention the nailing of the corpses to the wall of Beth-shean, but he states instead that "they fastened his skull in the temple of Dagon," a fact which is passed over in the account before us. From this we may see how both writers have restricted themselves to the principal points, or those which appeared to them of the greatest importance (*vid.* Bertheau on 1 Chron. x. 10).

Vers. 11–13. When the inhabitants of Jabesh in Gilead heard this, all the brave men of the town set out to Beth-shean, took down the bodies of Saul and his sons from the wall, brought them to Jabesh, and burned them there. "*But their bones they buried under the tamarisk at Jabesh, and fasted seven days,*" to mourn for the king their former deliverer (see ch. xi.). These statements are given in a very condensed form in the Chronicles (vers. 11, 12). Not only is the fact that "they went the whole night" omitted, as being of no essential importance to the general history; but the removal of the bodies from the town-wall is also passed over, because their being fastened there had not been mentioned, and also the burning of the bodies. The reason for the last omission is not to be sought for in the fact that the author of the Chronicles regarded burning as ignominious, according to Lev. xx. 14, xxi. 9, but because he did not see how to reconcile the burning of the bodies with the burial of the bones. It was not the custom in Israel to burn the corpse, but to bury it in the ground. The former was restricted to the worst criminals (see at Lev. xx. 14). Consequently the Chaldee interpreted the word "burnt" as relating to the burning of spices, a custom which we meet with afterwards as a special honour shown to certain of the kings of Judah on the occasion of their burial (2 Chron. xvi. 14, xxi. 19; Jer. xxxiv. 5). But this is expressed by שָׂרַף לוֹ שְׂרֵפָה, "to make a burning for him," whereas here it is stated distinctly that "they burnt them." The reason for the burning of the bodies in the case of Saul and his sons is to be sought for in the peculiarity of the circumstances; viz. partly in the fact that the bodies were mutilated by the removal of the heads, and therefore a regular burial of the dead was impossible, and partly in their anxiety lest, if the Philistines followed up their victory and came to Jabesh, they should desecrate the bodies still further. But even this was not a complete burning to ashes, but merely a burning of the skin and flesh; so that the bones still remained, and they were buried in the ground under a shady tree. Instead of "under the (well-known) tamarisk" (*eshel*), we have תַּחַת הָאֵלָה (under the strong tree) in 1 Chron. x. 11. David afterwards had them fetched away and buried in Saul's family grave at Zela, in the land of Benjamin (2 Sam. xxi. 11 sqq.). The seven days' fast kept by the Jabeshites was a sign of public and general mourning on the part of the inhabitants of that town at the death of the king, who had once rescued them from the most abominable slavery.

In this ignominious fate of Saul there was manifested the righteous judgment of God in consequence of the hardening of his heart. But the love which the citizens of Jabesh displayed in their treatment of the corpses of Saul and his sons, had reference not to the king as rejected by God, but to the king as anointed with the Spirit of Jehovah, and was a practical condemnation, not of the divine judgment which had fallen upon Saul, but of the cruelty of the enemies of Israel and its anointed. For although Saul had waged war almost incessantly against the Philistines, it is not known that in any one of his victories he had ever been guilty of such cruelties towards the conquered and slaughtered foe as could justify this barbarous revenge on the part of the uncircumcised upon his lifeless corpse.

THE SECOND BOOK OF SAMUEL.

THIS book contains the history of *David's* reign, arranged according to its leading features: viz. (1) the commencement of his reign as king of *Judah* at Hebron, whereas the other tribes of Israel adhered to the house of Saul (ch. i.-iv.); (2) his promotion to be king over all Israel, and the victorious extension of his sway (ch. v.-ix.); (3) the decline of his power in consequence of his adultery (ch. x.-xx.); (4) the close of his reign (ch. xxi.-xxiv.). Parallels and supplements to this history, in which the reign of David is described chiefly in its connection with the development of the kingdom of God under the Old Testament, are given in ch. xi.-xxviii. of the first book of Chronicles, where we have an elaborate description of the things done by David, both for the elevation and organization of the public worship of God, and also for the consolidation and establishment of the whole kingdom, and the general administration of government.

I. DAVID KING OVER JUDAH; AND ISHBOSHETH KING OVER ISRAEL.

When David received the tidings at Ziklag of the defeat of Israel and the death of Saul, he mourned deeply and sincerely for the fallen king and his noble son Jonathan (ch. i.). He then returned by the permission of God into the land of Judah, namely to Hebron, and was anointed king of Judah by the elders of that tribe; whereas Abner, the cousin and chief general of Saul, took Ishbosheth, the only remaining son of the fallen monarch, and made him king over the other tribes of Israel at Mahanaim (ch. ii. 1-11). This occasioned a civil war. Abner marched to Gibeon against David with the forces of Ishbosheth, but was defeated by Joab, David's commander-in-chief, and pursued to Mahanaim, in which pursuit Abner slew Asahel the brother of Joab, who was eagerly following him (ch. ii. 12-32). Nevertheless, the conflict between the house of David and the house of Saul continued for some time longer, but with the former steadily advancing and the latter declining, until at length Abner quarrelled with Ishbosheth, and persuaded the tribes that had hitherto adhered to him to acknowledge David as king over all Israel. After the negotiations with David for effecting this, he was assassinated by Joab on his return from Hebron,—an act at which David not only expressed his abhorrence by a solemn mourning for Abner, but declared it still more openly by cursing Joab's crime (ch. iii.). Shortly afterwards, Ishbosheth was assassinated in his own house by two Benjaminites; but this murder was also avenged by David, who ordered the murderers to be put to death, and the head of Ishbosheth, that had been delivered up to him, to be buried in Abner's tomb (ch. iv.). Thus the civil war and the threatened split in the kingdom were brought to an end, though without any complicity on the part of David, but rather against his will, viz. through the death of Abner, the author of the split, and of Ishbosheth, whom he had placed upon the throne, both of whom fell by treacherous hands, and received the reward of their rebellion against the ordinance of God. David himself, in his long school of affliction under Saul, had learned to put all his hope in the Lord his God; and therefore, when Saul was dead, he took no steps to grasp by force the kingdom which God had promised him, or to remove his rival out of the way by crime.

DAVID'S CONDUCT ON HEARING OF SAUL'S DEATH. HIS ELEGY UPON SAUL AND JONATHAN.—CHAP. I.

David received the intelligence of the defeat of Israel and the death of Saul in the war with the Philistines from an Amalekite, who boasted of having slain Saul and handed over to David the crown and armlet of the fallen king, but whom David punished with death for the supposed murder of the anointed of God (vers. 1-16). David mourned for the death of Saul and Jonathan, and poured out his grief in an elegiac ode (vers. 17-27). This account is closely connected with the concluding chapters of the first book of Samuel.

Vers. 1-16. *David receives the news of Saul's death.*—Vers. 1-4. After the death of Saul, and David's return to Ziklag from his campaign against the Amalekites, there came a man to David on the third day, with his clothes torn and earth strewed upon his head (as a sign of deep mourning: see at 1 Sam. iv. 12), who informed him of the flight and overthrow of the Israelitish army, and the death of Saul and Jonathan.—Ver. 1 may be regarded as the protasis to ver. 2, so far as the contents are concerned, although formally it is rounded off, and וַיֵּשֶׁב forms the apodosis to וַיְהִי : "*It came to pass after the death of Saul, David had returned from the slaughter of the Amalekites* (1 Sam. xxx. 1-26), *that David remained at Ziklag two days. And it came to pass on the third day*," etc. Both of these notices of the time refer to the day, on which David returned to Ziklag from the pursuit and defeat of the Amalekites. Whether the battle at Gilboa, in which Saul fell, occurred before or after the return of David, it is impossible to determine. All that follows from the juxtaposition of the two events in ver. 1, is that they were nearly contemporaneous. The man "*came from the army from with Saul*," and therefore appears to have kept near to Saul during the battle.—Ver. 4. David's inquiry, "*How did the thing happen?*" refers to the statement made by the messenger, that he had escaped from the army of Israel. In the answer, אֲשֶׁר serves, like כִּי in other passages, merely to introduce the words that follow, like our *namely* (vid. Ewald, § 338, *b*). "*The people fled from the fight; and not only have many of the people fallen, but Saul and Jonathan his son are also dead.*" וְגַם ... וְגַם : *not only ... but also.*—Vers. 5 sqq. To David's further inquiry how he knew this, the young man replied (vers. 6-10), "*I happened to come* (נִקְרֹה = נִקְרָא) *up to the mountains of Gilboa, and saw Saul leaning upon his spear; then the chariots* (the war-chariots for the charioteers) *and riders were pressing upon him, and he turned round and saw me, ... and asked me, Who art thou? and I said, An Amalekite; and he said to me, Come hither to me, and slay me, for the cramp* (שָׁבָץ *according to the Rabbins*) *hath seized me* (sc. so that I cannot defend myself, and must fall into the hands of the Philistines); *for my soul (my life) is still whole in me*. *Then I went to him, and slew him, because I knew that after his fall he would not live; and took the crown upon his head, and the bracelet upon his arm, and brought them to my lord*" (David). "After his fall" does not mean "after he had fallen upon his sword or spear" (Clericus), for this is neither implied in נֹפְלִי nor in נִשְׁעָן עַל־חֲנִיתוֹ ("supported, *i.e.* leaning upon his spear"), nor are we at liberty to transfer it from 1 Sam. xxxi. 4 into this passage; but "*after his defeat*,' *i.e.* so that he would not survive this calamity. This statement is at variance with the account of the death of Saul in 1 Sam. xxxi. 3 sqq.; and even apart from this it has an air of improbability, or rather of untruth in it, particularly in the assertion that Saul was leaning upon his spear when the chariots and horsemen of the enemy came upon him, without having either an armour-bearer or any other Israelitish soldier by his side, so that he had to turn to an Amalekite who accidentally came by, and to ask him to inflict the fatal wound. The Amalekite invented this, in the hope of thereby obtaining the better recompense from David. The only part of his statement which is certainly true, is that he found the king lying dead upon the field of battle, and took off the crown and armlet since he brought these to David. But it is by no means certain whether he was present when Saul expired, or merely found him after he was dead.—Vers. 11, 12. This information, the substance of which was placed beyond all doubt by the king's jewels that were brought, filled David with the deepest sorrow. As a sign of his pain he rent his clothes; and all the men with him did the same, and mourned with weeping and fasting until the evening "*for Saul and for Jonathan his son, for the people of Jehovah, and for the house of Israel, because they had fallen by the sword*" (*i.e.* in battle). "The people of Jehovah" and the "*house or people of Israel*" are distinguished from one another, according to the twofold attitude of Israel, which furnished a double ground for mourning. Those who had fallen were first of all members of the people of Jehovah, and secondly, fellow-countrymen. "They were therefore associated with them, both according to the flesh and according to the spirit, and for that reason they mourned the more" (Seb. Schmidt). "The only deep mourning for Saul, with the exception of that of the Jabeshites (1 Sam. xxxi. 11), proceeded from the man whom he had hated and persecuted for so many years even to the time of his death; just as David's successor wept over the fall of Jerusalem, even when it was about to destroy Himself" (O. v. Gerlach).—Ver. 13. David then asked the bringer of the news for further information concerning his own descent, and received the reply that he was the son of an Amalekite stranger, *i.e* of an Amalekite who had emigrated to Israel.—Ver. 14. David then reproached him for what he had done : "*How wast thou not afraid to stretch forth thine hand to destroy the Lord's anointed?*" and commanded one of his attendants to slay him (vers. 15 sqq.), passing sentence of death in these words : "*Thy blood come upon thy head* (cf. Lev. xx. 9, Josh. ii. 19) ; *for thy mouth hath testified against thee, saying, I have slain the Lord's anointed.*"[1] David regarded the statement of the Amalekite as a sufficient ground for condemnation, without investigating the truth any further ; though it was most probably untrue, as he could see through his design of securing a great reward as due to him for performing such a deed (*vid.* ch. iv. 10), and looked upon a man who could attribute such an act to himself from mere avarice as perfectly capable of committing it. Moreover, the king's jewels, which he had brought, furnished a practical proof that Saul had really been put to death. This punishment was by no means so severe as to render it necessary to "estimate its morality according to the times," or to defend it merely from the standpoint of political prudence, on the ground that as David was the successor of Saul, and had been pursued by him as his rival with constant suspicion and hatred, he ought not to leave the murder of the king unpunished, if only because the people, or at any rate his own opponents among the people, would accuse him of complicity in the murder of the king, if not of

---

[1] "*Thy mouth hath testified against thee*, and out of it thou art judged (Luke xix. 22), whether thou hast done it or not. If thou hast done it, thou receivest the just reward of thy deeds. If thou hast not done it, then throw the blame upon thine own lying testimony, and be content with the wages of a wicked flatterer ; for, according to thine own confession, thou art the murderer of a king, and that is quite enough to betray thine evil heart. David could see plainly enough that the man was no murderer : he would show by his example that flatterers who boast of such sins as these should get no hearing from their superiors."—*Berleb. Bible.*

actually instigating the murderer. David would never have allowed such considerations as these to lead him into unjust severity. And his conduct requires no such half vindication. Even on the supposition that Saul had asked the Amalekite to give him his death-thrust, as he said he had, it was a crime deserving of punishment to fulfil this request, the more especially as nothing is said about any such mortal wounding of Saul as rendered his escape or recovery impossible, so that it could be said that it would have been cruel under such circumstances to refuse his request to be put to death. If Saul's life was still "full in him," as the Amalekite stated, his position was not so desperate as to render it inevitable that he should fall into the hands of the Philistines. Moreover, the supposition was a very natural one, that he had slain the king for the sake of a reward. But slaying the king, the anointed of the Lord, was in itself a crime that deserved to be punished with death. What David might more than once have done, but had refrained from doing from holy reverence for the sanctified person of the king, this foreigner, a man belonging to the nation of the Amalekites, Israel's greatest foes, had actually done for the sake of gain, or at any rate pretended to have done. Such a crime must be punished with death, and that by David who had been chosen by God and anointed as Saul's successor, and whom the Amalekite himself acknowledged in that capacity, since otherwise he would not have brought him the news together with the royal diadem.

Vers. 17-27. *David's elegy upon Saul and Jonathan.*—An eloquent testimony to the depth and sincerity of David's grief for the death of Saul is handed down to us in the elegy which he composed upon Saul and his noble son Jonathan, and which he had taught to the children of Israel. It is one of the finest odes of the Old Testament; full of lofty sentiment, and springing from deep and sanctified emotion, in which, without the slightest allusion to his own relation to the fallen king, David celebrates without envy the bravery and virtues of Saul and his son Jonathan, and bitterly laments their loss. "*He said to teach*," *i.e.* he commanded the children of Judah to practise or learn it. קֶשֶׁת, *bow;* *i.e.* a song to which the title *Kesheth* or bow was given, not only because the bow is referred to (ver. 22), but because it is a martial ode, and the bow was one of the principal weapons used by the warriors of that age, and one in the use of which the Benjaminites, the tribe-mates of Saul, were particularly skilful: cf. 1 Chron. viii. 40, xii. 2 ; 2 Chron. xiv. 7, xvii. 17. Other explanations are by no means so natural; such, for example, as that it related to the melody to which the ode was sung; whilst some are founded upon false renderings, or arbitrary alterations of the text, *e.g.* that of Ewald (*Gesch.* i. p. 41), Thenius, etc. This elegy was inserted in "*the book of the righteous*" (see at Josh. x. 13), from which the author of the books of Samuel has taken it.

The ode is arranged in three strophes, which gradually diminish in force and sweep (viz. vers. 19-24, 25-26, 27), and in which the vehemence of the sorrow is gradually modified, and finally dies away. Each strophe opens with the exclamation, "*How are the mighty fallen!*" The *first* contains all that had to be said in praise of the fallen heroes; the deepest mourning for their death; and praise of their bravery, of their inseparable love, and of the virtues of Saul as king. The *second* commemorates the friendship between David and Jonathan. The *third* simply utters the last sigh, with which the elegy becomes silent. The *first* strophe runs thus :

Ver. 19. The ornament, O Israel, is slain upon thy heights!
 Oh how are the mighty fallen !
 20. Tell it not in Gath, publish it not in the streets of Askelon;
 Lest the daughters of the Philistines rejoice,
 Lest the daughters of the uncircumcised triumph !
 21. Ye mountains of Gilboa, let not dew or rain be upon you, or fields of first-fruit offerings :
 For there is the shield of the mighty defiled,
 The shield of Saul, not anointed with oil.
 22. From the blood of the slain, from the fat of the mighty,
 The bow of Jonathan turned not back,
 And the sword of Saul returned not empty.
 23. Saul and Jonathan, beloved and kind, in life
 And in death they are not divided.
 Lighter than eagles were they ; stronger than lions.
 24. Ye daughters of Israel, weep over Saul,
 Who clothed you in purple with delight ;
 Who put a golden ornament upon your apparel !

The first clause of ver. 19 contains the theme of the entire ode. הַצְּבִי does not mean the gazelle here (as the Syriac and Clericus and others render it), the only plausible support of which is the expression "upon thy heights," whereas the parallel גִּבּוֹרִים shows that by הַצְּבִי we are to understand the two heroes Saul and Jonathan, and that the word is used in the appellative sense of *ornament*. The king and his noble son were the ornament of Israel. They were slain upon the heights of Israel. Luther has given a correct rendering, so far as the sense is concerned (*die Edelsten*, the noblest), after the *inclyti* of the Vulgate. The pronoun "*thy* high places" refers to Israel. The reference is to the heights of the mountains of Gilboa (see ver. 21). This event threw Israel into deep mourning, which commences in the second clause.—Ver. 20. The tidings of this mourning were not to be carried out among the enemies of Israel, lest they should rejoice thereat. Such rejoicing would only increase the pain of Israel at the loss it had sustained. Only two of the cities of Philistia are mentioned by name, viz. Gath, which was near, and Askelon, which was farther off by the sea. The rejoicing of the daughters of the Philistines refers to the custom of employing women to celebrate the victories of their nation by singing and dancing (cf. 1 Sam. xviii. 6).—Ver. 21. Even nature is to join in the mourning. May God withdraw His blessing from the mountains upon which the heroes have fallen, that they may not be moistened by the dew and rain of heaven, but, remaining in eternal barrenness, be memorials of the horrible occurrence that has taken place upon them. הָרֵי בַגִּלְבֹּעַ is an address to them; and the preposition בְּ with the construct state is poetical: "*mountains in Gilboa*" (*vid.* Ewald, § 289, *b*). In עֲלֵיכֶם . . . אַל the verb יְהִי is wanting. The following words, וּשְׂדֵי תְרוּמֹת, are in apposition to the foregoing: "*and let not fields of first-fruit offerings be upon you*," i.e. fields producing fruit, from which offerings of first-fruits were presented. This is the simplest and most appropriate explanation of the words, which have been very differently, and in some respects very marvellously rendered. The reason for this cursing of the mountains of Gilboa was, that there the shield of the heroes, particularly of Saul, had been defiled with blood, namely the blood of those whom the shield ought to defend. נִגְעַל does not mean to throw away (Dietrich.), but to soil or defile (as in the Chaldee), then to abhor. "*Not anointed with oil*," i.e. not cleansed and polished with oil, so that the marks of Saul's blood still adhered to it. בְּלִי poetical for לֹא. The interpolation of the words "*as though*" (*quasi non esset unctus oleo*, Vulgate), cannot be sustained.—Ver. 22. Such was the ignominy experienced upon Gilboa by those who had always fought so bravely, that their bow and sword did not turn back until it was satisfied with the blood and fat of the slain. The figure upon which the passage is founded is, that arrows drink the blood of the enemy, and a sword devours their flesh (*vid.* Deut. xxxii. 42; Isa. xxxiv. 5, 6; Jer. xlvi. 10). The two principal weapons are divided between Saul and Jonathan, so that the bow is assigned to the latter and the sword to the former.—Ver. 23. In death as in life, the two heroes were not divided, for they were alike in bravery and courage. Notwithstanding their difference of character, and the very opposite attitude which they assumed towards David, the noble Jonathan did not forsake his father, although his fierce hatred towards the friend whom Jonathan loved as his own soul might have undermined his attachment to his father. The two predicates, נֶאֱהָב, loved and amiable, and נְעִים, affectionate or kind, apply chiefly to Jonathan; but they were also suitable to Saul in the earliest years of his reign, when he manifested the virtues of an able ruler, which secured for him the lasting affection and attachment of the people. In his mourning over the death of the fallen hero, David forgets all the injury that Saul has inflicted upon him, so that he only brings out and celebrates the more amiable aspects of his character. The light motion or swiftness of an eagle (cf. Hab. i. 8), and the strength of a lion (*vid.* ch. xvii. 10), were the leading characteristics of the great heroes of antiquity.—Lastly, in ver. 24, David commemorates the rich booty which Saul had brought to the nation, for the purpose of celebrating his heroic greatness in this respect as well. שָׁנִי was the scarlet purple (see at Ex. xxv. 4). " With delights," or with lovelinesses, *i.e.* in a lovely manner.

The *second* strophe (vers. 25 and 26) only applies to the friendship of Jonathan:

> Ver. 25. Oh how are the mighty fallen in the midst of the battle!
> Jonathan (is) slain upon thy heights!
> 26. I am distressed for thee, my brother Jonathan:
> Thou wast very kind to me:
> Stranger than the love of woman was thy love to me!

Ver. 25 is almost a verbal repetition of ver. 19. צַר (ver.

26) denotes the pinching or pressure of the heart consequent upon pain and mourning. נִפְלְאַתָה, *third pers. fem.*, like a verb ל"ה with the termination lengthened (*vid.* Ewald, § 194, *b*), to be wonderful or distinguished. אַהֲבָתְךָ, thy love to me. Comparison to the love of woman is expressive of the deepest earnestness of devoted love.

The *third* strophe (ver. 27) contains simply a brief aftertone of sorrow, in which the ode dies away:

Oh how are the mighty fallen,
The instruments of war perished!

"*The instruments of war*" are not the weapons; but the expression is a figurative one, referring to the heroes by whom war was carried on (*vid.* Isa. xiii. 5). Luther has adopted this rendering (*die Streitbaren*).

DAVID KING OVER JUDAH, AND ISHBOSHETH KING OVER ISRAEL. BATTLE AT GIBEON.—CHAP. II.

After David had mourned for the fallen king, he went, in accordance with the will of the Lord as sought through the Urim, to Hebron, and was there anointed king by the tribe of Judah. He then sent his thanks to the inhabitants of Jabesh, for the love which they had shown to Saul in burying his bones (vers. 1–7), and reigned seven years and a half at Hebron over Judah alone (vers. 10 and 11). Abner, on the other hand, put forward Ishbosheth the son of Saul, who still remained alive, as king over Israel (vers. 8 and 9); so that a war broke out between the adherents of Ishbosheth and those of David, in which Abner and his army were beaten, but the brave Asahel, the son-in-law of David, was slain by Abner (vers. 12–32). The promotion of Ishbosheth as king was not only a continuation of the hostility of Saul towards David, but also an open act of rebellion against Jehovah, who had rejected Saul and chosen David prince over Israel, and who had given such distinct proofs of this election in the eyes of the whole nation, that even Saul had been convinced of the appointment of David to be his successor upon the throne. But David attested his unqualified submission to the guidance of God, in contrast with this rebellion against His clearly revealed will, not only by not returning to Judah till he had received permission from the Lord, but also by the fact that after the tribe of Judah had acknowledged him as king, he did not go to war with Ishbosheth, but contented himself with resisting the attack made upon him by the supporters of the house of Saul, because he was fully confident that the Lord would secure to him in due time the whole of the kingdom of Israel.

Vers. 1–4a. *David's return to Hebron, and anointing as king over Judah.*—Ver. 1. "*After this*," *i.e.* after the facts related in ch. i., David inquired of the Lord, namely through the Urim, whether he should go up to one of the towns of Judah, and if so, to which. He received the reply, "*to Hebron*," a place peculiarly well adapted for a capital, not only from its situation upon the mountains, and in the centre of the tribe, but also from the sacred reminiscences connected with it from the olden time. David could have no doubt that, now that Saul was dead, he would have to give up his existing connection with the Philistines and return to his own land. But as the Philistines had taken the greater part of the Israelitish territory through their victory at Gilboa, and there was good reason to fear that the adherents of Saul, more especially the army with Abner, Saul's cousin, at its head, would refuse to acknowledge David as king, and consequently a civil war might break out, David would not return to his own land without the express permission of the Lord. Vers. 2–4a. When he went with his wives and all his retinue (*vid.* 1 Sam. xxvii. 2) to Hebron and the "*cities of Hebron,*" *i.e.* the places belonging to the territory of Hebron, the men of Judah came (in the persons of their elders) and anointed him king *over the house, i.e.* the tribe, *of Judah.* Just as Saul was made king by the tribes after his anointing by Samuel (1 Sam. xi. 15), so David was first of all anointed by Judah here, and afterwards by the rest of the tribes (ch. v. 3).

Vers. 4b–7. A new section commences with וַיַּגִּדוּ. The first act of David as king was to send messengers to Jabesh, to thank the inhabitants of this city for burying Saul, and to announce to them his own anointing as king. As this expression of thanks involved a solemn recognition of the departed king, by which David divested himself of even the appearance of a rebellion, the announcement of the anointing he had received contained an indirect summons to the Jabeshites to recognise him as their king now.—Ver. 6. "*And now,*" sc. that ye have shown this love to Saul your lord, "*may Jehovah show you grace and truth.*" "*Grace and truth*" are connected together, as in Ex. xxxiv. 6, as the two sides by which the goodness of God is manifested to men, namely in His forgiving grace, and in His trustworthiness, or the fulfilment of His promises (*vid.* Ps. xxv. 10). "*And I also show you this good,*" namely the prayer for the blessing of God (ver. 5), because ye have done this (to Saul). In ver. 7 there is attached to this the demand, that now that Saul their lord was dead, and the Judæans had anointed him (David) king, they would show themselves valiant, namely valiant in their reverence and fidelity towards David, who had become their king since the death of Saul. תֶּחֱזַקְנָה יְדֵיכֶם, *i.e.* be comforted, spirited (cf. Judg. vii. 11). It needed some resolution and courage to recognise David as king, because Saul's army had fled to Gilead, and there was good ground for apprehending opposition to David on the part of Abner. Ishbosheth, however, does not appear to have been proclaimed king yet; or at any rate the fact was not yet known to David. וְגַם does not belong to אֹתִי, but to the whole clause, as אֹתִי is placed first merely for the sake of emphasis.

Vers. 8-11. *Promotion of Ishbosheth to be king over Israel.* —The account of this is attached to the foregoing in the form of an antithesis: "*But Abner, the chief captain of Saul* (see at 1 Sam. xiv. 50), *had taken Ishbosheth the son of Saul, and led him over to Mahanaim.*" Ishbosheth had probably been in the battle at Gilboa, and fled with Abner across the Jordan after the battle had been lost. *Ishbosheth* (*i.e.* man of shame) was the fourth son of Saul (according to 1 Chron. viii. 33, ix. 39): his proper name was *Esh-baal* (*i.e.* fire of Baal, probably equivalent to destroyer of Baal). This name was afterwards changed into Ishbosheth, just as the name of the god Baal was also translated into *Bosheth* ("shame," Hos. ix 10, Jer. iii. 24, etc.), and Jerubbaal changed into Jerubbosheth (see at Judg. viii. 35). Ewald's supposition, that *bosheth* was originally employed in a good sense as well, like αἰδώς and פַּחַד (Gen. xxxi. 53), cannot be sustained. *Mahanaim* was on the eastern side of the Jordan, not far from the ford of Jabbok, and was an important place for the execution of Abner's plans, partly from its historical associations (Gen. xxxii. 2, 3), and partly also from its situation. There he made Ishbosheth king "*for Gilead*," *i.e.* the whole of the land to the east of the Jordan (as in Num. xxxii. 29, Josh. xxii. 9, etc.). "*For the Ashurites:*" this reading is decidedly faulty, since we can no more suppose it to refer to Assyria (Asshur) than to the Arabian tribe of the Assurim (Gen. xxv. 3) ; but the true name cannot be discovered.[1] "*And for Jezreel,*" *i.e.* not merely the city of that name, but the plain that was named after it (as in 1 Sam. xxix. 1). "*And for Ephraim, and Benjamin, and all* (the rest of) *Israel,*" of course not including Judah, where David had already been acknowledged as king.—Vers. 10, 11. *Length of the reigns of Ishbosheth over Israel, and David at Hebron.* The age of Ishbosheth is given, as is generally the case at the commencement of a reign. He was forty years old when he began to reign, and reigned *two years;* whereas David was king at Hebron over the house of Judah *seven years and a half.* We are struck with this difference in the length of the two reigns; and it cannot be explained, as Seb. Schmidt, Clericus, and others suppose, on the simple assumption that David reigned two years at Hebron over *Judah*, namely up to the time of the murder of Ishbosheth, and then five years and a half over *Israel,* namely up to the time of the conquest

---

[1] In the Septuagint we find Θασιρί or Θασούρ, an equally mistaken form. The Chaldee has "over the tribe of Asher," which is also unsuitable, unless we include the whole of the northern portion of Canaan, including the territory of Zebulun and Naphtali. But there is no proof that the name *Asher* was ever extended to the territory of the three northern tribes. We should be rather disposed to agree with Bachienne, who supposes it to refer to the city of Asher (Josh. xvii. 7) and its territory, as this city was in the southeast of Jezreel, and Abner may possibly have conquered this district for Ishbosheth with Gilead as a base, before he ventured to dispute the government of Israel with the Philistines, if only we could discover any reason why the inhabitants ("*the Ashurites*") should be mentioned instead of the city *Asher*, or if it were at all likely that one city should be introduced in the midst of a number of large districts. The Syriac and Vulgate have *Geshuri*, and therefore seem to have read or conjectured הַגְּשׁוּרִי ; and Thenius decides in favour of this, understanding the name *Geshur* to refer to the most northerly portion of the land on both sides of the Jordan, from Mount Hermon to the Lake of Gennesareth (as in Deut. iii. 14, Josh. xii. 5, xiii. 13, 1 Chron. ii. 23). But no such usage of speech can be deduced from any of these passages, as *Geshuri* is used there to denote the land of the Geshurites, on the north-east of Bashan, which had a king of its own in the time of David (see at ch. iii. 3), and which Abner would certainly never have thought of conquering.

of Jerusalem: for this is at variance with the plain statement in the text, that "David was king in Hebron over the house of Judah seven years and a half." The opinion that the two years of Ishbosheth's reign are to be reckoned up to the time of the war with David, because Abner played the principal part during the other five years and a half that David continued to reign at Hebron, is equally untenable. We may see very clearly from ch. iii.-v. not only that Ishbosheth was king to the time of his death, which took place after that of Abner, but also that after both these events David was anointed king over Israel in Hebron by all the tribes, and that he then went directly to attack Jerusalem, and after conquering the citadel of Zion, chose that city as his own capital. The short duration of Ishbosheth's reign can only be explained, therefore, on the supposition that he was not made king, as David was, immediately after the death of Saul, but after the recovery by Abner of the land which the Philistines had taken on this side the Jordan, which may have occupied five years.[1]

Vers. 12-32. *War between the supporters of Ishbosheth and those of David.*—Vers. 12, 13. When Abner had brought all Israel under the dominion of Ishbosheth, he also sought to make Judah subject to him, and went with this intention from Mahanaim to *Gibeon*, the present Jib, in the western portion of the tribe of Benjamin, two good hours to the north of Jerusalem (see at Josh. ix. 3), taking with him the servants, *i.e.* the fighting men, of Ishbosheth. There Joab, a son of Zeruiah, David's sister (1 Chron. ii. 16), advanced to meet him with the servants, *i.e.* the warriors of David; and the two armies met at

---

[1] From the fact that in vers. 10, 11, Ishbosheth's ascending the throne is mentioned before that of David, and is also accompanied with a statement of his age, whereas the age of David is not given till ch. v. 4, 5, when he became king over all Israel, Ewald draws the erroneous conclusion that the earlier (?) historian regarded Ishbosheth as the true king, and David as a pretender. But the very opposite of this is stated as distinctly as possible in vers. 4 sqq. (compared with ver. 8). The fact that Ishbosheth is mentioned before David in ver. 10 may be explained simply enough from the custom so constantly observed in the book of Genesis, of mentioning subordinate lines or subordinate persons first, and stating whatever seemed worth recording with regard to them, in order that the ground might be perfectly clear for relating the history of the principal characters without any interruption.

the pool of Gibeon, *i.e.* probably one of the large reservoirs that are still to be found there (see Rob. *Pal.* ii. pp. 135–6; Tobler, *Topogr. v. Jerusalem*, ii. pp. 515–6), the one encamping upon the one side of the pool and the other upon the other.—Vers. 14 sqq. Abner then proposed to Joab that the contest should be decided by single combat, probably for the purpose of avoiding an actual civil war. "*Let the young men arise and wrestle before us.*" שָׂחַק, to joke or play, is used here to denote the war-play of single combat. As Joab accepted this proposal, twelve young warriors for Benjamin and Ishbosheth, and twelve from David's men, went over, *i.e.* went out of the two camps to the appointed scene of conflict; "*and one seized the other's head, and his sword was* (immediately) *in the side of the other* (his antagonist), *so that they fell together.*" The clause וְחַרְבּוֹ בְּצַד רֵעֵהוּ is a circumstantial clause: and his sword (every one's sword) was in the side of the other, *i.e.* thrust into it. Sending the sword into the opponent's side is thus described as simultaneous with the seizure of his head. The ancient translators expressed the meaning by supplying a verb (ἐνέπηξαν, *defixit*: LXX., Vulg.). This was a sign that the young men on both sides fought with great ferocity, and also with great courage. The place itself received the name of *Helkath-hazzurim*, "*field of the sharp edges,*" in consequence (for this use of *zur*, see Ps. lxxxix. 44).—Ver. 17. As this single combat decided nothing, there followed a general and very sore or fierce battle, in which Abner and his troops were put to flight by the soldiers of David. The only thing connected with this, of which we have any further account, is the slaughter of Asahel by Abner, which is mentioned here (vers. 18–23) on account of the important results which followed. Of the three sons of Zeruiah, viz. Joab, Abishai, and Asahel, Asahel was peculiarly light of foot, like one of the gazelles; and he pursued Abner most eagerly, without turning aside to the right or to the left.—Vers. 20, 21. Then Abner turned round, asked him whether he was Asahel, and said to him, "*Turn to thy right hand or to thy left, and seize one of the young men and take his armour for thyself,*" *i.e.* slay one of the common soldiers, and take his accoutrements as booty, if thou art seeking for that kind of fame. But Asahel would not turn back from Abner. Then he repeated his command that he would depart, and added, "*Why should I smite thee to the ground, and how could I then lift up my face to Joab thy brother?*" from which we may see that Abner did not want to put the young hero to death, out of regard for Joab and their former friendship.—Ver. 23. But when he still refused to depart in spite of this warning, Abner wounded him in the abdomen with the hinder part, *i.e.* the lower end of the spear, so that the spear came out behind, and Asahel fell dead upon the spot. The lower end of the spear appears to have been pointed, that it might be stuck into the ground (*vid.* 1 Sam. xxvi. 7); and this will explain the fact that the spear passed through the body. The fate of the young hero excited such sympathy, that all who came to the place where he had fallen stood still to mourn his loss (cf. ch. xx. 12).—Ver. 24. But Joab and Abishai pursued Abner till the sun set, and until they had arrived at the hill *Ammah*, in front of *Giah*, on the way to the desert of *Gibeon*. Nothing further is known of the places mentioned here.—Vers. 25, 26. The Benjaminites then gathered in a crowd behind Abner, and halted upon the top of a hill to beat back their pursuers; and Abner cried out to Joab, "*Shall the sword then devour for ever* (shall there be no end to the slaughter)? *dost thou not know that bitterness arises at last? and how long wilt thou not say to the people, to return from pursuing their brethren?*" Thus Abner warns Joab of the consequences of a desperate struggle, and calls upon him to put an end to all further bloodshed by suspending the pursuit.—Ver. 27. Joab replied, "*If thou hadst not spoken* (*i.e.* challenged to single combat, ver. 14), *the people would have gone away in the morning, every one from his brother,*" *i.e.* there would have been no such fratricidal conflict at all. The first כִּי introduces the substance of the oath, as in 1 Sam. xxv. 34; the second gives greater force to it (*vid.* Ewald, § 330, *b*). Thus Joab threw all the blame of the fight upon Abner, because he had been the instigator of the single combat; and as that was not decisive, and was so bloody in its character, the two armies had felt obliged to fight it out. But he then commanded the trumpet to be blown for a halt, and the pursuit to be closed—Ver. 29. Abner proceeded with his troops through the *Arabah*, *i.e.* the valley of the Jordan, marching the whole night; and then crossing the river, went through the whole of *Bithron* back to Mahanaim. *Bithron* is a district upon the eastern side of the Jordan, which is only mentioned here. Aquila and the Vulgate identify it with *Bethhoron*;

but there is no more foundation for this than for the suggestion of Thenius, that it is the same place as *Bethharam*, the later *Libias*, at the mouth of the Nahr Hesbân (see at Num. xxxii. 36). It is very evident that *Bithron* is not the name of a city, but of a district, from the fact that it is preceded by the word *all*, which would be perfectly unmeaning in the case of a city. The meaning of the word is a cutting; and it was no doubt the name given to some ravine in the neighbourhood of the Jabbok, between the Jordan and Mahanaim, which was on the north side of the Jabbok.—Vers. 30, 31. Joab also assembled his men for a retreat. Nineteen of his soldiers were missing besides Asahel, all of whom had fallen in the battle. But they had slain as many as three hundred and sixty of Benjamin and of Abner's men. This striking disproportion in the numbers may be accounted for from the fact that in Joab's army there were none but brave and well-tried men, who had gathered round David a long time before; whereas in Abner's army there were only the remnants of the Israelites who had been beaten upon Gilboa, and who had been still further weakened and depressed by their attempts to recover the land which was occupied by the Philistines.—Ver. 32. On the way back, David's men took up the body of Asahel, and buried it in his father's grave at Bethlehem. They proceeded thence towards Hebron, marching the whole night, so that they reached Hebron itself at daybreak. "*It got light to them* (*i.e.* the day dawned) *at Hebron.*"

DAVID ADVANCES AND ISHBOSHETH DECLINES. ABNER GOES OVER TO DAVID, AND IS MURDERED BY JOAB.—CHAP. III.

Ver. 1. "*And the war became long* (was protracted) *between the house of Saul and the house of David; but David became stronger and stronger, and the house of Saul weaker and weaker.*" הָלַךְ, when connected with another verb or with an adjective, expresses the idea of the gradual progress of an affair (*vid.* Ges § 131, 3, Anm. 3). The historian sums up in these words the historical course of the two royal houses, as they stood opposed to one another. "*The war*" does not mean continual fighting, but the state of hostility or war in which they continued to stand towards one another. They concluded no peace, so that David was not recognised by Ishbosheth as king, any more than Ishbosheth by David. Not only is there nothing said about any continuance of actual warfare by Abner or Ishbosheth after the loss of the battle at Gibeon, but such a thing was very improbable in itself, as Ishbosheth was too weak to be able to carry on the war, whilst David waited with firm reliance upon the promise of the Lord, until all Israel should come over to him.

Vers. 2-5. GROWTH OF THE HOUSE OF DAVID.—Proof of the advance of the house of David is furnished by the multiplication of his family at Hebron. The account of *the sons who were born to David at Hebron* does not break the thread, as Clericus, Thenius, and others suppose, but is very appropriately introduced here, as a practical proof of the strengthening of the house of David, in harmony with the custom of beginning the history of the reign of every king with certain notices concerning his family (*vid.* ch. v. 13 sqq.; 1 Kings iii. 1, xiv. 21, xv. 2, 9, etc.). We have a similar list of the sons of David in 1 Chron. iii. 1-4. The first two sons were born to him from the two wives whom he had brought with him to Hebron (1 Sam. xxv. 42, 43). The *Chethibh* וילדו is probably only a copyist's error for וַיִּוָּלְדוּ, which is the reading in many Codices. From *Ahinoam*—the first-born, *Amnon* (called Aminon in ch. xiii. 20); from *Abigail*—the second, *Chileab*. The latter is also called *Daniel* in 1 Chron. iii. 1, and therefore had probably two names. The *lamed* before Ahinoam and the following names serves as a periphrasis for the genitive, like the German *von*, in consequence of the word *son* being omitted (*vid.* Ewald, § 292, *a*). The other four were by wives whom he had married in Hebron : *Absalom* by *Maachah*, the daughter of Talmai king of Geshur, a small kingdom in the north-east of Bashan (see at Deut. iii. 14); *Adonijah* by *Haggith*; *Shephatiah* by *Abital*; and *Ithream* by *Eglah*. The origin of the last three wives is unknown. The clause appended to Eglah's name, viz. "*David's wife*," merely serves as a fitting conclusion to the whole list (Bertheau on 1 Chron. iii. 3), and is not added to show that Eglah was David's principal wife, which would necessitate the conclusion drawn by the Rabbins, that Michal was the wife intended.

Vers. 6–39. DECLINE OF THE HOUSE OF SAUL.—Vers. 6–11. *Abner's quarrel with Ishbosheth.*—During the war between the house of Saul and the house of David, Abner adhered firmly to the house of Saul, but he appropriated one of Saul's concubines to himself. When Ishbosheth charged him with this, he fell into so violent a rage, that he at once announced to Ishbosheth his intention to hand over the kingdom to David. Abner had certainly perceived the utter incapacity of Ishbosheth for a very long time, if not from the very outset, and had probably made him king after the death of Saul, merely that he might save himself from the necessity of submitting to David, and might be able to rule in Ishbosheth's name, and possibly succeed in paving his own way to the throne. His appropriation of the concubine of the deceased monarch was at any rate a proof, according to Israelitish notions, and in fact those generally prevalent in the East, that he was aiming at the throne (*vid.* ch. xvi. 21; 1 Kings ii. 21). But it may gradually have become obvious to him, that the house of Saul could not possibly retain the government in opposition to David; and this may have led to his determination to persuade all the Israelites to acknowledge David, and thereby to secure for himself an influential post under his government. This will explain in a very simple manner Abner's falling away from Ishbosheth and going over to David.—Vers. 6 and 7 constitute one period, expanded by the introduction of circumstantial clauses, the וַיְהִי (it came to pass) of the protasis being continued in the וַיֹּאמֶר (he said) of ver. 7b. "*It came to pass, when there was war between the house of Saul and the house of David, and Abner showed himself strong for the house of Saul, and Saul had a concubine named Rizpah, the daughter of Aiah, that he* (Ishbosheth) *said to Abner, Why hast thou gone to my father's concubine?*" The subject to "*said*" is omitted in the apodosis; but it is evident from ver. 8, and the expression "*my father*," that *Ishbosheth* is to be supplied. Even in the second circumstantial clause, "*and Saul had a concubine,*" the reason why this is mentioned is only to be gathered from Ishbosheth's words. הִתְחַזֵּק בְּ: to prove one's self strong for, or with, a person, *i.e.* to render him powerful help. בּוֹא אֶל means "*to cohabit with.*" It was the exclusive right of the successor to the throne to cohabit with the concubines of the deceased king, who came down to him as part of the property which he inherited.—Ver. 8. Abner was so enraged at Ishbosheth's complaint, that he replied, "*Am I a dog's head, holding with Judah? To-day* (*i.e.* at present) *I show affection to the house of Saul thy father, towards his brethren and his friends, and did not let thee fall into the hand of David, and thou reproachest me to-day with the fault with the woman?*" "*Dog's head*" is something thoroughly contemptible. אֲשֶׁר לִיהוּדָה, *lit.* which (belongs) to Judah, *i.e.* holds with Judah.—Ver. 9. "*God do so to Abner, . . . as Jehovah hath sworn to David, so will I do to him.*" The repetition of כִּי serves to introduce the oath, as in ch. ii. 27. "*To take away the kingdom from the house of Saul, and set up the throne of David over Israel and over Judah, from Dan to Beersheba.*" We do not know of any oath with which God had promised the kingdom to David; but the promise of God in itself is equivalent to an oath, as God is the true God, who can neither lie nor deceive (1 Sam. xv. 29; Num. xxiii. 19). This promise was generally known in Israel. "*From Dan to Beersheba*" (as in Judg. xx. 1).—Ver. 11. Ishbosheth could make no reply to these words of Abner, "*because he was afraid of him.*"

Vers. 12–21. *Abner goes over to David.*—Ver. 12. Abner soon carried out his threat to Ishbosheth. He sent messengers to David *in his stead* (not "on the spot," or immediately, a rendering adopted by the Chaldee and Symmachus, but for which no support can be found) with this message: "*Whose is the land?*" *i.e.* to whom does it belong except to thee? and, "*Make a covenant with me; behold, so is my hand with thee* (*i.e.* so will I stand by thee), *to turn all Israel to thee.*"—Ver. 13. David assented to the proposal on this condition: "*Only one thing do I require of thee, namely, Thou shalt not see my face, unless thou first of all bringest me Michal, the daughter of Saul, when thou comest to see my face.*" כִּי אִם־לִפְנֵי הֲבִיאֲךָ, "*except before thy bringing,*" *i.e.* unless when thou hast first of all brought or delivered "Michal to me." This condition was imposed by David, not only because Michal had been unjustly taken away from him by Saul, after he had rightfully acquired her for his wife by paying the dowry demanded, and in spite of her love to him (1 Sam. xviii. 27, xix. 11, 12), and given to another man (1 Sam. xxv. 44), so that he could demand her back again with perfect justice, and Ishbosheth could not refuse to give her up to him, but probably on political grounds also, namely, because the renewal of his marriage to the king's daughter would show to all Israel that he cherished no hatred in his heart towards the fallen king.—Ver. 14. Thereupon, namely when Abner had assented to this condition, David sent messengers to Ishbosheth with this demand: "*Give* (me) *my wife Michal, whom I espoused to me for a hundred foreskins of the Philistines*" (see 1 Sam. xviii. 25, 27). David sent to Ishbosheth to demand the restoration of Michal, that her return might take place in a duly legal form, "that it might be apparent that he had dealt justly with Paltiel in the presence of his king, and that he had received his wife back again, and had not taken her by force from her husband" (Seb. Schmidt).—Ver. 15. Ishbosheth probably sent Abner to Gallim (1 Sam. xxv. 44) to fetch Michal from her husband Paltiel (see at 1 Sam. xxv. 44), and take her back to David. The husband was obliged to consent to this separation.—Ver. 16. When he went with his wife, weeping behind her, to Bahurim, Abner commanded him to turn back; "*and he returned.*" *Bahurim*, Shimei's home (ch. xix. 17; 1 Kings ii. 8), was situated, according to ch. xvi. 1, 5, and xvii. 18, upon the road from Jerusalem to Gilgal, in the valley of the Jordan, not far from the Mount of Olives, and is supposed by v. Schubert (*R.* iii. p. 70) to have stood upon the site of the present *Abu Dis*, though in all probability it is to be sought for farther north (see Rob. *Pal.* ii. p. 103). Paltiel had therefore followed his wife to the border of the tribe of Judah, or of the kingdom of David.—Vers. 17, 18. But before Abner set out to go to David, he had spoken to the elders of Israel (the tribes generally, with the exception of Benjamin (see ver. 19) and Judah): "*Both yesterday and the day before yesterday* (*i.e.* a long time ago), *ye desired to have David as king over you. Now carry out your wish: for Jehovah hath spoken concerning David, Through my servant David will I save my people Israel out of the power of the Philistines and all their enemies.*" הֹשִׁיעַ is an evident mistake in writing for אֹשִׁיעַ, which is found in many MSS., and rendered in all the ancient versions.—Ver. 19. Abner had spoken in the same way in the ears of Benjamin. He spoke to the Benjaminites more especially, because the existing royal family belonged to that tribe, and they had reaped many advantages in consequence (*vid.* 1 Sam. xxii. 7). The verb הָיָה in the circumstantial clause (ver. 17), and the verb וַיְדַבֵּר in ver. 19, which serves as a continuation of the circumstantial clause, must be translated as pluperfects, since Abner's interview with the elders of Israel and with Benjamin preceded his interview with David at Hebron. We may see from Abner's address to the elders, that even among the northern tribes the popular voice had long since decided for David. In 1 Chron. xii. we have historical proofs of this. The word of Jehovah concerning David, which is mentioned in ver. 18, is not met with anywhere in this precise form in the history of David as it has come down to us. Abner therefore had either some expression used by one of the prophets (Samuel or Gad) in his mind, which he described as the word of Jehovah, or else he regarded the anointing of David by Samuel in accordance with the command of the Lord, and the marvellous success of all that David attempted against the enemies of Israel, as a practical declaration on the part of God, that David, as the appointed successor of Saul, would perform what the Lord had spoken to Samuel concerning Saul (1 Sam. ix. 16), but what Saul had not fulfilled on account of his rebellion against the commandments of the Lord.—Ver. 19*b*. When Abner had gained over the elders of Israel and Benjamin to recognise David as king, he went to Hebron to speak in the ears of David "*all that had pleased Israel and the whole house of Benjamin,*" *i.e.* to make known to him their determination to acknowledge him as king. There went with him twenty men as representatives of all Israel, to confirm Abner's statements by their presence; and David prepared a meal for them all.—Ver. 21. After the meal, Abner said to David, "*I will rise and go and gather together all Israel to my lord the king, that they may make a covenant with thee* (*i.e.* do homage to thee before God as king), *and thou mayest become king over all that thy soul desireth,*" *i.e.* over all the nation of God; whereupon David took leave of him, and Abner went away in peace. The expression "*in peace*" serves to prepare the way for what follows. It is not stated, however, that David sent him away in peace (without avenging himself upon him), but that "David sent him away, and he went in peace." Apart altogether from the mildness of David's own character, he had no reason whatever for treating Abner as an enemy, now that he had given up all opposition to his reigning, and had brought all the Israelites over to him. What Abner had done for Ishbosheth, including his fighting against David, was indeed a sinful act of resistance to the will of Jehovah, which was not unknown to him, and according to which Samuel had both called and anointed David king over the nation; but for all that, it was not an ordinary act of rebellion against the person of David and his rightful claim to the throne, because Jehovah had not yet caused David to be set before the nation as its king by Samuel or any other prophet, and David had not yet asserted the right to reign over all Israel, which had been secured to him by the Lord and guaranteed by his anointing, as one which the nation was bound to recognise; but, like a true servant of God, he waited patiently till the Lord should give him the dominion over all His people.

Vers. 22-30. *Abner assassinated by Joab.*—Ver. 22. After Abner's departure, the servants of David returned with much booty from a marauding expedition, and Joab at their head. The singular בָּא may be explained from the fact that Joab was the principal person in the estimation of the writer. מֵהַגְּדוּד, *lit.* from the marauding host, *i.e.* from the work of a marauding host, or from a raid, which they had been making upon one of the tribes bordering upon Judah.—Ver. 23. When Joab learned (*lit. they told him*) that Abner had been with David, and he had sent him away again, he went to David to reproach him for having done so. " *What hast thou done? Behold, Abner came to thee; why then hast thou sent him away, and he is gone quite away?*" *i.e.* so that he could go away again without being detained (for this meaning of the *inf. abs.*, see Ewald, § 280, b). " *Thou knowest* (or more correctly as a question, Dost thou know?) *Abner, the son of Ner, that he came to persuade thee* (*i.e.* to make thee certain of his intentions), *and to learn thy going out and in* (*i.e.* all thine undertakings), *and to learn all that thou wilt do*" (*i.e.* all thy plans). Joab hoped in this way to prejudice David against Abner, to make him suspected as a traitor, that he might then be able to gratify his own private revenge with perfect impunity.—Ver. 26. For Abner had only just gone away from David, when Joab sent messengers after him, no doubt in David's name, though without his knowledge, and had him fetched back " from *Bor-hasirah,* i.e. the cistern of *Sirah.*" *Sirah* is a place which is quite unknown to us. According to

Josephus (*Ant.* vii. 1, 5), it was twenty stadia from Hebron, and called *Βησιρά*.—Ver. 27. When he came back, Joab "*took him aside into the middle of the gate, to talk with him in the stillness*," *i.e.* in private, and there thrust him through the body, so that he died "*for the blood of Asahel his brother*," *i.e.* for having put Asahel to death (ch. ii. 23).—Vers. 28, 29. When David heard this, he said, "*I and my kingdom are innocent before Jehovah for ever of the blood of Abner. Let it turn* (חוּל, to twist one's self, to turn or fall, *irruit*) *upon the head of Joab and all his father's house* (or so-called family)! *Never shall there be wanting* (אַל־יִכָּרֵת, let there not be cut off, so that there shall not be, as in Josh. ix. 23) *in the house of Joab one that hath an issue* (*vid.* Lev. xv. 2), *and a leper, and one who leans upon a stick* (*i.e.* a lame person or cripple; פֶּלֶךְ, according to the LXX. σκυτάλη, a thick round staff), *and who falls by the sword, and who is in want of bread.*" The meaning is: May God avenge the murder of Abner upon Joab and his family, by punishing them continually with terrible diseases, violent death, and poverty. To make the reason for this fearful curse perfectly clear, the historian observes in ver. 30, that Joab and his brother Abishai had murdered Abner, "*because he had slain their brother Asahel at Gibeon* in the battle" (ch. ii. 23). This act of Joab, in which Abishai must have been in some way concerned, was a treacherous act of assassination, which could not even be defended as blood-revenge, since Abner had slain Asahel in battle after repeated warnings, and only for the purpose of saving his own life. The principal motive for Joab's act was the most contemptible jealousy, or the fear lest Abner's reconciliation to David should diminish his own influence with the king, as was the case again at a later period with the murder of Amasa (ch. xx. 10).

Vers. 31–39. *David's mourning for Abner's death.*—Vers. 31, 32. To give a public proof of his grief at this murder, and his displeasure at the crime in the sight of all the nation, David commanded Joab, and all the people with him (David), *i.e.* all his courtiers, and the warriors who returned with Joab, to institute a public mourning for the deceased, by tearing their clothes, putting on sackcloth, *i.e.* coarse hairy mourning and penitential clothes, and by a funeral dirge for Abner; *i.e.* he commanded them to walk in front of Abner's bier mourning and in funeral costume, and to accompany the deceased to his resting-place, whilst David as king followed the bier.—Ver. 32 Thus they buried Abner at Hebron ; and David wept aloud at his grave, and all the people with him.—Vers. 33, 34. Although the appointment of such a funeral by David, and his tears at Abner's grave, could not fail to divest the minds of his opponents of all suspicion that Joab had committed the murder with his cognizance (see at ver. 37), he gave a still stronger proof of his innocence, and of the sincerity of his grief, by the ode which he composed for Abner's death :

Ver. 33. Like an ungodly man must Abner die !
34. Thy hands were not bound, and thy feet were not placed in fetters.
As one falls before sinners, so hast thou fallen !

The first strophe (ver. 33) is an expression of painful lamentation at the fact that Abner had died a death which he did not deserve. " *The fool*" (*nabal*) is " the ungodly," according to Israelitish ideas (*vid.* Ps. xiv. 1). The meaning of ver. 34 is : Thou hadst not made thyself guilty of any crime, so as to have to die like a malefactor, in chains and bonds ; but thou hast been treacherously murdered. This dirge made such an impression upon all the people (present), that they wept still more for the dead.—Ver. 35. But David mourned so bitterly, that when all the people called upon him to take some food during the day, he declared with an oath that he would not taste bread or anything else before the setting of the sun. הַבְרוֹת לֶחֶם does not mean, as in ch. xiii. 5, to give to eat, on account of the expression " *all the people*," as it can hardly be imagined that all the people, *i.e.* all who were present, could have come to bring David food, but it signifies to make him eat, *i.e.* call upon him to eat ; whilst it is left uncertain whether David was to eat with the people (cf. ch. xii. 17), *i.e.* to take part in the funeral meal that was held after the burial, or whether the people simply urged him to take some food, for the purpose of soothing his own sorrow. כִּי אִם are to be taken separately ; כִּי, ὅτι, introducing the oath, and אִם being the particle used in an oath : " *if*," *i.e.* assuredly not.—Ver. 36. " *And all the people perceived it* (*i.e.* his trouble), *and it pleased them, as everything that the king did pleased all the people.*"— Ver. 37. All the people (*sc.* who were with the king) and all

Israel discerned on that day (from David's deep and heartfelt trouble), that the death of Abner had not happened (proceeded) from the king, as many may probably at first have supposed, since Joab had no doubt fetched Abner back in David's name. —Vers. 38, 39. Finally, David said to his (confidential) servants: " *Know ye not* (*i.e.* ye surely perceive) *that a prince and great man has this day fallen in Israel?*" This sentence shows how thoroughly David could recognise the virtues possessed by his opponents, and how very far he was from looking upon Abner as a traitor, because of his falling away from Ishbosheth and coming over to him, that on the contrary he hoped to find in him an able general and a faithful servant. He would at once have punished the murderer of such a man, if he had only possessed the power. "*But*," he adds, "*I am this day* (still) *weak, and only anointed king; and these men, the sons of Zeruiah, are too strong for me. The Lord reward the doer of evil according to his wickedness.*" The expression " to-day" not only applies to the word " *weak*," or tender, but also to "*anointed*" (*to-day, i.e.* only just *anointed*). As David was still but a young sovereign, and felt himself unable to punish a man like Joab according to his deserts, he was obliged to restrict himself at first to the utterance of a curse upon the deed (ver. 29), and to leave the retribution to God. He could not and durst not forgive; and consequently, before he died, he charged Solomon, his son and successor, to punish Joab for the murder of Abner and Amasa (1 Kings ii. 5).

MURDER OF ISHBOSHETH, AND PUNISHMENT OF THE MURDERERS.—CHAP. IV.

Vers. 1-6. *Murder of Ishbosheth.*—Ver. 1. When the son of Saul heard of the death of Abner, " *his hands slackened,*" *i.e.* he lost the power and courage to act as king, since Abner had been the only support of his throne. " *And all Israel was confounded;*" *i.e.* not merely alarmed on account of Abner's death, but utterly at a loss what to do to escape the vengeance of David, to which Abner had apparently fallen a victim.— Vers. 2, 3. Saul's son had two leaders of military companies (for הָיוּ בְן־שָׁאוּל we must read שׁ לְבֶן הָיוּ): the one was named *Baanah*, the other *Rechab*, sons of *Rimmon* the Beerothite, " *of* the sons of Benjamin," i.e. belonging to them ; "*for Beeroth is also reckoned to Benjamin*" (עַל, over, above, added to). *Beeroth*, the present *Bireh* (see at Josh. ix. 17), was close to the western frontier of the tribe of Benjamin, to which it is also reckoned as belonging in Josh. xviii. 25. This remark concerning Beeroth in the verse before us, serves to confirm the statement that the Beerothites mentioned were Benjaminites ; but that statement also shows the horrible character of the crime attributed to them in the following verses. Two men of the tribe of Benjamin murdered the son of Saul, the king belonging to their own tribe.—Ver. 3. "*The Beerothites fled to Gittaim, and were strangers there unto this day.*" *Gittaim* is mentioned again in Neh. xi. 33, among the places in which Benjaminites were dwelling after the captivity, though it by no means follows from this that the place belonged to the tribe of Benjamin before the captivity. It may have been situated outside the territory of that tribe. It is never mentioned again, and has not yet been discovered. The reason why the Beerothites fled to Gittaim, and remained there as strangers until the time when this history was written, is also unknown ; it may perhaps have been that the Philistines had conquered Gittaim.—Ver. 4. Before the historian proceeds to describe what the two Beerothites did, he inserts a remark concerning Saul's family, to show at the outset, that with the death of Ishbosheth the government of this family necessarily became extinct, as the only remaining descendant was a perfectly helpless cripple. He was a son of Jonathan, *smitten* (*i.e.* lamed) *in his feet.* He was five years old when the tidings came from Jezreel of Saul and Jonathan, *i.e.* of their death. His nurse immediately took him and fled, and on their hasty flight he fell and became lame. His name was *Mephibosheth* (according to Simonis, for מִפְאָה בֹּשֶׁת, destroying the idol) ; but in 1 Chron. viii. 34 and ix. 40 he is called *Meribbaal* (Baal's fighter), just as Ishbosheth is also called *Eshbaal* (see at ch. ii. 8). On his future history, see ch. ix., xvi. 1 sqq., and xix. 25 sqq.—Ver. 5. The two sons of Rimmon went to Mahanaim, where Ishbosheth resided (ch. ii. 8, 12), and came in the heat of the day (at noon) into Ishbosheth's house, when he was taking his mid-day rest.—Ver. 6. "*And here they had come into the midst of the house, fetching wheat* (*i.e.* under the pretext of fetching wheat, probably for the soldiers in their companies), *and smote him in the abdomen; and Rechab and his brother escaped.*" The first clause in this verse is a circumstantial clause, which furnishes the explanation of the way in which it was possible for the murderers to find their way to the king. The second clause continues the narrative, and וַיַּכֻּהוּ is attached to וַיָּבֹאוּ (ver. 5).[1]

Vers. 7–12. *Punishment of the murderers by David.*—Ver. 7. As the thread of the narrative was broken by the explanatory remarks in ver. 6, it is resumed here by the repetition of the words וַיָּבֹאוּ וגו׳: "*They came into the house, as he lay upon his bed in his bed-chamber, and smote him, and slew him,*" for the purpose of attaching the account of the further progress of the affair, viz. that they cut off his head, took it and went by the way of the Arabah (the valley of the Jordan : see ch. ii. 29) the whole night, and brought the head of Ishbosheth unto David to Hebron with these words: "Behold (= there thou hast) the head of Ishbosheth, the son of Saul thine enemy,

---

[1] The LXX. thought it desirable to explain the possibility of Rechab and Baanah getting into the king's house, and therefore paraphrased the sixth verse as follows: καὶ ἰδοὺ ἡ θυρωρὸς τοῦ οἴκου ἐκάθαιρε πυροὺς καὶ ἐνύσταξε καὶ ἐκάθευδε, καὶ Ῥηχὰβ καὶ Βαανὰ οἱ ἀδελφοὶ διήλαθον (" and behold the doorkeeper of the house was cleaning wheat, and nodded and slept. And Rahab and Baana the brothers escaped, or went in secretly "). The first part of this paraphrase has been retained in the Vulgate, in the interpolation between vers. 5 and 6: *et ostiaria domus purgans triticum obdormivit*; whether it was copied by Jerome from the Itala, or was afterwards introduced as a gloss into his translation. It is very evident that this clause in the Vulgate is only a gloss, from the fact that, in all the rest of ver. 6, Jerome has closely followed the Masoretic text, and that none of the other ancient translators found anything about a doorkeeper in his text. When Thenius, therefore, attempts to prove the " evident corruption of the Masoretic text," by appealing to the " nonsense (*Unsinn*) of relating the murder of Ishbosheth and the flight of the murderers twice over, and in two successive verses (see ver. 7)," he is altogether wrong in speaking of the repetition as " nonsense " whereas it is simply tautology, and has measured the peculiarities of Hebrew historians by the standard adopted by our own. J. P. F. Königsfeldt has given the true explanation when he says: " The Hebrews often repeat in this way, for the purpose of adding something fresh, as for example, in this instance, their carrying off the head." Comp. with this ch. iii. 22, 23, where the arrival of Joab is mentioned twice, viz. in two successive verses ; or ch. v. 1–3, where the assembling of the tribes of Israel at Hebron is also referred to a second time,—a repetition at which Thenius himself has taken no offence,—and many other passages of the same kind.

who sought thy life; and thus hath Jehovah avenged my lord the king this day upon Saul and his seed." No motive is assigned for this action. But there can be little doubt that it was no other than the hope of obtaining a great reward from David. Thus they presumed "to spread the name of God and His providence as a cloak and covering over their villany, as the wicked are accustomed to do" (*Berleb. Bible*).—Vers. 9 sqq. But David rewarded them very differently from what they had expected. He replied, "*As Jehovah liveth, who hath redeemed my soul out of all adversity, the man who told me, Behold, Saul is dead, and thought he was a messenger of good to me, I seized and slew at Ziklag* (vid. i. 14, 15), *to give him a reward for his news: how much more when wicked men have murdered a righteous man in his house upon his bed, should I not require his blood at your hand, and destroy you from the earth?*" The several parts of this reply are not closely linked together so as to form one period, but answer to the excited manner in which they were spoken. There is first of all the oath, "*As truly as Jehovah liveth*," and the clause appended, "*who redeemed my soul*," in which the thought is implied that David did not feel it necessary to get rid of his enemies by the commission of crimes. After this (ver. 10) we have an allusion to his treatment of the messenger who announced Saul's death to him, and pretended to have slain him in order that he might obtain a good reward for his tidings. כִּי, like ὅτι, simply introduces the address. הַמַּגִּיד ... בְּעֵינָיו is placed at the head absolutely, and made subordinate to the verb by בּוֹ after וָאֹחֲזָה. לְתִתִּי־לוֹ, "*namely, to give him.*" אֲשֶׁר is employed to introduce the explanation, like our "*namely*" (vid. Ewald, § 338, *b*). בְּשׂרָה, good news, here "*the reward of news.*" The main point follows in ver. 11, beginning with אַף כִּי, "*how much more*" (vid. Ewald, § 354, *c*), and is introduced in the form of a climax. The words אֲנָשִׁים ... מִשְׁכָּבוֹ are also written absolutely, and placed at the head: "men have slain," for "how much more in this instance, when wicked men have slain." "*Righteous*" (*zaddik*), *i.e.* not guilty of any wicked deed or crime. The assumption of the regal power, which Abner had forced upon Ishbosheth, was not a capital crime in the existing state of things, and after the death of Saul; and even if it had been, the sons of Rimmon had no right to assassinate him. David's sentence then follows: "*And now that this is* the fact, that ye have murdered a righteous man, should I not," etc. בִּעֵר, to destroy by capital punishment, as in Deut. xiii. 6, etc. בִּקֵּשׁ דָּם (= דָּרַשׁ דָּם, Gen. ix. 5), to require the blood of a person, i.e. to take blood-revenge.—Ver. 12. David then commanded his servant to slay the murderers, and also to make the punishment more severe than usual. *" They cut off their hands and feet,"*—the hands with which they had committed the murder, and the feet which had run for the reward,—*" and hanged the bodies by the pool at Hebron"* for a spectacle and warning, that others might be deterred from committing similar crimes (cf. Deut. xxi. 22 ; J. H. Michaelis). In illustration of the fact itself, we may compare the similar course pursued by Alexander towards the murderer of king Darius, as described in Justin's history (xii. 6) and Curtius (vii. 5). They buried Ishbosheth's head in Abner's grave at Hebron. Thus David acted with strict justice in this case also, not only to prove to the people that he had neither commanded nor approved of the murder, but from heartfelt abhorrence of such crimes, and to keep his conscience void of offence towards God and towards man.

II. THE GOVERNMENT OF DAVID OVER ALL ISRAEL IN THE TIME OF ITS STRENGTH AND GLORY

CHAP. V.–IX.

After the death of Ishbosheth, David was anointed in Hebron by all the tribes as king over the whole of Israel (ch. v. 1–5). He then proceeded to attack the Jebusites in Jerusalem, conquered their fortress Zion, and made Jerusalem the capital of his kingdom ; fortifying it still further, and building a palace in it (ch. v. 6–16), after he had twice inflicted a defeat upon the Philistines (ch. v. 17–25). But in order that the chief city of his kingdom and the seat of his own palace might also be made the religious centre of the whole nation as a congregation of Jehovah, he first of all brought the ark of the covenant out of its place of concealment, and had it conveyed in a festal procession to Zion, and deposited there in a tent which had been specially prepared for it, as a place of worship for the whole congregation (ch. vi.). He then resolved to erect for the Lord in Jerusalem a temple fitted for His name; and the Lord gave him in return the promise of the eternal perpetuity of his throne (ch. vii.). To this there is appended a cursory account of David's wars with the neighbouring nations, by which not only his own sovereignty, but the Israelitish kingdom of God, was raised into a commanding power among the nations and kingdoms of the world. In connection with all this, David still maintained his affection and fidelity towards the fallen royal family of Saul, and showed compassion towards the last remaining descendant of that family (ch. ix.).

This account of the unfolding of the power and glory of the kingdom of Israel, through the instrumentality of David and during his reign, is so far arranged chronologically, that all the events and all the enterprises of David mentioned in this section occurred in the first half of his reign over the whole of the covenant nation. The chronological arrangement, however, is not strictly adhered to, so far as the details are concerned; but the standpoint of material resemblance is so far connected with it, that all the greater wars of David are grouped together in ch. viii. (see the introduction to ch. viii.). It is obvious from this, that the plan which the historian adopted was first of all to describe the internal improvement of the Israelitish kingdom of God by David, and then to proceed to the external development of his power in conflict with the opposing nations of the world.

DAVID ANOINTED KING OVER ALL ISRAEL. JERUSALEM TAKEN, AND MADE THE CAPITAL OF THE KINGDOM. VICTORIES OVER THE PHILISTINES.—CHAP. V.

Vers. 1-5. DAVID ANOINTED KING OVER ALL ISRAEL.— Vers. 1-3 (compare with this the parallel passages in 1 Chron. xi. 1-3). After the death of Ishbosheth, all the tribes of Israel (except Judah) came to Hebron in the persons of their representatives the elders (*vid.* ver. 3), in response to the summons of Abner (ch. iii. 17-19), to do homage to David as their king. They assigned three reasons for their coming: (1.) "*Behold, we are thy bone and thy flesh,*" *i.e.* thy blood-relations, inasmuch as all the tribes of Israel were lineal descendants of Jacob (*vid.*

Gen. xxix. 14; Judg. ix. 2). (2.) "*In time past, when Saul was king over us, thou wast the leader of Israel (thou leddest out and broughtest in Israel),*" *i.e.* thou didst superintend the affairs of Israel (see at Num. xxvii. 17; and for the fact itself, 1 Sam. xviii. 5). הָיִיתָה מוֹצִיא is an error in writing for הָיִיתָ הַמּוֹצִיא, and מֵבִי for מֵבִיא, with the א dropped, as in 1 Kings xxi. 21, etc. (*vid.* Olshausen, *Gr.* p. 69). (3.) They ended by asserting that Jehovah had called him to be the shepherd and prince over His people. The remarks which we have already made at ch. iii. 18 respecting Abner's appeal to a similar utterance on the part of Jehovah, are equally applicable to the words of Jehovah to David which are quoted here: "Thou shalt feed my people Israel," etc. On the *Piska*, see the note to Josh. iv. 1.—Ver. 3. "*All the elders of Israel came*" is a repetition of ver. 1a, except that the expression "all the tribes of Israel" is more distinctly defined as meaning "all the elders of Israel." "*So all the elders came; . . . and king David made a covenant with them in Hebron before the Lord* (see at ch. iii. 21): *and they anointed David king over* (all) *Israel.*" The writer of the Chronicles adds, "according to the word of the Lord through Samuel," *i.e.* so that the command of the Lord to Samuel, to anoint David king over Israel (1 Sam. xvi. 1, 12), found its complete fulfilment in this.—Vers. 4, 5. The age of David when he began to reign is given here, viz. thirty years old; also the length of his reign, viz. seven years and a half at Hebron over Judah, and thirty-three years at Jerusalem over Israel and Judah. In the books of Chronicles these statements occur at the close of David's reign (1 Chron. xxix. 27).

Vers. 6-10. CONQUEST OF THE STRONGHOLD OF ZION, AND CHOICE OF JERUSALEM AS THE CAPITAL OF THE KINGDOM (cf. 1 Chron. xi. 4, 9).—These parallel accounts agree in all the main points; but they are both of them merely brief extracts from a more elaborate history, so that certain things, which appeared of comparatively less importance, are passed over either in the one or the other, and the full account is obtained by combining the two. The conquest of the citadel Zion took place immediately after the anointing of David as king over all the tribes of Israel. This is apparent, not only from the fact that the account follows directly afterwards, but also from the circumstance that, according to ver. 5, David reigned in Jerusalem just as many years as he was king over all Israel.—Ver. 6. The king went with his men (*i.e.* his fighting men: the Chronicles have "all Israel," *i.e.* the fighting men of Israel) to Jerusalem to the Jebusites, the inhabitants of the land, *i.e.* the natives or Canaanites; "*and they said* (the singular וַיֹּאמֶר is used because הַיְבוּסִי is a singular form) *to David, Thou wilt not come hither* (*i.e.* come in), *but the blind and lame will drive thee away: to say* (*i.e.* by which they meant to say), *David will not come in.*" הֲסִירְךָ is not used for the infinitive, but has been rightly understood by the LXX., Aben Ezra, and others, as a perfect. The perfect expresses a thing accomplished, and open to no dispute; and the use of the singular in the place of the plural, as in Isa. xiv. 32, is to be explained from the fact that the verb precedes, and is only defined precisely by the subject which follows (*vid.* Ewald, § 319, *a*). The Jebusites relied upon the unusual natural advantages of their citadel, which stood upon Mount Zion, a mountain shut in by deep valleys on three different sides; so that in their haughty self-security they imagined that they did not even need to employ healthy and powerful warriors to resist the attack made by David, but that the blind and lame would suffice.—Ver. 7. However, David took the citadel Zion, *i.e.* "the city of David." This explanatory remark anticipates the course of events, as David did not give this name to the conquered citadel, until he had chosen it as his residence and capital (*vid.* ver. 9). צִיּוֹן (*Sion*), from צִיָּה, to be dry: the dry or arid mountain or hill. This was the name of the southern and loftiest mountain of Jerusalem. Upon this stood the fortress or citadel of the town, which had hitherto remained in the possession of the Jebusites; whereas the northern portion of the city of Jerusalem, which was upon lower ground, had been conquered by the Judæans and Benjaminites very shortly after the death of Joshua (see at Judg. i. 8).—In ver. 8 we have one circumstance mentioned which occurred in connection with this conquest. On that day, *i.e.* when he had advanced to the attack of the citadel Zion, David said, "Every one who smites the Jebusites, let him hurl into the waterfall (*i.e.* down the precipice) both the lame and blind, who are hateful to David's soul." This is most probably the proper interpretation of these obscure words of David, which have been very differently explained. Taking up the words of the Jebusites, David called all the defenders of the citadel of Zion "lame and blind," and ordered them to be cast down the precipice without quarter. צִנּוֹר signifies a waterfall (*catarracta*) in Ps. xlii. 8, the only other passage in which it occurs, probably from צָנַר, to roar. This meaning may also be preserved here, if we assume that at the foot of the steep precipice of Zion there was a waterfall probably connected with the water of Siloah. It is true we cannot determine anything with certainty concerning it, as, notwithstanding the many recent researches in Jerusalem, the situation of the Jebusite fortress and the character of the mountain of Zion in ancient times are quite unknown to us. This explanation of the word *zinnor* is simpler than Ewald's assumption that the word signifies the steep side of a rock, which merely rests upon the fact that the Greek word καταρράκτης originally signified a plunge.[1] וְיִגַּע should be pointed as a *Hiphil* יַגַּע. The Masoretic pointing וְיִגַּע arises from their mistaken interpretation of the whole sentence. The *Chethibh* שְׂנֻאוּ might be the *third pers. perf.*, "who hate David's soul;" only in that case the omission of אֲשֶׁר would be surprising, and consequently the *Keri* שְׂנֻאֵי is to be preferred. "From this," adds the writer, "the proverb arose, 'The blind and lame shall not enter the house;'" in which proverb the epithet "blind and lame," which David applied to the Jebusites who were hated by him, has the general signification of "repulsive persons," with whom one does not wish to have anything to do. In the Chronicles not only is the whole of ver. 7 omitted, with the proverb to which the occurrence gave rise, but also the allusion

---

[1] The earliest translators have only resorted to guesses. The Seventy, with their ἁπτέσθω ἐν παραξιφίδι, have combined צִנּוֹר with צִנָּה, which they render now and then μάχαιρα or ῥομφαία. This is also done by the Syriac and Arabic. The Chaldee paraphrases in this manner: "who begins to subjugate the citadel." Jerome, who probably followed the Rabbins, has *et tetigisset domatum fistulas* (and touched the *water-pipes*); and Luther, "*und erlanget die Dachrinnen*" (like the English version, "whosoever getteth up to the gutter:" Tr.). Hitzig's notion, that *zinnor* signifies ear ("whosoever boxes the ears of the blind and lame") needs no refutation; nor does that of Fr. Böttcher, who proposes to follow the Alexandrian rendering, and refer *zinnor* to a "sword of honour or marshal's staff," which David promised to the victor.

to the blind and lame in the words spoken by the Jebusites (ver. 6); and another word of David's is substituted instead, namely, that David would make the man who first smote the Jebusites, *i.e.* who stormed their citadel, *head and chief*;[1] and also the statement that Joab obtained the prize. The historical credibility of the statement cannot be disputed, as Thenius assumes, on the ground that Joab had already been chief (*sar*) for a long time, according to ch. ii. 13: for the passage referred to says nothing of the kind; and there is a very great difference between the commander of an army in the time of war, and a "head and chief," *i.e.* a commander-in-chief. The statement in ver. 8 with regard to Joab's part, the fortification of Jerusalem, shows very clearly that the author of the Chronicles had other and more elaborate sources in his possession, which contained fuller accounts than the author of our books has communicated.—Ver. 9. "*David dwelt in the fort,*" *i.e.* he selected the fort or citadel as his palace, "*and called it David's city.*" David may have been induced to select the citadel of Zion as his palace, and by so doing to make Jerusalem the capital of the whole kingdom, partly by the natural strength of Zion, and partly by the situation of Jerusalem, viz. on the border of the tribes of Benjamin and Judah, and tolerably near to the centre of the land. "*And David built, i.e.* fortified (the city of Zion), *round about from Millo and inwards.*" In the Chronicles we have עַד־הַסָּבִיב, "and to the environs or surroundings," *i.e.* to the encircling wall which was opposite to the Millo. The fortification "inwards" must have consisted in the enclosure of Mount Zion with a strong wall upon the north side, where Jerusalem joined it as a lower town, so as to defend the palace against hostile attacks on the north or town side, which had hitherto been left without fortifications. The "Millo" was at any rate some kind of fortification, probably a large tower or castle at one particular part of the surrounding wall (comp. Judg. ix. 6 with vers. 46 and 49, where *Millo* is used interchangeably with *Migdal*). The name ("the filling") probably originated in the fact that through this tower or castle the fortification of the city, or the surrounding wall, was *filled* or completed. The definite article before *Millo* indicates that

---

[1] This is also inserted in the passage before us by the translators of the English version: "he shall be chief and captain."—TR.

it was a well-known fortress, probably one that had been erected by the Jebusites. With regard to the situation of *Millo*, we may infer from this passage, and 1 Chron. xi. 8, that the tower in question stood at one corner of the wall, either on the north-east or north-west, "where the hill of Zion has the least elevation and therefore needed the greatest strengthening from without" (Thenius on 1 Kings ix. 15). This is fully sustained both by 1 Kings xi. 27, where Solomon is said to have closed the breach of the city of David by building (fortifying) Millo, and by 2 Chron. xxxii. 5, where Hezekiah is said to have built up all the wall of Jerusalem, and made *Millo* strong, *i.e.* to have fortified it still further (*vid.* 1 Kings ix. 15 and 24). —Ver. 10. And David increased in greatness, *i.e.* in power and fame, for Jehovah the God of hosts was with him.

Vers. 11–16.—DAVID'S PALACE, WIVES AND CHILDREN (comp. 1 Chron. xiv. 1–7).—King Hiram of Tyre sent messengers to David, and afterwards, by the express desire of the latter, cedar-wood and builders, carpenters and stone-masons, who built him a house, *i.e.* a palace. *Hiram* (*Hirom* in 1 Kings v. 32; *Huram* in the Chronicles; LXX. Χειράμ; *Josephus*, Εἴραμος and Εἴρωμος), king of Tyre, was not only an ally of David, but of his son Solomon also. He sent to the latter cedar-wood and builders for the erection of the temple and of his own palace (1 Kings v. 21 sqq.; 2 Chron. ii. 2 sqq.), and fitted out a mercantile fleet in conjunction with him (1 Kings ix. 27, 28; 2 Chron. ix. 10); in return for which, Solomon not only sent him an annual supply of corn, oil, and wine (1 Kings v. 24; 2 Chron. ii. 9), but when all the buildings were finished, twenty years after the erection of the temple, he made over to him twenty of the towns of Galilee (1 Kings ix. 10 sqq.). It is evident from these facts that Hiram was still reigning in the twenty-fourth, or at any rate the twentieth, year of Solomon's reign, and consequently, as he had assisted David with contributions of wood for the erection of his palace, that he must have reigned at least forty-five or fifty years; and therefore that, even in the latter case, he cannot have begun to reign earlier than the eighth year of David's reign over all Israel, or from six to ten years after the conquest of the Jebusite citadel upon Mount Zion. This is quite in harmony with the account given here; for it by no means follows, that because the arrival of an embassy from Hiram, and the erection of David's palace, are mentioned immediately after the conquest of the citadel of Zion, they must have occurred directly afterwards. The arrangement of the different events in the chapter before us is topical rather than strictly chronological. Of the two battles fought by David with the Philistines (vers. 17-25), the first at any rate took place before the erection of David's palace, as it is distinctly stated in ver. 17 that the Philistines made war upon David when they heard that he had been anointed king over Israel, and therefore in all probability even before the conquest of the fortress of the Jebusites, or at any rate immediately afterwards, and before David had commenced the fortification of Jerusalem and the erection of a palace. The historian, on the contrary, has not only followed up the account of the capture of the fortress of Zion, and the selection of it as David's palace, by a description of what David gradually did to fortify and adorn the new capital, but has also added a notice as to David's wives and the children that were born to him in Jerusalem. Now, if this be correct, the object of Hiram's embassy cannot have been "to congratulate David upon his ascent of the throne," as Thenius maintains; but after he had ascended the throne, Hiram sent ambassadors to form an alliance with this powerful monarch; and David availed himself of the opportunity to establish an intimate friendship with Hiram, and ask him for cedar-wood and builders for his palace.[1]—Ver. 12. "And David

[1] The statements of Menander of Ephesus in Josephus (c. *Ap.* i. 18), that after the death of *Abibal* his son *Hirom* (Εἴρωμος) succeeded him in the government, and reigned thirty-four years, and died at the age of fifty-three, are at variance with the biblical history. For, according to these statements, as Hiram was still reigning "at the end of twenty years" (according to 1 Kings ix. 10, 11), when Solomon had built his palaces and the house of the Lord, *i.e.* twenty-four years after Solomon began to reign, he cannot have ascended the throne before the sixty-first year of David's life, and the thirty-first of his reign. But in that case the erection of David's palace would fall somewhere within the last eight years of his life. And to this we have to add the repeated statements made by Josephus (*l.c.* and *Ant.* viii. 3, 1), to the effect that Solomon commenced the building of the temple in Hiram's twelfth year, or after he had reigned eleven years; so that Hiram could only have begun to reign seven years before the death of David (in the sixty-third year of his life), and the erection of the palace by David must have fallen later still, and his determination to build the

perceived (*sc.* from the success of his enterprises) that Jehovah had firmly established him king over Israel, and that He had exalted his kingdom for His people Israel's sake," *i.e.* because temple, which he did not form till he had taken possession of his house of cedar, *i.e.* the newly erected palace (ch. vii. 2), would fall in the very last years of his life, but a very short time before his death. As this seems hardly credible, it has been assumed by some that Hiram's father, Abibal, also bore the name of Hiram, or that Hiram is confounded with Abibal in the account before us (Thenius), or that Abibal's father was named Hiram, and it was he who formed the alliance with David (Ewald, *Gesch.* iv. 287). But all these assumptions are overthrown by the fact that the identity of the Hiram who was Solomon's friend with the contemporary and friend of David is expressly affirmed not only in 2 Chron. ii. 2 (as Ewald supposes), but also in 1 Kings v. 15. For whilst Solomon writes to Hiram in 2 Chron. ii. 3, " as thou didst deal with David my father, and didst send him cedars to build him an house to dwell therein," it is also stated 1 Kings v. 1 that " Hiram king of Tyre sent his servants unto Solomon; for he had heard that they had anointed him king in the room of his father: for *Hiram was a lover of David all days* (all his life)." Movers (*Phönizier* ii. 1, p. 147 sqq.) has therefore attempted to remove the discrepancy between the statements made in Josephus and the biblical account of Hiram's friendship with David and Solomon, by assuming that in the narrative contained in the books of Samuel we have a topical and not a chronological arrangement, and that according to this arrangement the conquest of Jerusalem by David is followed immediately by the building of the city and palace, and this again by the removal of the holy ark to Jerusalem, and lastly by David's resolution to build a temple, which really belonged to the close of his reign, and indeed, according to 2 Sam. vii. 2, to the period directly following the completion of the cedar palace. There is a certain amount of truth at the foundation of this, but it does not remove the discrepancy; for even if David's resolution to build a temple did not fall within the earlier years of his reign at Jerusalem, as some have inferred from the position in which it stands in the account given in this book, it cannot be pushed forward to the very last years of his life and reign. This is decidedly precluded by the fact, that in the promise given to David by God, his son and successor upon the throne is spoken of in such terms as to necessitate the conclusion that he was not yet born. This difficulty cannot be removed by the solution suggested by Movers (p. 149), "that the historian necessarily adhered to the topical arrangement which he had adopted for this section, because he had not said anything yet about Solomon and his mother Bathsheba:" for the expression "which shall proceed out of thy bowels" (ch. vii. 12) is not the only one of the kind; but in 1 Chron. xxii. 9, David says to his son Solomon, " The word of the Lord came to me, saying, A son *shall be* born to thee—Solomon—he shall build an house for my name;" from which it is very obvious, that Solomon was not born at the time when David determined to build the temple and received this promise from God in conse-

He had chosen Israel as His people, and had promised to make it great and glorious.

To the building of David's palace, there is appended in

quence of his intention. To this we have also to add 2 Sam. xi. 2, where David sees Bathsheba, who gave birth to Solomon a few years later, from the roof of his palace. Now, even though the palace is simply called "the king's house" in this passage, and not the "house of cedar," as in ch. vii. 2, and therefore the house intended might possibly be the house in which David lived before the house of cedar was built, this is a very improbable supposition, and there cannot be much doubt that the "king's house" is the palace (ch. v. 11, vii. 1) which he had erected for himself. Lastly, not only is there not the slightest intimation in the whole of the account given in ch. vii. that David was an old man when he resolved to build the temple, but, on the contrary, the impression which it makes throughout is, that it was the culminating point of his reign, and that he was at an age when he might hope not only to commence this magnificent building, but in all human probability to live to complete it. The only other solution left, is the assumption that there are errors in the chronological date of Josephus, and that Hiram lived longer than Menander affirms. The assertion that Solomon commenced the erection of the temple in the eleventh or twelfth year of Hiram's reign was not derived by Josephus from Phœnician sources; for the fragments which he gives from the works of Menander and Dius in the *Antiquities* (viii. 5, 3) and *c. Apion* (i. 17, 18), contain nothing at all about the building of the temple (*vid.* Movers, p. 141), but he has made it as the result of certain chronological combinations of his own, just as in *Ant.* viii. 3, 1, he calculates the year of the building of the temple in relation both to the exodus and also to the departure of Abraham out of Haran, but miscalculates, inasmuch as he places it in the 592d year after the exodus instead of the 480th, and the 1020th year from Abraham's emigration to Canaan instead of the 1125th. And in the present instance his calculation of the exact position of the same event in relation to Hiram's reign may be just as erroneous. His statement concerning the length of Hiram's reign was no doubt taken from Menander; but even in this the numbers may be faulty, since the statements respecting *Balezorus* and *Myttonus* in the very same extract from Menander, as to the length of the reigns of the succeeding kings of Tyre, can be proved to be erroneous, and have been corrected by Movers from Eusebius and Syncellus; and, moreover, the seven years of Hiram's successor, *Baleazar*, do not tally with Eusebius and Syncellus, who both give seventeen years. Thus the proof which Movers adduces from the synchronism of the Tyrian chronology with the biblical, the Egyptian, and the Assyrian, to establish the correctness of Menander's statements concerning Hiram's reign, is rendered very uncertain, to say nothing of the fact that Movers has only succeeded in bringing out the synchronism with the biblical chronology by a very arbitrary and demonstrably false calculation of the years that the kings of Judah and Israel reigned.

vers. 13-15 the account of the increase of his house by the multiplication of his wives and concubines, and of the sons who were born to him at Jerusalem (as in 1 Chron. xiv. 3 sqq.). Taking many wives was indeed prohibited in the law of the king in Deut. xvii. 17; but as a large harem was considered from time immemorial as part of the court of an oriental monarch, David suffered himself to be seduced by that custom to disregard this prohibition, and suffered many a heartburn afterwards in consequence, not to mention his fearful fall in consequence of his passion for Bathsheba. The concubines are mentioned before the wives, probably because David had taken many of them to Jerusalem, and earlier than the wives. In the Chronicles the concubines are omitted, though not "intentionally," as they are mentioned in 1 Chron. iii. 9; but as being of no essential importance in relation to the list of sons which follows, because no difference was made between those born of concubines and those born of wives. "Out of Jerusalem," *i.e.* away from Jerusalem: not that the wives were all born in Jerusalem, as the words which follow, "after he was come from Hebron," clearly show. In the Chronicles, therefore, it is explained as meaning "in Jerusalem." The sons are mentioned again both in 1 Chron. xiv. 5-7 and in the genealogy in 1 Chron. iii. 5-8. *Shammua* is called *Shimea* in 1 Chron. iii. 5, according to a different pronunciation. *Shammua, Shobab, Nathan,* and *Solomon* were sons of Bathsheba according to 1 Chron. iii. 5.—Ver. 15. *Elishua* is written incorrectly in 1 Chron. iii. 6 as *Elishama,* because *Elishama* follows afterwards. There are two names after *Elishua* in 1 Chron. iii. 6, 7, and xiv. 6, 7, viz. *Eliphalet* and *Nogah,* which have not crept into the text from oversight or from a wrong spelling of other names, because the number of the names is given as nine in 1 Chron. iii. 8, and the two names must be included in order to bring out that number. And, on the other hand, it is not by the mistake of a copyist that they have been omitted from the text before us, but it has evidently been done deliberately on account of their having died in infancy, or at a very early age. This also furnishes a very simple explanation of the fact, that the name *Eliphalet* occurs again at the end of the list, namely, because a son who was born later received the name of his brother who had died young. *Eliada,* the last but one, is called *Beeliada* in 1 Chron. xiv. 7, another form of the name, compounded with *Baal* instead of *El*. David had therefore nineteen sons, six of whom were born in Hebron (ch. iii. 2 sqq.), and thirteen at Jerusalem. Daughters are not mentioned in the genealogical accounts, because as a rule only heiresses or women who acquired renown from special causes were included in them. There is a daughter named *Thamar* mentioned afterwards in ch. xiii. 1.

Vers. 17-25. DAVID GAINS TWO VICTORIES OVER THE PHILISTINES (compare 1 Chron. xiv. 8-17). — Both these victories belong in all probability to the interval between the anointing of David at Hebron over all Israel and the conquest of the citadel of Zion. This is very evident, so far as the first is concerned, from the words, "When the Philistines heard that they had anointed David king over Israel" (ver. 17), not when David had conquered the citadel of Zion. Moreover, when the Philistines approached, David "went down to the hold," or mountain fortress, by which we cannot possibly understand the citadel upon Zion, on account of the expression "went down." If David had been living upon Zion at the time, he would hardly have left this fortification when the Philistines encamped in the valley of Rephaim on the west of Jerusalem, but would rather have attacked and routed the enemy from the citadel itself. The second victory followed very soon after the first, and must therefore be assigned to the same period. The Philistines evidently resolved, as soon as the tidings reached them of the union of all the tribes under the sovereignty of David, that they would at once resist the growing power of Israel, and smite David before he had consolidated his government.—Ver. 17. "*The Philistines went up to seek David*," i.e. to seek him out and smite him. The expression לְבַקֵּשׁ presupposes that David had not yet taken up his abode upon Zion He had probably already left Hebron to make preparations for his attack upon the Jebusites. When he heard of the approach of the Philistines, he went down into the mountain fortress. "The hold" cannot be the citadel of Zion (as in vers. 7 and 9), because this was so high that they had to go *up* to it on every side; and it is impossible to sustain the opinion advanced by Bertheau, that the verb יָרַד (to go down) is used for falling back into a fortification. הַמְּצוּדָה (*the hold*), with the definite article, is probably the mountain stronghold in the desert of Judah, into which David withdrew for a long time to defend himself from Saul (*vid.* ch. xxiii. 14 and 1 Chron. xii. 8). In ver. 18 the position of the Philistines is more minutely defined. The verse contains a circumstantial clause: "*The Philistines had come and spread themselves out in the valley of Rephaim,*" a valley on the west of Jerusalem, and only separated from the valley of Ben-hinnom by a narrow ridge of land (see at Josh. xv. 8). Instead of יִנָּטְשׁוּ the Chronicles have יִפְשְׁטוּ, they had invaded, which is perfectly equivalent so far as the sense is concerned.—Vers. 19, 20. David inquired of the Lord by the Urim whether he should go out against the foe, and whether God would give them into his hand;[1] and when he had received an answer in the affirmative to both these questions, he went to *Baal-perazim* (*lit.* into Baal-perazim), and smote them there, and said (ver. 20), "Jehovah hath broken mine enemies before me like a water-breach," *i.e.* has smitten them before me, and broken their power as a flood breaks through and carries away whatever opposes it. From these words of David, the place where the battle was fought received the name of *Baal-perazim, i.e.* "possessor of breaches" (equivalent to *Bruch-hausen* or *Brechendorf*, *Breach-ham* or *Break-thorpe*). The only other passage in which the place is mentioned is Isa. xxviii. 21, where this event is alluded to, but it cannot have been far from the valley of Rephaim.—Ver. 21. The Philistines left their idols behind them there. They had probably brought them to the war, as the Israelites once did their ark, as an auxiliary force. "*And David took them away.*" The Chronicles have "their gods" instead of "their idols," and "they were burned with fire" instead of וַיִּשָּׂאֵם, "he took them

---

[1] Through the express statement that David inquired of Jehovah (viz. by the Urim) in both these conflicts with the Philistines (vers. 19 and 23), Diestel's assertion, that after the death of Saul we do not read any more about the use of the holy lot, is completely overthrown, as well as the conclusion which he draws from it, namely, that "David probably employed it for the purpose of giving a certain definiteness to his command over his followers, over whom he had naturally but little authority (1 Sam. xxii. 2?), rather than because he looked upon it himself with any peculiar reverence."

away,"[1] took them as booty. The reading in the Chronicles gives the true explanation of the fact, as David would certainly dispose of the idols in the manner prescribed in the law (Deut. vii. 5, 25). The same reading was also most probably to be found in the sources employed by our author, who omitted it merely as being self-evident. In this way David fully avenged the disgrace brought upon Israel by the Philistines, when they carried away the ark in the time of Eli.—Vers. 22-25. Although thoroughly beaten, the Philistines soon appeared again to repair the defeat which they had suffered. As David had not followed up the victory, possibly because he was not sufficiently prepared, the Philistines assembled again in the valley of Rephaim.—Ver. 23. David inquired once more of the Lord what he was to do, and received this answer: "*Thou shalt not go up* (*i.e.* advance to meet the foe, and attack them in front); *turn round behind them, and come upon them* (attack them) *opposite to the Baca-shrubs.*" בְּכָאִים, a word which only occurs here and in the parallel passage in 1 Chron. xiv. 14, is rendered ἀπίους, pear-trees, by the LXX., and *mulberry-trees* by the Rabbins. But these are both of them uncertain conjectures. *Baca*, according to Abulfadl, is the name given in Arabic to a shrub which grows at Mecca and resembles the balsam, except that it has longer leaves and larger and rounder fruit, and from which, if a leaf be broken off, there flows a white pungent sap, like a white tear, which in all probability gave rise to the name בָּכָא = בָּכָה, to weep (*vid.* Celsii, *Hierob.* i. pp. 338 sqq., and Gesenius, *Thes.* p. 205).—Ver. 24. "*And when thou hearest the rush of a going in the tops of the baca-shrubs, then bestir thyself,*" or hasten; "*for Jehovah has gone out before thee, to smite the army of the Philistines.*" "The sound of a going," *i.e.* of the advance of an army, was a significant sign of the approach of an army of God, which would smite the enemies of Jehovah and of His servant David; like the visions of Jacob (Gen. xxxii. 2, 3) and Elisha (2 Kings vi. 17). "Then thou shalt bestir thyself," *lit.* be sharp, *i.e.* active, quick: this is paraphrased in the Chronicles by "then thou shalt go out to battle."—Ver. 25. David did this, and smote the Philistines from *Geba* to the neighbourhood of *Gezer*. In the Chronicles

---

[1] This is the marginal reading in the English version, though the text has "he burned them."—TR.

we find "from *Gibeon*" instead of from *Geba*. The former is unquestionably the true reading, and *Geba* an error of the pen: for *Geba*, the present *Jeba*, was to the north of Jerusalem, and on the east of *Ramah* (see at Josh. xviii. 24); so that it is quite unsuitable here. But that is not the case with *Gibeon*, the present *el Jib*, on the north-west of Jerusalem (see at Josh. ix. 3); for this was on the way to *Gezer*, which was four Roman miles to the north of *Amws*, and is probably to be sought for on the site of the present *el Kubab* (see at Josh. x. 33).[1]

REMOVAL OF THE ARK TO JERUSALEM.—CHAP. VI.

After David had selected the citadel of Zion, or rather Jerusalem, as the capital of the kingdom, he directed his attention to the organization and improvement of the legally established worship of the congregation, which had fallen grievously into decay since the death of Eli, in consequence of the separation of the ark from the tabernacle. He therefore resolved first of all to fetch out the ark of the covenant, as the true centre of the Mosaic sanctuary, from its obscurity and bring it up to Zion; and having deposited it in a tent previously prepared to receive it, to make this a place of worship where the regular worship of God might be carried on in accordance with the instructions of the law. That he should make the capital of his kingdom the central point of the worship of the whole congregation of Israel, followed so naturally from the nature of the kingdom of God, and the relation in which David stood, as the earthly

---

[1] There is no force in the objection brought by Bertheau against this view, viz. that "it is *a priori* improbable that the Philistines who were fighting against David and his forces, whose base of operations was Jerusalem, should have taken possession of the whole line from Gibeon to Gezer," as the improbability is by no means apparent, and has not been pointed out by Bertheau, whilst the assumption that Jerusalem was David's base of operations has no foundation whatever. Moreover, Bertheau's opinion, that *Geba* was the same as *Gibeah* in the tribe of Judah (Josh. xv. 57), is decidedly erroneous: for this *Gibeah* is not to be identified with the present village of *Jeba* on the south side of the Wady *Musurr*, half-way between Shocoh and Jerusalem, but was situated towards the desert of Judah (see at Josh. xv. 57); and besides, it is impossible to see how the Philistines, who had invaded the plain of Rephaim, could have been beaten from this Gibeah as far as to Gezer.

monarch of that kingdom, towards Jehovah the God-king, that there is no necessity whatever to seek for even a partial explanation in the fact that David felt it desirable to have the high priest with the Urim and Thummim always close at hand. But why did not David remove the Mosaic tabernacle to Mount Zion at Jerusalem at the same time as the ark of the covenant, and so restore the divinely established sanctuary in its integrity? This question can only be answered by conjectures. One of the principal motives for allowing the existing separation of the ark from the tabernacle to continue, may have been that, during the time the two sanctuaries had been separated, two high priests had arisen, one of whom officiated at the tabernacle at Gibeon, whilst the other, namely Abiathar, who escaped the massacre of the priests at Nob and fled at once to David, had been the channel of all divine communications to David during the time of his persecution by Saul, and had also officiated as high priest in his camp; so that he could no more think of deposing him from the office which he had hitherto filled, in consequence of the reorganization of the legal worship, than he could of deposing Zadok, of the line of Eleazar, the officiating high priest at Gibeon. Moreover, David may from the very first have regarded the service which he instituted in connection with the ark upon Zion as merely a provisional arrangement, which was to continue till his kingdom was more thoroughly consolidated, and the way had been thereby prepared for erecting a fixed house of God, and so establishing the worship of the nation of Jehovah upon a more durable foundation. David may also have cherished the firm belief that in the meantime the Lord would put an end to the double priesthood which had grown out of the necessities of the times, or at any rate give him some direct revelation as to the arrangements which he ought to make.

We have a parallel account of the removal of the ark of the covenant to Zion in 1 Chron. xiii. 15 and 16, which agrees for the most part *verbatim*, at all events in all essential points, with the account before us; but the liturgical side of this solemn act is very elaborately described, especially the part taken by the Levites, whereas the account given here is very condensed, and is restricted in fact to an account of the work of removing the ark from Kirjath-jearim to Jerusalem as carried out by

David. David composed the 24th Psalm for the religious cere-monies connected with the removal of the ark to Mount Zion.

Vers. 1-10. *The ark fetched from Kirjath-jearim.*—Ver. 1. "*David assembled together again all the chosen men in Israel, thirty thousand.*" יֹסֶף for יֹאסֶף is the *Kal* of אָסַף, as in 1 Sam. xv. 6, Ps. civ. 29. עוֹד, *again, once more*, points back to ch. v. 1 and 3, where all Israel is said to have assembled for the first time in Hebron to anoint David king. It is true that that assembly was not convened directly by David himself; but this was not the point in question, but merely their assembling a second time (see Bertheau on 1 Chron. xiii. 5). בָּחוּר does not mean "the young men" here (νεάνια, LXX.), or "the fighting men," but, according to the etymology of the word, "the picked men." Instead of thirty thousand, the LXX. have seventy chiliads, probably with an intentional exaggeration, because the number of men in Israel who were capable of bearing arms amounted to more than thirty thousand. The whole nation, through a very considerable body of representatives, was to take part in the removal of the ark. The writer of the Chronicles gives a more elaborate account of the preparations for these festivities (1 Chron. xiii. 1-5); namely, that David took counsel with the heads of thousands and hundreds, and all the leaders, *i.e.* all the heads of families and households, and then with their consent collected together the whole nation from the brook of Egypt to Hamath, of course not every individual, but a large number of heads of households as representatives of the whole. This account in the Chronicles is not an expansion of the brief notice given here; but the account before us is a condensation of the fuller description given in the sources that were employed by both authors.—Ver. 2. "*David went with all the people that were with him to Baale-Jehuda, to fetch up the ark of God from thence.*" The words מִבַּעֲלֵי יְהוּדָה cause some difficulty on account of the מִן, which is used instead of the accusative with ה *loc.*, like בַּעֲלָתָה in the Chronicles; yet the translators of the Septuagint, Chaldee, Vulgate, and other versions, all had the reading מִן in their text, and בַּעֲלֵי has therefore been taken as an appellative and rendered ἀπὸ τῶν ἀρχόντων Ἰουδά ("from the rulers of Judah"), or as Luther renders it, "from the citizens of Judah." This is decidedly incorrect, as the word "thence" which follows is perfectly unintelligible on any other supposition than that *Baale-Jehudah* is the name of a place. *Baale-Jehudah* is another name of the city of *Kirjath-jearim* (Josh. xv. 60, xviii. 14), which is called *Baalah* in Josh. xv. 9 and 1 Chron. xiii. 6, according to its Canaanitish name, instead of which the name *Kirjath-jearim* (city of the woods) was adopted by the Israelites, though without entirely supplanting the old name. The epithet "of Judah" is a contraction of the fuller expression "city of the children of Judah" in Josh. xviii. 14, and is added to distinguish this Baal city, which was situated upon the border of the tribe of Judah, from other cities that were also named after Baal, such as *Baal* or *Baalath-beer* in the tribe of Simeon (1 Chron. iv. 33, Josh. xix. 8), *Baalath* in the tribe of Dan (Josh. xix. 44), the present *Kuryet el Enab* (see at Josh. ix. 17). The מִ (from) is either a very ancient error of the pen that crept by accident into the text, or, if genuine and original, it is to be explained on the supposition that the historian dropped the construction with which he started, and instead of mentioning *Baale-Jehudah* as the place to which David went, gave it at once as the place from which he fetched the ark; so that the passage is to be understood in this way: "And David went, and all the people who were with him, out of Baale-Jehudah, to which they had gone up to fetch the ark of God" (Kimchi). In the sentence which follows, a difficulty is also occasioned by the repetition of the word שֵׁם in the clause אֲשֶׁר נִקְרָא . . . עָלָיו, "*upon which the name is called, the name of Jehovah of hosts, who is enthroned above the cherubim.*" The difficulty cannot be solved by altering the first שֵׁם into שָׁם, as Clericus, Thenius, and Bertheau suggest: for if this alteration were adopted, we should have to render the passage "where the name of Jehovah of hosts is invoked, who is enthroned above the cherubim (which are) upon it (*i.e.* upon the ark);" and this would not only introduce an unscriptural thought into the passage, but it would be impossible to find any suitable meaning for the word עָלָיו, except by making very arbitrary interpolations. Throughout the whole of the Old Testament we never meet with the idea that the name of Jehovah was invoked at the ark of the covenant, because no one was allowed to approach the ark for the purpose of invoking the name of the Lord there; and upon the great day of atonement the high priest was only allowed to enter the most holy place with the cloud of incense, to sprinkle the blood of the atoning sacrifice upon the ark. Moreover, the standing expression for "call upon the name of the Lord" is קָרָא בְשֵׁם יְיָ; whereas נִקְרָא שֵׁם יְיָ עַל signifies "the name of Jehovah is called above a person or thing." Lastly, even if עָלָיו belonged to יֹשֵׁב הַכְּרֻבִים, it would not only be a superfluous addition, occurring nowhere else in connection with יֹשֵׁב הכ׳, not even in 1 Chron. xiii. 6 (vid. 1 Sam. iv. 4; 2 Kings xix. 15; Isa. xxxvii. 16; Ps. xcix. 1), but such an addition if made at all would necessarily require אֲשֶׁר עָלָיו (vid. Ex. xxv. 22). The only way in which we can obtain a biblical thought and grammatical sense is by connecting עָלָיו with the אֲשֶׁר before נִקְרָא: "above which (ark) the name of Jehovah-Zebaoth is named," i.e. above which Jehovah reveals His glory or His divine nature to His people, or manifests His gracious presence in Israel. "The name of God denotes all the operations of God through which He attests His personal presence in that relation into which He has entered to man, i.e. the whole of the divine self-manifestation, or of that side of the divine nature which is turned towards men" (Oehler, Herzog's *Real-Encycl.* x. p. 197). From this deeper meaning of "the name of God" we may probably explain the repetition of the word שֵׁם, which is first of all written absolutely (as at the close of Lev. xxiv. 16), and then more fully defined as "the name of the Lord of hosts."—Vers. 3, 4. "*They set the ark of God upon a new cart, and took it away from the house of Abinadab.*" הִרְכִּיב means here "to put (load) upon a cart," and נָשָׂא to take away, i.e. drive off: for there are grammatical (or syntactical) reasons which make it impossible to render וַיִּשָּׂאֻהוּ as a pluperfect ("they had taken"), on account of the previous וירכבו.

The ark of the covenant had been standing in the house of Abinadab from the time when the Philistines had sent it back into the land of Israel, i.e. about seventy years (viz. twenty years to the victory at Ebenezer mentioned in 1 Sam. vii. 1 sqq., forty years under Samuel and Saul, and about ten years under David: see the chronological table in vol. iv. p. 289). The further statement, that "Uzzah and Ahio, sons of Abinadab, drove the cart," may easily be reconciled with this. These two sons were either born about the time when the ark was first taken to Abinadab's house, or at a subsequent period; or else the term *sons* is used, as is frequently the case, in the sense of grandsons. The words from חֲדָשָׁה (the last word in ver. 3) to *Gibeah* in ver. 4 are wanting in the Septuagint, and can only have been introduced through the error of a copyist, whose eye wandered back to the first עֲגָלָה in ver. 3, so that he copied a whole line twice over; for they not only contain a pure tautology, a merely verbal and altogether superfluous and purposeless repetition, but they are altogether unsuitable to the connection in which they stand. Not only is there something very strange in the repetition of the חֲדָשָׁה without an article after הָעֲגָלָה; but the words which follow, עִם אֲרוֹן ה' (with the ark of God), cannot be made to fit on to the repeated clause, for there is no sense whatever in such a sentence as this: "They brought it (the ark) out of the house of Abinadab, which is upon the hill, *with the* ark of God." The only way in which the words " with the ark " can be made to acquire any meaning at all, is by omitting the repetition referred to, and connecting them with the new cart in ver. 3: "Uzzah and Ahio ... drove the cart with the ark of God, and Ahio went before the ark." נָהַג, to drive (a carriage), is construed here with an accusative, in 1 Chron. xiii. 7 with בְּ, as in Isa. xi. 6.—Ver. 5. And David and all the house (people) of Israel were מְשַׂחֲקִים, sporting, *i.e.* they danced and played, before Jehovah. בְּכֹל עֲצֵי בְרוֹשִׁים, " with all kinds of woods of cypresses." This could only mean, with all kinds of instruments made of cypress wood; but this mode of expression would be a very strange one even if the reading were correct. In the Chronicles, however (ver. 8), instead of this strange expression, we find בְּכָל־עֹז וּבְשִׁירִים, " with all their might and with songs." This is evidently the correct reading, from which our text has sprung, although the latter is found in all the old versions, and even in the Septuagint, which really combines the two readings thus: ἐν ὀργάνοις ἡρμοσμένοις ἐν ἰσχύϊ καὶ ἐν ᾠδαῖς, where ἐν ὀργάνοις ἡρμοσμένοις is evidently the interpretation of בְּכֹל עֲצֵי בְרוֹשִׁים; for the text of the Chronicles cannot be regarded as an explanation of Samuel. Moreover, songs would not be omitted on such a festive occasion; and two of the instruments mentioned, viz. the *kinnor* and *nebel* (see at 1 Sam. x. 5), were generally played as accompaniments to singing. The *vav* before בְּשִׁירִים, and before the different instruments, corresponds to the Latin *et ... et*, both ... and. תֹּף, the timbrel. בִּמְנַעַנְעִים וּבְצֶלְצְלִים, *sistris et cymbalis*

(Vulg., Syr.), "with bells and cymbals" (Luther). מְנַעַנְעִים,
from נוּעַ, are instruments that are shaken, the σεῖστρα, *sistra*, of
the ancients, which consisted of two iron rods fastened together
at one end, either in a semicircle or at right angles, upon which
rings were hung loosely, so as to make a tinkling sound when
they were shaken. מְצִלְתַּיִם = צֶלְצְלִים are cymbals or castanets.
Instead of מְנַעַנְעִים, we find חֲצֹצְרוֹת, trumpets, mentioned in the
Chronicles in the last rank after the cymbals. It is possible
that *sistra* were played and trumpets blown, so that the two
accounts complete each other.—Vers. 6, 7. When the procession
had reached the threshing-floor of *Nachon*, Uzzah stretched out
his hand to lay hold of the ark, *i.e.* to keep it from falling
over with the cart, because the oxen slipped. And the wrath
of the Lord was kindled, and God slew Uzzah upon the spot.
Goren nachon means "the threshing-floor of the stroke" (*nachon*
from נָכָה, not from כּוּן); in the Chronicles we have *goren chidon*,
i.e. the threshing-floor of destruction or disaster (בְּידוֹן = כִּיד,
Job xxi. 20). *Chidon* is probably only an explanation of *nachon*,
so that the name may have been given to the threshing-floor,
not from its owner, but from the incident connected with the
ark which took place there. Eventually, however, this name
was supplanted by the name *Perez-uzzah* (ver. 8). The situation
of the threshing-floor cannot be determined, as all that we can
gather from this account is that the house of Obed-edom the
Gathite was somewhere near it; but no village, hamlet, or
town is mentioned.[1] Jerome paraphrases כִּי שָׁמְטוּ הַבָּקָר thus:
"Because the oxen kicked and turned it (the ark) over." But
שָׁמַט does not mean to kick; its true meaning is to let go, or
let lie (Ex. xxiii. 11; Deut. xv. 2, 3), hence to slip or stumble.
The stumbling of the animals might easily have turned the cart
over, and this was what Uzzah tried to prevent by laying hold
of the ark. God smote him there "on account of the offence"
(שַׁל, ἀπ. λεγ. from שָׁלָה, in the sense of erring, or committing a
fault). The writer of the Chronicles gives it thus: "Because

---

[1] If it were possible to discover the situation of Gath-rimmon, the home
of Obed-edom (see at ver. 10), we might probably decide the question
whether Obed-edom was still living in the town where he was born or not.
But according to the *Onom.*, Kirjath-jearim was ten miles from Jerusalem,
and Gath-rimmon twelve, that is to say, farther off. Now, if these statements are correct, Obed-edom's house cannot have been in Gath-rimmon.

he had stretched out his hand to the ark," though of course the text before us is not to be altered to this, as Thenius and Bertheau suggest.—Ver. 8. "And David was angry, because Jehovah had made a rent on Uzzah, and called the place *Perez-uzzah*" (rent of Uzzah). פָּרַץ פֶּרֶץ, to tear a rent, is here applied to a sudden tearing away from life. יִחַר לְ is understood by many in the sense of "he troubled himself;" but this meaning cannot be grammatically sustained, whilst it is quite possible to become angry, or fall into a state of violent excitement, at an unexpected calamity. The burning of David's anger was not directed against God, but referred to the calamity which had befallen Uzzah, or speaking more correctly, to the cause of this calamity, which David attributed to himself or to his undertaking. As he had not only resolved upon the removal of the ark, but had also planned the way in which it should be taken to Jerusalem, he could not trace the occasion of Uzzah's death to any other cause than his own plans. He was therefore angry that such misfortune had attended his undertaking. In his first excitement and dismay, David may not have perceived the real and deeper ground of this divine judgment. Uzzah's offence consisted in the fact that he had touched the ark with profane feelings, although with good intentions, namely to prevent its rolling over and falling from the cart. Touching the ark, the throne of the divine glory and visible pledge of the invisible presence of the Lord, was a violation of the majesty of the holy God. "Uzzah was therefore a type of all who with good intentions, humanly speaking, yet with unsanctified minds, interfere in the affairs of the kingdom of God, from the notion that they are in danger, and with the hope of saving them" (O. v. Gerlach). On further reflection, David could not fail to discover where the cause of Uzzah's offence, which he had atoned for with his life, really had lain, and that it had actually arisen from the fact that he (David) and those about him had decided to disregard the distinct instructions of the law with regard to the handling of the ark. According to Num. iv. the ark was not only to be moved by none but Levites, but it was to be carried on the shoulders, not in a carriage; and in ver. 15, even the Levites were expressly forbidden to touch it on pain of death. But instead of taking these instructions as their rule, they had followed the example of the Philistines when they sent back the ark (1 Sam. vi. 7 sqq.), and had placed it upon a new cart, and directed Uzzah to drive it, whilst, as his conduct on the occasion clearly shows, he had no idea of the unapproachable holiness of the ark of God, and had to expiate his offence with his life, as a warning to all the Israelites.— Vers. 9, 10. David's excitement at what had occurred was soon changed into fear of the Lord, so that he said, "How shall the ark of Jehovah come to me?" If merely touching the ark of God is punished in this way, how can I have it brought near me, up to the citadel of Zion? He therefore relinquished his intention of bringing it into the city of David, and placed it in the house of Obed-edom the Gathite. *Obed-edom* was a Levite of the family of the Korahites, who sprang from Kohath (compare Ex. vi. 21, xviii. 16, with 1 Chron. xxvi. 4), and belonged to the class of Levitical doorkeepers, whose duty it was, in connection with other Levites, to watch over the ark in the sacred tent (1 Chron. xv. 18, 24). He is called the *Gittite* or *Gathite* from his birthplace, the Levitical city of *Gath-rimmon* in the tribe of Dan (Josh. xxi. 24, xix. 45).

Vers. 11–19. *Removal of the ark of God to the city of David* (cf. 1 Chron. xv.).—Vers. 11, 12. When the ark had been in the house of Obed-edom for three months, and David heard that the Lord had blessed his house for the sake of the ark of God, he went thither and brought it up to the city of David with gladness, *i.e.* with festal rejoicing, or a solemn procession. (For שִׂמְחָה, in the sense of festal rejoicing, or a joyous fête, see Gen. xxxi. 27, Neh. xii. 43, etc.) On this occasion, however, David adhered strictly to the instructions of the law, as the more elaborate account given in the Chronicles clearly shows. He not only gathered together all Israel at Jerusalem to join in this solemn act, but summoned the priests and Levites, and commanded them to sanctify themselves, and carry the ark "according to the right," *i.e.* as the Lord had commanded in the law of Moses, and to offer sacrifices during the procession, and sing songs, *i.e.* psalms, with musical accompaniment. In the very condensed account before us, all that is mentioned is the carrying of the ark, the sacrificing during the march, and the festivities of the king and people. But even from these few facts we see that David had discovered his former mistake, and had given up the idea of removing the ark upon a carriage as a transgression of the law.—Ver. 13. The bearers of the ark are not particularly mentioned in this account; but it is very evident that they were Levites, as the Chronicles affirm, from the fact that the ark was carried this time, and not driven, as before. *" And it came to pass, when the bearers of the ark of Jehovah had gone six paces, he sacrificed an ox and a fatted calf"* (*i.e.* had them sacrificed). These words are generally understood as meaning, that sacrifices of this kind were offered along the whole way, at the distance of six paces apart. This would certainly have been a possible thing, and there would be no necessity to assume that the procession halted every six paces, until the sacrificial ceremony was completed, but the ark might have continued in progress, whilst sacrifices were being offered at the distances mentioned. And even the immense number of sacrificial animals that would have been required is no valid objection to such an assumption. We do not know what the distance really was: all that we know is, that it was not so much as ten miles, as Kirjath-jearim was only about twelve miles from Jerusalem, so that a few thousand oxen, and the same number of fatted calves, would have been quite sufficient. But the words of the text do not distinctly affirm that sacrifices were offered whenever the bearers advanced six paces, but only that this was done as soon as the bearers had taken the first six steps. So that, strictly speaking, all that is stated is, that when the procession had started and gone six paces, the sacrifice was offered, namely, for the purpose of inaugurating or consecrating the solemn procession. In 1 Chron. xv. this fact is omitted; and it is stated instead (ver. 26), that " when God helped the Levites that bare the ark of the covenant of the Lord, they offered seven bullocks and seven rams," *i.e.* at the close of the procession, when the journey was ended, to praise God for the fact that the Levites had been enabled to carry the ark of God to the place appointed for it, without suffering the slightest harm.[1]—Ver. 14. " *And David danced with all his might before*

---

[1] There is no discrepancy, therefore, between the two different accounts; but the one supplements the other in a manner perfectly in harmony with the whole affair,—at the outset, a sacrifice consisting of one ox and one fatted calf; and at the close, one of seven oxen and seven rams. Consequently there is no reason for altering the text of the verse before us, as Thenius proposes, according to the senseless rendering of the LXX., καὶ

the Lord (*i.e.* before the ark), *and was girded with a white ephod* (shoulder-dress)." Dancing, as an expression of holy enthusiasm, was a customary thing from time immemorial : we meet with it as early as at the festival of thanksgiving at the Red Sea (Ex. xv. 20) ; but there, and also at subsequent celebrations of the different victories gained by the Israelites, none but women are described as taking part in it (Judg. xi. 34, xxi. 19 ; 1 Sam. xviii. 6). The white ephod was, strictly speaking, a priestly costume, although in the law it is not prescribed as the dress to be worn by them when performing their official duties, but rather as the dress which denoted the priestly character of the wearer (see at 1 Sam. xxii. 18) ; and for this reason it was worn by David in connection with these festivities in honour of the Lord, as the head of the priestly nation of Israel (see at 1 Sam. ii. 18). In ver. 15 it is still further related, that David and all the house (nation) of Israel brought up the ark of the Lord with jubilee and trumpet-blast. תְּרוּעָה is used here to signify the song of jubilee and the joyous shouting of the people. In the Chronicles (ver. 28) the musical instruments played on the occasion are also severally mentioned. —Ver. 16. When the ark came (*i.e.* was carried) into the city of David, Michal the daughter of Saul looked out of the window, and there she saw king David leaping and dancing before Jehovah, and despised him in her heart. וְהָיָה, " and it came to pass," for וַיְהִי, because there is no progress made, but only another element introduced. בָּא is a perfect : " the ark had come, . . . and Michal looked through the window, . . . there she saw," etc. Michal is intentionally designated the daughter of Saul here, instead of the wife of David, because on this occasion she manifested her father's disposition rather than her husband's. In Saul's time people did not trouble themselves about the ark of the covenant (1 Chron. xiii. 3) ; public worship was neglected, and the soul for vital religion had died out in the family of the king. Michal possessed teraphim, and in

ἦσαν μετ' αὐτοῦ αἴροντες τὴν κιβωτὸν ἑπτὰ χοροί, καὶ θῦμα μόσχος καὶ ἄρνες (" with David there were bearers of the ark, seven choirs, and sacrifices of a calf and lambs"), which has also found its way into the Vulgate, though Jerome has rendered our Hebrew text faithfully afterwards (*i.e.* after the gloss, which was probably taken from the Itala, and inserted in his translation).

David she only loved the brave hero and exalted king: she therefore took offence at the humility with which the king, in his pious enthusiasm, placed himself on an equality with all the rest of the nation before the Lord.—Ver. 17. When the ark was brought to the place appointed for it upon Mount Zion, and was deposited in the tent which David had prepared for it, he offered burnt-offerings and thank-offerings before the Lord. " In its place" is still further defined as " in the midst of the tent which David," etc., *i.e.* in the Most Holy Place; for the tent would certainly be constructed according to the type of the Mosaic tabernacle. The burnt-offerings and peace-offerings were offered to consecrate the newly erected house of God.— Vers. 18, 19. When the offering of sacrifice was over, David blessed the people in the name of the Lord, as Solomon did afterwards at the dedication of the temple (1 Kings viii. 55), and gave to all the (assembled) people, both men and women, to every one a slice of bread, a measure (of wine), and a cake for a festal meal, *i.e.* for the sacrificial meal, which was celebrated with the *shelamim* after the offering of the sacrifices, and after the king had concluded the liturgical festival with a benediction. חַלַּת לֶחֶם is a round cake of bread, baked for sacrificial meals, and synonymous with כִּכַּר־לֶחֶם (1 Chron. xvi. 3), as we may see from a comparison of Ex. xxix. 23 with Lev. viii. 26 (see the commentary on Lev. viii. 2). But the meaning of the ἀπ λεγ. אֶשְׁפָּר is uncertain, and has been much disputed. Most of the Rabbins understand it as signifying a piece of flesh or roast meat, deriving the word from אֵשׁ and פַּר; but this is certainly false. There is more to be said in favour of the derivation proposed by L. de Dieu, viz. from the Ethiopic שפר, *netiri*, from which Gesenius and Roediger (Ges. *Thes.* p. 1470) have drawn their explanation of the word as signifying a measure of wine or other beverage. For אֲשִׁישָׁה, the meaning grape-cake or raisin-cake is established by Song of Sol. ii. 5 and Hos. iii. 1 (*vid.* Hengstenberg, *Christol.* on Hos. iii. 1). The people returned home after the festal meal.

Vers. 20–23. When David returned home to bless his house, as he had previously blessed the people, Michal came to meet him with scornful words, saying, *" How has the king of Israel glorified himself to-day, when he stripped himself before the eyes of the maids of his servants, as only one of the loose people strips him-*

self!" The unusual combination פְּהַגָּלוֹת נִגְלוֹת is explained by Ewald (§ 240, e, p. 607) in this manner, that whilst, so far as the sense of the clause is concerned, the second verb ought to be in the infinitive absolute, they were both written with a very slight change of form in the infinitive construct; whereas others regard נִגְלוֹת as an unusual form of the infinitive absolute (Ges. *Lehrgeb.* p. 430), or a copyist's error for נִגְלֹה (Thenius, Olsh. *Gr.* p. 600). The proud daughter of Saul was offended at the fact, that the king had let himself down on this occasion to the level of the people. She availed herself of the shortness of the priests' shoulder-dress, to make a contemptuous remark concerning David's dancing, as an impropriety that was unbecoming in a king. "Who knows whether the proud woman did not intend to sneer at the rank of the Levites, as one that was contemptible in her eyes, since their humble service may have looked very trivial to her?" (*Berleb. Bible.*)—Vers. 21, 22. David replied, "Before Jehovah, who chose me before thy father and all his house, to appoint me prince over the people of Jehovah, over Israel, before Jehovah have I played (*lit.* joked, given utterance to my joy). And I will be still more despised, and become base in my eyes: and with the maidens of whom thou hast spoken, with them will I be honoured." The copula *vav* before שִׂחַקְתִּי serves to introduce the apodosis, and may be explained in this way, that the relative clause appended to "before Jehovah" acquired the power of a protasis on account of its length; so that, strictly speaking, there is an anakolouthon, as if the protasis read thus: "Before Jehovah, as He hath chosen me over Israel, I have humbled myself before Jehovah" (for "before him"). With the words "who chose me before *thy father and all his house*," David humbles the pride of the king's daughter. His playing and dancing referred to the Lord, who had chosen him, and had rejected Saul on account of his pride. He would therefore let himself be still further despised before the Lord, *i.e.* would bear still greater contempt from men than that which he had just received, and be humbled in his own eyes (*vid.* Ps. cxxxi. 1): then would he also with the maidens attain to honour before the Lord. For whoso humbleth himself, him will God exalt (Matt. xxiii. 12). בְּעֵינַי is not to be altered into בְּעֵינֶיךָ, as in the Septuagint. This alteration has arisen from a total misconception of the nature of true humility, which is of no worth in its own eyes. The rendering given by De Wette is at variance with both the grammar and the sense (" with the maidens, ... with them will I magnify myself"); and so also is that of Thenius (" with them will I be honoured, *i.e.* indemnify myself for thy foolish contempt!").—Ver. 23. Michal was humbled by God for her pride, and remained childless to the time of her death

DAVID'S RESOLUTION TO BUILD A TEMPLE. THE PROMISED PERPETUITY OF HIS THRONE.—CHAP. VII.

To the erection of a sanctuary for the ark upon Mount Zion there is appended an account of David's desire to build a temple for the Lord. We find this not only in the text before us, but also in the parallel history in 1 Chron. xvii. When David had acquired rest from his enemies round about, he formed the resolution to build a house for the Lord, and this resolution was sanctioned by the prophet Nathan (vers. 1-3). But the Lord revealed to the prophet, and through him to David, that He had not required the building of a temple from any of the tribes of Israel, and that He would first of all build a house himself for His servant David, and confirm the throne to his seed for ever, and then he should build Him a temple (vers. 4-17). David then gave utterance to his thanksgiving for this glorious promise in a prayer, in which he praised the unmeasurable grace of God, and prayed for the fulfilment of this renewed promise of divine grace (vers. 18-29).[1]

[1] With regard to the historical authenticity of this promise, Tholuck observes, in his *Prophets and their Prophecies* (pp. 165-6), that "it can be proved, with all the evidence which is ever to be obtained in support of historical testimony, that David actually received a prophetic promise that his family should sit upon the throne for ever, and consequently an intimation of a royal descendant whose government should be eternal. Anything like a merely subjective promise arising from human combinations is precluded here by the fact that Nathan, acting according to the best of his knowledge, gave his consent to David's plan of building a temple; and that it was not till afterwards, when he had been instructed by a divine vision, that he did the very opposite, and assured him on the contrary that God would build *him* a house." Thenius also affirms that "there is no reason for assuming, as De Wette has done, that Nathan's prophecies were not composed till after the time of Solomon;" that "their historical credibility

Vers. 1-3 When David was dwelling in his house, *i.e.* the palace of cedar (ch. v. 11), and Jehovah had given him rest from all his enemies round about, he said to Nathan the prophet: " See now, I dwell in a house of cedar, and the ark of God dwelleth within the curtains." הַיְרִיעָה in the singular is used, in Ex. xxvi. 2 sqq., to denote the inner covering, com-

is attested by Ps. lxxxix. (vers. 4, 5, 20–38, and especially ver. 20), Ps. cxxxii. 11, 12, and Isa. lv. 3 ; and that, properly interpreted, they are also Messianic." The principal evidence of this is to be found in the prophetic utterance of David in ch. xxiii., where, as is generally admitted, he takes a retrospective glance at the promise, and thereby attests the historical credibility of Nathan's prophecy (Thenius, p. 245). Nevertheless, Gust. Baur maintains that "a closer comparison of this more elaborate and simple description (ch. vii.) with the brief and altogether unexampled *last words of David*, more especially with 2 Sam. xxiii. 5, can hardly leave the slightest doubt, that the relation in which the chapter before us stands to these words, is that of a later expansion to an authentic prophetic utterance of the king himself." For example, the distinct allusion to the birth of Solomon, and the building of the temple, which was to be completed by him, is said to have evidently sprung from a later development of the original promise after the time of Solomon, on account of the incongruity apparent in Nathan's prediction between the ideal picture of the Israelitish monarchy and the definite allusion to Solomon's building of the temple. But there is no such " incongruity" in Nathan's prediction ; it is only to be found in the naturalistic assumptions of Baur himself, that the utterances of the prophets contained nothing more than subjective and *ideal* hopes of the future, and not supernatural predictions. This also applies to Diestel's opinion, that the section vers. 4-16 does not harmonize with the substance of David's glorious prayer in vers. 18–29, nor the latter again with itself, because the advice given him to relinquish the idea of building the temple is not supported by any reasons that answer either to the character of David or to his peculiar circumstances, with which the allusion to his son would have been in perfect keeping ; but the prophet's dissuasion merely alludes to the fact that Jehovah did not stand in need of a stately house at all, and had never given utterance to any such desire. On account of this "obvious" fact, Diestel regards it as credible that the original dissuasion came from God, because it was founded upon an earlier view, but that the promise of the son of David which followed proceeded from Nathan, who no doubt looked with more favourable eyes upon the building of the temple. This discrepancy is also arbitrarily foisted upon the text. There is not a syllable about any " original dissuasion " in all that Nathan says ; for he simply tells the king that Jehovah had hitherto dwelt in a tent, and had not asked any of the tribes of Israel to build a stately temple, but not that Jehovah did not need a stately house at all.

Of the different exegetical treatises upon this passage, see *Christ. Aug Crusii Hypomnemata*, ii. 190-219, and Hengstenberg's *Christol.* i. 123 sqq.

posed of a number of lengths of tapestry sewn together, which was spread over the planks of the tabernacle, and made it into a dwelling, whereas the separate pieces of tapestry are called יְרִיעֹת in the plural; and hence, in the later writers, יְרִיעוֹת alternates sometimes with אֹהֶל (Isa. liv. 2), and at other times with אֹהָלִים (Song of Sol. i. 5; Jer. iv. 20, xlix. 29). Consequently הַיְרִיעָה refers here to the tent-cloth or tent formed of pieces of tapestry. " *Within* (*i.e.* surrounded by) *the tent-cloth:*" in the Chronicles we find "under curtains." From the words " when the Lord had given him rest from all his enemies round about," it is evident that David did not form the resolution to build the temple in the first years of his reign upon Zion, nor immediately after the completion of his palace, but at a later period (see the remarks on ch. v. 11, note). It is true that the giving of rest from all his enemies round about does not definitely presuppose the termination of *all* the greater wars of David, since it is not affirmed that this rest was a definitive one; but the words cannot possibly be restricted to the two victories over the Philistines (ch. v. 17-25), as Hengstenberg supposes, inasmuch as, however important the second may have been, their foes were not even permanently quieted by them, to say nothing of their being entirely subdued. Moreover, in the promise mentioned in ver. 9, God distinctly says, " I was with thee whithersoever thou wentest, and have cut off *all* thine enemies before thee." These words also show that at that time David had already fought against all the enemies round about, and humbled them. Now, as all David's principal wars are grouped together for the first time in ch. viii. and x., there can be no doubt that the history is not arranged in a strictly chronological order. And the expression "after this" in ch. viii. 1 is by no means at variance with this, since this formula does not at all express a strictly chronological sequence. From the words of the prophet, " Go, do all that is in thy heart, for the Lord is with thee," it is very evident that David had expressed the intention to build a splendid palatial temple. The word לֵךְ, *go* (equivalent to "quite right"), is omitted in the Chronicles as superfluous. Nathan sanctioned the king's resolution " from his own feelings, and not by divine revelation" (J. H Michaelis); but he did not "afterwards perceive that the time for carrying out this intention had not yet come," as Thenius and Berthean maintain; on the contrary, the Lord God revealed to the prophet that David was not to carry out his intention at all.

Vers. 4-17. *The revelation and promise of God.*—Ver. 4. "*That night,*" i.e. the night succeeding the day on which Nathan had talked with the king concerning the building of the temple, the Lord made known His decree to the prophet, with instructions to communicate it to the king. הָאַתָּה וגו׳, "*Shouldest thou build me a house for me to dwell in?*" The question involves a negative reply, and consequently in the Chronicles we find "thou shalt not."—Vers. 6, 7. The reason assigned for this answer: "I have not dwelt in a house from the day of the bringing up of Israel out of Egypt even to this day, but I was wandering about in a tent and in a dwelling." "*And in a dwelling*" (*mishcan*) is to be taken as explanatory, viz. in a tent which was my dwelling. As a tent is a traveller's dwelling, so, as long as God's dwelling was a tent, He himself appeared as if travelling or going from place to place. "In the whole of the time that I walked among all the children of Israel, . . . have I spoken a word to one of the tribes of Israel, whom I commanded to feed my people, saying, Wherefore have ye not built me a cedar house?" A "cedar house" is equivalent to a palace built of costly materials. The expression אַחַד שִׁבְטֵי יִשְׂרָאֵל ("one of the tribes of Israel") is a striking one, as the feeding of the nation does not appear to be a duty belonging to the "tribes," and in the Chronicles we have שֹׁפְטֵי (judges) instead of שִׁבְטֵי (tribes). But if שֹׁפְטֵי had been the original expression used in the text, it would be impossible to explain the origin and general acceptance of the word שִׁבְטֵי. For this very reason, therefore, we must regard שִׁבְטֵי as the original word, and understand it as referring to the *tribes*, which had supplied the nation with judges and leaders before the time of David, since the feeding, i.e. the government of Israel, which was in the hands of the judges, was transferred to the tribes to which the judges belonged. This view is confirmed by Ps. lxxviii. 67, 68, where the election of David as prince, and of Zion as the site of the sanctuary, is described as the election of the *tribe* of Judah and the rejection of the tribe of Ephraim. On the other hand, the assumption of Thenius, that שִׁבְטֵי, "shepherd-staffs," is used poetically for shepherds, cannot be established on the ground of Lev. xxvii. 32 and Micah vii. 14.

Jehovah gave two reasons why David's proposal to build Him a temple should not be carried out: (1) He had hitherto lived in a tent in the midst of His people; (2) He had not commanded any former prince or tribe to build a temple. This did not involve any blame, as though there had been something presumptuous in David's proposal, or in the fact that he had thought of undertaking such a work without an express command from God, but simply showed that it was not because of any negligence on the part of the former leaders of the people that they had not thought of erecting a temple, and that even now the time for carrying out such a work as that had not yet come.—Ver. 8. After thus declining his proposal, the Lord made known His gracious purpose to David: "Thus saith Jehovah of hosts" (not only *Jehovah*, as in ver. 5, but *Jehovah Sebaoth*, because He manifests himself in the following revelation as the God of the universe): "I have taken thee from the pasturage (grass-plat), behind the flock, to be prince over my people Israel; and was with thee whithersoever thou wentest, and exterminated all thine enemies before thee, and so made thee, וְעָשִׂיתִי (perfect with *vav* consec.), a great name, . . . and created a place for my people Israel, and planted them, so that they dwell in their place, and do not tremble any more (before their oppressors); and the sons of wickedness do not oppress them any further, as at the beginning, and from the day when I appointed judges over my people Israel: and I create thee rest from all thine enemies. And Jehovah proclaims to thee, that Jehovah will make thee a house." The words לְמִן הַיּוֹם . . . עַמִּי יִשׂ׳ are to be joined to בָּרִאשׁוֹנָה, "as in the beginning," *i.e.* in Egypt, and from the time of the judges; that is to say, during the rule of the judges, when the surrounding nations constantly oppressed and subjugated Israel. The plan usually adopted, of connecting the words with וַהֲנִיחֹתִי, does not yield any suitable thought at all, as God had not given David rest from the very beginning of the times of the judges; but the period of the judges was long antecedent to the time of David, and was not a period of rest for the Israelites. Again, וַהֲנִיחֹתִי does not resume what is stated in ver. 9, and is not to be rendered as a preterite in the sense of "I have procured thee rest," but as a perfect with *vav consec.*, "and I procure thee rest" from what is now about to come to pass. And וְהִגִּיד is to be taken in the same way: the Lord shows thee, first of all through His promise (which follows), and then through the fact itself, the realization of His word. וַהֲנִיחֹתִי refers to the future, as well as the building of David's house, and therefore not to the rest from all his enemies, which God had already secured for David, but to that which He would still further secure for him, that is to say, to the maintenance and establishment of that rest. The commentary upon this is to be found in Ps. lxxxix. 22-24. In the Chronicles (ver. 10) there is a somewhat different turn given to the last clauses: "and I bend down all thine enemies, and make it (the bending-down) known to thee (by the fact), and a house will Jehovah build for thee." The thought is not essentially changed by this; consequently there is no ground for any emendation of the text, which is not even apparently necessary, unless, like Bertheau, we misinterpret the words, and connect וְהִכְנַעְתִּי erroneously with the previous clause.

The connection between vers. 5-7 and 8-16 has been correctly indicated by Thenius as follows: Thou shalt not build a house for ME; but I, who have from the very beginning glorified myself in thee and my people (vers. 8-11), will build a house for thee; and thy son shall erect a house for me (ver. 13). This thought is not merely "a play upon words entirely in the spirit of prophecy," but contains the deep general truth that God must first of all build a man's house, before the man can build God's house, and applies it especially to the kingdom of God in Israel. As long as the quiet and full possession of the land of Canaan, which had been promised by the Lord to the people of God for their inheritance, was disputed by their enemies round about, even the dwelling-place of their God could not assume any other form than that of a wanderer's tent. The kingdom of God in Israel first acquired its rest and consolation through the efforts of David, when God had made all his foes subject to him and established his throne firmly, *i.e.* had assured to his descendants the possession of the kingdom for all future time. And it was this which ushered in the time for the building of a stationary house as a dwelling for the name of the Lord, *i.e.* for the visible manifestation of the presence of God in the midst of His people. The conquest of the citadel of Zion and the elevation of this fortress into the palace of the king, whom the Lord had given to His people, formed the commencement of the establishment of the kingdom of God. But this commencement received its first pledge of perpetuity from the divine assurance that the throne of David should be established for all future time. And this the Lord was about to accomplish: He would build David a house, and then his seed should build the house of the Lord. No definite reason is assigned why David himself was not to build the temple. We learn this first of all from David's last words (1 Chron. xxviii. 3), in which he says to the assembled heads of the nation, "God said to me, Thou shalt not build a house for my name, because thou art a man of wars, and hast shed blood." Compare with this the similar words of David to Solomon in 1 Chron. xxii. 8, and Solomon's statement in his message to Hiram, that David had been prevented from building the temple in consequence of his many wars. It was probably not till afterwards that David was informed by Nathan what the true reason was. As Hengstenberg has correctly observed, the fact that David was not permitted to build the temple on account of his own personal unworthiness, did not involve any blame for what he had done; for David stood in a closer relation to the Lord than Solomon did, and the wars which he waged were wars of the Lord (1 Sam. xxv. 28) for the maintenance and defence of the kingdom of God. But inasmuch as these wars were necessary and inevitable, they were practical proofs that David's kingdom and government were not yet established, and therefore that the time for the building of the temple had not yet come, and the rest of peace was not yet secured. The temple, as the symbolical representation of the kingdom of God, was also to correspond to the nature of that kingdom, and shadow forth the peace of the kingdom of God. For this reason, David, the man of war, was not to build the temple; but that was to be reserved for Solomon, the man of peace, the type of the Prince of Peace (Isa. ix. 5).

In vers. 12-16 there follows a more precise definition of the way in which the Lord would build a house for His servant David: "When thy days shall become full, and thou shalt lie with thy fathers, I will set up thy seed after thee, who shall come from thy body, and establish his kingdom. He will build a house for my name, and I shall establish the throne of his kingdom for ever." הָקִים, to set up, *i.e.* to promote to royal dignity. אֲשֶׁר יֵצֵא is not to be altered into אֲשֶׁר יָצָא, as Thenius and others maintain. The assumption that Solomon had already been born, is an unfounded one (see the note to ch. v. 11, p. 319); and it by no means follows from the statement in ver. 1, to the effect that God had given David rest from all his enemies, that his resolution to build a temple was not formed till the closing years of his reign.—Vers. 14 sqq. "*I will be a father to him, and he will be a son to me; so that if he go astray, I shall chastise him with rods of men, and with strokes of the children of men* (*i.e.* not 'with moderate punishment, such as parents are accustomed to inflict,' as Clericus explains it, but with such punishments as are inflicted upon all men who go astray, and from which even the seed of David is not to be excepted). *But my mercy shall not depart from him, as I caused it to depart from Saul, whom I put away before thee. And thy house and thy kingdom shall be established for ever before thee; thy throne shall be established for ever.*" It is very obvious, from all the separate details of this promise, that it related primarily to Solomon, and had a certain fulfilment in him and his reign. On the death of David, his son Solomon ascended the throne, and God defended his kingdom against the machinations of Adonijah (1 Kings ii. 12); so that Solomon was able to say, "The Lord hath fulfilled His word that He spoke; for I have risen up in the stead of my father David," etc. (1 Kings viii. 20). Solomon built the temple, as the Lord said to David (1 Kings v. 19, viii. 15 sqq.). But in his old age Solomon sinned against the Lord by falling into idolatry; and as a punishment for this, after his death his kingdom was rent from his son, not indeed entirely, as one portion was still preserved to the family for David's sake (1 Kings xi. 9 sqq.). Thus the Lord punished him with rods of men, but did not withdraw from him His grace. At the same time, however unmistakeable the allusions to Solomon are, the substance of the promise is not fully exhausted in him. The threefold repetition of the expression "for ever," the establishment of the kingdom and throne of David *for ever*, points incontrovertibly beyond the time of Solomon, and to the eternal continuance of the seed of David. The word *seed* denotes the posterity of a person, which may consist either in one son or in several children, or in a long line of successive generations. The idea of a number of persons living at the same time, is here precluded by the context of the promise, as only one of David's successors could sit upon the throne at a time. On the other hand, the idea of a number of descendants following one another, is evidently contained in the promise, that God would not withdraw His favour from the seed, even if it went astray, as He had done from Saul, since this implies that even in that case the throne should be transmitted from father to son. There is still more, however, involved in the expression "for ever." When the promise was given that the throne of the kingdom of David should continue "to eternity," an eternal duration was also promised to the seed that should occupy this throne, just as in ver. 16 the house and kingdom of David are spoken of as existing for ever, side by side. We must not reduce the idea of eternity to the popular notion of a long incalculable period, but must take it in an absolute sense, as the promise is evidently understood in Ps. lxxxix. 30: "I set his seed for ever, and his throne as the days of heaven." No earthly kingdom, and no posterity of any single man, has eternal duration like the heaven and the earth; but the different families of men become extinct, as the different earthly kingdoms perish, and other families and kingdoms take their place. The posterity of David, therefore, could only last for ever by running out in a person who lives for ever, *i.e.* by culminating in the Messiah, who lives for ever, and of whose kingdom there is no end. The promise consequently refers to the posterity of David, commencing with Solomon and closing with Christ: so that by the "seed" we are not to understand Solomon alone, with the kings who succeeded him, nor Christ alone, to the exclusion of Solomon and the earthly kings of the family of David; nor is the allusion to Solomon and Christ to be regarded as a double allusion to two different objects.

But if this is established,—namely, that the promise given to the seed of David that his kingdom should endure for ever only attained its ultimate fulfilment in Christ,—we must not restrict the building of the house of God to the erection of Solomon's temple. "The building of the house of the Lord goes hand in hand with the eternity of the kingdom" (Hengstenberg). As the kingdom endures for ever, so the house built for the dwelling-place of the Lord must also endure for ever, as Solomon said at the dedication of the temple (1 Kings viii. 13) : " I have surely built Thee an house to dwell in, a settled place for Thee to abide in for ever." The everlasting continuance of Solomon's temple must not be reduced, however, to the simple fact, that even if the temple of Solomon should be destroyed, a new building would be erected in its place by the earthly descendants of Solomon, although this is also implied in the words, and the temple of Zerubbabel is included as the restoration of that of Solomon. For it is not merely in its earthly form, as a building of wood and stone, that the temple is referred to, but also and chiefly in its essential characteristic, as the place for the manifestation and presence of God in the midst of His people. The earthly form is perishable, the essence eternal. This essence was the dwelling of God in the midst of His people, which did not cease with the destruction of the temple at Jerusalem, but culminated in the appearance of Jesus Christ, in whom Jehovah came to His people, and, as God the Word, made human nature His dwelling-place ($\dot{\epsilon}\sigma\kappa\dot{\eta}\nu\omega\sigma\epsilon\nu$ $\dot{\epsilon}\nu$ $\dot{\eta}\mu\hat{\iota}\nu$, John i. 14) in the glory of the only-begotten Son of the Father; so that Christ could say to the Jews, " Destroy this temple (*i.e.* the temple of His body), and in three days I will build it up again" (John ii. 19). It is with this building up of the temple destroyed by the Jews, through the resurrection of Jesus Christ from the dead, that the complete and essential fulfilment of our promise begins. It is perpetuated within the Christian church in the indwelling of the Father and Son through the Holy Ghost in the hearts of believers (John xiv. 23; 1 Cor. vi. 19), by which the church of Jesus Christ is built up a spiritual house of God, composed of living stones (1 Tim. iii. 15, 1 Pet. ii. 5; compare 2 Cor. vi. 16, Heb. iii. 6); and it will be perfected in the completion of the kingdom of God at the end of time in the new Jerusalem, which shall come down upon the new earth out of heaven from God, as the true tabernacle of God with men (Rev. xxi. 1–3).

As the building of the house of God receives its fulfilment first of all through Christ, so the promise, " I will be to him a father, and he shall be to me a son," is first fully realized in Jesus Christ, the only-begotten Son of the heavenly Father (*vid.* Heb. i. 5). In the Old Testament the relation between father and son denotes the deepest intimacy of love; and love is perfected in unity of nature, in the communication to the son of all that the father hath. The Father loveth the Son, and hath given all things into His hand (John iii. 35). Sonship therefore includes the government of the world. This not only applied to Christ, the only-begotten Son of God, but also to the seed of David generally, so far as they truly attained to the relation of children of God. So long as Solomon walked in the ways of the Lord, he ruled over all the kingdoms from the river (Euphrates) to the border of Egypt (1 Kings v. 1); but when his heart turned away from the Lord in his old age, adversaries rose up against him (1 Kings xi. 14 sqq., 23 sqq.), and after his death the greater part of the kingdom was rent from his son. The seed of David was chastised for its sins; and as its apostasy continued, it was humbled yet more and more, until the earthly throne of David became extinct. Nevertheless the Lord did not cause His mercy to depart from him. When the house of David had fallen into decay, Jesus Christ was born of the seed of David according to the flesh, to raise up the throne of His father David again, and to reign for ever as King over the house of Jacob (Luke i. 32, 33), and to establish the house and kingdom of David for ever.—In ver. 16, where the promise returns to David again with the words, "thy house and thy kingdom shall be established for ever," the expression לְפָנֶיךָ (before thee), which the LXX. and Syriac have arbitrarily changed into לְפָנַי (before me), should be particularly observed. David, as the tribe-father and founder of the line of kings, is regarded either "as seeing all his descendants pass before him in a vision," as O. v. Gerlach supposes, or as continuing to exist in his descendants.—Ver. 17. "*According to all these words . . . did Nathan speak unto David,*" *i.e.* he related the whole to David, just as God had addressed it to him in the night. The clause in apposition, "according to all this vision," merely introduces a more minute definition of the peculiar form of the revelation. God spoke to Nathan in a vision which he had in the night, *i.e.* not in a dream, but in a waking condition, and during the night; for חִזָּיוֹן=חָזוּת is constantly distinguished from חֲלוֹם, a revelation in a dream.

Vers. 18-29. *David's prayer and thanksgiving.*—Ver. 18. King David came, *i.e.* went into the sanctuary erected upon Zion, and remained before Jehovah. יָשַׁב, *remained, tarried* (as in Gen. xxiv. 55, xxix. 19, etc.), not "*sat;*" for the custom of sitting before the Lord in the sanctuary, as the posture assumed in prayer, cannot be deduced from Ex. xvii. 12, where Moses is compelled to sit from simple exhaustion. David's prayer consists of two parts,—thanksgiving for the promise (vers. 18b–24), and supplication for its fulfilment (vers. 25–29). The thanksgiving consists of a confession of unworthiness of all the great things that the Lord had hitherto done for him, and which He had still further increased by this glorious promise (vers. 18–21), and praise to the Lord that all this had been done in proof of His true Deity, and to glorify His name upon His chosen people Israel.—Ver. 18b. "*Who am I, O Lord Jehovah? and who my house* (*i.e.* my family), *that Thou hast brought me hitherto?*" These words recal Jacob's prayer in Gen. xxxii. 10, "I am not worthy of the least of all the mercies," etc. David acknowledged himself to be unworthy of the great mercy which the Lord had displayed towards him, that he might give the glory to God alone (*vid.* Ps. viii. 5 and cxliv. 3).—Ver. 19. "*And this is still too little in Thine eyes, O Lord Jehovah, and Thou still speakest with regard to the house of Thy servant for a great while to come.*" לְמֵרָחוֹק, *lit.* that which points to a remote period, *i.e.* that of the eternal establishment of my house and throne. "*And this is the law of man, O Lord Jehovah.*" "The law of man" is the law which determines or regulates the conduct of man. Hence the meaning of these words, which have been very differently interpreted, cannot, with the context immediately preceding it, be any other than the following: This—namely, the love and condescension manifested in Thy treatment of Thy servant—is the law which applies to man, or is conformed to the law which men are to observe towards men, *i.e.* to the law, Thou shalt love thy neighbour as thyself (Lev. xix. 18, compare Micah vi. 8). With this interpretation, which is confirmed by the parallel text of the Chronicles (in ver. 17), "Thou sawest (*i.e.* visitedst me, or didst deal with me) according to the manner of man," the words are expressive of praise of the condescending grace of the Lord. "When God the Lord, in His treatment of poor mortals, follows the rule which He has laid down for the conduct of men one towards another, when He shows himself kind and affectionate, this must fill with adoring amazement those who know themselves and God" (Hengstenberg). Luther is wrong in the rendering which he has adopted: "This is the manner of a man, who is God the Lord;" for "Lord Jehovah" is not an explanatory apposition to "man," but an address to God, as in the preceding and following clause.—Ver. 20. "*And what more shall David speak to Thee? Thou knowest Thy servant, Lord Jehovah.*" Instead of expressing his gratitude still further in many words, David appeals to the omniscience of God, before whom his thankful heart lies open, just as in Ps. xl. 10 (compare also Ps. xvii. 3).—Ver. 21. "*For Thy word's sake, and according to Thy heart* (and therefore not because I am worthy of such grace), *hast Thou done all this greatness, to make it known to Thy servant.*" The word, for the sake of which God had done such great things for David, must be some former promise on the part of God. Hengstenberg supposes it to refer to the word of the Lord to Samuel, "Rise up and anoint him" (1 Sam. xvi. 12), which is apparently favoured indeed by the parallel in the corresponding text of 1 Chron. xvii. 19, "for Thy servant's sake," *i.e.* because Thou hast chosen Thy servant. But even this variation must contain some special allusion which does not exclude a *general* interpretation of the expression "for Thy word's sake," viz. an allusion to the earlier promises of God, or the Messianic prophecies generally, particularly the one concerning Judah in Jacob's blessing (Gen. xlix. 10), and the one relating to the ruler out of Jacob in Balaam's sayings (Num. xxiv. 17 sqq.), which contain the germs of the promise of the everlasting continuance of David's government. For the fact that David recognised the connection between the promise of God communicated to him by Nathan and Jacob's prophecy in Gen. xlix. 10, is evident from 1 Chron. xxviii. 4, where he refers to his election as king as being the consequence of the election of Judah as ruler. "According to Thine own heart" is equivalent to "according to Thy love and grace; for God is gracious, merciful, and of great kindness and truth" (Ex. xxxiv. 6, compare Ps. ciii. 8). גְּדוּלָה does not mean great things, but greatness.

The praise of God commences in ver. 22: "*Wherefore Thou art great, Jehovah God; and there is not* (one) *like Thee, and no God beside Thee, according to all that we have heard with our ears.*" By the word "wherefore," *i.e.* because Thou hast done this, the praise of the singleness of God is set forth as the result of David's own experience. God is great when He manifests the greatness of His grace to men, and brings them to acknowledge it. And in these great deeds He proves the incomparable nature of His Deity, or that He alone is the true God. (For the fact itself, compare Ex. xv. 11; Deut. iii. 24, iv. 35.)—Ver. 23. "*And where is* (any) *like Thy people, like Israel, a nation upon earth, which God went to redeem as a people for himself, that He might make Him a name, and do great things for you, and terrible things for Thy land before Thy people, which Thou hast redeemed for Thee out of Egypt,* (out of the) *nations and their gods?*" מִי does not really mean *where,* but *who,* and is to be connected with the words immediately following, viz. גּוֹי אֶחָד (one nation); but the only way in which the words can be rendered into good English (*German in the original:* TR.) is, "where is there any people," etc. The relative אֲשֶׁר does not belong to הָלְכוּ, which follows immediately afterwards; but, so far as the sense is concerned, it is to be taken as the object to לִפְדּוֹת, "which Elohim went to redeem." The construing of *Elohim* with a plural arises from the fact, that in this clause it not only refers to the true God, but also includes the idea of the gods of other nations. The idea, therefore, is not, "Is there any nation upon earth to which the only true God went?" but, "Is there any nation to which the deity worshipped by it went, as the true God went to Israel to redeem it for His own people?" The rendering given in the Septuagint to הָלְכוּ, viz. ὡδήγησεν, merely arose from a misapprehension of the true sense of the words; and the emendation הוֹלִיךְ, which some propose in consequence, would only distort the sense. The stress laid upon the incomparable character of the things which God had done for Israel, is merely introduced to praise and celebrate the God who did this as the only true God. (For the thought itself, compare the original passage in Deut. iv. 7, 34.) In the clause וְלַעֲשׂוֹת לָכֶם, "and to do for you," David addresses the people of Israel with oratorical vivacity. Instead of saying "to do great things to (for) Israel," he says "to do great things to (for) *you.*" *For you* forms an antithesis to *him,* "to make Him a name, and to do great things for you (Israel)." The suggestion made by some, that לָכֶם is to be taken as a *dativ. comm.*, and referred to *Elohim*, no more needs a serious refutation than the alteration into לָהֶם. There have been different opinions, however, as to the object referred to in the suffix attached to לְאַרְצְךָ, and it is difficult to decide between them; for whilst the fact that נֹרָאוֹת לְאַרְצְךָ (terrible things to Thy land) is governed by לַעֲשׂוֹת (to do) favours the allusion to Israel, and the sudden transition from the plural to the singular might be accounted for from the deep emotion of the person speaking, the words which follow ("before Thy people") rather favour the allusion to God, as it does not seem natural to take the suffix in two different senses in the two objects which follow so closely the one upon the other, viz. "*for Thy land*," and "*before Thy people;*" whilst the way is prepared for a transition from speaking of God to speaking to God by the word לְכֶם (to you). The words of Deut. x. 21 floated before the mind of David at the time, although he has given them a different turn. (On the "terrible things," see the commentary on Deut. x. 21 and Ex. xv. 11.) The connection of נֹרָאוֹת (terrible things) with לְאַרְצְךָ (to Thy land) shows that David had in mind, when speaking of the acts of divine omnipotence which had inspired fear and dread of the majesty of God, not only the miracles of God in Egypt, but also the marvellous extermination of the Canaanites, whereby Israel had been established in the possession of the promised land, and the people of God placed in a condition to found a kingdom. These acts were performed *before* Israel, before the nation, whom the Lord redeemed to himself out of Egypt. This view is confirmed by the last words, "nations and their gods," which are in apposition to "from Egypt," so that the preposition כִּן should be repeated before גּוֹיִם (nations). The suffix to וֵאלֹהָיו (literally "and *its* gods") is to be regarded as distributive: "the gods of each of these heathen nations." In the Chronicles (ver. 21) the expression is simplified, and explained more clearly by the omission of "to Thy land," and the insertion of לְגָרֵשׁ, "to drive out nations from before Thy people." It has been erroneously inferred from this, that the text of our book is corrupt, and ought to be emended, or at any rate interpreted according to the Chronicles. But whilst לְאַרְצְךָ is certainly not to be altered into לְגָרֵשׁ, it is just as wrong to do as Hengstenberg proposes,—namely, to take the thought expressed in לְגָרֵשׁ

from the preceding לַעֲשׂוֹת by assuming a *zeugma*; for עָשָׂה, to do or make, has nothing in common with driving or clearing away.—Ver. 24. "*And Thou hast established to thyself Thy people Israel to be a people unto Thee for ever: and Thou, Jehovah, hast become a God to them.*" The first clause does not refer merely to the liberation of Israel out of Egypt, or to the conquest of Canaan alone, but to all that the Lord had done for the establishment of Israel as the people of His possession, from the time of Moses till His promise of the eternal continuance of the throne of David. Jehovah had thereby become God to the nation of Israel, *i.e.* had thereby attested and proved himself to be its God.

To this praise of the acts of the Lord there is attached in vers. 25 sqq. the prayer for the fulfilment of His glorious promise. Would Jehovah set up (*i.e.* carry out) the word which He had spoken to His servant that His name might be great, *i.e.* be glorified, through its being said, "The Lord of Sabaoth is God over Israel," and "the house of Thy servant will be firm before Thee." The prayer is expressed in the form of confident assurance.—Ver. 27. David felt himself encouraged to offer this prayer through the revelation which he had received. Because God had promised to build him a house, "therefore Thy servant hath found in his heart to pray this prayer," *i.e.* hath found joy in doing so.—Vers. 28, 29. David then briefly sums up the two parts of his prayer of thanksgiving in the two clauses commencing with וְעַתָּה, "and now."—In ver. 28 he sums up the contents of vers. 18*b*–24 by celebrating the greatness of the Lord and His promise; and in ver. 29 the substance of the prayer in vers. 25–27. הוֹאֵל וּבָרֵךְ, may it please Thee to bless (הוֹאִיל; see at Deut. i. 5). "*And from (out of) Thy blessing may the house of Thy servant be blessed for ever.*"

DAVID'S WARS, VICTORIES, AND MINISTERS OF STATE.—
CHAP. VIII.

To the promise of the establishment of his throne there is appended a general enumeration of the wars by which David secured the supremacy of Israel over all his enemies round about. In this survey all the nations are included with which war had ever been waged by David, and which he had conquered and rendered tributary: the Philistines and Moabites, the Syrians of Zobah and Damascus, Toi of Hamath, the Ammonites, Amalekites, and Edomites. It is very evident from this, that the chapter before us not only treats of the wars which David carried on after receiving the divine promise mentioned in ch. vii., but of all the wars of his entire reign. The only one of which we have afterwards a fuller account is the war with the Ammonites and their allies the Syrians (ch. x. and xi.), and this is given on account of its connection with David's adultery. In the survey before us, the war with the Ammonites is only mentioned quite cursorily in ver. 12, in the account of the booty taken from the different nations, which David dedicated to the Lord. With regard to the other wars, so far as the principal purpose was concerned,—namely, to record the history of the kingdom of God,—it was quite sufficient to give a general statement of the fact that these nations were smitten by David and subjected to his sceptre. But if this chapter contains a survey of all the wars of David with the nations that were hostile to Israel, there can be no doubt that the arrangement of the several events is not strictly regulated by their chronological order, but that homogeneous events are grouped together according to a material point of view. There is a parallel to this chapter in 1 Chron. xviii.

Ver. 1. SUBJUGATION OF THE PHILISTINES.—In the introductory formula, "*And it came to pass afterwards,*" the expression "*afterwards*" cannot refer specially to the contents of ch. vii., for reasons also given, but simply serves as a general formula of transition to attach what follows to the account just completed, as a thing that happened afterwards. This is incontestably evident from a comparison of ch. x. 1, where the war with the Ammonites and Syrians, the termination and result of which are given in the present chapter, is attached to what precedes by the same formula, "*It came to pass afterwards*" (cf. ch. xiii. 1). "*David smote the Philistines and subdued them, and took the bridle of the mother out of the hand of the Philistines,*" *i.e.* wrested the government from them and made them tributary. The figurative expression *Metheg-ammah*, "bridle of the mother," *i.e.* the capital, has been explained by Alb. Schultens (on Job xxx. 11) from an Arabic idiom, in which giving up one's bridle to another is equivalent to submitting to him. Gesenius also gives several proofs of this (*Thes.* p. 113). Others, for example Ewald, render it arm-bridle; but there is not a single passage to support the rendering "arm" for *ammah*. The word is a feminine form of אֵם, mother, and only used in a tropical sense. "*Mother*" is a term applied to the chief city or capital, both in Arabic and Phœnician (*vid.* Ges. *Thes.* p. 112). The same figure is also adopted in Hebrew, where the towns dependent upon the capital are called its daughters (*vid.* Josh. xv. 45, 47). In 1 Chron. xviii. 1 the figurative expression is dropped for the more literal one: "David took Gath and its daughters out of the hand of the Philistines," *i.e.* he wrested Gath and the other towns from the Philistines. The Philistines had really five cities, every one with a prince of its own (Josh. xiii. 3). This was the case even in the time of Samuel (1 Sam. vi. 16, 17). But in the closing years of Samuel, Gath had a *king* who stood at the head of all the princes of the Philistines (1 Sam. xxix. 2 sqq., cf. xxvii. 2). Thus Gath became the capital of the land of the Philistines, which held the bridle (or reins) of Philistia in its own hand. The author of the Chronicles has therefore given the correct explanation of the figure. The one suggested by Ewald, Bertheau, and others, cannot be correct,—namely, that David wrested from the Philistines the power which they had hitherto exercised over the Israelites. The simple meaning of the passage is, that David wrested from the Philistines the power which the capital had possessed over the towns dependent upon it, *i.e.* over the whole of the land of Philistia; in other words, he brought the capital (Gath) and the other towns of Philistia into his own power. The reference afterwards made to a king of Gath in the time of Solomon in 1 Kings ii. 39 is by no means at variance with this; for the king alluded to was one of the tributary sovereigns, as we may infer from the fact that Solomon ruled over all the kings on this side of the Euphrates as far as to Gaza (1 Kings v. 1, 4).

Ver. 2. SUBJUGATION OF MOAB.—"*He smote Moab* (*i.e.* the Moabites), *and measured them with the line, making them lie down upon the ground, and measured two lines* (*i.e.* two parts) *to put to death, and one line full to keep alive.*" Nothing further is known about either the occasion or the history of this war, with the exception of the cursory notice in 1 Chron. xi. 22, that Benaiah, one of David's heroes, smote two sons of the king of Moab, which no doubt took place in the same war. In the earliest period of his flight from Saul, David had met with a hospitable reception from the king of Moab, and had even taken his parents to him for safety (1 Sam. xxii. 3, 4). But the Moabites must have very grievously oppressed the Israelites afterwards, that David should have inflicted a severer punishment upon them after their defeat, than upon any other of the nations that he conquered, with the exception of the Ammonites (ch. xii. 31), upon whom he took vengeance for having most shamefully insulted his ambassadors (ch. x. 2 sqq.). The punishment inflicted, however, was of course restricted to the fighting men who had been taken prisoners by the Israelites. They were ordered to lie down in a row upon the earth; and then the row was measured for the purpose of putting two-thirds to death, and leaving one-third alive. The Moabites were then made "*servants*" to David (*i.e.* they became his subjects), "*bringing gifts*" (*i.e.* paying tribute).

Vers. 3-8. CONQUEST AND SUBJUGATION OF THE KING OF ZOBAH, AND OF THE DAMASCENE SYRIANS.—Ver. 3. The situation of *Zobah* cannot be determined. The view held by the Syrian church historians, and defended by Michaelis, viz. that *Zobah* was the ancient *Nisibis* in northern Mesopotamia, has no more foundation to rest upon than that of certain Jewish writers who suppose it to have been *Aleppo*, the present *Haleb*. *Aleppo* is too far north for *Zobah*, and *Nisibis* is quite out of the range of the towns and tribes in connection with which the name of Zobah occurs. In 1 Sam. xiv. 47, compared with ver. 12 of this chapter, Zobah, or *Aram Zobah* as it is called in ch. x. 6 and Ps. lx. 2, is mentioned along with Ammon, Moab, and Edom, as a neighbouring tribe and kingdom to the Israelites; and, according to vers. 3, 5, and 9 of the present chapter, it is to be sought for in the vicinity of Damascus and Hamath towards the Euphrates. These data point to a situation to the north-east of Damascus and south of Hamath, between the Orontes and Euphrates, and in fact extending as far as the latter according to ver. 3, whilst, according to ch. x. 16, it even reached beyond it with its vassal-chiefs into Mesopotamia itself. Ewald (*Gesch.* iii. p. 195) has therefore combined *Zobah*, which was no doubt the capital, and gave its name to the kingdom, with the *Sabe* mentioned in Ptol. v. 19,—a town in the same latitude as Damascus, and farther east towards the Euphrates. The king of Zobah at the time referred to is called *Hadadezer* in the text (*i.e.* whose help is *Hadad*); but in ch. x. 16–19 and throughout the Chronicles he is called *Hadarezer*. The first is the original form; for *Hadad*, the name of the sun-god of the Syrians, is met with in several other instances in Syrian names (*vid.* Movers, *Phönizier*). David smote this king "*as he was going to restore his strength at the river* (Euphrates)." הָשִׁיב יָדוֹ does not mean to turn his hand, but signifies to return his hand, to stretch it out again over or against any one, in all the passages in which the expression occurs. It is therefore to be taken in a derivative sense in the passage before us, as signifying to restore or re-establish his sway. The expression used in the Chronicles (ver. 3), הַצִּיב יָדוֹ, has just the same meaning, since establishing or making fast presupposes a previous weakening or dissolution. Hence the subject of the sentence "as he went," etc., must be Hadadezer and not David; for David could not have extended his power to the Euphrates before the defeat of Hadadezer. The Masoretes have interpolated *P'rath* (Euphrates) after "*the river*," as in the text of the Chronicles. This is correct enough so far as the sense is concerned, but it is by no means necessary, as the *nahar* (the river κ. ἐξ.) is quite sufficient of itself to indicate the Euphrates.

There is also a war between David and Hadadezer and other kings of Syria mentioned in ch. x.; and the commentators all admit that that war, in which David defeated these kings when they came to the help of the Ammonites, is connected with the war mentioned in the present chapter. But the connection is generally supposed to be this, that the first of David's Aramæan wars is given in ch. viii., the second in ch. x.; for no other reason, however, than because ch. x. stands after ch. viii. This view is decidedly an erroneous one. According to the chapter before us, the war mentioned there terminated in the complete subjugation of the Aramæan kings and kingdoms. Aram became subject to David, paying tribute (ver. 6). Now, though the revolt of subjugated nations from their conquerors is by no means a rare thing in history, and therefore it is perfectly conceivable in itself that the Aramæans should have fallen away from David when he was involved in the war with the Ammonites, and should have gone to the help of the Ammonites, such an assumption is precluded by the fact that there is nothing in ch. x. about any falling away or revolt of the Aramæans from David; but, on the contrary, these tribes appear to be still entirely independent of David, and to be hired by the Ammonites to fight against him. But what is absolutely decisive against this assumption, is the fact that the number of Aramæans killed in the two wars is precisely the same (compare ver. 4 with ch. x. 18) : so that it may safely be inferred, not only that the war mentioned in ch. x., in which the Aramæans who had come to the help of the Ammonites were smitten by David, was the very same as the Aramæan war mentioned in ch. viii., but of which the result only is given ; but also that all the wars which David waged with the Aramæans, like his war with Edom (vers. 13 sqq.), arose out of the Ammonitish war (ch. x.), and the fact that the Ammonites enlisted the help of the kings of Aram against David (ch. x. 6). We also obtain from ch. x. an explanation of the expression "as he went to restore his power (Eng. Ver. 'recover his border') at the river," since it is stated there that Hadadezer was defeated by Joab the first time, and that, after sustaining this defeat, he called the Aramæans on the other side of the Euphrates to his assistance, that he might continue the war against Israel with renewed vigour (ch. x. 13, 15 sqq.). The power of Hadadezer had no doubt been crippled by his first defeat; and in order to restore it, he procured auxiliary troops from Mesopotamia with which to attack David, but he was defeated a second time, and obliged to submit to him (ch. x. 17, 18). In this second engagement "*David took from him (i.e.* captured) *seventeen hundred horse-soldiers and twenty thousand foot*" (ver. 4, compare ch. x. 18). This decisive battle took place, according to 1 Chron. xviii. 3, in the neighbourhood of *Hamath, i.e.* Epiphania on the Orontes (see at Num. xiii. 21, and Gen. x. 18), or, according to ch. x. 18 of this book, at *Helam,*—a difference which may easily be reconciled by the simple assumption that the unknown Helam was somewhere near to Hamath. Instead of 1700 horse-soldiers, we find in the Chronicles (1, xviii. 4) 1000 chariots and 7000 horsemen. Consequently the word *receb* has no doubt dropped out after אֶלֶף in the text before us, and the numeral denoting a thousand has been confounded with the one used to denote a hundred; for in the plains of Syria seven thousand horsemen would be a much juster proportion to twenty thousand foot than seventeen hundred. (For further remarks, see at ch. x. 18.) "*And David lamed all the cavalry,*" *i.e.* he made the war-chariots and cavalry perfectly useless by laming the horses (see at Josh. xi. 6, 9),—"*and only left a hundred horses.*" The word *receb* in these clauses signifies the war-horses generally,—not merely the carriage-horses, but the riding-horses as well,—as the meaning cavalry is placed beyond all doubt by Isa. xxi. 7, and it can hardly be imagined that David would have spared the riding-horses.—Vers. 5, 6. After destroying the main force of Hadadezer, David turned against his ally, against *Aram-Damascus*, *i.e.* the Aramæans, whose capital was Damascus. *Dammesek* (for which we have *Darmesek* in the Chronicles according to its Aramæan form), *Damascus*, a very ancient and still a very important city of Syria, standing upon the *Chrysorrhoas* (*Pharpar*), which flows through the centre of it. It is situated in the midst of paradisaical scenery, on the eastern side of the Antilibanus, on the road which unites Western Asia with the interior. David smote 22,000 Syrians of Damascus, placed garrisons in the kingdom, and made it subject and tributary. נְצִיבִים are not governors or officers, but military posts, garrisons, as in 1 Sam. x. 5, xiii. 3.—Ver. 7. Of the booty taken in these wars, David carried the golden shields which he took from the servants, *i.e.* the governors and vassal princes, of Hadadezer, to Jerusalem.[1] *Shelet* signifies "a shield," according to the Targums

---

[1] The Septuagint has this additional clause: "And Shishak the king of Egypt took them away, when he went up against Jerusalem in the days of Rehoboam the son of Solomon," which is neither to be found in the Chronicles nor in any other ancient version, and is merely an inference drawn by the Greek translator, or by some copyist of the LXX., from 1 Kings xiv. 25-28, taken in connection with the fact that the application of the brass is given in 1 Chron. xviii. 8. But, in the first place, the author of this gloss has overlooked the fact that the golden shields of Rehoboam which Shishak carried away, were not those captured by David, but those

and Rabbins, and this meaning is applicable to all the passages in which the word occurs; whilst the meaning "equivalent" cannot be sustained either by the rendering πανοπλία adopted by Aquila and Symmachus in 2 Kings xi. 10, or by the renderings of the Vulgate, viz. *arma* in loc. and *armatura* in Song of Sol. iv. 4, or by an appeal to the etymology (*vid.* Gesenius' *Thes.* and Dietrich's *Lexicon*).—Ver. 8. And from the cities of *Betach* and *Berothai* David took very much brass, with which, according to 1 Chron. xviii. 8, Solomon made the brazen sea, and the brazen columns and vessels of the temple. The LXX. have also interpolated this notice into the text. The name *Betach* is given as *Tibhath* in the Chronicles; and for *Berothai* we have *Chun*. As the towns themselves are unknown, it cannot be decided with certainty which of the forms and names are the correct and original ones. מִבֶּטַח appears to have been written by mistake for מִטֶּבַח. This supposition is favoured by the rendering of the LXX., ἐκ τῆς Μετεβάκ; and by that of the Syriac also (viz. *Tebach*). On the other hand, the occurrence of the name *Tebah* among the sons of *Nahor the Aramæan* in Gen. xxii. 24 proves little or nothing, as it is not known that he founded a family which perpetuated his name; nor can anything be inferred from the fact that, according to the more modern maps, there is a town of *Tayibeh* to the north of Damascus in 35° north lat., as there is very little in common between the names *Tayibeh* and *Tebah*. Ewald connects *Berothai* with the *Barathena* of Ptol. v. 19 in the neighbourhood of Saba. The connection is a possible one, but it is not sufficiently certain to warrant us in founding any conclusions upon it with regard to the name *Chun* which occurs in the Chronicles; so that there is

which Solomon had had made, according to 1 Kings x. 16, for the retainers of his palace; and in the second place, he has not observed that, according to ver. 11 of this chapter, and also of the Chronicles, David dedicated to the Lord all the gold and silver that he had taken, *i.e.* put it in the treasury of the sanctuary to be reserved for the future temple, and that at the end of his reign he handed over to his son and successor Solomon all the gold, silver, iron, and brass that he had collected for the purpose, to be applied to the building of the temple (1 Chron. xxii. 14 sqq., xxix. 2 sqq.). Consequently the clause in question, which Thenius would adopt from the Septuagint into our own text, is nothing more than the production of a presumptuous Alexandrian, whose error lies upon the very surface, so that the question of its genuineness cannot for a moment be entertained.

no ground whatever for the opinion that it is a corruption of *Berothai*.

Vers. 9–12. After the defeat of the king of Zobah and his allies, Toi king of Hamath sought for David's friendship, sending his son to salute him, and conveying to him at the same time a considerable present of vessels of silver, gold, and brass. The name *Toi* is written *Tou* in the Chronicles, according to a different mode of interpretation; and the name of the son is given as *Hadoram* in the Chronicles, instead of *Joram* as in the text before us. The former is evidently the true reading, and *Joram* an error of the pen, as the Israelitish name *Joram* is not one that we should expect to find among Aramæans; whilst *Hadoram* occurs in 1 Chron. i. 21 in the midst of Arabic names, and it cannot be shown that the *Hadoram* or *Adoram* mentioned in 2 Chron. x. 18 and 1 Kings xii. 18 was a man of Israelitish descent. The primary object of the mission was to salute David (" to ask him of peace ;" cf. Gen. xliii. 27, etc.), and to congratulate him upon his victory (" to bless him because he had fought," etc.) ; for Toi had had wars with Hadadezer. " *A man of wars*". signifies a man who wages wars (cf. 1 Chron. xxviii. 3 ; Isa. xlii. 13). According to 1 Chron. xviii. 3, the territory of the king of Hamath bordered upon that of Hadadezer, and the latter had probably tried to make king Toi submit to him. The secret object of the salutation, however, was no doubt to secure the friendship of this new and powerful neighbour.—Vers. 11, 12. David also sanctified Toi's presents to the Lord (handed them over to the treasury of the sanctuary), together with the silver and gold which he had sanctified from all the conquered nations, from Aram, Moab, etc. Instead of אֲשֶׁר הִקְדִּישׁ the text of the Chronicles has אֲשֶׁר נָשָׂא, which he took, *i.e.* took as booty. Both are equally correct ; there is simply a somewhat different turn given to the thought.[1] In the enumeration of the conquered nations in ver. 12, the text of the Chronicles differs from that of the book before us. In the

---

[1] Bertheau erroneously maintains that אֲשֶׁר נָשָׂא, which he took, is at variance with 2 Sam. viii. 7, as, according to this passage, the golden shields of Hadadezer did not become the property of the Lord. But there is not a word to that effect in 2 Sam. viii. 7. On the contrary, his taking the shields to Jerusalem implies, rather than precludes, the intention to devote them to the purposes of the sanctuary.

first place, we find "*from Edom*" instead of "*from Aram;*" and secondly, the clause "*and of the spoil of Hadadezer, son of Rehob king of Zobah,*" is altogether wanting there. The text of the Chronicles is certainly faulty here, as the name of *Aram* (Syria) could not possibly be omitted. *Edom* could much better be left out, not "because the conquest of Edom belonged to a later period," as Movers maintains, but because the conquest of Edom is mentioned for the first time in the subsequent verses. But if we bear in mind that in ver. 12 of both texts not only are those tribes enumerated the conquest of which had been already noticed, but all the tribes that David ever defeated and subjugated, even the Ammonites and Amalekites, to the war with whom no allusion whatever is made in the present chapter, we shall see that *Edom* could not be omitted. Consequently "*from Syria*" must have dropped out of the text of the Chronicles, and "*from Edom*" out of the one before us; so that the text in both instances ran originally thus, "from Syria, and from Edom, and from Moab." For even in the text before us, "from Aram" (Syria) could not well be omitted, notwithstanding the fact that the booty of Hadadezer is specially mentioned at the close of the verse, for the simple reason that David not only made war upon Syria-Zobah (the kingdom of Hadadezer) and subdued it, but also upon Syria-Damascus, which was quite independent of Zobah.

Vers. 13, 14. "*And David made* (himself) *a name, when he returned from smiting* (*i.e.* from the defeat of) *Aram,* (and smote Edom) *in the valley of Salt, eighteen thousand men.*" The words enclosed in brackets are wanting in the Masoretic text as it has come down to us, and must have fallen out from a mistake of the copyist, whose eye strayed from אֶת־אֲרָם to אֶת־אֱדוֹם; for though the text is not "utterly unintelligible" without these words, since the passage might be rendered "after he had smitten Aram in the valley of Salt eighteen thousand men," yet this would be decidedly incorrect, as the Aramæans were not smitten in the *valley of Salt*, but partly at *Medeba* (1 Chron. xix. 7) and *Helam* (ch. x. 17), and partly in their own land, which was very far away from the Salt valley. Moreover, the difficulty presented by the text cannot be removed, as Movers supposes, by changing אֶת־אֲרָם (Syria) into אֶת־אֱדוֹם (Edom), as the expression בְּשֻׁבוֹ ("when he returned") would still be un explained. The facts were probably these: Whilst David, or rather Israel, was entangled in the war with the Ammonites and Aramæans, the Edomites seized upon the opportunity, which appeared to them a very favourable one, to invade the land of Israel, and advanced as far as the southern extremity of the Dead Sea. As soon, therefore, as the Aramæans were defeated and subjugated, and the Israelitish army had returned from this war, David ordered it to march against the Edomites, and defeated them in the valley of Salt. This valley cannot have been any other than the Ghor adjoining the Salt mountain on the south of the Dead Sea, which really separates the ancient territories of Judah and Edom (Robinson, *Pal.* ii. 483). There Amaziah also smote the Edomites at a later period (2 Kings xiv. 7). We gather more concerning this war of David from the text of the Chronicles (ver. 12) taken in connection with 1 Kings xi. 15, 16, and Ps. lx. 2. According to the Chronicles, it was Abishai the son of Zeruiah who smote the Edomites. This agrees very well not only with the account in ch. x. 10 sqq., to the effect that Abishai commanded a company in the war with the Syrians and Ammonites under the generalship of his brother Joab, but also with the heading to Ps. lx., in which it is stated that Joab returned after the defeat of Aram, and smote the Edomites in the valley of Salt, twelve thousand men; and with 1 Kings xi. 15, 16, in which we read that when David was in Edom, Joab, the captain of the host, came up to bury the slain, and smote every male in Edom, and remained six months in Edom with all Israel, till he had cut off every male in Edom. From this casual but yet elaborate notice, we learn that the war with the Edomites was a very obstinate one, and was not terminated all at once. The difference as to the number slain, which is stated to have been 18,000 in the text before us and in the Chronicles, and 12,000 in the heading to Ps. lx., may be explained in a very simple manner, on the supposition that the reckonings made were only approximative, and yielded different results;[1] and the fact that *David* is named

---

[1] Michaelis adduces a case in point from the Seven Years' War. After the battle of *Lissa*, eight or twelve thousand men were reported to have been taken prisoners; but when they were all counted, including those who fell into the hands of the conquerors on the second, third, and fourth days of the flight, the number amounted to 22,000.

as the victor in the verse before us, *Joab* in Ps. l.c., and *Abishai* in the Chronicles, admits of a very easy explanation after what has just been observed. The Chronicles contain the most literal account. Abishai smote the Edomites as commander of the men engaged, Joab as commander-in-chief of the whole army, and David as king and supreme governor, of whom the writer of the Chronicles affirms, " The Lord helped David in all his undertakings." After the defeat of the Edomites, David placed garrisons in the land, and made all Edom subject to himself.

Vers. 15-18. DAVID'S MINISTERS.—To the account of David's wars and victories there is appended a list of his official attendants, which is introduced with a general remark as to the spirit of his government. As king over all Israel, David continued to execute right and justice.—Ver. 16. The chief ministers were the following :—*Joab* (see at ch. ii. 18) was " *over the army*," *i.e.* commander-in-chief. *Jehoshaphat* the son of Ahilud, of whom nothing further is known, was *mazcir*, chancellor; not merely the national annalist, according to the Septuagint and Vulgate (ἐπὶ τῶν ὑπομνημάτων, ὑπομνηματόγραφος; *a commentariis*), *i.e.* the recorder of the most important incidents and affairs of the nation, but an officer resembling the *magister memoriæ* of the later Romans, or the *waka nuvis* of the Persian court, who keeps a record of everything that takes place around the king, furnishes him with an account of all that occurs in the kingdom, places his *visé* upon all the king's commands, and keeps a special protocol of all these things (*vid.* Chardin, *Voyages* v. p. 258, and Paulsen, *Regierung der Morgenländer*, pp. 279-80).—Ver. 17. *Zadok* the son of Ahitub, of the line of Eleazar (1 Chron. v. 34, vi. 37, 38), and *Ahimelech* the son of Abiathar, were *cohanim*, *i.e.* officiating high priests; the former at the tabernacle at Gibeon (1 Chron. xvi. 39), the latter probably at the ark of the covenant upon Mount Zion. Instead of *Ahimelech*, the Chronicles have *Abimelech*, evidently through a copyist's error, as the name is written *Ahimelech* in 1 Chron. xxiv. 3, 6. But the expression " *Ahimelech the son of Abiathar*" is apparently a very strange one, as Abiathar was a son of Ahimelech according to 1 Sam. xxii. 20, and in other passages *Zadok* and *Abiathar* are mentioned as the two high priests in the time of David (ch. xv. 24, 35, xvii. 15, xix. 12, xx. 25). This difference cannot be set aside, as Movers, Thenius, Ewald, and others suppose, by transposing the names, so as to read Abiathar the son of Ahimelech; for such a solution is precluded by the fact that, in 1 Chron. xxiv. 3, 6, 31, *Ahimelech* is mentioned along with Zadok as head of the priests of the line of Ithamar, and according to ver. 6 he was the son of Abiathar. It would therefore be necessary to change the name Ahimelech into Abiathar in this instance also, both in ver. 3 and ver. 6, and in the latter to transpose the two names. But there is not the slightest probability in the supposition that the names have been changed in so many passages. We are therefore disposed to adopt the view held by Bertheau and Oehler, viz. that Abiathar the high priest, the son of Ahimelech, had also a son named Ahimelech, as it is by no means a rare occurrence for grandfather and grandson to have the same names (*vid.* 1 Chron. v. 30–41), and also that this (the younger) Ahimelech performed the duties of high priest in connection with his father, who was still living at the commencement of Solomon's reign (1 Kings ii. 27), and is mentioned in this capacity, along with Zadok, both here and in the book of Chronicles, possibly because Abiathar was ill, or for some other reason that we cannot discover. As Abiathar was thirty or thirty-five years old at the time when his father was put to death by Saul, according to what has already been observed at 1 Sam. xiv. 3, and forty years old at the death of Saul, he was at least forty-eight years old at the time when David removed his residence to Mount Zion, and might have had a son of twenty-five years of age, namely the Ahimelech mentioned here, who could have taken his father's place in the performance of the functions of high priest when he was prevented by illness or other causes. The appearance of a son of Abiathar named Jonathan in ch. xv. 27, xvii. 17, 20, is no valid argument against this solution of the apparent discrepancy; for, according to these passages, he was still very young, and may therefore have been a younger brother of Ahimelech. The omission of any allusion to Ahimelech in connection with Abiathar's conspiracy with Adonijah against Solomon (1 Kings i. 42, 43), and the reference to his son Jonathan alone, might be explained on the supposition that

Ahimelech had already died. But as there is no reference to Jonathan at the time when his father was deposed, no stress is to be laid upon the omission of any reference to Ahimelech. Moreover, when Abiathar was deposed after Solomon had ascended the throne, he must have been about eighty years of age. *Seraiah* was a scribe. Instead of *Seraiah*, we have *Shavsha* in the corresponding text of the Chronicles, and *Sheva* in the parallel passage ch. xx. 25. Whether the last name is merely a mistake for Shavsha, occasioned by the dropping of שׁ, or an abbreviated form of Shisha and Shavsha, cannot be decided. *Shavsha* is not a copyist's error, for in 1 Kings iv. 3 the same man is unquestionably mentioned again under the name of Shisha, who is called Shavsha in the Chronicles, *Sheva* (שִׁיָא) in the text of ch. xx. 25, and here Seraiah. *Seraiah* also is hardly a copyist's error, but another form for Shavsha or Shisha. The *scribe* was a secretary of state; not a military officer, whose duty it was to raise and muster the troops, for the technical expression for mustering the people was not סָפַר, but פָּקַד (cf. ch. xxiv. 2, 4, 9; 1 Chron. xxi. 5, 6, etc.).

Ver. 18. *Benaiah* the son of Jehoiada, a very brave hero of Kabzeel (see at ch. xxiii. 20 sqq.), was over the *Crethi* and *Plethi*. Instead of וְהַכְּרֵתִי, which gives no sense, and must be connected in some way with 1 Kings i. 38, 44, we must read עַל הַכְּרֵתִי according to the parallel passage ch. xx. 23, and the corresponding text of the Chronicles. The *Crethi* and *Plethi* were the king's body-guard, σωματοφύλακες (Josephus, *Ant.* vii. 5, 4). The words are adjectives in form, but with a substantive meaning, and were used to indicate a certain rank, *lit.* the executioners and runners, like הַשָּׁלִישִׁי (ch. xxiii. 8). כְּרֵתִי, from כָּרַת, to cut down or exterminate, signifies *confessor*, because among the Israelites (see at 1 Kings ii. 25), as in fact throughout the East generally, the royal halberdiers had to execute the sentence of death upon criminals. פְּלֵתִי, from פָּלַט (to fly, or be swift), is related to פָּלַט, and signifies *runners*. It is equivalent to רָץ, a courier, as one portion of the halberdiers, like the ἄγγαροι of the Persians, had to convey the king's orders to distant places (*vid.* 2 Chron. xxx. 6). This explanation is confirmed by the fact that the epithet הַכָּרִי וְהָרָצִים was afterwards applied to the king's body-guard (2 Kings xi. 4, 19), and that הַכָּרִי for הַכְּרֵתִי occurs as early as ch. xx. 23. כָּרִי, from כּוּר,

fodit, perfodit, is used in the same sense.[1] And David's sons were כֹּהֲנִים ("confidants"); not priests, domestic priests, court chaplains, or spiritual advisers, as Gesenius, De Wette, and others maintain, but, as the title is explained in the corresponding text of the Chronicles, when the title had become obsolete, "the first at the hand (or side) of the king." The correctness

[1] Gesenius (*Thes. s. vv.*) and Thenius (on 1 Kings i. 38) both adopt this explanation; but the majority of the modern theologians decide in favour of Lakemacher's opinion, to which Ewald has given currency, viz. that the *Crethi* or *Cari* are Cretes or Carians, and the *Pelethi* Philistines (*vid.* Ewald, *Krit. Gramm.* p. 297, and *Gesch. des Volkes Israel*, pp. 330 sqq.; Bertheau, *zur Geschichte Israel*, p. 197; Movers, *Phönizier* i. p. 19). This view is chiefly founded upon the fact that the Philistines are called *C'rethi* in 1 Sam. xxx. 14, and *C'rethim* in Zeph. ii. 5 and Ezek. xxv. 16. But in both the passages from the prophets the name is used with special reference to the meaning of the word הִכְרִית, viz. to exterminate, cut off, as Jerome has shown in the case of Ezekiel by adopting the rendering *interficiam interfectores* (I will slay the slayers) for הִכְרַתִּי אֶת־כְּרֵתִים. The same play upon the words takes place in Zephaniah, upon which Strauss has correctly observed: "Zephaniah shows that this violence of theirs had not been forgotten, calling the Philistines *Crethim* for that very reason, *ut sit nomen et omen*." Besides, in both these passages the true name *Philistines* stands by the side as well, so that the prophets might have used the name *Crethim* (slayers, exterminators) without thinking at all of 1 Sam. xxx. 14. In this passage it is true the name *Crethi* is applied to a branch of the Philistine people that had settled on the south-west of Philistia, and not to the Philistines generally. The idea that the name of a portion of the royal body-guard was derived from the Cretans is precluded, *first* of all, by the fact of its combination with הַפְּלֵתִי (the Pelethites); for it is a totally groundless assumption that this name signifies the *Philistines*, and is a corruption of פְּלִשְׁתִּים. There are no such contractions as these to be found in the Semitic languages, as Gesenius observes in his *Thesaurus* (*l.c.*), "Quis hujusmodi contractionem in linguis Semiticis ferat?" *Secondly*, it is also precluded by the strangeness of such a combination of two synonymous names to denote the royal body-guard. "Who could believe it possible that two synonymous epithets should be joined together in this manner, which would be equivalent to saying Englishmen and Britons?" (Ges. *Thes.* p. 1107.) *Thirdly*, it is opposed to the title afterwards given to the body-guard, הַכָּרִי וְהָרָצִים (2 Kings xi. 4, 19), in which the *Cari* correspond to the *Crethi*, as in ch. xx. 23, and *ha-razim* to the *Pelethi*; so that the term *pelethi* can no more signify a particular tribe than the term *razim* can. Moreover, there are other grave objections to this interpretation. In the first place, the hypothesis that the Philistines were emigrants from Crete is merely founded upon the very indefinite statements

of this explanation is placed beyond the reach of doubt by
1 Kings iv. 5, where the *cohen* is called, by way of explanation,
"the king's friend." The title *cohen* may be explained from
the primary signification of the verb כָּהַן, as shown in the
corresponding verb and noun in Arabic ("*res alicujus gerere*,"
and "*administrator alieni negotii*"). These *cohanim*, therefore,
were the king's confidential advisers.

of Tacitus (*Hist.* v. 3, 2), "*Judæos Creta insula profugos novissima Libyæ
insedisse memorant*," and that of Steph. Byz. (*s. v.* Γαζά), to the effect that
the city of Gaza was once called *Minoa*, from *Minos* a king of Crete,—
statements which, according to the correct estimate of Strauss (*l.c.*), "have
all so evidently the marks of fables that they hardly merit discussion," at
all events when opposed to the historical testimony of the Old Testament
(Deut. ii. 23 ; Amos ix. 7), to the effect that the Philistines sprang from
Caphtor. And secondly, " it is *a priori* altogether improbable, that a man
with so patriotic a heart, and so devoted to the worship of the one God,
should have surrounded himself with a *foreign* and *heathen* body-guard"
(Thenius). This argument cannot be invalidated by the remark " that it
is well known that at all times kings and princes have preferred to commit
the protection of their persons to foreign mercenaries, having, as they
thought, all the surer pledge of their devotedness in the fact that they did
not spring from the nation, and were dependent upon the ruler alone "
(Hitzig). For, in the first place, the expression " at all times " is one that
must be very greatly modified ; and secondly, this was only done by kings
who did not feel safe in the presence of their own people, which was not
the case with David. And the Philistines, those arch-foes of Israel, would
have been the last nation that David would have gone to for the purpose
of selecting his own body-guard. It is true that he himself had met with
a hospitable reception in the land of the Philistines ; but it must be borne
in mind that it was not as king of Israel that he found refuge there, but as
an outlaw flying from Saul the king of Israel, and even then the chiefs of
the Philistines would not trust him (1 Sam. xxix. 3 sqq.). And when
Hitzig appeals still further to the fact, that according to ch. xviii. 2, David
handed over the command of a third of his army to a foreigner who had
recently entered his service, having emigrated from Gath with a company
of his fellow-countrymen (ch. xv. 19, 20, 22), and who had displayed the
greatest attachment to the person of David (ver. 21), it is hardly necessary
to observe that the fact of David's welcoming a brave soldier into his army,
when he had come over to Israel, and placing him over a division of the
army, after he had proved his fidelity so decidedly as Ittai had at the time
of Absalom's rebellion, is no proof that he chose his body-guard from the
Philistines. Nor can ch. xv. 18 be adduced in support of this, as the
notion that, according to that passage, David had 600 Gathites in his
service as body-guard, is simply founded upon a misinterpretation of the
passage mentioned.

DAVID'S KINDNESS TOWARDS MEPHIBOSHETH.—CHAP. IX.

When David was exalted to be king over all Israel, he sought to show compassion to the house of the fallen king, and to repay the love which his noble-minded friend Jonathan had once sworn to him before the Lord (1 Sam. xx. 13 sqq.; comp. xxiii. 17, 18). The account of this forms the conclusion of, or rather an appendix to, the first section of the history of his reign, and was intended to show how David was mindful of the duty of gratitude and loving fidelity, even when he reached the highest point of his regal authority and glory. The date when this occurred was about the middle of David's reign, as we may see from the fact, that Mephibosheth, who was five years old when Saul died (ch. iv. 4), had a young son at the time (ver. 12).

Vers. 1–8. When David inquired whether there was any one left of the house of Saul to whom he could show favour for Jonathan's sake (הֲכִי יֵשׁ־עוֹד: *is it so that there is any one?* = there is certainly some one left), a servant of Saul named *Ziba* was summoned, who told the king that there was a son of Jonathan living in the house of Machir at Lodebar, and that he was lame in his feet. הַאֶפֶס עוֹד אִישׁ, "*is there no one at all besides?*" The ל before בֵּית is a roundabout way of expressing the genitive, as in 1 Sam. xvi. 18, etc., and is obviously not to be altered into מִבֵּית, as Thenius proposes. "*The kindness of God*" is love and kindness shown in God, and for God's sake (Luke vi. 36). *Machir* the son of Ammiel was a rich man, judging from ch. xvii. 27, who, after the death of Saul and Jonathan, had received the lame son of the latter into his house. *Lodebar* (לוֹדְבָר, written לֹא דְבָר in ch. xvii. 27, but erroneously divided by the Masoretes into two words in both passages) was a town on the east of Mahanaim, towards Rabbath Amman, probably the same place as Lidbir (Josh. xiii. 26); but it is not further known.—Vers. 5 sqq. David sent for this son of Jonathan (*Mephibosheth*: cf. ch. iv. 4), and not only restored his father's possessions in land, but took him to his own royal table for the rest of his life. "*Fear not*," said David to Mephibosheth, when he came before him with the deepest obeisance, to take away any anxiety lest the king should intend to slay the descendants of the fallen king, according to the custom of eastern usurpers. It is evident from the words, "*I will restore thee all the land of Saul thy father*," that the landed property belonging to Saul had either fallen to David as crown lands, or had been taken possession of by distant relations after the death of Saul. "*Thou shalt eat bread at my table continually*," i.e. eat at my table all thy life long, or receive thy food from my table.—Ver. 8. Mephibosheth expressed his thanks for this manifestation of favour with the deepest obeisance, and a confession of his unworthiness of any such favour. On his comparison of himself to a "*dead dog*," see at 1 Sam. xxiv. 15.

Vers. 9-13. David then summoned Ziba the servant of Saul, told him of the restoration of Saul's possessions to his son Mephibosheth, and ordered him, with his sons and servants, to cultivate the land for the son of his lord. The words, "*that thy master's son may have food to eat*," are not at variance with the next clause, "*Mephibosheth shall eat bread alway at my table*," as bread is a general expression, including all the necessaries of life. Although Mephibosheth himself ate daily as a guest at the king's table, he had to make provision as a royal prince for the maintenance of his own family and servants, as he had children according to ver. 12 and 1 Chron. viii. 34 sqq. Ziba had fifteen sons and twenty servants (ver. 10), with whom he had probably been living in Gibeah, Saul's native place, and may perhaps have hitherto farmed Saul's land.—Ver. 11. Ziba promised to obey the king's command. The last clause of this verse is a circumstantial clause in form, with which the writer passes over to the conclusion of his account. But the words עַל שֻׁלְחָנִי, "*at my table*," do not tally with this, as they require that the words should be taken as David's own. This is precluded, however, not only by the omission of any intimation that David spoke again after Ziba, and repeated what he had said once already, and that without any occasion whatever, but also by the form of the sentence, more especially the participle אֹכֵל. There is no other course left, therefore, than to regard שֻׁלְחָנִי (my table) as written by mistake for שֻׁלְחַן דָּוִד: "*but Mephibosheth ate at David's table as one of the king's sons*." The further notices in vers. 12 and 13 follow this in a very simple manner. כֹּל מוֹשַׁב בֵּית, "*all the dwelling*," i.e. all the inhabitants of Ziba's house, namely his sons and servants, were servants of Mephibosheth, *i.e.* worked for him and cultivated his land, whilst he himself took up his abode at Jerusalem, to eat daily at the king's table, although he was lamed in both his feet.

III. DAVID'S REIGN IN ITS DECLINE.

Chap. x.–xx.

In the first half of David's reign he had strengthened and fortified the kingdom of Israel, both within and without, and exalted the covenant nation into a kingdom of God, before which all its enemies were obliged to bow; but in the second half a series of heavy judgments fell upon him and his house, which cast a deep shadow upon the glory of his reign. David had brought these judgments upon himself by his grievous sin with Bathsheba. The success of all his undertakings, and the strength of his government, which increased year by year, had made him feel so secure, that in the excitement of undisturbed prosperity, he allowed himself to be carried away by evil lusts, so as to stain his soul not only with adultery, but also with murder, and fell all the deeper because of the height to which his God had exalted him. This took place during the war with the Ammonites and Syrians, when Joab was besieging the capital of the Ammonites, after the defeat and subjugation of the Syrians (ch. x.), and when David had remained behind in Jerusalem (ch. xi. 1). For this double sin, the adultery with Bathsheba and the murder of her husband Uriah, the Lord announced as a punishment, that the sword should not depart from David's house, and that his wives should be openly violated; and notwithstanding the sincere sorrow and repentance of the king, when brought to see his sin, He not only caused the fruit of his sin, the child that was born of Bathsheba, to die (ch. xii.), but very soon afterwards allowed the threatened judgments to fall upon his house, inasmuch as Amnon, his first-born son, violated his half-sister Thamar, and was murdered in consequence by her own brother Absalom (ch. xiii.), whereupon Absalom fled to his father-in-law at Geshur; and when at length the king restored him to favour (ch. xiv.), he set on foot a rebellion, which nearly cost David his life and throne (ch. xv.–xvii. 23). And even after Absalom himself was dead (ch. xvii. 24–xix. 1), and David had been reinstated in his kingdom (ch. xix. 2–40), there arose the conspiracy set on foot by the Benjaminite Sheba, which was only stopped by the death of the chief conspirator, in the fortified city of Abel-Beth-Maachah (ch. xix. 41–xx. 26).

The period and duration of these divine visitations are not stated; and all that we are able to determine from the different data as to time, given in ch. xiii. 23, 38, xiv. 28, xv. 7, when taken in connection with the supposed ages of the sons of David, is that Amnon's sin in the case of Thamar did not take place earlier than the twentieth year of David's reign, and that Absalom's rebellion broke out seven or eight years later. Consequently the assumption cannot be far from the truth, that the events described in this section occupied the whole time between the twentieth and thirtieth years of David's reign. We are prevented from placing it earlier, by the fact that Amnon was not born till after David became king over Judah, and therefore was probably about twenty years old when he violated his half-sister Thamar. At the same time it cannot be placed later than this, because Solomon was not born till about two years after David's adultery; and he must have been eighteen or twenty years old when he ascended the throne on the death of his father, after a reign of forty years and a half, since, according to 1 Kings xiv. 21, compared with vers. 11 and 42, 43, he had a son a year old, named Rehoboam, at the time when he began to reign.

WAR WITH THE AMMONITES AND SYRIANS.—CHAP. X.

This war, the occasion and early success of which are described in the present chapter and the parallel passage in 1 Chron. xix., was the fiercest struggle, and, so far as the Israelitish kingdom of God was concerned, the most dangerous, that it ever had to sustain during the reign of David. The amount of distress which fell upon Israel in consequence of this war, and still more because the first successful battles with the Syrians of the south were no sooner over than the Edomites invaded the land, and went about plundering and devastating, in the hope of destroying the people of God, is shown very clearly in the two psalms which date from this period (the 44th and 60th), in which a pious Korahite and David himself pour out their lamentations before the Lord on account of the distress of their nation, and pray for His assistance; and not less clearly in Ps. lxviii., in which David foretels the victory of the God of Israel over all the hostile powers of the world.

Vers. 1–5. *Occasion of the war with the Ammonites.*—Ver. 1. On the expression "*it came to pass after this,*" see the remarks on ch. viii. 1. When *Nahash*, the king of the Ammonites, died, and *Hanun* his son reigned in his stead, David thought that he would show him the same kindness that Nahash had formerly shown to him. We are not told in what the love shown to David by Nahash consisted. He had most likely rendered him some assistance during the time of his flight from Saul. *Nahash* was no doubt the king of the Ammonites mentioned in 1 Sam. xi. 1, whom Saul had smitten at Jabesh. David therefore sent an embassy to Hanun, "*to comfort him for his father,*" *i.e.* to show his sympathy with him on the occasion of his father's death, and at the same time to congratulate him upon his ascent of the throne.—Ver. 3. On the arrival of David's ambassadors, however, the chiefs of the Ammonites said to Hanun their lord, "*Doth David indeed honour thy father in thine eyes* (*i.e.* dost thou really suppose that David intends to do honour to thy father), *because he has sent comforters to thee? Has David not sent his servants to thee with the intention of exploring and spying out the town, and* (then) *destroying it?*" The first question is introduced with הַֽ, because a negative answer is expected; the second with הֲלוֹא, because it requires an affirmative reply. הָעִיר is the capital *Rabbah*, a strongly fortified city (see at ch. xi. 1). The suspicion expressed by the chiefs was founded upon national hatred and enmity, which had probably been increased by David's treatment of Moab, as the subjugation and severe punishment of the Moabites (ch. viii. 2) had certainly taken place a short time before. King Hanun therefore gave credence to the suspicions expressed as to David's honourable intentions, and had his ambassadors treated in the most insulting manner.— Ver. 4. He had the half of their beard shaved off, and their clothes cut off up to the seat, and in this state he sent them away. "*The half of the beard*," *i.e.* the beard on one side. With the value universally set upon the beard by the Hebrews and other oriental nations, as being a man's greatest ornament,[1] the cutting off of one-half of it was the greatest insult that could have been offered to the ambassadors, and through them to David their king. The insult was still further increased by cutting off the long dress which covered the body; so that as the ancient Israelites wore no trousers, the lower half of the body was quite exposed. מַדְוֵיהֶם, from מַדּוּ or מַדְוֶה, the long robe reaching down to the feet, from the root מָדַד = מָדָה, to stretch, spread out, or measure.—Ver. 5. When David received information of the insults that had been heaped upon his ambassadors, he sent messengers to meet them, and direct them to remain in Jericho until their beard had grown again, that he might not have to set his eyes upon the insult they had received.

Ver. 6. When the Ammonites saw that they had made themselves stinking before David, and therefore that David would avenge the insult offered to the people of Israel in the persons of their ambassadors, they looked round for help among the powerful kings of Syria. They hired as auxiliaries (with a thousand talents of silver, *i.e.* nearly half a million of pounds sterling, according to 1 Chron. xix. 6) twenty thousand foot from *Aram-Beth-Rehob* and *Aram-Zoba*, and one thousand men from the king of *Maacah*, and twelve thousand troops from the men of *Tob*. *Aram-Beth-Rehob* was the Aramæan kingdom, the capital of which was *Beth-Rehob*. This Beth-Rehob, which is simply called *Rehob* in ver. 8, is in all probability the city of this name mentioned in Num. xiii. 21 and Judg. xviii. 28, which lay to the south of Hamath, but the exact position of which has not yet been discovered: for the castle of *Hunin*, in the ruins of which Robinson imagines that he has found Beth-Rehob

---

[1] "Cutting off a person's beard is regarded by the Arabs as an indignity quite equal to flogging and branding among ourselves. Many would rather die than have their beard shaved off" (Arvieux, *Sitten der Beduinen-araber*). Niebuhr relates a similar occurrence as having taken place in modern times. In the year 1764, a pretender to the Persian throne, named *Kerim Khan*, sent ambassadors to *Mir Mahenna*, the prince of Bendervigk, on the Persian Gulf, to demand tribute from him; but he in return cut off the ambassadors' beards. *Kerim Khan* was so enraged at this, that he went the next year with a large army to make war upon this prince, and took the city, and almost the whole of his territory, to avenge the insult.

(*Bibl. Researches*, p. 370), is to the south-west of Tell el Kadi, the ancient Laish-Dan, the northern boundary of the Israelitish territory; so that the capital of this Aramæan kingdom would have been within the limits of the land of Israel,—a thing which is inconceivable. *Aram-Naharaim* is also mentioned in the corresponding text of the Chronicles, and for that reason many have identified Beth-Rehob with Rehoboth, on "the river" (Euphrates), mentioned in Gen. xxxvi. 37. But this association is precluded by the fact, that in all probability the latter place is to be found in *Rachabe*, which is upon the Euphrates and not more than half a mile from the river (see Ritter, *Erdk.* xv. p. 128), so that from its situation it can hardly have been the capital of a separate Aramæan kingdom, as the government of the king of Zoba extended, according to ver. 16, beyond the Euphrates into Mesopotamia. On *Aram-Zoba*, see at ch. viii. 3; and for *Maacah* at Deut. iii. 14. אִישׁ־טוֹב is not to be taken as one word and rendered as a proper name, *Ish-Tob*, as it has been by most of the earlier translators; but אִישׁ is a common noun used in a collective sense (as it frequently is in the expression אִישׁ יִשְׂרָאֵל), "*the men of Tob.*" *Tob* was the district between Syria and Ammonitis, where Jephthah had formerly taken refuge (Judg. xi. 5). The corresponding text of the Chronicles (1 Chron. xix. 6, 7) is fuller, and differs in several respects from the text before us. According to the Chronicles, Hanun sent a thousand talents of silver to hire chariots and horsemen from Aram-Naharaim, Aram-Maacah, and Zobah. With this the Ammonites hired thirty-two thousand *receb* (*i.e.* chariots and horsemen: see at ch. viii. 4), and the king of Maacah and his people. They came and encamped before *Medeba*, the present ruin of *Medaba*, two hours to the south-east of Heshbon, in the tribe of Reuben (see at Num. xxi. 30, compared with Josh. xiii. 16), and the Ammonites gathered together out of their cities, and went to the war. The Chronicles therefore mention Aram-Naharaim (*i.e.* Mesopotamia) as hired by the Ammonites instead of Aram-Beth-Rehob, and leave out the men of Tob. The first of these differences is not to be explained, as Bertheau suggests, on the supposition that the author of the Chronicles took *Beth-Rehob* to be the same city as *Rehoboth of the river* in Gen. xxxvi. 37, and therefore substituted the well-known "*Aram* of the two rivers" as an interpretation of the rarer name *Beth-Rehob*, though hardly on good ground. For this conjecture does not help to explain the omission of "the men of Tob." It is a much simpler explanation, that the writer of the Chronicles omitted *Beth-Rehob* and *Tob* as being names that were less known, this being the only place in the Old Testament in which they occur as separate kingdoms, and simply mentioned the kingdoms of *Maacah* and *Zoba*, which frequently occur; and that he included "Aram of the two rivers," and placed it at the head, because the Syrians obtained succour from Mesopotamia after their first defeat. The account in the Chronicles agrees with the one before us, so far as the number of auxiliary troops is concerned. For twenty thousand men of Zoba and twelve thousand of Tob amount to thirty-two thousand, besides the people of the king of Maacah, who sent a thousand men according to the text of Samuel. But according to that of the Chronicles, the auxiliary troops consisted of chariots and horsemen, whereas only foot-soldiers are mentioned in our text, which appears all the more remarkable, because according to ch. viii. 4, and 1 Chron. xviii. 4, the king of Zoba fought against David with a considerable force of chariots and horsemen. It is very evident, therefore, that there are copyists' errors in both texts; for the troops of the Syrians did not consist of infantry only, nor of chariots and horsemen alone, but of foot-soldiers, cavalry, and war-chariots, as we may see very clearly not only from the passages already quoted in ch. viii. 4 and 1 Chron. xviii. 4, but also from the conclusion to the account before us. According to ver. 18 of this chapter, when Hadarezer had reinforced his army with auxiliaries from Mesopotamia, after losing the first battle, David smote seven hundred *receb* and forty thousand *parashim* of Aram, whilst according to the parallel text (1 Chron. xix. 18) he smote seven thousand *receb* and forty thousand foot. Now, apart from the difference between seven thousand and seven hundred in the case of the *receb*, which is to be interpreted in the same way as a similar difference in ch. viii. 4, the Chronicles do not mention any *parashim* at all in ver. 18, but foot-soldiers only, whereas in ver. 7 they mention only *receb* and *parashim*; and, on the other hand, there are no foot-soldiers given in ver. 18 of the text before us, but riders only, whereas in ver. 6 there are none but foot-soldiers mentioned, without any riders at all. It is evident that in both engagements the Syrians fought with all three (infantry, cavalry, and chariots), so that in both of them David smote chariots, horsemen, and foot.

Vers. 7–14. When David heard of these preparations and the advance of the Syrians into the land, he sent Joab and his brave army against the foe. הַגִּבּוֹרִים (*the mighty men*) is in apposition to כָּל־הַצָּבָא (*all the host*): the whole army, namely the heroes or mighty men, *i.e.* the brave troops that were well used to war. It is quite arbitrary on the part of Thenius to supply *vav* before הַגִּבּוֹרִים; for, as Bertheau has observed, we never find a distinction drawn between the *gibborim* and the whole army.—Ver. 8. On the other hand, the Ammonites came out (from the capital, where they had assembled), and put themselves in battle array before the gate. The Syrians were alone on the field, *i.e.* they had taken up a separate position on the broad treeless table-land (cf. Josh. xiii. 16) by Medeba. *Medeba* lay about four geographical miles in a straight line to the south-west of *Rabbath-Ammon*.—Ver. 9. When Joab saw that "the front of the war was (directed) against him both before and behind," he selected a picked body out of the Israelitish army, and posted them (the picked men) against the children of Aram (*i.e.* the Syrians). The rest of the men he gave to his brother Abishai, and stationed them against the Ammonites. "*The front of the battle:*" *i.e.* the face or front of the hostile army, when placed in battle array. Joab had this in front and behind, as the Ammonites had taken their stand before Rabbah at the back of the Israelitish army, and the Syrians by *Medeba* in their front, so that Joab was attacked both before and behind. This compelled him to divide his army. *He chose out, i.e.* made a selection. Instead of בְּחוּרֵי בְיִשְׂרָאֵל (the picked men in Israel) the Chronicles have בָּחוּר בְּיִשְׂרָאֵל (the men in Israel), the singular בָּחוּר being more commonly employed than the plural to denote the men of war. The בְּ before יִשְׂרָאֵל is not to be regarded as suspicious, although the early translators have not expressed it, and the Masoretes wanted to expunge it. "The choice of Israel" signifies those who were selected in Israel for the war, *i.e.* the Israelitish soldiers. Joab himself took up his station opposite to the Syrians with a picked body of men, because they were the stronger force of the two. He then made this arrangement with Abishai (ver. 11): "*If Aram becomes stronger than I* (i.e. overpowers me), *come to my help; and if the Ammonites should overpower thee, I will go to help thee.*" Consequently the attack was not to be made upon both the armies of the enemy simultaneously; but Joab proposed to attack the Aramæans (Syrians) first (cf. ver. 13), and Abishai was merely to keep the Ammonites in check, though there was still a possibility that the two bodies of the enemy might make their attack simultaneously.— Ver. 12. "*Be firm, and let us be firm* (strong) *for our people, and for the towns of our God: and Jehovah will do what seemeth Him good.*" Joab calls the towns of Israel the towns of our God, inasmuch as the God of Israel had given the land to the people of Israel, as being His own property. Joab and Abishai were about to fight, in order that Jehovah's possessions might not fall into the hands of the heathen, and become subject to their gods.—Ver. 13. Joab then advanced with his army to battle against Aram, and "*they fled before him.*"—Ver. 14. When the Ammonites perceived this, they also fled before Abishai, and drew back into the city (Rabbah); whereupon Joab returned to Jerusalem, probably because, as we may infer from ch. xi. 1, it was too late in the year for the siege and capture of Rabbah.

Vers. 15-19. The Aramæans, however, gathered together again after the first defeat, to continue the war; and Hadarezer, the most powerful of the Aramæan kings, sent messengers to Mesopotamia, and summoned it to war. It is very evident, not only from the words " he sent and brought out Aram, which was beyond the river," but also from the fact that Shobach, Hadarezer's general (*Shophach* according to the Chronicles), was at the head of the Mesopotamian troops, that the Mesopotamian troops who were summoned to help were under the supreme rule of Hadarezer. This is placed beyond all possible doubt by ver. 19, where the kings who had fought with Hadarezer against the Israelites are called his "servants," or vassals. וַיָּבֹאוּ חֵילָם (ver. 16) might be translated " and their army came;" but when we compare with this the וַיָּבֹא חֵלָאמָה of ver. 17, we are compelled to render it as a proper name (as in the Septuagint, Chaldee, Syriac, and Arabic)—"*and they* (the men from beyond the Euphrates) *came* (marched) *to Helam*"—and to take

חֵילָם as a contracted form of חֵלְאָם. The situation of this place has not yet been discovered. Ewald supposes it to be connected with the Syrian town *Alamatha* upon the Euphrates (Ptol. *Geogr.* v. 15); but this is not to be thought of for a moment, if only because it cannot be supposed that the Aramæans would fall back to the Euphrates, and wait for the Israelites to follow them thither before they gave them battle; and also on account of ch. viii. 4 and 1 Chron. xviii. 3, from which it is evident that *Helam* is to be sought for somewhere in the neighbourhood of Hamath (see p. 360). For וַיָּבֹא חֶלְאָמָה we find וַיָּבֹא אֲלֵיהֶם, "David came to them" (the Aramæans), in the Chronicles: so that the author of the Chronicles has omitted the unknown place, unless indeed אֲלֵיהֶם has been written by mistake for חֶלְאָם.—Vers. 17 sqq. David went with all Israel (all the Israelitish forces) against the foe, and smote the Aramæans at *Helam*, where they had placed themselves in battle array, slaying seven hundred charioteers and forty thousand horsemen, and so smiting (or wounding) the general *Shobach* that he died there, *i.e.* that he did not survive the battle (Thenius). With regard to the different account given in the corresponding text of the Chronicles as to the number of the slain, see the remarks on ver. 6 (pp. 376–7). It is a fact worthy of notice, that the number of men who fell in the battle (seven hundred *receb* and forty thousand *parashim*, according to the text before us; seven thousand *receb* and forty thousand *ragli*, according to the Chronicles) agrees quite as well with the number of Aramæans reported to be taken prisoners or slain, according to ch. viii. 4 and 1 Chron. xviii. 4, 5 (viz. seventeen hundred *parashim* or a thousand *receb*, and seven thousand *parashim* and twenty thousand *ragli* of Aram-Zoba, and twenty-two thousand of Aram-Damascus), as could possibly be expected considering the notorious corruption in the numbers as we possess them; so that there is scarcely any doubt that the number of Aramæans who fell was the same in both accounts (ch. viii. and x.), and that in the chapter before us we have simply a more circumstantial account of the very same war of which the result is given in ch. viii. and 1 Chron. xviii.—Ver. 19. "*And when all the kings, the vassals of Hadarezer, saw that they were smitten before Israel, they made peace with Israel, and became subject to them; and Aram was afraid to render any further help to the Ammonites.*" It might appear from the first half of this verse, that it was only the vassals of Hadarezer who made peace with Israel, and became subject to it, and that Hadarezer himself did not. But the last clause, " and the Aramæans were afraid," etc., shows very clearly that Hadarezer also made peace with the Israelites, and submitted to their rule ; so that the expression in the first half of the verse is not a very exact one.

SIEGE OF RABBAH. DAVID'S ADULTERY.—CHAP. XI.

Ver. 1 (cf. 1 Chron. xx. 1). SIEGE OF RABBAH.—"*And it came to pass at the return of the year, at the time when the kings marched out, that David sent Joab, and his servants with him, and all Israel; and they destroyed the Ammonites and besieged Rabbah: but David remained in Jerusalem.*" This verse is connected with ch. x. 14, where it was stated that after Joab had put to flight the Aramæans who came to the help of the Ammonites, and when the Ammonites also had fallen back before Abishai in consequence of this victory, and retreated into their fortified capital, Joab himself returned to Jerusalem. He remained there during the winter or rainy season, in which it was impossible that war should be carried on. At the return of the year, *i.e.* at the commencement of spring, with which the new year began in the month Abib (Nisan), the time when kings who were engaged in war were accustomed to open their campaign, David sent Joab his commander-in-chief with the whole of the Israelitish forces to attack the Ammonites once more, for the purpose of chastising them and conquering their capital. The *Chethibh* הַמְּלָאכִים should be changed into הַמְּלָכִים, according to the *Keri* and the text of the Chronicles. The א interpolated is a perfectly superfluous *mater lectionis*, and probably crept into the text from a simple oversight. The "*servants*" of David with Joab were not the men performing military service, or soldiers, (in which case "all Israel" could only signify the people called out to war in extraordinary circumstances,) but the king's military officers, the military commanders; and "*all Israel*," the whole of the military forces of Israel. Instead of "the children of Ammon" we find "the country of the children of Ammon," which explains the meaning more fully. But there was no necessity to insert אֶרֶץ (the land or country), as הִשְׁחִית is applied to men in other passages in the sense of "cast to the ground," or destroy (*e.g.* 1 Sam. xxvi. 15). *Rabbah* was the capital of Ammonitis (as in Josh. xiii. 25): the fuller name was *Rabbath* of the children of Ammon. It has been preserved in the ruins which still exist under the ancient name of *Rabbat-Ammân*, on the Nahr Ammân, *i.e.* the upper Jabbok (see at Deut. iii. 11). The last clause, "*but David sat* (remained) *in Jerusalem*," leads on to the account which follows of David's adultery with Bathsheba (vers. 2–27 and ch. xii. 1–25), which took place at that time, and is therefore inserted here, so that the conquest of Rabbah is not related till afterwards (ch. xii. 26–31).

Vers. 2–27. DAVID'S ADULTERY.—David's deep fall forms a turning-point not only in the inner life of the great king, but also in the history of his reign. Hitherto David had kept free from the grosser sins, and had only exhibited such infirmities and failings as simulation, prevarication, etc., which clung to all the saints of the Old Covenant, and were hardly regarded as sins in the existing stage of religious culture at that time, although God never left them unpunished, but invariably visited them upon His servants with humiliations and chastisements of various kinds. Among the unacknowledged sins which God tolerated because of the hardness of Israel's heart was polygamy, which encouraged licentiousness and the tendency to sensual excesses, and to which but a weak barrier had been presented by the warning that had been given for the Israelitish kings against taking many wives (Deut. xvii. 17), opposed as such a warning was to the notion so prevalent in the East both in ancient and modern times, that a well-filled harem is essential to the splendour of a princely court. The custom to which this notion gave rise opened a dangerous precipice in David's way, and led to a most grievous fall, that can only be explained, as O. v. Gerlach has said, from the intoxication consequent upon undisturbed prosperity and power, which grew with every year of his reign, and occasioned a long series of most severe humiliations and divine chastisements that marred the splendour of his reign, notwithstanding the fact that the great sin was followed by deep and sincere repentance.

Vers. 2–5. Towards evening David walked upon the roof

of his palace, after rising from his couch, *i.e.* after taking his mid-day rest, and saw from the roof a woman bathing, namely in the uncovered court of a neighbouring house, where there was a spring with a pool of water, such as you still frequently meet with in the East. " *The woman was beautiful to look upon.*" Her outward charms excited sensual desires.—Ver. 3. David ordered inquiry to be made about her, and found (וַיֹּאמֶר, " *he, i.e.* the messenger, *said;* " or indefinitely, " they said ") that she was Bathsheba, the wife of Uriah the Hethite. הֲלוֹא, *nonne,* is used, as it frequently is, in the sense of an affirmation, " it is indeed so." Instead of *Bathsheba* the daughter of Eliam, we find the name given in the Chronicles (1 Chron. iii. 5) as *Bathshua* the daughter of Ammiel. The form בַּת־שׁוּעַ may be derived from בַּת־שֶׁבַע, in which ב is softened into ו; for Bathsheba (with *beth*) is the correct and original form, as we may see from 1 Kings i. 11, 15, 28. *Eliam* and *Ammiel* have the same signification; the difference simply consists in the transposition of the component parts of the name. It is impossible to determine, however, which of the two forms was the original one.—Ver. 4. The information brought to him, that the beautiful woman was married, was not enough to stifle the sensual desires which arose in David's soul. " When lust hath conceived, it bringeth forth sin" (Jas. i. 15). David sent for the woman, and lay with her. In the expression "he took her, and she came to him," there is no intimation whatever that David brought Bathsheba into his palace through craft or violence, but rather that she came at his request without any hesitation, and offered no resistance to his desires. Consequently Bathsheba is not to be regarded as free from blame. The very act of bathing in the uncovered court of a house in the heart of the city, into which it was possible for any one to look down from the roofs of the houses on higher ground, does not say much for her feminine modesty, even if it was not done with an ulterior purpose, as some commentators suppose. Nevertheless in any case the greatest guilt rests upon David, that he, a man upon whom the Lord had bestowed such grace, did not resist the temptation to the lust of the flesh, but sent to fetch the woman. " *When she had sanctified herself from her uncleanness, she returned to her house.*" Defilement from sexual intercourse rendered unclean till the evening (Lev. xv. 18). Bathsheba thought it her duty to observe this statute most scrupulously, though she did not shrink from committing the sin of adultery. —Ver. 5. When she discovered that she was with child, she sent word to David. This involved an appeal to him to take the necessary steps to avert the evil consequences of the sin, inasmuch as the law required that both adulterer and adulteress should be put to death (Lev. xx. 10).

Vers. 6–13. David had Uriah the husband of Bathsheba sent to him by Joab, under whom he was serving in the army before Rabbah, upon some pretext or other, and asked him as soon as he arrived how it fared with Joab and the people (*i.e.* the army) and the war. This was probably the pretext under which David had had him sent to him. According to ch. xxiii. 39, Uriah was one of the *gibborim* ("mighty men") of David, and therefore held some post of command in the army, although there is no historical foundation for the statement made by Josephus, viz. that he was Joab's armour-bearer or aide-de-camp. The king then said to him, "*Go down to thy house* (from the palace upon Mount Zion down to the lower city, where Uriah's house was situated), *and wash thy feet;*" and when he had gone out of the palace, he sent a royal present after him. The Israelites were accustomed to wash their feet when they returned home from work or from a journey, to take refreshment and rest themselves. Consequently these words contained an intimation that he was to go and refresh himself in his own home. David's wish was that Uriah should spend a night at home with his wife, that he might afterwards be regarded as the father of the child that had been begotten in adultery. מַשְׂאֵת, a present, as in Amos v. 11, Jer. xl. 5, Esther ii. 18.—Ver. 9. But Uriah had his suspicions aroused. The connection between his wife and David may not have remained altogether a secret, so that it may have reached his ears as soon as he arrived in Jerusalem. "*He lay down to sleep before the king's house with all the servants of his lord* (*i.e.* the retainers of the court), *and went not down to his house.*" "Before, or at, the door of the king's house," *i.e.* in the court of the palace, or in a building adjoining the king's palace, where the court servants lived.—Ver. 10. When this was told to David (the next morning), he said to Uriah, "*Didst thou not come from the way* (*i.e.* from a journey)? *why didst thou not go down* (as men generally do when they return from a journey)?" Uriah replied (ver. 11), "*The ark* (ark of the covenant), *and Israel, and Judah, dwell in the huts, and my lord Joab and the servants of my lord encamp in the field; and should I go to my house to eat and to drink, and to lie with my wife? By thy life, and by the life of thy soul, I do no such thing!*" יֵשֵׁב בַּסֻּכּוֹת, to sit or sojourn in huts, is the same practically as being encamped in the field. Uriah meant to say: Whereas the ark, *i.e.* Jehovah with the ark, and all Israel, were engaged in conflict with the enemies of God and of His kingdom, and therefore encamped in the open country, it did not become a warrior to seek rest and pleasure in his own home. This answer expressed the feelings and the consciousness of duty which ought to animate one who was fighting for the cause of God, in such plain and unmistakeable terms, that it was well adapted to prick the king to the heart. But David's soul was so beclouded by the wish to keep clear of the consequences of his sin in the eyes of the world, that he did not feel the sting, but simply made a still further attempt to attain his purpose with Uriah. He commanded him to stop in Jerusalem all that day, as he did not intend to send him away till the morrow.—Ver. 13. The next day he invited him to his table and made him drunken, with the hope that when in this state he would give up his intention of not going home to his wife. But Uriah lay down again the next night to sleep with the king's servants, without going down to his house; for, according to the counsel and providence of God, David's sin was to be brought to light to his deep humiliation.

Vers. 14–27. When the king saw that his plan was frustrated through Uriah's obstinacy, he resolved upon a fresh and still greater crime. He wrote a letter to Joab, with which he sent Uriah back to the army, and the contents of which were these: "Set ye Uriah opposite to the strongest contest, and then turn away behind him, that he may be slain, and die."[1] David was so sure that his orders would be executed, that he

---

[1] "We may see from this how deep a soul may fall when it turns away from God, and from the guidance of His grace. This David, who in the days of his persecution would not even resort to means that were really plausible in order to defend himself, was now not ashamed to resort to the greatest crimes in order to cover his sin. O God! how great is our strength

did not think it necessary to specify any particular crime of which Uriah had been guilty.—Ver. 16. The king's wishes were fully carried out by Joab. "*When Joab watched* (*i.e.* blockaded) *the city, he stationed Uriah just where he knew that there were brave men*" (in the city).—Ver. 17. "*And the men of the city came out* (*i.e.* made a sally) *and fought with Joab, and some of the people of the servants of David fell, and Uriah the Hethite died also.*" The literal fulfilment of the king's command does not warrant us in assuming that Joab suspected how the matter stood, or had heard a rumour concerning it. As a general, who was not accustomed to spare human life, he would be a faithful servant of his lord in this point, in order that his own interests might be served another time.—Vers. 18-21. Joab immediately despatched a messenger to the king, to give him a report of the events of the war, and with these instructions: "When thou hast told all the things of the war to the king to the end, in case the anger of the king should be excited (חֵמָה, ascend), and he should say to thee, Why did ye advance so near to the city to fight? knew ye not that they would shoot from the wall? Who smote Abimelech the son of Jerubbosheth (*i.e.* Gideon, see at Judg. vi. 32)? did not a woman throw down a millstone from the wall, that he died in Thebez (Judg. ix. 53)? why went ye so nigh to the wall?' then only say, Thy servant Uriah the Hethite has perished." Joab assumed that David might possibly be angry at what had occurred, or at any rate that he might express his displeasure at the fact that Joab had sacrificed a number of warriors by imprudently approaching close to the wall: he therefore instructed the messenger, if such should be the case, to announce Uriah's death to the king, for the purpose of mitigating his wrath. The messenger seems to have known that Uriah was in disgrace with the king. At the same time, the words "thy servant Uriah is dead also" might be understood or interpreted as meaning that it was without, or even in opposition to, Joab's command, that Uriah went so far with his men,

when we lay firm hold of Thee! And how weak we become as soon as we turn away from Thee! The greatest saints would be ready for the worst of deeds, if Thou shouldst but leave them for a single moment without Thy protection. Whoever reflects upon this, will give up all thought of self-security and spiritual pride"—*Berleburg Bible.*

and that he was therefore chargeable with his own death and that of the other warriors who had fallen.—Vers. 22 sqq. The messenger brought to David all the information with which Joab had charged him (שָׁלַח with a double accusative, to send or charge a person with anything), but he so far condensed it as to mention Uriah's death at the same time. "When the men (of Rabbah) became strong against us, and came out to us into the field, and we prevailed against them even to the gate, the archers shot at thy servants down from the wall, so that some of the servants of the king died, and thy servant Uriah the Hethite is dead also." The א in the forms וַיִּרְאוּ הַמּוֹרְאִים instead of יָרוּ הַמּוֹרִים is an Aramaic mode of writing the words.—Ver. 25. David received with apparent composure the intelligence which he was naturally so anxious to hear, and sent this message back to Joab: "*Let not this thing depress thee, for the sword devours thus and thus. Keep on with the battle against the city, and destroy it.*" The construction of אַל־יֵרַע with אֵת *obj.* is analogous to the combination of a passive verb with אֵת: "Do not look upon this affair as evil" (disastrous). David then sent the messenger away, saying, "Encourage thou him" (*lit.* strengthen him, put courage into him), to show his entire confidence in the bravery and stedfastness of Joab and the army, and their ultimate success in the capture of Rabbah.—In ver. 26 the account goes back to its starting-point. When Uriah's wife heard of her husband's death, she mourned for her husband. When her mourning was over, David took her home as his wife, after which she bore him a son (the one begotten in adultery). The ordinary mourning of the Israelites lasted seven days (Gen. l. 10; 1 Sam. xxxi. 13). Whether widows mourned any longer we do not know. In the case before us Bathsheba would hardly prolong her mourning beyond the ordinary period, and David would certainly not delay taking her as his wife, in order that she might be married to the king as long as possible before the time of childbirth. The account of these two grievous sins on the part of David is then closed with the assurance that "the thing that David had done displeased the Lord," which prepares the way for the following chapter.

NATHAN'S REPROOF AND DAVID'S REPENTANCE. CONQUEST OF RABBAH.—CHAP. XII.

The Lord left David almost a whole year in his sin, before sending a prophet to charge the haughty sinner with his misdeeds, and to announce the punishment that would follow. He did this at length through Nathan, but not till after the birth of Bathsheba's child, that had been begotten in adultery (compare vers. 14, 15 with ch. xi. 27). Not only was the fruit of the sin to be first of all brought to light, and the hardened sinner to be deprived of the possibility of either denying or concealing his crimes, but God would first of all break his unbroken heart by the torture of his own conscience, and prepare it to feel the reproaches of His prophet. The reason for this delay on the part of God in the threatening of judgment is set forth very clearly in Ps. xxxii., where David describes most vividly the state of his heart during this period, and the sufferings that he endured as long as he was trying to conceal his crime. And whilst in this Psalm he extols the blessedness of a pardoned sinner, and admonishes all who fear God, on the ground of his own inmost experience after his soul had tasted once more the joy and confidence arising from the full forgiveness of his iniquities; in the fifty-first Psalm, which was composed after Nathan had been to him, he shows clearly enough that the promise of divine forgiveness, which the prophet had given him in consequence of his confession of his guilt, did not take immediate possession of his soul, but simply kept him from despair at first, and gave him strength to attain to a thorough knowledge of the depth of his guilt through prayer and supplication, and to pray for its entire removal, that his heart might be renewed and fortified through the Holy Ghost. But Nathan's reproof could not possibly have borne this saving fruit, if David had still been living in utter blindness as to the character of his sin at the time when the prophet went to him.

Vers. 1–14. NATHAN'S REPROOF.—Vers. 1 sqq. To ensure the success of his mission, viz. to charge the king with his crimes, Nathan resorted to a parable by which he led on the king to pronounce sentence of death upon himself. The parable is a very simple one, and drawn from life. Two men were living in a certain city: the one was rich, and had many sheep and oxen; the other was poor, and possessed nothing at all but one small lamb which he had bought and nourished (יְחַיֶּה, *lit.* kept alive), so that it grew up in his house along with his son, and was treated most tenderly and loved like a daughter. The custom of keeping pet-sheep in the house, as we keep lap-dogs, is still met with among the Arabs (*vid.* Bochart, *Hieroz.* i. p. 594). There came a traveller (הֵלֶךְ, a journey, for a traveller) to the rich man (לְאִישׁ without an article, the express definition being introduced afterwards in connection with the adjective הֶעָשִׁיר; *vid.* Ewald, § 293a, p. 741), and he grudged to take of his own sheep and oxen to prepare (*sc.* a meal) for the traveller who had come to his house; "and he took the poor man's lamb, and dressed it for the man that had come to him."—Vers. 5, 6. David was so enraged at this act of violence on the part of the rich man, that in the heat of his anger he pronounced this sentence at once: "*As the Lord liveth, the man who did this deserves to die; and the lamb he shall restore fourfold.*" The fourfold restoration corresponds to the law in Ex. xxi. 37. The culprit himself was also to be put to death, because the forcible robbery of a poor man's pet-lamb was almost as bad as man-stealing.—Vers. 7 sqq. The parable was so selected that David could not suspect that it had reference to him and to his sin. With all the greater shock therefore did the words of the prophet, "*Thou art the man,*" come upon the king. Just as in the parable the sin is traced to its root—namely, insatiable covetousness—so now, in the words of Jehovah which follow, and in which the prophet charges the king directly with his crime, he brings out again in the most unsparing manner this hidden background of all sins, for the purpose of bringing thoroughly home to his heart the greatness of his iniquity, and the condemnation it deserved. "*Jehovah the God of Israel hath said, I anointed thee king over Israel, and I delivered thee out of the hand of Saul, and I gave thee thy master's house and thy master's wives into thy bosom.*" These words refer to the fact that, according to the general custom in the East, when a king died, his successor upon the throne also succeeded to his harem, so that David was at liberty to take his predecessor's wives; though we cannot infer from this that he actually did so: in fact this is by no means probable, since, according to 1 Sam. xiv. 50, Saul had but one wife, and according to 2 Sam. iii. 7 only one concubine, whom Abner appropriated to himself. "*And gave thee the house of Israel and Judah;*" *i.e.* I handed over the whole nation to thee as king, so that thou couldst have chosen young virgins as wives from all the daughters of Judah and Israel. וְאִם מְעָט, "*and if (all this was) too little, I would have added to thee this and that.*" —Ver. 9. "*Why hast thou despised the word of Jehovah, to do evil in His eyes? Thou hast slain Uriah the Hethite with the sword, and taken his wife to be thy wife, and slain him with the sword of the Ammonites.*" The last clause does not contain any tautology, but serves to strengthen the thought by defining more sharply the manner in which David destroyed Uriah. הָרַג, to murder, is stronger than הִכָּה; and the fact that it was by the sword of *the Ammonites*, the enemies of the people of God, that the deed was done, added to the wickedness.—Vers. 10–12. The punishment answers to the sin. There is first of all (ver. 10) the punishment for the murder of Uriah: "*The sword shall not depart from thy house for ever, because thou hast despised me, and hast taken the wife,*" etc. "*For ever*" must not be toned down to the indefinite idea of a long period, but must be held firmly in its literal signification. The expression "thy house," however, does not refer to the house of David as continued in his descendants, but simply as existing under David himself until it was broken up by his death. The fulfilment of this threat commenced with the murder of Amnon by Absalom (ch. xiii. 29); it was continued in the death of Absalom the rebel (ch. xviii. 14), and was consummated in the execution of Adonijah (1 Kings ii. 24, 25).—Vers. 11, 12. But David had also sinned in committing adultery. It was therefore announced to him by Jehovah, "*Behold, I raise up mischief over thee out of thine own house, and will take thy wives before thine eyes, and give them to thy neighbour, that he may lie with thy wives before the eyes of this sun* (for the fulfilment of this by Absalom, see ch. xvi. 21, 22). *For thou hast done it in secret; but I will do this thing before all Israel, and before* (in the face of) *the sun.*" David's twofold sin was to be followed by a twofold punishment. For his murder he would have to witness the commission of murder in his own family, and for his adultery the violation of his wives, and both of them in an intensified form. As his sin began with adultery, and was consummated in murder, so the law of just retribution was also carried out in the punishment, in the fact that the judgments which fell upon his house commenced with Amnon's incest, whilst Absalom's rebellion culminated in the open violation of his father's concubines, and even Adonijah lost his life, simply because he asked for Abishag the Shunammite, who had lain in David's bosom to warm and cherish him in his old age (1 Kings ii. 23, 24).—Ver. 13. These words went to David's heart, and removed the ban of hardening which pressed upon it. He confessed to the prophet, "*I have sinned against the Lord.*" " The words are very few, just as in the case of the publican in the Gospel of Luke (xviii. 13). But that is a good sign of a thoroughly broken spirit. . . . There is no excuse, no cloaking, no palliation of the sin. There is no searching for a loophole, . . . no pretext put forward, no human weakness pleaded. He acknowledges his guilt openly, candidly, and without prevarication" (*Berleb. Bible*). In response to this candid confession of his sin, Nathan announced to him, " *The Lord also hath let thy sin pass by* (*i.e.* forgiven it). *Thou wilt not die. Only because by this deed thou hast given the enemies of the Lord occasion to blaspheme, the son that is born unto thee shall die.*" יָמוּת, *inf. abs. Piel*, with chirek, because of its similarity in sound to the following perfect (see Ewald, § 240, *c*). גַּם, with which the apodosis commences, belongs to the הַבֵּן which follows, and serves to give emphasis to the expression: "Nevertheless the son" (*vid.* Ges. § 155, 2, *a*). David himself had deserved to die as an adulterer and murderer. The Lord remitted the punishment of death, not so much because of his heartfelt repentance, as from His own fatherly grace and compassion, and because of the promise that He had given to David (ch. vii. 11, 12),—a promise which rested upon the assumption that David would not altogether fall away from a state of grace, or commit a mortal sin, but that even in the worst cases he would turn to the Lord again and seek forgiveness. The Lord therefore punished him for this sin with the judgments announced in vers. 10-12, as about to break upon him and his house. But as his sin had given occasion to the enemies of the Lord—*i.e.* not only to the heathen, but also to the unbelieving among the Israelites themselves—to blaspheme or ridicule his religion and that of all other believers also, the child that was begotten in adultery and had just been born should die; in order, on the one hand, that the father should atone for his adultery in the death of the son, and, on the other hand, that the visible occasion for any further blasphemy should be taken away: so that David was not only to feel the pain of punishment in the death of his son, but was also to discern in it a distinct token of the grace of God.

Vers. 15–25. DAVID'S PENITENTIAL GRIEF, AND THE BIRTH OF SOLOMON.—Ver. 15. The last-mentioned punishment was inflicted without delay. When Nathan had gone home, the Lord smote the child, so that it became very ill.—Vers. 16, 17. Then David sought God (in prayer) for the boy, and fasted, and went and lay all night upon the earth. וַיָּבֹא, "*he came*," not into the sanctuary of the Lord (ver. 20 is proof to the contrary), but into his house, or into his chamber, to pour out his heart before God, and bend beneath His chastising hand, and refused the appeal of his most confidential servants, who tried to raise him up, and strengthen him with food. "*The elders of his house*," judging from Gen. xxiv. 2, were the oldest and most confidential servants, "the most highly honoured of his servants, and those who had the greatest influence with him" (Clericus).—Ver. 18. On the seventh day, when the child died, the servants of David were afraid to tell him of its death; for they said (to one another), "Behold, while the child was still living, we spoke to him, and he did not hearken to our voice; how should we say to him, now the child is dead, that he should do harm?" (*i.e.* do himself an injury in the depth of his anguish.)—Vers. 19, 20. David saw at once what had happened from their whispering conversation, and asked whether the child was dead. When they answered in the affirmative, he rose up from the ground, washed and anointed himself, and changed his clothes; that is to say, he laid aside all the signs of penitential grief and mourning, went into the house of the Lord (the holy tent upon Mount Zion) and worshipped, and then returned to his house, and had food set before him.—Vers. 21 sqq. When his servants expressed their astonishment at all this, David replied, "*As long as the boy lived, I fasted and wept: for*

I thought (said), *Perhaps* (who knows) *the Lord may be gracious to me, that the child may remain alive. But now he is dead, why should I fast? can I bring him back again? I shall go to him, but he will not return to me.*" On this O. v. Gerlach has the following admirable remarks: " In the case of a man whose penitence was so earnest and so deep, the prayer for the preservation of his child must have sprung from some other source than excessive love of any created object. His great desire was to avert the stroke, as a sign of the wrath of God, in the hope that he might be able to discern, in the preservation of the child, a proof of divine favour consequent upon the restoration of his fellowship with God. But when the child was dead, he humbled himself under the mighty hand of God, and rested satisfied with His grace, without giving himself up to fruitless pain." This state of mind is fully explained in Ps. li., though his servants could not comprehend it. The form יחֻנַּי is the imperfect *Kal*, יְחָנֵּי according to the *Chethibh*, though the Masoretes have substituted as the *Keri* וְחַנַּנִי, the perfect with *vav consec.*—Ver. 23*b* is paraphrased very correctly by Clericus: " I shall go to the dead, the dead will not come to me."— Ver. 24. David then comforted his wife Bathsheba, and lived with her again; and she bare a son, whom he called *Solomon*, the man of peace (cf. 1 Chron. xxii. 9). David gave the child this name, because he regarded his birth as a pledge that he should now become a partaker again of peace with God, and not from any reference to the fact that the war with the Ammonites was over, and peace prevailed when he was born; although in all probability Solomon was not born till after the capture of Rabbah and the termination of the Ammonitish war. His birth is mentioned here simply because of its connection with what immediately precedes. The writer adds (in vers. 24, 25), "*And Jehovah loved him, and sent by the hand* (through the medium) *of Nathan the prophet; and he called his son Jedidiah* (*i.e.* beloved of Jehovah), *for Jehovah's sake.*" The subject to וַיִּשְׁלַח (he sent) cannot be David, because this would not yield any appropriate sense, but must be *Jehovah*, the subject of the clause immediately preceding. " To send by the hand," *i.e.* to make a mission by a person (*vid.* Ex. iv. 13, etc.), is equivalent to having a commission performed by a person, or entrusting a person with a commission to another. We learn from what follows, in what the commission with which Jehovah entrusted Nathan consisted : " *And he* (Nathan, not Jehovah) *called his* (the boy's) *name Jedidiah.*" And if Nathan is the subject to " called," there is nothing to astonish in the expression " because of the Lord." The idea is this : Nathan came to David according to Jehovah's instructions, and gave Solomon the name *Jedidiah* for Jehovah's sake, *i.e.* because Jehovah loved him. The giving of such a name was a practical declaration on the part of Jehovah that He loved Solomon, from which David could and was intended to discern that the Lord had blessed his marriage with Bathsheba. *Jedidiah*, therefore, was not actually adopted as Solomon's name.

Vers. 26-31. CONQUEST OF RABBAH, AND PUNISHMENT OF THE AMMONITES (comp. 1 Chron. xx. 1-3).—"*Joab fought against Rabbah of the children of Ammon, and took the king's city.*" עִיר הַמְּלוּכָה, the capital of the kingdom, is the city with the exception of the acropolis, as ver. 27 clearly shows, where the captured city is called " the water-city." *Rabbah* was situated, as the ruins of *Ammân* show, on both banks of the river (*Moiet*) *Ammân* (the upper Jabbok), in a valley which is shut in upon the north and south by two bare ranges of hills of moderate height, and is not more than 200 paces in breadth. " The northern height is crowned by the castle, the ancient acropolis, which stands on the north-western side of the city, and commands the whole city" (see Burckhardt, *Syria* ii. pp. 612 sqq., and Ritter, *Erdkunde* xv. pp. 1145 sqq.). After taking the water-city, Joab sent messengers to David, to inform him of the result of the siege, and say to him, " *Gather the rest of the people together, and besiege the city* (i.e. the acropolis, which may have been peculiarly strong), *and take it, that I may not take the city* (also), *and my name be named upon it*," *i.e.* the glory of the conquest be ascribed to me. Luther adopts this explanation in his free rendering, "and I have a name from it."
—Ver. 29. Accordingly David " *gathered together all the people*," —*i.e.* all the men of war who had remained behind in the land ; from which we may see that Joab's besieging army had been considerably weakened during the long siege, and at the capture of the water-city,—" *and fought against the acropolis, and took it.*"—Ver. 30. He then took their king's crown (" *their king,*"

viz. the king of the Ammonites) from off his (the king's) head; so that he had either been taken prisoner or slain at the capture of the city. The weight of the crown was " *a talent of gold, and precious stones*" (*sc.* were upon it): as the writer of the Chronicles has correctly explained it by supplying בָּהּ. The Hebrew talent (equal to 3000 shekels) was 83½ Dresden pounds. But the strongest man could hardly have borne a crown of this weight upon his head for however short a time; and David could scarcely have placed it upon his own head. We must therefore assume that the account of the weight is not founded upon actual weighing, but simply upon an approximative estimate, which is somewhat too high. David also took a great quantity of booty out of the city.—Ver. 31. He also had the inhabitants executed, and that with cruel tortures. "*He sawed them in pieces with the saw and with iron harrows.*" וַיָּשֶׂם בַּמְּגֵרָה, " he put them into the saw," does not give any appropriate sense; and there can be no doubt, that instead of וישם we should read וַיָּשַׂר (from שׂוּר) : " he cut (sawed) them in pieces." וּבְמְגֵרוֹת הַבַּרְזֶל, "*and with iron cutting tools.*" The meaning of the ἀπ. λεγ. מְגֵרוֹת cannot be more precisely determined. The current rendering, " axes or hatchets," is simply founded upon the circumstance that גָּזַר, to cut, is applied in 2 Kings vi. 4 to the felling of trees. The reading in the Chronicles, וּבַמְּגֵרוֹת, is evidently a copyist's error, as we have already had בַּמְּגֵרָה, " with the saw." The meaning of the next clause is a disputed point, as the reading itself varies, and the Masoretes read בַּמַּלְבֵּן instead of the *Chethibh* במלבן, " he made them go through brick-kilns," *i.e.* burnt them in brick-kilns, as the LXX. and Vulgate render it. On the other hand, Thenius takes the *Chethibh* under his protection, and adopts Kimchi's explanation : " he led them through *Malchan, i.e.* through the place where the Ammonites burned their children in honour of their idol." Thenius would therefore alter בְּמַלְבָּן into בְּמַלְכָּם or בַּמִּלֹּם : " he offered them as sacrifices in their image of Moloch." But this explanation cannot be even grammatically sustained, to say nothing of the arbitrary character of the alteration proposed; for the technical expression הֶעֱבִיר בָּאֵשׁ לַמֹּלֶךְ, " to cause to go through the fire for Moloch " (Lev. xviii. 21), is essentially different from הֶעֱבִיר בַּמֹּלֶךְ, to cause to pass through Moloch, an expression that we never meet with. Moreover, it is impossible to see how burning the Ammonites in the image of Moloch could possibly be "an obvious mode of punishing idolatry," since the idolatry itself consisted in the fact that the Ammonites burned their children to Moloch. So far as the circumstances themselves are concerned, the cruelties inflicted upon the prisoners are not to be softened down, as Daaz and others propose, by an arbitrary perversion of the words into a mere sentence to hard labour, such as sawing wood, burning bricks, etc. At the same time, the words of the text do not affirm that *all* the inhabitants of Rabbah were put to death in this cruel manner. הָעָם אֲשֶׁר בָּהּ (without כֹּל) refers no doubt simply to the fighting men that were taken prisoners, or at the most to the male population of the acropolis of Rabbah, who probably consisted of fighting men only. In doing this, David merely retaliated upon the Ammonites the cruelties with which they had treated their foes; since according to Amos i. 13 they ripped up women who were with child, and according to 1 Sam. xi. 2 their king Nahash would only make peace with the inhabitants of Jabesh upon the condition that the right eye of every one of them should be put out. It is sufficiently evident from this, that the Ammonites had aimed at the most shameful extermination of the Israelites. "*Thus did he unto all the cities of the Ammonites,*" *i.e.* to all the fortified cities that resisted the Israelites. After the close of this war, David returned to Jerusalem with all the men of war. The war with the Syrians and Ammonites, including as it did the Edomitish war as well, was the fiercest in which David was ever engaged, and was also the last great war of his life.

AMNON'S INCEST, AND ABSALOM'S FRATRICIDE.—CHAP. XIII.

The judgments threatened to king David in consequence of his sin with Bathsheba soon began to fall upon him and upon his house, and were brought about by sins and crimes on the part of his own sons, for which David was himself to blame, partly because of his own indulgence and want of discipline, and partly because of the bad example that he had set them. Having grown up without strict paternal discipline, simply under the care of their different mothers, who were jealous of one another, his sons fancied that they might gratify their own fleshly lusts, and carry out their own ambitious plans; and from this there arose a series of crimes, which nearly cost the king his life and throne. Amnon, David's eldest son, led the way with his forcible violation of his step-sister Tamar (vers. 1-22). The crime was avenged by her own brother Absalom, who treacherously assassinated Amnon, in consequence of which he was obliged to flee to Geshur and take refuge with his father-in-law (vers. 23-39).

Vers. 1-22. AMNON'S INCEST.—Vers. 1-14. The following occurrences are assigned in a general manner to the times succeeding the Ammonitish war, by the words "*And it came to pass after this;*" and as David did not marry Maacah the mother of Absalom and Tamar till after he had been made king at Hebron (see ch. iii. 3), they cannot well have taken place before the twentieth year of his reign. *Amnon*, the eldest son of David by *Ahinoam* the Jezreelite (ch. iii. 2), loved Tamar, the beautiful sister of his step-brother Absalom, so passionately that he became ill in consequence, because he could not get near to her as she was a virgin. Vers. 1 and 2 form one period. וַיֵּצֶר is a continuation of וַיְהִי אַחֲרֵי־כֵן; and the words from וּלְאַבְשָׁלוֹם to בֶּן־דָּוִד are a circumstantial clause. וַיֵּצֶר: literally "it became narrow (anxious) to Amnon, even to making himself ill," *i.e.* he quite pined away, not "he pretended to be ill" (Luther), for it was not till afterwards that he did this according to Jonadab's advice (ver. 5). הִתְחַלּוֹת: to make one's self ill, here to become ill, in ver. 5 to pretend to be ill. The clause כִּי בְתוּלָה הִיא is to be joined to the one which follows: "*because she was a virgin, and it seemed impossible to him to do anything to her.*" The maidenly modesty of Tamar evidently raised an insuperable barrier to the gratification of his lusts.—Vers. 3-5. Amnon's miserable appearance was observed by his cousin Jonadab, a very crafty man, who asked him what was the reason, and then gave him advice as to the way in which he might succeed in gratifying his desires. *Shimeah* is called *Shammah* in 1 Sam. xvi. 9.—Ver. 4. "*Why art thou so wasting away* (דַּל, thin, spare, here equivalent to wasting away, looking miserable), *king's son, from morning to morning?*" *i.e.* day by day. "The morning" is mentioned because sick persons look worst in the morning. The advice given in ver. 5,—viz. "Lay thee down upon thy bed, and pretend to be ill; and when thy father comes to visit thee, say to him, May my sister Tamar come to me, and give me to eat?" etc.,—was very craftily devised, as Amnon's wretched appearance would favour his pretence that he was ill, and it might be hoped that an affectionate father would gratify him, since even if the wish seemed a strange one, it might easily be accounted for from the marvellous desires of persons who are ill, particularly with regard to food,—desires which it is often very difficult to gratify. —Vers. 6 sqq. Amnon acted upon the advice, and begged his father, when he came to ask him how he was, to allow his sister Tamar to come and bake two heart-cakes for him before his eyes, which she very speedily did. לִבֵּב is a *denom.* from לְבִבוֹת, to make or bake heart-cakes. לְבִבוֹת is a heart-strengthening kind of pastry, a kind of pancake, which could be very quickly made. It is evident from these verses that the king's children lived in different houses. Probably each of the king's wives lived with her children in one particular compartment of the palace.—Vers. 9 sqq. "And she took the pan and shook out (what she had prepared) before him. The ἀπ. λεγ. מַשְׂרֵת signifies a frying-pan or sauce-pan, according to the ancient versions. The etymology is uncertain. But Amnon refused to eat, and, like a whimsical patient, he then ordered all the men that were with him to go out; and when this had been done, he told Tamar to bring the food into the chamber, that he might eat it from her hand; and when she handed him the food, he laid hold of her, and said, "Come, lie with me, my sister!"—Vers. 12, 13. Tamar attempted to escape by pointing to the wickedness of such a desire: "Pray, do not, my brother, do not humble me; for they do not such things in Israel: do not this folly." The words recal Gen. xxxiv. 7, where the expression "folly" (*nebalah*) is first used to denote a want of chastity. Such a sin was altogether out of keeping with the calling and holiness of Israel (*vid.* Lev. xx. 8 sqq.). "*And I, whither should I carry my shame?*" *i.e.* shame and contempt would meet me everywhere. "*And thou wouldst be as one of the fools in Israel.*" We should both of us reap nothing but shame from it. What Tamar still further said, "*Now therefore, I pray thee, speak to the king, for he will not refuse me to thee,*" is no doubt at variance with the law which prohibits marriage between step-brothers and sisters (Lev. xviii. 9, 11, xx. 17); but it by no means proves that the laws of Leviticus were not in existence at the time, nor does it even presuppose that Tamar was ignorant of any such law. She simply said this, as Clericus observes, "that she might escape from his hands by any means in her power, and to avoid inflaming him still more and driving him to sin by precluding all hope of marriage."[1] We cannot therefore even infer from these words of hers, that she really thought the king could grant a dispensation from the existing hindrances to their marriage.—Ver. 14. Amnon would not listen to her, however, but overpowered her, forced her, and lay with her.

Vers. 15-22. Amnon had no sooner gratified his animal passion, than his love to the humbled sister turned into hatred, which was even greater than his (previous) love, so that he commanded her to get up and go. This sudden change, which may be fully explained from a psychological point of view, and is frequently exemplified still in actual life, furnishes a striking proof that lust is not love, but simply the gratification of the animal passions.—Ver. 16. Tamar replied, "*Do not become the cause of this great evil,* (which is) *greater than another that thou hast done to me, to thrust me away,*" *i.e.* do not add to the great wrong which thou hast done me the still greater one of thrusting me away. This is apparently the only admissible explanation of the difficult expression אַל־אֹדוֹת, as nothing more is needed than to supply תְּהִי. Tamar calls his sending her away a greater evil than the one already done to her, because it would inevitably be supposed that she had been guilty of some shameful conduct herself, that the seduction had come from her; whereas she was perfectly innocent, and had done nothing but what affection towards a sick brother dictated, whilst it was impossible for her to call for help (as prescribed in Deut. xxii. 27), because Amnon had sent the servants away, and Tamar could not in any case expect assistance from them.—Ver. 17. Amnon then called the boy who waited upon him, and ordered him to put out this person (the sister he had humbled), and to bolt the door behind her, so that it had the appearance of her having made a shameful proposal to him.—Ver. 18. Before stating that this command was obeyed, the writer inserts this

---

[1] Josephus adopts this explanation: "This she said, as desirous to avoid her brother's violent passion at present" (*Ant.* viii. 8, 1).

remark: "*She* (Tamar) *wore a long dress with sleeves* (see Gen. xxxvii. 3); *for in this manner did the virgin daughters of the king dress themselves with mantles.*" מְעִילִים is an accusative belonging to תִּלְבַּשְׁנָה, and the meaning is that the king's daughters, who were virgins, wore long dresses with sleeves as cloaks. The *cetoneth passim* was not an ordinary under-garment, but was worn over the plain *cetoneth* or tunic, and took the place of the ordinary *meïl* without sleeves. Notwithstanding this dress, by which a king's daughter could at once be recognised, Amnon's servant treated Tamar like a common woman, and turned her out of the house.—Ver. 19. And Tamar took ashes upon her head, rent her sleeve-dress (as a sign of grief and pain at the disgrace inflicted upon her), laid her hand upon her head (as a sign that a grievous trouble had come upon her, that the hand of God was resting as it were upon her: *vid.* Jer. ii. 37), and "*went going and cried,*" *i.e.* crying aloud as she went along.—Ver. 20. Then Absalom said to her, namely when she came home mourning in this manner, "*Has Amnon thy brother been with thee?*" This was a euphemism for what had taken place (cf. Gen. xxxix. 10), as Absalom immediately conjectured. "*And now, my sister, be silent; it is thy brother, do not take this thing to heart.*" Absalom quieted the sister, because he was determined to take revenge, but wished to conceal his plan of vengeance for the time. So Tamar remained in her brother's house, "*and indeed desolate,*" *i.e.* as one laid waste, with the joy of her life hopelessly destroyed. It cannot be proved that שֹׁמֵם ever means single or solitary.—Vers. 21, 22. When David heard "all these things," he became very wrathful; but Absalom did not speak to Amnon "*from good to evil*" (*i.e.* either good or evil, not a single word: Gen. xxiv. 50), because he hated him for having humbled his sister. The LXX. add to the words "he (David) was very wroth," the following clause: "He did not trouble the spirit of Amnon his son, because he loved him, for he was his first-born." This probably gives the true reason why David let such a crime as Amnon's go unpunished, when the law enjoined that incest should be punished with death (Lev. xx. 17); at the same time it is nothing but a subjective conjecture of the translators, and does not warrant us in altering the text. The fact that David was contented to be simply angry is probably to be accounted for partly from his own consciousness of guilt, since he himself had been guilty of adultery; but it arose chiefly from his indulgent affection towards his sons, and his consequent want of discipline. This weakness in his character bore very bitter fruit.

Vers. 23-39. ABSALOM'S REVENGE AND FLIGHT.—Vers. 23, 24. Absalom postponed his revenge for two full years. He then "*kept sheep-shearing,*" which was celebrated as a joyous festival (see 1 Sam. xxv. 2, 8), "*at Baal-Hazor, near Ephraim,*" where he must therefore have had some property. The situation of *Baal-Hazor* cannot be precisely determined. The clause "*which* (was) *beside Ephraim*" points to a situation on the border of the tribe-territory of Ephraim (*juxta Ephraim,* according to the *Onom. s.v. Baalasor*); for the Old Testament never mentions any city of that name. This definition does not exactly tally with v. Raumer's conjecture (*Pal.* p. 149), that *Baal-Hazor* may have been preserved in *Tell Asûr* (Rob. *Pal.* ii. p. 151, iii. p. 79); for this Tell is about five Roman miles to the north-east of Bethel, *i.e.* within the limits of the tribe of Ephraim. There is greater probability in the suggestion made by Ewald and others, that Baal-Hazor is connected with the *Hazor* of Benjamin (Neh. xi. 33), though the situation of Hazor has not yet been thoroughly decided; and it is merely a conjecture of Robinson's that it is to be found in *Tell Asûr*. The following statement, that "*Absalom invited all the king's sons* (*sc.* to the feast), somewhat anticipates the course of events; for, according to ver. 24, Absalom invited the king himself, together with his courtiers; and it was not till the king declined the invitation for himself, that Absalom restricted his invitation to the royal princes.—Ver. 25. The king declined the invitation, that he might not be burdensome to Absalom. Absalom pressed him indeed, but he would not go, and blessed him, *i.e.* wished him a pleasant and successful feast (see 1 Sam. xxv. 14). —Ver. 26. Then Absalom said, "*And not* (*i.e.* if thou dost not go), *may my brother Amnon go with me?*" The king would not give his consent to this; whether from suspicion cannot be determined with certainty, as he eventually yielded to Absalom's entreaties and let Amnon and all the other king's sons go. From the length of time that had elapsed since Amnon's crime was committed, without Absalom showing any wish for revenge,

David might have felt quite sure that he had nothing more to fear. But this long postponement of revenge, for the purpose of carrying it out with all the more certainty, is quite in the spirit of the East.—Ver. 28. Absalom then commanded his servants to put Amnon to death without fear, as he had commanded, as soon as his heart should become merry with wine and he (Absalom) should tell them to smite him. The arrangement of the meal is passed over as being quite subordinate to the main purpose of the narrative; and the clause added by the LXX. at the close of ver. 27, καὶ ἐποίησεν Ἀβεσσαλὼν πότον κατὰ τὸν πότον τοῦ βασιλέως, is nothing more than an explanatory gloss, formed according to 1 Sam. xxv. 36. The words "Have not I commanded you?" implied that Absalom would take the responsibility upon himself.—Ver. 29. The servants did as he commanded, whereupon the other king's sons all fled upon their mules.—Ver. 30. But whilst they were on the road, the report of what Absalom had done reached the ears of the king, and, as generally happens in such cases, with very great exaggeration: "*Absalom hath slain all the king's sons, and there is not one of them left.*"—Ver. 31. The king rent his clothes with horror at such a deed, and sat down upon the ground, and all his servants (courtiers) stood motionless by, with their clothes rent as well. This is the rendering adopted by Böttcher, as נִצָּב has frequently the idea of standing perfectly motionless (*e.g.* Num. xxii. 23, 24; Ex. v. 20, etc.).—Ver. 32. Then Jonadab, the same person who had helped Amnon to commit his crime, said, "*Let not my lord say* (or think) *that they have slain all the young men the king's sons, but Amnon alone is dead; for it was laid upon the mouth of Absalom from the day that he forced his sister Tamar.*" The meaning is either "they might see it (the murder of Amnon) by his mouth," or "they might gather it from what he said." הָיְתָה שׂוּמָה: it was a thing laid down, *i.e.* determined (*vid.* Ex. xxi. 13). The subject, viz. the thing itself, or the intended murder of Amnon, may easily be supplied from the context. כִּי אִם is undoubtedly used in the sense of "*no but.*" The negation is implied in the thought: Let the king not lay it to heart, that they say all the king's sons are dead; it is not so, but only Amnon is dead. Jonadab does not seem to speak from mere conjecture; he is much too sure of what he says. He might possibly have heard expressions from Absalom's lips which made him certain as to how the matter stood.—Ver. 34. "And Absalom fled." This statement follows upon ver. 29. When the king's sons fled upon their mules, Absalom also took to flight.—Vers. 30-33 are a parenthesis, in which the writer describes at once the impression made upon the king and his court by the report of what Absalom had done. The apparently unsuitable position in which this statement is placed may be fully explained from the fact, that the flight of Absalom preceded the arrival of the rest of the sons at the king's palace. The alteration which Böttcher proposes to make in the text, so as to remove this statement altogether on account of its unsuitable position, is proved to be inadmissible by the fact that the account of Absalom's flight cannot possibly be left out, as reference is made to it again afterwards (vers. 37, 38, "Absalom had fled"). The other alterations proposed by Thenius in the text of vers. 34, 37, 38, are just as arbitrary and out of place, and simply show that this critic was ignorant of the plan adopted by the historian. His plan is the following: To the account of the murder of Amnon, and the consequent flight of the rest of the king's sons whom Absalom had invited to the feast (ver. 29), there is first of all appended a notice of the report which preceded the fugitives and reached the king's ears in an exaggerated form, together with the impression which it made upon the king, and the rectification of that report by Jonadab (vers. 30-33). Then follows the statement that Absalom fled, also the account of the arrival of the king's sons (vers. 34-36). After this we have a statement as to the direction in which Absalom fled, the king's continued mourning, and the length of time that Absalom's banishment lasted (vers. 37, 38), and finally a remark as to David's feelings towards Absalom (ver. 39).

Jonadab's assertion, that Amnon only had been slain, was very speedily confirmed (ver. 34). The young man, the spy, *i.e.* the young man who was looking out for the return of those who had been invited to the feast, "lifted up his eyes and saw," *i.e.* saw as he looked out into the distance, "much people (a crowd of men) coming from the way behind him along the side of the mountain." מִדֶּרֶךְ אַחֲרָיו, ἐν τῇ ὁδῷ ὄπισθεν αὐτοῦ (LXX.), *per iter devium* (Vulg.), is obscure; and אַחַר, "behind," is probably to be understood as meaning "to the west:" from

the way at the back of the spy, *i.e.* to the west of his station. The following words, מִצַּד הָהָר, also remain obscure, as the position of the spy is not given, so that the allusion may be to a mountain in the north-west of Jerusalem quite as well as to one on the west.[1] When the spy observed the crowd of men approaching, Jonadab said to the king (ver. 35), " Behold, the king's sons are coming: as thy servant said, so has it come to pass."—Ver. 36. Jonadab had hardly said this when the king's sons arrived and wept aloud, *sc.* as they related what had occurred; whereupon the king and all his retainers broke out in loud weeping.—Ver. 37. " Only Absalom had fled and gone to Talmai the son of Ammihud, the king of Geshur." These words form a circumstantial clause, which the writer has inserted as a parenthesis, to define the expression " the king's sons " more particularly. If we take these words as a parenthesis, there will be no difficulty in explaining the following word "mourned," as the subject (David) may very easily be supplied from the preceding words " the king," etc. (ver. 36). To the remark that David mourned all his life for his son (Amnon), there is attached, just as simply and quite in accordance with the facts, the more precise information concerning Absalom's flight, that he remained in Geshur three years. The repetition of the words " Absalom had fled and gone to Geshur " may be accounted for from the general diffuseness of the Hebrew style. *Talmai* the king of *Geshur* was the father of *Maacah*, Absalom's mother (ch. iii. 3). The LXX. thought it necessary expressly to indicate this by inserting εἰς γῆν Χαμαχάαδ (al. γῆν Μαχάδ).
—Ver. 39. " *And it* (this) *held king David back from going out*

---

[1] The LXX. have very comprehensive additions here: first of all, after ἐκ πλευρᾶς τοῦ ὄρους, they have the more precise definition ἐν τῇ καταβάσει, and then the further clause, " and the spy came and announced to the king," "Ἄνδρας ἑώρακα ἐκ τῆς ὁδοῦ τῆς ὠρωνὴν (?) ἐκ μέρους τοῦ ὄρους, partly to indicate more particularly the way by which the king's sons came, and partly to fill up a supposed gap in the account. But they did not consider that the statement in ver. 35, " and Jonadab said to the king, Behold, the king's sons are coming," does not square with these additions; for if the spy had already informed the king that his sons were coming, there was no necessity for Jonadab to do it again. This alone is sufficient to show that the additions made by the LXX. are nothing but worthless glosses, introduced according to subjective conjectures and giving no foundation for alterations of the text.

to Absalom, for he comforted himself concerning Amnon, because he was dead." In adopting this translation of the difficult clause with which the verse commences, we take וַתְּכַל in the sense of בָּלָא, as the verbs בלה and כלא frequently exchange their forms; we also take the third pers. fem. as the neuter impersonal, so that the subject is left indefinite, and is to be gathered from the context. Absalom's flight to Geshur, and his stay there, were what chiefly prevented David from going out to Absalom. Moreover, David's grief on account of Amnon's death gradually diminished as time rolled on. צֵאת אֶל־אבש׳ is used in a hostile sense, as in Deut. xxviii. 7, to go out and punish him for his wickedness. The כִּי before נִחַם might also be rendered "*but*," as after a negative clause, as the principal sentence implies a negation: "*He did not go out against Absalom, but comforted himself.*" There is not only no grammatical difficulty in the way of this explanation of the verse, but it also suits the context, both before and after. All the other explanations proposed are either at variance with the rules of the language, or contain an unsuitable thought. The old Jewish interpretation (adopted in the Chaldee version, and also by the Rabbins), viz. David longed (his soul pined) to go out to Absalom (*i.e.* to see or visit him), is opposed, as Gusset has shown (in his *Lex.* pp. 731-2), to the conduct of David towards Absalom as described in ch. xiv.,—namely, that after Joab had succeeded by craft in bringing him back to Jerusalem, David would not allow him to come into his presence for two whole years (ch. xiv. 24, 28). Luther's rendering, "and king David left off going out against Absalom," is not only precluded by the feminine תְּכַל, but also by the fact that nothing has been said about any pursuit of Absalom on the part of David. Other attempts at emendations there is no need whatever to refute.

ABSALOM'S RETURN, AND RECONCILIATION TO THE KING.—
CHAP. XIV.

As David did not repeal the banishment of Absalom, even after he had comforted himself for Amnon's death, Joab endeavoured to bring him back to Jerusalem by stratagem (vers. 1-20); and when this succeeded, he proceeded to effect his reconciliation to the king (vers. 21-33). He may have been induced to take these steps partly by his personal attachment to Absalom, but the principal reason no doubt was that Absalom had the best prospect of succeeding to the throne, and Joab thought this the best way to secure himself from punishment for the murder which he had committed. But the issue of events frustrated all such hopes. Absalom did not succeed to the throne, Joab did not escape punishment, and David was severely chastised for his weakness and injustice.

Vers. 1–20. When Joab perceived that the king's heart was against Absalom, he sent for a cunning woman from Tekoah, to work upon the king and change his mind, so that he might grant forgiveness to Absalom. Ver. 1 is understood by the majority of commentators, in accordance with the Syriac and Vulgate, as signifying that Joab learned that the king's heart was inclined towards Absalom, was well disposed towards him again. But this explanation is neither philologically sustained, nor in accordance with the context. לֵב, written with עַל and without any verb, so that הָיָה has to be supplied, only occurs again in Dan. xi. 28, where the preposition has the meaning "*against*." It is no argument against this meaning here, that if David had been ill disposed towards Absalom, there would have been no necessity to state that Joab perceived it; for we cannot see why Joab should only have perceived or noticed David's friendly feelings, and not his unfriendly feelings as well. If, however, Joab had noticed the re-awakening of David's good feelings towards Absalom, there would have been no necessity for him to bring the cunning woman from Tekoah to induce him to consent to Absalom's return. Moreover, David would not in that case have refused to allow Absalom to see his face for two whole years after his return to Jerusalem (ver. 24). *Tekoah*, the home of the prophet Amos, the present *Tekua*, two hours to the south of Bethlehem (see at Josh. xv. 59, LXX.). The "wise woman" was to put on mourning, as a woman who had been mourning for a long while for some one that was dead (הִתְאַבֵּל, to set or show herself mourning), and to go to the king in this attire, and say what Joab had put into her mouth.—Ver. 4. The woman did this. All the old translators have given as the rendering of וַתֹּאמֶר הָאִשָּׁה "the woman came (went) to the king," as if they had read וַתָּבֹא. This reading is actually found in some thirty *Codd.* of De Rossi, and is therefore regarded by Thenius and the majority of critics as the original one. But Böttcher has very justly urged, in opposition to this, that וַתֹּאמֶר cannot possibly be an accidental corruption of וַתָּבֹא, and that it is still less likely that such an alteration should have been intentionally made. But this remark, which is correct enough in itself, cannot sustain the conjecture which Böttcher has founded upon it, namely that two whole lines have dropt out of the Hebrew text, containing the answer which the woman of Tekoah gave to Joab before she went to the king, since there is not one of the ancient versions which contains a single word more than the Masoretic text. Consequently we must regard וַתֹּאמֶר as the original reading, and interpret it as a *hysteron-proteron*, which arose from the fact that the historian was about to relate at once what the woman said to the king, but thought it desirable to mention her falling down at the feet of the king before giving her actual words, "*Help, O king,*" which he introduces by repeating the word וַתֹּאמֶר.—Vers. 5 sqq. When the king asked her, "What aileth thee?" the woman described the pretended calamity which had befallen her, saying that she was a widow, and her two sons had quarrelled in the field; and as no one interposed, one of them had killed the other. The whole family had then risen up and demanded that the survivor should be given up, that they might carry out the avenging of blood upon him. Thus they sought to destroy the heir also, and extinguish the only spark that remained to her, so as to leave her husband neither name nor posterity upon the earth. The suffix attached to וַיַּכּוֹ, with the object following ("he smote him, the other," ver. 6), may be explained from the diffuseness of the style of ordinary conversation (see at 1 Sam. xxi. 14). There is no reason whatever for changing the reading into יַכּוּ, as the suffix וֹ, though unusual with verbs ל"ה, is not without parallel; not to mention the fact that the plural יַכּוּ is quite unsuitable. There is also quite as little reason for changing וְנִשְׁמִידָה into וְיַשְׁמִידוּ, in accordance with the Syriac and Arabic, as Michaelis and Thenius propose, on the ground that "the woman would have described her relatives as diabolically malicious men, if she had put into their mouths such words as these, 'We will destroy the heir also.'" It was the woman's intention to describe the conduct of the relations and their pursuit of blood-revenge in the harshest terms possible, in order that she might obtain help from the king. She begins to speak in her own name at the word וְכִבּוּ ("and so they shall quench and"), where she resorts to a figure, for the purpose of appealing to the heart of the king to defend her from the threatened destruction of her family, saying, "And so they shall quench the burning coal which is left." גַּחֶלֶת is used figuratively, like τὸ ζώπυρον, the burning coal with which one kindles a fresh fire, to denote the last remnant. לְבִלְתִּי שׂוּם : "*so as not to set,*" *i.e.* to preserve or leave name and remnant (*i.e.* posterity) to my husband.

This account differed, no doubt, from the case of Absalom, inasmuch as in his case no murder had taken place in the heat of a quarrel, and no avenger of blood demanded his death; so that the only resemblance was in the fact that there existed an intention to punish a murderer. But it was necessary to disguise the affair in this manner, in order that David might not detect her purpose, but might pronounce a decision out of pity for the poor widow which could be applied to his own conduct towards Absalom.—Ver. 8. The plan succeeded. The king replied to the woman, "*Go home, I will give charge concerning thee,*" *i.e.* I will give the necessary commands that thy son may not be slain by the avenger of blood. This declaration on the part of the king was perfectly just. If the brothers had quarrelled, and one had killed the other in the heat of the quarrel, it was right that he should be defended from the avenger of blood, because it could not be assumed that there was any previous intention to murder. This declaration therefore could not be applied as yet to David's conduct towards Absalom. But the woman consequently proceeded to say (ver. 9), "My lord, O king, let the guilt be upon me and upon my father's house, and let the king and his throne be guiltless." כִּסֵּא, the throne, for the government or reign. The meaning of the words is this: but if there should be anything wrong in the fact that this bloodshed is not punished, let the guilt fall upon me and my family. The king replied (ver. 10), "*Whosoever speaketh to thee, bring him to me; he shall not touch thee any more.*" אֵלַיִךְ does not stand for עָלַיִךְ, "against thee;" but the meaning is, whoever speaks to thee any more about this, *i.e.* demands thy son of thee again.—Ver. 11. The crafty woman was not yet satisfied with this, and sought by repeating her petition to induce the king to confirm his promise on oath, that she might bind him the more firmly. She therefore said still further: "*I pray thee, let the king remember Jehovah thy God, that the avenger of blood may no more prepare destruction, and that they may not destroy my son.*" The *Chethib* הרבית is probably a copyist's error for הַרְבּוֹת, for which the Masoretes would write הַרְבַּת, the construct state of הַרְבָּה,—a form of the inf. abs. which is not commonly used, and which may possibly have been chosen because הַרְבֵּה had become altogether an adverb (*vid.* Ewald, § 240, *e*). The context requires the inf. constr. הַרְבּוֹת: that the avenger of blood may not multiply (make much) to destroy, *i.e.* may not add to the destruction; and הַרְבִּית is probably only a verbal noun used instead of the infinitive. The king immediately promised on oath that her son should not suffer the least harm.—Vers. 12, 13. When the woman had accomplished so much, she asked permission to speak one word more; and having obtained it, proceeded to the point she wanted to reach: "*And wherefore thinkest thou such things against people of God? And because the king speaketh this word, he is as one inculpating himself, since the king does not let his own rejected one return.*" כְּאָשֵׁם, "like one who has laden himself with guilt," is the predicate to the clause וּמִדַּבֵּר וגו׳. These words of the woman were intentionally kept indefinite, rather hinting at what she wished to place before the king, than expressing it distinctly. This is more particularly applicable to the first clause, which needs the words that follow to render it intelligible, as חָשַׁבְתָּה כָּזֹאת is ambiguous; so that Dathe and Thenius are wrong in rendering it, "Why dost thou propose such things towards the people of God?" and understanding it as relating to the protection which the king was willing to extend to her and to her son. חָשַׁב with עַל does not mean to think or reflect "with regard to," but "*against*" a person. Ewald is quite correct in referring the word כָּזֹאת to what follows: such things, *i.e.* such thoughts as thou hast towards thy son, whose blood-guiltiness thou wilt not forgive. עַל־עַם אֱלֹהִים, without the article, is intentionally indefinite, "against people of God," *i.e.* against members of the congregation of God. "*This word*" refers to the decision which the king had pronounced in favour of the widow לְבִלְתִּי הָשִׁיב, literally, in not letting him return.

In order to persuade the king to forgive, the crafty woman reminded him (ver. 14) of the brevity of human life and of the mercy of God: "*For we must die, and* (are) *as water spilt upon the ground, which is not* (cannot be) *gathered up, and God does not take a soul away, but thinks thoughts, that He may not thrust from Him one expelled.*" Although these thoughts are intentionally expressed quite generally, their special allusion to the case in hand can easily be detected. We must all die, and when dead our life is irrevocably gone. Thou mightest soon experience this in the case of Absalom, if thou shouldst suffer him to continue in exile. God does not act thus; He does not deprive the sinner of life, but is merciful, and does not cast off for ever.—Ver. 15. After these allusions to David's treatment of Absalom, the woman returned again to her own affairs, to make the king believe that nothing but her own distress had led her to speak thus: "*And now that I have come to speak this word to the king my lord, was* (took place) *because the people have put me in fear* (sc. by their demand that I should give up my son to the avenger of blood); *thy handmaid said* (*i.e.* thought), *I will indeed go to the king, perhaps the king will do his handmaid's word,*" *i.e.* grant her request.—Ver. 16. "*Yea, the king will hear, to save his handmaid out of the hand of the man that would destroy me and my son from the inheritance of God.*" אֲשֶׁר must be supplied before לְהַשְׁמִיד: who is to destroy, *i.e.* who is seeking to destroy (*vid.* Gesenius, § 132, 3). "The inheritance of God" was the nation of Israel (as in 1 Sam. xxvi. 19; cf. Deut. xxxii. 9).—Ver. 17. "*Then thine handmaid thought, may the word of my lord the king be for rest* (*i.e.* tend to give me rest); *for as the angel of God* (the angel of the covenant, the mediator of the blessings of divine grace to the covenant-nation), *so is my lord the king to hear good and evil* (*i.e.* listening to every just complaint on the part of his subjects, and granting help to the oppressed), *and Jehovah thy God be with thee!*"—Vers. 18 sqq. These words of the woman were so well considered and so crafty, that the king could not fail to see both what she really meant, and also that she had not come with her petition of her own accord. He therefore told her to answer the question without disguise: whether the hand of Joab was with her in all this. She replied, "*Truly there is not* (אִם) *anything to the right hand or to the left of all that my lord the king saith,"* i.e. the king always hits the right point in everything that he says. *" Yea, thy servant Joab, he hath commanded me, and he hath put all these words into thy servant's mouth."* אֵשׁ is not a copyist's error, but a softer form of יֵשׁ, as in Micah vi. 10 (*vid.* Ewald, § 53c, and Olshausen, *Gramm.* p. 425).—Ver. 20. *" To turn the appearance of the king* (i.e. to disguise the affair in the finest way) *Joab hath done this; my lord* (i.e. the king), *however, is wise, like the wisdom of the angel of God, to know all that is* (happens) *upon earth."* She hoped by these flattering words to gain the king completely over.

Vers. 21-33. David then promised Joab, that the request which he had presented through the medium of the woman of Tekoah should be fulfilled, and commanded him to fetch Absalom back. The *Chethib* עָשִׂיתִי (ver. 21) is the correct reading, and the *Keri* עָשִׂיתָה has arisen from a misunderstanding. —Ver. 22. Joab thanked the king for this, and blessed him: *" To-day thy servant knoweth that I have found grace in thy sight, my lord, O king, in that the king hath fulfilled the request of his servant."* It is pretty evident from this, that Joab had frequently applied to David for Absalom's return, without any attention being paid to his application. David therefore suspected that Joab had instructed the woman of Tekoah. The *Chethib* עַבְדוֹ is not to be exchanged for the *Keri* עַבְדֶּךָ.— Ver. 23. Joab then went to *Geshur* (see ch. xiii. 37), and fetched Absalom back to Jerusalem.—Ver. 24. But David could not forgive Absalom altogether. He said to Joab, *" Let him turn to his own house, and my face he shall not see."* This half forgiveness was an imprudent measure, and bore very bitter fruit. The further account of Absalom is introduced in vers. 25-27 with a description of his personal appearance and family affairs.—Ver. 25. There was no man in all Israel so handsome as Absalom. לְהַלֵּל מְאֹד, *" to much praising,"* i.e. so that he was greatly praised. From the sole of the foot even to the crown of his head, there was no fault (מוּם, bodily blemish) in him.— Ver. 26. *" When he polled his head, and it took place from year to year that he polled it; for it became heavy upon him* (too heavy for him), *and so he polled it: they weighed the hair of his head, two hundred shekels by the king's weight."* A strong growth of hair was a sign of great manly power, and so far a proof of

Absalom's beauty. The statement as to the weight of the hair cut off, viz. two hundred shekels, is in any case a round number, and much too high, although we do not know what the difference between the royal and the sacred shekel really was According to the sacred reckoning, two hundred shekels would be about six pounds; so that if we were to assume that the royal shekel was about half the other, the number would be still much too high. It is evident, therefore, that there is an error in the text, such as we frequently meet with in the case of numbers, though we have no means of rectifying it, as all the ancient versions contain the same number.—Ver. 27. Unto Absalom there were born three sons, and one daughter named Tamar, who was beautiful in figure. Contrary to general usage, the names of the sons are not given, in all probability for no other reason than because they died in infancy. Consequently, as Absalom had no sons, he afterwards erected a pillar to preserve his name (ch. xviii. 18). The daughter's name is probably given as a proof of Absalom's great affection for his sister Tamar, whom Amnon had violated.[1]—Vers. 28–30. After Absalom had sat for two whole years in his house at Jerusalem without seeing the king's face, he sent to Joab that he might obtain for him the king's full forgiveness. But as Joab would not come to him, even after he had sent for him twice, Absalom commanded his servants to set fire to one of Joab's fields which adjoined his own and was then full of barley, for the purpose of compelling him to come, as he foresaw that Joab would not take this destruction of his property quietly, but would come to him to complain. אֶל יָדִי, literally "at my hand," i.e. by the side of my field or property. The *Chethib* וְהוֹצִיתִיהָ ("come, I will set it on fire") is a *Hiphil* formation, according to verbs יִ"פ, for which the *Keri* has וְהַצִּיתוּהָ, the ordinary *Hiphil* form of יָצַת in the second person plural, "go and set it on fire."— —Vers. 31, 32. When Joab came to Absalom's house in conse-

---

[1] The LXX. have this additional clause, καὶ γίνεται γυνὴ Ῥοβοὰμ υἱῷ Σαλωμὼν καὶ τίκτει αὐτῷ τὸν Ἀβιά (and she became the wife of Rehoboam the son of Solomon, and bore him a son named Abia). Although this is quite at variance with 1 Kings xv. 2, where it is stated that the wife of Rehoboam and mother of Abia (Abijam) was named *Maacah*, the clause has been adopted by Thenius, who regards it as original, though for reasons which Böttcher has shown to be worthless.

quence of this, and complained of it, Absalom said to him, "See, I have sent to thee, to say to thee, Come hither, and I will send thee to the king, to say to him, Wherefore have I come from Geshur? it were better for me that I were there still: and now I will see the king's face; and if there is any iniquity in me, let him put me to death." This half forgiving was really worse than no forgiveness at all. Absalom might indeed very properly desire to be punished according to the law, if the king could not or might not forgive him; although the manner in which he sought to obtain forgiveness by force manifested an evident spirit of defiance, by which, with the well-known mildness of David's temper, he hoped to attain his object, and in fact did attain it. For (ver. 33) when Joab went to the king, and announced this to him, the king sent for Absalom, and kissed him, as a sign of his restoration to favour. Nothing was said by Absalom about forgiveness; for his falling down before the king when he came into his presence, was nothing more than the ordinary manifestation of reverence with which a subject in the East approaches his king.

ABSALOM'S REBELLION AND DAVID'S FLIGHT.—
CHAP. XV.–XVI. 14.

After his restoration to favour, Absalom soon began to aspire to the throne, setting up a princely court, and endeavouring to turn the hearts of the people towards himself, by addressing in a friendly manner any who came to seek redress from the king in matters in dispute, and by saying things adapted to throw suspicion upon his father's rule (vers. 1–6). When he had succeeded in this, he asked permission from the king to take a journey to Hebron, under the pretence of wanting to fulfil a vow which he had made during his banishment; and when once there, he soon proceeded with his rebellious intentions (vers. 7–12). As soon as David heard of it, he determined to fly from Jerusalem, and crossed the Kidron with his faithful adherents. Having sent the priests with the ark of the covenant back to the city, he went up to the Mount of Olives, amidst the loud lamentations of the people. Hushai, who came to meet him, he sent to the city, to frustrate the counsel of Ahithophel, who was one of the conspirators, and to send information to him of what was going forward (vers. 13–37). When he reached the top, Ziba, Mephibosheth's servant, came to meet him with provisions and succour (ch. xvi. 1-4); whilst Shimei, a relation of the house of Saul, followed him with curses and stones (vers. 5–14).

With this rebellion the calamities which Nathan had predicted to David on account of his sin with Bathsheba began to burst upon him in all their fulness. The success of the rebellion itself may be accounted for, from the fact that the consciousness of his own fault not only made David weak towards his sons, but produced a want of firmness in his resolutions; whilst the imperfections and defects in the internal administration of the kingdom, when the time of the brilliant victories was past, became more and more perceptible to the people, and furnished occasion for dissatisfaction with his government, which Absalom was skilful enough to bend to his own purposes. During the time that this rebellion was in progress, David poured out his lamentations to the Lord (in Ps. xli. and lv.) as to the faithlessness of his most confidential councillors, and prayed for the judgment of retribution upon the conduct of this wicked band. After it had broken out, he uttered his longings to return to the sanctuary at Jerusalem, and his firm confidence that he should be delivered out of his distresses and reinstated in his kingdom, first of all in Ps. iii. and lxiii. during his flight in the desert of Judah, and in Ps. lxi. and lxii. during his stay in the land to the east of the Jordan.

Vers. 1-6. *Absalom seeks to secure the people's favour.*— Ver. 1. Soon afterwards (this seems to be the meaning of מֵאַחֲרֵי כֵן as distinguished from אַחֲרֵי כֵן; cf. ch. iii. 28) Absalom set up a carriage (*i.e.* a state-carriage; cf. 1 Sam. viii. 11) and horses, and fifty men as runners before him, *i.e.* to run before him when he drove out, and attract the attention of the people by a display of princely pomp, as Adonijah afterwards did (1 Kings i. 5). He then went early in the morning to the side of the road to the gate of the palace, and called out to every one who was about to go to the king " for judgment," *i.e.* seek justice in connection with any matter in dispute, and asked him, " Of what city art thou ?" and also, as we may see from the reply in ver. 3, inquired into his feelings towards the king, and then said, " Thy matters are good and right, but there is no hearer for thee with the king." שֹׁמֵעַ signifies the judicial officer, who heard complainants and examined into their different causes, for the purpose of laying them before the king for settlement. Of course the king himself could not give a hearing to every complainant, and make a personal investigation of his cause; nor could his judges procure justice for every complainant, however justly they might act, though it is possible that they may not always have performed their duty conscientiously.—Ver. 4. Absalom also said, "*Oh that I might be judge in the land, and every one who had a cause might come before me; I would procure him justice!*" מִי יְשִׂמֵנִי is a wish: "who might (*i.e.* oh that one might) appoint me judge," an analogous expression to מִי יִתֵּן (*vid.* Gesenius, § 136, 1, and Ewald, § 329, *c*). עָלַי placed before יָבֹא for the sake of emphasis, may be explained from the fact that a judge sat, so that the person who stood before him rose above him (comp. Ex. xviii. 13 with Gen. xviii. 8). הִצְדִּיק, to speak justly, or help to justice.—Ver. 5. *And when any one came near to him to prostrate himself before him, he took him by the hand and kissed him.* It was by conduct of this kind that Agamemnon is said to have secured the command of the Grecian army (Euripid. *Iphig. Aul.* v. 337 sqq.).—Ver. 6. Thus Absalom stole the heart of the men of Israel. גָּנַב לֵב does not mean to deceive or cheat, like גָּנַב לֵב in the *Kal* in Gen. xxxi. 20, but to steal the heart, *i.e.* to bring a person over to his side secretly and by stratagem.

Vers. 7–12. *Absalom's rebellion.*—Vers. 7, 8. After the lapse of forty (?) years Absalom said to the king, "*Pray I will go* (*i.e.* pray allow me to go) *and perform a vow in Hebron which I vowed to the Lord during my stay at Geshur*" (ver. 8). The number forty is altogether unsuitable, as it cannot possibly be understood either as relating to the age of Absalom or to the year of David's reign: for Absalom was born at Hebron after David had begun to reign, and David only reigned forty years and a half in all, and Absalom's rebellion certainly did not take place in the last few weeks of his reign. It is quite as inappropriate to assume, as the *terminus a quo* of the forty years, either the commencement of Saul's reign, as several of the Rabbins have done, as well as the author of the marginal note in *Cod.* 380 of De Rossi (למלכות שאול), or the anointing of David at Bethlehem, as Luther (in the marginal note) and Lightfoot do; for the word "*after*" evidently refers to some event in the life of Absalom, to which allusion has previously been made, namely, either to the time of his reconciliation with David (ch. xiv. 33), or (what is not so probable) to the period of his return from Geshur to Jerusalem (ch. xiv. 23). Consequently the reading adopted by the Syriac, Arabic, and Vulgate, also by Theodoret and others, viz. "*four* years," must certainly be the correct one, and not "forty days," which we find in Codd. 70 and 96 in Kennicott, since forty days would be far too short a time for maturing the rebellion. It is true, that with the reading אַרְבַּע we should expect, as a rule, the plural שָׁנִים. At the same time, the numbers from two to ten are sometimes construed with a singular noun (*e.g.* 2 Kings xxii. 1; cf. Gesenius, § 120, 2). The pretended vow was, that if Jehovah would bring him back to Jerusalem, he would serve Jehovah. עָבַד אֶת־יְהוָֹה, "to do a service to Jehovah," can only mean to offer a sacrifice, which is the explanation given by Josephus. The *Chethib* יָשִׁיב is not the infinitive, but the imperfect *Hiphil: si reduxerit, reduxerit me*, which is employed in an unusual manner instead of the *inf. absol.*, for the sake of emphasis. The *Keri* יָשׁוּב would have to be taken as an adverb "again;" but this is quite unnecessary.—Ver. 9. The king consented, and Absalom went to Hebron. Absalom had selected this city, probably assigning as the reason that he was born there, but really because his father David had been made king there, and also possibly because there may have been many persons there who had been displeased by the removal of the court to Jerusalem.—Ver. 10. When Absalom went to Hebron, he sent spies into all the tribes of Israel to say, "*When ye hear the sound of the trumpet, say, Absalom has become king in Hebron.*" We must suppose the sending of the spies to have been contemporaneous with the removal of Absalom to Hebron, so that וַיִּשְׁלַח is used quite regularly, and there is no reason for translating it as a pluperfect. The messengers sent out are called "spies," because they were first of all to ascertain the feelings of the people in the different tribes, and were only to execute their commission in places where they could reckon upon support. The conspiracy had hitherto been kept very secret, as we may see from the statement in ver. 11: "*With Absalom there had gone two hundred men out of Jerusalem, invited* (to the sacrificial festival), *and going in their simplicity, who knew nothing at all of the affair.*" (לֹא כָל־דָּבָר: nothing at all.)—Ver. 12. Moreover, Absalom sent for Ahithophel, David's councillor, to come from his own town Giloh, when he offered the sacrifices. The unusual construction of שָׁלַח אֶת with מֵעִירוֹ may be explained from the pregnant character of the expression: he sent and bade come, *i.e.* he summoned Ahithophel out of his city. *Giloh*, Ahithophel's home, was upon the mountains of Judah, to the south or south-west of Hebron (see at Josh. xv. 51). Ahithophel had no doubt been previously initiated into Absalom's plans, and had probably gone to his native city, merely that he might come to him with the greater ease; since his general place of abode, as king's councillor, must have been in Jerusalem. "*And the conspiracy became strong; for the people multiplied continually with Absalom*" (the latter is a circumstantial clause). These words give a condensed summary of the result of the enterprise.

Vers. 13–21. *David's flight from Jerusalem.*—Vers. 13, 14. When this intelligence reached David, "*The heart of the men of Israel is after Absalom*" (הָיָה אַחַר, as in ch. ii. 10, to be attached to a person as king; see at 1 Sam. xii. 14), he said to his servants that were with him in Jerusalem, "*Arise, let us flee, for there will be no escape for us from Absalom! Make speed to depart, lest he overtake us suddenly, and drive the calamity* (the judgment threatened in ch. xii. 10, 11) *over us, and smite the city with the edge of the sword.*" David was perhaps afraid that Jerusalem might fall into Absalom's power through treachery, and therefore resolved to fly as speedily as possible, not only in order to prevent a terrible massacre, but also to give his own faithful adherents time to assemble.— Vers. 15, 16. As his servants declared themselves ready to follow him, the king went out of the city with all his family in his train (*lit.* at his feet, as in Judg. iv. 10, 15, etc.), but left ten concubines behind to keep the palace.—Ver. 17. When outside the city the king and all the people in his suite (*i.e.* the royal family and their servants) halted at "the house of the distance." הַמֶּרְחָק is probably a proper name given to a house in the neighbourhood of the city and on the road to Jericho, which was called "the farthest house," viz. from the city.—

2 D

Ver. 18. And all his servants, *i.e.* his state officers and attendants, went along by his side, and the whole body-guard (the *Crethi* and *Plethi*: see at ch. viii. 18); and all the Gathites, namely the six hundred men who had come in his train from Gath, went along in front of the king. David directed the fugitives to fall into rank, the servants going by his side, and the body-guard and the six hundred old companions in arms, who probably also formed a kind of body-guard, marching in front. The verb עָבַר (passed on) cannot be understood as signifying to defile past on account of its connection with עַל־יָדוֹ (beside him, or by his side). The expression *Gittim* is strange, as we cannot possibly think of actual Gathites or Philistines from Gath. The apposition (the six hundred men, etc.) shows clearly enough that the six hundred old companions in arms are intended, the men who gathered round David on his flight from Saul and emigrated with him to Gath (1 Sam. xxvii. 2, 3), who afterwards lived with him in Ziklag (1 Sam. xxvii. 8, xxix. 2, xxx. 1, 9), and eventually followed him to Hebron and Jerusalem (ch. ii. 3, v. 6). In all probability they formed a separate company of well-tried veterans or a kind of body-guard in Jerusalem, and were commonly known as *Gathites*.[1]—Ver. 19. A military commander named *Ittai*, who had emigrated from Gath and come over to David not long before, also accompanied the king from the city. It is evident from ch. xviii. 2, where Ittai is said to have commanded a third part of the army sent against Absalom, and to have been placed on an equality with Joab and Abishai the most experienced generals, that Ittai was a Philistian general who had entered David's service. The reason for his going over to David is not known. According to ver. 22 of this chapter, Ittai did not come alone, but brought all his family with him (*taph*: the little ones). The opinion expressed by

---

[1] The Septuagint also has πάντες οἱ Γεθαῖοι, and has generally rendered the Masoretic text correctly. But כָּל־עֲבָדָיו has been translated incorrectly, or at all events in a manner likely to mislead, viz. πάντες οἱ παῖδες αὐτοῦ. But in the Septuagint text, as it has come down to us, another paraphrase has been interpolated into the literal translation, which Thenius would adopt as an emendation of the Hebrew text, notwithstanding the fact that the critical corruptness of the Alexandrian text must be obvious to every one.

Thenius, that he had come to Jerusalem as a hostage, is merely founded upon a false interpretation of the last two clauses of the verse before us. David said to Ittai, "*Wherefore goest thou also with us? return and stay with the king; for thou art a stranger, and also emigrating to thy place.*" There is no irony in the words "stay with the king," as Thenius and Clericus suppose (viz. "with the man who behaves as if he were king"); nor is there an acknowledgment of Absalom as king, which certainly could never have emanated from David. The words contain nothing more than the simple thought: Do you remain with whoever is or shall be king, since there is no necessity for you as a stranger to take sides at all. This is the explanation given by Seb. Schmidt: "It is not your place to decide this contest as to who ought to be king; but you may remain quiet and see whom God shall appoint as king, and whether it be I or Absalom, you can serve the one that God shall choose." This is the only way in which we can explain the reason assigned for the admonition, viz. "Thou art a stranger," and not an Israelite. There is some difficulty connected with the following words (rendered in the Eng. version "and also an exile"). In the Septuagint and Vulgate they are rendered καὶ ὅτι μετῴκησας σὺ ἐκ τοῦ τόπου σου, *et egressus es de loco tuo* (and thou hast gone out from thine own place); but in adopting this rendering the translators have not only passed over the גַּם (also), but have taken לִמְקוֹמְךָ for מִמְּקוֹמְךָ. Nevertheless Thenius proposes to bring the text into harmony with these versions for the purpose of bringing out the meaning, "and moreover thou art one carried away from his own home." But this is decidedly a mistake; for David would never have made a Philistine—who had just before been carried away from his own home, or, as Thenius understands it, who had been brought to Jerusalem as a hostage—the commander of a third of his army. The meaning is rather the following: "And thou hast still no fatherland," *i.e.* thou art still wandering about through the earth like an exile from his country: wherever thou findest a place, and art allowed to settle, there only canst thou dwell.—Ver. 20. "*Thy coming is yesterday* (from yesterday), *and should I disturb thee to-day to go with us, when I am going just where I go?*" *i.e.* wherever my way may lie (I go I know not whither; Chald.: cf. 1 Sam. xxiii. 13). The

Chethib אֲנִיעֲךָ is a copyist's error. The thought requires the *Hiphil* אֲנִיעֲךָ (*Keri*), as נוּעַ in the *Kal* has the intransitive meaning, to totter, sway about, or move hither and thither. "*Return and take thy brethren back; grace and truth be with thee.*" It is evidently more in accordance with the train of thought to separate עִמָּךְ from the previous clause and connect it with חֶסֶד וֶאֱמֶת, though this is opposed to the accents, than to adopt the adverbial interpretation, "take back thy brethren with thee in grace and truth," as Maurer proposes. (For the thought itself, see Prov. iii. 3.) The reference is to the grace and truth (faithfulness) of God, which David desired that Ittai should receive upon his way. In the Septuagint and Vulgate the passage is paraphrased thus: "Jehovah show thee grace and truth," after ch. ii. 6; but it by no means follows from this that יְהוָֹה יַעֲשֶׂה עִמָּךְ has fallen out of the Hebrew text. —Ver. 21. But Ittai replied with a solemn oath, "*Assuredly at the place where my lord the king shall be* (stay), *whether for death or life, there will thy servant be.*" כִּי אִם means "*only*," as in Gen. xl. 14, Job xlii. 8; here, in a declaration on oath, it is equivalent to *assuredly* (vid. Ewald, § 356, *b*). The *Chethib* is therefore correct, and the erasure of אִם in the *Keri* is a bad emendation. The כִּי in the apodosis is either an emphatic declaration, *yea*, or like ὅτι merely introduces a distinct assertion.—Ver. 22. After this assurance of his devotedness, David let Ittai do as he pleased. לֵךְ וַעֲבֹר, "go and pass on." עָבַר does not mean to pass by, but to go forward. Thus Ittai and his men and all his family that was with him went forward with the king. By "the little ones" (*taph*) we are to understand a man's whole family, as in many other instances (see at Ex. xii. 37).

Vers. 22–29. *The king crosses the Kidron, and sends the priests back with the ark to Jerusalem.*—Ver. 23. All the land (as in 1 Sam. xiv. 25) wept aloud when all the people went forward; and the king went over the brook Kidron, and all the people went over in the direction of (*lit.* in the face of) the way to the desert. The brook *Kidron* is a winter torrent, *i.e.* a mountain torrent which only flows during the heavy rains of winter (χείμαρρος τοῦ Κεδρών, John xviii. 1). It is on the eastern side of Jerusalem, between the city and the Mount of Olives, and derives its name from the appearance of the water when rendered muddy through the melting of the snow (cf. Job vi. 16). In summer it is nothing more than a dry channel in the valley of Jehoshaphat (see Robinson, *Pal.* i. 396, and v. Raumer, *Pal.* p. 309, note 81). " *The wilderness*" (*midbar*) is the northern part of the desert of Judah, through which the road to Jericho and the Jordan lay.—Ver. 24. Zadok the priest and all the Levites (who were in Jerusalem) left the city with the fugitive king, bearing the ark of the covenant: " *And they set down the ark of God, and Abiathar came up, till all the people had come completely over from the city.*" וַיַּעַל, ἀνέβη, *ascendit* (LXX., Vulg.), may probably be accounted for from the fact that Abiathar did not come to join the fugitives till the procession halted at the Mount of Olives; so that עָלָה, like ἀναβαίνειν, merely refers to his actually going up, and וַיַּעַל affirms that Abiathar joined them until all the people from the city had arrived. The rendering proposed by Michaelis and Böttcher ("he offered sacrifices") is precluded by the fact that עָלָה never means to sacrifice when written without עוֹלָה, or unless the context points distinctly to sacrifices, as in ch. xxiv. 22, 1 Sam. ii. 28. The ark of the covenant was put down, because those who went out with the king made a halt, to give the people who were still coming time to join the procession.— Vers. 25 sqq. Then the king said to Zadok, " *Take back the ark of God into the city! If I find favour in the eyes of Jehovah, He will bring me back and let me see Him* (i.e. himself: the reference is to God) *and His dwelling* (i.e. the ark of the covenant as the throne of the divine glory in the tent that had been set up for it). *But if He thus say, I have not delight in thee; behold, here am I, let Him do to me as seemeth good to Him.*" Thus David put his fate in believing confidence into the hand of the Lord, because he felt that it was the Lord who was chastising him for his sins through this rebellion.—Ver. 27. He also said still further to Zadok, " *Thou seer! return into the city in peace.*" הֲרוֹאֶה אַתָּה, with הֲ *interrog.*, does not yield any appropriate sense, as הֲ cannot stand for הֲלוֹא here, simply because it does not relate to a thing which the person addressed could not deny. Consequently the word must be pointed thus, הָרֹאֶה (with the article), and rendered as a vocative, as it has been by Jerome and Luther. רֹאֶה, seer, is equivalent to prophet. He applies this epithet to Zadok, as the high priest who received divine revelations by means of the Urim. The meaning is, Thou Zadok art equal to a prophet; therefore thy proper place is in Jerusalem (O. v. Gerlach). Zadok was to stand as it were upon the watch there with Abiathar, and the sons of both to observe the events that occurred, and send him word through their sons into the plain of the Jordan. "*Behold, I will tarry by the ferries of the desert, till a word comes from you to show me,*" sc. what has taken place, or how the things shape themselves in Jerusalem. Instead of בְּעַבְרוֹת, the earlier translators as well as the Masoretes adopted the reading בְּעַרְבוֹת, "in the steppes of the desert." The allusion in this case would be to the steppes of Jericho (2 Kings xxv. 5). But Böttcher has very properly defended the *Chethib* on the strength of ch. xvii. 16, where the *Keri* has עַרְבוֹת again, though עֲבָרוֹת is the true reading (cf. ch. xix. 19). The "ferries of the desert" are the places where the Jordan could be crossed, the fords of the Jordan (Josh. ii. 7; Judg. iii. 28).—Ver. 29. Zadok and Abiathar then returned to the city with the ark of God.

Vers. 30-37. *Ahithophel and Hushai.*—Vers. 30, 31. When David was going by the height of the olive-trees, *i.e.* the Mount of Olives, weeping as he went, with his head covered, and barefooted, as a sign of grief and mourning (see Esther vi. 12; Ezek. xxiv. 17), and with the people who accompanied him also mourning, he received intelligence that Ahithophel (see at ver. 12) was with Absalom, and among the conspirators. וְדָוִד הִגִּיד gives no sense; for David cannot be the subject, because the next clause, "and David said," etc., contains most distinctly an expression of David's on receiving some information. Thenius would therefore alter הִגִּיד into the *Hophal* הֻגַּד, whilst Ewald (§ 131, *a*) would change it into הֻגֵּיד, an unusual form of the *Hophal*, "David was informed," according to the construction of the *Hiphil* with the accusative. But although this construction of the *Hiphil* is placed beyond all doubt by Job xxxi. 37, xxvi. 4, and Ezek. xliii. 10, the *Hiphil* is construed as a rule, as the *Hophal* always is, with לְ of the person who receives information. Consequently דָּוִד must be altered into לְדָוִד, and הִגִּיד taken as impersonal, "they announced to David." Upon receipt of this intelligence David prayed to the Lord, that He would "turn the counsel of Ahithophel into foolishness," make it appear as folly, *i.e.* frustrate it,—a prayer which God answered (*vid.* ch. xvii. 1 sqq.).—Vers. 32, 33. On David's arrival at the height where people were accustomed to worship, *i.e.* upon the top of the Mount of Olives, the Archite *Hushai* came to meet him with his clothes rent and earth upon his head, that is to say, in the deepest mourning (see 1 Sam. iv. 12). It is evident from the words אֲשֶׁר־יִשְׁתַּחֲוֶה וגו׳ that there was a place of worship upon the top of the Mount of Olives, probably a *bamah*, such as continued to exist in different places throughout the land, even after the building of the temple. According to ver. 37, ch. xvi. 16, and 1 Chron. xxvii. 33, *Hushai* was רֵעֶה, a friend of David, *i.e.* one of his privy councillors. הָאַרְכִּי (the Archite), if we may judge from Josh. xvi. 2, was the name of a family whose possessions were upon the southern boundary of the tribe of Ephraim, between Bethel and Ataroth. *Hushai* was probably a very old man, as David said to him (vers. 33, 34), "If thou goest with me, thou wilt be a burden to me. But if thou returnest to the city and offerest Absalom thy services, thou canst bring for me the counsel of Ahithophel to nought. If thou sayest to Absalom, I will be thy servant, O king; servant of thy father (*i.e.* as regards this) I was that of old, but now I am thy servant." The ו before אֲנִי introduces the apodosis both times (*vid.* Ewald, § 348, *a*).—Vers. 35, 36. David then commissioned him to communicate to the priests Zadok and Abiathar all that he should hear of the king's house, and send word to him through their sons.—Ver. 37. So Hushai went into the city when Absalom came to Jerusalem. The ו before the second clause, followed by the imperfect יָבוֹא, indicates contemporaneous occurrence (*vid.* Ewald, § 346, *b*).

Ch. xvi. 1-4. *Ziba's faithless conduct towards Mephibosheth.* —Ver. 1. When David had gone a little over the height (of the Mount of Olives: הָרֹאשׁ points back to ch. xv. 32), Mephibosheth's servant Ziba came to meet him, with a couple of asses saddled, and laden with two hundred loaves, a hundred raisin-cakes, a hundred date or fig-cakes, and a skin of wine. The word קַיִץ corresponds to the Greek ὀπώρα, as the LXX. have rendered it in Jer. xl. 10, 12, and is used to signify summer fruits, both here and in Amos viii. 1 (Symm.). The early translators rendered it lumps of figs in the present passage (παλάθαι; cf. Ges. *Thes.* p. 1209). The Septuagint only has ἑκατὸν φοίνικες. The latter is certainly the more correct, as the dried lumps of figs or fig-cakes were called דְּבֵלִים (1 Sam xxv. 18); and even at the present day ripe dates, pressed together in lumps like cakes, are used in journeys through the desert, as a satisfying and refreshing food (vid. Winer, bibl. Realwörterbuch, i. 253).—Ver. 2. When the king asked him, "*What are these for thee?*" i.e. what art thou going to do with them? Ziba replied, "The asses are for the king's family to ride upon (to ride upon in turn), the bread and summer fruits for the young men (the king's servants) to eat, and the wine for those that are faint in the desert to drink" (see at ch. xv. 23). The *Chethib* וְלְהֹלְחֹם is evidently a copyist's error for וְהַלֶּחֶם.—Ver. 3. To the further question put by the king, "Where is thy lord (Mephibosheth)?" Ziba replied, "Behold, he sits (is staying) in Jerusalem; for he said, To-day will the house of Israel restore the kingship (government) of my father." The "*kingship of my father*," inasmuch as the throne would have passed to Jonathan if he had outlived Saul. It is obvious enough, apart altogether from ch. xix. 25 sqq., that Ziba was calumniating his master Mephibosheth, in the hope of getting possession of the lands that he was farming for him. A cripple like Mephibosheth, lame in both feet, who had never put in any claim to the throne before, could not possibly have got the idea now that the people of Israel, who had just chosen Absalom as king, would give the throne of Saul to such a cripple as he was. It is true that Ziba's calumny was very improbable; nevertheless, in the general confusion of affairs, it was not altogether an inconceivable thing that the oppressed party of Saul might avail themselves of this opportunity to make an attempt to restore the power of that house, which many greatly preferred to that of David, under the name of Mephibosheth.—Ver. 4. And in the excited state in which David then was, he was weak enough to give credence to Ziba's words, and to commit the injustice of promising the calumniator all that belonged to Mephibosheth,—a promise for which he most politely thanked him. הִשְׁתַּחֲוֵיתִי, "*I bow myself*," equivalent to, I lay myself at thy feet. "*May I find favour in the eyes of my lord the king!*" i.e. may the king grant me his favour (vid. 1 Sam. i. 18).

Vers. 5-14. *Shimei's cursing.*—Vers. 5, 6. When the king had come to *Bahurim*, on the other side of the Mount of Olives, but not far off (see at ch. iii. 16), there came out of that place a man of the family of the house of Saul, *i.e.* a distant relation of Saul, cursing him; and he pelted David and all his servants with stones, although all the people and all the heroes (the household troops and body-guard: ch. xv. 17, 18) were (marching) on the right and left of the king. The words " all the people," etc., are a circumstantial clause.—Vers. 7, 8. Shimei cursed thus: " *Out, out* (away, away), thou man of blood, and worthless man! Jehovah hath repaid thee (now) for all the blood of the house of Saul, in whose stead thou hast become king, and hath given the kingdom into the hand of Absalom thy son. Behold, now thou art in thy misfortune, for thou art a man of blood." אִישׁ דָּמִים, a man of drops of blood, *i.e.* one who has shed blood or committed murder. What Shimei meant by "*all the blood of the house of Saul*," which David had shed, and because of which he was a man of blood, it is impossible to determine with certainty. He may possibly have attributed to David the murder of Ishbosheth and Abner, notwithstanding the fact that David was innocent of the death of both (see ch. iii. 27 sqq., and 4, 6 sqq.). By "*in whose stead thou hast reigned*," he meant whose throne thou hast forcibly usurped; and by הִנְּךָ בְּרָעָתֶךָ, " it is for this that punishment hath overtaken thee now."—Vers. 9, 10. Abishai wanted to put an end to this cursing (on the expression " dead dog," see ch. ix. 8). " Let me go," said he to David, " and take away his head," *i.e.* chop off his head. But David replied, " What have I to do with you, ye sons of Zeruiah?" Joab probably joined with Abishai. The formula " what to me and you?" signifies that a person did not wish to have anything in common with the feelings and views of another (cf. 1 Kings xvii. 18, Josh. xxii. 24; and τί ἐμοὶ καὶ σοί, John ii. 4. For the thing itself, comp. Luke ix. 52-56). " If he curses, and if Jehovah hath said to him, Curse David, who shall then say, Wherefore hast thou done so?" For כִּי יְקַלֵּל וְכִי יה' (*Chethib*), the Masoretes give us the *Keri*, כֹּה יְקַלֵּל כִּי יה', " so let him curse, for Jehovah," etc. This thought lies at the foundation of the rendering adopted by the LXX., who have inserted, by way of explanation, καὶ ἄφετε αὐτὸν καὶ: so let him go, and so may he curse. The Vulgate is just the same: *dimittite eum ut maledicat*. This interpolation is taken from ver. 11, and, like the *Keri*, is nothing more than a conjecture, which was adopted simply because כִּי was taken as a causal particle, and then offence was taken at וְכִי. But כִּי signifies if, *quando*, in this passage, and the ו before the following וּמִי introduces the apodosis.—Vers. 11, 12. David said still further to Abishai and all his servants: "Behold, my own son seeketh after my life; how much more then the Benjaminite! (who belongs to a hostile race.) Let him curse, for Jehovah hath bidden him. Perhaps Jehovah will look upon my guilt, and Jehovah will requite me good for the curse which befals me this day." בַּעֲוֹנִי (*Chethib*) has been altered by the Masoretes into בְּעֵינִי, "upon mine eye," probably in the sense of "upon my tears;" and קִלְלָתִי into קִלְלָתוֹ,—from pure misapprehension. בַּעֲוֹנִי does not mean "upon my misery," for עָוֹן never has this meaning, but upon the guilt which really belongs to me, in contrast with that with which Shimei charges me; and קִלְלָתִי is the curse that has come upon me. Although David had committed no murder upon the house of Saul, and therefore Shimei's cursing was nothing but malicious blasphemy, he felt that it came upon him because of his sins, though not for the sin imputed to him. He therefore forbade their putting the blasphemer to death, and said Jehovah had commanded him to curse; regarding the cursing as the consequence of the wrath of God that was bringing him low (comp. the remarks on 1 Sam. xxvi. 19). But this consciousness of guilt also excited the assurance that the Lord would look upon his sin. When God looks upon the guilt of a humble sinner, He will also, as a just and merciful God, avert the evil, and change the suffering into a blessing. David founded upon this the hope, that the Lord would repay him with good for the curse with which Shimei was pursuing him now.—Ver. 13. "So David went with his men on the way, whilst Shimei went on the slope of the hill opposite to him, cursing continually, and pelted with stones over against him, and with earth." לְעֻמָּתוֹ means over against him in both instances. It is not expressly stated that Shimei threw stones and earth at David, but this is implied in the context.—Ver. 14. The king came with his train, pursued in this manner, to Ayephim, and refreshed himself there. The context requires that *Ayephim* should be taken as the name of a place. If it were an appellative, signifying weary, there would be no information as to the place to which

David came, and to which the word שָׁם (there) distinctly refers. Bahurim cannot be the place alluded to, for the simple reason that, according to ch. xvii. 18, the place where David rested was a considerable distance beyond Bahurim, towards the Jordan, as we may see from the fact that it is stated there that the priests' sons, who were sent to carry information to David of what was occurring in Jerusalem, hid themselves in a well at Bahurim from the officers who were following them, and consequently had to go still further in order to convey the news to David; so that it is out of the question to supply this name from ver. 5. It is true that we never meet with the name *Ayephim* again; but this applies to many other places whose existence is not called in question.[1]

ABSALOM'S ENTRANCE INTO JERUSALEM. ADVICE OF AHITHOPHEL AND HUSHAI.—CHAP. XVI. 15–XVII. 23.

Vers. 15-23. When Absalom and " all the people, the men of Israel," *i.e.* the people who had joined him out of all the tribes of Israel (ch. xv. 10), came to Jerusalem, and Ahithophel with him, Hushai the Archite also came and greeted him warmly as king, by exclaiming again and again, "Long live the king!"—Vers. 17. sqq. Absalom, apparently astonished at this, said to him, "Is this thy love to thy friend (David)? why wentest thou not with thy friend?" But Hushai replied, "No; but whom Jehovah hath chosen, and this people (*i.e.* the people who had entered Jerusalem with Absalom), and all the men of Israel (*i.e.* the whole nation), to him (לֹא for לוֹ, *Keri*) will I belong, and will remain with him. And again, whom should I serve? Is it not before his son? As I have served thy father, so will I be before thee" (*i.e.* serve thee). With great craftiness, Hushai declared at the very outset that Jehovah had chosen Absalom—at least he could not come to any other conclusion, judging from the results. And under such circum-

---

[1] The meaning of the word, wearied or weariness, does not warrant any conjectures, even though they should be more felicitous than that of Böttcher, who proposes to alter *Ayephim* into *Ephraim*, and assumes that there was a place of this name near Mahanaim, though without reflecting that the place where David rested was on this side of the Jordan, and somewhere near to Gilgal or Jericho (ch. xvii. 16 sqq. and 22).

stances he could not have any doubt as to whom it was his duty to serve. As he had formerly served the father, so now he would serve his son Absalom. In this way he succeeded in completely deceiving Absalom, so that he placed unbounded confidence in him.—Ver. 20. After taking possession of the capital of the kingdom, the next thing to do was to form the resolution to take and keep the throne. Absalom therefore turned to Ahithophel, and said, " Give ye counsel what we are to do." The plural הָבוּ (give ye) may be explained on the supposition that the other persons present were addressed as well as Ahithophel, as being capable of giving advice.—Ver. 21. Ahithophel gave the following counsel: " Go to thy father's concubines, whom he hath left behind to keep the house (*i.e.* lie with them: for בּוֹא אֶל, compare ch. iii. 7, etc.); so will all Israel hear that thou hast made thyself stinking with thy father, and the hands of all those who are with thee will strengthen themselves." This advice was sagacious enough. Lying with the king's concubines was an appropriation of the royal harem, and, as such, a complete usurpation of the throne (see at ch. iii. 7), which would render any reconciliation between Absalom and his father utterly impossible, and therefore would of necessity instigate the followers of Absalom to maintain his cause with all the greater firmness. This was what Ahithophel hoped to attain through his advice. For unless the breach was too great to be healed, with the affection of David towards his sons, which might in reality be called weakness, it was always a possible thing that he should forgive Absalom; and in that case Ahithophel would be the one to suffer. But under the superintendence of God this advice of Ahithophel was to effect the fulfilment, without any such intention on his part, of the threat held over David in ch. xii. 8.—Ver. 22. Absalom had a tent put up on the roof of the king's palace, that his going in to the concubines might be done publicly in the sight of all Israel. For (as the historian adds in ver. 23 by way of explanation) the counsel of Ahithophel, which he counselled in those days, was like a divine oracle both with David and with Absalom. The words from וַעֲצַת to הָהֵם are placed at the commencement absolutely: " and (as for) the counsel of Ahithophel, . . . as if one inquired the word of God, so was every counsel of Ahithophel." The Masoretes have supplied אִישׁ as the *Keri* to יִשְׁאַל. This is correct so far as the sense is concerned, but it is quite unnecessary, as יִשְׁאַל may be taken impersonally. שָׁאַל בִּדְבַר הָאֱלֹהִים is to be explained from the formula שָׁאַל בֵּאלֹהִים (see at Judg. i. 1).

Chap. xvii. 1-14. *Ahithophel's advice frustrated by Hushai.*
—Vers. 1-3. Ahithophel said still further to Absalom, " I will choose out twelve thousand men, and arise, and pursue after David this night; and fall upon him when he is exhausted and weak, and fill him with alarm: so shall all the people that are with him flee; and I will smite the king alone (when he is alone), and will bring back all the people to thee." הַלַּיְלָה, *the night*, is the night following the day of David's flight and Absalom's entrance into Jerusalem, as we may see very clearly from ver. 16. This advice was sagaciously conceived; for if David had been attacked that night by a powerful army, he might possibly have been defeated. אָשִׁיבָה, *to bring back*, may be explained on the supposition that Ahithophel regarded Absalom as king, and those who had fled with David as rebels, who were to be brought back under Absalom's sceptre. The following words, כְּשׁוּב הַכֹּל וגו׳, " *as the return of the whole* (the whole nation) *is the man*," *i.e.* the return of all is dependent upon David, for whom thou liest in wait, are somewhat difficult, though the meaning of Ahithophel is evident enough from what precedes: viz. if he is beaten, they will all come over to thee; "the whole nation will be at peace" (שָׁלוֹם is used adverbially).[1]
—Vers. 4, 5. Although this advice pleased Absalom and all the elders of Israel (present), Absalom sent for Hushai the Archite to hear his opinion. גַּם־הוּא serves to strengthen the suffix in בְּפִיו (cf. Ewald, § 311, *a*).—Vers. 6, 7. In answer to Absalom's inquiry, "Shall we do his word (*i.e.* follow Ahithophel's advice) or not?" Hushai said, "The advice is not good that Ahithophel hath given this time;" and then still further explained (ver. 8):

---

[1] Consequently no conjectures are needed as to the rendering of the words in the Septuagint, viz. καθὼς (*al.* ὃν τρόπον) ἐπιστρέφει ἡ νύμφη πρὸς τὸν ἄνδρα αὐτῆς· πλὴν ψυχὴν ἀνδρὸς ἑνὸς σὺ ζητεῖς, such as Ewald, Thenius, and Böttcher have attempted. For 't is very obvious that ἡ νύμφη πρὸς τὸν ἄνδρα αὐτῆς owes its origin simply to a false reading of הַכֹּל הָאִישׁ as הַכַּלָּה אִישׁ, and that πλὴν ψυχὴν ἀνδρὸς ἑνός has been interpolated by way of explanation from nothing but conjecture. No other of the ancient versions contains the slightest trace of a different reading from that given in the text.

"Thou knowest thy father and his men, that they are heroes, and of a ferocious disposition (like Judg. xviii. 25), like a bear in the field robbed of her young; and thy father is a man of war, and will not pass the night with the people," *sc.* so that it would be possible to come upon him unawares and slay him (לוֹ with אֶת, as in Job xix. 4). The idea that יָלִין is to be taken as a *Hiphil*, in the sense of "and does not let the people lodge for the night" (Böttcher), is quite untenable, since it does not tally with ver. 9, "Behold, he is hid now in one of the pits, or one of the places (פְּחָתִים are hiding-places that are strong by nature, מְקוֹמֹת are places rendered strong by art); and it comes to pass that he falls upon them at the first: so will men hear it, and say a defeat has taken place among the people that follow Absalom." נָפַל with בְּ, as in Josh. xi. 7, to fall upon a person. The subject to נָפֹל is David, but it is not mentioned as being evident enough from the context; so that there is no necessity for the emendation נִפְּלוּ, which Thenius proposes. The suffix בָּהֶם relates to those making the attack, the hosts of Absalom. Thenius has given the meaning correctly: "The report that David has made an attack will be sufficient to give rise to the belief that our men have sustained a severe defeat."—Ver. 10. "And even if he (the hearer, ver. 9) be a brave man, who has a lion's heart (lion-like courage), he will be thrown into despair, for all Israel knows that thy father is a hero, and brave men (are those) who are with him."—Ver. 11. "Yea (כִּי, *profecto*), I advise: let all Israel be gathered round thee from Dan to Beersheba (see at Judg. xx. 1), numerous as the sand by the sea; and thou thyself go into the war." פָּנֶיךָ, thy person, *i.e.* thou thyself be marching. The plural הֹלְכִים is used because of פָּנֶיךָ. For הָלַךְ בְּ, to enter into anything, see 1 Kings xix. 4, Isa. xlv. 16, xlvi. 2. קְרָב, war, the early translators have confounded with קָרֵב.—Ver. 12. "And come we to him (if we come upon him) in one of the places where he is found, we let ourselves down upon him, as the dew falls upon the earth; and of him and all the men with him there will not be one left." נַחְנוּ might be a contraction of אֲנַחְנוּ, as in Gen. xlii. 11, Ex. xvi. 7, 8, etc.: "so we upon him," equivalent to "so shall we come upon him." But if this were the meaning, we should expect וְהָיִינוּ עָלָיו. It is more correct, therefore, to take נַחְנוּ as the first pers. perf. of נוּחַ, as the early translators have done: so do we let ourselves down upon him. (For נוּחַ as applied to an army encamping, see Isa. vii. 2, 19; and as denoting the swarming of flies and grasshoppers, Isa. vii. 19 and Ex. x. 14.) In Ahithophel's opinion, it would be possible with a very small army to crush David and his little band, however brave his followers might be, and in fact to annihilate them altogether.—Ver. 13. "And if he draw back into a city, all Israel lays ropes to that city, and we drag it to the brook, till there is not even a little stone found there." עַד־הַנַּחַל: inasmuch as fortified cities were generally built upon mountains. צְרוֹר signifies a little stone, according to the ancient versions. Hushai speaks in hyperboles of the irresistible power which the whole nation would put forth when summoned together for battle, in order to make his advice appear the more plausible.—Ver. 14. And he secured his end. Absalom and all Israel thought his advice better than that of Ahithophel; for it was intended to commend itself to Absalom and his supporters. "The counsel appeared safe; at the same time it was full of a certain kind of boasting, which pleased the younger men" (Clericus). All that Hushai had said about the bravery and heroism of David and his followers, was well founded. The deception lay in the assumption that all the people from Dan to Beersheba would crowd around Absalom as one man; whereas it might easily be foreseen, that after the first excitement of the revolution was over, and greater calmness ensued, a large part of the nation and army would gather round David. But such a possibility as this never entered the minds of Absalom and his supporters. It was in this that the divine sentence referred to in ver. 14b was seen: "The Lord had commanded (appointed) it, to defeat the good counsel of Ahithophel, that he might bring the evil (intended) upon Absalom."

Vers. 15-23. *David is informed of what has occurred.*—Vers. 15, 16. Hushai communicated without delay to the priests Zadok and Abiathar the advice which had been given to Absalom both by Ahithophel and himself, and requested them to make it known to David as quickly as possible. "*Stay not the night*," he said, "*by the ferries* (עֲבָרוֹת, as in ch. xv. 28) *of the desert; but rather go over, lest the king and all the people with him be destroyed.*" וְגַם, "and indeed," or after a negative clause, "but rather." יְבֻלַּע לַמֶּלֶךְ is either "there will be a devouring," *i.e.* destruction, to the king, it will fall upon him, or if we supply the subject from the previous clause עֲבוֹר תַּעֲבוֹר, as Böttcher proposes, "that it (the crossing over) may not be swallowed up or cut off from the king." There is nothing to justify Ewald's explanation, "it (misfortune) is swallowed by him." Hushai recommended of course an immediate crossing of the Jordan; because he did not know whether Absalom would really act upon his advice, although he had expressed his approval of it, or whether he might not change his mind and follow Ahithophel's counsel.—Ver. 17. "Jonathan and Ahimaaz (the sons of the priests: ch. xv. 27) stood at the *Rogel* spring (the present well of Job or Nehemiah, at the south-east corner of Jerusalem: see at Job xv. 7), and the maid-servant (of one of the high priests) went and told them (Hushai's message), and they went and told it to king David; for they durst not let themselves be seen to come into the city." They had therefore been staying at the Rogel spring outside the city. After what had taken place publicly, according to ch. xv. 24 sqq., Absalom could not be in any doubt as to the views of the high priests. Consequently their sons could not come into the city, with the intention of leaving it again directly, to inform David of the occurrences that had taken place there as he had requested (ch. xv. 28). The clause "*and they went and told David*" anticipates the course of the affair, according to the general plan adopted by Hebrew historians, of communicating the result at the very outset wherever they possibly could.—Ver. 18. "*And a lad* (servant) *saw them, and told Absalom*." Absalom had most likely set spies to watch the priests and their sons. But the two sons who had noticed the spy hurried into the house of a man at Bahurim, who had a well (or cistern that was dry at the time) in his court, and went down into the well.—Ver. 19. And the man's wife spread a covering (הַמָּסָךְ, the covering which she had close at hand) over the well (over the opening into the cistern), and scattered groats (רִיפוֹת, peeled barley: Prov. xxvii. 22) upon it, so that nothing was noticed. The Vulgate explanation is a very good one: "*quasi siccans ptisanas*" (as if drying peeled barley).— Ver. 20. When Absalom's servants came and asked for the priest's sons, the woman said, They have gone over the little water-brook (מִיכַל הַמָּיִם, ἀπ. λεγ.), and thus led them wrong, so that they did not find them.—Vers. 21, 22. When they had gone away, the priest's sons came up out of the well and brought David the news, saying, "Go quickly over the water, for thus hath Ahithophel counselled against you;" whereupon David and all the people with him went hastily over the Jordan. "Till the morning dawn not one was missed who had not gone over." עַד אֶחָד, *lit.* even to one there was not any one missed.—Ver. 23. It is still further stated in conclusion, that when Ahithophel saw that his advice was not carried out, he saddled his ass and returned to his home, and there set his house in order and hanged himself, because he could foresee that Absalom would lose his cause through not taking his advice, and it would then be all over with himself. Thus was David's prayer (ch. xv. 31) fulfilled.

ABSALOM'S DEFEAT AND DEATH.—CHAP. XVII. 24–XIX. 1.

The account of the civil war, which terminated with Absalom's defeat and death, is introduced in vers. 24–26 with a description of the relative position of the two hostile parties. David had come to Mahanaim, a city, probably a fortified one, on the east of the Jordan, not far from a ford of the Jabbok (see at ch. ii. 8). Absalom had also gone over the Jordan, "he and all the men with him," *i.e.* all the fighting men that he had gathered together according to Hushai's advice, and encamped in the land of Gilead.—Ver. 25. Absalom had made Amasa captain over his army instead of Joab, who had remained true to David, and had gone with his king to Mahanaim. Amasa was the son of a man named *Jithra*, הַיִּשְׂרְאֵלִי, who had gone in to (*i.e.* had seduced) Abigail, the daughter of Nahash and sister of Zeruiah, Joab's mother. He was therefore an illegitimate cousin of Joab. The description given of *Jithra* as יִשְׂרְאֵלִי is very striking, since there was no reason whatever why it should be stated that Amasa's father was an *Israelite*. The Seventy have therefore given ὁ Ἰεζραηλίτης, *i.e.* sprung from Jezreel, where David's wife Ahinoam came from (1 Sam. xxvii. 3); but they have done so apparently from mere conjecture. The true reading is evidently הַיִּשְׁמְעֵאלִי, an Ishmaelite, according to 1 Chron. ii. 17, where the name is written Jether, a contracted form of Jithra. From the description given of Abigail as a daughter of Nahash and sister of Zeruiah, not of David, some of the earlier commentators have very justly concluded that Abigail and Zeruiah were only step-sisters of David, *i.e.* daughters of his mother by Nahash and not by Jesse.—Vers. 27-29. When David came to Mahanaim, some of the wealthier citizens of the land to the east of the Jordan supplied the men who were with him with provisions. This is mentioned as the first sign that the people had not all fallen away from David, but that some of the more distinguished men were still firm in their adherence. *Shobi*, the son of Nahash of *Rabbah*, the capital of the Ammonites (see ch. xi. 1), was possibly a son of Nahash the deceased king of the Ammonites, and brother of Hanun, who was defeated by David (ch. x. 1, 2), and one of those to whom David had shown favour and kindness when Rabbah was taken. At the same time, it is also quite possible that *Shobi* may have been an Israelite, who was merely living in the capital of the Ammonites, which had been incorporated into the kingdom of David, as it is evident from ver. 25 that Nahash was not an uncommon name among the Israelites. *Machir* the son of Ammiel of *Lodebar* (see at ch. ix. 4), and *Barsillai* of *Roglim* the Gileadite. *Roglim* was a town in Gilead, which is only mentioned once again, viz. in ch. xix. 32, and of which nothing further is known. They brought "bedding, basins, earthenware, and wheat, barley, meal, and parched grains, beans, lentils and *parched*." The position of the verb, which is not placed between the subject and the object of the sentence, but only at the close of the whole series of objects, is certainly unusual; but this does not warrant any alteration of the text. For if we were to supply a verb before מִשְׁכָּב, as having fallen out of the text, it would be necessary, since הִגִּישׁוּ follows without a copula, to divide the things enumerated into two classes, so as to connect one portion of the objects with הִגִּישׁוּ, which is obviously unnatural. The early translators who interpolate a verb before the objects have therefore also supplied the copula ו before הִגִּישׁוּ. There is still less ground for supplying the number 10, as having dropped out before מִשְׁכָּב and סַפּוֹת, as the LXX. have done, since none of the translators of the other ancient versions had any such reading. מִשְׁכָּב, couch or bed, is used here for bedding. סַפּוֹת, basins, probably field-kettles. The repetition of וְקָלִי is very striking; nevertheless the second must not be struck out without further ground as a supposed copyist's error. As they not only ate parched ears or grains of wheat (see at Lev. ii. 14), but were also in the habit of drying pulse, pease, and lentils before eating them (*vid.* Harmar, *Beobachtungen*, i. pp. 255-6), the second קָלִי may be understood as referring to parched pulse. The ἄπ. λεγ. שְׁפוֹת בָּקָר signifies, according to the Chaldee and the Rabbins, cheese of oxen (*i.e.* of cows), and according to the conjecture of Roediger (Ges. *Thes.* p. 1462), a peculiar kind of cheese, such as the *Aeneze* in the province of Nedjid still make,[1] and for which the term σαφὼθ βοῶν retained by the LXX. was probably the technical name. Theodotus, on the other hand, has γαλαθηνὰ μοσχάρια, milch-calves; and the Vulgate *pingues vitulos*,—both of them renderings which can certainly be sustained from the Arabic usage of speech, and would be more in accordance with the situation of the words, viz. after צָאן. כִּי אָמְרוּ, "for they said (or thought) the people have become hungry and faint and thirsty in the desert," *i.e.* in their flight to Mahanaim.

Chap. xviii. 1-5. *Preparation for war.*—Vers. 1, 2. David mustered the people that were with him, and placed over them captains of thousands and hundreds, and divided them into three companies, under the generals Joab, Abishai, and Ittai the Gathite, who had given such decided proofs, according to ch. xv. 21, 22, of his fidelity to David. שִׁלַּח בְּיַד, to leave to the hand of a person, *i.e.* to his power, is used here in the sense of placing under his direction. The people opposed in the most decided manner the wish of the king to go with them to the war, saying (ver. 3), "Thou shalt not go out: for if we flee, they will take no heed of us (*i.e.* attach no importance to this); and if half of us die, they will take no heed of us: for thou art as ten thousand of us (we must evidently read אַתָּה for עַתָּה, and עַתָּה has merely got into the text in consequence of וְעַתָּה following): and now it is good that thou be ready to give us help from the city" (the *Chethib* לַעְזִיר, *inf. Hiphil* for לְהַעְזִיר, is not to be disputed). David was to stay behind in the city with a reserve,

---

[1] According to Burckhardt's account (*Die Beduinen*, p. 48), "after they have taken the butter from the butter-milk, they beat the latter again till it coagulates, and then dry it till it is quite hard. It is then rubbed to pieces, and in the spring every family stores up two or three lasts of it, which they eat mixed with butter."

that he might be able to come to their relief in case of need.—
Vers. 4, 5. The king gave his consent to these proposals, and went to the side of the gate, whilst the people went out by hundreds and thousands; but in the hearing of all he commanded the principal generals, "*Mildly for me* (*i.e.* deal gently for my sake) *with the boy Absalom.*" לאט is not the imperative of לאט, to cover over, which would not suit the connection, and could not be construed with ל, but an adverb from אט, as in Isa. viii. 6, 1 Kings xxi. 27, Job xv. 11.

Vers. 6–18. *Battle in the wood of Ephraim, and death of Absalom.*—Vers. 6, 7. When the people, *i.e.* David's army, had advanced into the field against Israel (those who followed Absalom), a battle was fought " in the wood of Ephraim," when Israel was smitten by David's warriors and sustained a loss of 20,000 men. The question, where the " *wood of Ephraim*" was situated, is a disputed one. But both the name and the fact that, according to Josh. xvii 15, 16, the tribe-land of Ephraim abounded in forests, favour the idea that it was a wood in the inheritance of Ephraim, on this side of the Jordan; and this is in perfect harmony with the statement in ver. 23, that Ahimaaz took the way of the Jordan valley to bring the news of the victory to David, who was staying behind in Mahanaim. Nevertheless the majority of commentators have supposed that the place alluded to was a woody region on the other side of the Jordan, which had received the name of " wood Ephraim" probably after the defeat of the Ephraimites in the time of Jephthah (Judg. xii. 1–5). The reasons assigned are, *first*, that according to ch. xvii. 26, Absalom had encamped in Gilead, and it is not stated that he had crossed the Jordan again; *secondly*, that ver. 3 (" that thou succour us out of the city") presupposes that the battle took place in the neighbourhood of Mahanaim (Thenius); and *thirdly*, that after the victory the army returned to Mahanaim; whereas if the battle had been fought on this side of the Jordan, it would evidently have been much better for it to remain there and occupy Jerusalem (Ewald, *Gesch.* iii. p. 237). But neither of these reasons is decisive, and there is no force in the other arguments employed by Thenius. There was no necessity for an immediate occupation of Jerusalem by David's victorious army, since all Israel fled to their tents after the fall of Absalom and the defeat of his army (ver. 17 and ch. xix. 9); that is to say, such of Absalom's followers as had not fallen in or after the battle, broke up and returned home, and therefore the revolution was at an end. Consequently there was nothing left for David's army to do but to return to its king at Mahanaim, and fetch him back to Jerusalem, and reinstate him in his kingdom. The other two reasons might have some force in them, if the history before us contained a complete account of the whole course of the war. But even Ewald admits that it is restricted to a notice of the principal battle, which completely crushed the rebellion. There can be no doubt, however, that this was preceded, if not by other battles, yet by such military operations as accompany every war. This is clearly indicated in ver. 6, where it is stated that the army advanced into the field against Israel (ver. 6), which evidently refers to such an advance on the part of David's army as might compel Absalom to draw back from Gilead across the Jordan, until at length a decisive battle was fought, which ended in the complete destruction of his army and his own death. Ewald observes still further, that " it seems impossible, at any rate so far as the name is concerned, to assume that the wood of Ephraim was on the other side of the Jordan, whilst according to ch. xviii. 23, the messenger who reported the victory went from the field of battle towards the Jordan valley in order to get to David." But the way in which Ewald tries to set aside this important point, as bearing upon the conclusion that the battle took place on this side of the Jordan,—namely, by adopting this rendering of ver. 23, " he ran after the manner of *Kikkar*, running, and therefore overtook *Kushi*,"—is far too unnatural to meet with acceptance. Under all these circumstances, therefore, we decide in favour of the assumption that the wood of Ephraim is to be sought for in the tribe-territory of Ephraim.

The nature of the ground contributed a great deal to the utter defeat of Absalom.—Ver. 8. The conflict extended over the surface of the whole land, *i.e.* the whole of that region (the *Chethib* נפצות is not the plural נְפֹצוֹת, which would be quite unsuitable, but is most probably a noun, נְפָצוּת, signifying bursting asunder, or wild flight; the *Keri* נָפֹצֶת is a *Niphal* participle, fem. gen.); " and the wood devoured more of the people than the sword ate on the same day." The woody region was most likely full of ravines, precipices, and marshes, into which the flying foe was pursued, and where so many perished.—Ver. 9. "And Absalom was lighted upon (יָקָרֵא = יִקָּרֶה) by the servants of David, riding upon the mule; and the mule had come under the thick branches of the great terebinth, and his head fastened itself (remained hanging) on the terebinth, so that he was held (hung) between heaven and earth, as the mule under him went away." The imperfects, וַיָּבֹא ,וַיֶּחֱזַק, and וַיִּתֵּן, are only a combination of the circumstantial clause וְאַבְשָׁ׳ רכב. With regard to the fact itself, it is not clearly stated in the words that Absalom hung only by his hair, but simply that his hair entangled him in the thick branches, and his head was fastened in the terebinth, namely, by being jammed between the strong boughs. —Ver. 10. A man (one of David's men) saw him in this situation, and told Joab. Joab replied (ver. 11), "Behold, thou hast seen it, and wherefore hast thou not smitten him there to the ground? and it was for me to give thee ten silverlings and a girdle;" *i.e.* if thou hadst slain him, it would have been my duty to reward thee.—Ver. 12. But the man replied, "*And I ... not weighing a thousand shekels in my hand ... might not stretch out my hand to the king's son,*" *i.e.* I could not do it for a reward of a thousand shekels. This is the meaning of the *Chethib* וְלֹא; the Masoretes, on the other hand, have substituted וְלוּ, which is the reading adopted in most of the ancient versions, and the one preferred by the majority of expositors: "if I weighed ... I would not," etc. But there is no necessity for this alteration, as the *Chethib* is quite in accordance with the character of the words. "*For before our ears the king commanded*" (cf. ver. 5): שִׁמְרוּ מִי, "*take care whoever* (it be) *of the boy Absalom.*" On this use of מִי, see Ewald, § 104 *d, a.* The *Keri* לִי is merely a conjecture, notwithstanding the fact that all the versions follow it, and that one of the Codices in Kennicott has לִי. "*Or,*" continued the man (ver. 13), "*should I have acted deceitfully towards his life* (*i.e.* have slain him secretly, which he calls שֶׁקֶר, cheating, because it was opposed to the king's open command): *and nothing remains hidden from the king; ... thou wouldst have set thyself in opposition to me,*" *i.e.* have risen up against me before the king. The middle clause is a circumstantial one, as the fact that וְכָל־דָּבָר is placed first clearly shows; so that it cannot be regarded as introducing the apodosis, which really follows in the clause commencing with וְאַתָּה.—Ver. 14. Joab replied, "*Not so will I wait before thee,*" *i.e.* I will not leave the thing to thee. He then took three staffs in his hand, and thrust them into Absalom's heart. שְׁבָטִים is rendered by the LXX. and Vulgate, βέλη, *lanceas;* and Thenius would adopt שְׁלָחִים accordingly, as an emendation of the text. But in the earlier Hebrew שֶׁלַח only occurs in poetical writings in the sense of a missile or dart (Job xxxiii. 18, xxxvi. 12; Joel ii. 8); and it is not till after the captivity that we find it used to denote a weapon generally. There is no necessity, however, for altering the text. Joab caught up in his hurry the first thing that he found, namely pointed staffs, and pierced Absalom with them to the heart. This explains the reason for his taking *three*, whereas one javelin or dart would have been sufficient, and also the fact that Absalom was not slain, notwithstanding their being thrust at his heart. The last clause of the verse belongs to what follows: "*Still living* (*i.e.* as he was still alive) *in the midst of the terebinth, ten young men, Joab's armour-bearers, surrounded him, and smote him to death.*" —Ver. 16. Immediately afterwards Joab stopped any further pursuit, " for Joab spared the people," *i.e.* he wanted to spare them.—Ver. 17. But Absalom they cast into a great pit in the wood, and threw up over him a very large heap of stones, as an ignominious monument, like those thrown up over Achan (Josh. vii. 26) and the king of Ai (Josh. viii. 29). This was the end of Absalom and his rebellion. " All Israel (that had crowded round him) had fled, every one to his tent" (*i.e.* home: see at Deut. xvi. 7).—Ver. 18. Absalom had erected a monument to himself in the king's valley during his lifetime; " for he said, I have no son to preserve the remembrance of my name, and he called the monument by his own name; and so it was called hand (memorial) of Absalom unto this day." The לָקַח before וַיַּצֵּב is apparently pleonastic; but it belongs to the diffuse and circumstantial character of the antiquated Hebrew diction (as in Num. xvi. 1). מַצֶּבֶת, a memorial of stone; whether in the form of a column, or an obelisk, or a monolith, cannot be determined (*vid.* Gen. xxviii. 22, xxxi. 52). The king's valley, which received its name from the event narrated in Gen. xiv. 17, was two stadia from Jerusalem according to Josephus (*Ant.* vii. 10, 3), and therefore not " close to the

Dead Sea," or *in regione transjordanensi* (Ges. *Thes.* pp. 1045, 1377), or " in the Jordan valley in Ephraim" (Tuch and Winer). It was on the eastern side of Jerusalem, in the Kidron valley; though Absalom's pillar, which ecclesiastical tradition has transferred thither, a monument about forty feet in height and pointed like a pyramid, is not of early Hebrew, but of Grecian origin. On the words " I have no son," see at ch. xiv. 27.

Vers. 19–32. *David is informed of the victory, and of the death of Absalom.*—Vers. 19, 20. Ahimaaz, the son of Zadok, wanted to carry the news to David, that Jehovah had " procured the king justice out of the hand of his enemies" (שָׁפַט with מִ is a pregnant expression signifying to procure justice and deliver out of); but Joab, knowing how David would receive the tidings of the death of Absalom, replied, " Thou art no man of good tidings to-day; thou shalt take the news on another day, not on this, even because (כִּי עַל־בֵּן, see at Gen. xviii. 5) the king's son is dead." The *Keri* כִּי עַל־בֵּן is to be preferred to the *Chethib* בִּי־עַל; and בֵּן has no doubt been dropt out merely because of בֵּן which follows. The *Chethib* does not give any suitable sense; for the absence of the article before מֵת is decisive against the explanation proposed by Maurer, viz. " for (tidings have to be carried) concerning the king's son dead." If מֵת were to be construed as an adverb with בֶּן־מֶלֶךְ, it would of necessity have the article.—Ver. 21. Joab therefore entrusted *the Cushite* with the duty of conveying to David the announcement of what had occurred. It cannot be decided with certainty whether הַכּוּשִׁי or *Cushi* is the proper name of an Israelite, or whether it signifies the " Cushite," *i.e.* a descendant of Cush. The form of the name rather favours the latter view, in which case it would suggest the idea of a Moorish slave in the service of Joab.— Vers. 22, 23. As Ahimaaz still expressed a wish to hasten to the king, even after Cushi had been sent, and could not be induced to relinquish his purpose by the repeated expostulations of Joab, the latter at length permitted him to run. And he ran so fast, that he got before Cushi. וִיהִי מָה: let whatever will happen. וּלְכָה is the pronoun " to thee," as in Gen. xxvii. 37, and not the imperative of הָלַךְ, " thou mayest go." The meaning is, " and there is no striking message for thee," no message that strikes the mark, or affects anything. We must supply "he said" in thought before ver. 23. There was the less necessity to write it here (as in 1 Sam. i. 20), since it is perfectly obvious from the repetition of וַיְהִי מָה that it is Ahimaaz who is speaking. Ahimaaz then ran by the way of the plain, *i.e.* the way which lies through or across the plain of the Jordan. Now he could not possibly have taken this road, if the battle had been fought in a wood on the eastern side of the Jordan, and he had wanted to hurry from the scene of battle to Mahanaim; for in that case he would have taken a circuitous route two or three times the distance of the straight road, so that it would have been utterly impossible for him to get there before the Cushite, however quickly he might run. This notice therefore furnishes a decisive proof that the battle was fought upon the mountains of Ephraim, in the land to the west of the Jordan, since the straight road thence to Mahanaim would lie through the valley of the Jordan.—Ver. 24. David was sitting between the two gates of Mahanaim waiting for tidings of the result of the battle. The two gates are the outer and inner gate of the fortified city wall, between which there was a small court, where David was sitting. The watchman then went up to the roof of the gate by the wall, probably the outer gate in the city wall, and as he looked he saw a man running alone.— Ver. 25. When he announced this to the king, he said, "If he (is or comes) alone, there is good news in his mouth," namely, because several runners would have shown themselves if it had been a flight. As the first messenger came nearer and nearer, the watchman saw another man running, and shouted this into the gate (הַשֹּׁעֵר is wrongly pointed for הַשֹּׁעֵר, according to the LXX., Syr., and Vulgate); whereupon the king replied, "This is also a good messenger."—Ver. 27. When the watchman saw by the running of the first that it was Ahimaaz, recognising him probably by the swiftness of his running, and announced it to the king, he replied, "He is a good man, and cometh with good tidings," because Joab would not have selected him to bring any other than good news.—Ver. 28. Ahimaaz then called out to the king, "*Shalom*," *i.e. Hail!* and fell down before him to greet him reverentially, and said, "Blessed be Jehovah thy God, who hath given up the men that lifted up their hand against my lord the king."—Ver. 29. In answer to the king's inquiry, "Is it well with the young man Absalom?" Ahimaaz replied, "I saw the great tumult (that arose) when Joab sent off the king's servant, and thy servant, and know not what" (*sc.* had occurred). Ahimaaz spoke as if he had been sent off before Absalom's fate had been decided or could be known "*The king's servant*" is the Cushite, whom Ahimaaz saw just approaching, so that he could point to him. *Joab* is the subject, which is sometimes written after the object in the case of an infinitive construction (*vid.* Gesenius, § 133, 3 Anm.); and the expression "thy servant" is a conventional one for "me" (viz. Ahimaaz).—Ver. 30. And the king said, "Turn, and stand here," that he might hear the further news from the Cushite, who had just arrived.—Ver. 31. The Cushite said, "Let my lord the king receive good tidings, for Jehovah hath procured thee justice to-day out of the hand of all who have risen up against thee" (cf. ver. 19).—Ver. 32. When asked about the welfare of Absalom, the Cushite replied, "May it happen to the enemies of my lord the king, and all who have risen up against thee for evil (*i.e.* to do thee harm), as to the young man." The death of Absalom was indicated clearly enough in these words.

Ver. 33. The king understood the meaning of the words. He was agitated, and went up to the balcony of the gate (the room above the entrance) and wept, and said, walking about, "My son Absalom, my son, my son Absalom! Oh that I had died for thee, Absalom, my son, my son!" To understand this passionate utterance of anguish, we must bear in mind not only the excessive tenderness, or rather weakness, of David's paternal affection towards his son, but also his anger that Joab and his generals should have paid so little regard to his command to deal gently with Absalom. With the king's excitable temperament, this entirely prevented him from taking a just and correct view of the crime of his rebel son, which merited death, and of the penal justice of God which had been manifested in his destruction.

DAVID REINSTATED IN HIS KINGDOM.—CHAP. XIX. 1-39.

In his passionate and sinful sorrow on account of Absalom's death, David not only forgot altogether what it was his duty to do, in order to recover the affections of the people, so that Joab was obliged to remind him of this duty which was binding upon him as king (vers. 1-8); but he even allowed himself to be carried away into the most inconsiderate measures (vers. 9-14), and into acts of imprudence and injustice (vers. 16-23, 24-30), which could not contribute to the strengthening of his throne, however much the affection with which he wished to reward the old man Barzillai for his faithful services (vers. 31-40) might show that the king was anxious to promote the welfare of his subjects.

Vers. 1-8. *David's mourning, and Joab's reproof.*—Vers. 1-6. When Joab was told that the king was mourning and weeping for Absalom, he went to him into the house to expostulate with him. Ver. 5 introduces the continuation of ver. 1; vers. 2-4 contain parenthetical sentences, describing the impression made upon the people by the king's mourning. Through the king's deep trouble, the salvation (the victory) upon that day became mourning for all the people who had fought for David, and they went by stealth into the city (יִתְגַּנֵּב לָבוֹא: they stole to come, came by stealth), "as people steal away who have covered themselves with shame, when they flee in battle."—Ver. 4. But the king had covered his face, and cried aloud, "My son Absalom," etc.—Ver. 5. Then Joab went into the house to the king, and said to him, "Thou hast shamed this day the faces of all thy servants who have saved thy life, and the life of thy sons and daughters, thy wives and concubines" (covered them with shame, by deceiving their hope that thou wouldest rejoice in the victory).—Ver. 6. לְאַהֲבָה, "to love" (*i.e.* in that thou lovest) "those who hate thee, and hatest those who love thee; for thou hast given to know to-day (through thy conduct) that chiefs and servants (commanders and soldiers) are nothing (are worth nothing); for I have perceived to-day (or I perceive to-day) that if (לֹא for לוּ) Absalom were alive, and we had all perished, that it would be right in thine eyes."—Ver. 7. "And now rise up, go out and speak to the heart of thy servants (*i.e.* speak to them in a friendly manner: Gen. xxxiv. 3, l. 21, etc.): for I swear by Jehovah, if thou go not out, verily not a man will stay with thee to-night; and this will be worse to thee than all the evil that has come upon thee from thy youth until now." Joab was certainly not only justified, but bound in David's own interests, to expostulate with him upon his conduct, and to urge him to speak in a friendly manner to the people who had exposed their lives for him, inasmuch as his present conduct would necessarily stifle the affection of the people towards their king, and might be followed by the most serious results with reference to his throne. At the same time, he did this in so heartless and lordly a manner, that the king could not fail to be deeply hurt by his words.—Ver. 8. Nevertheless David was obliged to yield to his representations. "*The king rose up, and sat in the gate, and . . . all the people came before the king,*" *i.e.* the troops marched before the king, who (as we may supply from the context) manifested his good-will in both looks and words. But Israel, *i.e.* that portion of the people which had followed Absalom, had returned to its tents (*i.e.* gone home: cf. ch. xviii. 17). This sentence forms the transition to the account which follows.

Vers. 9–14. *Preliminaries to the return of David to Jerusalem.*—Vers. 9, 10. As the rebellion was entirely crushed by Absalom's death, and the dispersion of his followers to their respective homes, there arose a movement among all the tribes in favour of David. "All the people were disputing (נָדוֹן, casting reproaches at one another) in all the tribes of Israel, saying, The king has saved us out of the hand of our enemies, . . . and now he is fled out of the land before Absalom. But Absalom, whom we anointed over us, is dead in battle; and now why do ye keep still, to bring back the king?" This movement arose from the consciousness of having done an injustice to the king, in rising up in support of Absalom.—Vers. 11, 12. When these words of all Israel were reported to David, he sent to the priests Zadok and Abiathar, saying, "Speak to the elders of Judah, why will ye be the last to bring back the king to his palace? . . . Ye are my brethren, my bones and flesh (*i.e.* my blood relations): why then," etc.? The last clause of ver. 11, "*the speech of all Israel is come to the king, even to his house,*" is a circumstantial clause inserted in the midst of David's words, to explain the appeal to the men of Judah not to be the last. In the LXX., and some Codices of the Vulgate, this sentence occurs twice, viz. at the end of ver. 10, and also of ver. 11; and Thenius, Ewald, and Böttcher regard the clause at the end of ver. 10 as the original one, and the repetition of it at the close of ver. 11 as a gloss. But this is certainly a mistake: for if the clause, "and the speech of all Israel came to the king to his house (at Mahanaim)," ought to stand at the close of ver. 10, and assigns the reason for David's sending to Zadok and Abiathar, ver. 11 would certainly, or rather necessarily, commence with וַיִּשְׁלַח הַמֶּלֶךְ: "The word of all Israel came to the king, and then king David sent," etc. But instead of this, it commences with וְהַמֶּלֶךְ דָּוִד שָׁלַח, "But king David sent." This construction of the sentence decidedly favours the correctness of the Hebrew text; whereas the text of the Septuagint, apart altogether from the tautological repetition of the whole of the sentence in question, shows obviously enough that it is nothing more than a conjecture, by which the attempt was made to remove the difficulty occasioned by the striking position in which the circumstantial clause occurred. —Ver. 13. "And say ye to Amasa, Art thou not my bone and flesh? so shall God do to me, and so add, if thou shalt not be prince of the army (chief captain) before me continually in the place of Joab."—Ver. 14. Thus he (David) inclined the heart of all the people as of one man, and they sent to the king, saying, "Return thou, with all thy servants." The result of David's message to the priests is given summarily here. The subject to וַיֵּט is David, not Amasa or Zadok. So far as the fact itself is concerned, it was certainly wise of David to send to the members of his own tribe, and appeal to them not to be behind the rest of the tribes in taking part in his restoration to the kingdom, lest it should appear as though the tribe of Judah, to which David himself belonged, was dissatisfied with his victory, since it was in that tribe that the rebellion itself first broke out; and this would inevitably feed the jealousy between Judah and the rest of the tribes. But it was not only unwise, but unjust, to give to Amasa, the traitor-general of the rebels, a promise on oath that he should be commander-in-chief in the place of Joab; for even if the promise was only given privately at first, the fact that it had been given could not remain a secret from Joab very long, and would be sure to stir up his ambition, and lead him to the commission of fresh crimes, and in all probability the enmity of this powerful general would become dangerous to the throne of David. For however Joab might have excited David's anger by slaying Absalom, and by the offensive manner in which he had reproved the king for giving way to his grief,

David ought to have suppressed his anger in his existing circumstances, and ought not to have rendered evil for evil, especially as he was not only about to pardon Amasa's crime, but even to reward him as one of his faithful servants.

Vers. 15–30. *Return of the king; and occurrences at the crossing of the Jordan.*—Vers. 15–23. *Pardon of Shimei.*—Vers. 15, 16. When David reached the Jordan on his return, and Judah had come to Gilgal "to meet him, to conduct the king over the Jordan," *i.e.* to form an escort at the crossing, Shimei the Benjaminite hastened down from Bahurim (see ch. xvi. 5 sqq.) with the men of Judah to meet David.—Vers. 17 sqq. There also came along with Shimei a thousand men of Benjamin, and Ziba the servant of the house of Saul, with his fifteen sons and twenty servants (see ch. ix. 10); and they went over the Jordan before the king, viz. through a ford, and the ferry-boat had crossed over to carry over the king's family, and to do whatever seemed good to him, *i.e.* to be placed at the king's sole disposal. And Shimei fell down before the king, בְּעָבְרוֹ, *i.e.* "*when he* (David) *was about to cross over the Jordan,*" not " when Shimei had crossed over the Jordan;" for after what has just been stated, such a remark would be superfluous: moreover, it is very doubtful whether the infinitive with בְּ can express the sense of the pluperfect. Shimei said, "Let not my lord impute to me any crime, and do not remember how thy servant hath sinned."—Ver. 20. "For thy servant knoweth (*i.e.* I know) that I have sinned, and behold I have come to-day the first of the whole house of Joseph, to go to meet my lord the king." By "*the whole house of Joseph*" we are to understand the rest of the tribes with the exception of Judah, who are called "*all Israel*" in ver. 12. There is no reason for the objection taken by Thenius and Böttcher to the expression בֵּית־יוֹסֵף. The rendering of the LXX. (παντὸς ’Ισραὴλ καὶ οἴκου ’Ιωσήφ) does not prove that כָּל־יִשְׂרָאֵל was the original reading, but only that the translator thought it necessary to explain οἴκου ’Ιωσήφ by adding the gloss παντὸς ’Ισραήλ ; and the assertion that it was only in the oratorical style of a later period, when the kingdom had been divided, that Joseph became the party name of all that were not included in Judah, is overthrown by 1 Kings xi. 28. The designation of the tribes that opposed Judah by the name of the leading tribe (*Joseph:*

Josh. xvi. 1) was as old as the jealousy between these tribes and Judah, which did not commence with the division of the kingdom, but was simply confirmed thereby into a permanent distinction. Shimei's prayer for the forgiveness of his sin was no more a proof of sincere repentance than the reason which he adduced in support of his petition, namely that he was the first of all the house of Joseph to come and meet David. Shimei's only desire was to secure impunity for himself Abishai therefore replied (ver. 21), "Shall not Shimei be put to death for this (תַּחַת זֹאת, for this, which he has just said and done), because he hath cursed the anointed of Jehovah?" (vid. ch. xvi. 5 sqq.) But David answered (ver. 22), "What have I to do with you, ye sons of Zeruiah (cf. ch. xvi. 10), for ye become opponents to me to-day?" שָׂטָן, *an opponent*, who places obstacles in the way (Num. xxii. 22); here it signifies one who would draw away to evil. "Should any one be put to death in Israel to-day? for do I not know that I am this day king over Israel?" The reason assigned by David here for not punishing the blasphemer as he had deserved, by taking away his life, would have been a very laudable one if the king had really forgiven him. But as David when upon his deathbed charged his successor to punish Shimei for this cursing (1 Kings ii. 8, 9), the favour shown him here was only a sign of David's weakness, which was not worthy of imitation, the more especially as the king swore unto him (ver. 24) that he should not die.

Vers. 24-30. *David's conduct towards Mephibosheth* admits still less of justification.—Ver. 24. Mephibosheth, the son, *i.e.* grandson, of Saul, had also come down (from Jerusalem to the Jordan) to meet David, and had not "*made his feet and his beard,*" *i.e.* had not washed his feet or arranged his beard (עָשָׂה, as in Deut. xxi. 12), and had not washed his clothes—all of them signs of deep mourning (cf. Ezek. xxiv. 17)—since the day that the king had gone (*i.e.* had fled from Jerusalem) until the day that he came (again) in peace.—Ver. 25. "*Now when Jerusalem* (*i.e.* the inhabitants of the capital) *came to meet the king,*"[1] David said to him (*i.e.* to Mephibosheth, who was

[1] Dathe and Thenius propose to alter יְרוּשָׁלַיִם into מִירוּשָׁלַיִם (*from Jerusalem*), from a simple misunderstanding of the true meaning of the words; for, as Böttcher has observed, the latter (*from* Jerusalem) would

with the deputation from the capital which welcomed David at the Jordan), "*Why wentest thou not with me, Mephibosheth?*" David was justified in putting this question after what Ziba had told him concerning Mephibosheth (ch. xvi. 3).—Ver. 26. Mephibosheth replied, "My lord king, my servant hath deceived me: for thy servant thought I will have the ass saddled and go to the king; for thy servant is lame." If we understand אֶחְבְּשָׁה as signifying that Mephibosheth had the ass saddled by a servant, and not that he saddled it with his own hands, the meaning is obvious, and there is no ground whatever for altering the text. חָבַשׁ is certainly used in this sense in Gen. xxii. 3, and it is very common for things to be said to be done by a person, even though not done with his own hands. The rendering adopted by the LXX. and Vulgate, "Thy servant said to him (the servant), Saddle me the ass," is not true to the words, though correct so far as the sense is concerned. —Vers. 27, 28. "And he (Ziba) slandered thy servant to my lord the king." Mephibosheth had not merely inferred this from David's words, and the tone in which they were spoken, but had certainly found it out long ago, since Ziba would not delay very long to put David's assurance, that all the possessions of Mephibosheth should belong to him, in force against his master, so that Mephibosheth would discover from that how Ziba had slandered him. "And my lord the king is as the angel of God," *i.e.* he sees all just as it really is (see at ch. xiv. 17); "and do what is good in thy sight: for all my father's house (the whole of my family) were but men of death against my lord the king (*i.e.* thou mightest have had us all put to death), and thou didst set thy servant among thy companions at table

---

be quite superfluous, as it is already contained in the previous יָרַד. But Böttcher's emendation of בָּא into בְּאָה, because Jerusalem or the population of Jerusalem is a feminine notion, is equally unnecessary, since towns and lands are frequently construed as masculines when the inhabitants are intended (*vid.* Ewald, § 318, *a*). On the other hand, the rendering adopted by the LXX., and by Luther, Michaelis, and Maurer, in which יְרוּשָׁלַיִם is taken as an accusative in the sense of "when Mephibosheth came to Jerusalem to meet the king," is altogether wrong, and has been very properly given up by modern expositors, inasmuch as it is at variance not only with the word יָרַד, but also with ch. xvi. 3 and ix. 13, where Mephibosheth is said to have lived in Jerusalem.

(see ch. ix. 7, 11); and what right or (what) more have I still to cry (for help) to the king?" The meaning is, "I cannot assert any claims, but will yield to anything you decide concerning me." It must have been very evident to David from these words of Mephibosheth, that he had been deceived by Ziba, and that he had formed an unfounded prejudice against Mephibosheth, and committed an act of injustice in handing over his property to Ziba. He therefore replied, in evident displeasure (ver. 29), "Why talkest thou still of thine affairs? I have said, thou and Ziba shall divide the field?" to which Mephibosheth answered (ver. 30), "He may take the whole, since my lord the king has returned in peace to his own house." This reply shows very clearly that an injustice had been done to Mephibosheth, even if it is not regarded as an expression of wounded feeling on the part of Mephibosheth because of David's words, but, according to the view taken by Seb. Schmidt and others, as a vindication of himself, as said not to blame the king for the opinion he had formed, but simply to defend himself. But this completely overthrows the opinion held by Thenius and O. v. Gerlach, that David's words in ver. 30 contain nothing more than a revocation of his hasty declaration in ch. xvi. 4, and a confirmation of his first decision in ch. ix. 7–10, and are to be understood as signifying, "Let everything be as I settled it at first; hold the property jointly," inasmuch as Ziba and his sons had of course obtained their living from the produce of the land. Moreover, the words "thou and Ziba divide the land" are directly at variance with the promise in ch. ix. 7, "I will restore thee *all* the land of Saul thy father," and the statement in ch. ix. 9, "I have given unto thy master's son all that pertained to Saul, and to all his house." By the words, "*I have said, thou and Ziba divide the land*," David retracted the hasty decree in ch. xvi. 4, so as to modify to some extent the wrong that he had done to Mephibosheth, but he had not courage enough to retract it altogether. He did not venture to dispute the fact that Mephibosheth had really been calumniated by Ziba, which was placed beyond all doubt by his mourning during the whole period of David's flight, as described in ver. 24. There is no ground for Winer's statement, therefore, that "it is impossible now to determine whether Mephibosheth was really innocent or not."

Vers. 31-39. *Barzillai comes to greet David.*—Ver. 31. Barzillai the octogenarian "had also come down from Roglim and gone across the Jordan with the king, to escort him over the river." אֶת־הַיַּרְדֵּן is the portion in, or over, the Jordan. אֶת is the sign of the accusative, "the piece in the Jordan," and no further. This is the correct explanation as given by Böttcher, after Gesenius and Maurer; and the *Keri* הַיַּרְדֵּן is a bad emendation.—Vers. 32, 33. As Barzillai had supplied the king with provisions during his stay in Mahanaim (שִׂיבָה for יְשִׁיבָה, like צוֹאָה for יְצוֹאָה, and other words of the same kind), because he was very wealthy (*lit.* great), David would gladly have taken him with him to Jerusalem, to repay him there for his kindness; but Barzillai replied (vers. 34 sqq.), " How many days are there of the years of my life (*i.e.* how long shall I have yet to live), that I should go up with the king to Jerusalem? I am now eighty years old; can I (still) distinguish good and evil, or will thy servant taste what I eat and drink, or listen again to the voice of the singing men and singing women? and why should thy servant be yet a burden unto my lord the king? Thy servant would go over the Jordan with the king for a short time (*i.e.* could not remain long with him), and why does the king wish to repay me this favour?" יָשָׁב־נָא: "Let thy servant return, that I may die in my city (my home), at the grave of my parents; and behold thy servant Chimham (*i.e.* according to the explanation given by Josephus, Barzillai's son, who had come down with his father, as we may infer from 1 Kings ii. 7) may go over with my lord the king; and do to him what seemeth good to thee," *i.e.* show him favours at thy pleasure.—Ver. 38. David consented to this, and said, "All that thou desirest of me I will do to him." בָּחַר with עַל is a pregnant construction, signifying to choose and impose, "*choose upon me*," *i.e.* the thing for me to grant thee.—Ver. 39. Thus all the people went over the Jordan; and when the king had crossed over, he kissed Barzillai (to take leave of him: *vid.* Ruth i. 9); and he (Barzillai) blessed him, and turned to his place (returned home). Barzillai only escorted the king over the Jordan, and the conversation (vers. 31-38) probably took place as they were crossing.

DISCONTENT IN ISRAEL, AND SHEBA'S REBELLION.—
CHAP. XIX. 40–XX. 26.

Vers. 40–43. *Quarrel between Israel and Judah about the restoration of the king.*—Ver. 40. David went across to Gilgal (in the plain of the Jordan: Josh. iv. 19), and Chimham (*Chimhan* is a modified form for *Chimham:* ver. 37) had gone over with him, and all the people of Judah had brought the king over (the *Keri* הֶעֱבִירוּ is an easier reading than the *Chethib* יַעֲבִירוּ, "and as for the people, they had," etc.), and also "half the people of Israel," namely, beside the thousand Benjaminites who came with Shimei (ver. 17), other Israelites who dwelt in the neighbourhood.—Ver. 41. *All the men of Israel, i.e.* the representatives of the other tribes of Israel, came to meet the king in Gilgal; and being annoyed at the fact that the men of Judah had anticipated them, they exclaimed, "Why have our brethren the men of Judah stolen thee away?" *i.e.* fetched thee thus secretly without saying a word to us. "*All David's men*" were all his faithful adherents who had fled with him from Jerusalem (ch. xv. 17 sqq.).—Ver. 42. The men of Judah replied against (עַל) the men of Israel: "The king stands near to us" (inasmuch as he belonged to their tribe), "and wherefore then art thou angry at this matter? Have we eaten from the king (*i.e.* derived any advantage from our tribe-relationship to him, as the Benjaminites did from Saul, according to 1 Sam. xxii. 7), or received anything for ourselves therefrom?" נִשֵּׂאת is an infinitive *abs. Niph.* with a feminine termination, borrowed from ל״ה; literally, "*or has taking been taken for us.*"—Ver. 43. The Israelites were annoyed at this answer, and retorted, "I (Israel) have ten portions in the king, and also more than thou in David; and wherefore hast thou despised me?" They considered that they had ten shares in the king, because they formed ten tribes, in opposition to the one tribe of Judah, as the Levites did not come into consideration in the matter. Although David was of the tribe of Judah, he was nevertheless king of the whole nation, so that the ten tribes had a larger share than one tribe. הֱקִלֹּתַנִי refers to the fact, that Judah took no notice at all of the tribes of Israel when fetching back the king. וְלֹא־הָיָה וגו׳, "*and was not my speech the first to fetch back my king?*" (On the fact itself, see ch. xix. 10, 11.) לִי is an emphatic *dat. commodi*, and is to be taken in connection with לְהָשִׁיב, notwithstanding the accents. "And the speech of the men of Judah became fiercer (more violent) than the speech of the men of Israel." With these words the historian sums up briefly the further progress of the dispute, for the purpose of appending the account of Sheba's rebellion, to which it gave rise.

Chap. xx. 1-22. SHEBA'S REBELLION.—Ver. 1. There happened to be a worthless man there, named *Sheba*, a Benjaminite. He blew the trumpet, and said, "We have no part in David, nor inheritance in the son of Jesse. Every man to his tents, O Israel!" "*To his tents*," *i.e.* to his home, as in ch. xix. 9, etc.—Ver. 2. All the men of Israel responded to this call, and went up (to the mountains) away from David and after Sheba; but the men of Judah adhered to their king from the Jordan to Jerusalem. The construction of דָּבַק with וְעַד ... מִן is a pregnant one: they adhered to and followed him. The expression "*from Jordan*" does not prove that Sheba's rebellion broke out at the Jordan itself, and before David's arrival in Gilgal, but may be accounted for from the fact that the men of Judah had already fetched the king back across the Jordan.—Ver. 3. As soon as David returned to his palace at Jerusalem, he brought the ten concubines whom he had left behind, and with whom Absalom had lain, into a place of safety, and took care of them, without going in unto them any more. The masculine suffixes attached to יִתְּנֵם, יְכַלְכְּלֵם, and אֲלֵיהֶם are used, as they frequently are, as being the more general and indefinite, instead of the feminine, which is the more definite form. Thus were they shut up in lifelong widowhood until the day of their death. אַלְמְנוּת is an adverbial accusative, and חַיּוּת signifies "condition in life;" literally, in widowhood of life.—Ver. 4. David then ordered Amasa to call the men of Judah to pursue Sheba the rebel, and attack him within three days, and then to present himself to him again. This commission was intended as the commencement of the fulfilment of the promise which David had given to Amasa (ch. xix. 14). It was no doubt his intention to give him the command over the army that marched against Sheba, and after the defeat of the rebel to make him commander-in-chief. But this first step towards the fulfilment of the promise was a very imprudent act, like the promise itself, since Joab, who had been commander of the army for so many years, was grievously offended by it; and moreover, being a well-tried general, he had incomparably more distinction in the tribe of Judah than Amasa, who had taken part in Absalom's rebellion and even led the rebel army, could possibly have.—Vers. 5, 6. But when Amasa stayed out beyond the time fixed for the execution of the royal commission (the *Chethib* וייחר is the *Piel* וַיְיַחֵר, whilst the *Keri* is either the *Hiphil* וַיֹּחֶר, or the imperfect *Kal* of יָחַר = אָחַר, cf. תֹּחַז, ver. 9, and is quite unnecessary), probably because the men of Judah distrusted him, and were not very ready to respond to his summons, David said to Abishai, "Now will Sheba the son of Bichri be more injurious (more dangerous) to us than Absalom. Take thou the servants (soldiers) of thy lord and pursue after him, lest he reach fortified cities, and *tear out our eye*," *i.e.* do us a serious injury. This is the correct explanation given by Böttcher, who refers to Deut. xxxii. 10 and Zech. ii. 12, where the apple of the eye is the figure used to signify the most valuable possession; for the general explanation, "and withdraw from our eye," cannot be grammatically sustained.—Ver. 7. *Thus there went after him* (Abishai) *Joab's men* (the corps commanded by Joab), *and the Crethi and Plethi* (see at ch. viii. 18), out of Jerusalem, to pursue Sheba.—Ver. 8. "When they were by the great stone at Gibeon, and Amasa came to meet them (there), Joab was girded with his armour-coat as his clothing, and the girdle of the sword was bound over it upon his loins in its sheath, which came out, and it fell (*i.e.* the sheath came out of the sword-belt in which it was fastened, and the sword fell to the ground), Joab said to Amasa," etc. The eighth verse contains only circumstantial clauses, the latter of which (from וְיֹאָב onwards) are subordinate to the earlier ones, so that וַיֹּאמֶר (ver. 9) is attached to the first clause, which describes the meeting between the advancing army and Amasa.

There is something striking, however, in the fact that Joab appears among them, and indeed, as we see from what follows, as the commander of the forces; for according to ver. 6, David had commissioned Abishai, Joab's brother, to pursue Sheba, and even in ver. 7 Joab's men only are mentioned. This difficulty can hardly be solved in any other manner than by the simple assumption that David had told Abishai to go out with Joab, and that this circumstance is passed over in the brief account in ver. 6, in which the principal facts alone are given, and consequently the name of Joab does not occur there. Clericus adopts the following explanation. "Mention," he says, "has hitherto been made simply of the command given to Abishai, but this included an order to Joab to go as well; and there is nothing to preclude the supposition that Joab's name was mentioned by the king, although this is not distinctly stated in the brief account before us."[1]—Ver. 9. Joab asked Amasa how he was, and laid hold of his beard with his right hand to kiss him. And as Amasa took no heed of the sword in Joab's hand, he smote him with it in the paunch (abdomen), and shed out his bowels upon the ground, "*and repeated not* (the stroke) *to him*" (cf. 1 Sam. xxvi. 8). Laying hold of the beard to kiss is still customary among Arabs and Turks as a sign of friendly welcome (*vid.* Arvieux, *Merkwürdige Nachrichten*, iv. p. 182, and Harmar, *Beobachtungen*, ii. p. 61). The reason for this assassination was Joab's jealousy of Amasa. Joab and Abishai then followed Sheba.—Ver. 11. One of Joab's attendants remained standing by him (Amasa), no doubt at Joab's command, and said to the people who came thither, *i.e.* to the men of Judah who were collected together by Amasa (*vid.* ver. 4), "He that favoureth Joab, and he that (is) for David, let him (go) after Joab," *i.e.* follow him to battle against Sheba.— Vers. 12, 13. Amasa lay wallowing in blood in the midst of the road; and when the man (the attendant) saw that all the

---

[1] This difficulty cannot be removed by emendations of the text, inasmuch as all the early translators, with the exception of the Syriac, had our Hebrew text before them. Thenius does indeed propose to alter *Abishai* into *Joab* in ver. 6, after the example of Josephus and the Syriac; but, as Böttcher observes, if *Joab* had originally formed part of the text, it could not have been altered into Abishai either accidentally or intentionally, and the Syriac translators and Josephus have inserted *Joab* merely from conjecture, because they inferred from what follows that Joab's name ought to be found here. But whilst this is perfectly true, there is no ground for Böttcher's own conjecture, that in the original text ver. 6 read as follows: "Then David said to Joab, Behold, the three days are gone: shall we wait for Amasa?" and through the copyist's carelessness a whole line was left out. For this conjecture has no tenable support in the senseless reading of the *Cod. Vat.*, πρὸς Ἀμισσαί for Ἀβισαί.

people stood still (by the corpse), he turned (pushed) Amasa from the road to the field, and threw a cloth over him, whereupon they all passed by and went after Joab.—Ver. 14. But Joab "went through all the tribes of Israel to Abela, and Beth-Maacah, and all Berim." *Abela* (ver. 15), or *Abel* (ver. 18), has been preserved in the large Christian village of *Abil*, a place with ruins, and called *Abil-el-Kamh* on account of its excellent wheat (*Kamh*), which lies to the north-west of Lake Huleh, upon a Tell on the eastern side of the river *Derdára;* not in *Ibl-el-Hawa*, a place to the north of this, upon the ridge between *Merj Ayun* and *Wady et Teim* (*vid.* Ritter, *Erdk.* xv. pp. 240, 241; Robinson, *Bibl. Researches*, pp. 372–3; and v. de Velde, *Mem.* p. 280). *Beth-Maacah* was quite close to Abela; so that the names of the two places are connected together in ver. 15, and afterwards, as *Abel-Beth-Maacah* (*vid.* 1 Kings xv. 20, and 2 Kings xv. 29), also called *Abel-Maim* in 2 Chron. xvi. 4. *Berim* is the name of a district which is unknown to us; and even the early translators did not know how to render it. There is nothing, however, either in the πάντες ἐν χαρρί of the LXX or the *omnes viri electi* of the Vulgate, to warrant an alteration of the text. The latter, in fact, rests upon a mere conjecture, which is altogether unsuitable; for the subject to וַיִּקָּהֲלוּ cannot be כָּל־הַבֵּרִים on account of the *vav consec.*, but must be obtained from בְּכָל־שִׁבְטֵי יִשְׂרָאֵל. The *Chethib* ויקלהו is evidently a slip of the pen for וַיִּקָּהֲלוּ.—Ver. 15. They besieged him (Sheba) in Abel-Beth-Maacah, and *piled up a rampart against the city*, so that *it rose up by the town-moat* (חֵל, the moat with the low wall belonging to it); and *all the people with Joab destroyed to throw down the wall*.

Vers. 16 sqq. Then a wise woman of the city desired to speak to Joab, and said (from the wall) to him (ver. 18), "They were formerly accustomed to say, ask Abel; and so they brought (a thing) to pass." These words show that Abel had formerly been celebrated for the wisdom of its inhabitants. —Ver. 19. "I am of the peaceable, faithful in Israel: thou seekest to slay a city and mother in Israel; wherefore wilt thou destroy the inheritance of Jehovah?" The construing of אָנֹכִי with a predicate in the plural may be explained on the simple ground that the woman spoke in the name of the city as well as in its favour, and therefore had the citizens in her mind at the time, as is very evident from the figurative expression אֵם (mother) for mother-city or capital.[1] The woman gave Joab to understand, in the first place, that he ought to have asked the inhabitants of Abela whether they intended to fight for Sheba before commencing the siege and destruction of the town, according to the law laid down in Deut. xx. 10 sqq. with reference to the siege of foreign towns; and secondly, that he ought to have taken into consideration the peaceableness and fidelity of the citizens of Abela, and not to destroy peace-loving citizens and members of the nation of God.—Ver. 20. The woman's words made an impression upon Joab. He felt the truthfulness of her reproaches, and replied, "Far be it, far be it from me, to swallow up or destroy." אִם, as in the case of oaths: "*truly not*."—Ver. 21. "It is not so (*sc.* as thou sayest), but a man of the mountains of Ephraim (which extended into the tribe of Benjamin: see at 1 Sam. i. 1), Sheba the son of Bichri, hath lifted up his hand against the king David. Only give him up, and I will draw away from the city." The woman promised him this: "Behold, his head shall be thrown out to thee over the wall."—Ver. 22. She then came to all the people (*i.e.* the citizens of the town) "*with her wisdom*," *i.e.* with the wise counsel which she had given to Joab, and which he had accepted; whereupon the citizens cut off Sheba's head, and threw it out to Joab. Then Joab had a trumpet blown for a retreat, and the men disbanded, whilst he himself returned to Jerusalem to the king.

Vers. 23-26. DAVID'S MINISTERS OF STATE.—The second section of the history of David's reign closes, like the first (ch. viii. 16 sqq.), with a list of the leading ministers of state. The author evidently found the two lists in his sources, and included

---

[1] The correctness of the text is not to be called in question, as Thenius and Böttcher suppose, for the simple reason that all the older translators have followed the Hebrew text, including even the LXX. with their ἐγώ εἰμι εἰρηνικὰ τῶν στηριγμάτων ἐν Ἰσραήλ; whereas the words ἃ ἔθεντο οἱ πιστοὶ τοῦ Ἰσραήλ, which some of the MSS. contain at the close of ver. 18 after εἰ ἐξέλιπον, and upon which Thenius and Böttcher have founded their conjectures, are evidently a gloss or paraphrase of וּבֵן הָתֵמוּ, and of so little value on critical grounds, that Tischendorf did not even think the reading worth mentioning in his edition of the Septuagint.

them both in his work, for the simple reason that they belonged to different periods, as the difference in the names of some of the officers clearly shows, and that they supplemented one another. The list before us belongs to a later period of David's reign than the one in ch. viii. 16–18. In addition to the office-bearers mentioned in ch. viii., we find here *Adoram* over the tribute, and *Ira* the Jairite a confidential counsellor (*cohen* : see at ch. viii. 18), in the place of the sons of David noticed in ch. viii. 18. The others are the same in both lists. The *Chethib* הכרי is to be read הַכָּרִי (cf. 2 Kings xi. 4, 19), from בּוּר, *perfodit*, and is synonymous with הַכְּרֵתִי (see at ch. viii. 18). Adoram is the same person as Adoniram, who is mentioned in 1 Kings iv. 6 and v. 28 as overseer over the tributary service in the time of Solomon ; as we may see from the fact, that the latter is also called Adoram in 1 Kings xii. 18, and Hadoram in 2 Chron. x. 18. Hadoram is apparently only a contracted form of the name, and not merely a copyist's mistake for Adoniram. But when we find that, according to the passages cited, the same man filled this office under three kings, we must bear in mind that he did not enter upon it till the close of David's reign, as he is not mentioned in ch. viii. 16 sqq., and that his name only occurs in connection with Rehoboam's ascent of the throne ; so that there is no ground for assuming that he filled the office for any length of time under that monarch. הַמַּס does not mean *vectigal*, *i.e.* tribute or tributary service, but tributary labourers. The derivation of the word is uncertain, and has been disputed. The appointment of a special prefect over the tributary labourers can hardly have taken place before the closing years of David's reign, when the king organized the internal administration of the kingdom more firmly than before. On the tributary labourers, see at 1 Kings v. 27. Ira the Jairite is never mentioned again. There is no ground for altering *Jairi* (the Jairite) into *Jithri* (the Jithrite), as Thenius proposes, since the rendering given in the Syriac ("from Jathir") is merely an inference from ch. xxiii. 38 ; and the assumption upon which this conclusion is founded, viz. that *Ira*, the hero mentioned in ch. xxiii. 38, is the same person as *Ira* the royal *cohen*, is altogether unfounded.

IV. CLOSE OF DAVID'S REIGN.

Chap. XXI.-XXIV.

After the suppression of the rebellion headed by Sheba, David spent the remaining years of his reign in establishing the kingdom upon a firmer basis, partly by organizing the army, the administration of justice, and the general government of the realm, and partly by making preparations for the erection of the temple, and enacting rules for the service of the Levites; that he might be able to hand over the government in a firm and satisfactory state to his youthful son Solomon, whom the Lord had appointed as his successor. The account of these regulations and enactments fills up the whole of the last section of the history of David's reign in the first book of Chronicles. But in the book before us, several other things—(1) two divine punishments inflicted upon Israel, with the expiation of the sins that occasioned them (ch. xxi. 1-14, and ch. xxiv.); (2) David's psalm of praise for deliverance out of the hand of all his enemies (ch. xxii.), and his last prophetic words (ch. xxiii. 1-7); and (3) a few brief notices of victorious acts performed in the wars with the Philistines (ch. xxi. 15-22), and a longer list of David's heroes (ch. xxiii. 8-39)—form, as it were, a historical framework for these poetical and prophetic portions. Of the two divine visitations mentioned, the pestilence occasioned by the numbering of the people (ch. xxiv.) occurred undoubtedly in the closing years of David's reign; whereas the famine, and the expiation connected with it (ch. xxi. 1-14), happened most probably at an earlier period, and are merely introduced here because no fitting opportunity had presented itself before. The kernel and centre of this last section of the history of David is to be found unquestionably in the psalm of thanksgiving in ch. xxii., and the prophetic announcement of an exalted and blessed king. In the psalm of thanksgiving David looks back at the close of his life upon all the mercy and faithfulness which he had experienced throughout his reign, and praises the Lord his God for the whole. In his "last words" he looks forward into the time to come, and on the strength of the promise which he has received, of the eternal duration of the dominion of his house, sees in spirit the just Ruler, who will one day arise from his seed, and take the throne of his kingdom for ever. These two lyrical and prophetic productions of David, the ripest spiritual fruit of his life, form a worthy conclusion to his reign. To this there is appended the list of his heroes, in the form of a supplement (ch. xxiii. 8-39); and finally in ch. xxiv. the account of the numbering of the people, and the pestilence which fell upon Israel, as a punishment for this fault on the part of David. This account is placed at the close of the books of Samuel, merely because the altar which was built to expiate the wrath of God, together with the sacrifices offered upon it, served to consecrate the site for the temple, which was to be erected after David's death, in accordance with the divine promise (ch. vii. 13), by his son and successor Solomon.

THREE YEARS' FAMINE. HEROIC ACTS PERFORMED IN THE WARS WITH THE PHILISTINES.—CHAP. XXI.

Vers. 1-14. THREE YEARS' FAMINE.—A three years' famine in the land, the occasion of which, as Jehovah declared to the king, was Saul's crime with regard to the Gibeonites, was expiated by David's delivering up to the Gibeonites, at their own request, seven of Saul's descendants, who were then hung by them upon a mountain before Jehovah. This occurrence certainly did not take place in the closing years of David's reign; on the other hand, it is evident from the remark in ver. 7, to the effect that Mephibosheth was spared, that it happened after David had received tidings of Mephibosheth, and had taken him to his own table (ch. ix.). This is mentioned here as a practical illustration, on the one hand of the manner in which Jehovah visited upon the house of Saul, even after the death of Saul himself, a crime which had been committed by him; and, on the other hand, of the way in which, even in such a case as this, when David had been obliged to sacrifice the descendants of Saul to expiate the guilt of their father, he showed his tenderness towards him by the honourable burial of their bones.

Vers. 1-6a. A famine, which lasted for three successive years, induced David to seek the face of Jehovah, *i.e.* to approach God in prayer and ask the cause of this judgment which had fallen upon the land. The Lord replied, "Because of Saul, and because of the house of blood-guiltiness, because he hath slain the Gibeonites." The expression "because of the house of blood-guiltiness" is in apposition to "Saul," and determines the meaning more precisely: "because of Saul, and indeed because of the blood-guiltiness which rests upon his house." בֵּית הַדָּמִים signifies the house upon which blood that had been shed still rested as guilt, like עִיר הַדָּמִים in Ezek. xxii. 2, xxiv. 6, 9, and אִישׁ דָּמִים in Ps. v. 7, xxvi. 9, etc. Nothing further is known about the fact itself. It is simply evident from the words of the Gibeonites in ver. 5, that Saul, in his pretended zeal for the children of Israel, had smitten the Gibeonites, *i.e.* had put them to death. Probably some dissatisfaction with them had furnished Saul with a pretext for exterminating these Amoritish heathen from the midst of the people of God.—Ver. 2. In consequence of this answer from God, which merely indicated in a general manner the cause of the visitation that had come upon the land, David sent for the Gibeonites to ask them concerning the wrong that had been done them by Saul. But before the historian communicates their answer, he introduces an explanation respecting the Gibeonites, to the effect that they were not Israelites, but remnants of the Amorites, to whom Joshua had promised on oath that their lives should be preserved (*vid.* Josh. ix. 3 sqq.). They are called *Hivites* in the book of Joshua (ch. ix. 7); whereas here they are designated *Amorites*, according to the more general name which is frequently used as comprehending all the tribes of Canaan (see at Gen. x. 16 and xv. 16). David said to the Gibeonites, "What shall I do for you, and wherewith shall I expiate" (*sc.* the wrong done you), "that ye may bless the inheritance (*i.e.* the nation) of Jehovah?" On the use of the imperative וּבָרְכוּ to denote the certain consequences, see Ewald, § 347.—Ver. 4. The Gibeonites answered, "I have not to do with silver and gold concerning Saul and his house" (*lit.* it is not, does not stand, to me at silver and gold with Saul and his house), *i.e.* I have no money to demand of Saul, require no pecuniary payment as compensation for the blood which he shed among us (*vid.* Num. xxxv. 31). The *Chethib* לִי is not to be touched, notwithstanding the לָנוּ which follows. The use of the singular may be explained on the simple ground that the speaker thought of the Gibeonites as a corporation. "And it does not pertain to us to put any one to death in Israel" (*sc.* of our own accord). When David inquired still further, "What do you mean, then, that I should do to you?" they replied, "(As for) the man who consumed us, and who thought against us, that we should be destroyed (נִשְׁמַדְנוּ) without כִּי, subordinate to דִּמָּה, like אֲשֶׁר in the previous verse), so as not to continue in the whole of the territory of Israel, let seven men of his sons be given us, that we may crucify them to Jehovah at Gibeah of Saul, the chosen of Jehovah." אִישׁ אֲשֶׁר וגו׳ is placed at the head absolutely (cf. Gesenius, § 145, 2). On crucifixion as a capital punishment, see at Num. xxv. 4, where it has already been observed that criminals were not impaled or fastened to the cross alive, but were first of all put to death. Consequently the Gibeonites desired that the massacre, which had taken place among them by the command of Saul, should be expiated by the execution of a number of his sons—blood for blood, according to Num. xxxv. 31. They asked for the crucifixion for Jehovah, *i.e.* that the persons executed might be impaled, as a public exhibition of the punishment inflicted, before the face of the Lord (*vid.* ver. 9), as the satisfaction required to expiate His wrath. Seven was a sacred number, denoting the performance of a work of God. This was to take place in Gibeah, the home and capital of Saul, who had brought the wrath of God upon the land through his crime. There is a sacred irony in the epithet applied to Saul, "chosen of the Lord." If Saul was the chosen of Jehovah, his actions ought to have been in accordance with his divine election.

Vers. 6*b*–10. David granted the request, because, according to the law in Num. xxxv. 33, blood-guiltiness when resting upon the land could only be expiated by the blood of the criminal; but in delivering up the members of Saul's house for whom they asked, he spared Mephibosheth the son of Jonathan and grandson of Saul, for the sake of the bond of friendship which he had formed with Jonathan on oath (1 Sam. xviii. 3, xx. 8, 16), and gave up to the Gibeonites two sons of Rizpah, a concubine of Saul (*vid.* ver. 11 and ch. iii. 7), and five sons of Merab the daughter of Saul, whom she had borne to Adriel of Meholah. The name of *Michal*, which stands in the text, is founded upon an error of memory or a copyist's mistake; for it was not Michal, but *Merab*, Saul's eldest daughter, who was given to Adriel the Meholathite as his wife (1 Sam. xviii. 19). The Gibeonites crucified those who were delivered up to them upon the mountain at Gibeah before Jehovah (see the remarks on ver. 6). "*Thus fell seven at once.*" The *Chethib* שִׁבְעָתַיִם, at which the Masoretes took such offence that they wanted to change it into שִׁבְעָתָם, is defended by Böttcher very properly, on the ground that the dual of the numeral denotes what is uniformly repeated as if by pairing; so that here it expresses what was extraordinary in the event in a more pictorial manner than the *Keri*: "They fell sevenfold at once," *i.e.* seven in the same way. The further remark, "they were slain in the first days of harvest, at the beginning of the barley harvest," belongs to what follows, for which it prepares the way. The two *Keris*, וְהֵמָּה for וְהֵם, and בִּתְחִלַּת for תְּחִלַּת, are needless emendations. תְּחִלַּת is an adverbial accusative (*vid.* Ges. § 118, 2). The harvest began with the barley harvest, about the middle of Nisan, our April.—Ver. 10. And Rizpah took sackcloth, *i.e.* the coarse hairy cloth that was worn as mourning, and spread it out for herself by the rock—not as a tent, as Clericus supposes, still less as a covering over the corpses of those who had been executed, according to the exegetical handbook, but for a bed—"*from the beginning of the harvest till water was poured out upon them* (the crucified) *from heaven*," *i.e.* till rain came as a sign that the plague of drought that had rested upon the land was appeased; after which the corpses could be openly taken down from the stakes and buried,—a fact which is passed over in the account before us, where only the principal points are given. This is the explanation which Josephus has correctly adopted; but his assumption that the rain fell at once, and before the ordinary early rain, has no foundation in the text of the Bible. "And suffered not the birds of heaven to settle upon the corpses by day, or the wild beasts by night." Leaving corpses without burial, to be consumed by birds of prey and wild beasts, was regarded as the greatest ignominy that could befal the dead (see at 1 Sam. xvii. 44). According to Deut. xxi. 22, 23, persons executed were not to remain hanging through the night upon the stake, but to be buried before evening. This law, however, had no application whatever to the case before us, where the expiation of guilt that rested upon the whole land was concerned. In this instance the expiatory sacrifices were to remain exposed before Jehovah, till the cessation of the plague showed that His wrath had been appeased.

Vers. 11-14. When this touching care of Rizpah for the dead was told to David, he took care that the bones of the whole of the fallen royal house should be buried in the burial-place of Saul's family. He therefore sent for the bones of Saul and Jonathan, which the men of Jabesh had taken away secretly from the wall of Beisan, where the Philistines had fastened the bodies, and which had been buried in Jabesh (1 Sam. xxxi. 10 sqq.), and had the bones of the sons and grandsons of Saul who had been crucified at Gibeah collected together, and interred all these bones at Zela in the land of Benjamin, in the family grave of Kish the father of Saul. גָּנַב, to take away secretly. מֵרְחֹב בֵּית־שָׁן, from the *market-place* of Bethshan, does not present any contradiction to the statement in 1 Sam. xxxi. 10, that the Philistines fastened the body to the *wall* of Bethshan, as the *rechob* or market-place in eastern towns is not in the middle of the town, but is an open place against or in front of the gate (cf. 2 Chron. xxxii. 6; Neh. viii. 1, 3, 16). This place, as the common meeting-place of the citizens, was the most suitable spot that the Philistines could find for fastening the bodies to the wall. The *Chethib* תְּלוּם is the true Hebrew form from תָּלָה, whereas the *Keri* תְּלָאוּם is a formation resembling the Aramæan (cf. Ewald, § 252, *a*). The *Keri* שְׁמָּה פְלִשְׁתִּים is correct, however, as פְלִשְׁתִּים, being a proper name, does not take any article. In בְּיוֹם הַכּוֹת the literal meaning of יוֹם (day) must not be strictly pressed, but the expression is to be taken in the sense of "at the time of the smiting;" for the hanging up of the bodies did not take place till the day after the battle (1 Sam. xxxi. 8 sqq.).—In ver. 14 the account is abridged, and the bones of the crucified persons are not mentioned again. The situation of *Zela* is unknown (see at Josh. xviii. 28). After this had been carried out in accordance with the king's command, God suffered himself to be entreated for the land, so that the famine ceased.

Vers. 15-22. HEROIC ACTS PERFORMED IN THE WARS WITH THE PHILISTINES.—The brief accounts contained in these verses of different heroic feats were probably taken from a history of David's wars drawn up in the form of chronicles, and are introduced here as practical proofs of the gracious deliverance of David out of the hand of all his foes, for which he praises the Lord his God in the psalm of thanksgiving which follows, so that the enumeration of these feats is to be regarded as supplying a historical basis for the psalm.—Vers. 15–17. The Philistines had war with Israel again. עוֹד (again) refers generally to earlier wars with the Philistines, and has probably been taken without alteration from the chronicles employed by our author, where the account which follows was attached to notices of other wars. This may be gathered from the books of the Chronicles, where three of the heroic feats mentioned here are attached to the general survey of David's wars (*vid.* 1 Chron. xx. 4). David was exhausted in this fight, and a Philistian giant thought to slay him; but Abishai came to his help and slew the giant. He was called *Yishbo benob* (*Keri, Yishbi*), *i.e.* not *Yishbo* at *Nob*, but *Yishbobenob*, a proper name, the meaning of which is probably "his dwelling is on the height," and which may have been given to him because of his inaccessible castle. He was one of the descendants of Raphah, *i.e.* one of the gigantic race of Rephaim. *Raphah* was the tribe-father of the Rephaim, an ancient tribe of gigantic stature, of whom only a few families were left even in Moses' time (*vid.* Deut. ii. 11, iii. 11, 13, and the commentary on Gen. xiv. 5). The weight of his lance, *i.e.* of the metal point to his lance, was three hundred shekels, or eight pounds, of brass, half as much as the spear of Goliath (1 Sam. xvii. 7); "and he was girded with new armour." Böttcher has no doubt given the correct explanation of the word חֲדָשָׁה; he supposes the feminine to be used in a collective sense, so that the noun ("armour," כֵּלָיו) could be dispensed with. (For parallels both to the words and facts, *vid.* Judg. xviii. 11 and Deut. i. 41.) וַיֹּאמֶר, he said (*sc.* to himself), *i.e.* he thought.—Ver. 17. The danger into which the king had been brought in this war, and out of which he had been rescued solely by Abishai's timely help, induced his attendants to make him swear that he would not go into battle any more in person. נִשְׁבַּע לוֹ, administered an oath to him, *i.e.* fixed him by a promise on oath. וְלֹא תְכַבֶּה, "and shalt not extinguish the light of Israel." David had become the light of Israel from the fact that Jehovah was his light (ch. xxii. 29), or, according to the parallel passage in Ps. xviii. 29, that Jehovah had lighted his lamp and enlightened his darkness, *i.e.* had lifted him out of a state of humiliation and obscurity into one of honour and glory. The light (or lamp) is a figure used to represent the light of life as continually burning, *i.e.* life in prosperity and honour. David's regal life and actions were the light which the grace of God had kindled for the benefit of Israel. This light he was not to extinguish, namely by going into the midst of war and so exposing his valuable life to danger.—Ver. 18 (compare 1 Chron. xx. 4). In a second war, *Sibbechai* the Hushathite slew *Saph* the Rephaite at Gob. According to 1 Chron. xxvii. 11, *Sibbechai*, one of the *gibborim* of David (1 Chron. xi. 29), was the leader of the eighth division of the army (see at ch. xxiii. 27). הַחֻשָׁתִי is a patronymic from חוּשָׁה in 1 Chron. iv. 4. The scene of conflict is called *Gob* in our text, and *Gezer* in the Chronicles. As *Gob* is entirely unknown, Thenius supposes it to be a slip of the pen for Gezer; but this is improbable, for the simple reason that *Gob* occurs again in ver. 19. It may possibly have been a small place somewhere near to *Gezer*, which some suppose to have stood on the site of *el Kubab*, on the road from *Ramleh* to *Yalo* (see at Josh. x. 33). The name *Saph* is written *Sippai* in the Chronicles.—Ver. 19 (*vid.* 1 Chron. xx. 5). In another war with the Philistines at Gob, *Elhanan* the son of *Yaare-Orgim* of Bethlehem smote *Goliath* of Gath, whose spear was like a weaver's beam. In the Chronicles, however, we find it stated that "*Elhanan* the son of *Jair* smote *Lahmi* the brother of Goliath of Gath, whose spear," etc. The words of our text are so similar to those of the Chronicles, if we only leave out the word ארגים, which probably crept in from the next line through oversight on the part of a copyist, that they presuppose the same original text, so that the difference can only have arisen from an error in copying. The majority of the expositors (*e.g.* Piscator, Clericus, Michaelis, Movers, and Thenius) regard the text of the Chronicles as the true and original one, and the text before us as simply corrupt. But Bertheau and Böttcher maintain the opposite opinion, because it is impossible to see how the reading in 2 Sam. could grow out of that in the Chronicles; whereas the reading in the

Chronicles might have arisen through conscious alteration originating in the offence taken by some reader, who recalled the account of the conflict between David and Goliath, at the statement that Elhanan smote a giant named Goliath, and who therefore altered בית הלחמי את into את לחמי אחי. But apart from the question whether there were two Goliaths, one of whom was slain by David and the other by Elhanan, the fact that the conjecture of Bertheau and Böttcher presupposes a deliberate alteration of the text, or rather, to speak more correctly, an intentional falsification of the historical account, is quite sufficient to overthrow it, as not a single example of anything of the kind can be adduced from the whole of the Chronicles. On the other hand, the recollection of David's celebrated officer *Elhanan* of Bethlehem (ch. xxiii. 24; 1 Chron. xi. 26) might easily lead to an identification of the Elhanan mentioned here with that officer, and so occasion the alteration of את לחמי into בית הלחמי. This alteration was then followed by that of אחי גלית into את גלית, and all the more easily from the fact that the description of Lahmi's spear corresponds word for word with that of Goliath's spear in 1 Sam. xvii. 7. Consequently we must regard the reading in the Chronicles as the correct one, and alter our text accordingly; since the assumption that there were two Goliaths is a very improbable one, and there is nothing at all strange in the reference to a brother of Goliath, who was also a powerful giant, and carried a spear like Goliath. Elhanan the son of *Jairi* is of course a different person from Elhanan the Bethlehemite, the son of Dodo (ch. xxiii. 24). The Chronicles have יָעוּר instead of *Jairi* (the reading according to the *Chethib*), and the former is probably the correct way of writing the name.—Vers. 20, 21 (cf. 1 Chron. xx. 6, 7). In another war at Gath, a Philistian warrior, who had six fingers on each hand and six toes on each foot,[1] defied Israel, and was slain by Jonathan the son of Shimeah, the brother of David (see at ch. xiii. 3). The *Chethib* מדין is probably to be read מִדִּין, an archaic plural ("a man of measures,

---

[1] Men with six fingers and six toes have been met with elsewhere. Pliny (*h. nat.* xi. 43) speaks of certain *sedigiti* (six-fingered) Romans. This peculiarity is even hereditary in some families. Other examples are collected by Trusen (*Sitten, Gebräuche, und Krankheiten der alten Hebräer*, pp. 198–9, ed. 2) and Friedreich (*zur Bibel*, i. 298–9).

or extensions:" de Dieu, etc.); in the Chronicles we find the singular מִדָּה instead.—Ver. 22 (cf. 1 Chron. xx. 8). This verse contains a postscript, in which the previous verses are summed up. The accusative אֶת־אַרְבַּעַת may be explained from a species of attraction, *i.e.* from the fact that the historian had יֻבְּהוּ (ver. 21) still in his mind: " As for these four, they were born to *Rapha*," *i.e.* they were descendants of the Rephaite family at Gath, where remnants of the aboriginal Canaanitish tribes of gigantic stature were still to be found, as in other towns of the Philistines (*vid.* Josh. xi. 22). "They fell by the hand of David, and by the hand of his servants." "By the hand of David" refers to the fact that David had personally fought with *Yishbobenob* (ver. 16).

DAVID'S PSALM OF THANKSGIVING FOR VICTORY OVER ALL HIS ENEMIES.—CHAP. XXII.

In the following psalm of thanksgiving, David praises the Lord as his deliverer out of all dangers during his agitated life and conflicts with his foes (vers. 2-4). In the first half he pictures his marvellous deliverance out of all the troubles which he passed through, especially in the time of Saul's persecutions, under the image of an extraordinary theophany (vers. 5-20), and unfolds the ground of this deliverance (vers. 21-28). In the second half he proclaims the mighty help of the Lord, and his consequent victories over the foreign enemies of his government (vers. 29-46), and closes with renewed praise of God for all His glorious deeds (vers. 47-51). The psalm is thus arranged in two leading divisions, with an introductory and concluding strophe. But we cannot discover any definite system of strophes in the further arrangement of the principal divisions, as the several groups of thoughts are not rounded off symmetrically.

The contents and form of this song of praise answer to the fact attested by the heading, that it was composed by David in the later years of his reign, when God had rescued him from all his foes, and helped his kingdom to victory over all the neighbouring heathen nations. The genuineness of the psalm is acknowledged to be indisputable by all the modern critics, except J. Olshausen and Hupfeld,[1] who, with hypercritical scepticism, dispute the Davidic origin of the psalm on subjective grounds of æsthetic taste. This psalm is found in the Psalter as Ps. xviii., though with many divergences in single words and clauses, which do not, however, essentially affect the meaning. Commentators are divided in opinion as to the relation in which the two different forms of the text stand to one another. The idea that the text of 2 Sam. rests upon a careless copy and tradition must decidedly be rejected: for, on the one hand, by far the larger portion of the deviations in our text from that of the Psalter are not to be attributed to carelessness on the part of copyists, but are evidently alterations made with thoughtfulness and deliberation: *e.g.* the omission of the very first passage (ver. 1), "I will love Thee, O Lord, my strength;" the change of אֵלִי צוּרִי (my God, my strength, or rock) into אֱלֹהֵי צוּרִי (the God of my rock), as "the God of the rock" occurs again in ver. 47 of the text before us; or the substitution of וַיֵּרָא (He was seen, ver. 11) for וַיֵּדֶא (He did fly), etc. On the other hand, the original reading has undoubtedly been retained in many passages of our text, whilst simpler and more common forms have been substituted in that of the Psalms; *e.g.*

[1] Even Hitzig observes (*die Psalmen*, i. p. 95): "There is no ground whatever for calling in question the Davidic authorship of the psalm, and therefore the statement made in the heading; and, in fact, there is all the more reason for adhering to it, because it is attested twice. The recurrence of the psalm as one of Davidic origin in 2 Sam. xxii. is of some weight, since not the slightest suspicion attaches to any of the other songs or sayings attributed to David in the second book of Samuel (*e.g.* iii. 33, 34, v. 8, vii. 18-29, xxiii. 1-7). Moreover, the psalm is evidently ancient, and suited to the classical period of the language and its poetry. Ver. 31 is quoted as early as Prov. xxx. 5, and ver. 34 in Hab. iii. 19. The psalm was also regarded as Davidic at a very early period, as the '*diaskeuast*' of the second book of Samuel met with the heading, which attributes the psalm to David. No doubt this opinion might be founded upon ver. 51; and with perfect justice if it were: for if the psalm was not composed by David, it must have been composed in his name and spirit; and who could have been this contemporaneous and equal poet?" Again, after quoting several thoroughly Davidic signs, he says at p. 96: "It is very obvious with how little justice the words of ver. 51, relating to 2 Sam. vii. 12-16, 26, 29, have been pronounced spurious. Besides, the psalm can no more have concluded with לִמְשִׁיחוֹ (ver. 51) than with ver. 50; and if David refers to himself by name at the commencement in 2 Sam. xxiii. 1, and in the middle in ch. vii. 20, why should he not do the same at the close?"

in ver. 5, מִשְׁבְּרֵי מָוֶת instead of חֶבְלֵי מָוֶת; in ver. 8, מוֹסְדוֹת הַשָּׁמַיִם (the foundations of the heavens) for מוֹסְדֵי הָרִים (the foundations of the hills); in ver. 12, חַשְׁרַת־מַיִם for חֶשְׁכַת־מַיִם; in ver. 16, אֲפִיקֵי יָם for אֲפִיקֵי מַיִם; in ver. 28, וְעֵינֶיךָ עַל־רָמִים תַּשְׁפִּיל for וְעֵינַיִם רָמוֹת תַּשְׁפִּיל; in ver. 33, וַיַּתֵּר תָּמִים דַּרְכּוֹ for נָתַן תָּמִים דַּרְכִּי; and in ver. 44, תִּשְׁמְרֵנִי לְרֹאשׁ for תְּשִׂימֵנִי לְרֹאשׁ, and several others. In general, however, the text of the Psalms bears the stamp of poetical originality more than the text before us, and the latter indicates a desire to give greater clearness and simplicity to the poetical style. Consequently neither of the two texts that have come down to us contains the original text of the psalm of David unaltered; but the two recensions have been made quite independently of each other, one for the insertion of the psalm in the Psalter intended for liturgical use, and the other when it was incorporated into the history of David's reign, which formed the groundwork of our books of Samuel. The first revision may have been made by David himself when he arranged his Psalms for liturgical purposes; but the second was effected by the prophetic historian, whose object it was, when inserting David's psalm of praise in the history of his reign, not so much to give it with diplomatic literality, as to introduce it in a form that should be easily intelligible and true to the sense.

Ver. 1. The heading is formed precisely according to the introductory formula of the song of Moses in Deut. xxxi. 30, and was no doubt taken from the larger historical work employed by the author of our books. It was probably also adopted from this into the canonical collection of the Psalter, and simply brought into conformity with the headings of the other psalms by the alteration of וַיְדַבֵּר דָּוִד (and David said) into לְעֶבֶד יְהוָה לְדָוִד אֲשֶׁר דִּבֶּר (" of David, the servant of the Lord, who spake:" Eng. ver.), and the insertion of לַמְנַצֵּחַ ("to the chief musician:" Eng. ver.) at the head (see Delitzsch on the Psalms). "*In the day,*" *i.e.* at the time, "*when Jehovah had delivered him.*" Deliverance "*out of the hand of Saul*" is specially mentioned, not because this was the last, but because it was the greatest and most glorious,—a deliverance out of the deepest misery into regal might and glory. The psalm is opened by וַיֹּאמַר in both texts.—Vers. 2-4 form the introduction.

Ver. 2 Jehovah is my rock, my castle, and my deliverer to me;
3 My Rock-God, in whom I trust:
My shield and horn of my salvation, my fortress and my refuge,
My Saviour; from violence Thou redeemest me.
4 I call upon the praised one, Jehovah,
And I am saved from my enemies.

This introduction contains the sum and substance of the whole psalm, inasmuch as David groups the many experiences of divine deliverance in his agitated life into a long series of predicates, in all of which he extols God as his defence, refuge, and deliverer. The heaping up of these predicates is an expression both of liveliest gratitude, and also of hope for the future. The different predicates, however, are not to be taken as in apposition to *Jehovah*, or as vocatives, but are declarations concerning God, how He had proved himself faithful to the Psalmist in all the calamities of his life, and would assuredly do so still. David calls God סַלְעִי וּמְצֻדָתִי (my rock, and my castle) in Ps. xxxi. 4 as well (cf. Ps. lxxi. 4). The two epithets are borrowed from the natural character of Palestine, where steep and almost inaccessible rocks afford protection to the fugitive, as David had often found at the time when Saul was pursuing him (*vid.* 1 Sam. xxiv. 23, xxii. 5). But whilst David took refuge in rocks, he placed his hopes of safety not in their inaccessible character, but in God the Lord, the eternal spiritual rock, whom he could see in the earthly rock, so that he called Him his true castle. מְפַלְטִי לִי (my deliverer to me) gives the real explanation of the foregoing figures. The לִי (to me) is omitted in Ps. xviii. 2, and only serves to strengthen the suffix, "my, yea *my* deliverer." "*My Rock-God,*" equivalent to, God who is my Rock: this is formed after Deut. xxxii. 4, where Moses calls the Lord the Rock of Israel, because of His unchangeable faithfulness; for *zur*, a rock, is a figure used to represent immoveable firmness. In Ps. xviii. 3 we find אֵלִי צוּרִי, "my God" (strong one), "my rock," two synonyms which are joined together in our text, so as to form one single predicate of God, which is repeated in ver. 47. The predicates which follow, "*my horn and my salvation-shield,*" describe God as the mighty protector and defender of the righteous. A shield covers against hostile attacks. In this respect God was Abraham's shield (Gen. xv. 1), and the helping shield of Israel

(Deut. xxxiii. 29; cf. Ps. iii. 4, lix. 12). He is the "horn of salvation," according to Luther, because He overcomes enemies, and rescues from foes, and gives salvation. The figure is borrowed from animals, which have their strength and defensive weapons in their horns (see at 1 Sam. ii. 1). "*My fortress:*" *misgab* is a high place, where a person is secure against hostile attacks (see at Ps. ix. 10). The predicates which follow, viz. *my refuge*, etc., are not given in Ps. xviii. 3, and are probably only added as a rhythmical completion to the strophe, which was shortened by the omission of the introductory lines, "I love thee heartily, Jehovah" (Ps. xviii. 1). The last clause, "*My Saviour, who redeemest me from violence,*" corresponds to אֶרְחָמְךָ in the first hemistich. In ver. 4, David sums up the contents of his psalm of thanksgiving in a general sentence of experience, which may be called the theme of the psalm, for it embraces "the result of the long life which lay behind him, so full of dangers and deliverances." מְהֻלָּל, "*the praised one,*" an epithet applied to God, which occurs several times in the Psalms (xlviii. 2, xcvi. 4, cxiii. 3, cxlv. 3). It is in apposition to Jehovah, and is placed first for the sake of emphasis: "I invoke Jehovah as the praised one." The imperfects אֶקְרָא and אִוָּשֵׁעַ are used to denote what continually happens. In ver. 5 we have the commencement of the account of the deliverances out of great tribulations, which David had experienced at the hand of God.

> Ver. 5 For breakers of death had compassed me,
> Streams of wickedness terrified me.
> 6 Cords of hell had girt me about,
> Snares of death overtook me.
> 7 In my distress I called Jehovah,
> And to my God I called;
> And He heard my voice out of His temple,
> And my crying came into His ears.

David had often been in danger of death, most frequently at the time when he was pursued by Saul, but also in Absalom's conspiracy, and even in several wars (cf. ch. xxi. 16). All these dangers, out of which the Lord delivered him, and not merely those which originated with Saul, are included in vers. 5, 6. The figure "*breakers or waves of death*" is analogous to that of the "*streams of Belial.*" His distress is represented in both of them under the image of violent floods of water. In the psalm we find חֶבְלֵי מָוֶת, "snares of death," as in Ps. cxvi. 3, death being regarded as a hunter with a net and snare (cf. Ps. xci. 3): this does not answer so well to the parallel נַחֲלֵי, and therefore is not so good, since חַבְלֵי שְׁאוֹל follows immediately. בְּלִיַּעַל (*Belial*), *uselessness* in a moral sense, or *worthlessness*. The meaning "mischief," or injury in a physical sense, which many expositors give to the word in this passage on account of the parallel "death," cannot be grammatically sustained. *Belial* was afterwards adopted as a name for the devil (2 Cor. vi. 15). Streams of wickedness are calamities that proceed from wickedness, or originate with worthless men. קִדֵּם, to come to meet with a hostile intention, *i.e.* to fall upon (*vid.* Job xxx. 27). הֵיכָל, *the temple* out of which Jehovah heard him, was the heavenly abode of God, as in Ps. xi. 4; for, according to vers. 8 sqq., God came down from heaven to help him.

> Ver. 8 Then the earth swayed and trembled,
> The foundations of the heavens shook
> And swayed to and fro, because He was wroth.
> 9 Smoke ascended in His nose,
> And fire out of His mouth devoured,
> Red-hot coals burned out of Him.
> 10 And He bowed the heavens and came down,
> And cloudy darkness under His feet.

Jehovah came down from heaven to save His servant, as He had formerly come down upon Sinai to conclude His covenant with Israel in the midst of terrible natural phenomena, which proclaimed the wrath of the Almighty. The theophany under which David depicts the deliverance he had experienced, had its type in the miraculous phenomenon which accompanied the descent of God upon Sinai, and which suggested, as in the song of Deborah (Judg. v. 4, 5), the idea of a terrible storm. It is true that the deliverance of David was not actually attended by any such extraordinary natural phenomena; but the saving hand of God from heaven was so obviously manifested, that the deliverance experienced by him could be poetically described as a miraculous interposition on the part of God. When the Lord rises up from His heavenly temple to come down upon the earth to judgment, the whole world trembles at the fierceness of His wrath. Not only does the earth tremble, but the foundations of the heavens shake: the whole universe is moved. In the psalm we have "the foundations of the hills" instead of "*the foundations of the heavens*,"—a weaker expression, signifying the earth to its deepest foundations. The *Hithpael* יִתְגָּעַשׁ, *lit. to sway itself*, expresses the idea of continuous swaying to and fro. כִּי חָרָה לוֹ, "*for it* (sc. wrath) *burned to him*," it flamed up like a fire; cf. Deut. xxxii. 22, xxix. 19. "*Smoke*," the forerunner of fire, "*ascended in His nose.*" The figurative idea is that of snorting or violent breathing, which indicates the rising of wrath. Smoke is followed by fire, which devours out of the mouth, *i.e.* bursts forth devouring or consuming all that opposes it. The expression is strengthened still further by the parallel: "*red-hot coals come out of Him*," *i.e.* the flame of red-hot coals pours out of Him as out of a glowing furnace (cf. Gen. xv. 17). This description is based entirely upon Ex. xix. 18, where the Lord comes down upon Sinai in smoke and fire. We are not to picture to ourselves flashes of lightning; for all these phenomena are merely the forerunners of the appearance of God in the clouds, which is described in ver. 10, "He bowed the heavens" to come down. עֲרָפֶל, which is frequently connected with עָנָן, signifies cloudy darkness, or dark clouds. The substratum of this description is the fact that in a severe storm the heavens seem to sink down upon the earth with their dark clouds. The Lord draws near riding upon black thunder-clouds, "that the wicked may not behold His serene countenance, but only the terrible signs of His fierce wrath and punishment" (J. H. Michaelis).

> Ver. 11 He rode upon a cherub and flew hither,
> And appeared upon the wings of the wind.
> 12 He made darkness round about Him as pavilions,
> Water-gathering, thick clouds.
> 13 Out of the splendour before Him
> Burned red-hot coals of fire.

These three verses are a further expansion of ver. 10, and ver. 11 of ver. 10a. The *cherub* is not a personified earthly creature, for *cherubim* are angels around the throne of God (see at Gen. iii. 22). The poetical figure "riding upon the cherub" is borrowed from the fact that God was enthroned between the two cherubim upon the lid of the ark of the covenant, and above their outspread wings (Ex. xxv. 20, 21). As the idea of His "dwelling between the cherubim" (ch. vi. 2 ; 1 Sam. iv. 4, Ps. lxxx. 2) was founded upon this typical manifestation of the gracious presence of God in the Most Holy place, so here David depicts the descent of Jehovah from heaven as "riding upon a cherub," picturing the cherub as a throne upon which God appears in the clouds of heaven, though without therefore imagining Him as riding upon a sphinx or driving in a chariot-throne. Such notions as these are precluded by the addition of the term וַיָּעֹף, "did fly." The "*flying*" is also suggested by the wings of the cherubim. As the divine "*shechinah*" was enthroned above the ark of the covenant upon the wings of the cherubim, David in his poetical description represents the cherub and his wings as carrying the throne of God, to express the thought that Jehovah came down from heaven as the judge and saviour of His servants in the splendour of His divine glory, surrounded by cherubim who stand as His highest servants around His throne, just as Moses in his blessing (Deut. xxxiii. 2) speaks of Jehovah as coming out of myriads of His holy angels. The elementary substratum of this was the wings of the wind, upon which He appeared. In the psalm we have וַיֵּרָא, from דָּאָה, to soar (Deut. xxviii. 49; Jer. xlviii. 40), which suggests the idea of flying better than וַיֵּרָא (He was seen), though the latter gives the real explanation. In vers. 12 and 13, the "cloudy darkness under His feet" (ver. 10*b*) is still further expanded, so as to prepare the way for the description of thunder and lightning in vers. 14 sqq. God in His wrath withdraws His face from man. He envelopes himself in clouds. The darkness round about him is the black thunder-cloud which forms His hut or tent. The plural *succoth* is occasioned by the plural סְבִיבֹתָיו, "His surroundings:" it is used with indefinite generality, and is more probably the original term than סֻכָּתוֹ in the psalm. The "*darkness*" is still further explained in the second clause, חַשְׁרַת מַיִם, *water-gatherings*. חַשְׁרָה (ἅπ. λεγ.) signifies, according to the Arabic, a gathering or collection. The expression used in the psalm is חֶשְׁכַת מַיִם, *water-darkness*, which, if not less appropriate, is at any rate not the original term. עָבֵי שְׁחָקִים, *clouds of clouds, i.e.* the thickest clouds; a kind of superlative, in which a synonym is used instead of the same noun.—Ver. 13. The splendour of the divine nature enveloped in clouds breaks through the dark covering in burning coals of fire. The coals of fire which burst forth, *i.e.* which break out in flame from the dark clouds, are the lightning which shoots forth from the dark storm-clouds in streams of fire.

Ver. 14 Jehovah thundered from the heavens,
And the Most High gave His voice.
15 He sent arrows, and scattered them;
Lightning, and discomfited them.
16 Then the beds of the sea became visible;
The foundations of the world were uncovered,
Through the threatening of Jehovah,
By the snorting of the breath of His nostrils.

God sent lightning as arrows upon the enemies along with violent thunder, and threw them thereby into confusion. הָמַם, to throw into confusion, and thereby to destroy, is the standing expression for the destruction of the foe accomplished by the miraculous interposition of God (vid. Ex. xiv. 24, xxiii. 27; Josh. x. 10; Judg. iv. 15; 1 Sam. vii. 10). To the thunder there were added stormy wind and earthquake, as an effect of the wrath of God, whereby the foundations of the sea and land were laid bare, i.e. whereby the depth of the abyss and of the hell in the interior of the earth, into which the person to be rescued had fallen, were disclosed.[1]

Ver. 17 He reached out of the height, He laid hold of me;
Drew me out of great waters:
18 Saved me from my enemy strong;
From my haters, because they were too strong for me.
19 They fell upon me in my day of calamity:
Then Jehovah became my stay,
20 And led me out into a broad place;
Delivered me, because He had pleasure in me.

---

[1] In vers. 13-16 the text of the Psalms deviates greatly and in many instances from that before us. In ver. 13 we find עָבָיו עָבְרוּ בָּרָד וְגַחֲלֵי אֵשׁ instead of בָּעֲרוּ גַחֲלֵי אֵשׁ; and after ver. 14 בָּרָד וְגַחֲלֵי אֵשׁ is repeated in the psalm. In ver. 15 we have בָּרָק וּבְרָקִים רָב for בָּרָק, and in ver. 16 אֲפִיקֵי מַיִם for אֲפִיקֵי יָם. The other deviations are inconsiderable. So far as the repetition of בָּרָד וְגַחֲלֵי אֵשׁ at the end of ver. 14 is concerned, it is not only superfluous, but unsuitable, because the lightning following the thunder is described in ver. 15, and the words repeated are probably nothing more than a gloss that has crept by an oversight into the text. The אֲפִיקֵי מַיִם in ver. 16 is an obvious softening down of the אֲפִיקֵי יָם of the text before us. In the other deviations, however, the text of the Psalms is evidently the more original of the two; the abridgment of the second clause of ver. 13 is evidently a simplification of the figurative description in the psalm, and בְּרָקִים רָב in the 15th verse of the psalm is more poetical and a stronger expression than the mere בָּרָק of our text.

The Lord stretched His hand from the height into the deep abysses, which had been uncovered through the threatening of the wrath of God, and drew out the sinking man. יִשְׁלַח, without יָד is used to denote the stretching out of the hand, and in the sense of reaching out to a thing (as in ch. vi. 6). מַיִם רַבִּים (great waters) does not refer to the enemy, but to the calamities and dangers (waves of death and streams of Belial, ver. 5) into which the enemies of the Psalmist had plunged him. יַמְשֵׁנִי, from מָשָׁה (Ex. ii. 10), from which the name of *Moses* was derived, to whom there is probably an allusion made. As Moses was taken out of the waters of the Nile, so David was taken out of great (many) waters. This deliverance is still further depicted in more literal terms in vers. 18 sqq. אֹיְבִי עָז, my enemy strong, poetical for my strong enemy, does not refer to one single enemy, namely Saul; but, as the parallel " my haters " shows, is a poetical personification of all his enemies. They were stronger than David, therefore the Lord had to deliver him with an almighty hand. The "*day of calamity*" in which the enemy fell upon him (קֶדֶם : see at ver. 6) was the time when David wandered about in the desert helpless and homeless, fleeing from the pursuit of Saul. The Lord was then his support, or a staff on which he could support himself (*vid.* Ps. xxiii. 4), and led him out of the strait into the broad, *i.e.* into a broad space where he could move freely, because God had pleasure in him, and had chosen him in His grace to be His servant. This reason for his deliverance is carried out still further in what follows.

>Ver. 21 Jehovah rendered to me according to my righteousness,
>   According to the cleanness of my hands He recompensed me.
>22 For I have observed the ways of Jehovah,
>   And have not wickedly departed from my God.
>23 For all His rights are before my eyes;
>   And His statutes,—I do not depart from them.
>24 And I was innocent towards Him,
>   And kept myself from mine iniquity.

גָּמַל signifies to do to a person good or evil, like the Greek εὖ and κακῶς πράττειν τινά. The *righteousness* and *cleanness of hands*, *i.e.* the innocence, which David attributed to himself, were not perfect righteousness or holiness before God, but the righteousness of his endeavours and deeds as contrasted with the unrighteousness and wickedness of his adversaries and pursuers, and consisted in the fact that he endeavoured earnestly and sincerely to walk in the ways of God and to keep the divine commandments. רָשַׁע מִן, *to be wicked from*, is a pregnant expression, signifying to depart wickedly from God. לְנֶגְדִּי, *i.e.* as a standard before my eye. In the psalm we find תָּמִים עִמּוֹ, innocent in intercourse with the Lord, instead of תָּמִים לוֹ (see Deut. xviii. 13); and for the fact itself, David's own testimony in 1 Sam. xxvi. 23, 24, the testimony of God concerning him in 1 Kings xiv. 8, and the testimony of history in 1 Kings xv. 5. מֵעֲוֹנִי, from mine iniquity, *i.e.* from the iniquity which I might have committed.

Ver. 25 Thus Jehovah repaid me according to my righteousness,
According to my cleanness before His eyes.
26 Towards the pious Thou showest thyself pious,
Towards the perfectly innocent Thou showest thyself innocent.
27 Towards the genuine Thou showest thyself genuine,
And towards the perverse Thou showest thyself crooked.
28 And afflicted people Thou helpest,
And Thine eyes are against the haughty; them Thou humblest.

The motive for deliverance, which was expounded in vers. 21-24, is summed up briefly in ver. 25; and then in vers. 26 and 27 it is carried back to the general truth, that the conduct of God towards men is regulated according to the conduct of men towards God. The *vav cons.* in וַיָּשֶׁב expresses the logical consequence. כְּבֹרִי is used instead of כְּבֹר יָדַי in ver. 21, which is repeated in the psalm simply for the sake of variation. The truth that God treats every man in accordance with his conduct towards Him, is expounded in four parallel clauses, in which the conduct of God is expressed in verbs in the *Hithpael*, formed from the adjectives used to describe the conduct of men towards God. To the חָסִיד, the pious or devoted to God, He also shows himself pious; and innocent, blameless, to the גְּבוֹר תָּמִים, the man strong in innocence, who walks in perfect innocence. נָבָר, a *Niphal* participle, from בָּרַר, he who keeps himself pure, strives after purity of walk. תִּתָּבָר, an anomalous contraction of תִּתְבָּרַר (Ps.), analogous to the formation of נָבָר for נִבְרָר. The form תִּתַּפָּל for תִּתְפַּתָּל, to show one's self perverse or crooked, is still more anomalous. God shows himself so towards the perverse, by giving him up to his perverseness (Rom. i. 28)

This general truth is applied in ver. 28 to the congregation of God, in the contrast which it presents of humble and haughty, and is expounded from the conduct of God, as displayed in the history of Israel, towards these two classes of men, into which the nation was divided. In the psalm, therefore, we find כִּי אַתָּה, for which the simple ו is substituted here, because the verse does not contain any actual reason for what goes before. עַם עָנִי, afflicted people, is used to denote the pious and depressed in the nation; רָמִים, *the high, i.e.* the haughty, or godless rich and mighty in the nation. תַּשְׁפִּיל is to be taken as a relative: whom Thou humblest (see Ewald, § 332, *b*; and for the thought, Isa. ii. 11). In the psalm the unusual mode of expression in the second clause is changed into the more common phrase, "Thou bringest down high, *i.e.* proud looks" (cf. Prov. vi. 17, xxi. 4, xxx. 13; Ps. cxxxi. 1, etc.).

Ver. 29 commences the description of the help which David had already received from God in his conflict with the enemies of Israel, and which he would still receive.

> Ver. 29 For Thou art my lamp, O Jehovah!
> And Jehovah maketh my darkness bright.
> 30 For through Thee I run troops,
> And through my God I leap walls.
> 31 God—innocent is His way.
> The word of Jehovah is refined,
> A shield is He to all who trust in Him.

The explanatory כִּי, with which the new description of the divine mercy commences, refers to the thought implied in ver. 28, that David belonged to the "afflicted people," whom the Lord always helps. As the Lord delivered him out of the danger of death, because He took pleasure in him; so He also gave him power over all his enemies. For He was his lamp, *i.e.* He had lifted him out of a condition of depression and contempt into one of glory and honour (see at ch. xxi. 17), and would still further enlighten his darkness, *i.e.* "would cause the light of His salvation to shine upon him and his tribe in all the darkness of their distress" (Hengstenberg). In the psalm the verse reads thus: "For Thou lightest (makest bright) my lamp (or candle), Jehovah my God enlighteneth my darkness;" the bold figure "Jehovah the lamp of David" being more literally explained. The figure is analogous to the one in Ps.

xxvii. 1, "The Lord is my light;" whilst the form נֵיר is a later mode of writing נֵר.—Ver. 30. In the strength of his God he could run hostile troops and leap walls, *i.e.* overcome every hostile power. אָרֻץ, not from רָצַץ, to smash in pieces, but from רוּץ, to run; construed with the accusative according to the analogy of verbs of motion.—Ver. 31. He derives this confidence from the acts of God, and also from His word. הָאֵל (God) is written absolutely, like הַצּוּר in Deut. xxxii. 4. The article points back to בֵּאלֹהַי. Jehovah is *the* God (הָאֵל), whose way is perfect, without blemish; and His word is refined brass, pure silver (cf. Ps. xii. 7). He who trusts in Him is safe from all foes. The last two clauses occur again in Agur's proverbs (Prov. xxx. 5). The thought of the last clause is still further explained in vers. 32 sqq.

> Ver. 32 For who is God save Jehovah,
> And who a rock save our God?
> 33 This God is my strong fortress,
> And leads the innocent his way.
> 34 He makes my feet like the hinds,
> And setteth me upon my high places;
> 35 He teacheth my hands to fight,
> And my arms span brazen bows.

There is no true God who can help, except or by the side of Jehovah (cf. Deut. xxxii. 31; 1 Sam. ii. 2). צוּר, as in ver. 2. This God is "my strong fortress:" for this figure, comp. Ps. xxxi. 5 and xxvii. 1. חַיִל, strength, might, is construed with מָעוּזִי, by free subordination: "my fortress, a strong one," like מַחְסִי עֹז (Ps. lxxi. 7; cf. Ewald, § 291, *b*). יַתֵּר for יְתֵר, from תּוּר (*vid.* Ges. § 72; Olshausen, *Gram.* p. 579), in the sense of leading or taking round, as in Prov. xii. 26. God leads the innocent his way, *i.e.* He is his leader and guide therein. The *Keri* דַּרְכִּי rests upon a misunderstanding. There is an important difference in the reading of this verse in Ps. xviii., viz. "The God who girdeth me with strength, and makes my way innocent." The last clause is certainly an alteration which simplifies the meaning, and so is also the first clause, the thought of which occurs again, word for word, in ver. 40*a*, with the addition of לַמִּלְחָמָה. אַיָּלָה or אַיֶּלֶת, the hind, or female stag, is a figure of speech denoting swiftness in running. "*Like the hinds:*" a condensed simile for "like the hinds' feet," such as we frequently meet with in Hebrew (vid. Ges. § 144, Anm.). The reference is to swiftness in pursuit of the foe (vid. ch. ii. 18; 1 Chron. xii. 8). רַגְלַי, *his* feet, for רַגְלָי (*my* feet) in the psalm, may be accounted for from the fact, that David had spoken of himself in the third person as the innocent one. "*My high places*" were not the high places of the enemy, that became his by virtue of conquest, but the high places of his own land, which he maintained triumphantly, so that he ruled the land from them. The expression is formed after Deut. xxxii. 13, and is imitated in Hab. iii. 19. לִמֵּד is generally construed with a double accusative: here it is written with an accusative and לְ, and signifies to instruct for the war. נִחַת, in the psalm נִחֲתָה, on account of the feminine וְרוֹעֹתַי, is not the *Niphal* of חָתַת, to be broken in pieces, but the *Piel* of נָחַת, to cause to go down, to press down the bow, *i.e.* to set it. The bow of brass is mentioned as being the strongest: setting such a bow would be a sign of great heroic strength. The two verses (34 and 35) are simply a particularizing description of the power and might with which the Lord had endowed David to enable him to conquer all his foes.

>Ver. 36 And Thou reachest me the shield of my salvation,
>And Thy hearing makes me great.
>37 Thou makest my steps broad under me,
>And my ankles have not trembled.

The Lord bestows the true strength for victory in His salvation. The shield of salvation is the shield which consists of salvation, of the helping grace of the Lord. עֲנֹתְךָ, for which we find in the psalm עַנְוַתְךָ, thy humility, *i.e.* God's condescending grace, does not mean "thy humiliation," but "*thy hearkening*," *i.e.* that practical hearkening on the part of God, when called upon for help, which was manifested in the fact that God made his steps broad, *i.e.* provided the walker with a broad space for free motion, removing obstructions and stumblingblocks out of the way. God had done this for David, so that his ankles had not trembled, *i.e.* he had not been wanting in the power to take firm and safe steps. In this strength of his God he could destroy all his foes.

>Ver. 38 I will pursue my enemies and destroy them,
>I will not turn till they are consumed.

39 I will consume them and dash them in pieces, that they may not arise,
And may fall under my feet.
40 And Thou girdest me with strength for war,
Thou bowest mine adversaries under me.
41 And Thou makest mine enemies turn the back to me;
My haters, I root them out.

The optative form אֲרַדְּפָה serves to make the future signification of אֶרְדּוֹף (in the psalm) the more apparent. Consequently it is quite out of the question to take the other verbs as preterites. We are not compelled to do this by the interchange of imperfects *c. vav consec.* with simple imperfects, as the *vav consec.* is not used exclusively as expressive of the past. On the contrary, the substance of the whole of the following description shows very clearly that David refers not only to the victories he has already won, but in general to the defeat of all his foes in the past, the present, and the future; for he speaks as distinctly as possible not only of their entire destruction (vers. 38, 39, 43), but also of the fact that God makes him the head of the nations, and distant and foreign nations do him homage. Consequently he refers not only to his own personal dominion, but also, on the strength of the promise which he had received from God, to the increase of the dominion of the throne of his house, whilst he proclaims in the Spirit the ultimate defeat of all the enemies of the kingdom of God. This Messianic element in the following description comes out in a way that cannot be mistaken, in the praise of the Lord with which he concludes in vers. 47–51. וָאַשְׁמִידֵם, "*I destroy them,*" is stronger than וָאַשִּׂיגֵם, "I reach them" (in the psalm). In ver. 39 the words are crowded together, to express the utter destruction of all foes. In the psalm וָאֲכַלֵּם is omitted. וַתַּזְרֵנִי for וַתְּאַזְּרֵנִי in the psalm is not a poetical Syriasm, and still less a "careless solecism" (Hupfeld), but a simple contraction, such as we meet with in many forms: *e.g.* מַלְפֵנוּ for מְאַלְּפֵנוּ (Job xxxv. 11; cf. Ewald, § 232, *b*). The form תַּתָּה for נָתַתָּה (in the psalm) is unusual, and the aphæresis of the נ can only be accounted for from the fact that this much-used word constantly drops its נ as a radical sound in the imperfect (see Ewald, § 195, *c*). The phrase תַּתָּה לִּי עֹרֶף is formed after Ex. xxiii. 27. "Giving the enemy to a person's back" means causing them to turn the back, *i.e.* putting them to flight.

Ver. 42 They look out, but there is no deliverer;
For Jehovah, but He answereth them not.
43 And I rub in pieces as the dust of the earth,
Like the mire of the streets I crush them and stamp upon them.

The cry of the foe for help is not attended to; they are annihilated without quarter. יְשַׁוְּעוּ, to look out to God for help (with אֶל and עַל; *vid.* Isa. xvii. 7, 8), is more poetical than יְשַׁוֵּעוּ, "they cry" (in the psalm); and כַּעֲפַר־אָרֶץ is more simple than כְּעָפָר עַל־פְּנֵי־רוּחַ (in the psalm), "I crush them as dust before the wind," for the wind does not crush the dust, but carries it away. In the second clause of ver. 43, אֲדִקֵּם is used instead of אֲרִיקֵם in the psalm, and strengthened by אֶרְקָעֵם. אֲדִקֵּם, from דָּקַק, *to make thin*, to crush; so that instead of "I pour them out like mire of the streets which is trodden to pieces," the Psalmist simply says, "I crush and stamp upon them like mire of the streets." Through the utter destruction of the foe, God establishes the universal dominion to which the throne of David is to attain.

Ver. 44 And Thou rescuest me out of the strivings of my people,
Preservest me to be the head of the heathen.
People that I knew not serve me.
45 The sons of the stranger dissemble to me,
Upon hearsay they obey me.
46 The sons of the stranger despair,
And tremble out of their castles.

By "*the strivings of my people*" the more indefinite expression in the psalm, "strivings of the people," is explained. The words refer to the domestic conflicts of David, out of which the Lord delivered him, such as the opposition of Ishbosheth and the rebellions of Absalom and Sheba. These deliverances formed the prelude and basis of his dominion over the heathen. Consequently תִּשְׁמְרֵנִי (*Thou preservest me* to be the head of the nations) occurs quite appropriately in the second clause; and תְּשִׂימֵנִי, "Thou settest me," which occurs in the psalm, is a far less pregnant expression. עַם before לֹא יָדַעְתִּי is used indefinitely to signify foreign nations. *Toi* king of Hamath (ch. viii. 10) was an example, and his subjugation was a prelude of the future subjection of all the heathen to the sceptre of the Son of David, as predicted in Ps. lxxii. In ver. 45 the two clauses of the psalm are very appropriately transposed. The *Hithpael* יִתְכַּחֲשׁוּ, as compared with יְכַחֲשׁוּ, is the later form. In the primary passage (Deut. xxxiii. 29) the *Niphal* is used to signify the dissembling of friendship, or of involuntary homage on the part of the vanquished towards the victor. לִשְׁמוֹעַ אֹזֶן, "*by the hearing of the ear,*" i.e. by hearsay, is a simple explanation of לְשֵׁמַע אֹזֶן, at the rumour of the ears (*vid.* Job xlii. 5), i.e. at the mere rumour of David's victories. The foreign nations pine away, i.e. despair of ever being able to resist the victorious power of David. יַחְגְּרוּ, "*they gird themselves,*" does not yield any appropriate meaning, even if we should take it in the sense of equipping themselves to go out to battle. The word is probably a misspelling of יַחְרְגוּ, which occurs in the psalm, חָרַג being a ἁπ. λεγ. in the sense of being terrified, or trembling: they tremble out of their castles, i.e. they come trembling out of their castles (for the thought itself, see Micah vii. 17). It is by no means probable that the word חָגַר, which is so frequently met with in Hebrew, is used in this one passage in the sense of "*to limp,*" according to Syriac usage.

In conclusion, the Psalmist returns to the praise of the Lord, who had so highly favoured him.

> Ver. 47 Jehovah liveth, and blessed is my rock,
> And the God of my refuge of salvation is exalted.
> 48 The God who giveth me vengeance,
> And bringeth nations under me;
> 49 Who leadeth me out from mine enemies,
> And exalteth me above mine adversaries,
> Delivereth me from the man of violence.

The formula חַי־יְהוָֹה does not mean "let Jehovah live," for the word יְחִי would be used for that (*vid.* ch. xvi. 16, 1 Sam. x. 24), but is a declaration: "the Lord is living." The declaration itself is to be taken as praise of God, for "praising God is simply ascribing to Him the glorious perfections which belong to him; we have only to give Him what is His own" (Hengstenberg). The following clauses also contain simply declarations; this is evident from the word יָרוּם, since the optative יָרֹם would be used to denote a wish. The Lord is living or alive when He manifests His life in acts of omnipotence. In the last clause, the expression צוּר (rock) is intensified into אֱלֹהֵי צוּר יִשְׁעִי (the God of my refuge, or rock, of salvation), *i.e.* the God who is my saving rock (cf. ver. 3). In the predicates of God in vers. 48, 49, the saving acts depicted by David in vers. 5-20 and 29-46 are summed up briefly. Instead of מוֹרִיד, "He causes to go down under me," *i.e.* He subjects to me, we find in the psalm וַיַּדְבֵּר, "He drives nations under me," and מְפַלְּטִי instead of מוֹצִיאִי; and lastly, instead of אִישׁ חָמָס in the psalm, we have here אִישׁ חֲמָסִים, as in Ps. cxl. 2. Therefore the praise of the Lord shall be sounded among all nations.

> Ver. 50 Therefore will I praise Thee, O Jehovah, among the nations,
> And sing praise to Thy name.
> 51 As He who magnifies the salvation of His king,
> And showeth grace to His anointed,
> To David, and his seed for ever.

The grace which the Lord had shown to David was so great, that the praise thereof could not be restricted to the narrow limits of Israel. With the dominion of David over the nations, there spread also the knowledge, and with this the praise, of the Lord who had given him the victory. Paul was therefore perfectly justified in quoting the verse before us (ver. 50) in Rom. xvi. 9, along with Deut. xxxii. 43 and Ps. cxvii. 1, as a proof that the salvation of God was intended for the Gentiles also. The king whose salvation the Lord had magnified, was not David as an individual, but David and his seed for ever,—that is to say, the royal family of David which culminated in Christ. David could thus sing praises upon the ground of the promise which he had received (ch. vii. 12-16), and which is repeated almost verbatim in the last clause of ver. 51. The *Chethib* מגדיל is the *Hiphil* participle מַגְדִּיל, according to Ps. xviii. 51; and the *Keri* מִגְדּוֹל, "tower of the fulness of salvation," is a singular conjecture.

DAVID'S LAST WORDS.—CHAP. XXIII. 1-7.

The psalm of thanksgiving, in which David praised the Lord for all the deliverances and benefits that he had experienced throughout the whole of his life, is followed by the prophetic will and testament of the great king, unfolding the importance of his rule in relation to the sacred history of the future. And whilst the psalm may be regarded (ch. xxii.) as a great hallelujah, with which David passed away from the stage of life, these "last words" contain the divine seal of all that he has sung and prophesied in several psalms concerning the eternal dominion of his seed, on the strength of the divine promise which he received through the prophet Nathan, that his throne should be established for ever (ch. vii.). These words are not merely a lyrical expansion of that promise, but a prophetic declaration uttered by David at the close of his life and by divine inspiration, concerning the true King of the kingdom of God. "The aged monarch, who was not generally endowed with the gift of prophecy, was moved by the Spirit of God at the close of his life, and beheld a *just Ruler in the fear of God*, under whose reign blessing and salvation sprang up for the righteous, and all the wicked were overcome. The pledge of this was the eternal covenant which God had concluded with him" (Tholuck: *die Propheten und ihre Weissagungen*, p. 166). The heading "*these are the last words of David*" serves to attach it to the preceding psalm of thanksgiving.

Ver. 1 Divine saying of David the son of Jesse,
Divine saying of the man, the highly exalted,
Of the anointed of the God of Jacob,
And of the lovely one in the songs of praise of Israel.
2 The Spirit of Jehovah speaks through me,
And His word is upon my tongue.

This introduction to the prophetic announcement rests, both as to form and substance, upon the last sayings of Balaam concerning the future history of Israel (Num. xxiv. 3, 15). This not only shows to what extent David had occupied himself with the utterances of the earlier men of God concerning Israel's future; but indicates, at the same time, that his own prophetic utterance was intended to be a further expansion of Balaam's prophecy concerning the Star out of Jacob and the Sceptre out of Israel. Like Balaam, he calls his prophecy a נְאֻם, *i.e.* a *divine saying* or oracle, as a revelation which he had received directly from God (see at Num. xxiv. 3). But the recipient of this revelation was not, like Balaam the son of Beor, a man with closed eye, whose eyes had been opened by a vision of the Almighty, but "*the man who was raised up on high*" (עַל, adverbially "*above*," is, strictly speaking, a substantive, "*height*," used in an adverbial sense, as in Hos. xi. 7, and probably also ch. vii. 16), *i.e.* whom God had lifted up out of humiliation to be the ruler of His people, yea, even to be the head of the nations (ch. xxii. 44). Luther's rendering, " who is assured of the Messiah of the God of Jacob," is based upon the Vulgate, "*cui constitutum est de Christo Dei Jacob*," and cannot be grammatically sustained. David was exalted on the one hand as "*the anointed of the God of Jacob*," *i.e.* as the one whom the God of Israel had anointed king over His people, and on the other hand as "*the lovely one in Israel's songs of praise*," *i.e.* the man whom God had enabled to sing lovely songs of praise in celebration of His grace and glory. זְמִרָה = זְמִיר does not mean a song generally, but a song of praise in honour of God (see at Ex. xv. 2), like מִזְמוֹר in the headings to the psalms. As David on the one hand had firmly established the kingdom of God in an earthly and political respect as the anointed of Jehovah, *i.e.* as king, so had he on the other, as the composer of Israel's songs of praise, promoted the spiritual edification of that kingdom. The idea of נְאֻם is explained in ver. 2. The Spirit of Jehovah speaks through him; his words are the inspiration of God. The preterite דִּבֶּר relates to the divine inspiration which preceded the utterance of the divine saying. דִּבֶּר בְּ, literally to speak into a person, as in Hos. i. 2. The saying itself commences with ver. 3.

> Ver. 3 The God of Israel saith,
>   The Rock of Israel speaketh to me:
>   A Ruler over men, just,
>   A Ruler in the fear of God.
>   4 And as light of the morning, when the sun rises,
>   As morning without clouds:
>   From shining out of rain (springeth) green out of the earth.
>   5 For is not my house thus with God?
>   For He hath made me an everlasting covenant,
>   Provided with all, and attested;
>   For all my salvation and all good pleasure,
>   Should He then not cause it to grow?

As the prophets generally preface their saying with " thus saith the Lord," so David commences his prophetic saying with "*the God of Israel saith*," for the purpose of describing it most emphatically as the word of God. He designates God " *the*

God" and "*the Rock*" (as in ch. xxii. 3) of Israel, to indicate that the contents of his prophecy relate to the salvation of the people of Israel, and are guaranteed by the unchangeableness of God. The saying which follows bears the impress of a divine oracle even in its enigmatical brevity. The verbs are wanting in the different sentences of vers. 3*b* and 4. "*A ruler over men*," sc. "will arise," or there will be. בָּאָדָם does not mean "among men," but "*over men;*" for בְּ is to be taken as with the verb מָשַׁל, as denoting the object ruled over (cf. Gen. iii. 16, iv. 7, etc.). הָאָדָם does not mean certain men, but the human race, humanity. This ruler is "*just*" in the fullest sense of the word, as in the passages founded upon this, viz. Jer. xxiii. 5, Zech. ix. 9, and Ps. lxxii. 2. The justice of the ruler is founded in his "*fear of God.*" יִרְאַת אֱלֹהִים is governed freely by מוֹשֵׁל. (On the fact itself, see Isa. xi. 2, 3.) The meaning is, "A ruler over the human race will arise, a just ruler, and will exercise his dominion in the spirit of the fear of God."—Ver. 4 describes the blessing that will proceed from this ruler. The idea that ver. 4 should be connected with ver. 3*b* so as to form one period, in the sense of "when one rules justly over men (as I do), it is as when a morning becomes clear," must be rejected, for the simple reason that it overlooks Nathan's promise (ch. vii.) altogether, and weakens the force of the saying so solemnly introduced as the word of God. The ruler over men whom David sees in spirit, is not any one who rules righteously over men; nor is the seed of David to be regarded as a collective expression indicating a merely ideal personality, but, according to the Chaldee rendering, the Messiah himself, the righteous Shoot whom the Lord would raise up to David (Jer. xxiii. 5), and who would execute righteousness and judgment upon earth (Jer. xxxiii. 15).—Ver. 4 is to be taken by itself as containing an independent thought, and the connection between it and ver. 3 must be gathered from the words themselves: the appearance (the rise) of this Ruler will be "*as light of the morning, when the sun rises.*" At the same time, the Messiah is not to be regarded as the subject to אוֹר בֹּקֶר (the light of the morning), as though the ruler over men were compared with the morning light; but the subject compared to the morning light is intentionally left indefinite, according to the view adopted by Luther in his exposition, "In the time of the Messiah it will be like the light of the morning." We are precluded from regarding the Messiah as the subject, by the fact that the comparison is instituted not with the sun, but with the morning dawn at the rising of the sun, whose vivifying effects upon nature are described in the second clause of the verse. The words יִזְרַח שֶׁמֶשׁ are to be taken relatively, as a more distinct definition of the morning light. The clause which follows, "*morning without clouds*," is parallel to the foregoing, and describes more fully the nature of the morning. The light of the rising sun on a cloudless morning is an image of the coming salvation. The rising sun awakens the germs of life in the bosom of nature, which had been slumbering through the darkness of the night. "The state of things before the coming of the ruler resembles the darkness of the night" (Hengstenberg). The verb is also wanting in the second hemistich. "*From the shining from rain* (is, comes) *fresh green out of the earth.*" נֹגַהּ signifies the brightness of the rising sun; but, so far as the actual meaning is concerned, it relates to the salvation which attends the coming of the righteous ruler. מִמָּטָר is either subordinate to מִנֹּגַהּ, or co-ordinate with it. In the former case, we should have to render the passage, "from the shining of the sun which proceeds out of rain," or "from the shining after rain;" and the allusion would be to a cloudless morning, when the shining of the sun after a night's rain stimulates the growth of the plants. In the latter case, we should have to render it "from the shining (and) from the rain;" and the reference would be to a cloudless morning, on which the vegetation springs up from the ground through sunshine followed by rain. Grammatically considered, the first view (? the second) is the easier of the two; nevertheless we regard the other (? the first) as the only admissible one, inasmuch as rain is not to be expected when the sun has risen with a cloudless sky. The rays of the sun, as it rises after a night of rain, strengthen the fresh green of the plants. The rain is therefore a figurative representation of blessing generally (cf. Isa. xliv. 3), and the green grass which springs up from the earth after the rain is an image of the blessings of the Messianic salvation (Isa. xliv. 4, xlv. 8).

In Ps. lxxii. 6, Solomon takes these words of David as the basis of his comparison of the effects resulting from the government of the true Prince of peace to the coming down of the rain upon the mown grass.

In ver. 5, the prophecy concerning the coming of the just ruler is sustained by being traced back to the original promise in ch. vii., in which David had received a pledge of this. The first and last clauses of this verse can only be made to yield a meaning in harmony with the context, by being taken interrogatively: "*for is not my house so with God?*" The question is only indicated by the tone (כִּי הֲלֹא = כִּי לֹא: ch. xix. 23), as is frequently the case, even before clauses commencing with לֹא (*e.g.* Hos. xi. 5, Mal. ii. 15: cf. Ewald, § 324, *a*). לֹא־כֵן (not so) is explained by the following clause, though the כִּי which follows is not to be taken in the sense of "*that.*" Each of the two clauses contains a distinct thought. That of the first is, "Does not my house stand in such a relation to God, that the righteous ruler will spring from it?" This is then explained in the second: "for He hath made an everlasting covenant with me." David calls the promise in ch. vii. 12 sqq., that God would establish his kingdom to his seed for ever, a covenant, because it involved a reciprocal relation,—namely, that Jehovah would first of all found for David a permanent house, and then that the seed of David was to build the house of the Lord. This covenant is עֲרוּכָה בַכֹּל, "*equipped (or provided) with all*" that could help to establish it. This relates more especially to the fact that all eventualities were foreseen, even the falling away of the bearers of the covenant of God, so that such an event as this would not annul the covenant (ch. vii. 14, 15). וּשְׁמֻרָה, "*and preserved,*" *i.e.* established by the assurance that even in that case the Lord would not withdraw His grace. David could found upon this the certainty, that God would cause all the salvation to spring forth which had been pledged to his house in the promise referred to. כָּל־יִשְׁעִי, "*all my salvation,*" *i.e.* all the salvation promised to me and to my house. כָּל־חֵפֶץ, not "all my desire," but "*all the good pleasure*" of God, *i.e.* all the saving counsel of God expressed in that covenant. The כִּי before לֹא is an energetic repetition of the כִּי which introduces the explanatory thought, in the sense of a firm assurance: "*for all my salvation and all good pleasure, yea, should He not cause it to spring forth?*"

Ver. 6 But the worthless, as rejected thorns are they all;
For men do not take them in the hand.
7 And the man who touches them
Provides himself with iron and spear-shaft,
And they are utterly burned with fire where they dwell.

The development of salvation under the ruler in righteousness and the fear of God is accompanied by judgment upon the ungodly. The abstract בְּלִיַּעַל, *worthlessness*, is stronger than אִישׁ בְּלִיַּעַל, the worthless man, and depicts the godless as personified worthlessness. מֻנָד, in the *Keri* מֻנָּד, the *Hophal* of נוד or נָדַד, literally "*scared*" or hunted away. This epithet does not apply to the thorns, so well as to the ungodly who are compared to thorns. The reference is to thorns that men root out, not to those which they avoid on account of their prickles. בְּלָהֶם, an antiquated form for בָּלָם (see Ewald, § 247, *d*). To root them out, or clean the ground of them, men do not lay hold of them with the bare hand; but "*whoever would touch them equips himself* (יִמָּלֵא, sc. יָדוֹ, to '*fill the hand*' with any thing: 2 Kings ix. 24) *with iron, i.e.* with iron weapons, *and spear-shaft*" (*vid.* 1 Sam. xvii. 7). This expression also relates to the godless rather than to the thorns. They are consumed בַּשֶּׁבֶת, "*at the dwelling,*" *i.e.* as Kimchi explains, at the place of their dwelling, the place where they grow. For בַּשֶּׁבֶת cannot mean "on the spot" in the sense of without delay. The burning of the thorns takes place at the final judgment upon the ungodly (Matt. xiii. 30).

DAVID'S HEROES.—CHAP. XXIII. 8-39.

The following list of David's heroes we also find in 1 Chron. xi. 10-47, and expanded at the end by sixteen names (vers. 41-47), and attached in ver. 10 to the account of the conquest of the fortress of Zion by the introduction of a special heading. According to this heading, the heroes named assisted David greatly in his kingdom, along with all Israel, to make him king, from which it is evident that the chronicler intended by this heading to justify his appending the list to the account of the election of David as king over all the tribes of Israel (1 Chron. xi. 1), and of the conquest of Zion, which followed immediately afterwards. In every other respect the two lists agree with one another, except that there are a considerable number of errors of the text, more especially in the names, which are frequently corrupt in both texts, so that the true reading cannot be determined with certainty. The heroes enumerated are divided into three classes. The *first* class consists of three, viz. *Jashobeam, Eleazar,* and *Shammah,* of whom certain brave deeds are related, by which they reached the first rank among David's heroes (vers. 8–12). They were followed by *Abishai* and *Benaiah,* who were in the *second* class, and who had also distinguished themselves above the rest by their brave deeds, though they did not come up to the first three (vers. 18–23). The others all belonged to the *third* class, which consisted of thirty-two men, of whom no particular heroic deeds are mentioned (vers. 24–39). Twelve of these, viz. the five belonging to the first two classes and seven of the third, were appointed by David commanders of the twelve detachments into which he divided the army, each detachment to serve for one month in the year (1 Chron. xxvii.). These heroes, among whom we do not find Joab the commander-in-chief of the whole of the forces, were the king's aides-de-camp, and are called in this respect הַשָּׁלִשִׁי (ver. 8), though the term הַשְּׁלִשִׁים (the *thirty,* vers. 13, 23, 24) was also a very customary one, as their number amounted to thirty in a round sum. It is possible that at first they may have numbered exactly thirty; for, from the very nature of the case, we may be sure that in the many wars in which David was engaged, other heroes must have arisen at different times, who would be received into the corps already formed. This will explain the addition of sixteen names in the Chronicles, whether the chronicler made use of a different list from that employed by the author of the books before us, and one belonging to a later age, or whether the author of our books merely restricted himself to a description of the corps in its earlier condition.

Vers. 8–12. *Heroes of the first class.*—The short heading to our text, with which the list in the Chronicles also begins (1 Chron. xi. 11), simply gives the names of these heroes. But instead of "the *names* of the mighty men," we have in the Chronicles "the *number* of the mighty men." This variation is all the more striking, from the fact that in the Chronicles the total number is not given at the close of the list as it is in our text. At the same time, it can hardly be a copyist's error for מִבְחַר (*selection*), as Bertheau supposes, but must be attributable to the fact that, according to vers. 13, 23, and 24, these heroes constituted a corps which was named from the number of which it originally consisted. The first, *Jashobeam*, is called "the chief of the thirty" in the Chronicles. Instead of יָשָׁבְעָם (*Jashobeam*), the reading in the Chronicles, we have here יֹשֵׁב בַּשֶּׁבֶת (*Josheb-basshebeth*), unquestionably a spurious reading, which probably arose, according to Kennicott's conjecture, from the circumstance that the last two letters of ישבעם were written in one MS. under בַּשֶּׁבֶת in the line above (ver. 7), and a copyist took בשבת from that line by mistake for עם. The correctness of the reading *Jashobeam* is established by 1 Chron. xxvii. 2. The word תַּחְכְּמֹנִי is also faulty, and should be corrected, according to the Chronicles, into בֶּן־חַכְמוֹנִי (*Ben-hachmoni*); for the statement that Jashobeam was a son (or descendant) of the family of *Hachmon* (1 Chron. xxvii. 32) can easily be reconciled with that in 1 Chron. xxvii. 2, to the effect that he was a son of Zabdiel. Instead of רֹאשׁ הַשְּׁלִשִׁים (*head of the thirty*), the reading in the Chronicles, we have here רֹאשׁ הַשְּׁלִישִׁי (*head of the three*). Bertheau would alter our text in accordance with the Chronicles, whilst Thenius proposes to bring the text of the Chronicles into accordance with ours. But although the many unquestionable corruptions in the verse before us may appear to favour Bertheau's assumption, we cannot regard either of the emendations as necessary, or even warrantable. The proposed alteration of הַשְּׁלִישִׁי is decidedly precluded by the recurrence of רֹאשׁ הַשְּׁלִשִׁי in ver. 18, and the alteration of הַשְּׁלִשִׁים in the Chronicles by the repeated allusion to the שְׁלִשִׁים, not only in vers. 15, 42, ch. xii. 4, and ch. xxvii. 6 of the Chronicles, but also in vers. 13, 23, and 24 of the chapter before us. The explanation given of שָׁלִישׁ and שָׁלִשִׁים, as signifying chariot-warriors, is decidedly erroneous;[1] for the singular הַשָּׁלִישׁ is used in all the passages in which the word occurs to signify the royal aide-de-camp (2 Kings vii. 2, 17, 19, ix. 25,

---

[1] This explanation, which we find in Gesenius (*Thes.* and *Lex.*) and Bertheau, rests upon no other authority than the testimony of Origen, to the effect that an obscure writer gives this interpretation of τριστάτης, the rendering of שָׁלִישׁ, an authority which is completely overthrown by the writer of the gloss in *Octateuch*. (Schleussner, *Lex. in* LXX. t. v. p. 338).

xv. 25), and the plural שָׁלִישִׁים the royal body-guard, not only in 2 Kings x. 25, but even in 1 Kings ix. 22, and Ex. xiv. 7, xv. 4, from which the meaning chariot-warriors has been derived. Consequently רֹאשׁ הַשָּׁלִשִׁי is the head of the king's aides-de-camp, and the interchange of הַשָּׁלִשִׁי with the הַשְּׁלֹשִׁים of the Chronicles may be explained on the simple ground that David's thirty heroes formed his whole body of adjutants. The singular שְׁלִשִׁי is to be explained in the same manner as הִכְּרֵתִי (see at ch. viii. 18). Luther expresses the following opinion in his marginal gloss with regard to the words which follow (הוּא עֲדִינוֹ הָעֶצְנוֹ): "We believe the text to have been corrupted by a writer, probably from some book in an unknown character and bad writing, so that *orer* should be substituted for *adino*, and *ha-eznib* for *eth hanitho*;" that is to say, the reading in the Chronicles, "he swung his spear," should be adopted (cf. ver. 18). This supposition is certainly to be preferred to the attempt made by Gesenius (*Lex.*) and v. Dietrich (*s.v.* עָדִין) to find some sense in the words by assuming the existence of a verb עָדַן and a noun עֶצֶן, a spear, since these words do not occur anywhere else in Hebrew; and in order to obtain any appropriate sense, it is still necessary to resort to alterations of the text. "*He swung his spear over eight hundred slain at once.*" This is not to be understood as signifying that he killed eight hundred men at one blow, but that in a battle he threw his spear again and again at the foe, until eight hundred men had been slain. The Chronicles give three hundred instead of eight hundred; and as that number occurs again in ver. 18, in the case of Abishai, it probably found its way from that verse into this in the book of Chronicles.—Vers. 9, 10. "*After him (i.e.* next to him in rank) was *Eleazar* the son of *Dodai* the Ahohite, among the three heroes with David when they defied the Philistines, who had assembled there, and the Israelites drew near." The *Chethib* דדי is to be read דּוֹדַי, *Dodai*, according to 1 Chron. xxvii. 4, and the form דּוֹדוֹ (*Dodo*) in the parallel text (1 Chron. xi. 12) is only a variation in the form of the name. Instead of בֶּן־אֲחֹחִי (*the son of Ahohi*) we find הָאֲחוֹחִי (*the Ahohite*) in the

---

who gives this explanation of τριστάτας: τοὺς παρὰ χεῖρα τοῦ βασιλέως ἀριστερὰν τρίτης μοίρας ἄρχοντας. Suidas and Hesychius give the same explanation (*s.v.* τριστάται). Jerome also observes (ad Ezek. xxiii.): "It is the name of the second rank next to the king."

Chronicles; but the בֶּן must not be struck out on that account as spurious, for "the son of an Ahohite" is the same as "the Ahohite." For בִּשְׁלֹשָׁה נְבֹרִים we must read בִּשְׁלֹשָׁה הַגִּבֹּרִים, according to the *Keri* and the Chronicles. שְׁלֹשָׁה is not to be altered, since the numerals are sometimes attached to substantives in the absolute state (see *Ges.* § 120, 1). "*The three heroes*" are Jashobeam, Eleazar, and Shammah (ver. 11), who reached the first rank, according to ver. 19, among the heroes of David. Instead of בְּחָרְפָם בַּפְּלִשְׁתִּים (*when they defied the Philistines*), we find in the Chronicles בַּפַּס דַּמִּים וְהַפְּלִשְׁתִּים, "*at Pas-dammim*," *i.e.* most probably *Ephes-dammim* (1 Sam. xvii. 1), where the Philistines were encamped when Goliath defied the Israelites. Thenius, Bertheau, and Böttcher therefore propose to alter our text so as to make it correspond to that of the Chronicles, and adduce as the reason the fact that in other passages חָרַף is construed with the accusative, and that שָׁם, which follows, presupposes the previous mention of the place referred to. But the reasons are neither of them decisive. חָרַף is not construed with the accusative alone, but also with לְ (2 Chron. xxxii. 17), so that the construction with בְּ is quite a possible one, and is not at variance with the idea of the word. שָׁם again may also be understood as referring to the place, not named, where the Philistines fought with the Israelites. The omission of אֲשֶׁר before נֶאֶסְפוּ is more difficult to explain; and וְהַפְּלִשְׁתִּים, which we find in the Chronicles, has probably dropped out after בַּפְּלִשְׁתִּים. The reading in the Chronicles בַּפַּס דַּמִּים (בְּאֶפֶס) is probably only a more exact description of the locality, which is but obscurely indicated in our text by בְּחָרְפָם בַּפְּלִשְׁתִּים; for these words affirm that the battle took place where the Israelites had once been defied by the Philistines (1 Sam. xvii. 10), and where they repaid them for this defiance in a subsequent conflict. The Philistines are at any rate to be regarded as the subject to נֶאֶסְפוּ, and these words are a circumstantial clause: the Philistines had assembled together there to battle, and the Israelites had advanced to the attack. The heroic act of Eleazar is introduced with "he arose." He arose and smote the Philistines till his hand was weary and clave to his sword, *i.e.* was so cramped as to be stiffened to the sword. Through this Jehovah wrought a great salvation for Israel on that day, "and the people (the soldiers) turned after him only to plunder," *sc.*

because he had put the enemy to flight by himself. שׁוּב אַחֲרָיו does not mean to turn back from flight after him, but is the opposite of שׁוּב מֵאַחֲרֵי, to turn away from a person (1 Sam. xv. 11, etc.), so that it signifies "to turn to a person and follow behind him." Three lines have dropped out from the parallel text of the Chronicles, in consequence of the eye of a copyist having wandered from פְּלִשְׁתִּים נֶאֶסְפוּ in ver. 9 to וַיֵּאָסְפוּ פְלִשְׁתִּים in ver. 11.—Vers. 11, 12. The third leading hero was *Shammah*, the son of *Age* the Hararite (הָרָרִי is probably contracted from הַהֲרָרִי, ver. 33). He also made himself renowned by a great victory over the Philistines. The enemy had gathered together לַחַיָּה, "*as a troop*," or in a crowd. This meaning of חַיָּה (here and ver. 13, and possibly also in Ps. lxviii. 11) is thoroughly established by the Arabic (see Ges. *Thes.* p. 470). But it seems to have fallen into disuse afterwards, and in the Chronicles it is explained in ver. 13 by מִלְחָמָה, and in ver. 15 by מַחֲנֶה. "On a portion of a field of lentils there," *sc.* where the Philistines had gathered together, the people (of Israel) were smitten. Then Shammah stationed himself in the midst of the field, and יַצִּילֶהָ, "*wrested it*," from the foe, and smote the Philistines. Instead of עֲדָשִׁים, *lentils*, we find in the Chronicles שְׂעוֹרִים, barley, a very inconsiderable difference.

Vers. 13–17. To this deed there is appended a similar heroic feat performed by three of the thirty heroes whose names are not given. The *Chethib* שלשים is evidently a slip of the pen for שְׁלֹשָׁה (*Keri* and Chronicles). The thirty chiefs are the heroes named afterwards (see above at p. 491). As שְׁלֹשָׁה has no article, either in our text or the Chronicles, the three intended are not the three already mentioned (Jashobeam, Eleazar, and Shammah), but three others out of the number mentioned in vers. 24 sqq. These three came to David in the harvest time unto the cave of Adullam (see at 1 Sam. xxii. 1), when a troop of the Philistines was encamped in the valley of Rephaim, and David was on the mountain fortress, and a Philistian post was then in Bethlehem. And David longed for water, and said, "Oh that one would bring me water to drink out of the well of Bethlehem at the gate!" The encampment of the Philistines in the valley of Rephaim, and the position of David on the mountain fortress (בַּמְּצוּדָה), render it probable that the feat mentioned here took place in the war with the Philistines described in ch. v. 17 sqq. Robinson could not discover any well in Bethlehem, "especially none 'by the gate,' except one connected with the aqueduct on the south" (*Palestine*, vol. ii. p. 158). בַּשַּׁעַר need not be understood, however, as signifying that the well was *in* or *under* the gate; but the well referred to may have been at the gate outside the city. The well to which tradition has given the name of "David's well" (*cisterna David*), is about a quarter of an hour's walk to the north-east of Bethlehem, and, according to Robinson's description, is "merely a deep and wide cistern or cavern now dry, with three or four narrow openings cut in the rock." But Ritter (*Erdk*. xvi. p. 286) describes it as "deep with clear cool water, into which there are three openings from above, which Tobler speaks of as bored;" and again as a cistern "built with peculiar beauty, from seventeen to twenty-one feet deep, whilst a house close by is pointed out to pilgrims as Jesse's house."—Ver. 16. The three heroes then broke through the camp of the Philistines at Bethlehem, *i.e.* the outpost that occupied the space before the gate, fetched water out of the well, and brought it to David. He would not drink it, however, but poured it out upon the ground to the Lord, as a drink-offering for Jehovah. "He poured it out upon the earth, rendering Him thanks for the return of the three brave men" (Clericus). And he said, "Far be it from me, O Jehovah, to do this! The blood of the men who went with their lives (*i.e.* at the risk of their lives)," *sc.* should I drink it? The verb אֶשְׁתֶּה is wanting in our text, but is not to be inserted according to the Chronicles as though it had fallen out; the sentence is rather to be regarded as an *aposiopesis*. יהוָֹה after חָלִילָה לִּי is a vocative, and is not to be altered into מֵיהוָֹה, according to the מֵאֱלֹהַי of the Chronicles. The fact that the vocative does not occur in other passages after חָלִילָה לִּי proves nothing. It is equivalent to the oath חַי יְהוָֹה (1 Sam. xiv. 45). The chronicler has endeavoured to simplify David's exclamation by completing the sentence. בְּנַפְשׁוֹתָם, "*for the price of their souls*," *i.e.* at the risk of their lives. The water drawn and fetched at the risk of their lives is compared to the soul itself, and the soul is in the blood (Lev. xvii. 11). Drinking this water, therefore, would be nothing else than drinking their blood.

Vers. 18–23. *Heroes of the second class.*—Vers. 18, 19.

Abishai, Joab's brother (see 1 Sam. xxvi. 6), was also chief of the body-guard, like Jashobeam (ver. 8: the *Chethib* הַשְּׁלִשִׁי is correct; see at ver. 8). He swung his spear over three hundred slain. "He had a name among the three," *i.e.* the three principal heroes, Jashobeam, Eleazar, and Shammah. The following words, מִן־הַשְּׁלשָׁה, make no sense. הַשְּׁלשָׁה is an error in writing for הַשְּׁלִשִׁים, as ver. 23 shows in both the texts (ver. 25 of the Chronicles): an error the origin of which may easily be explained from the word שְׁלשָׁה, which stands immediately before. "He was certainly honoured before the thirty (heroes of David), and became their chief, but he did not come to the three," *i.e.* he was not equal to Jashobeam, Eleazar, and Shammah. הֲכִי has the force of an energetic assurance: "*is it so that,*" *i.e.* it is certainly so (as in ch. ix. 1; Gen. xxvii. 36, xxix. 15).— Vers. 20-23. *Benaiah*, the son of Jehoiada, "Jehoiada the priest" according to 1 Chron. xxvii. 5, possibly the one who was "prince for Aaron," *i.e.* of the family of Aaron, according to 1 Chron. xii. 27, was captain of the Crethi and Plethi according to ch. viii. 18 and xx. 23. He was the son of a brave man, rich in deeds (חַי is evidently an error for חַיִל in the Chronicles), of Kabzeel in the south of Judah (Josh. xv. 21). "*He smote the two Ariels of Moab.*" The Arabs and Persians call every remarkably brave man *Ariel*, or lion of God (*vid.* Bochart, *Hieroz.* ii. pp. 7, 63). They were therefore two celebrated Moabitish heroes. The supposition that they were sons of the king of the Moabites is merely founded upon the conjecture of Thenius and Bertheau, that the word בְּנֵי (sons of) has dropped out before Ariel. "He also slew the lion in the well on the day of the snow," *i.e.* a lion which had been driven into the neighbourhood of human habitations by a heavy fall of snow, and had taken refuge in a cistern. The *Chethib* הָאֲרִיֵה and בְּאֵר are the earlier forms for the *Keris* substituted by the Masoretes הָאֲרִי and הַבּוֹר, and consequently are not to be altered. He also slew an Egyptian of distinguished size. According to the *Keri* we should read אִישׁ מַרְאֶה (instead of אֲשֶׁר מַרְאֶה), "*a man of appearance,*" *i.e.* a distinguished man, or a man of great size, ἄνδρα ὁρατόν (LXX.); in the Chronicles it is simplified as אִישׁ מִדָּה, a man of measure, *i.e.* of great height. This man was armed with a spear or javelin, whereas Benaiah was only armed with a stick; nevertheless the latter smote him, took away his spear, and slew him with his own weapon. According to the Chronicles the Egyptian was five cubits high, and his spear like a weaver's beam. Through these feats Benaiah acquired a name among the three, though he did not equal them (vers. 22, 23, as in vers. 18, 19); and David made him a member of his privy council (see at 1 Sam. xxii. 14).

Vers. 24–39. *Heroes of the third class.*—Ver. 24. "*Asahel*, the brother of Joab, among the thirty," *i.e.* belonging to them. This definition also applies to the following names; we therefore find at the head of the list in the Chronicles, וְגִבּוֹרֵי הַחֲיָלִים, "and brave heroes (were)." The names which follow are for the most part not further known. *Elhanan*, the son of *Dodo* of Bethlehem, is a different man from the Bethlehemite of that name mentioned in ch. xxi. 19. *Shammah* the Harodite also must not be confounded with the Shammahs mentioned in vers. 11 and 33. In the Chronicles we find *Shammoth*, a different form of the name; whilst הַחֲרוֹרִי is an error in writing for הַחֲרֹדִי, *i.e.* sprung from *Harod* (Judg. vii. 1). This man is called *Shamhut* in 1 Chron. xxvii. 8; he was the leader of the fifth division of David's army. *Elika* of *Harod* is omitted in the Chronicles; it was probably dropped out in consequence of the *homoioteleuton* הַחֲרֹדִי.—Ver. 26. *Helez* the Paltite; *i.e.* sprung from *Beth-Pelet* in the south of Judah (Judg. xv. 27). He was chief of the seventh division of the army (compare 1 Chron. xxvii. 10 with 1 Chron. xi. 27, though in both passages הַפַּלְטִי is misspelt הַפְּלֹנִי). *Ira* the son of *Ikkesh* of Tekoah in the desert of Judah (ch. xiv. 2), chief of the sixth division of the army (1 Chron. xxvii. 9).—Ver. 27. *Abiezer* of Anathoth (Anata) in Benjamin (see at Josh. xviii. 24), chief of the ninth division of the army (1 Chron. xxvii. 12). *Mebunnai* is a mistake in spelling for *Sibbechai* the Hushathite (compare ch. xxi. 18 and 1 Chron. xi. 29). According to 1 Chron. xxvii. 11, he was chief of the eighth division of the army.—Ver. 28. *Zalmon* the Ahohite, *i.e.* sprung from the Benjaminite family of Ahoah, is not further known. Instead of *Zalmon* we find Ilai in the Chronicles (ver. 29); but which of the two names is the correct one it is impossible to decide. *Maharai* of *Netophah:* according to Ezra ii. 22 and Neh. vii. 26, Netophah was a place in the neighbourhood of Bethlehem, but it has not yet been discovered, as *Beit Nattif*, which might be thought of, is too far from Bethlehem (*vid.* Rob. *Pal.* ii. p. 344, and Tobler, *Dritte Wanderung*, pp. 117-8). According to 1 Chron. xxvii. 13, *Maharai* belonged to the Judahite family of Serah, and was chief of the tenth division of the army.—Ver. 29. *Cheleb*, more correctly *Cheled* (1 Chron. xi. 30; or *Cheldai*, 1 Chron. xxvii. 15), also of Netophah, was chief of the twelfth division of the army. *Ittai* (*Ithai* in the Chronicles), the son of Ribai of Gibeah of Benjamin, must be distinguished from *Ittai* the Gathite (ch. xv. 19). Like all that follow, with the exception of Uriah, he is not further known.—Ver. 30. *Benaiah* of *Phir'aton* in the tribe of Ephraim, a place which has been preserved in the village of *Fer'ata*, to the south-west of Nablus (see at Judg. xii. 13). *Hiddai* (wrongly spelt *Hudai* in the Chronicles), out of the valleys of *Gaash*, in the tribe of Ephraim by the mountain of *Gaash*, the situation of which has not yet been discovered (see at Josh. xxiv. 30).—Ver. 31. *Abi-Albon* (written incorrectly *Abiel* in the Chronicles) the Arbathite, *i.e.* from the place called *Beth-haarabah* or *Arabah* (Josh. xv. 61 and xviii. 18, 22) in the desert of Judah, on the site of the present *Kasr Hajla* (see at Josh. xv. 6). *Azmaveth* of *Bahurim*: see at ch. xvi. 5.—Vers. 32, 33. *Eliahba* of *Shaalbon* or *Shaalbin*, which may possibly have been preserved in the present *Selbit* (see at Josh. xix. 42). The next two names, בְּנֵי יָשֵׁן יְהוֹנָתָן and שַׁמָּה הַהֲרָרִי (*Bneyashen Jehonathan* and *Shammah the Hararite*), are written thus in the Chronicles (ver. 34), בְּנֵי הָשֵׁם הַגִּזוֹנִי יוֹנָתָן בֶּן־שָׁגֵא הַהֲרָרִי: "*Bnehashem the Gizonite, Jonathan the son of Sage the Hararite*." The text of the Chronicles is evidently the more correct of the two, as *Bne Jashen Jehonathan* does not make any sense. The only question is whether the form בְּנֵי הָשֵׁם is correct, or whether בְּנֵי has not arisen merely through a misspelling. As the name does not occur again, all that can be said is that *Bne hashem* must at any rate be written as one word, and therefore should be pointed differently. The place mentioned, *Gizon*, is unknown. שַׁמָּה for בֶּן־שָׁגֵא probably arose from ver. 11. *Ahiam* the son of *Sharar* or *Sacar* (Chron.) the Ararite (in the Chronicles the Hararite).—Ver. 34. The names in 34*a*, *Eliphelet ben-Ahasbai ben-Hammaacathi*, read thus in the Chronicles (vers. 35, 36): *Eliphal ben-Ur*; *Hepher hammecerathi*. We see from this that in *ben-Ahasbai ben* two names have been fused together; for the text as it lies before us is rendered suspicious partly by the fact that the names of both father and grandfather are given, which does not occur in connection with any other name in the whole list, and partly by the circumstance that בֶּן cannot properly be written with הַמַּעֲכָתִי, which is a *Gentile noun*. Consequently the following is probably the correct way of restoring the text, אֱלִיפֶלֶט בֶּן־אוּר חֵפֶר הַמַּעֲכָתִי, *Eliphelet* (a name which frequently occurs) *the son of Ur; Hepher the Maachathite, i.e.* of Maacah in the north-east of Gilead (see at ch. x. 6 and Deut. iii. 14). *Eliam* the son of Ahithophel the Gilonite, the clever but treacherous counsellor of David (see at ch. xv. 12). This name is quite corrupt in the Chronicles.—Ver. 35. *Hezro* the Carmelite, *i.e.* of Carmel in the mountains of Judah (1 Sam. xxv. 2). *Paarai* the Arbite, *i.e.* of Arab, also in the mountains of Judah (Josh. xv. 52). In the Chronicles we find *Naarai ben-Ezbi*: the latter is evidently an error in writing for *ha-Arbi;* but it is impossible to decide which of the two forms, *Paarai* and *Naarai,* is the correct one.—Ver. 36. *Jigal* the son of Nathan of Zoba (see at ch. viii. 3): in the Chronicles, Joel the brother of Nathan. *Bani* the Gadite: in the Chronicles we have *Mibhar* the son of Hagri. In all probability the names in the Chronicles are corrupt in this instance also.—Ver. 37. *Zelek* the Ammonite, *Nacharai* the Beerothite (of Beeroth : see at ch. iv. 2), the armour-bearer of Joab. Instead of נֹשְׂאֵי, the *Keri* and the Chronicles have נֹשֵׂא : the latter reading is favoured by the circumstance, that if more than one of the persons named had been Joab's armour-bearers, their names would most probably have been linked together by a copulative *vav.*—Ver. 38. *Ira* and *Gareb*, both of them Jithrites, *i.e.* sprung from a family in Kirjath-jearim (1 Chron. ii. 53). *Ira* is of course a different man from the *cohen* of that name (ch. xx. 26).—Ver. 39. *Uriah* the Hittite is well known from ch. xi. 3. "*Thirty and seven in all.*" This number is correct, as there were *three* in the first class (vers. 8–12), *two* in the second (vers. 18–23), and *thirty-two* in the third (vers. 24–39), since ver. 34 contains three names according to the amended text.

NUMBERING OF THE PEOPLE, AND PESTILENCE.—CHAP. XXIV.

For the purpose of ascertaining the number of the people, and their fitness for war, David ordered Joab, his commander-in-chief, to take a census of Israel and Judah. Joab dissuaded him from such a step; but inasmuch as the king paid no attention to his dissuasion, he carried out the command with the help of the military captains (vers. 1-9). David very speedily saw, however, that he had sinned; whereupon the prophet Gad went to him by the command of Jehovah to announce the coming punishment, and give him the choice of three different judgments which he placed before him (vers. 10-13). As David chose rather to fall into the hand of the Lord than into the hand of men, God sent a pestilence, which carried off seventy thousand men in one day throughout the whole land, and had reached Jerusalem, when the Lord stopped the destroying angel in consequence of the penitential prayer of David (vers. 14-17), and sent Gad to the king to direct him to build an altar to the Lord on the spot where the destroying angel had appeared to him (ver. 18). Accordingly David bought the threshing-floor of Araunah the Jebusite, built an altar upon it, and sacrificed burnt-offerings and thank-offerings, after which the plague was stayed (vers. 19-25).

This occurrence, which is introduced in the parallel history in 1 Chron. xxi. between David's wars and his arrangements for a more complete organization of the affairs of the nation, belongs undoubtedly to the closing years of David's reign. The mere taking of a census, as a measure that would facilitate the general organization of the kingdom, could not in itself be a sinful act, by which David brought guilt upon himself, or upon the nation, before God. Nevertheless it is not only represented in ver. 1 as a manifestation of the wrath of God against Israel, but in ver. 3 Joab seeks to dissuade the king from it as being a wrong thing; and in ver. 10 David himself admits that it was a grievous sin against God, and as a sin it is punished by the Lord (vers. 12 sqq.). In what, then, did David's sin consist? Certainly not in the fact that, when taking the census, "he neglected to demand the atonement money, which was to be raised, according to Ex. xxx. 12 sqq., from all who were numbered, because the numbering of the people was regarded in itself as an undertaking by which the anger of God might easily be excited," as Josephus and Bertheau maintain; for the Mosaic instructions concerning the atonement money had reference to the incorporation of the people into the army of

Jehovah (see at Ex. xxx. 13, 14), and therefore did not come into consideration at all in connection with the census appointed by David as a purely political measure. Nor can we imagine that David's sin consisted merely in the fact that he "entered upon the whole affair from pride and vain boasting," or that "he commanded the census from vanity, inasmuch as he wanted to have it distinctly set before his own eyes how strong and mighty he was" (Buddeus, Hengstenberg, and others); for although pride and vanity had something to do with it, as the words of Joab especially seem to indicate, David was far too great a man to allow us to attribute to him a childish delight in the mere number of souls in his kingdom. The census had certainly a higher purpose than this. It is very evident from 1 Chron. xxvii. 23, 24, where it is mentioned again that it was connected with the military organization of the people, and probably was to be the completion of it. David wanted to know the number of his subjects, not that he might be able to boast of their multitude, nor that he might be able to impose all kinds of taxes upon every town and village according to their houses and inhabitants, as Ewald maintains.; but that he might be fully acquainted with its defensive power, though we can neither attribute to him the definite purpose " of transforming the theocratic sacred state into a conquering world-state" (Kurtz), nor assume that through this numbering the whole nation was to be enrolled for military service, and that thirst for conquest was the motive for the undertaking. The true kernel of David's sin was to be found, no doubt, in self-exaltation, inasmuch as he sought for the strength and glory of his kingdom in the number of the people and their readiness for war. This sin was punished. "Because David was about to boast proudly and to glory in the number of his people, God determined to punish him by reducing their number either by famine, war, or pestilence" (Seb. Schmidt). At the same time, the people themselves had sinned grievously against God and their king, through the two rebellions headed by Absalom and Sheba.

Vers. 1–9. "Again the anger of Jehovah was kindled against Israel; and He moved David against them, saying, Go, number Israel and Judah." וַיֹּסֶף . . . לַחֲרוֹת points back to the manifestation of the wrath of God, which Israel had ex perienced in the three years' famine (ch. xxi.). Just as that plague had burst upon the land on account of the guilt which rested upon the people, so the kindling of the wrath of God against Israel a second time also presupposes guilt on the part of the nation; and as this is not expressly pointed out, we may seek for it generally in the rebellions of Absalom and Sheba against the divinely established government of David. The subject to "*moved*" is *Jehovah*, and the words "*against them*" point back to *Israel*. Jehovah instigated David against Israel to the performance of an act which brought down a severe judgment upon the nation. With regard to the idea that God instigates to sin, see the remarks on 1 Sam. xxvi. 19. In the parallel text of the Chronicles, Satan is mentioned as the tempter to evil, through whom Jehovah led David to number the people.—Ver. 2. David entrusted the task to his commander-in-chief Joab. אֲשֶׁר אִתּוֹ, "*who was with him:*" the meaning is, "when he was with him" (David). We are not warranted in attempting any emendations of the text, either by the expression אֲשֶׁר אִתּוֹ, or by the reading in the Chronicles, וְאֶל־שָׂרֵי הָעָם ("and to the rulers of the people"); for whilst the latter reading may easily be seen to be a simplification founded upon ver. 4, it is impossible to show how שַׂר־הַחַיִל אֲשֶׁר אִתּוֹ, which is supported by all the ancient versions (with the sole exception of the Arabic), could have originated in וְאֶל־שָׂרֵי הָעָם. "*Go now through all the tribes of Israel, from Dan to Beersheba* (see at Judg. xx. 1), *and muster the people.*" פָּקַד, to muster or number, as in Num. i. 44 sqq. The change from the singular שׁוּט to the plural פִּקְדוּ may be explained very simply, from the fact that, as a matter of course, Joab was not expected to take the census by himself, but with the help of several assistants.— Ver. 3. Joab discountenanced the thing: "Jehovah thy God add to the nation, as it is, a hundredfold as many, and may the eyes of my lord the king see it. But why doth my lord the king delight in this thing?" The ו before יוֹסֵף stands at the commencement, when what is said contains a sequel to something that has gone before (*vid.* Ges. § 255, 1, *a*). The thought to which Joab's words are appended as a sequel, is implied in what David said, "that I may know the number of the people;" and if expressed fully, his words would read somewhat as follows: "If thou hast delight in the greatness of the number of the people, may Jehovah," etc. Joab evidently saw through the king's intention, and perceived that the numbering of the people could not be of any essential advantage to David's government, and might produce dissatisfaction among the people, and therefore endeavoured to dissuade the king from his purpose. כָּהֵם וְכָהֵם, "*as they* (the Israelites) *just are*," *i.e.* in this connection, " just as many as there are of them." From a grammatical point of view, כָּהֵם is to be taken as the object to יֹסֵף, as in the parallel passages, Deut. i. 11, 2 Sam. xii. 8. Not only did he desire that God would multiply the nation a hundredfold, but that He would do it during the lifetime of David, so that his eyes might be delighted with the immense numbers.—Vers. 4, 5. But as the king's word prevailed against Joab and against the captains of the army, they (Joab and the other captains) went out to number Israel. יַּחֲנוּ, they encamped, *i.e.* they fixed their headquarters in the open field, because great crowds assembled together. This is only mentioned here in connection with the place where the numbering commenced; but it is to be understood as applying to the other places as well (Thenius). In order to distinguish *Aroer* from the place of the same name on the Arnon, in the tribe of Reuben (Josh. xii. 2; Num. xxxii. 34, etc.), it is defined more precisely as "the town in the brook-valley of Gad," *i.e.* Aroer of Gad before Rabbah (Josh. xiii. 25; Judg. xi. 33), in the Wady *Nahr Ammân*, to the north-east of Ammân (see at Josh. xiii. 25). וְאֶל־יַעְזֵר (and to *Jazer*): this is a second place of encampment, and the preposition אֶל is to be explained on the supposition that יָבֹאוּ (they came), which follows, was already in the writer's thoughts. *Jazer* is probably to be found in the ruins of *es Szir*, at the source of the *Nahr Szir* (see at Num. xxi. 32).—Ver. 6. "And they came to *Gilead*," *i.e.* the mountainous district on the two sides of the Jabbok (see at Deut. iii. 10). The words which follow, viz. " into the land חָדְשִׁי תַּחְתִּים," are quite obscure, and were unintelligible even to the earlier translators. The Septuagint has γῆν Ἐθαὼν Ἀδασαί, or γῆν Θαβασών (also γῆν χεττιείμ) ἥ ἐστιν Ἀδασαί. Symmachus has τὴν κατωτέραν ὁδόν; Jonathan לְאַרְעָא דָרוֹמָא לְחָדְשִׁי (" into the southland *Chodshi*"); and the Vulgate *in terram inferiorem*. The singular form תַּחְתִּים, and the fact that we never read of a land called *Chodshi*, render the conjecture a very probable one that the text is corrupt. But it is no longer possible to discover the correct reading. Ewald imagines that we should read *Hermon* instead of the unintelligible *Chodshi*; but this is not very probable. Böttcher supposes החתים to be a mistake in writing for תחת ים, "below the lake," namely the lake of Gennesareth, which might have been called *Chodshi* (the new-moon-like), since it had very much the appearance of a crescent when seen from the northern heights. This is ingenious, but incredible. The order of the places named points to the eastern side of the sea of Galilee; for they went thence to *Dan-Jaan*, i.e. the Dan in northern Peræa, mentioned in Gen. xiv. 14, to the south-west of Damascus, at that time probably the extreme north-eastern boundary of the kingdom of David, in the direction towards Syria (see at Gen. xiv. 14): " and round to *Sidon*," the extreme north-western boundary of the kingdom.—Ver. 7. Thence southwards to the fortress of *Zor*, i.e. Tyre (see at Josh. xix. 29), and " *into all the towns of the Hivites and Canaanites*," i.e. the towns in the tribes of Naphtali, Zebulun, and Issachar, or the (subsequent) province of Galilee, in which the Canaanites had not been exterminated by the Israelites, but had only been made tributary.—Vers. 8, 9. When they had traversed the whole land, they came back to Jerusalem, at the end of nine months and twenty days, and handed over to the king the number of the people mustered: viz. 800,000 men of Israel fit for military service, drawing the sword, and 500,000 men of Judah. According to the Chronicles (ver. 5), there were 1,100,000 Israelites and 470,000 Judæans. The numbers are not given by thousands, and therefore are only approximative statements in round numbers; and the difference in the two texts arose chiefly from the fact, that the statements were merely founded upon oral tradition, since, according to 1 Chron. xxvii. 4, the result of the census was not inserted in the annals of the kingdom. There is no ground, however, for regarding the numbers as exaggerated, if we only bear in mind that the entire population of a land amounts to about four times the number of those who are fit for military service, and therefore 1,300,000, or even a million and a half, would only represent a total population of five or six millions,—a number which could undoubtedly have been sustained in Palestine, according to thoroughly reliable testimony as to its unusual fertility (see the discussion of this subject at Num. i.–iv., vol. iii. pp. 4–13). Still less can we adduce as a proof of exaggeration the fact, that according to 1 Chron. xxvii. 1–15, David had only an army of 288,000; for it is a well-known fact, that in all lands the army, or number of men in actual service, is, as a rule, much smaller than the total number of those who are capable of bearing arms. According to 1 Chron. xxi. 6, the tribes of Levi and Benjamin were not numbered, because, as the chronicler adds, giving his own subjective view, " the word of the king was an abomination to Joab," or, as it is affirmed in 1 Chron. xxvii. 4, according to the objective facts, " because the numbering was not completed." It is evident from this, that in consequence of Joab's repugnance to the numbering of the people, he had not hurried with the fulfilment of the king's command; so that when David saw his own error, he revoked the command before the census was complete, and so the tribe of Benjamin was not numbered at all, the tribe of Levi being of course *eo ipso* exempt from a census that was taken for the sake of ascertaining the number of men who were capable of bearing arms.

Vers. 10–18. David's heart, *i.e.* his conscience, smote him, after he had numbered the people, or had given orders for the census to be taken. Having now come to a knowledge of his sin, he prayed to the Lord for forgiveness, because he had acted foolishly. The sin consisted chiefly in the self-exaltation which had led to this step (see the introductory remarks).— Vers. 11–13. When he rose up in the morning, after he had calmly reflected upon the matter during the night upon his bed, and had been brought to see the folly of his determination, the prophet Gad came to him by the command of God, pointed out to him his fault, and foretold the punishment that would come from God. " Shall seven years of famine come upon thy land, or three months of flight before thine oppressors that they may pursue thee, or shall there be three days of pestilence in thy land? Now mark and see what answer I shall bring to Him that sendeth me." These three verses form *one* period, in which וַיָּבֹא גָד (ver. 13) answers as the consequent to וַיָּקָם דָּוִד וגו' in ver. 11, and the words from וּדְבַר יְהוָה (ver. 11*b*) to וְאֶעֱשֶׂה־לָּךְ (ver. 12) form a circumstantial clause inserted between. וּדְבַר יְהוָה וגו': " and the word of the Lord had taken place (gone forth) to Gad, David's seer, saying, Go . . . thus saith Jehovah, I lay upon thee three (things or evils); choose thee one of them that I may do it to thee." Instead of נֹטֵל עַל, to lay upon, we find נֹטֶה in the Chronicles, "to turn upon thee." The three things are mentioned first of all in connection with the execution of Gad's commission to the king. Instead of *seven* years of famine, we find *three* years in the Chronicles; the Septuagint has also the number three in the passage before us, and apparently it is more in harmony with the connection, viz. *three* evils to choose from, and each lasting through *three* divisions of time. But this agreement favours the *seven* rather than the *three*, which is open to the suspicion of being intentionally made to conform to the rest. נֻסְךָ is an infinitive: "thy fleeing," for that thou fliest before thine enemies. In the Chronicles the last two evils are described more fully, but the thought is not altered in consequence.—Ver. 14. David replied, "I am in great trouble. Let us fall into the hand of the Lord, for His mercy is great; but let me not fall into the hand of men." Thus David chose the third judgment, since pestilence comes directly from God. On the other hand, in flight from the enemy, he would have fallen into the hands of men. It is not easy to see, however, how far this could apply to famine; probably inasmuch as it tends more or less to create dependence upon those who are still in possession of the means of life.—Ver. 15. God then gave (sent) a pestilence into (upon) Israel, "from the morning till the time of the assembly;" and there died of the people in the whole land (from Dan to Beersheba) seventy thousand men. "*From the morning:*" on which Gad had foretold the punishment. The meaning of וְעַד־עֵת מוֹעֵד is doubtful. The rendering "*to the time appointed,*" *i.e.* "till the expiration of the three days," in support of which the Vulgate (*ad tempus constitutum*) is wrongly appealed to, is precluded not only by the circumstance that, according to ver. 16, the plague was stayed earlier because God repented Him of the evil, so that it did not last so long as was at first appointed, but also by the grammatical difficulty that עֵת מוֹעֵד has no article, and can only be rendered "for *an* (not for *the*) appointed time." We meet with two different explanations in the ancient versions: one in the Septuagint, ἕως ὥρας ἀρίστου, "till the hour of breakfast," *i.e.*

till the sixth hour of the day, which is the rendering also adopted by the Syriac and Arabic as well as by Kimchi and several of the Rabbins; the other in the Chaldee (Jonathan), "from the time at which the sacrifice is commonly slain until it is consumed." Accordingly Bochart explains עֵת מוֹעֵד as signifying "the time at which the people came together for evening prayers, about the ninth hour of the day, *i.e.* the third hour in the afternoon" (*vid.* Acts iii. 1). The same view also lies at the foundation of the Vulgate rendering, according to the express statement of Jerome (*traditt. Hebr. in* 2 *libr. Regum*) : "He calls that the *time appointed*, in which the evening sacrifice was offered." It is true that this meaning of מוֹעֵד cannot be established by precisely analogous passages, but it may be very easily deduced from the frequent employment of the word to denote the meetings and festivals connected with the worship of God, when it generally stands without an article, as for example in the perfectly analogous יוֹם מוֹעֵד (Hos. ix. 5; Lam. ii. 7, 22); whereas it is always written with the article when it is used in the general sense of a fixed time, and some definite period is referred to.[1] We must therefore decide in favour of the latter. But if the pestilence did not last a whole day, the number of persons carried off by it (70,000 men) exceeded very considerably the number destroyed by the most violent pestilential epidemics on record, although they have not unfrequently swept off hundreds of thousands in a very brief space of time. But the pestilence burst upon the people in this instance with supernatural strength and violence, that it might be seen at once to be a direct judgment from God.—Ver. 16. The general statement as to the divine judgment and its terrible effects is followed by a more minute

---

[1] The objections brought against this have no force in them, viz. that, according to this view, the section must have been written a long time after the captivity (Clericus and Thenius), and that "the perfectly general expression '*the time of meeting*' could not stand for the time of the afternoon or evening meeting" (Thenius): for the former rests upon the assumption that the daily sacrifice was introduced after the captivity,—an assumption quite at variance with historical facts; and the latter is overthrown by the simple remark, that the indefinite expression derived its more precise meaning from the legal appointment of the morning and evening sacrifice as times of meeting for the worship of God, inasmuch as the evening meeting was the only one that could be placed in contrast with the morning.

description of the judgment itself, and the arrest of the plague. "When the destroying angel ('*the angel*' is defined immediately afterwards as '*the angel that destroyed the people*') stretched out his hand towards Jerusalem to destroy it, Jehovah repented of the evil (for this expression, see Ex. xxxii. 14, Jer. xxvi. 13, 19, etc.; and for the repentance of God, the remarks on Gen. vi. 6), and He commanded the angel, Enough! stay now thine hand." This implies that the progress of the pestilence was stayed before Jerusalem, and therefore that Jerusalem itself was spared. "*And the angel of Jehovah was at the threshing-floor of Aravnah the Jebusite.*" These words affirm most distinctly that the destroying angel was visible. According to ver. 17, David saw him there. The visible appearance of the angel was to exclude every thought of a natural land plague. The appearance of the angel is described more minutely in the Chronicles: David saw him standing by the threshing-floor of Aravnah between heaven and earth with a drawn sword in his hand, stretched out over Jerusalem. The drawn sword was a symbolical representation of the purpose of his coming (see at Num. xxii. 23 and Josh. v. 13). The threshing-floor of Aravnah was situated, like all other threshing-floors, outside the city, and upon an eminence, or, according to the more precise statement which follows, to the north-east of Zion, upon Mount Moriah (see at ver. 25). According to the *Chethib* of ver. 16, the name of the owner of the floor was הָאוֹרְנָה, of ver. 18 אֲרַנְיָה, and of ver. 20 (twice) אֲרַוְנָה. The last form also occurs in vers. 22, 23, and 24, and has been substituted by the Masoretes as the *Keri* in vers. 16 and 18. In the Chronicles, on the other hand, the name is always written אָרְנָן (*Ornan*), and hence in the Septuagint we find Ὄρνα in both texts. "The form אֲרַוְנָה (*Aravnah*) has not a Hebrew stamp, whereas *Orna* and *Ornan* are true Hebrew formations. But for this very reason *Aravnah* appears to be derived from an ancient tradition" (Bertheau).—Ver. 17. When David saw the angel, he prayed to the Lord (he and the elders being clothed in mourning costume: Chron.): "*Behold, I have sinned, and I have acted perversely; but these, the flock, what have they done? Let Thy hand come upon me and my house.*" The meaning is: I the shepherd of Thy people have sinned and transgressed, but the nation is innocent; *i.e.* not indeed free from every kind of blame, but only from the sin which God was punishing by the pestilence. It belongs to the very nature of truly penitential prayer, that the person praying takes all the blame upon himself, acknowledges before God that he alone is deserving of punishment, and does not dwell upon the complicity of others for the sake of palliating his own sin in the sight of God. We must not infer, therefore, from this confession on the part of David, that the people, whilst innocent themselves, had had to atone only for an act of transgression on the part of their king.—Ver. 18. David's prayer was heard. The prophet Gad came and said to him by command of Jehovah, "Go up, and erect an altar to the Lord upon the floor of Aravnah the Jebusite." This is all that is communicated here of the word of Jehovah which Gad was to convey to the king; the rest is given afterwards, as is frequently the case, in the course of the subsequent account of the fulfilment of the divine command (ver. 21). David was to build the altar and offer burnt-offerings and supplicatory-offerings upon it, to appease the wrath of Jehovah. The plague would then be averted from Israel.

Vers. 19-25. David went up to Aravnah according to the command of God.—Vers. 20, 21. When Aravnah saw the king coming up to him with his servants (וַיַּשְׁקֵף, "*he looked out*," viz. from the enclosure of the threshing-floor), he came out, bowed low even to the earth, and asked the king what was the occasion of his coming; whereupon David replied, "To buy the floor from thee, to build an altar to the Lord, that the plague may be turned away from the people."—Ver. 22. Aravnah replied, "Let my lord the king take and offer up what seemeth good unto him: behold (*i.e.* there thou hast) the ox for the burnt-offering, and the threshing-machine, and the harness of the ox for wood" (*i.e.* for fuel). הַבָּקָר, the *pair of oxen* yoked together in front of the threshing-machine. כְּלֵי הַבָּקָר, the *wooden yokes*. "*All this giveth Aravnah, O king, to the king.*" הַמֶּלֶךְ is a vocative, and is simply omitted by the LXX., Vulgate, Syriac, and Arabic, because the translators regarded it as a nominative, which is quite unsuitable, as Aravnah was not a king. When Thenius, on the other hand, objects to this, for the purpose of throwing suspicion upon the passage, that the sentence is thus stamped as part of Aravnah's address to the king, and that in that case the words that follow, " and Aravnah said," would be altogether superfluous; the former remark is correct enough, for the words " all this giveth Aravnah ... to the king" must form part of what Aravnah said, inasmuch as the remark, " all this gave Aravnah to the king," if taken as the historian's own words, would be in most glaring contradiction to what follows, where the king is said to have bought the floor and the oxen from Aravnah. And the words that follow (" and Aravnah said") are not superfluous on that account, but simply indicate that Aravnah did not proceed to say the rest in the same breath, but added it after a short pause, as a word which did not directly bear upon the question put by the king. וַיֹּאמֶר (and he said) is often repeated, where the same person continues speaking (see for example ch. xv. 4, 25, 27). " Jehovah thy God accept thee graciously," *i.e.* fulfil the request thou presentest to Him with sacrifice and prayer.—Ver. 24. The king did not accept the offer, however, but said, " No; but I will buy it of thee at a price, and will not offer burnt-offerings to the Lord my God without paying for them." Thus David bought the threshing-floor and the oxen for fifty shekels of silver. Instead of this, the Chronicles give "shekels of gold, in weight six hundred." This difference cannot be reconciled by assuming that David paid his fifty shekels in gold coin, which would have been worth as much as six hundred shekels of silver, since gold was worth twelve times as much as silver. For there is nothing about gold shekels in our text; and the words of the Chronicles cannot be interpreted as meaning that the shekels of gold were worth six hundred shekels of silver. No other course is left, therefore, than to assume that the number must be corrupt in one of the texts. Apparently the statement in the Chronicles is the more correct of the two: for if we consider that Abraham paid four hundred shekels of silver for the site of a family burial-place, at a time when the land was very thinly populated, and therefore land must certainly have been much cheaper than it was in David's time, the small sum of fifty shekels of silver (about £6) appears much too low a price; and David would certainly pay at least fifty shekels of gold. But we are not warranted in any case in speaking of the statement in the Chronicles, as Thenius does, as " intentionally exaggerated."

This style of criticism, which carries two kinds of weights and measures in its bag, explaining the high numbers in the books of Samuel and Kings as corruptions of the text, and those in the Chronicles as intentional exaggerations on the part of the chronicler, is sufficiently dealt with by the remark of Bertheau, that " this (*i.e.* the charge of exaggeration) could only be sustained if it were perfectly certain that the chronicler had our present text of the books of Samuel before him at the time."—Ver. 25. After acquiring the threshing-floor by purchase, David built an altar to the Lord there, and offered burnt-offerings and supplicatory-offerings (*shelamim*: as in Judg. xx. 26, xxi. 4; 1 Sam. xiii. 9) upon it to the Lord. " So Jehovah was entreated, and the plague was turned away from Israel."

This remark brings to a close not only the account of this particular occurrence, but also the book itself; whereas in the Chronicles it is still further stated that Jehovah answered David with fire from heaven, which fell upon the burnt-offering; and that after his prayer had been answered thus, David not only continued to offer sacrifice upon the floor of Aravnah, but also fixed upon it as the site for the temple which was afterwards to be built (1 Chron. xxi. 27, xxii. 1); and to this there is appended, in ch. xxii. 2 sqq., an account of the preparations which David made for the building of the temple. It is not affirmed in the Chronicles, however, that David fixed upon this place as the site for the future temple in consequence of a revelation from God, but simply that he did this, because he saw that the Lord had answered him there, and because he could not go to Gibeon, where the tabernacle was standing, to seek the Lord there, on account of the sword of the angel, *i.e.* on account of the pestilence. The command of God to build an altar upon the threshing-floor of Aravnah, and offer expiatory sacrifices upon it, when connected with His answering his prayer by turning away the plague, could not fail to be taken as a distinct intimation to David, that the site of this altar was the place where the Lord would henceforth make known His gracious presence to His people; and this hint was quite sufficient to determine the site for the temple which his son Solomon was to build.

T. and T. Clark's Publications.

NEW SERIES
OF THE
FOREIGN THEOLOGICAL LIBRARY.

The Issue for 1882 *comprises—*
DORNER'S SYSTEM OF CHRISTIAN DOCTRINE. Vols. III. and IV. (completion).
WEISS'S BIBLICAL THEOLOGY OF THE NEW TESTAMENT. Vol. I.
MARTENSEN'S CHRISTIAN ETHICS. (Social Ethics.)

1880.—GODET'S COMMENTARY ON THE EPISTLE OF ST. PAUL TO THE ROMANS. Vol. I.
HAGENBACH'S HISTORY OF DOCTRINES. Vols. I. and II.
DORNER'S SYSTEM OF CHRISTIAN DOCTRINE. Vol. I.

1881.—GODET'S COMMENTARY ON THE EPISTLE OF ST. PAUL TO THE ROMANS. Vol. II.
DORNER'S SYSTEM OF CHRISTIAN DOCTRINE. Vol. II.
MARTENSEN'S CHRISTIAN ETHICS. (Individual Ethics.)
HAGENBACH'S HISTORY OF DOCTRINES. Vol. III. (completion).

The FOREIGN THEOLOGICAL LIBRARY was commenced in 1846, and from that time to this Four Volumes yearly (or 148 in all) have appeared with the utmost regularity.

The Publishers decided to begin a NEW SERIES with 1880, and so give an opportunity to many to subscribe who are possibly deterred by the extent of the former Series.

With this view, Messrs. CLARK beg to announce as in preparation
DR. KEIL'S HANDBOOK OF BIBLICAL ARCHÆOLOGY.
GOEBEL'S PARABLES OF JESUS.
REUSCH'S BIBLE AND NATURE.
WEISS'S LIFE OF CHRIST.

From time to time other works will be added to this list; but the Publishers are sanguine enough to believe that a Series containing the works of writers so eminent, upon the most important subjects, cannot fail to secure support.

The Binding of the Series is modernized, so as to distinguish it from the former Series.

The Subscription Price will remain as formerly, 21s. annually for Four Volumes, payable in advance.

A SELECTION OF TWENTY VOLUMES
FOR FIVE GUINEAS

May be had from the Volumes issued previously to New Series, viz. :—
Works mentioned on pages 2, 3, 4.

[*See pages* 2, 3, 4.

MESSRS. CLARK allow a SELECTION of TWENTY VOLUMES (*or more at the same ratio*) from the Volumes issued previously to New Series (*see below*),

At the Subscription Price of Five Guineas.

NON-SUBSCRIPTION PRICES WITHIN BRACKETS.

Dr. Hengstenberg.—Commentary on the Psalms. By E. W. HENGSTENBERG, D.D., Professor of Theology in Berlin. In Three Vols. 8vo. (33s.)

Dr. Gieseler.—Compendium of Ecclesiastical History. By J. C. L. GIESELER, D.D., Professor of Theology in Göttingen. Five Vols. 8vo. (£2, 12s. 6d.)

Dr. Olshausen.—Biblical Commentary on the Gospels and Acts. Adapted especially for Preachers and Students. By HERMANN OLSHAUSEN, D.D., Professor of Theology in the University of Erlangen. In Four Vols. 8vo. (£2, 2s.)—Commentary on the Romans. In One Vol. 8vo. (10s. 6d.)—Commentary on St. Paul's First and Second Epistles to the Corinthians. In One Vol. 8vo. (9s.)—Commentary on St. Paul's Epistles to the Philippians, to Titus, and the First to Timothy. In continuation of the Work of Olshausen. By LIC. AUGUST WIESINGER. In One Vol. 8vo. (10s. 6d.)

Dr. Neander.—General History of the Christian Religion and Church. By AUGUSTUS NEANDER, D.D. Nine Vols. 8vo. (£3, 7s. 6d.)

Prof. H. A. Ch. Hävernick.—General Introduction to the Old Testament. By Professor HÄVERNICK. One Vol. 8vo. (10s. 6d.)

Dr. Müller.—The Christian Doctrine of Sin. By Dr. JULIUS MÜLLER. Two Vols. 8vo. (21s.) New Edition.

Dr. Hengstenberg.—Christology of the Old Testament, and a Commentary on the Messianic Predictions. By E. W. HENGSTENBERG, D.D. Four Vols. (£2, 2s.)

Dr. M. Baumgarten.—The Acts of the Apostles; or, The History of the Church in the Apostolic Age. By M. BAUMGARTEN, Ph.D. Three Vols. (£1, 7s.)

Dr. Stier.—The Words of the Lord Jesus. By RUDOLPH STIER, D.D., Chief Pastor and Superintendent of Schkeuditz. In Eight Vols. 8vo. (£4, 4s.)

Dr. Carl Ullmann.—Reformers before the Reformation, principally in Germany and the Netherlands. Two Vols. 8vo. (£1, 1s.)

Professor Kurtz.—History of the Old Covenant; or, Old Testament Dispensation. By Professor KURTZ of Dorpat. In Three Vols. (£1, 11s. 6d.)

Dr. Stier.—The Words of the Risen Saviour, and Commentary on the Epistle of St. James. By RUDOLPH STIER, D.D. One Vol. (10s. 6d.)

Professor Tholuck.—Commentary on the Gospel of St. John. One Vol. (9s.)

Professor Tholuck.—Commentary on the Sermon on the Mount. One Vol. (10s. 6d.)

Dr. Hengstenberg.—On the Book of Ecclesiastes. To which are appended: Treatises on the Song of Solomon; the Book of Job; the Prophet Isaiah; the Sacrifices of Holy Scripture; and on the Jews and the Christian Church. In One Vol. 8vo. (9s.)

Dr. Ebrard.—Commentary on the Epistles of St. John. By Dr. JOHN H. A. EBRARD, Professor of Theology. In One Vol. (10s. 6d.)

Dr. Lange.—Theological and Homiletical Commentary on the Gospels of St. Matthew and Mark. By J. P. LANGE, D.D. Three Vols. (10s. 6d. each.)

Dr. Dorner.—History of the Development of the Doctrine of the Person of Christ. By Dr. I. A. DORNER, Professor of Theology in the University of Berlin. Five Vols. (£2, 12s. 6d.)

Lange and Dr. J. J. Van Oosterzee.—Theological and Homiletical Commentary on the Gospel of St. Luke. Two Vols. (18s.)

Dr. Ebrard.—The Gospel History: A Compendium of Critical Investigations in support of the Historical Character of the Four Gospels. One Vol. (10s. 6d.)

Lange, Lechler, and Gerok.—Theological and Homiletical Commentary on the Acts of the Apostles. Edited by Dr. LANGE. Two Vols. (21s.)

Dr. Hengstenberg.—Commentary on the Gospel of St. John. Two Vols. (21s.)

Professor Keil.—Biblical Commentary on the Pentateuch. Three Vols. (31s. 6d.)

CLARK'S FOREIGN THEOLOGICAL LIBRARY—*Continued.*

Professor Keil.—Commentary on Joshua, Judges, and Ruth. One Vol. (10s. 6d.)
Professor Delitzsch.—A System of Biblical Psychology. One Vol. (12s.)
Dr. C. A. Auberlen.—The Divine Revelation. 8vo. (10s. 6d.)
Professor Delitzsch.—Commentary on the Prophecies of Isaiah. Two Vols. (21s.)
Professor Keil.—Commentary on the Books of Samuel. One Vol. (10s. 6d.)
Professor Delitzsch.—Commentary on the Book of Job. Two Vols. (21s.)
Bishop Martensen.—Christian Dogmatics. A Compendium of the Doctrines of Christianity. One Vol. (10s. 6d.)
Dr. J. P. Lange.—Commentary on the Gospel of St. John. Two Vols. (21s.)
Professor Keil.—Commentary on the Minor Prophets. Two Vols. (21s.)
Professor Delitzsch.—Commentary on Epistle to the Hebrews. Two Vols. (21s.)
Dr. Harless.—A System of Christian Ethics. One Vol. (10s. 6d.)
Dr. Hengstenberg.—Commentary on Ezekiel. One Vol. (10s. 6d.)
Dr. Stier.—The Words of the Apostles Expounded. One Vol. (10s. 6d.)
Professor Keil.—Introduction to the Old Testament. Two Vols. (21s.)
Professor Bleek.—Introduction to the New Testament. Two Vols. (21s.)
Professor Schmid.—New Testament Theology. One Vol. (10s. 6d.)
Professor Delitzsch.—Commentary on the Psalms. Three Vols. (31s. 6d.)
Dr. Hengstenberg.—The Kingdom of God under the Old Covenant. Two Vols. (21s.)
Professor Keil.—Commentary on the Books of Kings. One Volume. (10s. 6d.)
Professor Keil.—Commentary on the Book of Daniel. One Volume. (10s. 6d.)
Professor Keil.—Commentary on the Books of Chronicles. One Volume. (10s. 6d.)
Professor Keil.—Commentary on Ezra, Nehemiah, and Esther. One Vol. (10s. 6d.)
Professor Keil.—Commentary on Jeremiah. Two Vols. (21s.)
Winer (Dr. G. B.)—Collection of the Confessions of Christendom. One Vol. (10s. 6d.)
Bishop Martensen.—Christian Ethics. One Volume. (10s. 6d.)
Professor Delitzsch.—Commentary on the Proverbs of Solomon. Two Vols. (21s.)
Professor Oehler.—Biblical Theology of the Old Testament. Two Vols. (21s.)
Professor Christlieb.—Modern Doubt and Christian Belief. One Vol. (10s. 6d.)
Professor Godet.—Commentary on St. Luke's Gospel. Two Vols. (21s.)
Professor Luthardt.—Commentary on St. John's Gospel. Three Vols. (31s. 6d.)
Professor Godet.—Commentary on St. John's Gospel. Three Vols. (31s. 6d.)
Professor Keil.—Commentary on Ezekiel. Two Vols. (21s.)
Professor Delitzsch.—Commentary on Song of Solomon and Ecclesiastes. One Vol. (10s. 6d.)
Gebhardt (H.)—Doctrine of the Apocalypse. One Vol. (10s. 6d.)
Steinmeyer (Dr. F. L.)—History of the Passion and Resurrection of our Lord. One Vol. (10s. 6d.)
Haupt (E.)—Commentary on the First Epistle of St. John. One Vol. (10s. 6d.)
Hagenbach (Dr. K. R.)—History of the Reformation. Two Vols. (21s.)
Philippi (Dr. F. A.)—Commentary on Romans. Two Vols. (21s.)

And, in connection with the Series—

Murphy's Commentary on the Book of Psalms. *To count as Two Volumes.* (12s.)
Alexander's Commentary on Isaiah. Two Volumes. (17s.)
Ritter's (Carl) Comparative Geography of Palestine. Four Volumes. (32s.)
Shedd's History of Christian Doctrine. Two Volumes. (21s.)
Macdonald's Introduction to the Pentateuch. Two Volumes. (21s.)
Gerlach's Commentary on the Pentateuch. 8vo. (10s. 6d.)
Dr. Hengstenberg.—Dissertations on the Genuineness of Daniel, etc. One Vol.

The series, in 155 Volumes (including 1882), price £40, 13s. 9d., forms an *Apparatus* without which it may be truly said *no Theological Library can be complete;* and the Publishers take the liberty of suggesting that no more appropriate gift could be presented to a Clergyman than the Series, in whole or in part.

⁎⁎* No DUPLICATES *can be included in the Selection of Twenty Volumes; and it will save trouble and correspondence if it be distinctly understood that* NO LESS *number than Twenty can be supplied, unless at non-subscription price.*

Subscribers' Names received by all Retail Booksellers.
LONDON: (*For Works at Non-subscription price only*) HAMILTON, ADAMS, & CO.

FOREIGN THEOLOGICAL LIBRARY.

ANNUAL SUBSCRIPTION: One Guinea for Four Volumes, Demy 8vo.

N.B.—Any *two* Years in this Series can be had at Subscription Price. *A single Year's Books* (except in the case of the current Year) *cannot be supplied separately.* Non-subscribers, price 10s. 6d. each volume, with exceptions marked.

1864—Lange on the Acts of the Apostles. Two Volumes.
Keil and Delitzsch on the Pentateuch. Vols. I. and II.

1865—Keil and Delitzsch on the Pentateuch. Vol. III.
Hengstenberg on the Gospel of John. Two Volumes.
Keil and Delitzsch on Joshua, Judges, and Ruth. One Volume.

1866—Keil and Delitzsch on Samuel. One Volume.
Keil and Delitzsch on Job. Two Volumes.
Martensen's System of Christian Doctrine. One Volume.

1867—Delitzsch on Isaiah. Two Volumes.
Delitzsch on Biblical Psychology. (12s.) One Volume.
Auberlen on Divine Revelation. One Volume.

1868—Keil's Commentary on the Minor Prophets. Two Volumes.
Delitzsch's Commentary on Epistle to the Hebrews. Vol. I.
Harless' System of Christian Ethics. One Volume.

1869—Hengstenberg on Ezekiel. One Volume.
Stier on the Words of the Apostles. One Volume.
Keil's Introduction to the Old Testament. Vol. I.
Bleek's Introduction to the New Testament. Vol. I.

1870—Keil's Introduction to the Old Testament. Vol. II.
Bleek's Introduction to the New Testament. Vol. II.
Schmid's New Testament Theology. One Volume.
Delitzsch's Commentary on Epistle to the Hebrews. Vol. II.

1871—Delitzsch's Commentary on the Psalms. Three Volumes.
Hengstenberg's Kingdom of God under the Old Testament. Vol. I.

1872—Keil's Commentary on the Books of Kings. One Volume.
Keil's Commentary on the Book of Daniel. One Volume.
Keil's Commentary on the Books of Chronicles. One Volume.
Hengstenberg's History of the Kingdom of God. Vol. II.

1873—Keil's Commentary on Ezra, Nehemiah, and Esther. One Volume.
Winer's Collection of the Confessions of Christendom. One Volume.
Keil's Commentary on Jeremiah. Vol. I.
Martensen on Christian Ethics.

1874—Christlieb's Modern Doubt and Christian Belief. One Vol.
Keil's Commentary on Jeremiah. Vol. II.
Delitzsch's Commentary on Proverbs. Vol. I.
Oehler's Biblical Theology of the Old Testament. Vol. I.

1875—Godet's Commentary on St. Luke's Gospel. Two Volumes.
Oehler's Biblical Theology of the Old Testament. Vol. II.
Delitzsch's Commentary on Proverbs. Vol. II.

1876—Keil's Commentary on Ezekiel. Two Volumes.
Luthardt's Commentary on St. John's Gospel. Vol. I.
Godet's Commentary on St. John's Gospel. Vol. I.

1877—Delitzsch's Commentary on Song of Solomon and Ecclesiastes.
Godet's Commentary on St. John's Gospel. Vols. II. and III.
Luthardt's Commentary on St. John's Gospel. Vol. II.

1878—Gebhardt's Doctrine of the Apocalypse.
Luthardt's Commentary on St. John's Gospel. Vol. III.
Philippi's Commentary on the Romans. Vol. I.
Hagenbach's History of the Reformation. Vol. I.

1879—Philippi's Commentary on the Romans. Vol. II.
Hagenbach's History of the Reformation. Vol. II.
Steinmeyer's History of the Passion and Resurrection of our Lord.
Haupt's Commentary on the First Epistle of St. John. One Volume.

⁎ *For New Series commencing with* 1880, *see page* 1.

T. and T. Clark's Publications.

In Twenty Handsome 8vo Volumes, SUBSCRIPTION PRICE £5, 5s.,

MEYER'S
Commentary on the New Testament.

'Meyer has been long and well known to scholars as one of the very ablest of the German expositors of the New Testament. We are not sure whether we ought not to say that he is unrivalled as an interpreter of the grammatical and historical meaning of the sacred writers. The Publishers have now rendered another seasonable and important service to English students in producing this translation.'—*Guardian.*

(Yearly Issue of Four Volumes, 21s.)
Each Volume will be sold separately at (on an average) 10s. 6d. *to Non-Subscribers.*

CRITICAL AND EXEGETICAL
COMMENTARY ON THE NEW TESTAMENT.
By Dr. H. A. W. MEYER,
OBERCONSISTORIALRATH, HANNOVER.

The portion contributed by Dr. MEYER has been placed under the editorial care of Rev. Dr. DICKSON, Professor of Divinity in the University of Glasgow; Rev. Dr. CROMBIE, Professor of Biblical Criticism, St. Mary's College, St. Andrews; and Rev. Dr. STEWART, Professor of Biblical Criticism, University of Glasgow.

- **1st Year**—Romans, Two Volumes.
  Galatians, One Volume.
  St. John's Gospel, Vol. I.
- **2d Year**—St. John's Gospel, Vol. II.
  Philippians and Colossians, One Volume.
  Acts of the Apostles, Vol. I.
  Corinthians, Vol. I.
- **3d Year**—Acts of the Apostles, Vol. II.
  St. Matthew's Gospel, Two Volumes.
  Corinthians, Vol. II.
- **4th Year**—Mark and Luke, Two Volumes.
  Ephesians and Philemon, One Volume.
  Thessalonians. (*Dr. Lünemann.*)
- **5th Year**—Timothy and Titus. (*Dr. Huther.*)
  Peter and Jude. (*Dr. Huther.*)
  Hebrews. (*Dr. Lünemann.*)
  James and John. (*Dr. Huther.*)

The series, as written by Meyer himself, is completed by the publication of Ephesians with Philemon in one volume. But to this the Publishers have thought it right to add Thessalonians and Hebrews, by Dr. Lünemann, and the Pastoral and Catholic Epistles, by Dr. Huther. So few, however, of the Subscribers have expressed a desire to have Dr. Düsterdieck's Commentary on Revelation included, that it has been resolved in the meantime not to undertake it.

'I need hardly add that the last edition of the accurate, perspicuous, and learned commentary of Dr. Meyer has been most carefully consulted throughout; and I must again, as in the preface to the Galatians, avow my great obligations to the acumen and scholarship of the learned editor.'—BISHOP ELLICOTT *in Preface to his 'Commentary on Ephesians.'*

'The ablest grammatical exegete of the age.'—PHILIP SCHAFF, D.D.

'In accuracy of scholarship and freedom from prejudice, he is equalled by few.'—*Literary Churchman.*

'We have only to repeat that it remains, of its own kind, the very best Commentary of the New Testament which we possess.'—*Church Bells.*

'No exegetical work is on the whole more valuable, or stands in higher public esteem. As a critic he is candid and cautious; exact to minuteness in philology; a master of the grammatical and historical method of interpretation.'—*Princeton Review.*

In Twenty-four Handsome 8vo Volumes, Subscription Price £6, 6s. 0d.,

Ante-Nicene Christian Library.

A COLLECTION OF ALL THE WORKS OF THE FATHERS OF THE CHRISTIAN CHURCH PRIOR TO THE COUNCIL OF NICÆA.

EDITED BY THE

REV. ALEXANDER ROBERTS, D.D., AND JAMES DONALDSON, LL.D.

MESSRS. CLARK are now happy to announce the completion of this Series. It has been received with marked approval by all sections of the Christian Church in this country and in the United States, as supplying what has long been felt to be a want, and also on account of the impartiality, learning, and care with which Editors and Translators have executed a very difficult task.

The Publishers do not bind themselves to *continue* to supply the Series at the Subscription price.

The Works are arranged as follow :—

FIRST YEAR.

APOSTOLIC FATHERS, comprising Clement's Epistles to the Corinthians; Polycarp to the Ephesians; Martyrdom of Polycarp; Epistle of Barnabas; Epistles of Ignatius (longer and shorter, and also the Syriac version); Martyrdom of Ignatius; Epistle to Diognetus; Pastor of Hermas; Papias; Spurious Epistles of Ignatius. In One Volume.
JUSTIN MARTYR; ATHENAGORAS. In One Volume.
TATIAN; THEOPHILUS; THE CLEmentine Recognitions. In One Volume.
CLEMENT OF ALEXANDRIA, Volume First, comprising Exhortation to Heathen; The Instructor; and a portion of the Miscellanies.

SECOND YEAR.

HIPPOLYTUS, Volume First; Refutation of all Heresies, and Fragments from his Commentaries.
IRENÆUS, Volume First.
TERTULLIAN AGAINST MARCION.
CYPRIAN, Volume First; the Epistles, and some of the Treatises.

THIRD YEAR.

IRENÆUS (completion); HIPPOLYTUS (completion); Fragments of Third Century. In One Volume.
ORIGEN: De Principiis; Letters; and portion of Treatise against Celsus.

CLEMENT OF ALEXANDRIA, Volume Second; Completion of Miscellanies.
TERTULLIAN, Volume First; To the Martyrs; Apology; To the Nations, etc.

FOURTH YEAR.

CYPRIAN, Volume Second (completion); Novatian; Minucius Felix; Fragments.
METHODIUS; ALEXANDER OF LYcopolis; Peter of Alexandria; Anatolius; Clement on Virginity; and Fragments.
TERTULLIAN, Volume Second.
APOCRYPHAL GOSPELS, ACTS, AND Revelations; comprising all the very curious Apocryphal Writings of the first three Centuries.

FIFTH YEAR.

TERTULLIAN, Volume Third (completion).
CLEMENTINE HOMILIES; APOSTOlical Constitutions. In One Volume.
ARNOBIUS.
DIONYSIUS; GREGORY THAUMAturgus; Syrian Fragments. In One Volume.

SIXTH YEAR.

LACTANTIUS; Two Volumes.
ORIGEN, Volume Second (completion). 12s. to Non-Subscribers.
EARLY LITURGIES AND REMAINing Fragments. 9s. to Non-Subscribers.

Single Years cannot be had separately, unless to complete sets; but any Volume may be had separately, price 10s. 6d.,—with the exception of ORIGEN, Vol. II., 12s.; and the EARLY LITURGIES, 9s.

In Fifteen Volumes, demy 8vo, Subscription Price £3, 19s.
(*Yearly issues of Four Volumes, 21s.*)

The Works of St. Augustine.

EDITED BY MARCUS DODS, D.D.

SUBSCRIPTION:

Four Volumes for a Guinea, *payable in advance* (24s. when not paid in advance).

FIRST YEAR.

THE 'CITY OF GOD.' Two Volumes.

WRITINGS IN CONNECTION WITH the Donatist Controversy. In One Volume.

THE ANTI-PELAGIAN WORKS OF St. Augustine. Vol. I.

SECOND YEAR.

'LETTERS.' Vol. I.

TREATISES AGAINST FAUSTUS the Manichæan. One Volume.

THE HARMONY OF THE EVANgelists, and the Sermon on the Mount. One Volume.

ON THE TRINITY. One Volume.

THIRD YEAR.

COMMENTARY ON JOHN. Two Volumes.

ON CHRISTIAN DOCTRINE, ENCHIRIDION, ON CATECHIZING, and ON FAITH AND THE CREED. One Volume.

THE ANTI-PELAGIAN WORKS OF St. Augustine. Vol. II.

FOURTH YEAR.

'LETTERS.' Vol. II.

'CONFESSIONS.' With Copious Notes by Rev. J. G. PILKINGTON.

ANTI-PELAGIAN WRITINGS. Vol. III.

Messrs. CLARK believe this will prove not the least valuable of their various Series. Every care has been taken to secure not only accuracy, but elegance.

It is understood that Subscribers are bound to take at least the issues for two years. Each volume is sold separately at 10s. 6d.

'For the reproduction of the "City of God" in an admirable English garb we are greatly indebted to the well-directed enterprise and energy of Messrs. Clark, and to the accuracy and scholarship of those who have undertaken the laborious task of translation.'
—*Christian Observer.*

'The present translation reads smoothly and pleasantly, and we have every reason to be satisfied both with the erudition and the fair and sound judgment displayed by the translators and the editor.'—*John Bull.*

SELECTION FROM
ANTE-NICENE LIBRARY
AND
ST. AUGUSTINE'S WORKS.

THE Ante-Nicene Library being now completed in 24 volumes, and the St. Augustine Series being also complete (*with the exception of the* 'LIFE') in 15 volumes, Messrs. CLARK will, as in the case of the Foreign Theological Library, give a Selection of 20 Volumes from both of those series at the *Subscription Price* of FIVE GUINEAS (or a larger number at same proportion).

LANGE'S COMMENTARIES.

(Subscription price, nett), 15s. each.

THEOLOGICAL AND HOMILETICAL COMMENTARY ON THE OLD AND NEW TESTAMENTS. Specially designed and adapted for the use of Ministers and Students. By Prof. JOHN PETER LANGE, D.D., in connection with a number of eminent European Divines. Translated, enlarged, and revised under the general editorship of Rev. Dr. PHILIP SCHAFF, assisted by leading Divines of the various Evangelical Denominations.

OLD TESTAMENT—14 VOLUMES.

I. **GENESIS.** With a General Introduction to the Old Testament. By Prof. J. P. LANGE, D.D. Translated from the German, with Additions, by Prof. TAYLER LEWIS, LL.D., and A. GOSMAN, D.D.

II. **EXODUS.** By J. P. LANGE, D.D. **LEVITICUS.** By J. P. LANGE, D.D. With GENERAL INTRODUCTION by Rev. Dr. OSGOOD.

III. **NUMBERS AND DEUTERONOMY. NUMBERS.** By Prof. J. P. LANGE, D.D. **DEUTERONOMY.** By W. J. SCHROEDER.

IV. **JOSHUA.** By Rev. F. R. FAY. **JUDGES** and **RUTH.** By Prof. PAULUS CASSELL, D.D.

V. **SAMUEL, I. and II.** By Professor ERDMANN, D.D.

VI. **KINGS.** By KARL CHR. W. F. BAHR, D.D.

VII. **CHRONICLES, I. and II.** By OTTO ZÖCKLER. **EZRA.** By FR. W. SCHULTZ. **NEHEMIAH.** By Rev. HOWARD CROSBY, D.D., LL.D. **ESTHER.** By FR. W. SCHULTZ.

VIII. **JOB.** With an Introduction and Annotations by Prof. TAYLER LEWIS, LL.D. A Commentary by Dr. OTTO ZÖCKLER, together with an Introductory Essay on Hebrew Poetry by Prof. PHILIP SCHAFF, D.D.

IX. **THE PSALMS.** By CARL BERNHARDT MOLL, D.D. With a new Metrical Version of the Psalms, and Philological Notes, by T. J. CONANT, D.D.

X. **PROVERBS.** By Prof. OTTO ZÖCKLER, D.D. **ECCLESIASTES.** By Prof. O. ZÖCKLER, D.D. With Additions, and a new Metrical Version, by Prof. TAYLER LEWIS, D.D. **THE SONG OF SOLOMON.** By Prof. O. ZÖCKLER, D.D.

XI. **ISAIAH.** By C. W. E. NAEGELSBACH.

XII. **JEREMIAH.** By C. W. E. NAEGELSBACH, D.D. **LAMENTATIONS.** By C. W. E. NAEGELSBACH, D.D.

XIII. **EZEKIEL.** By F. W. SCHRÖDER, D.D. **DANIEL.** By Professor ZÖCKLER, D.D.

XIV. **THE MINOR PROPHETS.** HOSEA, JOEL, and AMOS. By OTTO SCHMOLLER, Ph.D. OBADIAH and MICAH. By Rev. PAUL KLEINERT. JONAH, NAHUM, HABAKKUK, and ZEPHANIAH. By Rev. PAUL KLEINERT. HAGGAI. By Rev. JAMES E. M'CURDY. ZECHARIAH. By T. W. CHAMBERS, D.D. MALACHI. By JOSEPH PACKARD, D.D.

THE APOCRYPHA. *(Just published.)* By E. C. BISSELL, D.D. One Volume.

NEW TESTAMENT—10 VOLUMES.

I. **MATTHEW.** With a General Introduction to the New Testament. By J. P. LANGE, D.D. Translated, with Additions, by PHILIP SCHAFF, D.D.

II. **MARK.** By J. P. LANGE, D.D. **LUKE.** By J. J. VAN OOSTERZEE.

III. **JOHN.** By J. P. LANGE, D.D.

IV. **ACTS.** By G. V. LECHLER, D.D., and Rev. CHARLES GEROK.

V. **ROMANS.** By J. P. LANGE, D.D., and Rev. F. R. FAY.

VI. **CORINTHIANS.** By CHRISTIAN F. KLING.

VII. **GALATIANS.** By OTTO SCHMOLLER, Ph.D. **EPHESIANS** and **COLOSSIANS.** By KARL BRAUNE, D.D. **PHILIPPIANS.** By KARL BRAUNE, D.D.

VIII. **THESSALONIANS.** By Drs. AUBERLIN and RIGGENBACH. **TIMOTHY.** By J. J. VAN OOSTERZEE, D.D. **TITUS.** By J. J. VAN OOSTERZEE, D.D. **PHILEMON.** By J. J. VAN OOSTERZEE, D.D. **HEBREWS.** By KARL B. MOLL, D.D.

IX. **JAMES.** By J. P. LANGE, D.D., and J. J. VAN OOSTERZEE, D.D. **PETER** and **JUDE.** By G. F. C. FRONMÜLLER, Ph.D. **JOHN.** By KARL BRAUNE, D.D.

X. **THE REVELATION OF JOHN.** By Dr. J. P. LANGE. Together with double Alphabetical Index to all the Ten Volumes on the New Testament, by JOHN H. WOODS.

CHEAP RE-ISSUE OF
STIER'S WORDS OF THE LORD JESUS.

To meet a very general desire that this now well-known Work should be brought more within the reach of all classes, both Clergy and Laity, Messrs. CLARK are now issuing, for a limited period, the *Eight* Volumes, handsomely bound in *Four*, at the *Subscription Price* of

TWO GUINEAS

As the allowance to the Trade must necessarily be small, orders sent either direct or through Booksellers must *in every case* be accompanied with a Post Office Order for the above amount.

'The whole work is a treasury of thoughtful exposition. Its measure of practical and spiritual application, with exegetical criticism, commends it to the use of those whose duty it is to preach as well as to understand the Gospel of Christ.'—*Guardian.*

New and Cheap Edition, in Four Vols., demy 8vo, *Subscription Price* 28s.,

THE LIFE OF THE LORD JESUS CHRIST:

A Complete Critical Examination of the Origin, Contents, and Connection of the Gospels. Translated from the German of J. P. LANGE, D.D., Professor of Divinity in the University of Bonn. Edited, with additional Notes, by MARCUS DODS, D.D.

'We have arrived at a most favourable conclusion regarding the importance and ability of this work—the former depending upon the present condition of theological criticism, the latter on the wide range of the work itself; the singularly dispassionate judgment of the Author, as well as his pious, reverential, and erudite treatment of a subject inexpressibly holy. . . . We have great pleasure in recommending this work to our readers. We are convinced of its value and enormous range.'—*Irish Ecclesiastical Gazette.*

BENGEL'S GNOMON—CHEAP EDITION.
GNOMON OF THE NEW TESTAMENT.

By JOHN ALBERT BENGEL. Now first translated into English. With Original Notes, Explanatory and Illustrative. Edited by the Rev. ANDREW R. FAUSSET, M.A. The Original Translation was in Five Large Volumes, demy 8vo, averaging more than 550 pages each, and the very great demand for this Edition has induced the Publishers to issue the *Five* Volumes bound in *Three*, at the *Subscription Price* of

TWENTY-FOUR SHILLINGS.

They trust by this still further to increase its usefulness.

'It is a work which manifests the most intimate and profound knowledge of Scripture, and which, if we examine it with care, will often be found to condense more matter into a line than can be extracted from many pages of other writers.'—*Archdeacon* HARE.

'In respect both of its contents and its tone, Bengel's Gnomon stands alone. Even among laymen there has arisen a healthy and vigorous desire for scriptural knowledge, and Bengel has done more than any other man to aid such inquirers. There is perhaps no book every word of which has been so well weighed, or in which a single technical term contains so often far-reaching and suggestive views. . . . The theoretical and practical are as intimately connected as light and heat in the sun's ray.'—*Life of Perthes.*

Just published, in demy 4to, Third Edition, price 25s.,

BIBLICO-THEOLOGICAL LEXICON OF NEW TESTAMENT GREEK.

By HERMANN CREMER, D.D.,
PROFESSOR OF THEOLOGY IN THE UNIVERSITY OF GREIFSWALD.

TRANSLATED FROM THE GERMAN OF THE SECOND EDITION

(WITH ADDITIONAL MATTER AND CORRECTIONS BY THE AUTHOR)

By WILLIAM URWICK, M.A.

'Dr. Cremer's work is highly and deservedly esteemed in Germany. It gives with care and thoroughness a complete history, as far as it goes, of each word and phrase that it deals with. . . . Dr. Cremer's explanations are most lucidly set out.'—*Guardian*.

'It is hardly possible to exaggerate the value of this work to the student of the Greek Testament. . . . The translation is accurate and idiomatic, and the additions to the later edition are considerable and important.'—*Church Bells*.

'A valuable addition to the stores of any theological library. . . . It is what it claims to be, a Lexicon, both biblical and theological, and treats not only of words, but of the doctrines inculcated by those words.'—*John Bull*.

'We very heartily commend this goodly volume to students of biblical literature.'—*Evangelical Magazine*.

'We cannot find an important word in our Greek New Testament which is not discussed with a fulness and discrimination which leaves nothing to be desired.'—*Nonconformist*.

'Cremer's Lexicon is, and is long likely to be, indispensable to students whether of theology or of the Bible, and must always bear witness to his scholarship, erudition, and diligence.'—*Expositor*.

'A work of immense erudition.'—*Freeman*.

'This noble edition in quarto of Cremer's Biblico-Theological Lexicon quite supersedes the translation of the first edition of the work. Many of the most important articles have been re-written and re-arranged. . . . We heartily congratulate Mr. Urwick on the admirable manner in which he has executed his task, revealing on his part adequate scholarship, thorough sympathy, and a fine choice of English equivalents and definitions.'—*British Quarterly Review*.

'As an aid in our search, we warmly commend the honest and laborious New Testament Lexicon of Dr. Cremer.'—*London Quarterly Review*.

'The judiciousness and importance of Dr. Cremer's design must be obvious to all students of the New Testament; and the execution of that design, in our judgment, fully establishes and justifies the translator's encomiums.'—*Watchman*.

'A majestic volume, admirably printed and faultlessly edited, and will win gratitude as well as renown for its learned and Christian Author, and prove a precious boon to students and preachers who covet exact and exhaustive acquaintance with the literal and theological teaching of the New Testament.'—*Dickinson's Theological Quarterly*.

Second Edition in preparation,

FINAL CAUSES.

By PAUL JANET, Member of the Institute, Paris.

Translated from the French by William Affleck, B.D.

CONTENTS.—PRELIMINARY CHAPTER—The Problem. BOOK I.—The Law of Finality. BOOK II.—The First Cause of Finality. APPENDIX.

'This very learned, accurate, and, within its prescribed limits, exhaustive work. . . . The book as a whole abounds in matter of the highest interest, and is a model of learning and judicious treatment.'—*Guardian.*

'Illustrated and defended with an ability and learning which must command the reader's admiration.'—*Dublin Review.*

'A great contribution to the literature of this subject. M. Janet has mastered the conditions of the problem, is at home in the literature of science and philosophy, and has that faculty of felicitous expression which makes French books of the highest class such delightful reading; . . . in clearness, vigour, and depth it has been seldom equalled, and more seldom excelled, in philosophical literature.'—*Spectator.*

'A wealth of scientific knowledge and a logical acumen which will win the admiration of every reader.'—*Church Quarterly Review.*

Just published, in demy 8vo, price 10s. 6d.,

THE BIBLE DOCTRINE OF MAN.

(Seventh Series of Cunningham Lectures.)

By JOHN LAIDLAW, D.D.,

Professor of Systematic Theology, New College, Edinburgh.

'An important and valuable contribution to the discussion of the anthropology of the sacred writings, perhaps the most considerable that has appeared in our own language.'—*Literary Churchman.*

'The work is a thoughtful contribution to a subject which must always have deep interest for the devout student of the Bible.'—*British Quarterly Review.*

'Dr. Laidlaw's work is scholarly, able, interesting, and valuable. . . . Thoughtful and devout minds will find much to stimulate, and not a little to assist, their meditations in this learned and, let us add, charmingly printed volume.'—*Record.*

'On the whole, we take this to be the most sensible and reasonable statement of the Biblical psychology of man we have met.'—*Expositor.*

'The book will give ample material for thought to the reflective reader; and it holds a position, as far as we know, which is unique.'—*Church Bells.*

'The Notes to the Lectures, which occupy not less than 130 pages, are exceedingly valuable. The style of the lecturer is clear and animated; the critical and analytical judgment predominates.'—*English Independent.*

Just published, Second Edition, demy 8vo, 10s. 6d.,

THE HUMILIATION OF CHRIST,

IN ITS PHYSICAL, ETHICAL, AND OFFICIAL ASPECTS.

By A. B. BRUCE, D.D.,

PROFESSOR OF DIVINITY, FREE CHURCH COLLEGE, GLASGOW.

'Dr. Bruce's style is uniformly clear and vigorous, and this book of his, as a whole, has the rare advantage of being at once stimulating and satisfying to the mind in a high degree.'—*British and Foreign Evangelical Review.*

'This work stands forth at once as an original, thoughtful, thorough piece of work in the branch of scientific theology, such as we do not often meet in our language. . . . It is really a work of exceptional value; and no one can read it without perceptible gain in theological knowledge.'—*English Churchman.*

'We have not for a long time met with a work so fresh and suggestive as this of Professor Bruce. . . . We do not know where to look at our English Universities for a treatise so calm, logical, and scholarly.'—*English Independent.*

By the same Author.

Just published, Second Edition, demy 8vo, 10s. 6d.,

THE TRAINING OF THE TWELVE;

OR,

Exposition of Passages in the Gospels exhibiting the Twelve Disciples of Jesus under Discipline for the Apostleship.

'Here we have a really great book on an important, large, and attractive subject—a book full of loving, wholesome, profound thoughts about the fundamentals of Christian faith and practice.'—*British and Foreign Evangelical Review.*

'It is some five or six years since this work first made its appearance, and now that a second edition has been called for, the Author has taken the opportunity to make some alterations which are likely to render it still more acceptable. Substantially, however, the book remains the same, and the hearty commendation with which we noted its first issue applies to it at least as much now.'—*Rock.*

'The value, the beauty of this volume is that it is a unique contribution to, because a loving and cultured study of, the life of Christ, in the relation of the Master of the Twelve.'—*Edinburgh Daily Review.*

WORKS BY THE LATE
PATRICK FAIRBAIRN, D.D.,
PRINCIPAL AND PROFESSOR OF THEOLOGY IN THE FREE CHURCH COLLEGE, GLASGOW.

In crown 8vo, price 6s.,

PASTORAL THEOLOGY: A Treatise on the Office and Duties of the Christian Pastor. With a Biographical Sketch of the Author.

'This treatise on the office and duties of a Christian pastor, by the late Professor Fairbairn, is well deserving thoughtful perusal. Throughout the volume, however, there is a tone of earnest piety and practical good sense, which finds expression in many profitable counsels, embodying the result of large experience and shrewd observation. . . . Much of the volume is devoted to the theory and practice of preaching, and this part we can most heartily commend; it is replete with valuable suggestions, which even those who have had some experience in the ministry will find calculated to make them more attractive and efficient preachers.'—*Christian Observer.*

In crown 8vo, price 7s. 6d.,

THE PASTORAL EPISTLES. The Greek Text and Translation. With Introduction, Expository Notes, and Dissertations.

'We cordially recommend this work to ministers and theological students.'—*Methodist Magazine.*
'We have read no book of his with a keener appreciation and enjoyment than that just published on the Pastoral Epistles.'—*Nonconformist.*

In Two Volumes, demy 8vo, price 21s., Sixth Edition,

THE TYPOLOGY OF SCRIPTURE, viewed in connection with the whole Series of the Divine Dispensations.

In demy 8vo, price 10s. 6d., Fourth Edition,

EZEKIEL, AND THE BOOK OF HIS PROPHECY: An Exposition. With a new Translation.

In demy 8vo, price 10s. 6d., Second Edition,

PROPHECY, viewed in its Distinctive Nature, its Special Functions, and Proper Interpretation.

In demy 8vo, price 10s. 6d.,

HERMENEUTICAL MANUAL; or, Introduction to the Exegetical Study of the Scriptures of the New Testament.

In demy 8vo, price 10s. 6d.,

THE REVELATION OF LAW IN SCRIPTURE, considered with respect both to its own Nature and to its Relative Place in Successive Dispensations. (The Third Series of the 'Cunningham Lectures.')

PROFESSOR GODET'S WORKS.

In Three Volumes, 8vo, price 31s. 6d.,
A COMMENTARY ON
THE GOSPEL OF ST. JOHN.
By F. GODET, D.D.,
PROFESSOR OF THEOLOGY, NEUCHATEL.

'This work forms one of the battle-fields of modern inquiry, and is itself so rich in spiritual truth that it is impossible to examine it too closely; and we welcome this treatise from the pen of Dr. Godet. We have no more competent exegete, and this new volume shows all the learning and vivacity for which the Author is distinguished.'—*Freeman.*

In Two Volumes, 8vo, price 21s.,
THE GOSPEL OF ST. LUKE.
Translated from the Second French Edition.

'Marked by clearness and good sense, it will be found to possess value and interest as one of the most recent and copious works specially designed to illustrate this Gospel.'—*Guardian.*

In Two Volumes, 8vo, price 21s.,
ST. PAUL'S EPISTLE TO THE ROMANS.

'We have looked through it with great care, and have been charmed not less by the clearness and fervour of its evangelical principles than by the carefulness of its exegesis, its fine touches of spiritual intuition, and its appositeness of historical illustration.'—*Baptist Magazine.*

Just published, in crown 8vo, price 6s.,
DEFENCE OF THE CHRISTIAN FAITH.
TRANSLATED BY THE
HON. AND REV. CANON LYTTELTON, M.A.,
RECTOR OF HAGLEY.

'This volume is not unworthy of the great reputation which Professor Godet enjoys. It shows the same breadth of reading and extent of learning as his previous works, and the same power of eloquent utterance.'—*Church Bells.*

'Professor Godet is at once so devoutly evangelical in his spirit and so profoundly intelligent in his apprehension of truth, that we shall all welcome these contributions to the study of much debated subjects with the utmost satisfaction.'—*Christian World.*

Just published, in demy 8vo, Fourth Edition, price 10s. 6d.,
MODERN DOUBT AND CHRISTIAN BELIEF.
A Series of Apologetic Lectures addressed to Earnest Seekers after Truth.
By THEODORE CHRISTLIEB, D.D.,
UNIVERSITY PREACHER AND PROFESSOR OF THEOLOGY AT BONN.

Translated, with the Author's sanction, chiefly by the Rev. H. U. WEITBRECHT, Ph.D., and Edited by the Rev. T. L. KINGSBURY, M.A.

'We recommend the volume as one of the most valuable and important among recent contributions to our apologetic literature. . . . We are heartily thankful both to the learned Author and to his translators.'—*Guardian.*

'We express our unfeigned admiration of the ability displayed in this work, and of the spirit of deep piety which pervades it; and whilst we commend it to the careful perusal of our readers, we heartily rejoice that in those days of reproach and blasphemy so able a champion has come forward to contend earnestly for the faith which was once delivered to the saints.'—*Christian Observer.*

DR. LUTHARDT'S WORKS.

In Three handsome crown 8vo Volumes, price 6s. each.

'We do not know any volumes so suitable in these times for young men entering on life, or, let us say, even for the library of a pastor called to deal with such, than the three volumes of this series. We commend the whole of them with the utmost cordial satisfaction. They are altogether quite a specialty in our literature.'—*Weekly Review.*

APOLOGETIC LECTURES
ON THE
FUNDAMENTAL TRUTHS OF CHRISTIANITY.
Fifth Edition.

BY C. E. LUTHARDT, D.D., LEIPZIG.

'From Dr. Luthardt's exposition even the most learned theologians may derive invaluable criticism, and the most acute disputants supply themselves with more trenchant and polished weapons than they have as yet been possessed of.'—*Bell's Weekly Messenger.*

APOLOGETIC LECTURES
ON THE
SAVING TRUTHS OF CHRISTIANITY.
Fourth Edition.

'Dr. Luthardt is a profound scholar, but a very simple teacher, and expresses himself on the gravest matters with the utmost simplicity, clearness, and force.'—*Literary World.*

APOLOGETIC LECTURES
ON THE
MORAL TRUTHS OF CHRISTIANITY.
Third Edition.

'The ground covered by this work is, of course, of considerable extent, and there is scarcely any topic of specifically moral interest now under debate in which the reader will not find some suggestive saying. The volume contains, like its predecessors, a truly wealthy apparatus of notes and illustrations.'—*English Churchman.*

In Three Volumes, 8vo, price 31s. 6d.,

ST. JOHN'S GOSPEL DESCRIBED AND EXPLAINED ACCORDING TO ITS PECULIAR CHARACTER.

'Full to overflowing with a ripe theology and a critical science worthy of their great theme.'—*Irish Ecclesiastical Gazette.*

Just published, in demy 8vo, price 9s.,

ST. JOHN THE AUTHOR OF THE FOURTH GOSPEL.
BY PROFESSOR C. E. LUTHARDT,
Author of 'Fundamental Truths of Christianity,' etc.

Translated and the Literature enlarged by C. R. GREGORY, Leipzig.

'A work of thoroughness and value. The translator has added a lengthy Appendix, containing a very complete account of the literature bearing on the controversy respecting this Gospel. The indices which close the volume are well ordered, and add greatly to its value.'—*Guardian.*

'There are few works in the later theological literature which contain such a wealth of sober theological knowledge and such an invulnerable phalanx of objective apologetical criticism.'—*Professor Guericke.*

Crown 8vo, 5s.,

LUTHARDT, KAHNIS, AND BRÜCKNER.
The Church: Its Origin, its History, and its Present Position.

'A comprehensive review of this sort, done by able hands, is both instructive and suggestive.'—*Record.*

HANDBOOKS FOR BIBLE CLASSES.

'These volumes are models of the *multum in parvo* style. We have long desired to meet with a Series of this kind—Little Books on Great Subjects.'—*Literary World.*

THE EPISTLE OF ST. PAUL TO THE GALATIANS.
With Introduction and Notes [Price 1s. 6d.
By the Rev. Professor JAMES MACGREGOR, D.D.

THE POST-EXILIAN PROPHETS— HAGGAI, ZECHARIAH, MALACHI.
With Introduction and Notes [Price 2s.
By MARCUS DODS, D.D.

'Thoughtful, suggestive, and finely analytical.'—*Evangelical Magazine.*

THE LIFE OF CHRIST.
By Rev. JAMES STALKER, M.A. [Price 1s. 6d.

'As a succinct, suggestive, beautifully written exhibition of the life of our Lord, we are acquainted with nothing that can compare with it.'—*Christian World.*

THE CHRISTIAN SACRAMENTS.
By Professor JAMES S. CANDLISH, D.D. [Price 1s. 6d.

'An admirable manual; sound, clear, suggestive, and interesting.'—*Free Church Record.*

THE BOOKS OF CHRONICLES.
By Rev. Professor MURPHY, Belfast. [Price 1s. 6d.

'We know no Commentary on the Chronicles to compare with this, considering the small size and cost.'—*Wesleyan Methodist Magazine.*

THE WESTMINSTER CONFESSION OF FAITH.
With Introduction and Notes [Price 2s.
By Rev. JOHN MACPHERSON, M.A.

'This volume is executed with learning, discrimination, and ability.'—*British Messenger.*

THE BOOK OF JUDGES.
By Rev. Principal DOUGLAS. [Price 1s. 3d.

'This volume is as near perfection as we can hope to find such a work.'—*Church Bells.*

THE BOOK OF JOSHUA.
By Rev. Principal DOUGLAS. [Price 1s. 6d.

THE EPISTLE TO THE HEBREWS.
By Rev. Professor A. B. DAVIDSON. [Price 2s. 6d.

SCOTTISH CHURCH HISTORY.
By Rev. NORMAN L. WALKER, M.A. [Price 1s. 6d.

THE CHURCH.
By Rev. Professor WM. BINNIE, D.D., [Price 1s. 6d.

www.ingramcontent.com/pod-product-compliance
Lightning Source LLC
Chambersburg PA
CBHW031945290426
44108CB00011B/679